The Consumer Society Reader

Edited by Juliet B. Schor and Douglas B. Holt

The New Press

New York

Published in the United States by The New Press, New York, 2000
Distributed by W.W. Norton & Company, Inc., New York

LIBRARY OF CONGRESS CATALOGING-IN-PUBLICATION DATA

The consumer society reader / edited by Juliet B. Schor and Douglas B. Holt.
    p.   cm.
    ISBN 1–56584–532–3 (hc.)
    ISBN 1–56584–598–6 (pbk.)
    1. Consumption (Economics)   2. Consumer behavior.   I. Schor, Juliet B.   II. Holt,
Douglas B.
    HC79.C6C6552000
    658.8'342–dc21   00–028255

The New Press was established in 1990 as a not-for-profit alternative to the large, commercial
publishing houses currently dominating the book publishing industry. The New Press operates
in the public interest rather than for private gain, and is committed to publishing, in innovative ways, works of educational, cultural, and community value that are often deemed
insufficiently profitable.

www.thenewpress.com

Printed in Canada

9 8 7

Contents

Acknowledgments

We would like to thank a number of people who helped us along the way: Diane Wachtell, who originally suggested the idea of an anthology; Gerry McCauley, our wonderful agent; Matt Weiland, our editor, and Tim Roberts, our production editor, both at The New Press; Susan Bordo, Robert Goldman, and Tom O'Guinn, who provided photos for us; Elisheva Lambert and Jim McNeill, who provided dedicated research assistance; Eric Hall, who secured permissions; and Prosannun Parthasarathi and Tuba Üstüner. We are especially grateful to those publishers and authors who allowed us to reprint their work free of charge or at reduced rates.

INTRODUCTION
Douglas B. Holt and Juliet B. Schor
DO AMERICANS CONSUME TOO MUCH?

Global warming, the conspicuous spending of the newly wealthy, excessive advertising, and, most recently, the "Battle of Seattle" have all conspired to put the question of our consumer lives back into public view. Consumer society—the "air we breathe," as George Orwell has described it—disappears during economic downturns and political crises. It becomes visible again when prosperity seems secure, cultural transformation is too rapid, or environmental disasters occur. Such is the time in which we now find ourselves. As the roads clog with gas-guzzling SUVs and McMansions proliferate in the suburbs, the nation is once again asking fundamental questions about lifestyle. Has "luxury fever," to use Robert Frank's phrase, gotten out of hand? Are we really comfortable with the "Brand Is Me" mentality? Have we gone too far in pursuit of the almighty dollar, to the detriment of our families, communities, and natural environment? Even politicians, ordinarily impermeable to questions about consumerism, are voicing doubts. A year ago, Hillary Clinton got the attention of the world by worrying that the export of American entertainment and consumer products was destroying indigenous cultures; and recently, Vice President Al Gore suggested that Americans should focus less on earning money and spend more time with their families. Polls suggest majorities of Americans feel the country has become too materialistic, too focused on getting and spending, and increasingly removed from long-standing nonmaterialist values.

Why are doubts about consumer society reemerging at the end of the twentieth century? Three factors have combined to create the current disquiet. Perhaps most obvious is the new inequality—the top 1 percent of households now own about 40 percent of all wealth, and the top 20 percent are responsible for half the country's consumer spending. The long boom of the 1990s has resulted in a dazzling display among the nation's newly rich to outdo one another in ostentatious spending. Each twist and turn of this Veblen-esque competition is duly reported on by the national media, whether it's thousand-dollar bedsheets, ten-thousand-square-foot homes, or hundred thousand dollar vehicles. The entire nation becomes privy to the ins and outs of hiring butlers and erecting stone walls. The onlookers are alternately attracted and repelled, disliking the values driving the conspicuous consumption but at the same time fearful of falling too far behind in this accelerated race. Households of ordinary means console themselves with affordable luxuries, but all is not well in the kingdom of plastics.

On the one hand, the sheer disparities of wealth, income, and situation grow harder to justify, particularly as prosperity feels more assured. Homelessness, hunger, and child poverty continue to nag at Americans' consciences. Furthermore, the upscaling of the wealthy puts pressure on others to follow suit. Many households find themselves stretched thin, as incomes for the majority have not kept pace with rising consumer standards. Savings rates have fallen, while credit card debt and bankruptcies have skyrocketed. Not only money but also time is in short supply. As lifestyle norms require two earners, and jobs become increasingly demanding, time for family and community is squeezed. The acceleration of daily life, often for purposes of consuming, contributes to a feeling that things are out of control. People look back to an earlier era when there *was* time enough, even if living standards were less opulent. Many long for a simpler, more authentic, less materialist past. "Balance" has become a defining mantra.

The second trend is the relentless commodification of all areas of social life, and the rise of market values. Perhaps the most striking aspect of this trend is the marketization of a wide variety of goods and services that had hitherto been outside the profit nexus. Most prominent among these are the services produced in the household economy, where self-provision had been the norm. Today, as married women are more devoted to paid employment, they begin "outsourcing"—hiring baby-sitters, accountants, gardeners, grocery delivery, and personal shoppers. Households that can afford it substitute time for money. Less and less of daily life is produced at home; more and more of what we consume is commodified, i.e., produced for sale on the market.

This commodification of daily life is also occurring in other areas. Health care and education, which were previously provided as public goods to citizens, are given over to private corporations who produce them for profit, as if they were ordinary consumer goods. Public services such as welfare and prisons are run by corporations for the purpose of making money.

The production of news, culture, sports, and entertainment is also increasingly commodified. Twenty-five years ago, the public good aspect of book and newspaper publishing coexisted with the need to make money. Now, a handful of megaconglomerates have taken over all the major media. Profitability and reproducing the political legitimacy of the system have become the dominant criteria for cultural production. The mouse is truly eating the world.

Indeed, virtually no aspect of social life appears to be immune from these trends. "Personal style" is now a hot market commodity. Trend spotters scour the nation's inner cities, searching for the successors to the hip-hop innovators of the 1980s. They scrutinize the walk, the talk, the way one's pants are worn. At lightning speed, style moves from inner city to suburb and back again, a marketed commodity. But it's not just youth culture that is being replicated and sold. Business gurus urge everyone to perfect their personal style. Brand and market yourself, whomever you are.

The relentless drive to commodify is also evident in the commercialization of public space and culture. Advertising and marketing appear almost everywhere—in museums, on public television and radio, in doctor's offices, on subway platforms, and on restaurant menus. Sports arenas, previously named for communities, now sport corporate logos. Movies are replete with product placements. Public schools, once relatively isolated from corporate advertisers, became their new frontier during the 1990s, as marketers strived for "share of mind" among six-year-olds. Many of the nation's children now watch commercials in their classrooms (via Channel One), learn from corporate-written curricula, look at advertising on the Internet, or drink the official school soft drink (Coke or Pepsi).

Indeed, our deepest personal connections are increasingly dominated by market transactions, whether it's through surrogate motherhood, the sale of one's DNA, the booming trade in sex for hire, or the commercialization of religion and spirituality. Little remains sacred, and separate from the world of the commodity. As a result people become ever more desperate to sacralize the profane consumer world around them, worshiping celebrities, collections, and brand logos.

The third major development that is reigniting criticism of consumer society is the rapid globalization of the world economy. Beginning with the French general strike of December 1995, grassroots opposition to globalization has begun to intensify. The most dramatic example has been the Battle of Seattle, a mesmerizing confrontation between the agents of corporate globalization (represented by the World Trade Organization) and a coalition of labor, environmental, church, student, and anticonsumerist activists.

Protesters in Seattle attacked not only, or even mainly, the export of American jobs, but rather the corporate vision of global consumerism. They questioned the very desirability of the WTO's stated purpose of increasing incomes through global trade. Rejecting the current system of cheap commodities based on exploiting labor and natural resources, they offered alternative visions of local economies built on sustainable agriculture, locally controlled manufacturing and retailing, and limited material desires. It is significant that the protesters went after Nike, Starbucks, and other mega-brands. They stood against corporate consumerism, in favor of locally owned small businesses; they rejected the idea that one's personhood is defined by the logo on the shoe; and they argued against the impoverishment of small farmers and producers that globalization has wrought.

Perhaps most important has been the link between the spread of consumerism and the ongoing devastation of the natural environment—the connections between air travel and carbon accumulation; the demand for exotic hardwoods and species extinction; meat consumption and soil erosion; toxics and human health hazards. Recent years have been the warmest of the century. Weather patterns have turned extreme, and crocuses are appearing in December. As the planet warms up, so too must the debate about our consumption, the ultimate cause of climate change.

Within the academy, a parallel discussion is taking place. Scholars are becoming more attentive to questions about the nature and desirability of consumer society, engaging in an ongoing academic conversation. As they have always been, the public and academic debates are dialectically connected. Sometimes scholars anticipate broader cultural changes; in other moments, such as the current one, political movements have set the agenda for the academic dialogue. In the pages that follow, we've selected essays that provide an entry point into these discussions.

THE ECONOMIC CRITIQUES:
CAPITALISM NEEDS CONSUMERS

What drives consumer society? Is it corporations, who by their marketing and advertising campaigns ultimately determine what consumers want? Or is it consumers, whom producers must satisfy in order to stay in business? This deceptively simple question has been at the heart of much of the scholarly literature, and continues to preoccupy both supporters and detractors of consumer society.

Throughout the middle decades of the century, from the 1940s until the 1980s, the theme of corporate influence was dominant in the scholarly literature. One of the most influential contributions was the 1944 classic essay "The Culture Industry: Enlightenment as Mass Deception," by Theodor Adorno and Max Horkheimer, prominent members of the Frankfurt School. Drawing on Marx's theory of alienation in the workplace, Adorno and Horkheimer argue that employers' needs for objectified and submissive workers created a parallel need for dominated, passive consumers. Creativity and subjectivity, the hallmarks of the artisanal economy, are simply incompatible with the de-skilling and repetitiveness of mass-production industry. Culture, once brilliant, demanding, and intellectually challenging, becomes soothing, banal, familiar, and entertaining. With astonishing prescience, Adorno and Horkheimer predicted the "dumbing down" of art and culture, the concentration of cultural producers, and the spread of an entertainment society.

For Adorno and Horkheimer, the objectification of labor requires the objectification of the consumer. This "paramount position of production" was to assume a central role in other influential critiques of consumer society, such as John Kenneth Galbraith's *The Affluent Society*. Galbraith was also posing the question of compatability between production and consumption, but in ways more Keynesian than Marxian. In particular, the phenomenal increases in productivity that fueled mass production had to be accompanied by similarly phenomenal increases in consumer demand. But how to ensure that the endless stream of cars, appliances, and other products would actually be sold?

Galbraith's answer—the dependence effect—is that "the institutions of advertising and salesmanship . . . create desires." The corporation both creates the want, and satisfies it. Compatibility is ensured because the same institution controls both sides of the market.

This was to prove a potent theme in the fifties and early sixties, as the ascendance of Madison Avenue and its turn to ever more sophisticated psychological approaches alarmed many. Books such as Vance Packard's *The Hidden Persuaders* and Herbert Marcuse's *One Dimensional Man* stressed the seamlessness of the system. In 1963 Betty Friedan produced a brilliant gynocentric companion piece to Adorno and Horkheimer's androcentric analysis. For the latter, production means factories and male workers; for Friedan, the relevant labor process is the household economy and occupation: housewife. But in both, work is boring, repetitive, unskilled, mundane. Friedan argues that *the feminine mystique*, and its attendant confinement of women to the home, was driven mainly by the need to sell products. Combing through the motivation research of Ernest Dichter, Friedan reconstructs the marketers' view of women. They were the backbone of the consumer economy, but career women did not care to spend their lives doing something as trivial and unsatisfying as shopping. Capitalism needed housewives, stunted in their careers, driven to purchase discerningly, manipulated into channeling their considerable creative potential into cake mixes, washing powders, and the choice of breakfast cereal rather than more significant accomplishments in the world of work.

Of course marketers promise more than the mundane world of the kitchen. As Stuart Ewen argues in his piece on style, Madison Avenue also offers commodities as the route to pleasure and sexuality, through their ability to create identity, freedom, "fascination and enchantment," beauty, and style. Consumers are seduced by sophisticated advertising to adopt a host of superfluous preferences for products, which are at heart advertisers' fictions: Buy style in the marketplace and you can be whoever you want to be.

While they differed in many ways, these critical accounts shared certain themes—they described false and true needs, a superficial, surface world of commodities versus an underlying realm of authentic life. Furthermore, in these accounts, the standard defense of the system became illegitimate, for if corporations *created* needs, particularly in insidious ways, they could hardly be credited for meeting them. There was a better, more authentic, and less consumerist way to live. But it was blocked by corporate power.

A second critique was aesthetic. Mass production was derided as lacking quality, taste, and creativity. Thus, consumer society produced neither the good, the true, nor the beautiful. It was a great con game.

THE CULTURAL CRITIQUES: MANUFACTURING MEANINGS

The economic critiques explain how the profit motive leads to the organization of consumption. They are less compelling in their descriptions of why consumers go along with corporate designs. One answer is that advertisers have been successful because they have been able to embed valued meanings in products. If correct, this argument leads to the important conclusion that meaning does not necessarily emanate from the material or functional aspects of products.

As anthropology has been particularly good at showing, human understandings and experiences of what are seemingly objective properties are actually cultural constructions. Goods have symbolic meanings in all societies. However, capitalism poses a new problem—imbuing functionally and materially similar products with different symbolic meanings. The marketer needs to induce the consumer to pay a premium for products that are mere commodities (i.e., mass-produced, identical goods).

Despite their emphasis on manipulation, Adorno and Horkheimer understood the importance of symbolic meanings with their recognition that consumers could use consumer goods and marketed imagery to create categories of social difference. It is with Jean Baudrillard, however, that we begin to find a fully articulated theory of the production of social meaning through commodities. The primary target of his damning essays is the argument of most defenders of consumer society—the idea that commodities are produced to respond to individual needs and wants. Such tautological formulations beg the question: How are these needs and wants produced?

Baudrillard's answer is that individual desires are disguised expressions of social differences in a system of cultural meanings that is produced through commodities. This "fashion system" is a code—an infinitely variable set of social differences—that people access through consumption. It is not meaningful to talk about authentic versus false needs in Baudrillard's model, only the extent to which people have been absorbed into the fashion logic. One of the most important implications of this view is that if consumer society is premised upon the production of difference through commodities, then the system is extremely resilient. How can a social movement challenge consumer society without falling prey to the further expansion of fashionable difference through its opposition?

Building upon Baudrillard, Roland Barthes, and Judith Williamson's pioneering discourse analyses of advertisements as mythological systems, Robert Goldman and his coauthor Stephen Papson explicate the ways in which cultural meanings are sold. By positing a set of equivalences, ads reframe public meanings in order to enhance the meanings of "commodity-signs." From this approach, which is based on detailed analyses of the semiotic mechanics of ads, a new critique emerges. Rather than wants and needs, the conceptual building blocks are meaning and identity. The critic now has ammunition for challenging the meanings of commodities.

Susan Bordo uses this method to powerful effect in her analyses of how advertisements work as "gender ideology." Gendered advertisements represent the idealized woman as thin without having to struggle to be so, and frequently exploit many women's struggles to take control of their appetites and hunger. Advertising, in Bordo's argument, is a compelling symbolic arena in which patriarchal ideology, which seeks to maintain control over women's bodies and sexuality, is continually reproduced as an unintended consequence of advertisers' seeking out meanings that will sell product.

CONSUMERS' LIVED EXPERIENCES

The economic and cultural critiques are functionalist arguments in which consumers are imbricated into systems of superfluous benefits and commodified meanings, respectively. But how is it that people—whom we presume to be reasonably smart, industrious, diverse, and increasingly reflexive and cynical about marketing—allow this to happen? How do their actions as consumers work in concert with marketers' efforts to reproduce the system? The foregoing approaches do not provide fully satisfactory accounts of that process. A tradition of research initiated by the Centre for Contemporary Cultural Studies at the University of Birmingham (known as the "Birmingham School" or, more broadly, "British Cultural Studies"), pursued the question of how such structures play out in everyday life. Using detailed historical and ethnographic case studies this work links structuralist theories (such as Baudrillard's) with anthropological accounts of the production of meaning. The Birmingham School's most influential studies (including those by Stuart Hall, Paul Willis, Dick Hebdige, and others) examine how the everyday cultural practices found in British youth subcultures serve to reproduce class boundaries. This style of analysis is readily extended to broader questions about the organization of consumption in advanced capitalist societies. The essays in this volume offer vivid and nuanced depictions of the ways in which people use commodities to experience, challenge, and transform dominant cultural meanings.

Hebdige's chapter on Italian motor scooters is the most explicit examination of the ways in which commodities are used in everyday life while simultaneously locating these practices within "larger networks of relationships." His chronicle of the meanings of motor scooters begins with their introduction in Italy as a gendered (for the "new Italian woman"), cosmopolitan, and youthful mode of transportation. Migrating to Great Britain after World War II, the scooters' design elements, combined with their "Italianness," make them read as very feminine. These meanings were taken up by the emerging scooter clubs as well as movies (one of the early product-placement successes). This rearticulation produced the scooter as the perfect raw semiotic material for yet another movement, the Mods. The Mods were a highly stylized male youth subculture that fancied accouterments that screamed modern and (slightly) effeminate (in opposition to the vulgarities of the "rockers"). Hebdige continues the structuralist emphasis on meaning embedded in relational oppositions but, in the poststructuralist spirit, demonstrates how these meanings shift dramatically across place and time.

Janice Radway's famous ethnographic study shows how women use romance reading to manage their pleasures and identities within patriarchical relations. Digging beneath the common observation that women read romances "to escape," she describes the ways in which women bracket their demanding family and household care responsibilities—patriarchal constructs naturalized as what women are born to do—in order to gain emotional respite. By entering a fantasy world in which a heroine with burdens similar to her own gets her emotional and identity needs met, the romance reader is able to experience vicariously the pleasures of receiving the care that often goes unreciprocated in her own family. Romances are "exercises in extrapolation . . . experiments [that] explore the meaning and consequences of behavior accepted by contemporary society as characteristically masculine." In other words, the romances act as little mythologies, providing miraculous resolutions to the contradictory and often emotionally punishing nature of living in a culture dominated by men's interests. Radway's analysis, often considered only within the context of gender studies, offers an excellent treatment of the ways in which commodity logic works to capture powerful ideologies and pleasures. In a manner rather opposite that suggested by Galbraith and Ewen, the book market has evolved a carefully tailored formula to provide novels that will deliver the emotional safety valve demanded by women. This analysis entails a critique of consumer culture that addresses how the contradictions produced by patriarchy get channeled into the commodification process rather than generating political, legal, and cultural efforts to push for an egalitarian family structure.

Tom O'Guinn's study of the Central Midwest Barry Manilow Fan Club delves into a central phenomenon of consumer society: the consumption of celebrity. Informed primarily by cultural anthropology, O'Guinn views celebrity fandom as a modern-day religion. Barry Manilow fans go to great lengths to "touch greatness," that is, to develop a relationship with the star. While O'Guinn does not explicitly develop the societal implications of this pervasive and intensive type of activity, we think it provides an illuminating example of consumer society at work. As sociologists have long argued, modern social relations tend to drain absolutist faith. However, the need for the metaphysical moorings that religion provides does not disappear. Consumer society, as perhaps the most powerful locus of cultural meanings now available (along with the nation-state), has become a prime site for the rearticulation of religiosity. Thus, as O'Guinn documents, people from all walks of life engage in a new form of religious practice via famous actors, sports stars and teams, and other media-anointed icons.

As a group, these essays push for a more complicated critique of consumer society. If commodities are an important site through which the most consequential discourses of our time move, then they surely cannot be dismissed as superfluous needs, or even as mere constellations of social difference. A compelling critique must focus not on only on the quantity of consumption, but also on what happens when the primary structures of social difference and inequality (gender, nation, race, and class) are channeled through commodities. It is to those questions that we now turn.

THE REPRODUCTION OF SOCIAL INEQUALITY

Perhaps the most influential statement of the view that consumption structures social difference is Thorstein Veblen's 1899 *Theory of the Leisure Class*. With trenchant wit, Veblen argued that in modern society, wealth (rather than military prowess) had become the basis of social esteem. However, wealth is difficult to measure. Therefore, visible expenditure and the display of idleness become the primary means to communicate the possession of riches. The wealthiest display most ostentatiously, and new consumer trends appear first at the top. Then they trickle down the hierarchy. Of course, social hierarchies are not static. Veblen was writing in a time like our own—great fortunes were being made, and the nouveaux riches used luxury consumption (carriages, elaborately dressed servants, fancy dinner parties) to raise their social position. Central to Veblen's analyses were the ideas that consuming is a means of social communication; that it communicates class and income differences; and that within a society the valuations of goods are widely shared.

These premises also underlie Pierre Bourdieu's monumental work, *Distinction: A Social Critique of the Judgement of Taste*. Bourdieu, using French consumer surveys, went beyond showing the class patterning of consumption to argue that the very notion of taste is an important aspect of reproducing class differences. For Veblen, it was the cost of an item that was the crucial differentiator. Bourdieu showed that differentiation extended to areas where cost was hardly a factor, as in styles of art, music, decor, and film, and to how, rather than simply what, one consumed. Consumer tastes varied in predictable ways, and depended on "cultural capital"—family upbringing and formal education as well as economic resources. At each place in the social hierarchy, individuals were inculcated into specific taste groups. Bourdieu showed that the class patterning of consumption had become far more sophisticated and complex. Those in the higher reaches of the hierarchy used their superior taste to create "distinction" for themselves, and to distance themselves from those of inferior tastes. Thus, the possession of "good" taste became a mechanism whereby individuals assured their social and economic position; consumption, then, was an integral part of the reproduction of inequality. In Bourdieu's account, one gained the authority to be a manager, or a professional, not merely by specific skills but also by one's style of life. Consumption was no longer innocent, trivial, personal, or apolitical, but was directly linked to inequalities in production. Changing how people consume would be a necessary part of any egalitarian social transformation.

The contributions by Douglas Holt and Alex Kotlowitz build on these ideas. Holt's article is the first general application of Bourdieu's theories to the United States; previous research (e.g., David Halle) had looked at individual cultural forms, such as painting, and concluded that Bourdieu was wrong. By contrast, Holt finds clear class differences among his informants, which are expressed in the ways in which they consume (even more than what they choose). Those high in cultural capital apply a formal aesthetic sensibility to their consumption of food, decor, and mass media, in contrast to the functional aesthetic (emphasis on qualities such as durability) of low cultural capital consumers. Cultural elites also display more cosmopolitanism and connoisseurship in their choice of foods, travel, reading material, and decor. They seek out idiosyncratic consumer opportunities because they are much more sensitive about constructing a distinctive individual style. Those low in cultural capital remain willing participants in mass culture and mass taste. Kotlowitz, writing from a more Veblenian tradition, describes how the same labels and styles are now coveted by very different people—the impoverished African-American youth of inner-city Chicago and middle-class suburban kids both demand Hilfiger, Coach, Nike, and Hush Puppies. Veblen's simple trickle down from rich to poor has been inverted, even exploded, but visible symbols of status are alive and well. Returning to the theme of the earlier critiques, Kotlowitz argues that the fashion bond between the ghetto and suburban youth is a false one, as the economic deprivation, racism, and social isolation of the urban poor leaves them substantively miles away from the middle-class kids.

Ann duCille's penetrating piece also takes up the theme of racial differences. Looking at the history of how the Mattel corporation has introduced "multicultural" Barbies, duCille makes a sophisticated argument about the ways in which consumer society constructs categories of race. A "black" Barbie can have certain features ("pearly white teeth"), but not others (short or uncombable hair). As Mattel has moved into the lucrative "ethnic" market, it has done so in highly constrained and stereotypical ways, permitting only the "discursively familiar." Ethnic Barbies retain the bodies and class status of the normative (white) Barbie. The currently trendy commodification of "difference," duCille reminds us, is both an "impossible space," and an "anti-matter." Barbies remain mired in a relational hierarchy—as little girls put it, the white Barbie is the real one.

CONSUMING AS LIBERATION

Nearly all the premises of critics of consumer society were challenged in the academic debates of the 1980s and 1990s. Veblen, whose influence in the American literature had been profound, was a ritual target of attack. Academics argued that consumption was not a form of social communication, that people were unable to read the "code" of consumer meanings, that advertisers had little control over how consumers constructed meaning. The old social hierarchies were dead; consumption had become a democratic exercise in which anybody could be anything merely by donning the right outfit or car or style. These accounts challenged the Veblenian idea that consumer innovation flowed from top to bottom, they argued against the view that group identities were formed through consumer patterns, and they emphasized the use of commodities to construct individual, creative selves. Instead of being a passive form of mass conformity, consuming was seen as a resistant, liberatory, and creative act. Scholars wrote about the pleasure, enjoyment, escape, and fantasy of consuming. Bourdieu's hierarchies of taste were seen to have broken down, as high art collapsed into mass culture. It was an anything-goes, chaotic world. Some argued that production and consumption were no longer part of a unified structure; consumption had eclipsed production as the driving force, with production relegated to a relatively minor and adaptive role. The classic critiques were denounced as elitist, moralistic, ascetic, puritanical, mechanical, and out of touch with the consumer experience. (This is the position represented by James

Twitchell.) In a related, but more critical vein, a wide variety of work in mass communication and cultural studies has advocated a liberatory view, suggesting that many progressive political possibilities germinate in popular consumption. Elizabeth Wilson and John Fiske represent this view.

One of the most common arguments against consumer critics is that they are ascetic (often academic) elites whose status is constructed in opposition to hedonic pleasures. Therefore they aim to deny the bounty of capitalism to the hoi polloi. James Twitchell has become a witty, if not always persuasive, debunker of this anti-hedonist bias among consumer critics. In some ways, his argument is similar to that found in influential anthropological accounts, such as those of Mary Douglas and Douglas Isherwood or Grant McCracken, which take the view that material goods are the primary vehicle for experiencing meaning. What Twitchell adds is a positive spin on this manufactured meaning system, a pure consumer attitude: we love to spend, stuff is our new religion, it makes us happy, it gives us purpose, and, besides, it's our nature to be materially acquisitive. Forget the dour, puritanical attitudes to spending. The consumer is king and virtually anything goes. Relax and enjoy the ride.

Elizabeth Wilson stakes out a feminist politics of fashion that can be readily generalized to a politics of consumption. Wilson argues against an unproductive division between a puritanical moralism that labels as oppressive any normative pressures to be fashionable and a liberal populism that welcomes all forms of pleasure (à la Twitchell). She demonstrates, in arguments that are closely aligned to those of Baudrillard and Barthes, the impossibility of escaping the fashion system either through "feminist style" or through expressing "personal preferences." Like Bourdieu, she locates feminist style in its appropriate milieu as the dress of cultural elites. Her arguments—that fashion is always impregnated with social meanings and aesthetic considerations, and that it can be played for pleasure as much as for social position—make fashion a form of aesthetic agency that allows for sociopolitical critique as well as a search for alternative ways of living. The pointlessness of fashion, which Veblen hated, is precisely what makes it valuable. It is in this marginalized area of the contingent, the decorative, and the futile, that not simply a new aesthetic but a new cultural order may seed itself. Out of the "cracks in the pavement of cities grow the weeds that begin to rot the fabric, i.e., aesthetic creativity."

John Fiske is frequently cited as offering the most celebratory view of the ways in which structures of social domination can be resisted through consumption. Drawing upon Antonio Gramsci and Michel de Certeau, Fiske analyzes a variety of consumer activities—shopping, watching television, fashion, listening to rock music—to view "tactical raids" on patriarchal capitalism. Fiske finds that subordinated groups (women, people of color, the working class) use commodities to pursue their own socio-cultural interests, albeit in ways that will never threaten the political-economic underpinnings of the system. In the analysis of mall shopping we excerpt, a careful reading will reveal that Fiske's arguments are more subtle than he is often given credit for. Fiske is concerned with redressing the structuralist emphasis on consumer society as an oppressive system that tends to avoid any consideration of how the oppressed are actually managing their lives within this oppression. To his credit, Fiske demands that elite critics recognize that the oppressed use cultural strategies to compensate for what they are denied economically and politically. What Fiske does not address, however, is the political and economic effects of the pursuit of interest through sociocultural identity.

EVERYTHING A COMMODITY?
THE POSTMODERN MARKET

Much of the debate about consumer society has centered on questions of quantity—excessive consumption, proliferation of new needs. But a second theme, stemming from Marx and Georg Lukacs, emphasizes that at the center of consumer society is a process—goods become commodities, moving through a "circuit" specific to capitalist economies. While this process has occurred since the beginnings of capitalism, vast new arenas are now being commodified—from education and health care to culture itself.

The papers in this section reveal the ways in which culture, embodied in concepts such as personal identity, alterity, dissent, and style, have all become grist for the marketer's mill. These are the new commodities that the market is capitalizing on. In a prescient and sophisticated contribution on this theme, bell hooks analyzes the ways in which racial and cultural differences are sold in contemporary America, through a "consumer cannibalism" in which white middle-class consumers want to "eat" the commodified other: white college boys aspire to be transformed by erotic sexual encounters with black women's bodies; bored suburbanites crave the exotic primitive sold in apparel catalogues. Blackness and primitiveness stand in for true pleasure, which consumer culture, despite its hedonistic tendencies, is now unable to deliver. While hooks acknowledges that these trends represent an opening that does challenge white supremacy and gender structures, she also warns that they often contain new, subtle messages of racism and sexism. Malcolm Gladwell's essay describes how the consumption of otherness is now occurring through the search for the newest, coolest trends, a search carried out largely in the inner cities and in youth subcultures. This account of contemporary marketing practices reveals how much the market has changed in the last forty years.

In a forthcoming paper, one of us (Holt) has argued that this post-modern marketplace differs in fundamental ways from the world that the earlier critical thinkers were responding to. In the accounts of Adorno and Horkheimer, Galbraith, Friedan, Baudrillard, and others, marketers possessed tremendous "cultural authority." They were able to inscribe products with meanings, and convince people they needed those products and meanings. While the literature has tended to treat these arguments in absolutist terms (as either true or false), it is important to remember their historic context. Beginning in the 1920s, marketing emerged as a profession, with a self-confident project of social transformation. Marketing gurus, of whom Ernest Dichter with his "motivation research" is the most infamous example, presented their techniques as scientific. When viewed from within the zeitgeist of the period—the success of Hitler and Mussolini in using propaganda, the zenith of belief in positivist science, and the widespread belief in the possibility of social engineering through behaviorism, Freudian psychology, and the like—the idea that marketers could actually "organize" consumers must have been irresistible.

But such an era was not to last. As the social engineering approach became public, it encountered great resistance. (After all, who wants to be manipulated and programmed?) There ensued a broad attack on the deadening conformity of mass culture—witness the popularity of such authors as Galbraith, Packard, Friedan, Marcuse, and William Whyte. By the early 1960s the cultural authority of the market was under siege. As Thomas Frank's piece shows, Madison Avenue was not to take this siege lying down. With a flexibility that shows how truly resilient consumer culture can be, Madison Avenue was able to turn the critique of itself into another advertising strategy. Frank's contribution looks at how the Volkswagen bug was positioned as a statement against corporate conformity. In effect Madison Avenue was able to mobilize popular resentment against itself to reproduce itself. This was a trend that would continue for decades, in various ways, ending with countercultural icons such as William Burroughs, Jack Kerouac, and the Beatles showing up in commercials for Nike, the Gap, and Apple Computers.

Marketing learned a lesson from this attack: People must experience consumption as a volitional site of personal development, achievement, and self-creation, not as a place in which they are simply mapping their lives on some advertiser's template. Over time the field evolved away from a top-down approach toward one in which consumers provide the innovation for new trends and meanings (c.f., the "coolhunt," described by Gladwell). Thus, marketers realize that they no longer need to create meaning, they only need to mobilize it. The logic of branding today is that Nike, for instance, does not aim to attach particular meanings to its product; it just needs to attach the swoosh to any person, place, or thing that is granted cultural value in the world of sport. Thus, monopolizing the public channels of meaning creation is becoming more important than monopolizing *particular* meanings. Two developments made this change feasible. On the one hand, the increasing role of brands, which often differentiate functionally equivalent products, elevated the importance of symbolism. Second, new more flexible production technologies allow a proliferation of customized products and niche markets, which grants the consumer far more choice (and "creativity"). Mass production is no longer so "mass."

And yet the profitability of consumer corporations appears unassailable. They were able to relinquish certain forms of control to consumers while still retaining market power over other phases of the circuit of capital. Gladwell's street-level innovators capture very little of the value they produce. Furthermore, and this is the enduring wisdom of the earlier critiques, particularly that of Adorno and Horkheimer, the postmodern marketplace retains the idea that subjectivity is created, and naturalized, through consuming. Indeed, the commodity form continues to gain stature as the preeminent site through which people experience and express the social world, even as the worlds that are channeled through it are orchestrated less by marketers than by consumers.

In this contemporary marketplace, escaping the commodity form becomes increasingly difficult. Difference, dissent, resistance, opposition— they all resurface as consumables, whether through the purchase of a black Barbie, a Working Assets telephone card, or a Patagonia organic t-shirt. A recent popular anticonsumer manifesto by Naomi Klein has its own "NoLogo" logo; opposition ads are another form of ad. Is it possible to escape a world of such ubiquitous commodification?

ALTERNATIVES TO CONSUMER SOCIETY

The contributions in the last section of the book provide an optimistic answer to this question and offer a variety of stances from which to challenge consumer culture. Taken together, they are a rough roadmap of most of the forces that are now arrayed in an emergent anticonsumerist movement: environmentalists, spiritualists engaged in lives of voluntary simplicity, culture jammers, labor-oriented feminists, critics of capitalist production, and advocates for a new quality of life politics.

The section begins with an excerpt from Duane Elgin's classic book *Voluntary Simplicity*. This perspective has gained many adherents in recent years, as millions of Americans have begun searching for more meaning, spirituality, intentionality, and simplicity in their lives. While most have not gone as far as Elgin advocates, downshifting has been one of the fastest-growing trends of the 1990s. Elgin's strategy might be somewhat flippantly described as the rejection of "just do it" in favor of "just say no" to consumerism.

By contrast, Kalle Lasn advocates a far more radical, and oppositional, strategy. Building on the politics of the French Situationists, who believed in staging dramatic social moments that would illuminate the alienating nature of the "society of the spectacle," Lasn has catalyzed a growing movement of "culture jammers." Culture jammers are using sub-vertising, de-marketing, and the "un-cooling" of everything from fashion to fast food to auto transport. Through their own sophisticated marketing, employing the consumer culture itself, they de-legitimate the premise of "I consume, therefore I am," which lies at the core of the postmodern marketplace. In their view, true subjectivity arises only through an invigorating encounter with consumer culture.

Angela McRobbie and Frithjof Bergmann, each in their own way, tie changes in consumption to new structures of production. McRobbie's essay addresses the exploitation of female garment workers in the small workshops of London, and she argues that a neighborhood-based system linking fashion designers, local customers, and well-paid workers could provide a new, relational economic model in which the forging of community creates security, a decent standard of living, and a measure of consumer and producer sovereignty. Her piece is especially innovative in its linking of feminist perspectives, economic development, and consumer concerns. Bergmann argues for a thorough overhauling of current production systems in favor of what he has termed "New Work." The New Work movement, now gaining adherents in many countries, emphasizes the importance of work as a calling, dramatically curtailed hours of labor, and economic self-sufficiency through self-provisioning with sophisticated new technologies. Arguing strongly that consumption is mainly compensatory—a doomed attempt to deal with the painful alienation of modern life—Bergmann believes that when work is empowering, people will lose interest in high-consumption lifestyles. De-marketing will proceed virtually automatically.

Betsy Taylor and David Tilford provide a damning ecological critique of middle-class lifestyles. On the basis of an extensive review of the literature, they conclude that we cannot continue to consume stocks of natural resources and devastate renewable resources at current levels. This environmental critique is among the most compelling ever leveled at consumer society, and has gained tremendous resonance in recent years. Finally, Juliet Schor, in her call for a new politics of consumption, attacks the paralyzing logic of noninterference in consumer markets, arguing that the basic premises of that view are not supportable by the evidence. She believes that erosion in the quality of life for many middle-class consumers is creating the conditions for an emerging anticonsumerist coalition.

Thus, we conclude the volume hopefully, for at least two reasons. First, while acknowledging the difficulty of remaining un-co-opted in the postmodern marketplace, these contributions affirm the possibility that politically self-conscious individuals and movements can take truly oppositional stances toward consumer society. Second, we see tremendous potential in the newly forged alliances among trade unionists, environmentalists, culture jammers, simple livers, and other opponents of consumer society. It is our hope that this volume, by helping to elucidate the dynamics and structures of that society, may prove useful in the struggle.

A NOTE ABOUT OUR SELECTIONS

The literature on consumer society is vast. To produce a collection of reasonable length, we have had to exclude many articles, authors, and topics. The most glaring of these omissions is undoubtedly the debate about the globalization of consumer culture. Because this literature is so large and varied, we believe it deserves a volume of its own. Hence, the perspective of this collection is heavily North American.

PART ONE

The Consumer Society Critique

Theodor W. Adorno and Max Horkheimer
"THE CULTURE INDUSTRY: ENLIGHTENMENT AS MASS DECEPTION"
(1944)

The sociological theory that the loss of the support of objectively established religion, the dissolution of the last remnants of precapitalism, together with technological and social differentiation or specialization, have led to cultural chaos is disproved every day; for culture now impresses the same stamp on everything. Films, radio and magazines make up a system which is uniform as a whole and in every part. Even the aesthetic activities of political opposites are one in their enthusiastic obedience to the rhythm of the iron system. The decorative industrial management buildings and exhibition centers in authoritarian countries are much the same as anywhere else. The huge gleaming towers that shoot up everywhere are outward signs of the ingenious planning of international concerns, toward which the unleashed entrepreneurial system (whose monuments are a mass of gloomy houses and business premises in grimy, spiritless cities) was already hastening. Even now the older houses just outside the concrete city centers look like slums, and the new bungalows on the outskirts are at one with the flimsy structures of world fairs in their praise of technical progress and their built-in demand to be discarded after a short while like empty food cans. Yet the city housing projects designed to perpetuate the individual as a supposedly independent unit in a small hygienic dwelling make him all the more subservient to his adversary—the absolute power of capitalism. Because the inhabitants, as producers and as consumers, are drawn into the center in search of work and pleasure, all the living units crystallize into well-organized complexes. The striking unity of microcosm and macrocosm presents men with a model of their culture: the false identity of the general and the particular. Under monopoly all mass culture is identical, and the lines of its artificial framework begin to show through. The people at the top are no longer so interested in concealing monopoly: as its violence becomes more open, so its power grows. Movies and radio need no longer pretend to be art. The truth that they are just business is made into an ideology in order to justify the rubbish they deliberately produce. They call themselves industries;

and when their directors' incomes are published, any doubt about the social utility of the finished products is removed.

Interested parties explain the culture industry in technological terms. It is alleged that because millions participate in it, certain reproduction processes are necessary that inevitably require identical needs in innumerable places to be satisfied with identical goods. The technical contrast between the few production centers and the large number of widely dispersed consumption points is said to demand organization and planning by management. Furthermore, it is claimed that standards were based in the first place on consumers' needs, and for that reason were accepted with so little resistance. The result is the circle of manipulation and retroactive need in which the unity of the system grows ever stronger. No mention is made of the fact that the basis on which technology acquires power over society is the power of those whose economic hold over society is greatest. A technological rationale is the rationale of domination itself. It is the coercive nature of society alienated from itself. Automobiles, bombs, and movies keep the whole thing together until their leveling element shows its strength in the very wrong which it furthered. It has made the technology of the culture industry no more than the achievement of standardization and mass production, sacrificing whatever involved a distinction between the logic of the work and that of the social system. This is the result not of a law of movement in technology as such but of its function in today's economy. The need which might resist central control has already been suppressed by the control of the individual consciousness. The step from the telephone to the radio has clearly distinguished the roles. The former still allowed the subscriber to play the role of subject, and was liberal. The latter is democratic: it turns all participants into listeners and authoritatively subjects them to broadcast programs which are all exactly the same. No machinery of rejoinder has been devised, and private broadcasters are denied any freedom. They are confined to the apocryphal field of the "amateur," and also have to accept organization from above. But any trace of spontaneity from the public in official broadcasting is controlled and absorbed by talent scouts, studio competitions and official programs of every kind selected by professionals. Talented performers belong to the industry long before it displays them; otherwise they would not be so eager to fit in. The attitude of the public, which ostensibly and actually favors the system of the culture industry, is a part of the system and not an excuse for it. If one branch of art follows the same formula as one with a very different medium and content; if the dramatic intrigue of broadcast soap operas becomes no more than useful material for showing how to master technical problems at both ends of the scale of musical experience—real jazz or a cheap imitation; or if a movement from a Beethoven symphony is crudely "adapted" for a film sound-track in the same way as a Tolstoy novel is garbled in a film script: then the claim that this is done to satisfy the spontaneous wishes of the public is no more than hot air. We are closer to the facts if we explain these phenomena as inherent in the technical and personnel apparatus which, down to its last cog, itself forms part of the economic mechanism of selection. In addition there is the agreement—or at least the determination—of all executive authorities not to produce or sanction anything that in any way differs from their own rules, their own ideas about consumers, or above all themselves.

In our age the objective social tendency is incarnate in the hidden subjective purposes of company directors, the foremost among whom are in the most powerful sectors of industry—steel, petroleum, electricity, and chemicals. Culture monopolies are weak and dependent in comparison. They cannot afford to neglect their appeasement of the real holders of power if their sphere of activity in mass society (a sphere producing a specific type of commodity which anyhow is still too closely bound up with easygoing liberalism and Jewish intellectuals) is not to undergo a series of purges. The dependence of the most powerful broadcasting company on the electrical industry, or of the motion picture industry on the banks, is characteristic of the whole sphere, whose individual branches are themselves economically interwoven. All are in such close contact that the extreme concentration of mental forces allows demarcation lines between different firms and technical branches to be ignored. The ruthless unity in the culture industry is evidence of what will happen in politics. Marked differentiations such as those of A and B films, or of stories in magazines in different price ranges, depend not so much on subject matter as on classifying, organizing, and labeling consumers. Something is provided for all so that none may escape; the distinctions are emphasized and extended. The public is catered for with a hierarchical range of mass-produced products of varying quality, thus advancing the rule of complete quantification. Everybody must behave (as if spontaneously) in accordance with his previously determined and indexed level, and choose the category of mass product turned out for his type. Consumers appear as statistics on research organization charts, and are divided by income groups into red, green, and blue areas; the technique is that used for any type of propaganda.

How formalized the procedure is can be seen when the mechanically differentiated products prove to be all alike in the end. That the difference between the Chrysler range and General Motors products is basically illusory strikes every child with a keen interest in varieties. What connoisseurs discuss as good or bad points serve only to perpetuate the semblance of competition and range of choice. The same applies to the Warner Brothers and Metro Goldwyn Mayer productions. But even the differences between the more expensive and cheaper models put out by the same firm steadily diminish: for automobiles, there are such differences as the number of cylinders, cubic capacity, details of patented gadgets; and for films there are the number of stars, the extravagant use of technology, labor, and equipment, and the introduction of the latest psychological formulas. The universal criterion of merit is the amount of "conspicuous production," of blatant cash investment. The varying budgets in the culture industry do not bear the slightest relation to factual values, to the meaning of the products themselves. Even the technical media are relentlessly forced into uniformity. Television aims at a synthesis of radio and film, and is held up only because the interested parties have not yet reached agreement, but its consequences will be quite enormous and promise to intensify the impoverishment of aesthetic matter so drastically, that by tomorrow the thinly veiled identity of all industrial culture products can come triumphantly out into the open, derisively fulfilling the Wagnerian dream of the *Gesamtkunstwerk*—the fusion of all the arts in one work. The alliance of word, image, and music is all the more perfect than in *Tristan* because the sensuous elements which all approvingly reflect the surface of social reality are in principle embodied in the same technical process, the unity of which becomes its distinctive content. This process integrates all the elements of the production, from the novel (shaped with an eye to the film) to the last sound effect. It is the triumph of invested capital, whose title as absolute master is etched deep into the hearts of the dispossessed in the employment line; it is the meaningful content of every film, whatever plot the production team may have selected.

The man with leisure has to accept what the culture manufacturers offer him. Kant's formalism still expected a contribution from the individual, who was thought to relate the varied experiences of the senses to fundamental concepts; but industry robs the individual of his function. Its prime service to the customer is to do his schematizing for him. Kant said that there was a secret mechanism in the soul which prepared direct intuitions in such a way that they could be fitted into the system of pure reason. But today that secret has been deciphered. While the mechanism is to all appearances planned by those who serve up the data of experience, that is, by the culture industry, it is in fact forced upon the latter by the power of society, which remains irrational, however we may try to rationalize it; and this inescapable force is processed by commercial agencies so that they give an artificial impression of being in command. There is nothing left for the consumer to classify. Producers have done it for him. Art for the masses has destroyed the dream but still conforms to the tenets of that dreaming idealism which critical idealism balked at. Everything derives from consciousness: for Malebranche and Berkeley, from the consciousness of God; in mass art, from the consciousness of the production team. Not only are the hit songs, stars, and soap operas cyclically recurrent and rigidly invariable types, but the specific content of the entertainment itself is derived from them and only appears to change. The details are interchangeable. The short interval sequence which was effective in a hit song, the hero's momentary fall from grace (which he accepts as good sport), the rough treatment which the beloved gets from the male star, the latter's rugged defiance of the spoilt heiress, are, like all the other details, ready-made clichés to be slotted in anywhere; they never do anything more than fulfill the purpose allotted them in the overall plan. Their whole *raison d'être* is to confirm it by being its constituent parts. As soon as the film begins, it is quite clear how it will end, and who will be rewarded, punished, or forgotten. In light music, once the trained ear has heard the first notes of the hit song, it can guess what is coming and feel flattered when it does come. The average length of the short story has to be rigidly adhered to. Even gags, effects, and jokes are calculated like the setting in which they are placed. They are the responsibility of special experts and their narrow range makes it easy for them to be apportioned in the office. The development of the culture industry has led to the predominance of the effect, the obvious touch, and the technical detail over the work itself—which once expressed an idea, but was liquidated together with the idea. When the detail won its freedom, it became rebellious and, in the period from Romanticism to Expressionism, asserted itself as free expression, as a vehicle of protest against the organization. In music the single harmonic effect obliterated the awareness of form as a whole; in painting the individual color was stressed at the expense of pictorial composition; and in the novel psychology became more important than structure. The totality of the culture industry has put an end to this. Though concerned exclusively with effects, it crushes their insubordination and makes them subserve the formula, which replaces the work. The same fate is inflicted on whole and parts alike. The whole inevitably bears no relation to the details—just like the career of a successful man into which everything is made to fit as an illustration or a proof, whereas it is nothing more than the sum of all those idiotic events. The so-called dominant idea is like a file which ensures order but not coherence. The whole and the parts are alike; there is no antithesis and no connection. Their prearranged harmony is a mockery of what had to be striven after in the great bourgeois works of art. In Germany the graveyard stillness of the dictatorship already hung over the gayest films of the democratic era.

The whole world is made to pass through the filter of the culture industry. The old experience of the movie-goer, who sees the world outside as an extension of the film he has just left (because the latter is intent upon reproducing the world of everyday perceptions), is now the producer's guideline. The more intensely and flawlessly his techniques duplicate empirical objects, the easier it is today for the illusion to prevail that the outside world is the straightforward continuation of that presented on the screen. This purpose has been furthered by mechanical reproduction since the lightning takeover by the sound film.

Real life is becoming indistinguishable from the movies. The sound film, far surpassing the theater of illusion, leaves no room for imagination or reflection on the part of the audience, who is unable to respond within the structure of the film, yet deviate from its precise detail without losing the thread of the story; hence the film forces its victims to equate it directly with reality. The stunting of the mass-media consumer's powers of imagination and spontaneity does not have to be traced back to any psychological mechanisms; he must ascribe the loss of those attributes to the objective nature of the products themselves, especially to the most characteristic of them, the sound film. They are so designed that quickness, powers of observation, and experience are undeniably needed to apprehend them at all; yet sustained thought is out of the question if the spectator is not to miss the relentless rush of facts. Even though the effort required for his response is semi-automatic, no scope is left for the imagination. Those who are so absorbed by the world of the movie—by its images, gestures, and words—that they are unable to supply what really makes it a world, do not have to dwell on particular points of its mechanics during a screening. All the other films and products of the entertainment industry which they have seen have taught them what to expect: they react automatically. The might of industrial society is lodged in men's minds. The entertainments manufacturers know that their products will be consumed with alertness even when the customer is distraught, for each of them is a model of the huge economic machinery which has always sustained the masses, whether at work or at leisure—which is akin to work. From every sound film and every broadcast program the social effect can be inferred which is exclusive to none but is shared by all alike. The culture industry as a whole has molded men as a type unfailingly reproduced in every product. All the agents of this process, from the producer to the women's clubs, take good care that the simple reproduction of this mental state is not nuanced or extended in any way.

The art historians and guardians of culture who complain of the extinction in the West of a basic style-determining power are wrong. The stereotyped appropriation of everything, even the inchoate, for the purposes of mechanical reproduction surpasses the rigor and general currency of any "real style," in the sense in which cultural *cognoscenti* celebrate the organic precapitalist past. No Palestrina could be more of a purist in eliminating every unprepared and unresolved discord than the jazz arranger in suppressing any development which does not conform to the jargon. When jazzing up Mozart he changes him not only when he is too serious or too difficult but when he harmonizes the melody in a different way, perhaps more simply, than is customary now. No medieval builder can have scrutinized the subjects for church windows and sculptures more suspiciously than the studio hierarchy scrutinizes a work by Balzac or Hugo before finally approving it. No medieval theologian could have determined the degree of the torment to be suffered by the damned in accordance with the *ordo* of divine love more meticulously than the producers of shoddy epics calculate the torture to be undergone by the hero or the exact point to which the leading lady's hemline shall be raised. The explicit and implicit, exoteric and esoteric catalog of the forbidden and tolerated is so extensive that it not only defines the area of freedom but is all-powerful inside it. Everything down to the last detail is shaped accordingly. Like its counterpart, avant-garde art, the entertainment industry determines its own language, down to its very syntax and vocabulary, by the use of anathema. The constant pressure to produce new effects (which must conform to the old pattern) serves merely as another rule to increase the power of the conventions when any single effect threatens to slip through the net. Every detail is so firmly stamped with sameness that nothing can appear which is not marked at birth, or does not meet with approval at first sight. And the star performers, whether they produce or reproduce, use this jargon as freely and fluently and with as much gusto as if it were the very language which it silenced long ago. Such is the ideal of what is natural in this field of activity, and its influence becomes all the more powerful, the more technique is perfected and diminishes the tension between the finished product and everyday life. The paradox of this routine, which is essentially travesty, can be detected and is often predominant in everything that the culture industry turns out. A jazz musician who is playing a piece of serious music, one of Beethoven's simplest minuets, syncopates it involuntarily and will smile superciliously when asked to follow the normal divisions of the beat. This is the "nature" which, complicated by the ever-present and extravagant demands of the specific medium, constitutes the new style and is a "system of non-culture, to which one might even concede a certain 'unity of style' if it really made any sense to speak of stylized barbarity."[1]

The universal imposition of this stylized mode can even go beyond what is quasi-officially sanctioned or forbidden; today a hit song is more readily forgiven for not observing the 32 beats or the compass of the ninth than for containing even the most clandestine melodic or harmonic detail which does not conform to the idiom. Whenever Orson Welles offends against the tricks of the trade, he is forgiven because his departures from the norm are regarded as calculated mutations which serve all the more strongly to confirm the validity of the system. The constraint of the technically-conditioned idiom which stars and directors have to produce as "nature" so that the people can appropriate it, extends to such fine nuances that they almost attain the subtlety of the devices of an avant-garde work as against those of truth. The rare capacity minutely to fulfill the obligations of the natural idiom in all branches of the culture industry becomes the criterion of efficiency. What and how they say it must be measurable by everyday language, as in logical positivism. The producers are experts. The idiom demands an astounding productive power, which it absorbs and squanders. In a diabolical way it has overreached the culturally conservative distinction between genuine and artificial style. A style might be called artificial which is imposed from without on the refractory impulses of a form. But in the culture industry every element of the subject matter has its origin in the same apparatus as that jargon whose stamp it bears. The quarrels in which the artistic experts become involved with sponsor and censor about a lie going beyond the bounds of credibility are evidence not so much of an inner aesthetic tension as of a divergence of interests. The reputation of the specialist, in which a last remnant of objective independence sometimes finds refuge, conflicts with the business politics of the Church, or the concern which is manufacturing the cultural commodity. But the thing itself has been essentially objectified and made viable before the established authorities began to argue about it. Even before Zanuck acquired her, Saint Bernadette was regarded by her latter-day hagiographer as brilliant propaganda for all interested parties. That is what became of the emotions of the character. Hence the style of the culture industry, which no longer has to test itself against any refractory material, is also the negation of style. The reconciliation of the general and particular, of the rule and the specific demands of the subject matter, the achievement of which alone gives essential, meaningful content to style, is futile because there has ceased to be the slightest tension between opposite poles: these concordant extremes are dismally identical; the general can replace the particular, and vice versa.

Nevertheless, this caricature of style does not amount to something beyond the genuine style of the past. In the culture industry the notion of genuine style is seen to be the aesthetic equivalent of domination. Style considered as mere aesthetic regularity is a romantic dream of the past. The unity of style not only of the Christian Middle Ages but of the Renaissance expresses in each case the different structure of social power, and not the obscure experience of the oppressed in which the general was enclosed. The great artists were never those who embodied a wholly flawless and perfect style, but those who used style as a way of hardening themselves against the chaotic expression of suffering, as a negative truth. The style of their works gave what was expressed that force without which life flows away unheard. Those very art forms which are known as classical, such as Mozart's music, contain objective trends which represent something different to the style which they incarnate. As late as Schönberg and Picasso, the great artists have retained a mistrust of style, and at crucial points have subordinated it to the logic of the matter. What Dadaists and Expressionists called the untruth of style as such triumphs today in the sung jargon of a crooner, in the carefully contrived elegance of a film star, and even in the admirable expertise of a photograph of a peasant's squalid hut. Style represents a promise in every work of art. That which is expressed is subsumed through style into the dominant forms of generality, into the language of music, painting, or words, in the hope that it will be reconciled thus with the idea of true generality. This promise held out by the work of art that it will create truth by lending new shape to the conventional social forms is as necessary as it is hypocritical. It unconditionally posits the real forms of life as it is by suggesting that fulfillment lies in their aesthetic derivatives. To this extent the claim of art is always ideology too. However, only in this confrontation with tradition of which style is the record can art express suffering. That factor in a work of art which enables it to transcend reality certainly cannot be detached from style; but it does not consist of the harmony actually realized, of any doubtful unity of form and content, within and without, of individual and society; it is to be found in those features in which discrepancy appears: in the necessary failure of the passionate striving for identity. Instead of exposing itself to this failure in which the style of the great work of art has always achieved self-negation, the inferior work has always relied on its similarity with others—on a surrogate identity.

In the culture industry this imitation finally becomes absolute. Having ceased to be anything but style, it reveals the latter's secret: obedience to the social hierarchy. Today aesthetic barbarity completes what has threatened the creations of the spirit since they were gathered together as culture and neutralized. To speak of culture was always contrary to culture. Culture as a common denominator already contains in embryo that schematization and process of cataloging and classification which bring culture within the sphere of administration. And it is precisely the industrialized, the consequent, subsumption which entirely accords with this notion of culture. By subordinating in the same way and to the same end all areas of intellectual creation, by occupying men's senses from the time they leave the factory in the evening to the time they clock in again the next morning with matter that bears the impress of the labor process they themselves have to sustain throughout the day, this subsumption mockingly satisfies the concept of a unified culture which the philosophers of personality contrasted with mass culture. . . .

. . . The culture industry perpetually cheats its consumers of what it perpetually promises. The promissory note which, with its plots and staging, it draws on pleasure is endlessly prolonged; the promise, which is actually all the spectacle consists of, is illusory: all it actually confirms is that the real point will never be reached, that the diner must be satisfied with the menu. In front of the appetite stimulated by all those brilliant names and images there is finally set no more than a commendation of the depressing everyday world it sought to escape. Of course works of art were not sexual exhibitions either. However, by representing deprivation as negative, they retracted, as it were, the prostitution of the impulse and rescued by mediation what was denied. The secret of aesthetic sublimation is its representation of fulfillment as a broken promise. The culture industry does not sublimate; it represses. By repeatedly exposing the objects of desire, breasts in a clinging sweater or the naked torso of the athletic hero, it only stimulates the unsublimated forepleasure which habitual deprivation has long since reduced to a masochistic semblance. There is no erotic situation which, while insinuating and exciting, does not fail to indicate unmistakably that things can never go that far. The Hays Office merely confirms the ritual of Tantalus that the culture industry has established anyway. Works of art are ascetic and unashamed; the culture industry is pornographic and prudish. Love is downgraded to romance. And, after the descent, much is permitted; even license as a marketable speciality has its quota bearing the trade description "daring." The mass production of the sexual automatically achieves its repression. Because of his ubiquity, the film star with whom one is meant to fall in love is from the outset a copy of himself. Every tenor voice comes to sound like a Caruso record, and the "natural" faces of Texas girls are like the successful models by whom Hollywood has typecast them. The mechanical reproduction of beauty, which reactionary cultural fanaticism wholeheartedly serves in its methodical idolization of individuality, leaves no room for that unconscious idolatry which was once essential to beauty. The triumph over beauty is celebrated by humor—the *Schadenfreude* that every successful deprivation calls forth. There is laughter because there is nothing to laugh at. Laughter, whether conciliatory or terrible, always occurs when some fear passes. It indicates liberation either from physical danger or from the grip of logic. Conciliatory laughter is heard as the echo of an escape from power; the wrong kind overcomes fear by capitulating to the forces which are to be feared. It is the echo of power as something inescapable. Fun is a medicinal bath. The pleasure industry never fails to prescribe it. It makes laughter the instrument of the fraud practiced on happiness. Moments of happiness are without laughter; only operettas and films portray sex to the accompaniment of resounding laughter. But Baudelaire is as devoid of humor as Hölderlin. In the false society laughter is a disease which has attacked happiness and is drawing it into its worthless totality. To laugh at something is always to deride it, and the life which, according to Bergson, in laughter breaks through the barrier, is actually an invading barbaric life, self-assertion prepared to parade its liberation from any scruple when the social occasion arises. Such a laughing audience is a parody of humanity. Its members are monads, all dedicated to the pleasure of being ready for anything at the expense of everyone else. Their harmony is a caricature of solidarity. What is fiendish about this false laughter is that it is a compelling parody of the best, which is conciliatory. Delight is austere: *res severa verum gaudium*. The monastic theory that not asceticism but the sexual act denotes the renunciation of attainable bliss receives negative confirmation in the gravity of the lover who with foreboding commits his life to the fleeting moment. In the culture industry, jovial denial takes the place of the pain found in ecstasy and in asceticism. The supreme law is that they shall not satisfy their desires at any price; they must laugh and be content with laughter. In every product of the culture industry, the permanent denial imposed by civilization is once again unmistakably demonstrated and inflicted on its victims. To offer and to deprive them of something is one and the same. This is what happens in erotic films. Precisely because it must never take place, everything centers upon copulation. In films it is more strictly forbidden for an illegitimate relationship to be admitted without the parties being punished than for a millionaire's future son-in-law to be active in the labor movement. In contrast to the liberal era, industrialized as well as popular culture may wax indignant at capitalism, but it cannot renounce the threat of castration. This is fundamental. It outlasts the organized acceptance of the uniformed seen in the films which are produced to that end, and in reality. What is decisive today is no longer puritanism, although it still asserts itself in the form of women's organizations, but the necessity inherent in the system not to leave the customer alone, not for a moment to allow him any suspicion that resistance is possible. The principle dictates that he should be shown all his needs as capable of fulfillment, but that those needs should be so predetermined that he feels himself to be the eternal consumer, the object of the culture industry. Not only does it make him believe that the deception it practices is satisfaction, but it goes further and implies that, whatever the state of affairs, he must put up with what is offered. The escape from everyday drudgery which the whole culture industry promises may be compared to the daughter's abduction in the cartoon: the father is holding the ladder in the dark. The paradise offered by the culture industry is the same old drudgery. Both escape and elopement are predesigned to lead back to the starting point. Pleasure promotes the resignation which it ought to help to forget.

Amusement, if released from every restraint, would not only be the antithesis of art but its extreme role. The Mark Twain absurdity with which the American culture industry flirts at times might be a corrective of art. The more seriously the latter regards the incompatibility with life, the more it resembles the seriousness of life, its antithesis; the more effort it devotes to developing wholly from its own formal law, the more effort it demands from the intelligence to neutralize its burden. In some revue films, and especially in the grotesque and the funnies, the possibility of this negation does glimmer for a few moments. But of course it cannot happen. Pure amusement in its consequence, relaxed self-surrender to all kinds of associations and happy nonsense, is cut short by the amusement on the market: instead, it is interrupted by a surrogate overall meaning which the culture industry insists on giving to its products, and yet misuses as a mere pretext for bringing in the stars. Biographies and other simple stories patch the fragments of nonsense into an idiotic plot. We do not have the cap and bells of the jester but the bunch of keys of capitalist reason, which even screens the pleasure of achieving success. Every kiss in the revue film has to contribute to the career of the boxer, or some hit song expert or other whose rise to fame is being glorified. The deception is not that the culture industry supplies amusement but that it ruins the fun by allowing business considerations to involve it in the ideological clichés of a culture in the process of self-liquidation. Ethics and taste cut short unrestrained amusement as "naïve"—naïveté is thought to be as bad as intellectualism—and even restrict technical possibilities. The culture industry is corrupt: not because it is a sinful Babylon but because it is a cathedral dedicated to elevated pleasure. On all levels, from Hemingway to Emil Ludwig, from Mrs. Miniver to the Lone Ranger, from Toscanini to Guy Lombardo, there is untruth in the intellectual content taken ready-made from art and science. The culture industry does retain a trace of something better in those features which bring it close to the circus, in the self-justifying and nonsensical skill of riders, acrobats and clowns, in the "defense and justification of physical as against intellectual art."[2] But the refuges of a mindless artistry which represents what is human as opposed to the social mechanism are being relentlessly hunted down by a schematic reason which compels everything to prove its significance and effect. The consequence is that the nonsensical at the bottom disappears as utterly as the sense in works of art at the top.

The fusion of culture and entertainment that is taking place today leads not only to a depravation of culture, but inevitably to an intellectualization of amusement. This is evident from the fact that only the copy appears: in the movie theater, the photograph; on the radio, the recording. In the age of liberal expansion, amusement lived on the unshaken belief in the future: things would remain as they were and even improve. Today this belief is once more intellectualized; it becomes so faint that it loses sight of any goal and is little more than a magic-lantern show for those with their backs to reality. It consists of the meaningful emphases which, parallel to life itself, the screen play puts on the smart fellow, the engineer, the capable girl, ruthlessness disguised as character, interest in sport, and finally automobiles and cigarettes, even where the entertainment is not put down to the advertising account of the immediate producers but to that of the system as a whole. Amusement itself becomes an ideal, taking the place of the higher things of which it completely deprives the masses by repeating them in a manner even more stereotyped than the slogans paid for by advertising interests. Inwardness, the subjectively restricted form of truth, was always more at the mercy of the outwardly powerful than they imagined. The culture industry turns it into an open lie. It has now become mere twaddle which is acceptable in religious bestsellers, psychological films, and women's serials as an embarrassingly agreeable garnish, so that genuine personal emotion in real life can be all the more reliably controlled. In this sense amusement carries out that purgation of the emotions which Aristotle once attributed to tragedy and Mortimer Adler now allows to movies. The culture industry reveals the truth about catharsis as it did about style.

The stronger the positions of the culture industry become, the more summarily it can deal with consumers' needs, producing them, controlling them, disciplining them, and even withdrawing amusement: no limits are set to cultural progress of this kind. But the tendency is immanent in the principle of amusement itself, which is enlightened in a bourgeois sense. If the need for amusement was in large measure the creation of industry, which used the subject as a means of recommending the work to the masses—the oleograph by the dainty morsel it depicted, or the cake mix by a picture of a cake—amusement always reveals the influence of business, the sales talk, the quack's spiel. But the original affinity of business and amusement is shown in the latter's specific significance: to defend society. To be pleased means to say Yes. It is possible only by insulation from the totality of the social process, by desensitization and, from the first, by senselessly sacrificing the inescapable claim of every work, however inane, within its limits to reflect the whole. Pleasure always means not to think about anything, to forget suffering even where it is shown. Basically it is helplessness. It is flight; not, as is asserted, flight from a wretched reality, but from the last remaining thought of resistance. The liberation which amusement promises is freedom from thought and from negation. The effrontery of the rhetorical question "What do people want?" lies in the fact that it is addressed—as if to reflective individuals—to those very people who are deliberately to be deprived of this individuality. Even when the public does—exceptionally—rebel against the pleasure industry, all it can muster is that feeble resistance which that very industry has inculcated in it. Nevertheless, it has become increasingly difficult to keep people in this condition. The rate at which they are reduced to stupidity must not fall behind the rate at which their intelligence is increasing. In this age of statistics the masses are too sharp to identify themselves with the millionaire on the screen, and too slow-witted to ignore the law of the largest number. Ideology conceals itself in the calculation of probabilities. Not everyone will be lucky one day—but the person who draws the winning ticket, or rather the one who is marked out to do so by a higher power—usually by the pleasure industry itself, which is represented as unceasingly in search of talent. Those discovered by talent scouts and then publicized on a vast scale by the studio are ideal types of the new dependent average. Of course, the starlet is meant to symbolize the typist in such a way that the splendid evening dress seems meant for the actress as distinct from the real girl. The girls in the audience not only feel that they could be on the screen, but realize the great gulf separating them from it. Only one girl can draw the lucky ticket, only one man can win the prize, and if, mathematically, all have the same chance, yet this is so infinitesimal for each one that he or she will do best to write it off and rejoice in the other's success, which might just as well have been his or hers, and somehow never is. Whenever the culture industry still issues an invitation naïvely to identify, it is immediately withdrawn. No one can escape from himself anymore. Once a member of the audience could see his own wedding in the one shown in the film. Now the lucky actors on the screen are copies of the same category as every member of the public, but such equality only demonstrates the insurmountable separation of the human elements. The perfect similarity is the absolute difference. The identity of the category forbids that of the individual cases. Ironically, man as a member of a species has been made a reality by the culture industry. Now any person signifies only those attributes by which he can replace everybody else: he is interchangeable, a copy. As an individual he is completely expendable and utterly insignificant, and this is just what he finds out when time deprives him of this similarity. This changes the inner structure of the religion of success—otherwise strictly maintained. Increasing emphasis is laid not on the path *per aspera ad astra* (which presupposes hardship and effort), but on winning a prize. The element of blind chance in the routine decision about which song deserves to be a hit and which extra a heroine is stressed by the ideology. Movies emphasize chance. By stopping at nothing to ensure that all the characters are essentially alike, with the exception of the villain, and by excluding nonconforming faces (for example, those which, like Garbo's, do not look as if you could say "Hello sister!" to them), life is made easier for moviegoers at first. They are assured that they are all right as they are, that they could do just as well and that nothing beyond their powers will be asked of them. But at the same time they are given a hint that any effort would be useless because even bourgeois luck no longer has any connection with the calculable effect of their own work. They take the hint. Fundamentally they all recognize chance (by which one occasionally makes his fortune) as the other side of planning. Precisely because the forces of society are so deployed in the direction of rationality that anyone might become an engineer or manager, it has ceased entirely to be a rational matter who the one will be in whom society will invest training or confidence for such functions. Chance and planning become one and the same thing, because, given men's equality, individual success and failure—right up to the top—lose any economic meaning. Chance itself is planned, not because it affects any particular individual but precisely because it is believed to play a vital part. It serves the planners as an alibi, and makes it seem that the complex of transactions and measures into which life has been transformed leaves scope for spontaneous and direct relations between man. This freedom is symbolized in the various media of the culture industry by the arbitrary selection of average individuals. In a magazine's detailed accounts of the modestly magnificent pleasure-trips it has arranged for the lucky person, preferably a stenotypist (who has probably won the competition because of her contacts with local bigwigs), the powerlessness of all is reflected. They are mere matter—so much so that those in control can take someone up into their heaven and throw him out again: his rights and his work count for nothing. Industry is interested in people merely as customers and employees, and has in fact reduced mankind as a whole and each of its elements to this all-embracing formula. According to the ruling aspect at the time, ideology emphasizes plan or chance, technology or life, civilization or nature. As employees, men are reminded of the rational organization and urged to fit in like sensible people. As customers, the freedom of choice, the charm of novelty, is demonstrated to them on the screen or in the press by means of the human and personal anecdote. In either case they remain objects.

The less the culture industry has to promise, the less it can offer a meaningful explanation of life, and the emptier is the ideology it disseminates. Even the abstract ideals of the harmony and beneficence of society are too concrete in this age of universal publicity. We have even learned how to identify abstract concepts as sales propaganda. Language based entirely on truth simply arouses impatience to get on with the business deal it is probably advancing. The words that are not means appear senseless; the others seem to be fiction, untrue. Value judgments are taken either as advertising or as empty talk. Accordingly ideology has been made vague and noncommittal, and thus neither clearer nor weaker. Its very vagueness, its almost scientific aversion from committing itself to anything which cannot be verified, acts as an instrument of domination. It becomes a vigorous and prearranged promulgation of the status quo. The culture industry tends to make itself the embodiment of authoritative pronouncements, and thus the irrefutable prophet of the prevailing order. It skillfully steers a winding course between the cliffs of demonstrable misinformation and manifest truth, faithfully reproducing the phenomenon whose opaqueness blocks any insight and installs the ubiquitous and intact phenomenon as ideal. Ideology is split into the photograph of stubborn life and the naked lie about its meaning—which is not expressed but suggested and yet drummed in. To demonstrate its divine nature, reality is always repeated in a purely cynical way. Such a photological proof is of course not stringent, but it is overpowering. Anyone who doubts the power of monotony is a fool. The culture industry refutes the objection made against it just as well as that against the world which it impartially duplicates. The only choice is either to join in or to be left behind: those provincials who have recourse to eternal beauty and the amateur stage in preference to the cinema and the radio are already—politically—at the point to which mass culture drives its supporters. It is sufficiently hardened to deride as ideology, if need be, the old wish-fulfillments, the father-ideal and absolute feeling. The new ideology has as its objects the world as such. It makes use of the worship of facts by no more than elevating a disagreeable existence into the world of facts in representing it meticulously. This transference makes existence itself a substitute for meaning and right. Whatever the camera reproduces is beautiful. The disappointment of the prospect that one might be the typist who wins the world trip is matched by the disappointing appearance of the accurately photographed areas which the voyage might include. Not Italy is offered, but evidence that it exists. A film can even go so far as to show the Paris in which the American girl thinks she will still her desire as a hopelessly desolate place, thus driving her the more inexorably into the arms of the smart American boy she could have met at home anyhow. That this goes on, that, in its most recent phase, the system itself reproduces the life of those of whom it consists instead of immediately doing away with them, is even put down to its credit as giving it meaning and worth. Continuing and continuing to join in are given as justification for the blind persistence of the system and even for its immutability. What repeats itself is healthy, like the natural or industrial cycle. The same babies grin eternally out of the magazines; the jazz machine will pound away forever. In spite of all the progress in reproduction techniques, in controls and the specialities, and in spite of all the restless industry, the bread which the culture industry offers man is the stone of the stereotype. It draws on the life cycle, on the well-founded amazement that mothers, in spite of everything, still go on bearing children and that the wheels still do not grind to a halt. This serves to confirm the immutability of circumstances. The ears of corn blowing in the wind at the end of Chaplin's *The Great Dictator* give the lie to the anti-Fascist plea for freedom. They are like the blond hair of the German girl whose camp life is photographed by the Nazi film company in the summer breeze. Nature is viewed by the mechanism of social domination as a healthy contrast to society, and is therefore denatured. Pictures showing green trees, a blue sky, and moving clouds make these aspects of nature into so many cryptograms for factory chimneys and service stations. On the other hand, wheels and machine components must seem expressive, having been degraded to the status of agents of the spirit of trees and clouds. Nature and technology are mobilized against all opposition; and we have a falsified memento of liberal society, in which people supposedly wallowed in erotic plush-lined bedrooms instead of taking open-air baths as in the case today, or experiencing breakdowns in prehistoric

Benz models instead of shooting off with the speed of a rocket from A (where one is anyhow) to B (where everything is just the same). The triumph of the gigantic concern over the initiative of the entrepreneur is praised by the culture industry as the persistence of entrepreneurial initiative. The enemy who is already defeated, the thinking individual, is the enemy fought. The resurrection in Germany of the anti-bourgeois "Haus Sonnenstösser," and the pleasure felt when watching *Life with Father*, have one and the same meaning. . . .

ENDNOTES

1. Nietzsche, *Unzeitgemässe Betrachtungen, Werke*, Vol. 1 (Leipzig, 1917), p. 187.
2. Frank Wedekind, *Gesammelte Werke*, Vol. IX (Munich, 1921), p. 426.

2
John Kenneth Galbraith
"The Dependence Effect"
(1958)*

The notion that wants do not become less urgent the more amply the individual is supplied is broadly repugnant to common sense. It is something to be believed only by those who wish to believe. Yet the conventional wisdom must be tackled on its own terrain. Intertemporal comparisons of an individual's state of mind do rest on technically vulnerable ground. Who can say for sure that the deprivation which afflicts him with hunger is more painful than the deprivation which afflicts him with envy of his neighbor's new car? In the time that has passed since he was poor, his soul may have become subject to a new and deeper searing. And where a society is concerned, comparisons between marginal satisfactions when it is poor and those when it is affluent will involve not only the same individual at different times but different individuals at different times. The scholar who wishes to believe that with increasing affluence there is no reduction in the urgency of desires and goods is not without points for debate. However plausible the case against him, it cannot be proven. In the defense of the conventional wisdom, this amounts almost to invulnerability.

However, there is a flaw in the case. If the individual's wants are to be urgent, they must be original with himself. They cannot be urgent if they must be contrived for him. And above all, they must not be contrived by the process of production by which they are satisfied. For this means that the whole case for the urgency of production, based on the urgency of wants, falls to the ground. One cannot defend production as satisfying wants if that production creates the wants.

Were it so that a man on arising each morning was assailed by demons which instilled in him a passion sometimes for silk shirts, sometimes for kitchenware, sometimes for chamber pots, and sometimes for orange squash, there would be every reason to applaud the effort to find the goods, however odd, that quenched this flame. But should it be that his passion was the result of his first having cultivated the demons, and

* Updated 1969, 1976, and 1998.

should it also be that his effort to allay it stirred the demons to ever greater and greater effort, there would be question as to how rational was his solution. Unless restrained by conventional attitudes, he might wonder if the solution lay with more goods or fewer demons.

So it is that if production creates the wants it seeks to satisfy, or if the wants emerge *pari passu* with the production, then the urgency of the wants can no longer be used to defend the urgency of the production. Production only fills a void that it has itself created.

II

The point is so central that it must be pressed. Consumer wants can have bizarre, frivolous or even immoral origins, and an admirable case can still be made for a society that seeks to satisfy them. But the case cannot stand if it is the process of satisfying wants that creates the wants. For then the individual who urges the importance of production to satisfy these wants is precisely in the position of the onlooker who applauds the efforts of the squirrel to keep abreast of the wheel that is propelled by his own efforts.

That wants are, in fact, the fruit of production will now be denied by few serious scholars. And a considerable number of economists, though not always in full knowledge of the implications, have conceded the point. Keynes noted that needs of "the second class," i.e., those that are the result of efforts to keep abreast or ahead of one's fellow being, "may indeed be insatiable; for the higher the general level, the higher still are they."[1] And emulation has always played a considerable role in the views of other economists of want creation. One man's consumption becomes his neighbor's wish. This already means that the process by which wants are satisfied is also the process by which wants are created. The more wants that are satisfied, the more new ones are born.

However, the argument has been carried farther. A leading modern theorist of consumer behavior, Professor James Duesenberry, has stated explicitly that "ours is a society in which one of the principal social goals is a higher standard of living . . . [This] has great significance for the theory of consumption . . . the desire to get superior goods takes on a life of its own. It provides a drive to higher expenditure which may even be stronger than that arising out of the needs which are supposed to be satisfied by that expenditure."[2] The implications of this view are impressive. The notion of independently established need now sinks into the background. Because the society sets great store by ability to produce a high living standard, it evaluates people by the products they possess. The urge to consume is fathered by the value system which emphasizes the ability of the society to produce. The more that is produced, the more that must be owned in order to maintain the appropriate prestige. The latter is an important point, for, without going as far as Duesenberry in reducing goods to the role of symbols of prestige in the affluent society, it is plain that his argument fully implies that the production of goods creates the wants that the goods are presumed to satisfy.[3]

III

The even more direct link between production and wants is provided by the institutions of modern advertising and salesmanship. These cannot be reconciled with the notion of independently determined desires, for their central function is to create desires—to bring into being wants that previously did not exist.[4] This is accomplished by the producer of the goods or at his behest. A broad empirical relationship exists between what is spent on production of consumer goods and what is spent in synthesizing the desires for that production. A new consumer product must be introduced with a suitable advertising campaign to arouse an interest in it. The path for an expansion of output must be paved by a suitable expansion in the advertising budget. Outlays for the manufacturing of a product are not more important in the strategy of modern business enterprise than outlays for the manufacturing of demand for the product. None of this is novel. All would be regarded as elementary by the most retarded student in the nation's most primitive school of business administration. The cost of this want formation is formidable. In 1987, total advertising expenditure—though, as noted, not all of it may be assigned to the synthesis of wants—amounted to approximately one hundred and ten billion dollars. The increase in previous years was by an estimated six billion dollars a year. Obviously, such outlays must be integrated with the theory of consumer demand. They are too big to be ignored.

But such integration means recognizing that wants are dependent on production. It accords to the producer the function both of making the goods and of making the desires for them. It recognizes that production, not only passively through emulation, but actively through advertising and related activities, creates the wants it seeks to satisfy.

The businessman and the lay reader will be puzzled over the emphasis which I give to a seemingly obvious point. The point is indeed obvious. But it is one which, to a singular degree, economists have resisted. They have sensed, as the layman does not, the damage to established ideas which lurks in these relationships. As a result, incredibly, they have closed their eyes (and ears) to the most obtrusive of all economic phenomena, namely, modern want creation.

This is not to say that the evidence affirming the dependence of wants on advertising has been entirely ignored. It is one reason why advertising has so long been regarded with such uneasiness by economists. Here is something which cannot be accommodated easily to existing theory. More pervious scholars have speculated on the urgency of desires which are so obviously the fruit of such expensively contrived campaigns for popular attention. Is a new breakfast cereal or detergent so much wanted if so much must be spent to compel in the consumer the sense of want? But there has been little tendency to go on to examine the implications of this for the theory of consumer demand and even less for the importance of production and productive efficiency. These have remained sacrosanct. More often, the uneasiness has been manifested in a general disapproval of advertising and advertising men, leading to the occasional suggestion that they shouldn't exist. Such suggestions have usually been ill received in the advertising business.

And so the notion of independently determined wants still survives. In the face of all the forces of modern salesmanship, it still rules, almost undefiled, in the textbooks. And it still remains the economist's mission—and on few matters is the pedagogy so firm—to seek unquestionably the means for filling these wants. This being so, production remains of prime urgency. We have here, perhaps, the ultimate triumph of the conventional wisdom in its resistance to the evidence of the eyes. To equal it, one must imagine a humanitarian who was long ago persuaded of the grievous shortage of hospital facilities in the town. He continues to importune the passersby for money for more beds and refuses to notice that the town doctor is deftly knocking over pedestrians with his car to keep up the occupancy.

And in unraveling the complex, we should always be careful not to overlook the obvious. The fact that wants can be synthesized by advertising, catalyzed by salesmanship, and shaped by the discreet manipulations of the persuaders shows that they are not very urgent. A man who is hungry need never be told of his need for food. If he is inspired by his appetite, he is immune to the influence of Messrs. Batten, Barton, Durstine & Osborn. The latter are effective only with those who are so far removed from physical want that they do not already know what they want. In this state alone, men are open to persuasion.

IV

The general conclusion of these pages is of such importance for this essay that it had perhaps best be put with some formality. As a society becomes increasingly affluent, wants are increasingly created by the process by which they are satisfied. This may operate passively. Increases in consumption, the counterpart of increases in production, act by suggestion or emulation to create wants. Expectation rises with attainment. Or producers may proceed actively to create wants through advertising and salesmanship. Wants thus come to depend on output. In technical terms, it can no longer be assumed that welfare is greater at an all-round higher level of production than a lower one. It may be the same. The higher level of production has, merely, a higher level of want creation necessitating a higher level of want satisfaction. There will be frequent occasion to refer to the way wants depend on the process by which they are satisfied. It will be convenient to call it the Dependence Effect.

We may now contemplate briefly the conclusions to which this analysis has brought us.

Plainly, the theory of consumer demand is a peculiarly treacherous friend of the present goals of economics. At first glance, it seems to defend the continuing urgency of production and our preoccupation with it as a goal. The economist does not enter into the dubious moral arguments about the importance or virtue of the wants to be satisfied. He doesn't pretend to compare mental states of the same or different people at different times and to suggest that one is less urgent than another. The desire is there. That for him is sufficient. He sets about in a workmanlike way to satisfy desire, and accordingly, he sets the proper store by the production that does. Like woman's, his work is never done.

But this rationalization, handsomely though it seems to serve, turns destructively on those who advance it once it is conceded that wants are themselves both passively and deliberately the fruits of the process by which they are satisfied. Then the production of goods satisfies the wants that the consumption of these goods creates or that the producers of goods synthesize. Production induces more wants and the need for more production. So far, in a major tour de force, the implications have been ignored. But this obviously is a perilous solution. It cannot long survive discussion.

Among the many models of the good society, no one has urged the squirrel wheel. Moreover, the wheel is not one that revolves with perfect smoothness. Aside from its dubious cultural charm, there are serious structural weaknesses which may one day embarrass us. For the moment, however, it is sufficient to reflect on the difficult terrain which we are traversing. We have seen how deeply we are committed to production for reasons of economic security. Not the goods but the employment provided by their production was the thing by which we set ultimate store. Now we find our concern for goods further undermined. It does not arise in spontaneous consumer need. Rather, the dependence effect means that it grows out of the process of production itself. If production is to increase, the wants must be effectively contrived. In the absence of the contrivance, the increase would not occur. This is not true of all goods, but that it is true of a substantial part is sufficient. It means that since the demand for this part would not exist, were it not contrived, its utility or urgency, *ex* contrivance, is zero. If we regard this production as marginal, we may say that the marginal utility of present aggregate output, *ex* advertising and salesmanship, is zero. Clearly the attitudes and values which make production the central achievement of our society have some exceptionally twisted roots.

Perhaps the thing most evident of all is how new and varied become the problems we must ponder when we break the nexus with the work of Ricardo and face the economics of affluence of the world in which we live. It is easy to see why the conventional wisdom resists so stoutly such change. It is far, far better and much safer to have a firm anchor in nonsense than to put out on the troubled seas of thought.

ENDNOTES

1. J. M. Keynes, *Essays in Persuasion*, "Economic Possibilities for Our Grand-children" (London: Macmillan, 1931), p. 365.

2. James S. Duesenberry, *Income, Saving and the Theory of Consumer Behavior* (Cambridge, Mass.: Harvard University Press, 1949), p. 28.

3. A more recent and definitive study of consumer demand has added even more support. Professors Houthakker and Taylor, in a statistical study of the determinants of demand, found that for most products price and income, the accepted determinants, were less important than past consumption of the product. This "psychological stock," as they called it, concedes the weakness of traditional theory; current demand cannot be explained without recourse to past consumption. Such demand nurtures the need for its own increase. H. S. Houthakker and L. D. Taylor, *Consumer Demand in the United States*, 2nd ed., enlarged (Cambridge, Mass.: Harvard University Press, 1970).

4. Advertising is not a simple phenomenon. It is also important in competitive strategy and want creation is, ordinarily, a complementary result of efforts to shift the demand curve of the individual firm at the expense of others or (less importantly, I think) to change its shape by increasing the degree of product differentiation. Some of the failure of economists to identify advertising with want creation may be attributed to the undue attention that its use in purely competitive strategy has attracted. It should be noted, however, that the competitive manipulation of consumer desire is only possible, at least on any appreciable scale, when such need is not strongly felt.

3
Betty Friedan
"THE SEXUAL SELL"
(1963)

Some months ago, as I began to fit together the puzzle of women's retreat to home, I had the feeling I was missing something. I could trace the routes by which sophisticated thought circled back on itself to perpetuate an obsolete image of femininity; I could see how that image meshed with prejudice and misinterpreted frustrations to hide the emptiness of "Occupation: housewife" from women themselves.

But what powers it all? If, despite the nameless desperation of so many American housewives, despite the opportunities open to all women now, so few have any purpose in life other than to be a wife and mother, somebody, something pretty powerful must be at work. The energy behind the feminist movement was too dynamic merely to have trickled dry; it must have been turned off, diverted, by something more powerful than that underestimated power of women.

There are certain facts of life so obvious and mundane that one never talks about them. Only the child blurts out: "Why do people in books never go to the toilet?" Why is it never said that the really crucial function, the really important role that women serve as housewives is *to buy more things for the house*. In all the talk of femininity and woman's role, one forgets that the real business of America is business. But the perpetuation of house-wifery, the growth of the feminine mystique, makes sense (and dollars) when one realizes that women are the chief customers of American business. Somehow, somewhere, someone must have figured out that women will buy more things if they are kept in the underused, nameless-yearning, energy-to-get-rid-of state of being housewives.

I have no idea how it happened. Decision-making in industry is not as simple, as rational, as those who believe the conspiratorial theories of history would have it. I am sure the heads of General Foods, and General Electric, and General Motors, and Macy's and Gimbel's and the assorted directors of all the companies that make detergents and electric mixers, and red stoves with rounded corners, and synthetic furs, and waxes, and hair coloring, and patterns for home sewing and home carpentry, and lotions for detergent hands, and bleaches to keep the towels pure white, never sat down around a mahogany conference table in a board room on Madison Avenue or Wall Street and voted on a motion: "Gentlemen, I move, in the interests of all, that we begin a concerted fifty-billion dollar campaign to stop this dangerous movement of American women out of the home. We've got to keep them housewives, and let's not forget it."

A thinking vice-president says: "Too many women getting educated. Don't want to stay home. Unhealthy. If they all get to be scientists and such, they won't have time to shop. But how can we keep them home? They want careers now."

"We'll liberate them to have careers at home," the new executive with horn-rimmed glasses and the Ph.D. in psychology suggests. "We'll make home-making creative."

Of course, it didn't happen quite like that. It was not an economic conspiracy directed against women. It was a byproduct of our general confusion lately of means with ends; just something that happened to women when the business of producing and selling and investing in business for profit—which is merely the way our economy is organized to serve man's needs efficiently—began to be confused with the purpose of our nation, the end of life itself. No more surprising, the subversion of women's lives in America to the ends of business, than the subversion of the sciences of human behavior to the business of deluding women about their real needs. It would take a clever economist to figure out what would keep our affluent economy going if the housewife market began to fall off, just as an economist would have to figure out what to do if there were no threat of war.

It is easy to see why it happened. I learned *how* it happened when I went to see a man who is paid approximately a million dollars a year for his professional services in manipulating the emotions of American women to serve the needs of business. This particular man got in on the ground floor of the hidden-persuasion business in 1945, and kept going. The headquarters of his institute for motivational manipulation is a baronial mansion in upper Westchester. The walls of a ballroom two-stories high are filled with steel shelves holding a thousand-odd studies for business and industry, 300,000 individual "depth interviews," mostly with American housewives.[1]

He let me see what I wanted, said I could use anything that was not confidential to a specific company. Nothing there for anyone to hide, to feel guilty about—only, in page after page of those depth studies, a shrewd cheerful awareness of the empty, purposeless, uncreative, even sexually joyless lives that most American housewives lead. In his own unabashed terms, this most helpful of hidden persuaders showed me the function served by keeping American women housewives—the reservoir that their lack of identity, lack of purpose, creates, to be manipulated into dollars at the point of purchase.

Properly manipulated ("if you are not afraid of that word," he said), American housewives can be given the sense of identity, purpose, creativity, the self-realization, even the sexual joy they lack—by the buying of things. I suddenly realized the significance of the boast that women wield seventy-five percent of the purchasing power in America. I suddenly saw American women as *victims* of that ghastly gift, that power at the point of purchase. The insights he shared with me so liberally revealed many things. . . .

The dilemma of business was spelled out in a survey made in 1945 for the publisher of a leading women's magazine on the attitudes of women toward electrical appliances. The message was considered of interest to all the companies that, with the war about to end, were going to have to make consumer sales take the place of war contracts. It was a study of "the psychology of housekeeping"; "a woman's attitude toward housekeeping appliances cannot be separated from her attitude toward homemaking in general," it warned.

On the basis of a national sample of 4,500 wives (middle-class, high-school or college-educated), American women were divided into three categories. "The True Housewife Type," "The Career Woman," and "The Balanced Homemaker." While 51 percent of the women then fitted "The True Housewife Type" ("From the psychological point of view, housekeeping is this woman's dominating interest. She takes the utmost pride and satisfaction in maintaining a comfortable and well-run home for her family. Consciously or subconsciously, she feels that she is indispensable and that no one else can take over her job. She has little, if any, desire for a position outside the home, and if she has one it is through force or circumstances or necessity"), it was apparent that this group was diminishing, and probably would continue to do so as new fields, interests, education were now open to women.

The largest market for appliances, however, was this "True Housewife"—though she had a certain "reluctance" to accept new devices that had to be recognized and overcome. ("She may even fear that they [appliances] will render unnecessary the old-fashioned way of doing things that has always suited her.") After all, housework was the justification for her whole existence. ("I don't think there is any way to make housework easier for myself," one True Housewife said, "because I don't believe that a machine can take the place of hard work.")

The second type—The Career Woman or Would-Be Career Woman—was a minority, but an extremely "unhealthy" one from the sellers' standpoint; advertisers were warned that it would be to their advantage not to let this group get any larger. For such women, though not necessarily job-holders, "do not believe that a woman's place is primarily in the home." ("Many in this group have never actually worked, but their attitude is: 'I think housekeeping is a horrible waste of time. If my youngsters were old enough and I were free to leave the house, I would use my time to better advantage. If my family's meals and laundry could be taken care of, I would be delighted to go out and get a job.' ") The point to bear in mind regarding career women, the study said, is that, while they buy modern appliances, they are not the ideal type of customer. *They are too critical.*

The third type—"The Balanced Homemaker"—is "from the market standpoint, the ideal type." She has some outside interests, or has held a job before turning exclusively to homemaking; she "readily accepts" the help mechanical appliances can give—but "does not expect them to do the impossible" because she needs to use her own executive ability "in managing a well-run household."

The moral of the study was explicit: "Since the Balanced Homemaker represents the market with the greatest future potential, it would be to the advantage of the appliance manufacturer to make more and more women aware of the desirability of belonging to this group. Educate them through advertising that it is possible to have outside interests and become alert to wider intellectual influences (without becoming a Career Woman). The art of good homemaking should be the goal of every normal woman."

The problem—which, if recognized at that time by one hidden persuader for the home-appliance industry, was surely recognized by others with products for the home—was that "a whole new generation of women is being educated to do work outside the home. Furthermore, an increased desire for emancipation is evident." The solution, quite simply, was to encourage them to be "modern" housewives. The Career or Would-Be Career Woman who frankly dislikes cleaning, dusting, ironing, washing clothes, is less interested in a new wax, a new soap powder. Unlike "The True Housewife" and the "Balanced Homemaker" who prefer to have sufficient appliances and do the housework themselves, the Career Woman would "prefer servants—housework takes too much time and energy." She buys appliances, however, whether or not she has servants, but she is "more likely to complain about the service they give," and to be "harder to sell."

It was too late—impossible—to turn these modern could-or-would-be career women back into True Housewives, but the study pointed out, in 1945, the potential for Balanced House-wifery—the home career. Let them "want to have their cake and eat it too . . . save time, have more comfort, avoid dirt and disorder, have mechanized supervision, yet not want to give up the feeling of personal achievement and pride in a well-run household, which comes from 'doing it yourself.' As one young housewife said: 'It's nice to be modern—it's like running a factory in which you have all the latest machinery.' "

But it was not an easy job, either for business or advertisers. New gadgets that were able to do almost all the housework crowded the market; increased ingenuity was needed to give American women that "feeling of achievement," and yet keep housework their main purpose in life. Education, independence, growing individuality, everything that made them ready for other purposes had constantly to be countered, channeled back to the home.

The manipulator's services became increasingly valuable. In later surveys, he no longer interviewed professional women; they were not at home during the day. The women in his samples were deliberately True or Balanced Housewives, the new suburban housewives. Household and consumer products are, after all, geared to women; seventy-five percent of all consumer advertising budgets is spent to appeal to women; that is, to housewives, the women who are available during the day to be interviewed, the women with the time for shopping. Naturally, his depth interviews, projective tests, "living laboratories," were designed to impress his clients, but more often than not they contained the shrewd insights of a skilled social scientist, insights that could be used with profit.

His clients were told they had to do something about this growing need of American women to do creative work—"the major unfulfilled need of the modern housewife." He wrote in one report, for example:

> Every effort must be made to sell X Mix, as a base upon which the woman's creative effort is used.
> The appeal should emphasize the fact that X Mix aids the woman in expressing her creativity because it takes the drudgery away. At the same time, stress should be laid upon the cooking manipulations, the fun that goes with them, permitting you to feel that X Mix baking is real baking.

But the dilemma again: how to make her spend money on the mix that takes some of the drudgery out of baking by telling her "she can utilize her energy where it really counts"—and yet keep her from being "too busy to bake"? ("I don't use the mix because I don't do any baking at all. It's too much trouble. I live in a sprawled-out apartment and what with keeping it clean and looking after my child and my part-time job, I don't have time for baking.") What to do about their "feeling of disappointment" when the biscuits come out of the oven, and they're really only bread and there is no feeling of creative achievement? ("Why should I bake my own biscuits when there are so many good things on the market that just need to be heated up? It just doesn't make any sense at all to go through all the trouble of mixing your own and then greasing the tin and baking them.") What to do when the woman doesn't get the feeling her mother got, when the cake *had* to be made from scratch? ("The way my mother made them, you had to sift the flour yourself and add the eggs and the butter and you knew you'd really made something you could be proud of.")

The problem can be handled, the report assured:

> By using X Mix the woman can prove herself as a wife and mother, not only by baking, but by spending more time with her family. . . . Of course, it must also be made clear that home-baked foods are in every way preferable to bakery-shop foods . . .

Above all, give X Mix "a therapeutic value" by downplaying the easy recipes, emphasizing instead "the stimulating effort of baking." From an advertising viewpoint, this means stressing that "with X Mix in the home, you will be a different woman . . . a happier woman."

Further, the client was told that a phrase in his ad "and you make that cake the easiest, laziest way there is" evoked a "negative response" in American housewives—it hit too close to their "underlying guilt." ("Since they never feel that they are really exerting sufficient effort, it is certainly wrong to tell them that baking with X Mix is the lazy way.") Supposing, he suggested, that this devoted wife and mother behind the kitchen stove, anxiously preparing a cake or pie for her husband or children "is simply indulging her own hunger for sweets." The very fact that baking is work for the housewife helps her dispel any doubts that she might have about her real motivations.

But there are even ways to manipulate the housewives' guilt, the report said:

> It might be possible to suggest through advertising that not to take advantage of all 12 uses of X Mix is to limit your efforts to give pleasure to your family. A transfer of guilt might be achieved. Rather than feeling guilty about using X Mix for dessert food, the woman would be made to feel guilty if she doesn't take advantage of this opportunity to give her family 12 different and delicious treats. "Don't waste your skill; don't limit yourself."

By the mid-fifties, the surveys reported with pleasure that the Career Woman ("the woman who clamored for equality—almost for identity in every sphere of life, the woman who reacted to 'domestic slavery' with indignation and vehemence") was gone, replaced by the "less worldly, less sophisticated" woman whose activity in PTA gives her "broad contacts with the world outside her home," but who "finds in housework a medium of expression for her femininity and individuality." She's not like the old-fashioned self-sacrificing housewife; she considers herself the equal of man. But she still feels "lazy, neglectful, haunted by guilt feelings" because she doesn't have enough work to do. The advertiser must manipulate her need for a "feeling of creativeness" into the buying of his product.

> After an initial resistance, she now tends to accept instant coffee, frozen foods, precooked foods, and labor-saving items as part of her routine. But she needs a justification and she finds it in the thought that "by using frozen foods I'm freeing myself to accomplish other important tasks as a modern mother and wife."

Creativeness is the modern woman's dialectical answer to the problem of her changed position in the household. Thesis: I'm a housewife. Antithesis: I hate drudgery. Synthesis: I'm creative!

This means essentially that even though the housewife may buy canned food, for instance, and thus save time and effort, she doesn't let it go at that. She has a great need for "doctoring up" the can and thus prove her personal participation and her concern with giving satisfaction to her family.

The feeling of creativeness also serves another purpose: it is an outlet for the liberated talents, the better taste, the freer imagination, the greater initiative of the modern woman. It permits her to use at home *all the faculties that she would display in an outside career.*

The yearning for creative opportunities and moments is a major aspect of buying motivations.

The only trouble, the surveys warned, is that she "tries to use her own mind and her own judgment. She is fast getting away from judging by collective or majority standards. She is developing dependent standards." ("Never mind the neighbors. I don't want to 'live up' to them or compare myself to them at every turn.") She can't always be reached now with "keep up with the Joneses"—the advertiser must appeal to her *own* need to live.

Appeal to this thirst. . . . Tell her that you are adding more zest, more enjoyment to her life, that it is within her reach now to taste new experiences and that she is entitled to taste these experiences. Even more positively, you should convey that you are giving her "lessons in living."

"House cleaning should be fun," the manufacturer of a certain cleaning device was advised. Even though his product was, perhaps, less efficient than the vacuum cleaner, it let the housewife use more of her own energy in the work. Further, it let the housewife have the illusion that she has become "a professional, an expert in determining which cleaning tools to use for specific jobs."

This professionalization is a psychological defense of the housewife against being a general "cleaner-upper" and menial servant for her family in a day and age of general work emancipation.

The role of expert serves a two-fold emotional function: (1) it helps the housewife achieve status, and (2) she moves beyond the orbit of her home, into the world of modern science in her search for new and better ways of doing things.

As a result, there has never been a more favorable psychological climate for household appliances and products. The modern housewife . . . is actually aggressive in her efforts to find those household products which, in her expert opinion, really meet her need. This trend accounts for the popularity of different waxes and polishes for different materials in the home, for the growing use of floor polishers, and for the variety of mops and cleaning implements for floors and walls.

The difficulty is to give her the "sense of achievement" of "ego enhancement" she has been persuaded to seek in the housewife "profession," when, in actuality, "her time-consuming task, housekeeping, is not only endless, it is a task for which society hires the lowliest, least-trained, most trod-upon individuals and groups. . . . Anyone with a strong enough back (and a small enough brain) can do these menial chores." But even this difficulty can be manipulated to sell her more things:

One of the ways that the housewife raises her own prestige as a cleaner of her home is through the use of specialized products for specialized tasks. . . .

When she uses one product for washing clothes, a second for dishes, a third for walls, a fourth for floors, a fifth for venetian blinds, etc., rather than an all-purpose cleaner, she feels less like an unskilled laborer, more like an engineer, an expert.

A second way of raising her own stature is to "do things my way"—to establish an expert's role for herself by creating her own "tricks of the trade." For example, she may "always put a bit of bleach in all my washing—even colored, to make them *really* clean!"

Help her to "justify her menial task by building up her role as the protector of her family—the killer of millions of microbes and germs," this report advised. "Emphasize her kingpin role in the family . . . help her be an expert rather than a menial worker . . . make housework a matter of knowledge and skill, rather than a matter of brawn and dull, unremitting effort." An effective way of doing this is to bring out a *new* product. For, it seems, there's a growing wave of housewives "who look forward to new products which not only decrease their daily work load, but actually engage their emotional and intellectual interest in the world of scientific development outside the home."

One gasps in admiration at the ingenuity of it all—the housewife can participate in science itself just by buying something new—or something old that has been given a brand new personality.

Besides increasing her professional status, a *new* cleaning appliance or product increases a woman's feeling of economic security and luxury, just as a new automobile does for a man. This was reported by 28 percent of the respondents, who agreed with this particular sentiment: "I like to try out new things. I've just started to use a new liquid detergent—and somehow it makes me feel like a queen."

The question of letting the woman use her mind and even participate in science through housework is, however, not without its drawbacks. Science should not relieve housewives of too much drudgery; it must concentrate instead on creating the *illusion* of that sense of achievement that housewives seem to need.

To prove this point, 250 housewives were given a depth test: they were asked to choose among four imaginary methods of cleaning. The first was a completely automatic dust- and dirt-removal system which operated continuously like a home-heating system. The second, the housewife had to press a button to start. The third was portable; she had to carry it around and point it at an area to remove the dirt. The fourth was a brand new, modern object with which she could sweep the dirt away herself. The housewives spoke up in favor of this last appliance. If it "appears new, modern" she would rather have the one that lets her work herself, this report said. "One compelling reason is her desire to be a participant, not just a button-pusher." As one housewife remarked, "As for some magical push-button cleaning system, well, what would happen to my exercise, my feeling of accomplishment, and what would I do with my mornings?"

This fascinating study incidentally revealed that a certain electronic cleaning appliance—long considered one of our great laborsavers—actually made "housekeeping more difficult than it need be." From the response of eighty percent of those housewives, it seemed that once a woman got this appliance going, she "felt compelled to do cleaning that wasn't really necessary." The electronic appliance actually dictated the extent and type of cleaning to be done.

Should the housewife then be encouraged to go back to that simple cheap sweeper that let her clean only as much as she felt necessary? No, said the report, of course not. Simply give that old-fashioned sweeper the "status" of the electronic appliance as a "labor-saving necessity" for the modern housewife "and then indicate that the modern homemaker would, naturally, own both."

No one, not even the depth researchers, denied that housework was endless, and its boring repetition just did not give that much satisfaction, did not require that much vaunted expert knowledge. But the endlessness of it all was an advantage from the seller's point of view. The problem was to keep at bay the underlying realization which was lurking dangerously in "thousands of depth interviews which we have conducted for dozens of different kinds of house-cleaning products"—the realization that, as one housewife said, "It stinks! I have to do it, so I do it. It's a necessary evil, that's all." What to do? For one thing, put out more and more products, make the directions more complicated, make it really necessary for the housewife to "be an expert." (Washing clothes, the report advised, must become more than a matter of throwing clothes into a machine and pouring in soap. Garments must be carefully sorted, one load given treatment A, a second load treatment B, some washed by hand. The housewife can then "take great pride in knowing just which of the arsenal of products to use on each occasion.")

Capitalize, the report continued, on housewives' "guilt over the hidden dirt" so she will rip her house to shreds in a "deep cleaning" operation, which will give her a "sense of completeness" for a few weeks.

("The times of thorough cleaning are the points at which she is most willing to try new products and 'deep clean' advertising holds out the promise of completion.")

The seller must also stress the joys of completing each separate task, remembering that "nearly all housekeepers, even those who thoroughly detest their job, paradoxically find escape from their endless fate by accepting it—by 'throwing myself into it,' as she says."

> Losing herself in her work—surrounded by all the implements, creams, powders, soaps, she forgets for a time how soon she will have to redo the task. In other words, a housewife permits herself to forget for a moment how rapidly the sink will again fill with dishes, how quickly the floor will again be dirty, and she seizes the moment of completion of a task as a moment of pleasure as pure as if she had just finished a masterpiece of art which would stand as a monument to her credit forever.

This is the kind of creative experience the seller of things can give the housewife. In one housewife's own words:

> I don't like housework at all. I'm a lousy houseworker. But once in a while I get pepped up and I'll really go to town . . . When I have some new kind of cleaning material—like when Glass Wax first came out or those silicone furniture polishes—I got a real kick out of it, and I went through the house shining everything. I like to see the things shine. I feel so good when I see the bathroom just glistening.

And so the manipulator advised:

> Identify your product with the physical and spiritual rewards she derives from the almost religious feeling of basic security provided by her home. Talk about her "light, happy, peaceful feelings"; her "deep sense of achievement." . . . But remember she doesn't really want praise for the sake of praise . . . also remember that her mood is not simply "gay." She is tired and a bit solemn. Superficially cheerful adjectives or colors will not reflect her feelings. She will react much more favorably to simple, warm and sincere messages.

In the fifties came the revolutionary discovery of the teenage market. Teenagers and young marrieds began to figure prominently in the surveys. It was discovered that young wives, who had only been to high school and had never worked, were more "insecure," less independent, easier to sell. These young people could be told that, by buying the right things, they could achieve middle-class status, without work or study. The keep-up-with-the-Joneses sell would work again; the individuality and independence which American women had been getting from education and work outside the home was not such a problem with the teenage brides. In fact, the surveys said, if the pattern of "happiness through things" could be established when these women were young enough, they could be safely encouraged to go out and get a part-time job to help their husbands pay for all the things they buy. The main point now was to convince the teenagers that "happiness through things" is no longer the prerogative of the rich or the talented; it can be enjoyed by all, if they learn "the right way," the way the others do it, if they learn the embarrassment of being different.

In the words of one of these reports:

> 49 percent of the new brides were teenagers, and more girls marry at the age of 18 than at any other age. This early family formation yields a larger number of young people who are on the threshold of their own responsibilities and decision-making in purchases . . .
>
> But the most important fact is of a psychological nature: Marriage today is not only the culmination of a romantic attachment; more consciously and more clear-headedly than in the past, it is also a decision to create a partnership in establishing a comfortable home, equipped with a great number of desirable products.
>
> In talking to scores of young couples and brides-to-be, we found that, as a rule, their conversations and dreams centered to a very large degree around their future homes and their furnishings, around shopping "to get an idea," around discussing the advantages and disadvantages of various products. . . .
>
> The modern bride is deeply convinced of the unique value of married love, of the possibilities of finding real happiness in marriage and of fulfilling her personal destiny in it and through it.
>
> But the engagement period today is a romantic, dreamy and heady period only to a limited extent. It is probably safe to say that the period of engagement tends to be a rehearsal of the material duties and responsibilities of marriage. While waiting for the nuptials, couples work hard, put aside money for definite purchases, or even begin buying on an installment plan.
>
> What is the deeper meaning of this new combination of an almost religious belief in the importance and beauty of married life on the one hand, and the product-centered outlook, on the other? . . .
>
> The modern bride seeks as a conscious goal that which in many cases her grandmother saw as a blind fate and her mother as slavery: to belong to a man, to have a home and children of her own, to choose among all possible careers the career of wife-mother-homemaker.

The fact that the young bride now seeks in her marriage complete "fulfillment," that she now expects to "prove her own worth" and find all the "fundamental meanings" of life in her home, and to participate through her home in "the interesting ideas of the modern era, the future," has enormous "practical applications," advertisers were told. For all these meanings she seeks in her marriage, even her fear that she will be "left behind," can be channeled into the purchase of products. For example, a manufacturer of sterling silver, a product that is very difficult to sell, was told:

Reassure her that only with sterling can she be fully secure in her new role
... it symbolizes her success as a modern woman. Above all, dramatize
the fun and pride that derive from the job of cleaning silver. Stimulate the
pride of achievement. "How much pride you get from the brief task that's
so much fun . . ."

Concentrate on the very young teenage girls, this report further advised.
The young ones will want what "the others" want, even if their mothers
don't. ("As one of our teenagers said: 'All the gang has started their
own sets of sterling. We're real keen about it—compare patterns and
go through the ads together. My own family never had any sterling and
they think I'm showing off when I spend my money on it—they think
plated's just as good. But the kids think they're way off base.' ") Get
them in schools, churches, sororities, social clubs; get them through
home-economics teachers, group leaders, teenage TV programs and
teenage advertising. "This is the big market of the future and word-of-
mouth advertising, along with group pressure, is not only the most potent influence but in the absence of tradition, a most necessary one."

As for the more independent older wife, that unfortunate tendency to
use materials that require little care—stainless steel, plastic dishes, paper
napkins—can be met by making her feel guilty about the effects on the
children. ("As one young wife told us: 'I'm out of the house all day
long, so I can't prepare and serve meals the way I want to. I don't like
it that way—my husband and the children deserve a better break. Sometimes I think it'd be better if we tried to get along on one salary and
have a real home life but there are always so many things we need.' ")
Such guilt, the report maintained, can be used to make her see the product, silver, as a means of holding the family together; it gives "added
psychological value." What's more, the product can even fill the housewife's need for identity: "Suggest that it becomes truly a part of *you*,
reflecting *you*. Do not be afraid to suggest mystically that sterling will
adapt itself to any house and any person."

The fur industry is in trouble, another survey reported, because
young high school and college girls equate fur coats with "uselessness" and "a kept woman." Again the advice was to get to the very
young before these unfortunate connotations have formed. ("By introducing youngsters to positive fur experiences, the probabilities of eas-
ing their way into garment purchasing in their teens is enhanced.")
Point out that "the wearing of a fur garment actually establishes femininity and sexuality for a woman." ("It's the kind of thing a girl
looks forward to. It means something. It's feminine." "I'm bringing
my daughter up right. She always wants to put on 'mommy's coat.'
She'll want them. She's a real girl.") But keep in mind that "mink has
contributed a negative feminine symbolism to the whole fur market."

Unfortunately, two out of three women felt mink-wearers were "predatory . . . exploitative . . . dependent . . . socially nonproductive . . ."

Femininity today cannot be so explicitly predatory, exploitative, the report said; nor can it have the old high-fashion "connotations of stand-out-from-the-crowd, self-centeredness." And so fur's "ego-orientation" must be reduced and replaced with the new femininity of the housewife, for whom ego-orientation must be translated into togetherness, family-orientation.

> Begin to create the feeling that fur is a necessity—a delightful necessity . . . thus providing the consumer with moral permission to purchase something she now feels is ego-oriented. . . . Give fur femininity a broader character, developing some of the following status and prestige symbols . . . an emotionally happy woman . . . wife and mother who wins the affection and respect of her husband and her children because of the kind of person she is, and the kind of role she performs. . . .
>
> Place furs in a family setting; show the pleasure and admiration of a fur garment derived by family members, husband and children; their pride in their mother's appearance, in her ownership of a fur garment. Develop fur garments as "family" gifts—enable the whole family to enjoy that garment at Christmas, etc., thus reducing its ego-orientation for the owner and eliminating her guilt over her alleged self-indulgence.

Thus, the only way that the young housewife was supposed to express herself, and not feel guilty about it, was in buying products for the home-and-family. Any creative urges she may have should also be home-and-family oriented, as still another survey reported to the home sewing industry.

> Such activities as sewing achieve a new meaning and a new status. Sewing is no longer associated with absolute need. . . . Moreover, with the moral elevation of home-oriented activities, sewing, along with cooking, gardening, and home decorating—is recognized as a means of expressing creativity and individuality and also as a means of achieving the "quality" which a new taste level dictates.

The women who sew, this survey discovered, are the active, energetic, intelligent modern housewives, the new home-oriented modern American women, who have a great unfulfilled need to create, and achieve, and realize their own individuality—which must be filled by some home activity. The big problem for the home-sewing industry was that the "image" of sewing was too "dull"; somehow it didn't achieve the feeling of creating something important. In selling their products, the industry must emphasize the "lasting creativeness" of sewing.

But even sewing can't be too creative, too individual, according to the advice offered to one pattern manufacturer. His patterns required some intelligence to follow, left quite a lot of room for individual expression, and the manufacturer was in trouble for that very reason; his patterns implied that a woman "would know what she likes and would probably have definite ideas." He was advised to widen this "far too limited fashion personality" and get one with "fashion conformity"—appeal to the "fashion-insecure woman," "the conformist element in fashion," who feels "it is not smart to be dressed too differently." For, of course, the manufacturer's problem was not to satisfy woman's need for individuality, for expression or creativity, but to sell more patterns—which is better done by building conformity.

Time and time again, the surveys shrewdly analyzed the needs, and even the secret frustrations of the American housewife; and each time if these needs were properly manipulated, she could be induced to buy more "things." In 1957, a survey told the department stores that their role in this new world was not only to "sell" the housewife but to satisfy her need for "education"—to satisfy the yearning she has, alone in her house, to feel herself a part of the changing world. The store will sell her more, the report said, if it will understand that the real need she is trying to fill by shopping is not anything she can buy there.

> Most women have not only a material need, but a psychological compulsion to visit department stores. They live in comparative isolation. Their vista and experiences are limited. They know that there is a vaster life beyond their horizon and they fear that life will pass them by.
>
> Department stores break down that isolation. The woman entering a department store suddenly has the feeling she knows what is going on in the world. Department stores, more than magazines, TV, or any other medium of mass communication, are most women's main source of information about the various aspects of life . . .

There are many needs that the department store must fill, this report continued. For one, the housewife's "need to learn and to advance in life."

> We symbolize our social position by the objects with which we surround ourselves. A woman whose husband was making $6,000 a few years ago and is making $10,000 now needs to learn a whole new set of symbols. Department stores are her best teachers of this subject.

For another, there is the need for achievement, which for the new modern housewife, is primarily filled by a "bargain."

> We have found that in our economy of abundance, preoccupation with prices is not so much a financial as a psychological need for the majority of women. . . . Increasingly a "bargain" means not that "I can now buy something which I could not afford at a higher price"; it mainly means "I'm doing a good job as a housewife; I'm contributing to the welfare of the family just as my husband does when he works and brings home the paycheck."

The price itself hardly matters, the report said:

Since buying is only the climax of a complicated relationship, based to a large extent on the woman's yearning to know how to be a more attractive woman, a better housewife, a superior mother, etc., use this motivation in all your promotion and advertising. Take every opportunity to explain how your store will help her fulfill her most cherished roles in life . . .

If the stores are women's school of life, ads are the textbooks. They have an inexhaustible avidity for these ads which give them the illusion that they are in contact with what is going on in the world of inanimate objects, objects through which they express so much of so many of their drives . . .

Again, in 1957, a survey very correctly reported that despite the "many positive aspects" of the "new home-centered era," unfortunately too many needs were now centered on the home—that home was not able to fill. A cause for alarm? No indeed; even these needs are grist for manipulation.

The family is not always the psychological pot of gold at the end of the rainbow of promise of modern life as it has sometimes been represented. In fact, psychological demands are being made upon the family today which it cannot fulfill. . . .

Fortunately for the producers and advertisers of America (and also for the family and the psychological well-being of our citizens) much of this gap may be filled, and is being filled, by the acquisition of consumer goods.

Hundreds of products fulfill a whole set of psychological functions that producers and advertisers should know of and use in the development of more effective sales approaches. Just as producing once served as an outlet for social tension, now consumption serves the same purpose.

The buying of things drains away those needs which cannot really be satisfied by home and family—the housewives' need for "something beyond themselves with which to identify," "a sense of movement with others toward aims that give meaning and purpose to life," "an unquestioned social aim to which each individual can devote his efforts."

Deeply set in human nature is the need to have a meaningful place in a group that strives for meaningful social goals. Whenever this is lacking, the individual becomes restless. Which explains why, as we talk to people across the nation, over and over again, we hear questions like these: "What does it all mean?" "Where am I going?" "Why don't things seem more worth while and when we all work so hard and have so darn many things to play with?"

The question is: Can your product fill this gap?

"The frustrated need for privacy in the family life," in this era of "togetherness" was another secret wish uncovered in a depth survey. This need, however, might be used to sell a second car. . . .

In addition to the car the whole family enjoys together, the car for the husband and wife separately—"Alone in the car, one may get the breathing spell one needs so badly and may come to consider the car as one's castle, or the instrument of one's reconquered privacy." Or "individual" "personal" toothpaste, soap, shampoo.

Another survey reported that there was a puzzling "desexualization of married life" despite the great emphasis on marriage and family and sex. The problem: what can supply what the report diagnosed as a "missing sexual spark"? The solution: the report advised sellers to "put the libido back into advertising." Despite the feeling that our manufacturers are trying to sell everything through sex, sex as found on TV commercials and ads in national magazines is too tame, the report said, too narrow. "Consumerism," is desexing the American libido because it "has failed to reflect the powerful life forces in every individual which range far beyond the relationship between the sexes." The sellers, it seemed, have sexed the sex out of sex.

> Most modern advertising reflects and grossly exaggerates our present national tendency to downgrade, simplify and water down the passionate turbulent and electrifying aspects of the life urges of mankind. . . . No one suggests that advertising can or should become obscene or salacious. The trouble lies with the fact that through its timidity and lack of imagination, it faces the danger of becoming libido-poor and consequently unreal, inhuman and tedious.

How to put the libido back, restore the lost spontaneity, drive, love of life, the individuality, that sex in America seems to lack? In an absent-minded moment, the report concludes that "love of life, as of the other sex, should remain unsoiled by exterior motives . . . let the wife be more than a housewife . . . a woman . . ."

One day, having immersed myself in the varied insights these reports have been giving American advertisers for the last fifteen years, I was invited to have lunch with the man who runs this motivational research operation. He had been so helpful in showing me the commercial forces behind the feminine mystique, perhaps I could be helpful to him. Naively I asked why, since he found it so difficult to give women a true feeling of creativeness and achievement in housework, and tried to assuage their guilt and disillusion and frustrations by getting them to buy more "things"—why didn't he encourage them to buy things for all they were worth, so they would have time to get out of the home and pursue truly creative goals in the outside world.

"But we have helped her rediscover the home as the expression of her creativeness," he said. "We help her think of the modern home as the artist's studio, the scientist's laboratory. Besides," he shrugged, "most of the manufacturers we deal with are producing things which have to do with homemaking."

"In a free enterprise economy," he went on, "we have to develop the need for new products. And to do that we have to liberate women to desire these new products. We help them rediscover that homemaking is more creative than to compete with men. This can be manipulated. We sell them what they ought to want, speed up the unconscious, move it along. The big problem is to liberate the woman not to be afraid of what is going to happen to her, if she doesn't have to spend so much time cooking, cleaning."

"That's what I mean," I said. "Why doesn't the pie-mix ad tell the woman she could use the time saved to be an astronomer?"

"It wouldn't be too difficult," he replied. "A few images—the astronomer gets her man, the astronomer as the heroine, make it glamorous for a woman to be an astronomer . . . but no," he shrugged again. "The client would be too frightened. He wants to sell pie mix. The woman has to want to stay in the kitchen. The manufacturer wants to intrigue her back into the kitchen—and we show him how to do it the right way. If he tells her that all she can be is a wife and mother, she will spit in his face. But we show him how to tell her that it's creative to be in the kitchen. We liberate her need to be creative in the kitchen. If we tell her to be an astronomer, she might go too far from the kitchen. Besides," he added, "if you wanted to have a campaign to liberate women to be astronomers, you'd have to find somebody like the National Education Association to pay for it."

The motivational researchers must be given credit for their insights into the reality of the housewife's life and needs—a reality that often escaped their colleagues in academic sociology and therapeutic psychology, who saw women through the Freudian-functional veil. To their own profit, and that of their clients, the manipulators discovered that millions of supposedly happy American housewives have complex needs which home-and-family, love-and-children, cannot fill. But by a morality that goes beyond the dollar, the manipulators are guilty of using their insights to sell women things which, no matter how ingenious, will never satisfy those increasingly desperate needs. They are guilty of persuading housewives to stay at home, mesmerized in front of a television set, their nonsexual human needs unnamed, unsatisfied, drained by the sexual sell into the buying of things.

The manipulators and their clients in American business can hardly be accused of creating the feminine mystique. But they are the most powerful of its perpetuators; it is their millions which blanket the land with persuasive images, flattering the American housewife, diverting her guilt and disguising her growing sense of emptiness. They have done this so successfully, employing the techniques and concepts of modern social science, and transposing them into those deceptively simple, clever, outrageous ads and commercials, that an observer of the American scene today accepts as fact that the great majority of American women have no ambition other than to be housewives. If they are not solely responsible for sending women home, they are surely responsible for keeping them there. Their unremitting harangue is hard to escape in this day of mass communications; they have seared the feminine mystique deep into every woman's mind, and into the minds of her husband, her children, her neighbors. They have made it part of the fabric of her everyday life, taunting her because she is not a better housewife, does not love her family enough, is growing old.

> Can a woman ever feel right cooking on a dirty range? Until today, no range could ever be kept really clean. Now new RCA Whirlpool ranges have oven doors that lift off, broiler drawers that can be cleaned at the sink, drip pans that slide out easily. . . . The first range that any woman can keep completely clean easily . . . and make everything cooked taste better.

> Love is said in many ways. It's giving and accepting. It's protecting and selecting . . . knowing what's safest for those you love. Their bathroom tissue is Scott tissue always. . . . Now in four colors and white.

How skillfully they divert her need for achievement into sexual phantasies which promise her eternal youth, dulling her sense of passing time. They even tell her that she can make time stand still:

> Does she . . . or doesn't she? She's as full of fun as her kids—and just as fresh looking! Her naturalness, the way her hair sparkles and catches the light—as though she's found the secret of making time stand still. And in a way she has . . .

With increasing skill, the ads glorify her "role" as an American housewife—knowing that her very lack of identity in that role will make her fall for whatever they are selling.

> Who is she? She gets as excited as her six-year-old about the opening of school. She reckons her days in trains met, lunches packed, fingers bandaged, and 1,001 details. She could be you, needing a special kind of clothes for your busy, rewarding life.

> Are you this woman? Giving your kids the fun and advantages you want for them? Taking them places and helping them do things? Taking the part that's expected of you in church and community affairs . . . developing your talents so you'll be more interesting? You can be the woman you yearn to be with a Plymouth all your own. . . . Go where you want, when you want in a beautiful Plymouth that's yours and nobody else's . . .

But a new stove or a softer toilet paper do not make a woman a better wife or mother, even if she thinks that's what she needs to be. Dyeing her hair cannot stop time; buying a Plymouth will not give her a new identity; smoking a Marlboro will not get her an invitation to bed, even if that's what she thinks she wants. But those unfulfilled promises can keep her endlessly hungry for things, keep her from ever knowing what she really needs or wants.

A full-page ad in the *New York Times*, June 10, 1962, was "Dedicated to the woman who spends a lifetime living up to her potential!" Under the picture of a beautiful woman, adorned by evening dress and jewels and two handsome children, it said: "The only totally integrated program of nutrient make-up and skin care—designed to lift a woman's good looks to their absolute peak. The woman who uses 'Ultima' feels a deep sense of fulfillment. A new kind of pride. For this luxurious Cosmetic Collection is the *ultimate* . . . beyond it there is nothing."

It all seems so ludicrous when you understand what they are up to. Perhaps the housewife has no one but herself to blame if she lets the manipulators flatter or threaten her into buying things that fill neither her family's needs nor her own. But if the ads and commercials are a clear case of caveat emptor, the same sexual sell disguised in the editorial content of a magazine or a television program is both less ridiculous and more insidious. Here the housewife is often an unaware victim. I have written for some of the magazines in which the sexual sell is inextricably linked with the editorial content. Consciously or unconsciously, the editors know what the advertiser wants.

> The heart of X magazine is service—complete service to the whole woman who is the American homemaker; service in all the areas of greatest interest to advertisers, who are also business men. It delivers to the advertiser a strong concentration of serious, conscientious, dedicated homemakers. Women more interested in the home and products for the home. Women more willing and able to pay . . .

A memo need never be written, a sentence need never be spoken at an editorial conference; the men and women who make the editorial decisions often compromise their own very high standards in the interests of the advertising dollar. Often, as a former editor of *McCall's* recently revealed,[2] the advertiser's influence is less than subtle. The kind of home pictured in the "service" pages is dictated in no uncertain terms by the boys over in advertising.

And yet, a company has to make a profit on its products; a magazine, a network needs advertising to survive. But even if profit is the only motive, and the only standard of success, I wonder if the media are not making a mistake when they give the client what they think he wants. I wonder if the challenge and the opportunities for the American economy and for business itself might not in the long run lie in letting women grow up, instead of blanketing them with the youth-serum that keeps them mindless and thing-hungry.

The real crime, no matter how profitable for the American economy, is the callous and growing acceptance of the manipulator's advice "to get them young"—the television commercials that children sing or recite even before they learn to read, the big beautiful ads almost as easy as "Look, Sally, Look," the magazines deliberately designed to turn teenage girls into housewife buyers of things before they grow up to be women:

> She reads X Magazine from beginning to end . . . She learns how to market, to cook and to sew and everything else a young woman should know. She plans her wardrobe 'round X Magazine's clothes, heeds X Magazine's counsel on beauty and beaus . . . consults X Magazine for the latest teen fads . . . and oh, how she buys from those X Magazine ads! Buying habits start in X Magazine. It's easier to START a habit than to STOP one! (Learn how X Magazine's unique publication, X Magazine-at-school, carries your advertising into high school home economics classrooms.)

Like a primitive culture which sacrificed little girls to its tribal gods, we sacrifice our girls to the feminine mystique, grooming them ever more efficiently through the sexual sell to become consumers of the things to whose profitable sale our nation is dedicated. Two ads recently appeared in a national news magazine, geared not to teenage girls but to executives who produce and sell things. One of them showed the picture of a boy:

> I am *so* going to the moon . . . and you can't go, 'cause you're a girl! Children are growing faster today, their interests can cover such a wide range—from roller skates to rockets. X company too has grown, with a broad spectrum of electronic products for worldwide governmental, industrial and space application.

The other showed the face of a girl:

> Should a gifted child grow up to be a housewife? Educational experts estimate that the gift of high intelligence is bestowed upon only one out of every 50 children in our nation. When that gifted child is a girl, one question is inevitably asked: "Will this rare gift be wasted if she becomes a housewife?" Let these gifted girls answer that question themselves. Over 90 percent of them marry, and the majority find the job of being a housewife challenging and rewarding enough to make full use of all their intelligence, time and energy. . . . In her daily roles of nurse, educator, economist and just plain housewife, she is constantly seeking ways to improve her family's life. . . . Millions of women—shopping for half the families in America—do so by saving X Stamps.

If that gifted girl-child grows up to be a housewife, can even the manipulator make supermarket stamps use all of her human intelligence, her human energy, in the century she may live while that boy goes to the moon?

Never underestimate the power of a woman, says another ad. But that power was and is underestimated in America. Or rather, it is only estimated in terms that can be manipulated at the point of purchase. Woman's human intelligence and energy do not really figure in. And yet, they exist, to be used for some higher purpose than housework and thing-buying—or wasted. Perhaps it is only a sick society, unwilling to face its own problems and unable to conceive of goals and purposes equal to the ability and knowledge of its members, that chooses to ignore the strength of women. Perhaps it is only a sick or immature society that chooses to make women "housewives," not people. Perhaps it is only sick or immature men and women, unwilling to face the great challenges of society, who can retreat for long, without unbearable distress, into that thing-ridden house and make it the end of life itself.

ENDNOTES

1. The studies upon which this chapter is based were done by the Staff of the Institute for Motivational Research, directed by Dr. Ernest Dichter. They were made available to me through the courtesy of Dr. Dichter and his colleagues, and are on file at the Institute, in Croton-on-Hudson, New York.

2. Harrison Kinney, *Has Anybody Seen My Father?*, New York, 1960.

4
Stuart Ewen
"... IMAGES WITHOUT BOTTOM ..."
(1988)

Style, hard to define ... but easy to recognize.

—MAGAZINE ADVERTISEMENT FOR HATHAWAY BLOUSE

Each week on television, a taut-faced woman named Elsa Klensch hosts a program titled "Style." The prime focus of the show revolves around the new designer collections, transporting us to major fashion shows around the world, but there is more.

Some features center on the homes of the people in the world of fashion design: castles in the countryside near Rome; converted farm houses in rural Connecticut; fabulous playpens overlooking Paris. Still other items deal with the daily lives of people employed in the "world" (one dare not call it *industry!*) of fashion. We follow a tawny Milanese mannequin through her regular two-hour body and facial treatment at Sergio Valente. We observe a busy New York model, rollerskating and taking tap-dance lessons; intimately sharing her longing to "make it" in the musical theater. We glide through the byways of Tokyo with Toko, a slender fashion model with "the most famous Japanese face in the world." Her spare time, we learn, is divided between shopping for her new apartment and practicing traditional Japanese Buddhism. Materialism and its spiritual rejection coexist without conflict.

Accompanying commercials blend right in, telling us of the slimming value of Tab cola, or of the way that Henry Grethel clothing will lead us into accidental and anonymous romantic encounters with beautiful women—or men—in elegant hotel rooms.

We see that style is about beautiful mouth-watering surfaces, but we see more. Beyond displaying surfaces, the uninterrupted message of the television program is that style makes up a way of life, a utopian way of life marked by boundless wealth. The people we view apparently inhabit a universe of bounty. They wear dresses costing thousands. They live in castles. Their encounters with interior designers lead to unrestrained flights of fancy. Their desires, their fantasies, their whims are painlessly translated into objective forms. There are no conflicts. In the name of "good taste," there is no mention of cost. There is no anxiety about affordability.

This way of life is marked by an endless succession of material objects, yet it is a life that curiously seems to float beyond the terms of the real world. This is essential to the magic of style, its fascination and enchantment. Part of the promise of style is that it will lift us out of the dreariness of necessity.

At the other end of the tunnel of television, however, sits the viewer: cheaper clothes; no castles; bills piling up; no stranger to the anxieties of desire placed within the constraints of possibility. The viewer sits, watches, embedded in the finite terms of daily life. From this vantage point, the viewer is engaged in a relationship with style. It is a relationship that offers a pledge, a pledge repeated across the panorama of American consumer culture again and again, day in and day out. Everyday life in its details (clothing, house, routine objects, and activities) can, through the sorcery of style, be transformed. Without ever saying so explicitly, the media of style offer to lift the viewer out of his or her life and place him or her in a utopian netherworld where there are no conflicts, no needs unmet; where the ordinary is—by its very nature—extraordinary.

Style today is an incongruous cacophony of images, strewn across the social landscape. Style may be borrowed from any source and turn up in a place where it is least expected. The stylish person may look like a duchess one week, a murder victim the next. Style can hijack the visual idiom of astronauts, or poach from the ancient pageantry of Guatemalan peasant costumes.

An advertisement for Neiman-Marcus (1984), one of the most fashionable department stores in the United States, reveals style's ability to constitute what Herbert Marcuse once described as a "unity of opposites." In an ad for women's clothing, the newspaper display offers readers a choice between two stylistic polarities.

One possible direction is "Attitude," a cool and self-confident expression of aristocratic taste. The typeface here is elegant and conservative. Above is a photograph of a woman, a poised Parisian, perhaps, wearing a broad-brimmed *chapeau* and *haute couture* coat. Her delicate hand caresses the brim of her hat; her skin is milky white; her eyes are passive, and vacant. Below her, the words:

ATTITUDE IS disposition with regard to people or things.

ATTITUDE IS wearing the correct thing at the correct hour.

ATTITUDE IS a seam.

ATTITUDE IS exactly sized. ("I wear a size 6")

ATTITUDE IS a mode.

ATTITUDE IS dressing to please someone else.

ATTITUDE IS an evaluation.

ATTITUDE IS strolling the avenue.

ATTITUDE IS Neiman-Marcus.

On the same page, on the other side of a sharp, jagged line, lies another vision of style: "Latitude." Far from the "cultured" refinement of the aristocrat, this is about breaking the rules, violating taboos. The typeface here is scrawled, in bold graffiti strokes. Above is a picture of another woman, a languid and brooding Semitic type, wearing the head scarf of a Palestinian and a loose-fitting desert caftan. She reclines; her arms fall back above her head. Her skin is olive, glistening with moisture, and her dark eyes look off to the side, gazing in the direction of forbidden desires. Below her, the words:

LATITUDE IS freedom from narrow restrictions permitting freedom of action.

LATITUDE IS changing the structure of a garment, however, whenever, the mood hits.

LATITUDE IS a slash.

LATITUDE IS whatever feels comfortable.

LATITUDE IS a mood.

LATITUDE IS dressing to please yourself.

LATITUDE IS an evolution.

LATITUDE IS loving the street life.

and, once more,

LATITUDE IS Neiman-Marcus.

Colliding world views are translated into style, images to be purchased. As disembodied images, they can be easily reconciled, both available from the same source. As the ad concludes, we are instructed that style may fall on "the left or right" of a "strongly defined line," yet depending on the "moment or imagination," either may be appropriate. Style makes statements, yet has no convictions. "Our stocks," the advertisement concludes, "are full of both looks. Ask any N-M salesperson for a little direction—or just say the word. Attitude. Or Latitude." Obedience or self-determination, conservative or radical, Brahmin or Untouchable, Superego or Id; any of these dualities may be purchased, simultaneously, in the world of style.

· · ·

If the style market constitutes a presentation of a way of life, it is a way of life that is unattainable for most, nearly all, people. Yet this doesn't mean that style isn't relevant to most people. It is very relevant. It is the most common realm of our society in which the need for a better, or different way of life is acknowledged, and expressed on a material level, if not met. It constitutes a politics of change, albeit a "change" that resides wholly on the surface of things. The surfaces, themselves, are lifted from an infinite number of sources.

The imagery of elite culture is an ongoing aspect of style. A magazine advertisement for Benson & Hedges "Deluxe Ultra Lights" places two large, gold-edged packages of cigarettes in front of a sweeping spiral staircase, draped in muted tones of ivory and pink. Halfway up the stairs a woman in a beaded evening gown, dragging a white mink stole up thickly carpeted stairs, has her cigarette lit by an elegant gent in a black tuxedo. Meanwhile, in another ad in the same magazine, an unseen hand pours Chivas Regal scotch into a sparkling crystal slipper. Each image reeks of money, offering the consumer a democratic promise of limitless possibility while, at the same time, projecting the sheltered prerogatives of an elite few. Assuming the iconography or "attitude" of elites may, for some, represent a change for the better, an elevation of status. More and more, however, style offers other visions of change, drawn from an endless repository of images.

ELLE magazine presents a photo-feature entitled "Paramilitary Mode." Sultry, daring members of a "pricey platoon" display the potential allure of military gear. "Wake up to the fun of fatigues," challenges the text, as an enticing woman, preparing for "combat," removes her button-fly pants, revealing camouflage panties upon her forward-thrust hip.

TAXI, a slick magazine on "fashion, trends and leisure living," presents a profile of Ennio Capasa, a "rising star" among fashion designers. His "Japanese-influenced collection," comments the magazine (quoting the *New York Times*), "looks like what one imagines a rebel against totalitarianism would do to make drab clothes individual and the stultifying sexy." Political transformation and liberation come through "with energy and force," part of a bold, sensual new look.

An advertisement for Esprit jeans argues that "denim and jeans-wear" are "social equalizers." Warring on the elitist tyranny of "silks and satin," the ad continues, Esprit jeans offer an "Elegance" that is "anti-fashion and anti-luxury." To underscore the political egalitarianism of the product, the jeans are modeled by two "real" young women—not professional models—whose credentials are listed to create an atmosphere of intelligence, physical and spiritual health, and firm social commitments. Both blond and blue-eyed—conforming to the Aryan, photogenic ideals of the fashion trade—these two *really care.* Cara

Schanche of Berkeley, California (another symbol of youthful idealism), is an "English Literature Student, Part-time Waitress, Anti-Racism Activist, Beginning Windsurfer, Friend of the Dalai Lama." Her soulmate in style, Ariel O'Donnell of San Francisco, is a "Waitress/Bartender, Non-professional AIDS Educator, Cyclist, Art Restoration Student, Anglophile, Neo-Feminist." In the world of style, ideas, activities, and commitments become ornaments, adding connotation and value to the garment while they are, simultaneously, eviscerated of meaning.

Another ad, for Bloomingdale's "Fall '87 Collection," draws its idiom from an indiscriminate clatter of social, political, and artistic references. "Courage comrades," begins the ad. "Back-to-School's anything but a bore for young Post-constructivists. We condone conspicuous clothes with working-class conviction. . . . And a fundamentalist belief in French Connection, The Fall '87 Collection. . . . Juniors moves into a new age at Bloomingdale's. From counter culture to sophisticated, sexy, fast forward fashion for progressive thinkers." Ideas and concepts—socialism, fundamentalism, conspicuous consumption, new age—meld into an effervescent swirl of inchoate activity, a fashion statement, implying everything, signifying nothing. Here, amid the polymorphous collage, we are tantalized by empty promises of transgression.

If the "life-style" of style is not realizable in life, it is nevertheless the most constantly available lexicon from which many of us draw the visual grammar of our lives. It is a behavioral model that is closely interwoven with modern patterns of survival and desire. It is a "hard to define . . . but easy to recognize" element in our current history.

Often silently, at times unacknowledged, style works on the ways that people understand and relate to the world around them. Its influence can be seen within the insecure, but nonetheless formative, boundaries of adolescence, when the search for *identity* accelerates. Anita A——, now a twenty-four-year-old college student, confides,

> When I was in high school I cut out an advertisement from a magazine and hung it on my wall. The ad read "Create An Image" in big bold white letters. . . . I don't remember what the ad was for, and I never really cared. . . . I simply wanted to remind myself to work on my style. . . . I used to be really taken by someone who could cause that intense silence just by entering a room. I was often captured by their style.[1]

Lisa E——, twenty, feels that style "is closely related to advertising." "My elements of style," she readily admits, "are what's spread across the pages of *Vogue, Elle* and *Glamour* magazines." She explains,

> Right now I'm in the middle of a style change. I'm making myself miserable as I wait for my hair to grow out from an extremely short, close shaven cut. That haircut was my favorite. It was easy to care for. It looked great on me. I was always complimented . . . so why change it? The an-

drogenous, short-haired look of Annie Lennox has been replaced by the more feminine locks of Paulina Porizkova. Her image is everywhere nowadays. It's her image that is making me desire longer hair. So I will add that to me.[2]

For others, style is seen as a powerful mode of self-expression, a way in which people establish themselves in relation to others. Michael H———, who grew up in the South Bronx, spent much of his childhood and adolescence playing basketball. For him, style was an essential part of the game, part of winning:

> I played the game from sun-up till sundown. It's never enough to just score the ball in the basket, or to simply block someone's shot. There's got to be style added to it ... finesse, control, aggression. When a basketball is dunked in the basket, especially while an opponent is present, it says a statement and a sense of style. "Get off of me, and take this!" is the clear message. To block an opponent's shot and send the ball into another area of the park or gym is very threatening and shows style.

Michael's sense of "style" has been shaped by the choreography and competition of basketball, but it has also been mediated by items from the marketplace. Michael discusses the use of commodities in the process of establishing and expressing cultural meanings:

> When I grew up I wore basketball sneakers and *Lee* jeans. I wore my hair sometimes in braids or in waves, and I walked with a bop. It's a cultural statement that my friends and I identified with while growing up. . . . It's the "thing" to wear basketball sneakers in the ghetto.[3]

For a newcomer to the United States, the preponderance of marketplace style can initiate a moment of personal crisis. For Linda M———, a young woman who grew up in Peru, in a culture that she describes as "traditional," her encounter with "style" in metropolitan New York accentuated a fissure of meaning. In Peru, she explains, style was understood as "the way in which the inner being of someone is expressed." Here, in the United States, style has a "very different meaning . . . which comes from the external world rather than from the inner one":

> Not only tastes are being shaped, . . . but also perceptions of one's own self. . . . The interaction of people and environment is being turned inside out.
>
> My personal experience has been a difficult one. There are ways in which I feel anachronic in a modern society. . . . I found a tremendous difference in my perspectives of life and that of most people in a commercialized society. . . . Only now I seem to begin to understand why life seems so meaningless to many people in a big society up to the point where they prefer to drug themselves not to bear with an empty reality which displays a glamour of images without bottom, without real meaning. . . .
>
> If style . . . has become something people think they could buy, then

what we are losing is man himself. We are betraying our own self, we are selling our own inner being and replacing it for a more suitable one for "modern society."[4]

The phenomenon of style within contemporary American society is varied and complex. It registers different meanings to different people, or among different communities. Yet what Linda M——says, about "a glamour of images without bottom," cannot help but strike a chord with anyone who has observed, or lived in, the shadow of the managed image. In so many arenas of life, style has become the *legal tender*.

Style, more and more, has become the official idiom of the marketplace.* In advertising, packaging, product design, and corporate *identity*, the power of provocative surfaces speaks to the eye's mind, overshadowing matters of quality or substance. Style, moreover, is an intimate component of subjectivity, intertwined with people's aspirations and anxieties. Increasingly, style has emerged as a decisive component of politics; political issues and politicians are regularly subjected to the cosmetic sorcery of image managers, providing the public with a telegenic commodity. Democratic choice, like grocery shopping, has become a question of which product is most attractively packaged, which product is most imaginatively merchandised. How has this ubiquitous primacy of style come about?

Precisely because style deals in surface impressions, it is difficult to concretize, to discern its definitions. It forms a chimerical, yet highly visible corridor between the world of things and human consciousness. Investing profane things with sacred meanings, however, is an ancient activity, a universal preoccupation of our species. This, in and of itself, does not define style, nor does it situate style within the particular conditions and contradictions of contemporary life.

The ornamentation of life has been practiced within traditional cultures for millennia; the tendency to invest such embellishments with intricate, powerful, and often mysterious webs of interpretation has also been common. Often interwoven within mythological and magical belief systems, decorative objects asserted astonishing powers. They could explain the world as it was, ratify established patterns of kinship and power, or express visions of something beyond the conventional terms of existence: a horror or a consolation.

Yet within such traditional societies, the role of imagery and decoration differed significantly from the volatile phenomenon of *style* in modern life. Traditional imagery stood for an unchanging or cyclical world, frozen in time and space, hierarchical and static, where everyone knew his or her assigned place in the "great chain of being." Modern

---

* The term *marketplace* is employed as a euphemism for commerce. Today, as the market is often indistinguishable from society itself, there is no longer a market-*place* in its original and localized sense.

style speaks to a world where change is the rule of the day, where one's place in the social order is a matter of perception, the product of diligently assembled illusions. Today, style is one way by which we perceive a world in flux, moving—apparently—ever forward, whereas traditional societies' use of imagery invoked a sense of perpetuity, which conformed to a general outlook on life.

The power of style, and its emergence as an increasingly important feature in people's lives, cannot be separated from the evolution and sensibility of modernity. Style is a visible reference point by which we have come to understand life *in progress*. People's devotion to the acceleration of varying styles allows them to be connected to the "reality" of a given moment. At the same time they understand that this given moment will give way to yet another, and another, and that as it does, styles will change, again and again. A sense of rootedness or permanency is elusive in the world of style, and it is perhaps this quality, more than any other, that locates style in the modern world. On the one hand, style speaks for the rise of a democratic society, in which who one wishes to become is often seen as more consequential than who one is. On the other hand, style speaks for a society in which coherent meaning has fled to the hills, and in which drift has provided a context of continual discontent.

But the question of style cannot be limited to the realm of subjectivity. Style is also a significant element of power. Style, today, is inextricably woven into the fabric of social, political, and economic life. It is the product of a vast and seamless network of industries. The production of sumptuous images, for the very few, was once limited to the sacred workshops of the medieval monasteries; now, the production and marketing of style is global, touching the lives and imaginations of nearly everyone. Design, of one sort or another, is affixed to almost every conceivable commodity, and style is now "ladled out" from what the art critic Herbert Read once disparagingly termed a continuous and "glorified soup kitchen." It is to the historic development of that "soup kitchen," and to its implications, that we now must turn.

ENDNOTES

1. Style Project, written testimony A6.
2. Ibid., written testimony A9.
3. Ibid., written testimony A10.
4. Ibid., written testimony A2.

PART TWO

The Social Organization of Symbols

Jean Baudrillard
"The Ideological Genesis of Needs"[1]
(1969)

The rapturous satisfactions of consumption surround us, clinging to objects as if to the sensory residues of the previous day in the delirious excursion of a dream. As to the logic that regulates this strange discourse—surely it compares to what Freud uncovered in *The Interpretation of Dreams*? But we have scarcely advanced beyond the explanatory level of naive psychology and the medieval dreambook. We believe in "Consumption": we believe in a real subject, motivated by needs and confronted by real objects as sources of satisfaction. It is a thoroughly vulgar metaphysic. And contemporary psychology, sociology and economic science are all complicit in the fiasco. So the time has come to deconstruct all the assumptive notions involved—object, need, aspiration, *consumption* itself—for it would make as little sense to theorize the quotidian from surface evidence as to interpret the manifest discourse of a dream: it is rather the dream-work and the dream-processes that must be analyzed in order to recover the unconscious logic of a more profound discourse. And it is the workings and processes of an unconscious social logic that must be retrieved beneath the consecrated ideology of consumption.

1. CONSUMPTION AS A LOGIC OF SIGNIFICATIONS

The empirical "object," given in its contingency of form, color, material, function and discourse (or, if it is a cultural object, in its aesthetic finality) is a myth. How often it has been wished away! But the object is *nothing*. It is nothing but the different types of relations and significations that converge, contradict themselves, and twist around it, as such—the hidden logic that not only arranges this bundle of relations, but directs the manifest discourse that overlays and occludes it.

THE LOGICAL STATUS OF OBJECTS

Insofar as I make use of a refrigerator as a machine, it is not an object. It is a refrigerator. Talking about refrigerators or automobiles in terms of "objects" is something else. That is, it has nothing to do with them in their "objective" relation to keeping things cold or transportation. It is to speak of the object as functionally decontextualized:

1. Either as an object of psychic investment[2] and fascination, of passion and projection—qualified by its exclusive relation with the subject, who then cathects it as if it were his own body (a borderline case). Useless and sublime, the object then loses its common name, so to speak, and assumes the title of Object as generic proper name. For this reason, the collector never refers to a statuette or a vase as a beautiful statuette, vase, etc., but as "a beautiful Object." This status is opposed to the generic dictionary meaning of the word, that of the "object" plain and simple: "Refrigerator: an object that refrigerates . . ."

2. Or (between the Object, as proper name and projective equivalent of the subject, and the object, with the status of a common name and implement) as an object specified by its trademark, charged with differential connotations of status, prestige and fashion. *This is* the "object of consumption." It can just as easily be a vase as a refrigerator, or, for that matter, a whoopee cushion. Properly speaking, it has no more existence than a phoneme has an absolute meaning in linguistics. This object does not assume meaning either in a symbolic relation with the subject (the Object) or in an operational relation to the world (object-as-implement): it finds meaning with other objects, in difference, according to a hierarchical code of significations. This alone, at the risk of the worst confusion, defines the object of consumption.

OF SYMBOLIC EXCHANGE "VALUE"

In symbolic exchange, of which the gift is our most proximate illustration, the object is not an object: it is inseparable from the concrete relation in which it is exchanged, the transferential pact that it seals between two persons: it is thus not independent as such. It has, properly speaking, neither use value nor (economic) exchange value. The object given has symbolic exchange value. This is the paradox of the gift: it is on the one hand (relatively) arbitrary: it matters little what object is involved. Provided it is given,[3] it can fully signify the relation. On the other hand, once it has been given—and *because* of this—it is *this* object and not another. The gift is unique, specified by the people exchanging and the unique moment of the exchange. It is arbitrary, and yet absolutely singular.

As distinct from language, whose material can be disassociated from the subjects speaking it, the material of symbolic exchange, the objects given, are not autonomous, hence not codifiable as signs. Since they do not depend on economic exchange, they are not amenable to systematization as commodities and exchange value.

What constitutes the object as value in symbolic exchange is that one separates himself from it in order to give it, to throw it at the feet of the other, under the gaze of the other (*ob-jicere*); one divests himself as if of a part of himself—an act which is significant in itself as the basis, simultaneously, of both the mutual presence of the terms of the relationship, and their mutual absence (their distance). The ambivalence of all symbolic exchange material (looks, objects, dreams, excrement) derives from this: the gift is a medium of relation and distance; it is always love and aggression.[4]

FROM SYMBOLIC EXCHANGE TO SIGN VALUE

It is from the (theoretically isolatable) moment when the exchange is no longer purely transitive, when the object (the material of exchange) is immediately presented as such, that it is reified into a sign. Instead of abolishing itself in the relation that it establishes, and thus assuming symbolic value (as in the example of the gift), the object becomes autonomous, intransitive, opaque, and so begins to signify the abolition of the relationship. Having become a sign object, it is no longer the mobile signifier of a lack between two beings, it is 'of' and 'from' the reified relation (as is the commodity at another level, in relation to reified labor power). Whereas the symbol refers to lack (to absence) as a virtual relation of desire, the sign object only refers to the absence of relation itself, and to isolated individual subjects.

The sign object is neither given nor exchanged: it is appropriated, withheld and manipulated by individual subjects as a sign, that is, as coded difference. Here lies the object of consumption. And it is always of and from a reified, abolished social relationship that is "signified" in a code.

What we perceive in the symbolic object (the gift, and also the traditional, ritual and artisanal object) is not only the concrete manifestation of a total relationship (ambivalent, and total because it is ambivalent) of desire; but also, through the singularity of an object, the transparency of social relations in a dual or integrated group relationship. In the commodity, on the other hand, we perceive the opacity of social relations of production and the reality of the division of labor. What is revealed in the contemporary profusion of sign objects, objects of consumption, is precisely this opacity, the *total constraint of the code* that governs social value: it is the specific weight of *signs* that regulates the social logic of exchange.

The object-become-sign no longer gathers its meaning in the concrete relationship between two people. It assumes its meaning in its differential relation to other people. It assumes its meaning in its differential relation to other signs. Somewhat like Lévi-Strauss' myths, sign-objects exchange among themselves. Thus, only when objects are autonomized as differential signs and thereby rendered systematizable can one speak of consumption and of objects of consumption.

A LOGIC OF SIGNIFICATION

So it is necessary to distinguish the logic of consumption, which is a logic of the sign and of difference, from several other logics that habitually get entangled with it in the welter of evidential considerations. (This confusion is echoed by all the naive and authorized literature on the question.) Four logics would be concerned here:

1. A functional logic of use value;

2. An economic logic of exchange value;

3. A logic of symbolic exchange;

4. A logic of sign value.

The first is a logic of practical operations, the second one of equivalence, the third, ambivalence, and the fourth, difference.

Or again: a logic of utility, a logic of the market, a logic of the gift, and a logic of status. Organized in accordance with one of the above groupings, the object assumes respectively the status of an *instrument*, a *commodity*, a *symbol*, or a *sign*.

Only the last of these defines the specific field of consumption. Let us compare two examples:

The wedding ring: This is a unique object, symbol of the relationship of the couple. One would neither think of changing it (barring mishap) nor of wearing several. The symbolic object is made to last and to witness in its duration the permanence of the relationship. Fashion plays as negligible a role at the strictly symbolic level as at the level of pure instrumentality.

The ordinary ring is quite different: it does not symbolize a relationship. It is a non-singular object, a personal gratification, a sign in the eyes of others. I can wear several of them. I can substitute them. The ordinary ring takes part in the play of my accessories and the constellation of fashion. It is an object of consumption.

Living accommodations: The house, your lodgings, your apartment: these terms involve semantic nuances that are no doubt linked to the advent of industrial production or to social standing. But, whatever one's social level in France today, one's domicile is not necessarily perceived as a "consumption" good. The question of residence is still very closely associated with patrimonial goods in general, and its symbolic scheme remains largely that of the body. Now, for the logic of consumption to penetrate here, the exteriority of the sign is required. The residence must cease to be hereditary, or interiorized as an organic family space. One must avoid the appearance of filiation and identification if one's debut in the world of fashion is to be successful.

In other words, domestic practice is still largely a function of determinations, namely: symbolic (profound emotional investment, etc.), and economic (scarcity).

Moreover, the two are linked: only a certain "discretionary income" permits one to play with objects as status signs—a stage of fashion and the "game" where the symbolic and the utilitarian are both exhausted. Now, as to the question of residence—in France at least—the margin of free play for the mobile combinatory of prestige or for the game of substitution is limited. In the United States, by contrast, one sees living arrangements indexed to social mobility, to trajectories of careers and status. Inserted into the global constellation of status, and subjugated to the same accelerated obsolescence of any other object of luxury, the house truly becomes an object of consumption.

This example has a further interest: it demonstrates the futility of any attempt to define the object empirically. Pencils, books, fabrics, food, the car, curios—are these objects? Is a house an object? Some would contest this. The decisive point is to establish whether the symbolism of the house (sustained by the shortage of housing) is irreducible, or if even this can succumb to the differential and reified connotations of fashion logic: for if this is so, then the home becomes an object of consumption—as any other object will, if it only answers to the same definition: being, cultural trait, ideal, gestural pattern, language, etc.—anything can be made to fit the bill. The definition of an object of consumption is entirely independent of objects themselves and *exclusively a function of the logic of significations*.

An object is not an object of consumption unless it is released from its psychic determinations as *symbol*; from its functional determinations as *instrument*; from its commercial determinations as *product*; and is thus *liberated as a sign* to be recaptured by the formal logic of fashion, i.e., by the logic of differentiation.

THE ORDER OF SIGNS AND SOCIAL ORDER

There is no object of consumption before the moment of its substitution, and without this substitution having been determined by the social law, which demands not only the renewal of distinctive material, but the obligatory registration of individuals on the scale of status, through the mediation of their group and as a function of their relations with other groups. *This scale is properly the social order*, since the acceptance of this hierarchy of differential signs and the interiorization by the individual of signs in general (i.e., of the norms, values, and social imperatives that signs are) constitutes the fundamental, decisive form of social control—more so even than acquiescence to ideological norms.

It is now clear that there is no autonomous problematic of objects, but rather the much more urgent need for a theory of social logic, and of the codes that it puts into play (sign systems and distinctive material).

THE COMMON NAME, THE PROPER NAME, AND THE BRAND NAME

Let us recapitulate the various types of status of the object according to the specific and (theoretically) exhaustive logics that may penetrate it:

1. The refrigerator is specified by its function and irreplaceable in this respect. There is a necessary relation between the object and its function. The arbitrary nature of the sign is not involved. But all refrigerators are interchangeable in regard to this function (their objective "meaning").

2. By contrast, if the refrigerator is taken as an element of comfort or of luxury (standing), then in principle any other such element can be substituted for it. The object tends to the status of sign, and each social status will be signified by an entire constellation of exchangeable signs. No necessary relation to the subject or the world is involved. There is only a systematic relation obligated to all other signs. And in this combinatory abstraction lie the elements of a code.

3. In their symbolic relationship to the subject (or in reciprocal exchange), all objects are potentially interchangeable. Any object can serve as a doll for the little girl. But once cathected, it is *this* one and not another. The symbolic material is relatively arbitrary, but the subject-object relation is fused. Symbolic discourse is an idiom.

The functional use of the object occurs in relation to its technical structure and its practical manipulation. It relates to the common name: e.g., refrigerator. The use of the symbol-object occurs in the context of its concrete presence and through the proper name proper to it. Possession and passion baptize the object (in the metaphorical name of the subject), affixing their seal to it. The "consumption of" the object occurs in the context of its brand name, which is not a proper name, but a sort of generic Christian name.[5]

2. CONSUMPTION AS A STRUCTURE OF EXCHANGE AND DIFFERENTIATION

OF THE INVALIDITY OF THE NOTION OF THE OBJECT AND NEED

We can see now that objects have no meaning except in those logical contexts that can mingle, often contradictorily, on the plane of one object alone; and that these various significations depend on the index and modalities of *commutation* possible within the framework of each logic. And so what possible meaning can any classification, definition, or categorization of objects in themselves have when the object (once again taken in the widest sense of the term) is commutable according to many rules (the rules of equivalence in the functional and economic domain;

the rules of difference in the domain of signs; the rule of ambivalence in that of the symbolic)? Is it when the discourse of the conscious and the unconscious gets entangled in the object—the full discourse of denotation, the parallel discourse of connotation, the internal discourse of the subject and social discourse of relationship—even the entirely latent discourse, in the object, of the symbolic absence of the subject from himself and the other?[6] And what possible foundation could there be for all the possible theories of needs, more or less indexed as they are to these would-be categories and classifications of objects? In such an area of flux, empirical formalizations are devoid of meaning. The situation is reminiscent of Borges' zoological classification: "Animals are divided into: (a) belonging to the Emperor; (b) embalmed, (c) tame, (d) suckling pigs, (e) sirens, (f) fabulous, (g) stray dogs, (h) included in the present classification, etc., etc., ..."[7] All classifications of objects and needs are neither more logical nor less surrealist than this.

NEED AND MANA

To reduce the conceptual entity "object" is, by the same token, to deconstruct the conceptual entity "need." We could explode that of the subject as well.

Subject, object, need: the mythological structure of these three ideas is identical, triply elaborated in terms of the naive factuality and the schemas of a primary level psychology.

What speaks in terms of need is magical thinking. The subject and the object having been posited as autonomous and separated entities—as specular[8] and distinct myths—it then becomes necessary to establish their relation. This is accomplished, of course, with the concept of need. Incidentally—all else remaining equal—the concept resembles that of *mana*.[9] Conceiving exchange as an operation between two separated terms, each existing in isolation prior to the exchange, one has to establish the existence of the exchange itself in a double obligation: that of giving and that of returning. Thus it is necessary to imagine (as Mauss and the native apparently do) an immanent power in the object, the *hau*, whose force haunts the recipient of the object and incites him to divest himself of it. The insurmountable opposition between the terms of the exchange is thus reduced at the price of a tautological, artificial, magical, supplementary concept, of which Lévi-Strauss, in his critique, has worked out the economics in positing exchange directly as structure. Thus, the psychologist, economist, etc., having provided themselves with a subject and an object, can barely rejoin them but for the grace of need. But this concept can only explain the subject-object relation in terms of adequation, the functional response of subjects to objects, and vice versa. It amounts to a kind of functionalist nominalism, which precipitates the whole psycho-economic ideology of optimality, equilibrium, functional regulation and adaptation of needs.

In fact, the operation amounts to defining the subject by means of the object and the object in terms of the subject. It is a gigantic tautology of which the concept of need is the consecration. Metaphysics itself has never done anything else and, in Western thought, *metaphysics and economic science* (not to mention traditional psychology) *demonstrate a profound solidarity*, mentally and ideologically, in the way they posit the subject and tautologically resolve its relation to the world. *Mana*, vital force, instincts, needs, choices, preferences, utilities, motivations: it is always a question of the same magical copula, the equal sign in "A = A." Metaphysics and economics jostle each other at the same impasses, over the same aporias, the same contradictions and dysfunctions, condemning each from the start to unlimited circular speculation by positing the autonomy of the subject and its specular reflection in the autonomy of the object.

THE "CIRCLE" OF POWER

But we know that the tautology is never innocent—no more than the finalism that underlies the entire mythology of needs. Such run-arounds are always the rationalizing ideology of a system of power: the dormant virtue of opium, the refrains of "Que Sera Sera": like Borges' animal categories ("included in the present classification"), or like the theological pronouncement: "When a given subject purchases such and such an object, this behavior is a function of his particular choices and preferences." At bottom, under the umbrella of the logical principle of identity, such admirable metaphors for the void sanction the circular principle of a system of power, the reproductive finality of the order of production. This is why economic science does not dispense with the concept of need. It could easily do so, for its calculations operate at the level of statistical demand. But the notion is urgently required for ideological support.

The *legitimacy* of production rests on a *petitio principii*, i.e., that people discover a posteriori and almost miraculously that they need what is produced and offered at the marketplace (and thus, in order that they should experience this or any particular need, the need must already exist inside people as a virtual postulation). And so it appears that this begging of the question—this forced rationalization—simply masks the *internal finality* of the order of production. To become an end in itself, every system must dispel the question of its real teleology. Through the meretricious legitimacy of needs and satisfactions, the entire question of the social and political finality of productivity is repressed.

One could object that this is not a forced rationalization, since the discourse of needs is the subject's spontaneous form of interpreting his relation to objects and to the world. But this is precisely the problem. In his attempt to recapture this discourse, the analyst of modern society reproduces the misconstruction of naive anthropology: *he naturalizes the processes of exchange and signification.*

Thus social logic itself escapes him. It is true that all magical thinking draws a certain measure of efficacy from the empirical manipulation and theoretical misunderstanding of its own procedures. Thus, speculation on needs converges with the long tradition of speculation on *mana*. It is mythical thought that reflects in the mirror of economic "rationality."

INTERDISCIPLINARY NEO-HUMANISM, OR PSYCHO-SOCIAL ECONOMICS

It thus proves necessary to reconstruct social logic entirely. Nothing is more instructive in this regard than the adulterous relations that obtain between the economic and the social sciences. Virtuous thinkers have done their utmost for a generation now to reconcile these estranged disciplines (in the name of Man, their dada). They have striven to attenuate all that is profoundly inadmissible—*obscene*—for their disciplines in the very existence of the others and in the haunting memory of a knowledge that escapes them. Economics in particular can only delay the eruption, in the midst of its calculations, of a psychological logic of the unconscious or of an equally unconscious logic of social structures. The logic of ambivalence on the one hand, of difference on the other, are incompatible with the logic—sacred to economics—of equivalence. To foil their literally destructive influence, "economic science" will throw in its lot with desiccated and inoffensive forms of psychology and sociology, i.e., the latter as traditional disciplines—all in the name of pious interdisciplinary study. One never thinks, from this viewpoint, of introducing social or psychological dimensions of a specific nature: rather, one simply adds to the criteria of individual utility ("rational" economic variables) a pinch of "irrational" *individual* psychology (motivational studies, depth psychology) and some interpersonal social psychology (the individual *need* for prestige and status)—or simply a kind of global socio-culture. In short, one looks for *context*.

Some examples: certain studies (Chombart de Lauwe) reveal in the lower orders an abnormal consumption of meat: too little, or too much. As long as one consumes meat along the mean, one partakes of economic rationality. No problems. Otherwise, one produces the psychological: the need for prestige, conspicuous under- or over-consumption, etc. Hence, the social and the psychological are defined as the "economically pathological"! Another social analyst, Katona, discovers his "discretionary income" and his cultural implications with relish: he explores, beyond purchasing power, a "propensity to buy that reflects the motivations, the tendencies and the expectations of the clientele!"[10] Such are the maudlin illuminations of psycho-economics.

Or sometimes it is observed (when it becomes impossible to ignore) that the individual is never alone, that he is determined by his relation to others. And so Robinsonades are abandoned for micro-sociological *bricolage*. American sociology has somehow been arrested at this point. Even Merton, with his theory of the reference group, always works on groups that in fact are empirically given and with the empirical notion of aspiration as a lubricant of the social dynamic.

Psychologism goes hand in hand with culturalism, another benign version of a sociology that refuses to live dangerously: needs are functions of the particular history and culture of each society. This is the zenith of liberal analysis, beyond which it is congenitally incapable of thinking. The postulate of man endowed with needs and a natural inclination to satisfy them is never questioned. It is simply immersed in a historical and cultural dimension (very often defined in advance, and by other means): and then, by implication, impregnation, interaction, articulation or osmosis, it is recontextualized in a social history or a culture that is understood really as a second nature! All this culminates in overblown "character structures," cultural types writ large that are given as structures, though they are only empirical totalizations of distinctive traits, and—again—basically gigantic tautologies, since the "model" is composed of an admixture of the characteristic traits it is intended to explain.

Tautology is at work everywhere. Thus, in the theory of "consumption models": social situations can be as important as taste in determining the level of consumption (in France, sweets are inseparable from their use by parents as instruments of education). "It would thus be possible, when one got acquainted with the sociological significance of products, to paint the portrait of a society with the aid of the products that correspond to these norms. Reference groups and membership groups could be understood at the level of consumer behavior." Or, again, the concept of "role" in the work of Lazarsfeld and others: the good housekeeper is supposed to do the washing herself, use a sewing machine, and refrain from using instant coffee. The "role" plays the same function in the relation of the subject to social norms as need does in relation to objects. The same circle and the same white magic.

In the end, it is discovered that you can break down the purchase of a car into a whole constellation of possible motivations: biographical, technical, utilitarian, psychosymbolic (overcompensation, aggressiveness), sociological (group norms, desire for prestige, conformism or originality). The worst of it all is that every one of these is equally valid. It would be difficult to imagine a case where any one wouldn't apply. Often they formally contradict each other: the need for security versus the need to take risks; the desire to conform versus the need to be distinctive, etc. And which are determinant? How do you structure or rank them? In an ultimate effort, our thinkers strain to make their tautology dialectical: they talk about ongoing interaction (between the individual and the group, from one group to another, from one motivation to another). But the economists, hardly fond of dialectical variables, quickly retreat to their measurable utilities.

The confusion is quite irreparable, in fact. Without entirely lacking in interest, the results obtained at these different levels of abstraction (needs, social aspirations, roles, models of consumption, reference groups, etc.) are partial and misleading. Psycho-social economics is a sort of near-sighted, cross-eyed hydra. But it surveys and defends something, for all that. It exorcises the danger of a radical analysis, whose object would be neither the group nor the individual subject at the conscious level, but social logic itself, for which it is necessary to create a *principle* of analysis.

We have already asserted that this logic is a logic of differentiation. But this is not a question, as should be clear by now, of treating prestige, status, distinction, etc., as motivations, a level that has been largely thematized by contemporary sociology. At any rate, it is little more than a para-sociological extension of the traditional psychological givens. There is no doubt that individuals (or individuated groups) are consciously or subconsciously in quest of social rank and prestige and, of course, this level of the object should be incorporated into the analysis. But the fundamental level is that of *unconscious* structures that organize the social production of differences.

THE LOGIC OF SIGN EXCHANGE:
THE PRODUCTION OF DIFFERENCES

Even before survival has been assured, every group or individual experiences a vital pressure to produce themselves meaningfully in a system of exchange and relationships. Concurrently with the production of goods, there is a push to elaborate significations, meaning—with the result that the one-for-the-other exists before the one *and* the other exist for themselves.

The logic of exchange is thus primordial. In a way, the individual is non-existent (like the object of which we spoke at the beginning). At any rate, a certain language (of words, women, or goods) is prior to the individual. This language is a social form in relation to which there can properly speaking be no individuals, since it is an exchange structure. This structure amounts to a logic of differentiation on two simultaneous planes:

1. It differentiates the human terms of the exchange into partners, not individuated, but nevertheless distinct, and bound by the rules of exchange.

2. It differentiates the exchange material into distinct and *thus significant* elements.

This is true of language communication. It applies also to goods and products. Consumption is exchange. A consumer is never isolated, any more than a speaker. It is here that total revolution in the analysis of consumption must intervene: *Language cannot be explained by postulating an individual need to speak* (which would pose the insoluble double problem of establishing this need on an individual basis, and then of articulating it in a possible exchange). Before such questions can even be put, there is, simply, language—not as an absolute, autonomous *system*, but as a structure of exchange contemporaneous with meaning itself, and on which is articulated the individual intention of speech. Similarly, consumption does not arise from an objective need of the consumer, a final intention of the subject toward the object; rather, there is social production, in a system of exchange, of a material of differences, a code of significations and invidious (*statuaire*) values. The functionality of goods and individual needs only follows on this, adjusting itself to, rationalizing, and in the same stroke repressing these fundamental structural mechanisms.

The origin of meaning is never found in the relation between a subject (given a priori as autonomous and conscious) and an object produced for rational ends—that is, properly, the *economic* relation, rationalized in terms of choice and calculation. It is to be found, rather, in difference, systematizable in terms of a code (as opposed to private calculation)— a differential structure that establishes the social relation, and not the subject as such.

Veblen and Invidious Distinction

We should refer at this point to Veblen, who, even if he posited the logic of differentiation more in terms of individuals than of classes, of prestige interaction rather than of exchange structure, nevertheless offers in a way far superior to those who have followed him and who have pretended to surpass him the discovery of a principle of total social analysis, the basis of a radical logic, in the mechanisms of differentiation. This is not a superadded, contextual variable, situationally given, but a relational variable of structure. All of Veblen's work illustrates how the production of a social classification (class distinctions and statutory rivalry) is the fundamental law that arranges and subordinates all the other logics, whether conscious, rational, ideological, moral, etc.

Society regulates itself by means of the production of distinctive material: "The end of acquisition is conveniently held to be the consumption of the goods accumulated . . . but it is only in a sense far removed from its native meaning that consumption of goods can be said to afford the incentive from which accumulation proceeds. . . . Possession of wealth confers honors: it is an invidious distinction."[11]

Leisure

"Conspicuous abstention from labor becomes the conventional index of reputability."[12] Productive labor is degrading: the tradition never dies; it is only reinforced as social differentiation increases in complexity. In the end, it takes on the axiomatic authority of an absolute prescription—even alongside the moral reprobation of idleness and the reactive valorization of labor so strong in the middle classes (and today recuperated ideologically by the ruling class itself): a *président directeur général* works a fifteen-hour day, devotedly—it is his token of *affected* servitude. In fact, this reaction-formation proves, to the contrary, the power of leisure-nobility value as a deep-seated, unconscious representation.

Leisure is thus not a function of a need for leisure in the current sense of enjoying free time and functional repose. It can be invested in activities, provided they do not involve economic necessity. Leisure may be defined as any consumption of unproductive time. Now, this has nothing to do with passivity: it is an *activity*, an *obligatory* social phenomenon. Time is not in this instance "free," it is sacrificed, wasted; it is the moment of a production of value, of an invidious production of status, and the social individual is not free to escape it. No one needs leisure, but everyone is called upon to provide evidence of his availability for *unproductive* labor. The consumption of empty time is a form of potlatch. Here, free time is a material of exchange and signification. Like Bataille's "accursed share,"[13] it assumes value in the exchange itself—or in destruction—and leisure is the locus of this symbolic operation.[14]

The style of contemporary leisure provides a kind of experimental verification: left to himself, the conditions for creative freedom at last realized, the man of leisure looks desperately for a nail to hammer, a motor to dismantle. Outside the competitive sphere, there are no autonomous needs. Spontaneous motivation doesn't exist. But for all that, he can't permit himself to do nothing. At a loss for something to do with his free time, he nevertheless urgently "needs" to do nothing (or nothing useful), since this has distinctive social value.

Even today, what claims the average individual, through the holidays and during his free time, is not the liberty to "fulfill" himself (in terms of what? What hidden essence will surge to the fore?). He must verify the uselessness of his time—temporal surplus as sumptuous capital, as wealth. Leisure time, like consumption time in general, becomes emphatic, trade-marked social time—the dimension of social salvation, productive of value, but not of economic survival.[15]

Veblen pushed the law of distinctive value very far: "the canon of honorific waste may, immediately or remotely, influence the sense of duty, the sense of beauty, the sense of utility, the sense of devotional or ritualistic fitness, and the scientific sense of truth."[16]

THE LAW OF DISTINCTIVE VALUE AND ITS PARADOX

This law of value can play on wealth or on destitution. Conspicuous luxury or conspicuous austerity answer to the same fundamental rule.

What appears as an insoluble formal contradiction at the level of the empirical theory of needs falls into place, arranged according to this law, in a general theory of distinctive material.

Thus, churches are traditionally more sumptuous in the fashionable districts, but class imperative can impose a type of ascetic religiosity: Catholic pomp becomes the fact of the lower classes whereas, among Protestants, the spareness of the chapel only testifies to the greater glory of God (and establishes the distinctive sign of the class as well). There are innumerable examples of this paradox of value—of spartan wealth. People manipulate the subtle starkness of modern interiors. You pay through the nose to eat practically nothing. To deny oneself is a luxury! This is the sophistry of consumption, for which the refusal to validate a value is merely a hierarchical nuance in its formal verification.[17]

It is important to grasp that behind all these alleged finalities—functional, moral, aesthetic, religious and their contradictions—a logic of difference and super-difference is at work. But it is always repressed, since it belies the ideal finality of all the corresponding behavior. This is social reason, social logic. It transverses all values, all materials of exchange and communication.

In principle, nothing is immune to this structural logic of value. Objects, ideas, even conduct are not solely practiced as use values, by virtue of their "objective" meaning, in terms of their official discourse—for they can never escape the fact that they may be potentially exchanged as signs, i.e., assume another kind of value entirely in the very act of exchange and in the differential relation to the other that it establishes. The differential function of sign exchange always overdetermines the manifest function of what is exchanged, sometimes entirely contradicting it, repossessing it as an alibi, or *even producing it as an alibi*. This explains how the differential function materializes indifferently in opposite or contradictory terms: the beautiful or the ugly, the moral or the immoral, the good or the bad, the ancient or the new. The logic of difference cuts across all formal distinctions. It is equivalent to the primary process and the dream work: it pays no heed to the principle of identity and non-contradiction.[18]

FASHION

This deep-seated logic is akin to that of fashion. Fashion is one of the more inexplicable phenomena, so far as these matters go: its compulsion to innovate signs, its apparently arbitrary and perpetual production of meaning—a kind of meaning drive—and the logical mystery of its cycle are all in fact of the essence of what is sociological. The logical processes of fashion might be extrapolated to the dimension of "culture" in general—to all social production of signs, values and relations.

To take a recent example: neither the long skirt nor the mini-skirt has an absolute value in itself—only their differential relation acts as a criterion of meaning. The mini-skirt has nothing whatsoever to do with sexual liberation; it has no (fashion) value except in opposition to the long skirt. This value is, of course, reversible: the voyage from the mini- to the maxi-skirt will have the same distinctive and selective fashion value as the reverse; and it will precipitate the same effect of "beauty."

But it is obvious that this "beauty" (or any other interpretation in terms of chic, taste, elegance, or even distinctiveness) is nothing but the exponential function—the rationalization—of the fundamental processes of production and reproduction of distinctive material. Beauty ("in itself") has nothing to do with the fashion cycle.[19] In fact, it is inadmissible. Truly beautiful, definitively beautiful clothing would put an end to fashion. The latter can do nothing but deny, repress and efface it—*while conserving, with each new outing, the alibi of beauty.*

Thus fashion continually fabricates the "beautiful" on the basis of a radical denial of beauty, by reducing beauty to the logical equivalent of ugliness. It can impose the most eccentric, dysfunctional, ridiculous traits as eminently distinctive. This is where it triumphs—imposing and legitimizing the irrational according to a logic deeper than that of rationality.

3. THE SYSTEM OF NEEDS AND OF CONSUMPTION AS A SYSTEM OF PRODUCTIVE FORCES

It would appear that a "theory of needs" has no meaning. Only a theory of the *ideological concept* of need would make any sense. Before certain false problems have been overcome and radically reformulated, any reflection on the genesis of needs would have as little foundation as, for example, a history of the will. A form of the chimerical dialectic of being and appearance, soul and body still persists in the subject-object of dialectic of need. Ideological speculation of this sort has always appeared as a "dialectical" game of ceaseless interaction in a mirror: when it is impossible to determine which of two terms engenders the other and one is reduced to making them reflect or produce each other reciprocally, it is a sure sign that the terms of the problem itself must be changed.

So it proves necessary to examine how economic science—and behind it, the political order—operates the concept of need.

THE MYTH OF PRIMARY NEEDS

The legitimacy of the concept is rooted in the alleged existence of a vital anthropological minimum that would be the dimension of "primary needs"—an irreducible zone where the individual chooses himself, since he knows what he wants: to eat, to drink, to sleep, to make love, to find shelter, etc. At this level, he cannot, it is supposed, be alienated in his need as such: only deprived of the means to satisfy it.

This bio-anthropological postulate directly launches the insoluble dichotomy of primary and secondary needs: beyond the threshold of survival, man no longer knows what he wants. And it is here that he becomes properly "social" for the economist: i.e., vulnerable to alienation, manipulation, mystification. On one side of the imaginary line, the economic subject is prey to the social and the cultural; on the other, he is an autonomous, inalienable essence. Note that this distinction, by conjuring away the socio-cultural in secondary needs, permits the recuperation, behind the functional alibi of survival-need, of a level of individual essence: a human essence grounded in nature. Moreover, this all proves quite versatile as an ideology. It has a spiritualist as well as a rationalist version. Primary and secondary needs can be separated in order to refer the former back to animality, the latter to the immaterial.[20] Or one can simply reverse the whole procedure by positing primary needs as (alone) objectively grounded (thus rational), and treat the others as subjectively variable (hence irrational). But this ideology is quite coherent in its overall features, because it always defines man a priori as an essence (or a rationality) that the social merely obscures.

In fact, the "vital anthropological minimum" doesn't exist: in all societies, it is determined residually by the fundamental urgency of an excess: the divine or sacrificial share, sumptuous discharge, economic profit. It is this pre-dedication of luxury that negatively determines the level of survival, and not the reverse (which is an idealist fiction). Advantages, profits, sacrifice (in the sense of social wealth) and "useless" expenditures are all deducted in advance. And the priority of this claim works everywhere at the expense of the functional side of the balance sheet—at the expense, where necessary, of minimal subsistence.

There have never been "societies of scarcity" or "societies of abundance," since the expenditures of a society (whatever the objective volume of its resources) are articulated in terms of a structural surplus, and an equally structural deficit. An enormous surplus can coexist with the worst misery. In all cases, a certain surplus coexists with a certain poverty. But the crucial point is that it is always the production of this surplus that regulates the whole. The survival threshold is never determined from below, but from above. Eventually, one might hypothesize, there will be no survival at all, if social imperatives demand it: the newborn will be liquidated (like prisoners of war, before a new constellation of productive forces made slavery profitable). The Siane of New Guinea, enriched through contact with Europeans, squandered everything in feasts, without ceasing to live below the "vital minimum." It is impossible to isolate an abstract, "natural" stage of poverty or to determine absolutely "what men need to survive." It may please one fellow to lose everything at poker and to leave his family starving to death. We know it is often the most disadvantaged who squander in the most "irrational" way. The game flourishes in direct relation to underdevelopment. There is even a narrow correlation between underdevelopment, the size of the poor classes, and the tentacular spread of the church, the military, domestic personnel, and expensive and useless sectors in general.

Conversely, just as survival can fall well below the vital minimum if the production of surplus value requires it, the threshold of *obligatory* consumption can be set well above the strictly necessary—always as a function of the production of surplus value: this is the case in our societies, where no one is free to live on raw roots and fresh water. From which follows the absurdity of the concept of "discretionary income" (the complement of the "vital minimum" concept): "the portion of his income the individual is free to spend as he pleases." In what way am I more free buying clothing or a car than buying my food (itself very sophisticated)? And how am I free *not* to choose? Is the purchase of an automobile or clothing "discretionary" when it is the unconscious substitute for an unrealistic desire for certain living accommodations? The vital minimum today, the minimum of imposed consumption, is the standard package.[21] Beneath this level, you are an outcast. Is loss of status—or social non-existence—less upsetting than hunger?

In fact, discretionary income is an idea rationalized at the discretion of entrepreneurs and market analysts. It justifies their manipulation of secondary needs, since, in their view, these don't touch on the essential. The line of demarcation between essential and inessential has quite a precise double function:

1. To establish and preserve a sphere of individual human essence, which is the keystone of the system of ideological values.

2. To obscure behind the anthropological postulate the actual productivist definition of "survival": during the period of (capital) accumulation, what is "essential" is what is strictly necessary for the reproduction of the labor force. In the growth phase, however, it is what is necessary to maintain the rate of growth and surplus value.

THE EMERGENCE OF CONSUMMATIVITY:[22] NEED-PRODUCTIVE FORCE

One can generalize this conclusion by saying that needs—such as they are—can no longer be defined adequately in terms of the naturalist-idealist thesis—as innate, instinctive power, spontaneous craving, anthropological potentiality. Rather, they are better defined as a *function* induced (in the individual) by the internal logic of the system: more precisely, *not as a consummative force liberated* by the affluent society, but *as a productive force* required by the functioning of the system itself, by its process of reproduction and survival. In other words, there are only needs because the system needs them.

And the needs invested by the individual consumer today are just as essential to the order of production as the capital invested by the capitalist entrepreneur and the labor power invested by the wage laborer. It is *all* capital.

Hence, there is a compulsion to need and a compulsion to consume. One can imagine laws sanctioning such constraint one day (an obligation to change cars every two years).[23]

To be sure, this systematic constraint has been placed under the sign of choice and "liberty," and hence appears as entirely opposed to the labor process as the pleasure principle is to the reality principle. In fact, the "liberty" to consume is of the same order as the freedom offered by the labor market. The capitalist system was erected on this liberty—on the formal emancipation of the labor force (and not on the concrete autonomy of work, which it abolishes). Similarly, consumption is only possible in the abstraction of a system based on the "liberty" of the consumer. It is *necessary* that the individual user have a choice, and become through his choice free at last to enter as a productive force in a production calculus, exactly as the capitalist system frees the laborer to sell, at last, his labor power.

And just as the fundamental concept of this system is not, strictly speaking, that of production, but of *productivity* (labor and production disengage themselves from all ritual, religious, and subjective connotations to enter the historical process of rationalization); so, one must speak not of consumption, but of *consummativity*: even if the process is far from being as rationalized as that of production, the parallel tendency is to move from subjective, contingent, concrete enjoyment to an indefinite calculus of growth rooted in the abstraction of needs, on which the system this time imposes its coherence—a coherence that it literally produces as a by-product of its productivity.[24]

Indeed, just as concrete work is abstracted, little by little, into labor power in order to make it homogeneous with the means of production (machines, energy, etc.) and thus to multiply the homogeneous factors into a growing productivity—so desire is abstracted and atomized into needs, in order to make it homogeneous with the means of satisfaction (products, images, sign-objects, etc.) and thus to multiply consummativity.

The same process of rationalization holds (atomization and unlimited abstraction), but the ideological role of the concept of need is expanded: with all its hedonist illusions, *need-pleasure* masks the objective reality of *need-productive force*. Needs and labor[25] are therefore two modalities of the same exploitation[26] of productive forces. The saturated consumer appears as the spellbound avatar of the wage laborer.

Thus it should not be said that "consumption is entirely a function of production": rather, *it is consummativity that is a structural mode of productivity*. On this point, nothing has really changed in the historical passage from an emphasis on "vital" needs to "cultural" needs, or "primary" needs to "secondary" ones. The slave's only assurance that he would eat was that the system needed slaves to work. The only chance that the modern citizen may have to see his "cultural" needs satisfied lies in the fact that the system needs his needs, and that the individual is no longer content just to eat. In other words, if there had been, for the order of production, any means whatever of assuring the survival of the anterior mode of brutal exploitation, there would never have been much question of needs.[27] Needs are curbed as much as possible. But when it proves necessary, they are instigated as a means of repression.[28]

CONTROLLED DESUBLIMATION

The capitalist system has never ceased to make women and children work *first* (to whatever extent possible). Under absolute constraint, it eventually "discovered" the great humanitarian and democratic principles. Schooling was only conceded piece by piece, and it was not generalized until it had imposed itself on the system—like universal suffrage—as a powerful means of social control and integration (or as a means of acculturation to industrial society). During the phase of industrialization, the last pennyworth of labor power was extorted without compunction. To extract surplus value, it was hardly necessary to prime the pump with needs. Then capital, confronted by its own contradictions (over-production, falling rate of profit), tried at first to surmount them by totally restructuring its accumulation through destruction, deficit budgeting and bankruptcy. It thus averted a redistribution of wealth, which would have placed the existing relations of production and structures of power seriously in question. But as soon as the threshold of rupture had been reached, capital was already unearthing the individual *qua* consumer. He was no longer simply the slave as labor power. This was truly a "production." And in bringing it off, capital was only delivering up a new kind of serf: the individual as consumption power.[29]

This is the point of departure for an analysis of consumption at the political level: it is necessary to overcome the ideological understanding of consumption as a process of craving and pleasure, as an extended metaphor on the digestive functions—where the whole issue is naturalized according to the primary scheme of the oral drive. It is necessary to surpass this powerful imaginary preconception in order to define consumption *not only structurally as a system of exchange and of signs, but strategically as a mechanism of power*. Now, the question of consumption is not clarified by the concept of needs, nor by theories of their qualitative transformation, or their massive extension: these phenomena are no more than the characteristic effect, at the individual level, of a certain monopolistic productivity, of a totalitarian economy (capitalist or socialist) driven to conjuring up leisure, comfort, luxury, etc.; briefly, they are the ultimate realization of the private individual as a productive force. The system of needs must wring liberty and pleasure from him as so many functional elements of the reproduction of the system of production and the relations of power that sanction it. It gives rise to these private functions according to the same principle of abstraction and radical "alienation" that was formerly (and still today) the case for his labor power. In this system, the "liberation" of needs, of consumers, of women, of the young, the body, etc., is always really the *mobilization* of needs, consumers, the body. . . . It is never an explosive liberation, but a controlled emancipation, a mobilization whose end is competitive exploitation.

It would appear that even the most deep-seated forces, the unconscious instincts, can be mobilized in this way by the "strategy of desire." We are now at the very heart of the concept of controlled desublimation (or "repressive desublimation," as Marcuse would say). At the limit, retranscribed in this primary psychoanalysis, the consumer appears as a knot of drives (future productive forces) repressed by the system of ego defense functions. These functions must be "desublimated"—hence, the deconstruction of the *ego* functions, the conscious moral and individual functions, to the benefit of a "liberation" of the id and the super-ego as factors of integration, participation and consumption—to the benefit of a kind of total consuming immorality in which the individual finally submerges himself in a pleasure principle entirely controlled by production planning.

To sum up: man is not simply *there* first, equipped with his needs, and designated by nature to fulfill and finalize himself *qua* Man. This proposition, which smacks of spiritualist teleology, in fact defines the individual function in our society—the functional myth of productivist society. The whole system of individual values—this religion of spontaneity, liberty, creativity, etc.—is bloated with the productivist option. Even the vital functions are immediately "functions" of the system.

We must reverse the terms of the analysis, and abolish the cardinal reference to the individual, for even that is the product of this social logic. We must abandon the constitutive social structure of the individual, and even his lived perception of himself: for man never really does come face to face with his own needs. This is not only true of "secondary" needs (where the individual is reproduced according to the finalities of production considered as consumption power). It applies equally well to "survival" needs. In this instance, man is not reproduced as man: he is simply regenerated as a survivor (a surviving productive force). If he eats, drinks, lives somewhere, reproduces himself, it is because the system requires his self-production in order to reproduce itself: it needs men. If it could function with slaves, there would be no "free" workers. If it could function with asexual mechanical robots, there would be no sexual reproduction.[30] If the system could function without feeding its workers, there would be no bread. It is in this sense that we are all, in the framework of this system, survivors. Not even the instinct of self-preservation is fundamental: it is a social tolerance or a social imperative. When the system requires it, it cancels this instinct and people get excited about dying (for a sublime cause, evidently).

We do not wish to say that "the individual is a product of society" at all. For, as it is currently understood, this culturalist platitude only masks the much more radical truth that, in its totalitarian logic, a system of productivist growth (capitalist, but not exclusively) can only produce and reproduce men—even in their deepest determinations: in their liberty, in their needs, in their very unconscious—as productive forces. The system can only produce and reproduce individuals as elements of the system. It cannot tolerate exceptions.

GENERALIZED SIGN EXCHANGE AND THE TWILIGHT OF "VALUES"

So today everything is "recuperable."[31] But it is too simple to argue that first there are needs, authentic values, etc., and then they are alienated, mystified, recuperated, or what have you. This humanitarian Manicheanism explains nothing. If everything is "recuperable," it is because everything in monopoly capitalist society[32]—goods, knowledge, technique, culture, men, their relations and their aspirations—everything is reproduced, from the outset, immediately, as an element of the system, as an integrated variable.

The truth is—and this has been recognized for a long time in the area of economic production—that use value no longer appears anywhere in the system. The determining logic of exchange value is, however, as ubiquitous as ever. This must be recognized today as the truth of the sphere of "consumption" and the cultural system in general. In other words, everything, even artistic, intellectual, and scientific production, even innovation and transgression, is immediately produced as sign and exchange value (relational value of the sign).

A structural analysis of consumption is possible to the extent that "needs," consumption behavior and cultural behavior are not only recuperated, but systematically induced and produced as productive forces. Given this abstraction and this tendency toward total systematization, such an analysis is entirely possible, if it in turn is based on an analysis of the social logic of production and the *generalized exchange* of signs.

ENDNOTES

1. This piece first appeared in *Cahiers Internationaux de Sociologie*, 1969. It was then published in France as *For a Critique of the Political Economy of the Sign* in 1979 and again, in its current form, in 1981 by Telos Press, translation Charles Levin.

2. *Investissement*: this is the standard, and literal, French equivalent of Freud's *Besetzung*, which also means investment in ordinary German. The English, however, have insisted on rendering this concept by coining a word that sounds more technical: cathexis, to cathect, etc. The term has been used here mainly to draw attention to the psychoanalytic sense, which varies in intensity and precision, of Baudrillard's *investissement, investir*. Loosely, Freud's concept involves the quantitative transfer of psychic energy to parts of the psyche, images, objects, etc.—*Trans*.

3. *Not* epistemologically given!—*Trans*.

4. Thus the structure of exchange (cf. Lévi-Strauss) is never that of simple reciprocity. It is not two simple terms, but two *ambivalent* terms that exchange, and the exchange establishes their relationship as ambivalent.

5. In the logic of the commodity, all goods or objects become universally commutable. Their (economic) practice occurs through their price. There is no relationship either to the subject or to the world, but only a relation to the market.

6. The same goes for food: as a "functional need," hunger is not symbolic. Its objective is satiation. The food object is not substitutable. But it is well known that eating can satisfy an oral drive, being a neurotic substitute for lack of love. In this second function, eating, smoking, collecting objects, obsessive memorization can all be equivalent: the symbolic paradigm is radically different from the functional paradigm. Hunger as such is not signified, it is appeased. Desire, on the other hand, is signified throughout an entire chain of signifiers. And when it happens to be a desire for something experienced as lost, when it is a lack, an absence on which the objects that signify it have come to be inscribed, does it make any sense to treat such objects literally, as if they were merely what they are? And what can the notion of need possibly refer to, in these circumstances?

7. Borges, cited in Michel Foucault, *The Order of Things* (New York: Vintage, 1970). p. xv.

8. *Speculaire*: The adjective specular and the noun specularity occur often in Baudrillard's analyses of ideology. They deliberately recall the mirror-like relations of the Imaginary order, which is opposed to the Symbolic order in Lacanian psychoanalysis. For the best introduction to Lacan in English, see Anthony Wilden, *The Language of the Self* (New York: 1968) and *System and Structure* (London: 1972). The latter work is less informative with respect to Lacan specifically, but attempts a curious synthesis that may fruitfully be compared with Baudrillard's work. Wilden is more sympathetic toward traditional Marxist assumptions and to mainstream social science in the form of cybernetics, systems theory, etc. With the work of Lévi-Strauss, Lacan and others behind them, both have in common a concern for the apparently special or traditionally unaccountable status of *symbolic* exchange, a critique of the "digital bias" (Wilden) in the Western *episteme* (which, by definition, would include the 19th-century revolutionary critique of or version of political economy); and both attempt to reexamine such basic concepts as need, desire, the subject, object, etc.—*Trans*.

9. According to Marcel Mauss in *The Gift* (London: Routledge, 1970).

10. Chombart de Lauwe, *Pour une Sociologie des Aspirations* (Paris: Gonthier, 1969) and George Katona, *The Society of Mass Consumption* (New York: McGraw Hill, 1964).

11. Thorstein Veblen, *The Theory of the Leisure Class* (New York: Mentor, 1953), p. 35.

12. *Ibid.*, p. 43.

13. Georges Bataille, *La Part Maudite* (Paris: Les Editions de Minuit, 1967).

14. See the analysis of an analogous type of operation in the chapter on The Art Auction in *For a Critique of the Political Economy of the Sign* (New York: Telos, 1981).

15. "Free" time brings together the "right" to work and the "liberty" to consume in the framework of the same system: *it is necessary* for time to be "liberated" in order to become a sign-function and take on social exchange value, whereas labor time, which is constrained time, possesses only economic exchange value. Cf. Part I of this essay: one could add a definition of symbolic time to that of the object. It would be that which is neither economically constrained nor "free" as sign-function, but *bound*, that is, inseparable from the concrete act of exchange—a rhythm.

16. Veblen, *op. cit.*, p. 88.

17. Cf. "universal" furniture (or "universal" clothing in Roland Barthes' study of fashion): as the epitome of all functions, it becomes once again opposable to them, and thus simply one more term in the paradigm. Its value isn't universal, but derived from relative distinction. Thus all the "universal" values (ideological, moral, etc.) become again—indeed, perhaps are produced from the outset as—differential values.

18. In relation to this one, the other functions are secondary processes. They certainly constitute part of the sociological domain. But the logic of difference (like the primary process) constitutes the proper object of genuine social science.

19. Any more than originality, the specific value, the objective merit is belonging to the aristocratic or bourgeois class. This is defined by signs, to the exclusion of "authentic" values. See Goblot, *La Barrière et le Niveau: Etude Sociologique sur la Bourgeoisie Francaise Moderne* (Paris: Presse Universitaire de France, 1967).

20. On this point, see Ruyer, *La Nutrition Psychique*.

21. English in the original.—*Trans.*

22. *Consommativité*: Baudrillard's neologism obviously suggests a parallel with the term "productivity," and all that connotes.—*Trans.*

23. It is so true that consumption is a productive force that, by significant analogy, it is often subsumed under the notion of profit: "Borrowing makes money." "Buy, and you will be rich." It is exalted not as expenditure, but as investment and profitability.

24. Hence, it is vain to oppose consumption and production, as is so often done, in order to subordinate one to the other, or vice versa, in terms of causality or influence. For in fact we are comparing two heterogeneous sectors: productivity, that is, and abstract and generalized exchange value system where labor and concrete production are occluded in laws—the modes and relations of production: secondly, a logic, and a sector, that of consumption, which is entirely conceived in terms of motivations and individual, contingent, concrete satisfactions. So, properly speaking, it is illegitimate to confront the two. On the other hand, if one conceives of consumption as production, the production of signs, which is also in the process of systematization on the basis of a generalization of exchange value (of signs), then the two spheres are homogeneous—though, at the same time, not comparable in terms of causal priority, but homologous from the viewpoint of structural modalities. The structure is that of the mode of production.

25. Cf. *besoin* and *besogne*. Baudrillard here draws attention to the etymological connection between the French term for need and the archaic word *besogne*, which commonly referred to labor, a heavy burden, etc., as well as meaning to need.—*Trans.*

26. In both senses of the term: technical and social.

27. A hypothesis: labor itself did not appear as a productive force until the social order (the structure of privilege and domination) absolutely needed it to survive, since the power based on personal and hierarchical relations was no longer sufficient by itself. The exploitation of labor is a last resort for the social order. Access to work is still refused to women as socially subversive.

28. Nonetheless, this emergence of needs, however formal and subdued, is never without danger for the social order—as is the liberation of any productive

force. Apart from being the dimension of exploitation, it is also the origin of the most violent social contradictions, of class struggle. Who can say what historical contradictions the emergence and exploitation of this new productive force—that of needs—holds in store for us?

29. There is no other basis for aid to underdeveloped countries.

30. Robots remain the ultimate and ideal phantasm of a total productivist system. Still better, there is integrated automation. However, cybernetic rationality is devouring itself, for men are necessary for any system of social order and domination. Now, in the final analysis, this amounts nonetheless to the aim of all productivity, which is a *political* goal.

31. The term itself has been "recuperated," for it presupposes an original purity and delineates the capitalist system as a maleficent instance of perversion, revealing yet another moralizing vision.

32. Or, more simply, in a system of generalized exchange.

6

Robert Goldman and Stephen Papson
"Advertising in the Age of Accelerated Meaning"
(1996)

We've seen them thousands of times. They are commodity signs. The most familiar include the Coke insignia, the McDonald's arches, the Levi's 501 emblem, the Nike "swoosh." Commodity signs find their source in advertisements.

Today most television viewers have long since become acclimated to advertisements. We take them for granted. We decipher ads routinely, automatically, even absentmindedly, in what Walter Benjamin once called a "state of distraction." Ordinarily, little attention is paid to the codes that enable us to make sense of advertisements. Yet the transparency of these advertising codes is critical to our daily routine of reading and deciphering ads.

When we as viewers step back from this process of making and taking meaning from ads, it becomes apparent to us that the process depends on how we understand the advertisement itself as a framework for telling a particular kind of story. Once the commercial narrative framework is accepted as unproblematic, we are able to routinely decipher and evaluate the combinations of meanings that commercials advance as potential sign currency. We rarely pause to consider the assumptions imposed by the advertising framework since our attention is usually fixed on solving the particular riddle of each ad as it passes before us on the screen; just as importantly, our attention is usually fixed on the question of whether or not we like the ad. The vast majority of ads offer viewers few satisfactions from deciphering; but the few ads that do excite decoding pleasures place their products in line to realize profitable sign values.

Stripped of its glamour, advertising is a kind of cultural mechanics for constructing commodity signs. Advertisements are structured to boost the value of commodity brand names by attaching them to images that possess social and cultural value: brand-name commodity + meaning of image = a commodity sign. Constructing this currency of commodity images requires that advertisements take the form of semiotic equations into which disconnected signifiers and signifieds are entered and then recombined to create new equivalencies. Ads invite viewers to perceive an exchange between otherwise incommensurate meaning systems, and they must be structured to steer interpretation in that direction if they are to fulfill their purpose.

Advertisements are always commodity narratives. John Berger and Judith Williamson have each described the general curve of the commodity narrative expressed through the advertisement. According to Berger, "The spectator-buyer is meant . . . to imagine herself transformed by the product into an object of envy for others, an envy which will then justify her loving herself."[1] Consumer ads typically tell stories of success, desire, happiness, and social fulfillment in the lives of the people who consume the right brands. Interpreting the stories that ads tell is always conditional on how they address, or "hail," us—how we are positioned, how the commodity is positioned. When ads hail us, they *appellate* us, naming us and inviting us to take up a position in relation to the advertisements. Consumer ads greet us as individual viewers with what seem to be our own (*already*) ideological assumptions and personalities.[2]

Judith Williamson, in her pathbreaking book *Decoding Advertisements*, cracked open the operation of the advertising framework. She calls this the *metastructure*, "where meaning is not just 'decoded' within one structure, but transferred to create another."[3] This metastructure sets up tacit rules guiding these transfers; the metastructure is the framework within which sign currencies are assembled. Within this framework, advertisers attempt to engineer the transfers of meanings and values necessary to generate commodity signs. The *commodity sign* is formed at the intersection between a brand name and a meaning system summarized in an image.

We are socialized into recognition of sign values at an early age. A 1991 study of 6-year-old children confirmed the potential potency of sign values when it reported that children were as familiar with Joe Camel's link to cigarettes as they were with the Mickey Mouse logo and its connection to the Disney Channel.[4] In today's consumer-goods markets, products require signs that add value to them. Product standardization makes it imperative that products attach themselves to signs that carry an additional element of value. Nike captured a larger market share of the sneaker industry than Reebok did between 1986 and 1993 because Nike effectively harnessed the power of Michael Jordan's image while Reebok failed to counter with a superior or even an equal stream of imagery. In this kind of industry, everything depends on having a potent, differentiated image.

In the hotly competitive advertising industry, advertisers struggle to differentiate their images. For years, advertisers relied on a formula for joining the meaning of a brand-name product to the meaning of a socially charged image, vying for viewer attention by devising visually

This Special K ad told of a relationship between eating cereal and gaining the look (body shape) you want. The narrative is a slightly modified version of the "envy and desire" script iterated in Berger's quote above. This concluding scene defined the Special K sign in terms of the arched foot and calf of the model. The product sign now stands for the object of desire that supposedly comes with purchase of the product. Notice how the sign is literally formed as a combination of meaning systems: half product lettering and half product outcome. The calf is transformed into a marker of desire realized through the sign of Special K. Because of the relationship between the viewer and the object of desire, the calf portion of the sign functions as a closing form of appellation.

Like the Special K image, these Citicorp images offer a study in the formation of a commodity sign. Here the sign is formed by joining an image of the Citicorp Tower with the reflection of portraits of people who are labled as "Americans" (like ourselves) who "want to succeed."

distinctive styles of joining meanings. The formula's success led to expanded usage until it began to provoke sustained consumer resistance. Late 1970s polling data registered rising consumer complaint about feeling "manipulated" and "insulted" by ads. In the late 1980s, advertisers responded with a wave of more "realist looks" in ads. But the problem of advertising clutter continued unabated and eventually pressured advertisers to adopt advertising narratives that were more abbreviated, oblique, and ambiguous. By the late 1980s, a new cultural cutting edge of advertising emerged as advertisers began to indulge in self-reflective banter to win back the favor of disenchanted viewers. An avant-garde of advertisers—most notably Wieden & Kennedy and Chiat/Day—bypassed the clutter by stylistically differentiating their methods of narrative representation. What advertisers once sought to conceal in their ads, they now boldly compete to utter aloud. Where advertisers once sought to maximize the transparency of the framework, they now try to jar viewers into interpretive quandaries as a way of keeping them engaged in the ads. Some ads now humorously caution viewers to remember that a sign is just a sign, and not the product itself. Replicas already abound. For example, a current, extra-hip Sprite commercial has jumped on the bandwagon to position its sign against other folks' advertising claims that soda pop can make you popular, give you athletic ability, or "make me more attractive to the opposite sex, though I wish it would." "If I need a badge I'll become a security guard," declares the youthful, black, inner-city narrator. "If I need a refreshing drink, I'll obey my thirst. Image is nothing!"

Advertising campaigns have even attempted to disrupt the taken-for-granted semiotic framework that supports the usual advertising as-

Sprite's campaign lampoons the typical advertising hype that one can secure athletic accomplishments, sex appeal, popularity, or status badges by consuming commodity signs.

sumptions concerning the correspondence between commodities and social outcomes.[5] Already, imitators have adopted the tactic of disregarding coding rules associated with video editing, so that sequences of images are not ordered according to conventional narrative expectations. But how far can advertisers go in creating narrative confusion without undermining the goals of advertising? What happens when viewers can no longer figure out what the point of an ad is? Ambiguous and oblique ads may temporarily solve problems of clutter, but how effective are such ads in establishing commodity signs? In today's consumer-goods markets, the competition in images has evolved into a stage that we call *sign wars*. Today, advertisers seem caught between the Scylla of fetishized formulas that annoy and alienate viewers, and the Charybdis of clever self-reflexivity that regains viewer attention at the risk of blowing apart the whole system of sign value.

SIGN WARS: CONSTRUCTING SIGN VALUES

Corporate competition in selling consumer commodities has become centered on the image, the look, the sign. The sign value of the commodity gives a brand name its zip, its meaning. Over the years the cycle of this sign competition has begun to race along, while its density and intensity has escalated. Our study of sign wars explores what happens when meaning is systematically commodified and becomes subject to an economic circuit of exchange and devaluation.

We look at consumer-goods ads as exercises in sign construction. We view advertising as a system of sign values. A sign value is generally equal to the desirability of an image. A sign value establishes the relative value of a brand where the functional difference between products is minimal. Contemporary ads operate on the premise that signifiers and signifieds that have been removed from context can be rejoined to other similarly abstracted signifiers and signifieds to build new signs of identity. This is the heart of the commodity sign machine. No cultural analysis of advertising today can ignore the mercurial process of recombining meaning systems in order to generate additional value and desirability for brand-name commodities.

The necessity of differentiating products motivates sign competition.

The competition to build images that stand out in the media markets is based on a process of routinely unhinging signifiers from signifieds so that new signifier-signified relationships can be fashioned. This process occurs with such rapidity and frequency that we scarcely notice it anymore. But, slow down the videotape and the process becomes blatant as advertisers associate meaning systems that otherwise would not occupy the same space: for example, the sleek, phallic grace and power of a fighter jet in a steep climb is joined to an image of a female diver in a Diet Coke ad. The fighter jet is unhinged from its usual context and some of its connotations—sleekness, phallic grace, and power—can now be rehinged to the signified of the cola via the signifier of the gracefully arched female form. Stating the process in this linear march-step fashion makes it seem very mechanistic and formulaic, and to a certain extent it is.

Ads ask us to choose and construct our identities out of our consumption choices. What are the cultural consequences of continuously unhinging and recombining signifiers and signifieds to hail these identities? And what happens when the process of hinging and unhinging accelerates? By the mid-1980s, the average duration of television ad campaigns decreased to less than 13 weeks, as images were taken up and abandoned at an increasingly frenetic pace. That pace has not abated, and viewers are no longer surprised by the MTV-style of mutating images—a style based on an overfamiliarity with media formulas and clichés, and a frenzy of images thrown at us at ever-accelerating speeds until the speed itself is the primary signifier. As Moore remarks:

> Advertising is picking up speed. After more than 45 years of watching television commercials, after more than a decade of MTV and video games, viewers are used to a barrage of visual stimuli. In fact, younger viewers demand it. So television commercials move blindingly fast: Sometimes hundreds of images are crammed into 30 seconds. To follow the story in Nike's 1993 Super Bowl ad, in which [Michael] Jordan and Bugs Bunny battle Marvin the Martian and his flock of giant green chickens, you probably needed super-slow motion on your VCR. . . . What's pushing this frenetic pace? . . . Zapping. Viewers armed with remote controls can, and will, zap an ad that doesn't hold their interest. They also flash among channels, following the action on several. "They look at little snippets. Then they lean on that thing [the remote control] and they do their own editing at home. They're able to glean the content of six shows instead of one." As a result, commercials have started to skip around, too. "In the past [ad producers] paid the minutest attention to continuity. Now you can shorthand a lot," Sann says. In fact, if you don't, "you're going to bore people and they're going to shut you off."[6]

The appetite of advertising—what we call the commodity sign industry—for new meanings and styles is voracious. The production and reproduction of competitive sign values require the continuous search for cultural matter that might have fresh value. The economy of images drives cultural turnover, eroding the premise that anything carries lasting value (except perhaps the famous iconic trinity of Elvis, Marilyn, and James Dean).

Ads vary widely in the stylistic strategies used to compete in the field of sign value. In the jeans industry, ads for Bongo jeans or Shawnee jeans or Steel jeans are structured by mechanical formulas for making sign values out of fetishized glamour looks. At the other end of the spectrum, Diesel jeans ads construct convoluted, angry, and self-conscious images about cynical and jaded consumption, yet continue to tease with the fetish character of glamour. Practices of sign production have grown more extreme with each passing season in parity industries like the fashion and footwear industries, where jeans and sneakers are distinguished mostly by their signs. With brand names like Get Used or Damaged or Request jeans the sign is the primary commodity—where the commodity, the social relation, and the sign are collapsed into a single signifying field.

In a mature sign economy, allusions to previous ad campaigns become rampant and imagery is fashioned out of bits and pieces of previous signs and media representations, including ads, TV shows, movies, and music videos. When this logic of sign articulation escalates too far, it results in absurd campaigns that race along on the pure logic of pastiche—drawing together and combining meanings that otherwise seem ludicrous in the same sentence. Case in point: Miller Lite's 1993 campaign combines meanings that do not go together—for example, sumo wrestlers with competition divers; rodeo bulldogging and divorce lawyers; recliner ski jumping; drag-strip racing and Wiener dogs—to create a unifying image that functions as an analogy for the combination of meanings that Miller Lite takes as its sign: "Tastes Great" and "Less Filling." While ads like this may seem brain-dead, they illustrate how the logic of constructing novel sign values edges us toward a postmodern world where recombining meanings to construct differentiated sign values results in a "wild and wacky" TV image world composed of a cut-and-paste culture.

The "look" has become an essential element of currency production because escalating market competition has made it renewable, ephemeral, and disposable. In 1990, Nike's advertising sign machine created a spin-off commodity—a commodity based solely on sign value; a commodity whose sign value eclipsed its use value. Nike put out a new line of T-shirts featuring images drawn from their successful TV ads starring Michael Jordan, Spike Lee, and Bo Jackson. The product targeted teen and preteen boys in a market defined by the circulation of images. Every six weeks, Nike released a new T-shirt with another "hot" image from their ad campaign.[7] This truly is planned obsolescence in the sign industry. This constant refreshing of signs illustrates the imperative of finding new spaces for signs and circulating them as quickly as possible. The same process reveals a fundamental social instability of sign value in a mature political economy of sign value.

THE LOGIC OF APPROPRIATION

Advertising continuously appropriates meanings, which it chews up in the process of recontextualizing those meanings to fit commodities or corporations. Think of it as a giant harvesting machine—but instead of harvesting wheat, it harvests signifiers and signifieds of meaning. This harvest of uprooted meanings is delivered to a film editing studio, where it is reorganized according to the "scripts" (and agendas) of the advertiser. Advertising contributes in this way to a postmodern condition in which disconnected signs circulate at ever increasing rates, in which signifiers become detached from signifieds and reattached to still other signifieds.

Constructing a sign value retraces the path of meaning Roland Barthes describes as the transformation of language into myth.[8] It may be useful to walk through his formal grid for tracking the signifier, using an example from a Reebok campaign for the Blacktop shoe. The campaign drew on the referent system of "the blacktop"—a social and cultural space where inner-city youth play basketball. Appropriating signifiers for the purpose of constructing sign values tends to fetishize the signifier. What does this mean? Reebok's Blacktop campaign lifted the photographic image of the chain-link fence and turned it into a signifier of inner-city alienation. Similarly, Reebok has stolen and hollowed out rapper images in the form of the MC and the DJ and the "fatboys." When Reebok took the name of the so-

The DJ,

the chain-link fence,

and the fatboys

are turned into reified signifiers of Reebok's appropriation of the "hood," a.k.a. the "Blacktop."

cially structured space of the asphalt basketball court—the blacktop—and appropriated it as the name for their shoe, they not only sought to inflate the sign value of their shoe, they also turned the blacktop as a social and cultural space into what Barthes called a second-order signifier. Inside the semiotic space of the Reebok ads, the Blacktop (as defined by the chain-link image, the stylized MC image, etc.) has been turned into a reified signifier that marks the "place where legends are made" by Reebok.

Producing marketable commodity signs depends on how effectively advertisers are able to colonize and appropriate referent systems. Few referent systems are immune to this process, although the Bush White House aggressively combated consumer-goods advertising usage of the presidency because of its "sacred" status. Any referent system can be tapped, but remember that advertisers appropriate referent systems for the purpose of generating sign value, so they dwell on referent systems that they calculate might have value to their target audience. Celebrities are usually sought because they have high potential sign value. The referent systems that can pay off most handsomely when properly appropriated involve lifestyle and subcultures. In recent years advertising has appropriated nostalgia, hip-hop music, grunge, and feminist sensibilities. At our current stage of consumer culture, references to the images of these subcultures are drawn from the mass media more often than from daily life.

There exists no finite list of referent systems available for ads; there are as many as humans are capable of subjectively expressing. However, at any given moment, audiences will not be receptive to, and cannot recall, an infinite array of referent systems linked to brand names. At any rate, the issue is not whether all meaning systems will be used up, but rather how the sphere of cultural meaning has been turned over to the service of sustaining a system of commodities. The value-production process is insatiable as meaning systems are abstracted, appropriated, and carved up to fit the agendas of semiotic formulas necessary to fuel the engines of commodity sign production. Over the years, the velocity of this process of meaning circulation has accelerated, and the process of extracting sign value from any given meaning system has become subject to marginally diminishing returns. Ceaseless repetition of this circuit, the ceaseless replacement of images, has led to a rising cultural sensibility that meaning is insubstantial and ephemeral. Much of what has been written in marketing and reporting circles under the rubric of "Generation X" (members of the post-baby-boom generation) chronicles the culture of cynicism that has grown up in response to a cultural world characterized by the constant turnover of superficial meanings.

Sign values depend, then, on a system of cultural cannibalism. Though methods for producing sign values resist capsulation, we can distinguish some general approaches to appropriation. A common approach starts with the positive or "mimetic" appropriation of value. This frequently involves appropriating an image—a celebrity, a style, or the like—that is "hot" in terms of its potential market value. A second route relies on the negative signifier and the practice of counterpositioning, so that a sign value or a sign identity is established by sharply contrasting it with what it is not. A third maneuver adds the self-referential and media-referential domain. Here we enter into the logic of sign and code differentiation. A well-known combination of these strategies is the Energizer Bunny ad campaign, which is premised on using parody to harness the negative value of overused and irritating advertising genres. Like any system of currency, sign values only exist in relation to other values. Because sign values are constructed out of meaning, they must be articulated with reference to another system of value—a meaning system that is external to, and different from, the product. More and more frequently the referent system that is cannibalized to construct a new image comes from the land of television itself.

Effective sign values are rarely manufactured out of thin air. There are, of course, exceptions to this rule—for instance, Spuds MacKenzie for Bud Light. However, the risks associated with inventing an image are considerable, as Burger King (with Herb the Nerd) and Reebok (with its "UBU" campaign) found out. In each case the effort to invent a signifying image or gesture for their signs failed. Inventing a signifier without any basis in daily life (e.g., the Pepsi "summer chillout" gesture) is generally a recipe for sign failure in the contemporary era.

VALUE ADDED

Once upon a time, the Nike swoosh symbol possessed no intrinsic value as a sign, but value was added to the sign by drawing on the name and image value of celebrity superstars like Michael Jordan. Michael Jordan possesses value in his own right—the better his performances, the higher his value. The sign of Nike acquired additional value when it joined itself to the image of Jordan. Similarly, when Nike introduced a new shoe line named "Air Huarache" and wanted to distinguish its sign from those of other shoe lines, Nike adopted John Lennon's song "Instant Karma" as a starting point for the shoe's sign value. Nike justified drawing on Lennon's classic song by insisting that it was chosen because it dovetailed with Nike's own message of "self-improvement: making yourself better."[9]

No less common than drawing upon the value of a commodity classic like a famous song is the adoption of a subcultural style or image that has captured the popular imagination; the most pervasive current example of a signifying style appropriated for its sign value is rap or hip-hop music. This is almost invariably based on a cultural trickle-up process in which value is appropriated (it trickles up) while the critical ideological force of the style is dissipated (it trickles away). We emphasize that the mimetic approach to producing sign value works by sponging off other values.

Effective appropriation of a cultural moment or style is contingent on how the ad appellates (hails) its target audience members. An excellent example of appellation can be found in a series of McDonald's ads that hailed the viewer with a dude who speaks in the tongue and intonation of Southern California surfer-valley dudes immortalized and cleaned up in the movie *Bill & Ted's Excellent Adventure*. The "Excellent" campaign, by Leo Burnett USA of Chicago, offers viewers a permanently stoned, long-haired youth who wears the layered garb that signals membership in this subcultural totem group. In one ad he shares with viewers his analysis of navigation:

> *"In the past, when ancient old dudes cruised, they used the stars to lead their way. This was not a very excellent system because they were lost all day and ended up living in bogus caves. But luckily we dudes of today have a most excellent number of highways and very many busy streets, and even more excellent than that—they've all been built right next to a McDonald's."*

Another ad has him acting as a tourist guide, sitting astride a stone wall in front of a mansion as he discourses about the site. The content of his monologues is unimportant; it is the style with which they are delivered that defines the ads and their attitude.

> *"We have here a major casa. Home of seriously rich dudes. Now I know rich dudes have the most excellent manners. If we ask politely, well they're sure to invite us in. [He turns toward the mansion and yells out:] Yo, seriously rich dudes. May we come in and see your most excellent stuff? [When there is no reply, he turns back to us with a shrug:] Not home. Must've gone to McDonald's for apple pie or something."*

These ads begin and end with a wildly painted yellow "M" that extends beyond a red block. From its position in the lower right corner of the screen it is obvious that this replaces the ubiquitous golden arches logo of the fast-food giant. A change of this sort in a semiotic building block like the corporate logo should not be taken lightly. McDonald's here shows their moral flexibility to modify their corporate insignia to fit with the aesthetic preferences of a different target audience. Presenting this emblem at the start of the ad is as much a part of the hailing process as the youth who addresses us.

Generation X has recently become the hot topic in the advertising and marketing industries. It's risky hailing youth like this because if the representation does not ring true, then the advertiser has antagonized and estranged the viewer. Young and Rubicam Advertising's director of consumer research advises that when targeting youth, "You need to speak to them in their language and on their terms . . . Contrived 'hip' is the kiss of death with young people."[10] Constructing sign value by appropriating linguistic usage or gestures or music or clothing style also requires careful attention to the process of restylizing, which deletes—"airbrushes"—negative moments. Ads that build on a borrowed speech usage or a gesture or a look are based on the tacit acknowledgment that subcultures are the source of authentic—read: desirable—signs. Authenticity must have a referent system to back it up. Whether it is rap or Generation X or punk or grunge, this process of producing sign value makes images palatable by stripping out—extracting—the essential political ideology that initially drove the expression of these discourses. What is left is mere surface.

Driven by the logic of hailing, the practice of cultural appropriation when situated within the framework of the advertisement seems to magically unfold into an equivalency between brand and cultural icon. In an attempt to appeal to the "twentysomething" audience, Chevrolet has recently laid claim to the history of rock 'n' roll as represented by the music of Jimi Hendrix. Chevrolet justified this act of appropriation as "a natural combination. Camaro and rock 'n' roll truly grew up together. For a quarter century, the car and music have been the life of the party." Chevrolet cements this new equivalency with the slogan "From the country that invented rock 'n' roll."[11]

Once a sign is appropriated it circulates between advertising discourse and everyday life in a stylized form—this kind of mediation invariably changes the sign's cultural meanings and associations. Whether or not these signifying efforts are successful in marketing terms, the signs thus produced tend to be reified images of social relations. Despite this, our critique of commodity signs cannot end with the simple assertion that these signs are nothing more than the alienated relations and desires denied people in their production relations. Historically, the cultural emphasis on consuming, owning, and wearing signs as an indicator of personal identity was well under way by the 1920s. Since then, the commodity self has offered an identity assembled out of the sign-objects that a person consumes. Individuals may seek to present an identity through the commodity signs they possess and wear.

Signwork has evolved as a key practice of what Erving Goffman termed "face-work" in an impersonal urban society. The commodity self based on the packaging of self as a collection or ensemble of commodity signs is predicated on a certain degree of plasticity. At the very least, advertising has established the premise that the most gratifying social relations are those associated with the confident, and discriminating, sign user. While this contributes to rampant pseudoindividualism,[12] it is also true that commodity signs provide people with real social indicators of identity—after all, consumers do use signs to construct identities and to make invidious distinctions between themselves and others. This is one social consequence of positioning spectator-buyers to step into the advertising mirror.

Two generations ago, Sennett and Cobb examined how wearing badges to earn respect in our urban class-based society resulted in an array of social-psychological injuries.[13] Hebdige tracked how this, in turn, contributed to subcultural resistance to fashion codes, as youth bent the "approved" signs to suit their meanings (signs of disapproval). Hebdige adapted the concept of "bricolage" to describe the act of wearing meaning-laden objects (signs) in ways that seem to violate the cosmology (the moral hierarchies) of consumerism that binds the many signs into a cultural system.[14] As working-class political opposition has become closed off, opposition in the society of the spectacle is most readily expressed through the category of style. Though the code of commodity culture has always been able to reabsorb opposition and turn it into new commodity styles, the punk subculture's efforts at bricolage upped the ante, and advertisers eventually responded by appropriating and restyling the bricolaged look, and then turning it back into yet another commodity sign. Levi's advertising led the way, and others followed, into a period of "counterbricolage."[15]

This movement between bricolage and commodity counterbricolage has in its own right been a form of sign wars. Today, the appropriation process has grown so rapid that it can exploit and exhaust a subcultural movement before it has had time to develop—grunge is a case in point. Grunge has not only been thoroughly appropriated, its style stolen in a media blitz, the term itself has been adopted by the culture industry as a metaphor for what cultural analysts like ourselves call *bricolage*. Grunge has become a mass-media metaphor for the new style of mixing things that don't go together. In this brave new world of hyperappropriation, anything goes—retrolooks from any decade are thrown into the blender, as are the political sensibilities of any marginalized subculture—and everything becomes a mishmash.

FLOATING SIGNIFIERS AND THE IMAGE BANK

The perpetual abstraction and recombination of images in pursuit of new currency has logically led to the creation of "image banks." Image banks are an institutionally rationalized approach to managing a marketplace of images for the construction of commodity signs in a stage of advanced sign competition. Banks deal in currency. The name *image bank* is indicative of the fact that images have become a free-floating and interchangeable currency. Image banks deal in stock photos—of mountain tops, sunsets, farm scenes, sea birds, and so on—that have been severed from meaningful context. Advertising agencies work with image banks because they provide a cost-cutting measure. Bankable images, catalogued and filed, are a reminder that signifiers and signifieds are no longer conceived of as necessarily or naturally conjoint. The same image or scenic representation may appear in multiple and diverse commodity narratives—for example, the same shot of flamingo-like waterbirds in flight appears in a Du Pont ad to signify nature-not-yet-destroyed, while in a Kodak film commercial it signifies superior image quality. The image bank also signals a world where there is no necessary material ground—no necessary correspondence between image and referent system. The arbitrariness of the relationship between image signifiers and signifieds has reached a new plateau. A humorous instance of image bank abstraction gone haywire is illustrative. The advertising agency BBDO created a newspaper ad for Apple Computer that proved embarrassing when it discovered that the stock photo of an office building used in the ad was actually an image of the IBM Tower in Atlanta.[16]

SPIRALS OF REFERENTIALITY, SPEED, AND REFLEXIVITY

In the past, most ad campaigns (failures as well as successes) aimed at conveying a coherent and memorable symbolic value for their product by connecting it with an object of desire. But as these symbolic contests have escalated over the years, the turnover of images and symbols has accelerated and the reliance on media intertextuality has increased. This has contributed to an important cultural shift, the "substitution of referential density for narrative coherence."[17] Referential density means that frames become packed with multiple referents minus unifying threads that give the viewer clues about their relationships. Texts become defined not so much by the story they tell, but by the referential combinations they style. Style overwhelms story. Accelerated editing, a refusal to obey sequencing conventions, and a devotion to supermagnified close-ups—all place greater emphasis on the isolated signifier whose meaningfulness is now divorced from the contexts that initially gave meaning to it. Referential density is becoming a prominent characteristic of our cultural landscape, the result of a seemingly endless process of cannibalizing and lifting isolated images from previous media references and reassembling them in pastiche form. Indeed, advertising has shifted from an emphasis on narrative coherence such as that described by Roland Marchand as the "social tableaux"—stories about how to successfully live and act in modern society through the proper use of commodities—to visual fascination. While narrative coherence has hardly vanished in the world of ads, its importance has diminished and the old stories have been abbreviated into tacit assumptions.

More and more today, ads either refer to other ads or are about the subject of advertising itself as a method of positioning the commodity brand name. This process is usually referred to as "media self-referentiality" and "intertextuality." Spirals of referentiality are a function of the continuous process of lifting meanings from one context and placing them into the advertising framework where they become associated with another meaning system. Each time this occurs, meanings are modified and chains of signification are constructed. Let's take an apparently simple example of a bell. Initially, a bell may have meaning to you because it is located in the church near your home and you associate its ringing with the time of day when your mother called you home for dinner. In other words, its meaning was linked to its location and to your relationships with others. But as Walter Benjamin and John Berger have both shown, when a bell is photographed, the image is freed from its context and can be put to almost any service. Now the image can be used to signify a brand of tomatoes or it can be used to indicate "not-suburbia." Today, such an image has been used in a generic way to signify tourism or Europeanness, what we call a "Euro-signifier." We have just described what Barthes meant by second-order signifiers—that is, the bell now stands for Europeanness. Barthes understood that in the modern era this process of hinging and unhinging signifiers and signifieds could go on and on as the image of the bell gets lifted from its new context of generic tourism for use in yet another way. In this sense, advertising contributes to a world littered by second-order signifiers. The circuit of sign-value production is predicated on the diffusion of second-order signifiers. In advertising, harnessing the power of splitting the sign (much like an atom) releases significant potential energy as each signifying valence is steered toward recombination with another split sign to produce a new sign value. But this process also produces cultural by-products. In advertising, one result is an abnormally high level of second-order signifiers—what Barthes saw as the fundamental element of myth.

For decades, advertisers sought to avoid raising the subject of their ad's agenda or the power dynamic going on between text and viewer. Instead, the focus was on the glitter of the spectacular moment. But after decades of this, audiences have matured, become more media-literate, media-saturated, and media-cynical. The arbitrariness of the process eventually rises to the surface and can no longer be ignored. By the latter 1980s there emerged a genre of ads that played at being self-reflexive about the arbitrary process of meaning construction in ads. A new spiral emerged in which advertisers tried to top one an-

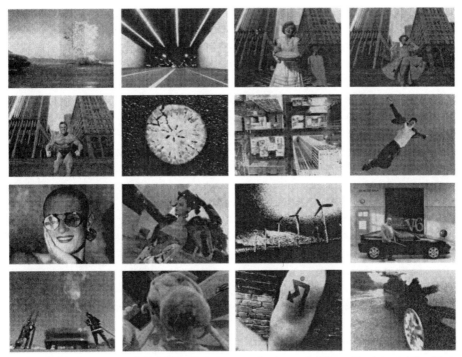

As commercials increase in referential density, images can be thrown together without any relationship to the image that comes before or after. These are but a few of the arbitrary images that populate a 1992 Mazda ad. No order is implied by our layout.

other in how outrageous they can be in their self-reflexive acknowledgments.

CULTURAL CRISIS AND CONTRADICTION

Where does this conversation about advertising culture fit in relation to changes in culture, the economy, and society? How are the spirals of speed, referential density, and media reflexivity related to the larger goings-on of our culture? We have previously argued that advertising has upheld culturally predominant ways of seeing things. Predominant ways of seeing are, however, almost always being contested or stretched by opposing social forces and relations. For example, in American society, patriarchy's long hegemony has recently been effectively contested by women who find patriarchal ways of seeing as too confining and repressive to meet their interests.

Saying that advertising tends to further the hegemony of commodity and market relations does not mean that advertisers are a wily ideological bunch intent on manipulating us politically. When we look at ads as an ideological site, we see ads as ideological in all the following senses: (1) as discourses that socially and culturally construct a world; (2) as discourses that disguise and suppress inequalities, injustices, irrationalities, and contradictions; (3) as discourses that promote a nor-mative vision of our world and our relationships; and (4) as discourses that reflect the logic of capital. In this sense, ideology refers to the "meaning made necessary by the conditions of our society while helping to perpetuate those conditions."[18] Ads are ideological insofar as they construct socially necessary illusions and normalize distorted commu-nication.[19] We are studying ads, then, because we think ads reveal some inner cultural contradictions of a commodity culture.

Advertisements offer rich social texts for investigating the socially constructed nature of hegemony because they are situated at the inter-section of conflicting economic and cultural demands: on the one hand, advertisements must devote themselves to reproducing commodity re-lations (selling more products); on the other hand, they must engage the attention and interpretive participation of consumers by hailing them with images of their own "alreadyness." Ads thus can be made to reveal not only a dominant mode of representation, but also the self-contradictory representations of commodity culture.

We have focused on two sides of the same coin: on sign wars, battles over the currency of images, and on the cultural contradictions of a political economy of sign value. As ideological discourses for under-standing these cultural contradictions, ads can be made to speak a cer-tain kind of truth about the commodity culture that produces them. To the extent that ads must give us back some sense of ourselves, they also unintentionally capture our cultural contradictions. Insofar as advertis-ers today feel the pressure to efficiently hail finely targeted audience segments, they must include signifiers of the self-contradictions mani-fested by this or that target group "persona" in their representations. In the last few years, in addition to the many ads that either try to suppress or disguise contradictions, we now have ads that literally swim in their self-reflexive awareness of issues of domination and power in commod-ity culture. Indeed, some ads now flaunt their own contradictoriness, or that of our culture, to gain attention for themselves. Today the practice of cultural criticism seems to be sponsored by commodity interests.

Herbert Marcuse's *One-Dimensional Man*, written in 1964, is the classic statement of the culture industry's capacity for containing op-position.[20] Marcuse argued that when culture was turned into commod-ity form it could contain contradictions and blunt critical alternative ways of seeing. He felt the process of commodifying language purged the vernacular of "class" from mass-mediated discourses, even though it remained an animating force in the landscape of everyday work life. Thirty years later, class has indeed been erased from public discourse, supplanted by the category of individual life-style; but the culture in-dustry's capacity to contain crisis and contradiction has become disen-gaged from its capacity to redirect the language of resistance and opposition. While the evidence is compelling that advertising is able to appropriate and incorporate the language and visual representations of resistance, we are less convinced by the capacity of advertising to contain crisis tendencies.

Ironically, in a world where advertisers are forever struggling to stylistically differentiate themselves, more than ever before they depend on symbols of cultural opposition to drive the sign–value circuit. In fact, we have come to believe that while some advertising is aimed at containing contradictions (e.g., the environmental consequences of capitalist growth), advertising has itself become the site of new cultural crisis tendencies and emergent cultural contradictions, not the least of which is a profoundly privatized cynicism.

Advertising is in crisis, yet somehow it remains the voice of commodity hegemony. Its formulas have antagonized viewers. Its cultural products no longer merely incorporate opposition to produce images of harmony, although god knows there are plenty of advertisers who still try. While the advertising form has historically functioned as a site for ideologically masking social and cultural contradictions, the neat, clean, and tidy categories of the past have been sublated.

Our argument emphasizes not the particular ad, but the system of ads—the sheer abundance of ads driven by the logic of capital and the reproduction of commodities. As a system, advertising produces sign wars, and sign wars will have real cultural consequences. Indeed, perhaps we should begin by asking what collective crises of meaning lie in store for a culture and society characterized by an increasing circulation velocity of images made necessary by sign wars.

ENDNOTES

1. Berger, John (1972). *Ways of Seeing*. New York: Penguin, p. 134.

2. Williamson, Judith. (1978). *Decoding Advertisements*. London: Marion Boyars; see also Hall, Stuart. (1980). "Encoding/Decoding." Pp. 128–138, in Stuart Hall, et al. (eds.), *Culture Media and Language*. London: Hutchinson & Co.

3. Williamson, 1978, p. 43.

4. Fischer, P.M., M.P. Schwartz, J.W. Richards Jr., A.O. Goldstein, T.H. Rojas. (1991). "Brand logo recognition by children aged 3 to 6 years. Mickey Mouse and Old Joe the Camel," *JAMA*. Dec 11, 266 (22): 3145–8.

5. Semiotics is well suited to the tasks of both constructing and deconstructing sign values because it mimics the structural mechanics of both the commodity form and the advertising form. The "preferred" interpretive conventions of the advertising form reproduce the logic of the commodity form. The latter consists of three intertwined moments: (1) abstraction, the removal of a meaningful action or relationship from its context; (2) equivalence exchange, the formal relation of universal exchangeability between items that are otherwise not comparable; and (3) reification, the conversion of human attributes and relations into the characteristics of objects or things. Advertisements routinely abstract meaning systems from their contexts, place them into relations of formal exchange, engineer a transfer of meanings to construct an equivalency, and propose a reified commodity sign. In this sense, we see the advertising framework replicating the logic of the commodity form.

6. Moore, Martha T. "Visual Overload: Fleeting ad images catch viewers," *USA Today*, June 15, 1993, p. 1B.

7. Baker, Nena. "If Nike lost a shoe, it'd still have T-shirt for its back," *The Oregonian*, April 28, 1991, p. K1, 5.

8. Barthes, Roland. (1972). *Mythologies*. New York: Hill and Wang.

9. Baker, Nena. "Nike's ready to go all out to promote latest sneaker," *The Oregonian*, March 14, 1992, p. B1.

10. Elliott, Stuart. "Hey, Dude, That's One Serious Pitch," *The New York Times*, May 10, 1991, p. D1.

11. " '93 Camaro Advertising Arrives with Rock 'n' Roll Beat," *PR Newswire*, March 29, 1993.

12. See Adorno, Theodor. (1941). "On Popular Music," *Studies in Philosophy and Social Science*, (9): 117–148; Gendron, Bernard. (1986). "Theodor Adorno Meets the Cadillacs," pp. 18–36 in Tania Modleski (ed.) *Studies in Entertainment*. Bloomington: Indiana University Press.

13. Sennett, Richard and Jonathan Cobb. (1972). *The Hidden Injuries of Class*. New York: Vintage.

14. Hebdige, Dick. (1979). *Subculture: The Meaning of Style*. London: Methuen.

15. See Goldman, Robert and Steve Papson. (1991). "Levi's & the Knowing Wink." *Current Perspectives in Social Theory*. Greenwich, CT: JAI Press, pp. 69–95.

16. Horovitz, Bruce. "Cost-conscious agencies turn to rental photos," *Los Angeles Times*, July 16, 1991, p. D6.

17. Hebdige, Dick. (1998). *Hiding in the Light: on images & things*. London: Routledge, p. 237.

18. Williamson, p. 13.

19. See Eagleton, Terry. (1991). *Ideology, an introduction*. New York: Verso, p. 1

20. Marcuse, Herbert. (1964). *One Dimensional Man*. Boston: Beacon.

7
Susan Bordo
"Hunger as Ideology"
(1993)

THE WOMAN WHO DOESN'T EAT MUCH

In a television commercial, two little French girls are shown dressing up in the feathery finery of their mother's clothes. They are exquisite little girls, flawless and innocent, and the scene emphasizes both their youth and the natural sense of style often associated with French women. (The ad is done in French, with subtitles.) One of the girls, spying a picture of the other girl's mother, exclaims breathlessly, "Your mother, she is so slim, so beautiful! Does she eat?" The daughter, giggling, replies: "Silly, just not so much," and displays her mother's helper, a bottle of FibreThin. "Aren't you jealous?" the friend asks. Dimpling, shy yet self-possessed, deeply knowing, the daughter answers, "Not if I know her secrets."

Admittedly, women are continually bombarded with advertisements and commercials for weight-loss products and programs, but this commercial makes many of us particularly angry. On the most obvious level, the commercial affronts with its suggestion that young girls begin early in learning to control their weight, and with its romantic mystification of diet pills as part of the obscure, eternal arsenal of feminine arts to be passed from generation to generation. This romanticization, as often is the case in American commercials, trades on our continuing infatuation with (what we imagine to be) the civility, tradition, and savoir-faire of "Europe" (seen as the stylish antithesis to our own American clumsiness, aggressiveness, crudeness). The little girls are fresh and demure, in a way that is undefinably but absolutely recognizably "European"—as defined, that is, within the visual vocabulary of popular American culture. And FibreThin, in this commercial, is nothing so crass and "medical" and pragmatic (read: American) as a diet pill, but a mysterious, prized (and, it is implied, age-old) "secret," known only to those with both history and taste.

But we expect such hype from contemporary advertisements. Far more unnerving is the psychological acuity of the ad's focus, not on the size and shape of bodies, but on a certain *subjectivity*, represented by the absent but central figure of the mother, the woman who eats, only "not so much." We never see her picture; we are left to imagine her ideal beauty and slenderness. But what she looks like is not important, in any case; what is important is the fact that she has achieved what we might call a "cool" (that is, casual) relation to food. She is not starving herself (an obsession, indicating the continuing power of food), but neither is she desperately and shamefully binging in some private corner. Eating has become, for her, no big deal. In its evocation of the lovely French mother who doesn't eat much, the commercial's metaphor of European "difference" reveals itself as a means of representing that enviable and truly foreign "other": the woman for whom food is merely ordinary, who can take it or leave it.

Another version, this time embodied by a sleek, fashionable African American woman, playfully promotes Virginia Slims Menthol (Figure 1). This ad, which appeared in *Essence* magazine, is one of a series specifically targeted at the African American female consumer. In contrast to the Virginia Slims series concurrently appearing in *Cosmo* and *People*, a series which continues to associate the product with historically expanded opportunities for women ("You've come a long way, baby" remains the motif and slogan), Virginia Slims pitches to the *Essence* reader by mocking solemnity and self-importance *after* the realization of those opportunities: "Why climb the ladder if you're not going to enjoy the view?" "Big girls don't cry. They go shopping." And, in the variant depicted in Figure 1: "Decisions are easy. When I get to a fork in the road, I eat."

Arguably, the general subtext meant to be evoked by these ads is the failure of the dominant, white culture (those who *don't* "enjoy the view") to relax and take pleasure in success. The upwardly mobile black consumer, it is suggested, will do it with more panache, with more cool—and of course with a cool, Virginia Slims Menthol in hand. In this particular ad, the speaker scorns obsessiveness, not only over professional or interpersonal decision-making, but over food as well. Implicitly contrasting herself to those who worry and fret, she presents herself as utterly "easy" in her relationship with food. Unlike the FibreThin mother, she eats anytime she wants. But *like* the FibreThin mother (and this is the key similarity for my purposes), she has achieved a state beyond craving. Undominated by unsatisfied, internal need, she eats not only freely but without deep desire and without apparent consequence. It's "easy," she says. Presumably, without those forks in the road she might forget about food entirely.

The Virginia Slims woman is a fantasy figure, her cool attitude toward food as remote from the lives of most contemporary African American women as from any others. True, if we survey cultural attitudes toward women's appetites and body size, we find great variety—a variety

FIGURE 1

shaped by ethnic, national, historical, class, and other factors. My eighty-year-old father, the child of immigrants, asks at the end of every meal if I "got enough to eat"; he considers me skinny unless I am plump by my own standards. His attitude reflects not only memories of economic struggle and a heritage of Jewish-Russian preference for zaftig women, but the lingering, well into this century, of a once more general Anglo-Saxon cultural appreciation for the buxom woman. In the mid-nineteenth century, hotels and bars were adorned with Bouguereau-inspired paintings of voluptuous female nudes; Lillian Russell, the most photographed woman in America in 1890, was known and admired for her hearty appetite, ample body (over two hundred pounds at the height of her popularity), and "challenging, fleshly arresting" beauty.[1] Even as such fleshly challenges became less widely appreciated in the twentieth century, men of Greek, Italian, Eastern European, and African descent, influenced by their own distinctive cultural heritages, were still likely to find female voluptuousness appealing. And even in the late 1960s and early 1970s, as Twiggy and Jean Shrimpton began to set a new norm for ultra-slenderness, lesbian cultures in the United States continued to be accepting—even celebrating—of fleshy, space-claiming female bodies.

Even more examples could be produced, of course, if we cast our glance more widely over the globe and back through history. Many cultures, clearly, have revered expansiveness in women's bodies and appetites. Some still do. But in the 1980s and 1990s an increasingly universal equation of slenderness with beauty and success has rendered the competing claims of cultural diversity ever feebler. Men who were teenagers from the mid-seventies on, whatever their ethnic roots or economic class, are likely to view long, slim legs, a flat stomach, and a firm rear end as essentials of female beauty. Unmuscled heft is no longer as acceptable as it once was in lesbian communities. Even Miss Soviet Union has become lean and tight, and the robust, earthy actresses who used to star in Russian films have been replaced by slender, Westernized types.

Arguably, a case could once be made for a contrast between (middle-class, heterosexual) white women's obsessive relations with food and a more accepting attitude toward women's appetites within African American communities. But in the nineties, features on diet, exercise, and body-image problems have grown increasingly prominent in magazines aimed at African American readers, reflecting the cultural reality that for most women today—whatever their racial or ethnic identity, and increasingly across class and sexual-orientation differences as well—free and easy relations with food are at best a relic of the past. (More frequently in *Essence* than in *Cosmo*, there may be a focus on health problems associated with overweight among African Americans, in addition to the glamorization of slenderness.) Almost all of us who can afford to be eating well are dieting—and hungry—almost all of the time.

It is thus Dexatrim, not Virginia Slims, that constructs the more realistic representation of women's subjective relations with food. In Dexatrim's commercial that shows a woman, her appetite-suppressant worn off, hurtling across the room, drawn like a living magnet to the breathing, menacing refrigerator, hunger is represented as an insistent, powerful force with a life of its own. This construction reflects the physiological reality of dieting, a state the body is unable to distinguish from starvation.[2] And it reflects its psychological reality as well; for dieters, who live in a state of constant denial, food is a perpetually beckoning

presence, its power growing ever greater as the sanctions against gratification become more stringent. A slender body may be attainable
through hard work, but a "cool" relation to food, the true "secret" of
the beautiful "other" in the FibreThin commercial, is a tantalizing reminder of what lies beyond the reach of the inadequate and hungry self.
(Of course, as the ads suggest, a psychocultural transformation remains
possible, through FibreThin and Virginia Slims.)

PSYCHING OUT THE FEMALE CONSUMER

Sometimes, when I am analyzing and interpreting advertisements and
commercials in class, students accuse me of a kind of paranoia about
the significance of these representations as carriers and reproducers of
culture. After all, they insist, these are just images, not "real life"; any
fool knows that advertisers manipulate reality in the service of selling
their products. I agree that on some level we "know" this. However,
were it a meaningful or *usable* knowledge, it is unlikely that we would
be witnessing the current spread of diet and exercise mania across racial
and ethnic groups, or the explosion of technologies aimed at bodily
"correction" and "enhancement."

Jean Baudrillard offers a more accurate description of our cultural
estimation of the relation and relative importance of image and "reality." In *Simulations*, he recalls the Borges fable in which the cartogra-
phers of a mighty empire draw up a map so detailed that it ends up
exactly covering the territory of the empire, a map which then frays and
disintegrates as a symbol of the coming decline of the empire it perfectly
represents. Today, Baudrillard suggests, the fable might be inverted: it
is no longer the territory that provides the model for the map, but the
map that defines the territory; and it is the *territory* "whose shreds are
slowly rotting across the map." Thinking further, however, he declares
even the inverted fable to be "useless." For what it still assumes is precisely that which is being lost today—namely, the distinction between
the territory and its map, between reality and appearance. Today, all
that we experience as meaningful are appearances.[3]

Thus, we all "know" that Cher and virtually every other female star
over the age of twenty-five is the plastic product of numerous cosmetic
surgeries on face and body. But, in the era of the "hyperreal" (as Baudrillard calls it), such "knowledge" is as faded and frayed as the old map
in the Borges tale, unable to cast a shadow of doubt over the dazzling,
compelling, authoritative images themselves. Like the knowledge of our
own mortality when we are young and healthy, the knowledge that
Cher's physical appearance is fabricated is an empty abstraction; it simply does not compute. It is the created image that has the hold on our
most vibrant, immediate sense of what *is*, of what matters, of what we
must pursue for ourselves.

In *constructing* the images, of course, continual use is made of knowledge (or at least what is imagined to be knowledge) of consumers' lives. Indeed, a careful reading of contemporary advertisements reveals continual and astute manipulation of problems that psychology and the popular media have targeted as characteristic dilemmas of the "contemporary woman," who is beset by conflicting role demands and pressures on her time. "Control"—a word that rarely used to appear in commercial contexts—has become a common trope in advertisements for products as disparate as mascara ("Perfect Pen Eyeliner. Puts *you* in control. And isn't that nice for a change?") and cat-box deodorant ("Control. I strive for it. My cat achieves it"). "*Soft felt tip gives you absolute control of your line*" (Figure 2). It is virtually impossible to glance casually at this ad without reading "line" as "life"—which is, of course, the subliminal coding such ads intend. "Mastery" also frequently figures in ads for cosmetics and hair products: "Master your curls with new Adaptable Perm." The rhetoric of these ads is interestingly contrasted to the rhetoric of mastery and control directed at male consumers. Here, the message is almost always one of mastery and control over *others* rather than the self: "Now it's easier than ever to achieve a position of power in Manhattan" (an ad for Manhattan health club), or "Don't just serve. Rule" (an ad for Speedo tennis shoes).

Advertisers are aware, too, of more specific *ways* in which women's lives are out of control, including our well-documented food disorders; they frequently incorporate the theme of food obsession into their pitch. The Sugar Free Jell-O Pudding campaign exemplifies a typical commercial strategy for exploiting women's eating problems while obscuring their dark realities. (The advertisers themselves would put this differently, of course.) In the "tip of my tongue" ad (Figure 3), the obsessive mental state of the compulsive eater is depicted fairly accurately, guaranteeing recognition from people with that problem: "If I'm not eating dessert, I'm talking about it. If I'm not talking about it, I'm eating it. And I'm always thinking about it . . . It's just always on my mind."

These thoughts, however, belong to a slender, confident, and—most important—decidedly not depressed individual, whose upbeat, open, and accepting attitude toward her constant hunger is far from that of most women who eat compulsively. "The inside of a binge," Geneen Roth writes, "is deep and dark. At the core . . . is deprivation, scarcity, a feeling that you can never get enough."[4] A student described her hunger as "a black hole that I had to fill up." In the Sugar Free Jell-O ad, by contrast, the mental state depicted is most like that of a growing teenage boy; to be continually hungry is represented as a normal, if somewhat humorous and occasionally annoying, state with no disastrous physical or emotional consequences.

The use of a male figure is one strategy, in contemporary ads, for representing compulsive eating as "natural" and even lovable. Men are

FIGURE 2

supposed to have hearty, even voracious, appetites. It is a mark of the manly to eat spontaneously and expansively, and manliness is a frequent commercial code for amply portioned products: "Manwich," "Hungry Man Dinners," "Manhandlers." Even when men advertise diet products (as they more frequently do, now that physical perfection is increasingly being demanded of men as well as women), they brag about their appetites, as in the Tommy Lasorda commercials for Slim-Fast, which feature three burly football players (their masculinity beyond reproach) declaring that if Slim-Fast can satisfy *their* appetites, it can satisfy anyone's. The displacement of the female by a male figure (displacement

FIGURE 3

when the targeted consumer is in fact a woman) thus dispels thoughts of addiction, danger, unhappiness, and replaces them with a construction of compulsive eating (or thinking about food) as benign indulgence of a "natural" inclination. Consider the ad shown in Figure 4, depicting a male figure diving with abandon into the "tempered-to-full-flavor-consistency" joys of Häagen-Dazs deep chocolate.

Emotional heights, intensity, love, and thrills: it is women who habitually seek such experiences from food and who are most likely to be

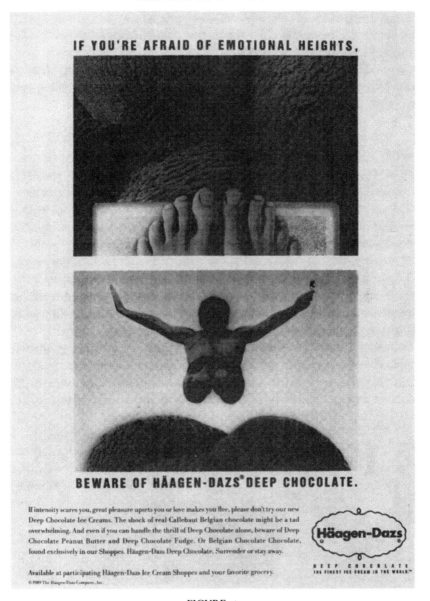

FIGURE 4

overwhelmed by their relationship to food, to find it dangerous and frightening (especially rich, fattening, soothing food like ice cream). The marketers of Häagen-Dazs know this; they are aware of the well-publicized prevalence of compulsive eating and binge behaviors among women. Indeed, this ad exploits, with artful precision, exactly the sorts of associations that are likely to resonate with a person for whom eating is invested with deep emotional meaning. Why, then, a male diver? In part, as I have been arguing, the displacement is necessary to insure that the grim actualities of women's eating problems remain obscured; the point, after all, is to sell ice cream, not to remind people of how dangerous food actually *is* for women. Too, the advertisers may reckon that women might enjoy seeing a man depicted in swooning surrender to ice cream, as a metaphor for the emotional surrender that so many women crave from their husbands and lovers.

FOOD, SEXUALITY, AND DESIRE

I would argue, however, that more than a purely profit-maximizing, ideologically neutral, Madison Avenue mentality is at work in these ads. They must also be considered as gender ideology—that is, as specifically (consciously or unconsciously) servicing the cultural reproduction of gender difference and gender inequality, quite independent of (although at times coinciding with) marketing concerns. As gender ideology, the ads I have been discussing are not distinctively contemporary but continue a well-worn representational tradition, arguably inaugurated in the Victorian era, in which the depiction of women eating, particularly in sensuous surrender to rich, exciting food, is taboo.[5]

In exploring this dimension, we might begin by attempting to imagine an advertisement depicting a young, attractive woman indulging as freely, as salaciously as the man in the Post cereal ad shown in Figure 5. Such an image would violate deeply sedimented expectations, would be experienced by many as disgusting and transgressive. When women are positively depicted as sensuously voracious about food (almost never in commercials, and only very rarely in movies and novels), their hunger for food is employed solely as a metaphor for their sexual appetite. In the eating scenes in *Tom Jones* and *Flashdance*, for example, the heroines' unrestrained delight in eating operates as sexual foreplay, a way of prefiguring the abandon that will shortly be expressed in bed. Women are permitted to lust for food itself only when they are pregnant or when it is clear they have been near starvation—as, for example, in *McCabe and Mrs. Miller*, in the scene in which Mrs. Miller, played by Julie Christie,

FIGURE 5

wolfs down half a dozen eggs and a bowl of beef stew before the amazed eyes of McCabe. Significantly, the scene serves to establish Mrs. Miller's "manliness"; a woman who eats like this is to be taken seriously, is not to be trifled with, the movie suggests.

The metaphorical situation is virtually inverted in the representation of male eaters. Although voracious eating may occasionally code male sexual appetite (as in *Tom Jones*), we frequently also find *sexual* appetite operating as a metaphor for eating pleasure. In commercials that feature male eaters, the men are shown in a state of wild, sensual transport over heavily frosted, rich, gooey desserts. Their total lack of control is portrayed as appropriate, even adorable; the language of the background jingle is unashamedly aroused, sexual and desiring:

I'm thinking about you the whole day through [crooned to a Pillsbury cake]. I've got a passion for you.

You're my one and only, my creamy deluxe [Betty Crocker frosting].

You butter me up, I can't resist, you leave me breathless [Betty Crocker frosting].

Your brownies give me fever. Your cake gives me chills [assorted Betty Crocker mixes].

I'm a fool for your chocolate. I'm wild, crazy, out of control [assorted Betty Crocker mixes].

I've got it bad, and I should know, 'cause I crave it from my head right down to my potato [for Pillsbury Potatoes Au Gratin].

Can't help myself. It's Duncan Hines [assorted cake mixes] and nobody else.

In these commercials food is constructed as a sexual object of desire, and eating is legitimated as much more than a purely nutritive activity. Rather, food is *supposed* to supply sensual delight and succor—not as metaphorically standing for something else, but as an erotic experience in itself. Women are permitted such gratification from food only in measured doses. In another ad from the Diet Jell-O series, eating is metaphorically sexualized: "I'm a girl who just can't say no. I insist on dessert," admits the innocently dressed but flirtatiously posed model (Figure 6). But at the same time that eating is mildly sexualized in this ad, it is also contained. She is permitted to "feel good about saying 'Yes' "—but ever so demurely, and to a harmless low-calorie product. Transgression beyond such limits is floridly sexualized, as an act of "cheating" (Figure 7). Women may be encouraged (like the man on the Häagen-Dazs high board) to "dive in"—not, however, into a dangerous pool of Häagen-Dazs Deep Chocolate, but for a "refreshing dip" into Weight Watchers linguini (Figure 8). Targeted at the working woman ("Just what you need to revive yourself from the workday routine"),

"I'm a girl who just can't say no. I insist on dessert."

The way I see it, every woman is entitled to her just desserts. Just as long as dessert is Sugar Free Jell-O® Gelatin. It's light and fruity and fun. And it's only 8 calories, 'cause it's made with all NutraSweet.® Kind of makes you feel good about saying 'Yes.'

The dessert you don't have to desert.

FIGURE 6

this ad also exploits the aquatic metaphor to conjure up images of female independence and liberation ("Isn't it just like us to make waves?").

All of this may seem peculiarly contemporary, revolving as it does around the mass marketing of diet products. But in fact the same metaphorical universe, as well as the same practical prohibitions against female indulgence (for, of course, these ads are not only selling products but teaching appropriate behavior) were characteristic of Victorian gender ideology. Victorians did not have *Cosmo* and television, of course.

You'll think
you're cheating
But you know you're not...
It's Wonder® Light bread.
Should you tell?
    Should you tell your
friend that each full-size slice
of great tasting Wonder
Light is only 40 calories?
    You can't just let her
suffer through carrot sticks
and rice cakes...Can you?

WONDER
LIGHT

WONDER
LIGHT

The lighter slice
of America.

FIGURE 7

But they did have conduct manuals, which warned elite women of the dangers of indulgent and overstimulating eating and advised how to consume in a feminine way (as little as possible and with the utmost precaution against unseemly show of desire). *Godey's Lady's Book* warned that it was vulgar for women to load their plates; young girls were admonished to "be frugal and plain in your tastes."[6] Detailed lexicons offered comparisons of the erotic and cooling effects of various foods, often with specific prescriptions for each sex.[7] Sexual metaphors permeate descriptions of potential transgression:

> Every luxurious table is a scene of temptation, which it requires fixed principles and an enlightened mind to withstand. . . . Nothing can be more seducing to the appetite than this arrangement of the viands which compose a feast; as the stomach is filled, and the natural desire for food subsides, the palate is tickled by more delicate and relishing dishes until it is betrayed into excess.[8]

Today, the same metaphors of temptation and fall appear frequently in advertisements for diet products (see Figure 9). And in the Victorian era, as today, the forbiddenness of rich food often resulted in private binge behavior, described in *The Bazaar Book of Decorum* (1870) as the "secret luncheon," at which "many of the most abstemious at the open dinner are the most voracious . . . swallowing cream tarts by the dozen, and caramels and chocolate drops by the pound's weight."[9]

  The emergence of such rigid and highly moralized restrictions on female appetite and eating are, arguably, part of what Bram Dijkstra has interpreted as a nineteenth-century "cultural ideological counteroffensive" against the "new woman" and her challenge to prevailing

Dive in.

Just what you need to revive yourself from the workday routine. A refreshing dip into our new Seafood Linguini. Generous chunks of seafood with whole shrimp, together with tender cuts of broccoli florets, carrots and zucchini. All in a light garlic sauce, and served amid a sea of linguini. Weight Watchers Seafood Linguini. Something deliciously different to add to your schedule. Isn't it just like us to make waves?

Weight Watchers.
This is living!

FIGURE 8

gender arrangements and their constraints on women.[10] Mythological, artistic, polemical, and scientific discourses from many cultures and eras certainly suggest the symbolic potency of female hunger as a cultural metaphor for unleashed female power and desire, from the blood-craving Kali (who in one representation is shown eating her own entrails) to the *Malleus Malificarum* ("For the sake of fulfilling the mouth of the womb, [witches] consort even with the devil") to Hall and Oates's contemporary rock lyrics: "Oh, oh, here she comes, watch out boys, she'll chew you up."[11]

In *Tom Jones* and *Flashdance*, the trope of female hunger as female sexuality is embodied in attractive female characters; more frequently, however, female hunger as sexuality is represented by Western culture in misogynist images permeated with terror and loathing rather than affection or admiration. In the figure of the man-eater the metaphor of the devouring woman reveals its deep psychological underpinnings. Eating is not really a metaphor for the sexual act; rather, the sexual act, when initiated and desired by a woman, is imagined as itself an act of eating, of incorporation and destruction of the object of desire. Thus, women's sexual appetites must be curtailed and controlled, because they threaten to deplete and consume the body and soul of the male. Such imagery, as Dijkstra has demonstrated, flourishes in the West in the art of the late nineteenth century. Arguably, the same cultural backlash (if not in the same form) operates today—for example, in the ascendancy of popular films that punish female sexuality and independence by rape and dismemberment (as in numerous slasher films), loss of family and children (*The Good Mother*), madness and death (*Fatal Attraction, Presumed Innocent*), and public humiliation and disgrace (*Dangerous Liaisons*).

Of course, Victorian prohibitions against women eating were not *only* about the ideology of gender. Or, perhaps better put, the ideology of gender contained other dimensions as well.

FIGURE 9

The construction of "femininity" had not only a significant moral and sexual aspect (femininity as sexual passivity, timidity, purity, innocence) but a class dimension. In the reigning body symbolism of the day, a frail frame and lack of appetite signified not only spiritual transcendence of the desires of the flesh but *social* transcendence of the laboring, striving "economic" body. Then, as today, to be aristocratically cool and unconcerned with the mere facts of material survival was highly fashionable. The hungering bourgeois wished to appear, like the aristocrat, above the material desires that in fact ruled his life. The closest he could come was to possess a wife whose ethereal body became a sort of fashion statement of *his* aristocratic tastes. If he could not be or marry an aristocrat, he could have a wife who looked like one, a wife whose nonrobust beauty and delicate appetite signified her lack of participation in the taxing "public sphere."[12]

AUTHOR'S NOTE

This essay grew out of a shorter piece, "How Television Teaches Women to Hate Their Hungers," in *Mirror Images* (Newsletter of Anorexia Bulimia Support, Syracuse, N.Y.) 4, no. 1(1986): 8–9. An earlier version was delivered at the 1990 meetings of the New York State Sociological Association, and some of the analysis has been presented in various talks at Le Moyne and other colleges and community organizations. I owe thanks to all my students who supplied examples.

ENDNOTES

1. Journalist Beatrice Fairfax, quoted in Lois Banner, *American Beauty* (Chicago: University of Chicago Press, 1984), p. 136.

2. "Starvation Stages in Weight-loss Patients Similar to Famine Victims," *International Obesity Newsletter* 3 (April 1989).

3. Jean Baudrillard, *Simulations* (New York: Semiotext(e), 1983), pp. 1–3; quotation is on p. 2.

4. Geneen Roth, *Feeding the Hungry Heart* (New York: New American Library, 1982), p. 15.

5. See Helena Mitchie, *The Flesh Made Word* (New York: Oxford University Press, 1987), for an extremely interesting discussion of this taboo in Victorian literature.

6. Quoted from *Godey's* by Joan Jacobs Brumberg, *Fasting Girls* (Cambridge: Harvard University Press, 1988), p. 179.

7. Mitchie, *The Flesh Made Word*, p. 15. Not surprisingly, red meat came under especial suspicion as a source of erotic inflammation. As was typical for the era, such anxieties were rigorously scientized: for example, in terms of the heat-producing capacities of red meat and its effects on the development of the sexual organs and menstrual flow. But, clearly, an irresistible associational overdetermination—meat as the beast, the raw, the primitive, the masculine—was the true inflammatory agent here. These associations survive today, put to commercial use by the American Beef Association, whose television ads feature James Garner and Cybill Shepard promoting "Beef: Real Food for Real People." Here the nineteenth-century link between meat aversion, delicacy, and refinement is exploited, this time in favor of the meat-eater, whose down-to-earth gutsiness is implicitly contrasted to the prissiness of the weak-blooded vegetarian.

8. Mrs. H. O. Ward, *The Young Lady's Friend* (Philadelphia: Porter and Coates, 1880), p. 162, quoted in Mitchie, *The Flesh Made Word*, pp. 16–17.

9. Quoted in Mitchie, *The Flesh Made Word*, p. 193.

10. Bram Dijkstra, *Idols of Perversity* (New York: Oxford University Press, 1986), pp. 30–31.

11. *Malleus Malificarum* quoted in Brian Easlea, *Witch-Hunting, Magic, and the New Philosophy* (Atlantic Highlands, N.J.: Humanities Press, 1980), p. 8; Hall and Oates, "Man-Eater."

12. Women were thus warned that "gluttonous habits of life" would degrade their physical appearance and ruin their marriageability. "Gross eaters" could develop thick skin, broken blood vessels on the nose, cracked lips, and an unattractively "superanimal" facial expression (Brumberg, *Fasting Girls*, p. 179). Of course, the degree to which actual women were able to enact any part of these idealized and idolized constructions was highly variable (as it always is); but *all* women, of all classes and races, felt their effects as the normalizing measuring rods against which their own adequacy was judged (and, usually, found wanting).

PART THREE

Consumption and Lived Experience

8
Dick Hebdige
"OBJECT AS IMAGE: THE ITALIAN SCOOTER CYCLE"
(1988)

One of the difficulties of sociological discourse lies in the fact that like all discourse, it unfolds in strictly linear fashion whereas, to escape over-simplification and one-sidedness one needs to be able to recall at every point the whole network of relationships found there.

—PIERRE BOURDIEU, LA DISTINCTION, 1979

Nowhere do we encounter "networks of relationships" more familiar and "material" yet more elusive and contradictory than those in which material objects themselves are placed and have meaning(s). If linearity is an effect of all discourse then the world of things seems especially resistant to coherent exegesis. And one of the central paradoxes facing those who write about product design must be that the more "material" the object—the more finite its historical and visual appearance—the more prodigious the things that can be said about it, the more varied the analyzes, descriptions and histories that can be brought to bear upon it.

In a sense, each essay in Roland Barthes' *Mythologies* is an equation which depends for its impact on the initial recognition of this perverse formula and Barthes handles the paradox with a relish which alternates between the comic and the macabre ("What I claim is to live to the full the contradiction of my time, which may well make sarcasm the condition of truth"[1]). In "The New Citroen," Barthes describes how the "tangible" is made to intersect with the "ethereal," the "material" with the "spiritual" through the convention of the annual motor show where the industry's new product is miraculously "unveiled" before the public. He refers to the mystique of the object: the dual mystery of its appearance—its magical lines, its "classical" body and the unanswerable riddle (unanswerable at least for Barthes, the aesthete) of how it came to be made in the first place—to religious myths and archetypes. Here a set of contemporary wonders—the transubstantiation of labor power into things, the domestication of the "miracle" in use—is intimated by

Barthes through the manipulation of a single pun: the Citroen DS19 (short for "diffusion Special") is pronounced *"Déesee"* (Goddess) in French.

The essay is, then, a kind of trial by catachresis. It might be argued that that is precisely Barthes' "method"; that Barthes would have been the first to insist on the validity of constructing an analysis on the strength of a single word—on what it evokes and makes possible for the mythologist. Indeed, for Barthes it is only through "displacements" of this kind that writing is exalted into Literature:

> ... for the text is the very outcropping of speech, and it is within speech that speech must be fought, led astray—not by the message of which it is the instrument, but by the play of words of which it is the theater ... The forces of freedom which are in literature depend not on the writer's civil person, nor on his political commitment ... nor do they even depend on the doctrinal content of his work, but rather on the labor of displacement he brings to bear upon the language ... [2]

To be Barthesian, writing is the only practice in which the writer has a "presence" in which, about which he or she is qualified to speak:

> The paradox is that the raw material, having become in some ways its own end, literature is basically a tautological activity ... the *ecrivain* is one who absorbs the why of the world radically into a how to write ... [3]

And for Barthes, that writing which would claim to deal with representation, with myth and the "doxa" must satisfy certain conditions. It must be self-returning and sensitive to the plurality of verbal signs. It must be capable of "sarcasm." A pun is therefore valued insofar as it opens up and undermines the strictures of a "natural" (i.e., "bourgeois") speech. So Barthes renders the Citroen back into its "real" premythical components. He recreates it using purely linguistic materials. Barthes' "New Citroen" is powered on a figure of speech. Nonetheless the subversive rationale of this replacement is not necessarily visible to everyone who picks up a copy of *Mythologies*. Like the DS revolving slowly on its dais, the argument is simply "exhibited," turned by a mechanism which remains hidden from the wondering eyes of the reader (even, in all likelihood, from the eyes of the reader who appreciates the pun):

> It is obvious that the new Citroen has fallen from the sky inasmuch as it appears at first sight as a superlative object. We must not forget that an object is the best messenger of a world above that of nature: one can easily see in an object a perfection and an absence of origin, a closure and a brilliance—a transformation of life into matter ... and in a word a silence which belongs to fairy tales. [4]

If writing is regarded as a "narcissistic activity" [5] as Barthes would have it, then the gross illusion that language is transparent (what has recently been dubbed the "realist fallacy") is certainly avoided. But the "new" position has its own attendant fantasies: when language becomes a mirror for the narcissist, other illusions are, of course, possible. We could say that what is "misrecognised" in (this kind of) language is the depth of perception (the depth of the reflection). To put it another way, what is "misrecognised" is the illusory "materiality" of language itself.

For Barthes, the real can only be inserted into language as a "silence"—"a silence which belongs to fairy tales." But instead of the "silence" of the object, we might like to stress its solidity, its materiality, the simple fact of its "being there." And it might be more accurate to say that the problem of representing the material world remains paramount in Barthes and is depicted in that form—i.e., as the relationship of speech to silence—because that problem is itself material: Barthes was, after all, a litterateur. Had he been an engineer or a traveling sales rep. who yearned to own a car capable of impressing potential clients ("actualising (perhaps) . . . the very essence of petit-bourgeois advancement"[6]), then the "problem" would have been differently conceived and differently presented. And if he had shared the interest in mechanics and "progress" (mechanics as a metaphor for progress) which no doubt informed the ecstatic response of many of the supplicants who filed past the Citroen stand in 1955 and wanted, themselves, to possess the Goddess, then, no doubt, we too would have been confronted with a different object, a different alienation. For, far from being silent, the number of voices which speak through and for "dumb things" are legion. The enigma of the object resides for us less in its "silence," its imagined essence than in the babble which proliferates around it.

THREE "MOMENTS"

The variability of significance rather than the persistence of qualities should be at the forefront of analysis . . .
— FRAN HANNAH AND TIM PUTNAM,
TAKING STOCK IN DESIGN HISTORY, BLOCK 3

How then can we hope to provide a comprehensive and unified account of all the multiple values and meanings which accumulate around a single object over time, the different symbolic and instrumental functions it can serve for different groups of users separated by geographical, temporal and cultural location? The problem Bourdieu outlines and Barthes embodies in *Mythologies* has already been acknowledged: there is a tendency amongst those who aspire toward a "materialist" conception of design to question the adequacy of the object as the basic unit of analysis and to substitute instead design practice as a more satisfactory point of entry. But this shift in emphasis and the quest for epistemological rigour which motivates it carries its own price. For in the case of design history, there can be no subject without objects. All design practice has as its ultimate ideal and actual destination a tangible result, a real set of objects. Indeed, in design the thing itself is the ideal.

How then is it possible to talk simultaneously about objects and the practices which shape them, determine or delimit their uses, their meanings and their values without losing sight of the larger networks of relationships into which those objects and practices are inserted? The task becomes still more daunting if we acknowledge first that there can be no absolute symmetry between the "moments" of design/production and consumption/use and, further, that advertising stands between these two instances—a separate moment of mediation: marketing, promotion, the construction of images and markets, the conditioning of public response. It is tempting when writing about design either to run these three moments together or to give undue prominence to one of them so that production, mediation or consumption becomes the "determining instance" which dictates the meaning of the object in every other context. In either case, the result is more or less the same—a delicately (un)balanced sequence of relationships is reduced to a brutal set of aphorisms, e.g., masses consume what is produced in mass (where production is regarded as determining); desire is a function of the advertising image (where mediation is regarded as the determining instance); people remain human and "authentic," untouched by the appeal of either images or objects (where consumption or the refusal of consumption is seen as determining). Clearly none of these models is sufficient in itself though each may seem appropriate in particular circumstances when applied to particular objects. It would be preferable to find a way of holding all three instances together so that we can consider the transformations effected on the object as it passes between them. But we are still left with the problem of constructing a language in which that passage can be adequately represented.

If we abandon those solutions to the problem which limit the production of significance to the immanent logic of the object itself—as an internal organisation of elements or as a latent essence—if, in other words, we abandon the formalist option and if we also discard the no less abstract language of pure function: "uses," "gratification" and so on, then the criteria for excluding and organising information become increasingly uncertain. We are in a field without fences left with an intractable mass: "cultural significance."

To reconstruct the full "cultural significance" of the DS Citroen we would have to do more than merely "demystify" its reception in the marketplace at the point where, as Barthes would have it, the Goddess is "mediatised" from "the heaven of Metropolis" and brought within the range of some people's pockets and everybody else's aspirations. If we were to produce a comprehensive analysis we would have to take into account the kinds of significance generated as the object passes through a maze of independent but interlocking frames—drawing back at every point to consider the structures in which each individual frame is housed.

We could trace the passage of the Citroen, then, from its inception/ conception through the various preparatory stages: market research, motivational research, design—engineering, styling (division of labor within the design team; relationship of team to management infrastructure), modifications in conception at design stages, constraints of available technological resources on DS design, adaptation of existing Citroen plant to accommodate the new product, production of prototypes and models; production (labor relations, labor processes), exhibitions and launch of new product, press conferences, press releases and handouts, reviews in trade press, advertising campaign (target group), distribution of finished product: retail arrangements, distribution of foreign licences, provision of servicing facilities, price, sales figures (consumer profile of target group), formation and composition of the Citroen user groups, etc., etc. Finally we would have to place the DS alongside other cars available in 1955 in order to assess its difference from equivalent products—the extent of its stylistic and technical "advances" or departures, its potential for "prestige," etc.

The "cultural significance" of the Citroen DS 19 might be defined as the sum total of all the choices and fixings made at each stage in the passage of the object from conception, production and mediation to mass-circulation, sale and use. Nor do the connotations accumulate in an orderly progression from factory to consumer. In the production of significance, time is reversible and each stage in the sequence (production-mediation-consumption) can predominate at different times in determining meaning.

For instance, to take a more topical example, the meaning of the Mini Metro is overdetermined by the uncertainty surrounding its production and the reputation for "bloodymindedness" of the British Leyland workforce—a reputation constructed through Press and television coverage of industrial disputes. This in turn enables the Metro to function contradictorily in the news media both as a symbol of "Britain's hope" and as a symptom of the "British disease" (where production hold-ups and technical faults are cited as evidence of Britain's decline as an industrial power which, to complete the circle, is "explained" by reference to the "problem" of the British workforce). The entire history of British Leyland labor relations is reified in the Mini Metro's public image. The advertising campaign mobilises that history (the memory of strikes hovers just behind the copy just as in the Hovis television ads the memory of the Depression looms out of the conjunction of sound and image— the melancholy strains of a northern brass band, the black and white image of "noble" cloth-capped workers). The Mini Metro advertising campaign overlays two forms of patriotic optimism—that Britain can make it, that British Leyland can go on making it (and supplying the spares) across the more generalised faith in the future which purchasing a new car normally implies. The potential purchaser is invited to make all three investments simultaneously—in the future of Britain, in the future of British Leyland, and in his or her own personal future. And newspaper reports make it clear that whenever a dispute threatens production of the Metro, then all three investments are endangered. In this way every reader's stake (as a taxpayer) in the British Leyland Motor Company is realized in the image of the Metro (the car for little people), in the image of the Metro in jeopardy and a number of parallel interpellations become possible: "you" the reader/taxpayer/consumer/car-owner/Briton/patriot/non-striker. The place of the Mini Metro in the present scheme of things is thus defined by a double address in time—back to British Leyland's past and forward toward a dream of trouble-free consumption, a purified economy and a disciplined, docile working class . . .

That, of course, does not exhaust the "meaning" of the Mini Metro for all time or for all people. It is merely an attempt to isolate some of the themes which already in 1981 have begun to congregate around what we might term the "official" fixing of the Mini Metro image—a fixing which brings us back to Barthes and myths and second-order significations. And the degree to which that reading of the Metro image proves convincing and even intelligible depends on the reader's prior knowledge of and place within a nexus of political issues and cultural codes which are historically particular and lie quite outside the scope of the list I compiled in relation to the 1955 Citroen. We come back, then, to the original problem: not one object but many objects at different "moments" (the moments, for instance, of design, assembly and use), at different (real and mythical) times (in different conjunctures in relation to imagined pasts and futures) seen from different perspectives for different purposes. How can all these different times, purposes and perspectives be reconciled so that they can be depicted? One solution might be to turn from the object to the text in order to find a more fragmentary mode of representation in which the object can be brought back "into touch" with that larger, less tangible and less coherent "network of relationships" which alone can give it order and significance . . .

The rest of this paper consists of a "dossier" on one particular genre of commodities: the Italian motor scooter. The sequence of the narrative corresponds loosely to the progression of the object from design/production through mediation into use though there is a good deal of cross-referencing between different "moments." Theoretical models have been introduced to frame the material and the narrative has been interrupted at certain points so that sections dealing with larger economic and social developments can be inserted. It is hoped that by presenting the "history of the motor scooter" in this way, some indication of the extent of the variability in its significance can be given as "echoes" and "rhymes" build up within the text. The text itself is "variable" because there is no one "voice" speaking through it. The same or similar information may be relayed through a different "voice" in a different section, i.e., its significance may vary according to its placement. In the same way, for the same reason, any "echoes" which do accumulate cannot be closed off, summed up, reduced to a "silence" or amplified into a thunderous conclusion.

What follows is premissed on the assumption—itself hardly novel— that the facts do not speak for themselves. They are already "spoken for" . . .

THE SCOOTER AS SEXED OBJECT: EARLY DAYS

The first motor scooters were manufactured in Europe in the years immediately after the First World War (though there are recorded examples of machines called "scooters" being sold even earlier than this in the United States). From the outset, the word "scooter" denoted a small, two-wheeled vehicle with a flat, open platform and an engine mounted over the rear wheel. The scooter was further characterised by its low engine capacity: the Autoglider (1921) had a two-and-a-half hp engine. Together these features distinguished the scooter from other categories of two-wheeled transport and marked it off especially from its more powerful, more "primitive" (i.e., of earlier origin, more "functional" and "aggressive") antecedent: the motor cycle. The demarcation between motorcycle and motorscooter coincided with and reproduced the boundary between the masculine and the feminine.

The earliest scooters were designed to meet the imagined needs of the female motor cyclist. For instance, it was possible for women to stand while driving the Scootamotor (1920) thus preserving decorum and the line of their long skirts. (How could the designer have predicted the flattening out of the female silhouette in the women's fashions of the 1920s? How could he have foreseen the vogue for trousers, breeches and strictly tailored suits which, as Lisa Tickner suggests, were to provide such provocative metaphors for the emancipation of women?[7]) Long before the mass production of Italian Vespas and Lambrettas began to threaten the supremacy of the British motorcycle industry in the 1950s and 1960s, the scooter was interpreted as an alien intrusion—a threat to the masculine culture of the road. It was seen as an absurd omen of a much more general process: the feminisation of the public domain (women over thirty were enfranchised in 1918 and one year later the Sex Disqualification Removal Act was passed giving women access to the professions). The machine's lowly status and its vulnerability to ridicule were further reinforced by its visible resemblance to a child's toy scooter. The Zutoped, for instance, was modelled directly on the original toy. Despite modifications in design over the years, the over-all conception and placement of the scooter—its projected market, its general shape, its public image—remained fixed in the formula—motor cycles:scooters as men:women and children.

Scooters were permanently wedded to motorcyles in a relation of in-feriority and dependence:

> The scooter is a device that we refuse to grace with the description of motorcycle and which, therefore, has no place in this work.
> —RICHARD HOUGH, A HISTORY OF THE
> WORLD'S MOTORCYCLES, ALLEN & UNWIN, 1973

THE GENDER OF MACHINERY

> The operative value of the system of naming and classifying commonly called the totemic drives derives from their formal character: they are codes suitable for conveying messages which can be transposed into other codes and for expressing messages received by means of different codes in terms of their own system . . . totemism, or what is referred to as such, corresponds to certain modalities arbitrarily isolated from a formal system, the function of which is to guarantee the controvertibility of ideas between different levels of social reality . . .
> CLAUDE LÉVI-STRAUSS, THE SAVAGE MIND

If we start the scooter cycle by following the lead established in 1962 by Lévi-Strauss we do not approach isolated phenomena as the imagi-nary bearers of substance and meaning but are driven to focus instead on how those phenomena are arranged conceptually and semantically; on what signifying power they possess as elements or functions within codes which are themselves organised into symbolic systems. For the structuralist,

> the term totemism covers relations, posed ideologically between two series, one *natural* the other *cultural* . . . [where] the natural series comprises on the one hand *categories*, on the other *particulars*; the cultural series com-prises *groups* and *persons*.
> LÉVI-STRAUSS, TOTEMISM (1962)

In "primitive" societies, elements from the natural world—flora and fauna—are made to perform these totemic functions. Through the prin-ciples of metaphor and metonymy, they guarantee the controvertibility of formal codes into moral, aesthetic and ideological categories. Ma-chines on the other hand, are for Roland Barthes "superlative object(s)" invested with a super-natural aura ("We must not forget that an object is the best messenger of a world above that of nature . . ."). They are brought down to earth ("mediatised") by being made to function as differential elements—as markers of identity and difference—organised into meaningful relations through their location within cultural/ideological codes. The first marker of identity is sexual difference. The sexing of the object is the first move in its descent from "the heaven of *Metropolis*" to its "proper" place in the existing (i.e. mortal and imperfect) order of things. In advanced industrial societies, the transposition of gender characteristics onto inanimate objects is peculiarly marked. Typically the qualities and status ascribed to the gender of the "ideal" user are transferred onto the object itself. Paul Willis's study of a Birmingham motorcycle gang provides an interesting example of this kind of "anthropomorphisation":

> The motor cycle boys accepted the motor bike and allowed it to reverberate right through into the world of human concourse. The lack of the helmet allowed long hair to blow freely back in the wind, and this, with the studded and ornamented jackets, and the aggressive style of riding, gave the motorbike boys a fearsome look which amplified the wildness, noise, surprise and intimidation of the motorbike. The motorbikes themselves were modified to accentuate these features. The high cattlehorn handlebars, the chromium-plated mudguards gave the bikes an exaggerated look of fierce power.[8]

This is merely an extreme localised instance of a much more widespread assumption that equates motorcycles with masculinity, machismo with what Barthes has called the "bestiary of power."[9] Once it has been sexed, the machine functions as a material sign of (realises) imagined gender differences: mechanical sexism.

Advertisements adjudicate in the settling of gender differences. Sometimes the object is split, janus-like, into its two opposed aspects: his and hers. His: functional, scientific, useful. Hers: decorative, aesthetic, gratifying. The distinction corresponds to the separation of design functions: his/engineering; hers/styling. Relations of dominance/subordination inscribed in the sexual division of labor are transposed so that engineering is perceived as superordinate and necessary (masculine/productive), styling as secondary and gratuitous (feminine/non-productive).

These transpositions can color critical perception of the broadest social and economic developments. For instance, the transition from a production (puritan) economy to a consumer (pagan) one is often condensed in books on economic history into a single image: the image of General Motors' growing ascendancy from the mid-1920s onwards over the Ford Motor Company. The success of General Motors is represented as the triumph of sophisticated marketing strategies (obsolescence of desirability—the annual model; massive advertising; "consumer financing" [the "trade in," hire purchase]; exotic styling) over Ford's more sober approach ("honest" competition in terms of quality and price). Styling is seen as the key to the popularity of General Motors' products: whereas Ford's Model T design remained virtually the same for decades but became relatively cheaper to purchase and produce, G.M. designers introduced ostentatious styling features to distinguish between markets on status grounds. The development of the modern advertising industry is frequently associated either with the increased spending power of the female consumer or with the growing influence which women are felt to exert over household expenditure. Vance Packard, writing in the late 1950s, quotes the chairman of Allied Stores Corporation to "illustrate" women's progressive colonisation of the consumption sphere:

> It is our job to make women unhappy with what they have. We must make them so unhappy that their husbands can find no happiness or peace in their excessive savings . . . [10]

The "spread of consumerism" is understood by reference to woman's essential gullibility and improvidence. Packard's triple invective against *The Wastemakers* (1960)—the Detroit motor industry; *The Status-Seekers* (1959)—the new breed of consumer; and *The Hidden Persuaders* (1957)—saturation and "subliminal" advertising—is carried along on a series of analogies between the decline of the "real" solid/masculine/functional aspects of American industrial design which symbolise the pioneer spirit, and the complementary rise of the "fantastic"/feminine/decorative elements which symbolise consumer decadence. The fact that terms taken from women's fashion are beginning to infiltrate the language of automobile design is cited as evidence of a more general decline in standards: a car parts dealer from Illinois is quoted as describing a car as a "woman's fashion item" and Packard claims that in professional design argot, product styling is now referred to as the "millinery aspect" and designing a new car shell is called "putting a dress on a model."[11] The sinister nature of these developments is inferred through the connection between General Motors' success and the investment in styling which is itself indicative of the "feminisation" or "emasculation" of American society. Throughout the book, indeed throughout much of the critical writing on product design produced in the 1950s, a certain type of car, a certain type of styling functions totemically to duplicate category distinctions which are collectively predicated on the denial or dismissal of the "female" and the "feminine." Misogynist values are thus relayed mechanically through the medium of objects and attitudes towards objects. The marking out of sexual difference moves along a chain which is constantly slipping: man/woman: work/pleasure: production/consumption: function/form, for example:

> . . . women have escaped the sphere of production only to be absorbed the more entirely by the sphere of consumption, to be captivated by the immediacy of the commodity world no less than men are transfixed by the immediacy of profit . . . [12]

This characterisation of the "masculine" and "feminine" domains and the priorities it encapsulates have been institutionalised in education in the distinction between "hard" and "soft" subjects: engineering is installed in universities as a scientific discipline (and seems relatively protected from the cuts?); fashion/fashion history is doubly subordinate—it is only an "applied art"—and is eminently dispensable.

The patriarchal inflection cuts across the entire field of academic discourse. It is this implicit bias which, at a deep level, orders the marxian distinction between "phenomenal forms" and "real relations." It is no coincidence that Althusser, in his parody of "vulgar marxism," should refer to the "economic base" as "His Imperial Majesty":

> . . . when the Time comes, (the superstructures) as his pure phenomena . . . scatter before His Majesty the Economy as he strides along the royal road of the Dialectic . . . [13]

Hairdrier: motorcyclists' slang for an Italian scooter

THE 1946 VESPA

Scooter
A machine of less than 250cc engine capacity with body work giving considerable weather protection and having a smart, clean appearance.

J. SIMMONDS: DESIGN NO 94., 1957

In 1946 and 1947, two new Italian scooters appeared which eclipsed all previous models in terms of sales and served to fix the design concept of the contemporary scooter—the Vespa (Wasp) appeared first and was designed by Corriando D'Ascanio for Piaggio, formerly Piaggio Air, the company which during the War had produced Italy's only heavy bomber, the P108 B. (It was not particularly successful. Mussolini's son, Bruno, was killed piloting an early test flight.)

In 1943, the works at Pontedera were completely destroyed by Allied bombing and a new factory was built with facilities geared towards peace-time production. (Piaggio later diversified into machine tools.) The scooter was originally conceived as a small-scale project which was intended to make maximum usage of available plant, materials and design expertise and to fill a gap in the market, supplying the demand on the part of consumers deprived during the War years of visually attractive, inexpensive luxury goods, for a cheap, stylish form of transport capable of negotiating Italy's war-damaged roads.

D'Ascanio, who had previously specialised in helicopter design, incorporated airplane motifs into the original Vespa. The air-cooled engine and stressed skin framework were commonplace enough in aircraft design but their application to two-wheeled transport was regarded as a major innovation. Equally novel was the idea of mounting the wheels on stub-axles rather than between forks. This made them easier to detach—and thus easier to repair—than motorcycle wheels. D'Ascanio was said to have adapted the idea from the mountings used on airplane landing gear though stub-axles were, of course, a standard feature of car design. But the spot-welded, sheet-metal frame represented the most noticeable departure from the conventional idea of the motorcycle. The two-stroke engine was concealed behind removable metal cowlings and the platform frame, which was attached to the central spine, extended upwards almost to the handlebars, providing foot support and protection from the weather. Speed was hardly a consideration: the 98cc engine (subsequently 130cc) had a top speed of only 35mph but the low fuel consumption (approximately 120mpg) and the ease with which the gear and clutch controls could be mastered, acted as compensatory incentives. (D'Ascanio had substituted handlebar controls for the foot pedals favored by the motorcycle industry.) The two-stroke engine which was mounted over the rear wheel was chosen for its simplicity and, without complicated valve gear or pump lubrication, driving was reduced to a basic set of operations which could be assimilated quickly even by people with no prior motorcycling experience.

The design, then, made concessions to the rider's comfort, convenience and vanity (the enveloping of machine parts meant that the scooterist was not obliged to wear specialist protective clothing). In addition, the Vespa made a considerable visual impact. It was streamlined and self-consciously "contemporary." There was a formal harmony and a fluency of line which was completely alien to the rugged functionalism of traditional motorcycle designs.

The Vespa was launched at the 1946 Turin show and was an immediate commercial success though reactions in the motorcycle trade were varied. While the novel styling was on the whole regarded favorably, at least in design circles, attention was drawn to basic engineering faults (the suspension was considered too "soft" and the sparking was sometimes erratic), and the scooter was criticised on the grounds of general safety (it was unstable at speed, and the eight-inch wheels were considered too small to give adequate road grip, especially in wet or slippery conditions). Piaggio, for their part, argued that these criteria were simply not appropriate: the machine was designed as a small, "gadabout" vehicle suitable for travelling short distances at low speeds. In other words, the Vespa was to be presented to the public not as a poor relation of the motorcycle but as the principal term in a new transport category, as a machine in its own right with its own singular qualities, its own attractions and its own public.

D'Ascanio's Vespa established the pattern for all subsequent scooter designs and its general shape changed little over the years (the headlamp was later moved from the mudguard to the handlebars but this was the only major styling alteration). It combined three innovations—the stub-axles, open frame, and enclosed engine—which were reproduced over the next twenty years by manufacturers in France, Germany and Britain so that, by 1966, one journalist could state authoritatively that "there is hardly a scooter built today which does not incorporate two out of these three distinctive features."[14] This fixing of the design concept was made possible through the phenomenal sales (by 1960, 1,000,000 Vespas had been sold, and after a slack period in the late 1960s, the oil crisis led to a market revival and in 1980 Piaggio were reported to be producing 450,000 scooters a year [see *Guardian*, 21 February, 1981]). Domination of the market led to domination of the image: the field was secured so effectively that by the mid-1960s the words "Vespa" and "scooter" were interchangeable in some European languages. (Traffic signs in Paris still stipulate the times when "Vespas" can be parked.)

THE 1947 LAMBRETTA

In design history, the monopoly exerted by the Vespa design over definitions of the scooter has tended to obscure the fact that Piaggio were not the only engineering company in Italy to recognise the emergence of the new "mood" and market. When the Vespa was entered for the 1946 Milan show, it appeared alongside a range of new lightweight motorcycles and mopeds and no fewer than seventeen auxiliary motors for powering pedal-cycles (see Hough, *The History of the Motor Cycle*). Moreover, the car industry was just as concerned to make inroads into the revitalised working-class and teenaged markets. By 1953, the Vespa was competing against a peculiarly Continental hybrid: the Isetta three-wheeler, the first of the "bubble cars." D'Ascanio was, then, merely the victor in the race to find a metaphor for the *ricostruzione*, to develop a "popular" commodity capable of translating the more inchoate desire for mobility and change—a desire associated with the re-establishment of parliamentary democracy and given a material boost in the form of Marshall Aid—into a single object, a single image.

In 1947, another scooter appeared which in its basic concept, scale and price, bore a close resemblance to the Piaggio prototype—the Lambretta produced by Innocenti of Milan. For almost twenty-five years, until Innocenti's scooter section was bought outright by the Indian Government in the early 1970s, the Lambretta range offered the most serious threat to Piaggio's lead in terms of international sales and trade recognition. By 1950, Piaggio and Innocenti had between them opened up a completely new market for cheap motorised transport. Early advertising campaigns were directed at two emergent consumer groups—teenagers and women—neither of which had been considered worthwhile targets for this class of goods before the War. A new machine had been created and inscribed in its design was another new "invention": the ideal scooterist—young, socially mobile, conscious of his or her appearance. The scooter was defined by one sympathetic journalist as "a comfortable, nicely designed little vehicle for people who do not care too much about the mechanical side of things."[15]

As the two companies competed for the same markets, the design of Lambretta and Vespa scooters drew closer together until, by the late 1960s, they were, in styling if not in performance and engineering detail, virtually identical. However, there were marked differences between the Lambretta model A and the D'Ascanio Vespa. Once again, the Lambretta design was a feat of *bricolage*—the material resources: expertise, plant and production processes—of the two component firms (Innocenti SpA which specialised in steel tube manufacture had amalgamated after the War with the Trussi coachbuilding concern) were adapted and diverted into scooter production. The model A chassis was based on a double steel tube structure (similar to the one used on the earlier British Corgi); the front wheel was carried on a fork, the rear wheel on a stub-axle and, as with the Vespa, there was a footboard for the rider. But the Lambretta differed from the Vespa in that it had a larger (125cc) engine and a pillion seat for passengers; on the model A there were footpedal changes for the gears and the clutch, the legshields were shorter and narrower and, most significantly, at least most conspicuously, the engines of the early models were open. Though for safety reasons, the gear and clutch controls were subsequently transferred to the handlebars, the Lambretta engine remained fully exposed until 1951 when the C and CL models were introduced. On the C model, the double tube chassis was replaced by a single tube frame and the prospective buyer was confronted with a choice between two different machines: the "dressed" (CL) or the "undressed" (C) scooter. Demand for the "dressed" model (which also offered superior weather protection with broader, higher legshields based on the D'Ascanio design) was so great that Innocenti were soon forced to withdraw open Lambrettas from production. Inevitably, the addition of the sleek, protective side panels drew the Lambretta closer to its rival. A pattern of parallel growth emerged: the production of a new model by Innocenti would force a similar design response from Piaggio and vice versa. By 1953, both companies were offering 125 and 150cc models. During the mid- and late-1950s, two factors: the demand for sturdier, high performance scooters suitable for long-distance touring and the appearance of powerful German machines—the Heinkel, the Bella, the TWN Contessa—led to adjustments in the engine and wheel sizes of both Vespa and Lambretta models: Piaggio introduced the four-speed GS (*Gran Sport*) and SS (*Super Sport*), Innocenti countered with the Lambretta 175cc TV series.

But throughout, the basic scooter "silhouette" remained more or less unchanged: the word "scooter" became synonymous with a streamlined shape and legshields. By the end of the 1950s, most of the successful designs for scooters in the popular 125–150cc ranges—the Italian Iso Milano, the French Moby, the German NSU Prima—made clear visual references to the Piaggio original. When British motorcycle manufacturers finally, and with considerable reluctance (see section entitled "The Reception in Britain"), capitulated to local demand and began producing their own (resolutely unsuccessful) scooters, they tended to turn to Italian models, even, occasionally, to Italian designers (e.g., Vincent

Piatti designed a scooter for Cyclemaster in the mid-1950s). The extent to which Continental scooters had penetrated the international motor-cycle market was to lead (for a brief period) to an inversion of the traditional hierarchy. Motorcycle designers began adopting the "effem-inate" practice of enclosing the machine parts. With the Ariel Leader the engine at last slipped out of sight . . .

THE PRODUCTION OF CONSUMERS

This convergence of form in the designs for machines in related cate-gories is not in itself remarkable. After all, design innovations are meant to set trends. However, the encasement of mechanical parts in metal or plastic "envelopes"—a development associated historically with the emergence of streamlining—signalled more than just a change in the look of things. It marked a general shift in production processes, in the scale and rate of capital accumulation, in the relationship between com-modity production and the market. The drift towards a more systematic "packaging" of objects, itself linked to the growth of the consultancies, coincided with a much broader development—the rise of the giant cor-porations—the modern conglomerates and multi-nationals with the con-centration of power and resources into larger and larger units, a movement which in turn had required a fundamental reorganisation of social and cultural life: the translation of masses into markets.

The economist Paul Sweezey has outlined some of the changes asso-ciated with the development of monopoly capitalism in the post-War period: the automation of the work process; increased specialisation and diversification (spreading of risk over a wider product range); expansion of the white-collar sector; control of distribution networks; market shar-ing between corporations; price fixing (the self-imposed limitation of growth in productive capacity to keep prices pegged at an "acceptable" level); imperialism (exploitation of Third World resources, domination of Third World markets); the displacement of competition from the field of price to the field of sales promotion; increased expenditure on re-search, design and "market preparation." All these developments were motivated by need: "the profound need of the modern corporation to dominate and control all the conditions and variables which affect its viability."[16]

It is in this context that the massive expansion of the advertising and marketing industries during the period can be most clearly understood. Given the huge costs involved in producing a new line of goods, if crip-pling losses were to be avoided, the consumer had to be as carefully primed as the materials used in the manufacturing process. The expe-dient was, on the face of it, quite simple: the element of risk was to be eliminated through the preparation and control of the market. It was not just the careful monitoring of current market trends that could help to guarantee profits. What was required was a more structured supervision of consumer demands according to the principles of what was later called "want formation."[17] In other words, corporate viability was seen to rely increasingly upon the regulation of desire.

It was during this period that design became consolidated as a "scientific" practice with its own distinctive functions and objectives. From now on, the shape and look of things were to play an important part in aligning two potentially divergent interests: production for profit, and consumption for pleasure. The investment on a previously unimagined scale in the visual aspects of design from the 1930s onward indicated a new set of priorities on the part of manufacturers and marked another stage in a more general (and more gradual) process: the intercession of the image between the consumer and the act of consumption.

These developments were, of course, already well advanced by the time Piaggio's Vespa appeared on the scene. In America there was a thriving, highly-organised advertising industry by the mid-1920s and advertising personnel were already formulating policy on the basis of sociological and psychological research (according to Stuart Ewen, the work of the early symbolic interactionists which placed the emphasis squarely on the social construction of personal identity was particularly influential[18]). The elaborate cynicism and self-consciously shark-like image of the post-War advertising executive were already fully in evidence by the end of the decade. The following passage appeared in 1930 in *Printer's Ink*, the advertising trade journal:

> ... advertising helps to keep the masses dissatisfied with their mode of life, discontented with the ugly things around them. Satisfied customers are not as profitable as discontented ones.[19]

And by 1958, the equivalence between the amounts of money spent on the construction of products and the production of consumers had become so systematised that J. K. Galbraith could present it to his readers as an economic law:

> A broad empirical relationship exists between what is spent on the production of consumer goods and what is spent in synthesizing the desires for that production. The path for an expansion of output must be paved by a suitable expansion in advertising budget.[20]

With the pressure on designers to provide "product identity" and "corporate image," a further refinement became possible: a single commodity could be used to promote a range of visually compatible objects produced by different divisions of the same corporation. An Olivetti typewriter or an IBM computer was an advertisement for itself and the company which produced it. The form functioned tautologically: it was a trademark in three dimensions. It "looked its best" in a "totally designed environment."

Developments such as these brought the practical aims of product and graphic design into a close proximity and this tendency to merge design functions became even more pronounced as multidisciplinary approaches—ergonomics and "management science"—emerged to displace the notion of designer "intuition" (see *The Practical Idealists*, J. P. A. Blake, Lund Humphries, 1969). By the end of the 1950s, the language of contemporary design, peppered with analogies from cybernetics and systems theory, was beginning to reflect the preoccupations with teamwork, integration and total planning which were to provide the dominant themes of the 1960s design boom. The dream of achieving a perfect symmetry between collective desires and corporate designs seemed at last on the point of fruition. An exaggerated formalism took root. The object itself would mediate between the needs of capital and the will of the masses: the consumer would be made over in the image of the object. In an article called "The Persuasive Image," which appeared in *Design* magazine in 1960, Richard Hamilton wrote:

> . . . the media . . . the publicists who not only understand public motivations but who play a large part in directing the public response to imagery . . . should be the designer's closest allies, perhaps more important in the team than researchers or sales managers. Ad man, copy writer and feature editor need to be working together with the designer at the initiation of a programme instead of as a separated group with the task of finding the market for a completed product. The time lag can be used to design a consumer to the product and he can be "manufactured" during the production span. Then producers should not feel inhibited, need not be disturbed by doubts about the reception their products may have by an audience they do not trust, the consumer can come from the same drawing board . . . [21]

MEDIATION

Both Innocenti and Piaggio invested in aggressive advertising campaigns supervised by their own publicity departments. By the early 1950s, both companies were publishing their own magazines (in three or four European languages) and had formed their own scooter clubs with massive national, later international memberships. Through these clubs they organised mass rallies and festivals. They mounted exhibitions, sponsored (sometimes in conjunction with Via Secura, the Italian Road Safety Organisation) tours, trials, races, hill climbs, competitions. Against those interests which sought to discredit the scooter's performance, Innocenti and Piaggio set out to display its versatility and range, its resilience, its androgynous qualities ("feminine" and sleek but also able to climb mountains, cross continents . . .)

More than this, by controlling the structures within which the scooter was to be perceived and used, they were attempting to penetrate the realm of the "popular." The duty of manufacturers to the market was to extend far beyond the mere maintenance of production standards, the meeting of delivery dates. Now they were to preside over the creation of new forms of social identity, and leisure, a new consumer relation to the "look of things." The tests and trials, the spectacles, displays and exhibitions, the social clubs and magazines were part of a more general will—linked, as we have seen, to the expansion of productive forces—to superimpose the image of the factory on the world.

The four sections which follow deal with public representations of the scooter. Most of the detail is drawn from material put out by Innocenti during the 1950s and 1960s—promotional films, advertisements, copies of *Lambretta Notizario*, etc. This simply reflects the availability of sources—Piaggio's campaigns were no less intensive and incorporated similar themes.

The way in which the material itself has been organised is not entirely arbitrary: the narrative is ordered according to the dictates of an economic principle: the circulation of the Image precedes the selling of the Thing. Before looking at what the scooter came to mean in use, it is necessary to consider how it was made to appear before the market . . .

The Dematerialisation of the Object

The Age of the Product ended after World War 2 with industrial design's search to disperse, miniaturise and dematerialise consumer goods.
    Ann Ferebee, A History of Design from the Victorian Era, *1970*

Innocenti's decision to launch the ("dressed") CL and ("undressed") C Lambrettas simultaneously in 1951 determined once and for all the direction in which consumer preferences were moving in the transport field. It amounted to an unofficial referendum on the issues of styling and taste and the results were unequivocal: the scooter-buying public voted overwhelmingly for convenience, looks, an enclosed engine. The success of the CL merely confirmed the growing trend in product design toward "sheathing"—defined by one design historian as the encasement of "complex electronic parts in boxes that are as unobtrusive and easy to operate as possible."[22]

All these themes were foregrounded in the advertising campaigns and marketing strategies employed by Innocenti and Piaggio. Scooters were presented to the public as clean, "social appliances"[23] which imposed few constraints on the rider. Design features were cited to reinforce these claims: the panels enclosing scooter engines were easy to remove and the engines themselves were spread out horizontally to facilitate cleaning and the replacement of spares. The stub-axles made it simpler to remove the wheels, and by the 1960s most scooters were designed to accommodate a spare. Elegance and comfort were selected as particularly strong selling points: the Lambretta was marketed in Britain as the "sports car on two wheels" and a variety of accessories—windscreens, panniers, bumpers, clocks, even radios and glove compartments were available to lend substance to the luxurious image. Innocenti's promotion policies tended to center directly on the notion of convenience: an international network of service stations manned by trained mechanics was set up to cater for the needs of a new class of scooterists who were presumed to have little interest in even the most routine maintenance (though the stereotype of the "effeminate," "impractical" scooterist was resisted by the scooter clubs, which encouraged their members to acquire rudimentary mechanical skills, to carry tool boxes, etc.). The concept of "trouble free scootering" was taken even further in Spain. At the height of the Continental touring craze in the late 1950s, Innocenti introduced a special mobile rescue unit called the Blue Angels to cope with Lambretta breakdowns and consumer complaints.

All these support structures can be regarded as extensions of the original design project: to produce a new category of machines, a new type of consumer. The provision of a comprehensive after-sales service can be referred back ultimately to the one basic element which distinguished the D'Ascanio Vespa from its competitors—the disappearance of the engine behind a sleek metal cowling. The sheathing of machine parts placed the user in a new relation to the object—one which was more remote and less physical—a relationship of ease. As such it formed part of what Barthes described in 1957 as the general "sublimation of the utensil which we also find in the design of contemporary household equipment"[24]—a sublimation effected through the enveloping skin which served to accentuate the boundary between the human and the technical, the aesthetic and the practical, between knowledge and use. The metal skin or clothing added another relay to the circuit linking images to objects. It was another step toward an ideal prospect—the dematerialisation of the object; the conversion of consumption into life style.

The following description of an advertisement incorporates many of the themes explored in the last two sections:

A machine, suspended on a circle of glass, is seen through a shop window. The voyeuristic relation is now a familiar one, familiar through the investment made by commerce in the Image, through the reiteration in similar advertisements of the same visual structure. (This is an early example of the genre. It is almost quaint. Almost innocent. The conventions have yet to be refined, obscured.) We look at them looking. We circle around from "her" to "him" to "her," from the "girl" to the "boy" to the "mother" (that, surely, is implied). We have all come by now to recognise the indirect address: desire by proxy. We are all now visionary consumers. Placed through the geometry of looks in a precise relation to the dream machine—a revelation in mechanical parts, we gaze with them from "outside" at "her," the object of desire—the scooter/girl poised on their adjacent pedestals. The girl's posture is classical. It is Diana, naked, surprised in the wood: the heel slightly lifted, the mouth slightly open (provocative, ashamed). The model is "undressed." But a pane of glass intercedes between "her" and the boy. Its function is to mediate. This, at least, is made perfectly clear because the cleaning fluid masks it, makes it visible, opaque. The boy's hands, pressed against the glass, mark it as a barrier. Our glance is directed around a circle of glass, through the girl, through the glass, through the boy and his "mother," through a reflection of a scooter on a circle of glass. All looks are turned at last towards the center of the image where the engine stands exposed—a still point at the centre of reflection. This is the place where we can all meet—"her" and "her" and "him" and "her" and you and I—the place where we can come into contact at a distance. A place where we can find contentment (where we can find the "content" of the "message"). The transference from "her" to "her," from the object-girl to the fetishised object—has taken place. At last— the object that was lost is found . . .

The mechanism which motivates our gaze is as naked as the machine which motivates the ad. The devices are laid bare: the caption reads: "A world of dreams is revealed in the shop-window." A historical transition is arrested in the composition of a single image: the dematerialisation of the object, the emergence of what Henri Lefebvre has called the "Display Myth":

> Consuming of displays, displays of consuming, consuming of displays of consuming, consuming of signs, signs of consuming. . . .[25]

FASHION AND THE FEMININE

Sound: "The air hostess can become the pilot herself . . ."
image: air hostess sprints across runway from plane to Lambretta;
sound: " . . . and there's plenty of room on that pillion for a friend!"
image: man in pilot's uniform leaps on behind her
SEQUENCE FROM TRAVEL FAR, TRAVEL WIDE, *PROMOTIONAL FILM,*
INNOCENTI FOR G.B., *1954*

When Innocenti first began exporting Lambrettas to New York in the early 1960s (a time when, according to Vance Packard, the New York *cognoscenti* were turning from Detroit to Europe for their cars seeking that "Continental, squared off boxy look"[26]) scooters were displayed (and sometimes sold) not in car or motorcycle showrooms but in exclusive "ladies" fashion shops. They were thought to be a good thing to dress a window with, regarded less as a means of transport than as chic metal accessories, as jewellry on wheels.

Fashion items appeared regularly in issues of *Lambretta Notizario* (e.g., "one is all-too-frequently tormented by the sight of badly trousered women on motor scooters [sic] . . . Hats? Any hat—provided it is practical and above all else—elegant."). A series of advertisements in the same magazine showed young women seated on scooters in a variety of contexts: the captions ran "On a Pic-nic," "Shopping," "In the Country," "By the Sea," "In the Busy City," etc. A reciprocal effect is achieved through the elision scooter/girl: the scooter's versatility is used to advertise the freedom enjoyed by "modern" young Italian women and vice versa (i.e., look at all the places "she" can visit, all the things "she" can do). These two creations—the new Italian woman (an image fixed and disseminated internationally by the post-War Italian film industry through stars like Anna Magnani, Silvano Mangano and Sophia Loren) and the new Italian scooter are run together completely in an article which appeared in the British weekly magazine *Picture Post* entitled "A New Race of Girls" (5 September, 1954). The two inventions—"untamed, unmanicured, proud, passionate, bitter Italian beauties" and the "clean, sporting Vespa scooter"—are together alleged to have "given Italians the same sort of 'lift' that the creation of the Comet gave the British." The article is illustrated by a photograph of Gina Lollabrigida on a Vespa.

The scooter is singled out (along with "beauty competitions and films") as a catalyst in the "emancipation" of the new Italian woman ("the motor scooter gave her new horizons" . . .). And it is held directly responsible for successive changes in Italian women's fashion since the War:

> The pocket handkerchief fashion which swept the women's world in 1949 was devised to keep a pillion girl's hair tidy at speed. The following winter, the headkerchief was developed by the Florentine designer, Emilio Pucci, into a woollen headscarf. Next year, the blown hair problem was solved by the urchin cut. The narrowing of the new look skirt was dictated in order to prevent it getting tangled up with the wheels. The slipper shoe was created for footplate comfort. The turtle neck sweater and the neckerchief were designed against drafts down the neck . . . [27]

The final sentence reads:

> By such means as this was the Italian girl's appearance transformed, and her emancipation consummated.

TOURISM AND THE INTERNATIONAL CONTEXT

> The entire world becomes a setting for the fulfillment of publicity's promise of the good life. The world smiles at us. It offers itself to us. And because everywhere is imagined as offering itself to us, everywhere is more or less the same.
>
> JOHN BERGER, WAYS OF SEEING, 1972

By 1951, Vespas were being manufactured under licence in Germany, France and Britain. Innocenti had a factory at Serveta in Spain and the motorcycle company NSU held the licence for Lambrettas in Germany until 1955. As the domestic market reached saturation point (by 1956 there were 600,000 two- and three-wheelers in Italy), Innocenti and Piaggio directed their attention toward Europe and the Third World. (Ironically enough, when Innocenti were forced to sell their scooter operation in 1972 [according to business history sources because of industrial disputes], it was taken over by Scooters India, a state-funded project based in Lucknow which still produces the "classic" Lambretta models of the 1960s.) By 1977, Vespa were exporting 289,000 scooters a year to 110 countries.

These new horizons were inevitably translated into advertising imagery. During the late 1950s, Innocenti ran a series of posters entitled "The Whole World in Lambretta," which showed scooters posed against Buddhist temples or busy London streets. The caption beneath a photograph depicting a group of Ghanaian scooterists in "folk costume" invoked the then-fashionable notion of youth/style-as-a-universal: "Wearing a continental suit or a native dress does not change young people's taste for scooters." It was through strategies such as these that Innocenti and Piaggio could appropriate new markets and convert them into visual capital. One promotion ploy exemplifies the process clearly:

In 1962, Innocenti mounted a "world wide photographs" competition. Entrants were instructed to submit "holiday style" snaps of Lambrettas in "representative" national settings:

> For example: a street in Las Vegas with the signboards of the famous gambling houses, a picture of a Lambretta amidst the intense traffic of a street of a great metropolis like London, New York, Paris, etc., or against a background of forests, exotic countries, natives in their traditional costumes, wild animals, monuments, and antique vestiges [sic] etc. . . .

Other conditions were stipulated: the Lambrettas should dominate the frame, be "well centreed . . . if possible taken in close up." The "boys and girls" photographed on or directly adjacent to the scooter should be "young and sports looking" (sic). All photographs and negatives were to be retained "in INNOCENTI files as documentation" and could be used in any future "advertising exploit considered by INNOCENTI suitable for its purposes."

The competition rules lay out in a precise, accessible form, the criteria which shaped Innocenti advertising policy. The scooter was to be loosely located within a range of connotations—youth, tourism, sport—which were so open-ended that they could be mobilised literally anywhere in the world. In this way, it was possible to reconcile the different practical and symbolic functions which the scooter was likely to serve for different national markets. Ultimately Innocenti ads recognise only one collectivity: the "international brotherhood" of "boys and girls": they interpellate the world.

A film produced for Innocenti in 1954 (*Travel Far, Travel Wide*) equates "freedom" with physical mobility, with the freedom to "go where you please." Made against a background of sponsored global marathons and long-distance rallies (one, organised by Innocenti in 1962 went from Trieste to Istanbul), the film was designed to promote the touring potential of the larger "sporting" scooters. The closing image shows a group of young scooterists approaching a frontier. The voice-over reads:

> A frontier. And on the other side, a completely different way of life. But whatever country you go to in the world today, you'll find Lambrettas and Lambretta service stations.

This is the paradigm of tourism (everywhere is anywhere, everywhere is different) but here it is especially contradictory. On the one hand, the need for "national markets" and the impetus to travel demand that national characteristics, "different ways of life" be accentuated. On the other hand, trouble-free touring (complete with every modern convenience) and the construction of homogenous "modern" markets require the suppression of national differences and traditional cultures. "Youth" and "progress" mediate between these two demands: it is natural for youth to be different, it is the destiny of science to generate change. The scooter serves as the material bridge between different generations, different cultures, different epochs, between contradictory desires. It is a sign of progress. It is for the "young or young at heart." It is a passport to the future. Freedom in space becomes freedom in time: "with a Lambretta you're part of the changing scene."[28]

THE IMAGE OF THE FACTORY

The image of the Innocenti works in Milan appeared as a logo on many of the early Lambretta ads. The image of the factory itself is the final mediation—the moment of production recalled at point of sale. The photograph, taken from an airplane, reduces an entire industrial complex to the status of a diagram (the reduction is a display of power in itself). We are left with an abstract "modern" pattern signifying progress, technology, resources: an echo of the image of the scooter.

The idealisation of production and production processes and the related image of the factory-as-microcosm are not of course confined to Innocenti's publicity campaigns. The same motifs can be found in the tradition which led to the development of Italian corporatism under Mussolini and to the "progressivism" of Giovanni Agnelli, head of Fiat during the period immediately after World War I. They lay behind Adriano Olivetti's attempts to establish "factory communities" and worker welfare schemes after World War II; they provided the moral and aesthetic basis for Olivetti's concept of "integrated design." And the images themselves derived originally from Marinetti, Sant'Elia and the futurists . . .

A promotion film called *We carry on*, made in 1966 soon after Innocenti's death, clearly draws on this native tradition. (The film won first prize in the non-fiction class at Cannes in 1967. The pressure to enter an impressive ["artistic"] product must have been intensified after 1961 when Piaggio won the same award.)

. . . The slow aerial surveillance of the huge Innocenti plant which opens the film suddenly cuts to the production area. The camera work is determinedly "modern" and avant-garde. A scooter is assembled before our eyes. As it moves along the line each stage in its construction is dramatised through the use of expressionist lighting, jump cuts and skewed camera angles. On the soundtrack, harsh *musique concrete* further reinforces the image of inhuman automation and industrial power. The voice-over alternates between the sober recital of statistical facts (. . . "the production line is one mile long and one-third of a mile wide . . .") and "poetic" descriptions of technical processes. The style of the latter is "futurist baroque":—"The factory is a hothouse in which the flowers are pieces of machinery . . . the electro-magnetic test bed is the altar of destruction on which will be sacrificed the body of a Lambretta" . . . At one point, there is a montage sequence which recalls the earlier "World in Lambretta" series but the rapid juxtaposition of shots—a scooter parked near an oasis, in a city street, on a Mediterranean beach—marks the conjunction of scooter and landscape as "bizarre." The contrasts are deliberately violent. (Surrealism in the service of industry: the film seems to have helped determine the stylistic conventions and the "strangeness" of many present-day [prestige] advertising films, e.g., the Benson and Hedges's "desert" series.) After an elegiac tribute to Innocenti (the camera circling respectfully around a plinth mounted with a bust of "our founder") the film ends with another aerial shot as the camera sweeps across the workers' swimming pool and tennis courts to rest, at last, above the enormous central tower/panopticon. There is a slow final scan along the ranks of completed scooters waiting for dispatch on the factory forecourt . . . "machines which carry one name and one name only—a name which dominates the whole world." The soundtrack is dominated by the wail of a siren on top of the tower "calling his [i.e., Innocenti's] people to work. . . . He is gone but we shall carry on . . ."

THE SCOOTER IN USE

The final sections are designed to explore some of the "cultural meanings" which became attached to the scooter as it was used in Britain.

THE RECEPTION IN BRITAIN

a) The Motorcycle Industry

Look, here's a beauty for you. She buys a scooter for a hundred and forty pounds and then she wants to know where the spark comes from.
MOTORCYCLE DEALER, QUOTED IN JAN STEVENS, SCOOTERING, *1966*

Imports of foreign motorcycles and scooters into Great Britain for the first six months of 1954—3,318; for the first six months of 1956—21,125.
FIGURES FROM J. SYMONDS, "WHERE ARE THE BRITISH SCOOTERS,"
DESIGN *NO. 94, 1957*

The first Italian scooters appeared in Britain in the early 1950s. Innocenti and Piaggio opted for different distribution strategies. Piaggio granted a manufacturing licence to the Bristol-based Douglas Motorcycle Company in 1951 and, in the same year, P. J. Agg and Son were registered as the Lambretta Concessionaires importing Innocenti's scooters from the Continent. Sales and marketing were also handled differently by the two companies. Innocenti advertising tended to be pitched more directly at the image-conscious youth market and by 1960 the Agg concessionaires had established a nationwide network of over 1,000 service stations and, for the first time in Europe, had secured a market lead for Innocenti over Piaggio.

By the mid-1950s the Italian scooter was beginning to represent a threat to the British motorcycle industry which until World War II had dominated the international market. Demand for the traditionally heavy, high performance machines which British manufacturers produced had been declining steadily since 1945. Within ten years, the trend had become pronounced: at the 1955 Earl's Court Motor Cycle Show, three motorcycles were on a display competing against fifty new scooters.

British manufacturers were eventually forced into scooter production though the transition from heavy, utilitarian vehicles to light, "visually attractive" ones was never satisfactorily accomplished. (The BSA Dandy, for instance, had narrow legshields and footboard, and there was none of what Stephen Bayley has described as the "beautiful clothing"[29] of the Vespa or Lambretta.) However, the initial response was one of scorn and dismissal. All the criticisms levelled by the Italian motorcycle industry in the 1940s were revived. Scooters were defined as "streamlined" and "effete." The original sales line—that this was a form of transport which (even) women could handle—was turned against itself. Scooters were not only physically unsafe, they were morally suspect. They were unmanly. They ran counter to the ethos of hard work, self-sufficiency and amateur mechanics upon which the success of the British motorcycle industry and the prevailing definitions of masculinity—the "preferred readings" of manhood—were based.

These objections, formed at least partly in response to commercial pressure, percolated down throughout the motorcycle producer, retail and user cultures. Motorcycle shops, many of them owned by former TT veterans, refused to stock the "gimmicky" new machines, to finance service facilities, or to employ mechanics. The reluctance to legitimate scooters and scooterists lingered on within the motorcycling fraternity. The scooter remained, for "committed" motorcyclists, a sexed (and inferior) object. As recently as 1979, an article appeared in *Motorcycle Sport* which invoked all the old categories and prejudices. The article, entitled "Is the Scooter Making a Comeback?" consists of an apparently neutral assessment of scooter performance. The writer endorses only the more powerful machines. The German Maicolette (known in the early 1960s as the "dustbin" amongst those British scooterists with Italianate tastes) is praised for "its beefy two-stroke engine. It could romp along at a confident 70mph holding the road like a motorcycle . . . it went like a rocket."[30] The author concludes by extracting the "essence" of "motorcycling sport"—its complexity, "depth," power, its solitary nature—and contrasting these qualities against the "superficial," "social" "fun" of scootering: "Naturally," the gender of the ideal motorcyclist is beyond question.

> . . . motorcycling is a much more complex sport than scootering . . . the enjoyment springs from the pure isolation aboard a fast solo when the rider, for a brief spell, is beyond authority and is in control of his own destiny. Motorcycling is fun of a multi-dimensional variety. Scootering is pleasure of the more superficial sort.[31]

b) Design

> Somewhere on the lower slopes of clique acceptance was the popular Italian craze which dominated British taste in the later 1950s and which found expression in the vogue for products like motor scooters . . . Olivetti typewriters . . . Espresso coffee machines . . .
> STEPHEN BAYLEY, IN GOOD SHAPE, 1979

Those "superficial" qualities which were interpreted negatively by the motorcycling industry—the social aspects and the look of the scooter—were regarded as positive assets by those working in the design field, at least by those young enough to appreciate the beauty of a mass-produced but "well-shaped" machine. The emergent Modern consensus in design which was to become dominant during the 1960s closed more or less unanimously around the Italian scooter and held it up to British industrialists as an example of what a good design should look like. As an everyday artefact invested with some standards of style and utility but which still managed to satisfy all the key criteria: elegance, serviceability, popularity and visual discretion—the scooter fulfilled all the modern ideals.

At least that was the opinion circulated amongst the "select band of glossy monthly magazines" which, as Banham puts it, decides "who shall see what"[32] in the design world. Indeed, the first article in the inaugural issue of one of the most influential of the post-War journals was entirely devoted to the "Italian look." Writing in *Design* (January, 1949), F. K. Henrion compiled a list of tasteful artefacts which "have together transformed the appearance" of Italian city life. He singled out cars, furniture, ceramics and a Gio Ponti coffee machine. But the Vespa scooter—"a virtual institution"—was especially commended:

> ... the most important of all new Italian design phenomena is without doubt the Vespa. This miniature motorcycle, streamlined and extremely pleasant to look at, has become an important factor in Italian village and town life.[33]

Henrion drew attention to the scooter's flexibility in use and its capacity for bridging markets:

> ... you see businessmen with briefcases, commercial travellers with boxes of samples on the vast floorspace. In the evenings, you see young couples ... at weekends, mother, child and father on picnics. You see these machines parked side by side in front of Ministries and it is surprising how many people afford them at a price equivalent to £80.[34]

Finally he placed the significance of the Vespa in the context of an overall "Italian style," as part of the "second Italian renaissance":

> I seemed to sense a similarity of aesthetic values amongst different products—a similarity which, seen from a distance of many years, might be called the style of the mid 20th Century.[35]

Throughout the 1950s and early 1960s, Italy tended to epitomise for young, trendsetting British designers, everything that was chic and modern and "acceptable," particularly in automobile and (through magazines like *Domus*) interior design. The cult of the individual designer-as-genius—as a modern Renaissance man blending mathematical skills and artistic flair—seems to have grown up largely around a few Italian names—Ponti, Ghia, Pininfarina, Nizzoli, etc. Sometimes the "superiority" of the Italian design is "explained" through its relationship to fine art (e.g., futurism). Ann Ferebee, for instance, compares streamlined Italian products to Boccioni's *Unique Forms of Continuity in Space* and praises "sheathed" Italian transport for its "sculptural elegance."[36] And always the "refinement ... and purity ... of line"—in this case of Pininfarina's 1947 Cisitalia Coupe—is valorised because it sets "alternative standards against the baroque styles [then] emerging in America."[37] All these qualities and effects have been attributed at different times to the

Italian scooter. It has become installed in the mythology of good Italian taste. It has now become an "object lesson": it is the only entry for 1946 in Stephen Bayley's *In Good Shape*—it stands in for its time.

A clash, then, between two "official" versions of the scooter, between two divergent interests. A "clash of opinion" between, on the one hand, a declining heavy engineering industry with a vested interest in preserving the market as it stands, with a fixed conception of both product and market, with material resources geared towards the reproduction of that market, the production of a particular design genre, with a set of established cultural values to mobilise in its defense; on the other, a design industry on the point of boom, with a vested interest in transforming the market, in aestheticising products and "educating" consumers, with material resources geared toward the production of a new commodity— Image—with an emergent set of cultural values (a new formation of desire) to articulate and bring to fruition. The Italian origins of the scooter function differentially within the two systems. In the first, "Italianness" defines the scooter as "foreign competition" and doubles its effeminacy (Italy: the home of "male narcissism"). In the second, it defines the scooter as "the look of the future" and doubles its value as a well-designed object (Italy: the home of "good taste").

The object splits. And is re-assembled in use . . .

THE SCOOTER CLUBS

By the mid-1950s, there were British branches of the Lambretta and Vespa user clubs, co-ordinated from separate offices in Central London and sponsored by the Douglas Company and the Agg Concessionaires. Both provided monthly magazines (*Vespa News, Lambretta Leader*, later *Jet-Set*). While these organisations were clearly modelled on the lines of the Italian clubs and served a promotional and public relations function, they tended to be less rigidly centralised and local branches, run by amateur enthusiasts, were allowed to organise their own affairs. Moreover, some of the larger branches had their own names—the "Bromley Innocents," the "Vagabonds," the "Mitcham Goons"—their own pennants, badges and colors and, in their informal character, and strong regional affiliations, they bore some resemblance to the pre-War cycling clubs. In the 1950s and early '60s the mass rallies and organised scooter runs were a major attraction for club members. As many as 3,000 scooterists would converge on Brighton and Southend for the National Lambretta Club's annual rally where, at the service marquee, set, according to one enthusiast, amidst "banners and flags, bunting and a Carnival atmosphere . . . your Lambretta would be repaired and serviced entirely free of charge."[38] During the evenings, there would be barbecues, fancy dress competitions and dances (". . . this was the day of Rock and Roll . . . Marty Wilde, Tommy Steele, Adam Faith . . .").[39]

One of the socially cohesive elements at these events, at least for many of the younger club members, was a shared prediliction for Italy and "Italianate" culture. The clubs organised "Italy in Britain" weeks to foster the connection. At the Lambretta Concessionaires' headquarters in Wimbledon, an espresso coffee machine dispensed "free frothy coffee" for club members who brought their machines in to be serviced.[40] One of the records played at the Southend rally dances in the early 1960s was an Italian hit entitled the "Lambretta Twist" . . .

As more scooters came onto the market (by 1963, there were twenty-two different firms selling scooters in Britain), the emphasis shifted on to the competitive events, which tended to be dismissed by the motor-cycling contingent as "rally-type stuff of an endurance nature."[41] It seems likely that the British scooter clubs were particularly receptive to the idea of competition because it offered a means of counteracting the stigma (of "effeminacy" and "shallowness") which had been attached to the sport in its earlier "social" phase. Innocenti developed the 200cc Lambretta specifically to meet the demands of the Isle of Man Scooter Rally which, by the late 1950s, had become the most important event of its kind in Europe. Quite apart from the racing and the track events, there were scooter expeditions to the Arctic Circle, non-stop runs from London to Milan, ascents of Snowdon on a scooter with a side-car: feats of lone heroism which were intended to display the toughness and stamina of both rider and machine. Some of these gestures had a positively epic quality: one scooterist crossed the English Channel using a Vespa to operate paddles fitted to floats.[42] Club scootering became more muscular, scooter runs longer, trials more arduous. Scooter Tours, an extension of the Lambretta Club of Great Britain, provided couriers to lead "snakes" of up to forty scooters to Switzerland, Austria and Germany.

As the demand for scooters began to level out (i.e., around 1959), the pressure to win races and break records grew more intense. "Friendly competition" sometimes gave way to open rivalry and these tensions tended to filter down from the works teams to the ordinary badge-wearing members. The younger, more ardent club supporters began marking out their loyalties in dress. The "blue boys," for instance, wore sharply cut suits in royal blue—the Lambretta club color. These rivalries were underscored by the distribution policies of the two firms: dealers were licenced to sell only Vespas or Lambrettas.

Nonetheless, competitiveness never totally dislodged the frame which had been imposed upon the sport at its inception: the "social aspects" with their attendant connotations of health, open air and cheerful camaraderie. This ideal was reflected in the actual composition of the clubs themselves. Subscriptions were not restricted to a single class or age group (though it seems plausible that there was a bias toward relatively young people [i.e. sixteen to thirty-five] from "respectable" working-class and lower-middle-class backgrounds). Female scooterists figured as prominently as the men, at least on the non-competitive circuit . . .

Piaggio and Innocenti publicity departments regarded the inclusion of a Vespa or Lambretta in a feature film as a major advertising coup. Film directors were solicited to promote the firms' products. Stars were photographed on set (sometimes in period costume) seated on the latest scooter model.

In the early 1960s, two films appeared both of which were, in a sense, made around the Italian scooter (and Cliff Richard): *Wonderful Life* (which featured the Vespa) and *Summer Holiday* (which co-starred the Lambretta). These films articulate precisely the ideal of the "fun-loving" collective which hovers over the literature, the rallies and the "socials" of the early scooter clubs, and they recapitulate many of the themes encountered in the scooter ads: "tourism," "youth," "freedom" and "fashion." All these categories were brought together in the image of Cliff Richard and a group of "zany," "up-to-date" but good-hearted youngsters off on their scooters in search of a continental coast-line, a holiday romance . . .

THE MODS

During the mid-1960s, Italian scooters became wedded, at least as far as the British press and television were concerned, to the image of the mods (and rockers)—to the image of "riotous assembly" at the coastal resorts of Southern England. (The marriage has yet to be dissolved: a feature made in 1979 for the television programme *About Anglia* on the Lambretta Preservation Society [a "respectable" offshoot of the old scooter clubs] began, as a matter of course, with documentary footage of the clashes in 1964 at Margate and Brighton.) The words "social scootering" had formerly summoned up the image of orderly mass rallies. Now it was suddenly linked to a more sinister collective: an army of youth, ostensibly conformist—barely distinguishable as individuals from each other or the crowd—and yet capable of concerted acts of vandalism. The mods and the scooter clubs, the "Battle of Brighton," 1964, and the Brighton runs of the 1950s, were connected and yet mutually opposed. They shared the same space like the recto and verso of a piece of paper. After the "social aspects," the "anti-social"; after *Summer Holiday, My Generation* . . .

THE "DRESSED" IMAGE

Everyone was trying to look like a photograph, as smooth and as flat as a page in a magazine . . . Everyone wanted to catch the light . . .

JOAN BUCK, WHATEVER HAPPENED TO THE BRITISH MODEL?,
HARPERS & QUEEN, 1980

... and even here in this Soho, the headquarters of the adult mafia you could everywhere see the signs of the un-silent teenage revolution. The disc shops with those lovely sleeves set in their windows ... and the kids inside them purchasing guitars or spending fortunes on the songs of the Top Twenty. The shirt-stores and bra-stores with cine-star photos in the window, selling all the exclusive teenage drag ... The hair-style salons ... The cosmetic shops ... Scooters and bubble-cars driven madly down the roads by kids, who, a few years ago were pushing toy ones on the pavement ... Life is the best film for sure, if you can see it as a film ...

COLIN MACINNES, ABSOLUTE BEGINNERS, *1959*

The first wave of modernist youth emerged in or around London in the late 1950s. Most commentators agree on certain basic themes: that Mod was predominantly working class, male-dominated and centreed on an obsessive clothes-consciousness which involved a fascination with American and Continental styles. The endorsement of Continental products was particularly marked.

The Dean in Colin MacInnes's *Absolute Beginners* (1959) is a "typical" (i.e., ideal) early modernist:

College-boy smooth crop hair with burned-in parting, neat white Italian rounded-collared shirt, short Roman jacket very tailored (two little vents, three buttons) no turn-up narrow trousers with seventeen-inch bottoms absolute maximum, pointed toe shoes, and a white mac folded by his side ...[43]

His (unnamed) girl friend is described in similar detail:

... short hem lines, seamless stockings, pointed toe high-heeled stiletto shoes, crepe nylon rattling petticoat, short blazer jacket, hair done up into the elfin style. Face pale-corpse colour with a dash of mauve, plenty of mascara ...[44]

But here the absence of precise calibration (no twos or threes or seventeens) pinpoints her position within the signifying systems of both the novel and the subculture itself. In the same way, though her style is rooted in the Italian connection, derived in all likelihood from the "new race of [Italian] girls," this isn't stated. The Dean, on the other hand, is defined through a geography of dress. He is English by birth, Italian by choice.

According to sociological and marketing sources, Mod was largely a matter of commodity selection.[45] It was through commodity choices that mods marked themselves out as mods, using goods as "weapons of exclusion"[46] to avoid contamination from the other alien worlds of teen-aged taste that orbited around their own (the teds, beats and later the rockers).

Mods exploited the expressive potential within commodity choice to its logical conclusion. Their "furious consumption programme"—clothes, clubs, records, hair styles, petrol and drinamyl pills—has been described as "a grotesque parody of the aspirations of [their] parents"—the people who lived in the new towns or on the new housing estates, the post-War working and lower-middle-class . . . [47] The mods converted themselves into objects, they "chose" (in order) to make themselves into mods, attempting to impose systematic control over the narrow domain which was "theirs," and within which they saw their "real" selves invested—the domain of leisure and appearance, of dress and posture. The transference of desire (". . . their parents' . . . aspirations . . .") on to dress is familiar enough. Here the process is auto-erotic: the self, "its self" becomes the fetish.

When the Italian scooter was first chosen by the mods as an identity-marker (around 1958–9 according to eye witness accounts[48]), it was lifted into a larger unity of taste—an image made up out of sartorial and musical preferences—which in turn was used to signal to others "in the know" a refinement, a distance from the rest—a certain way of seeing the world. Value was conferred upon the scooter by the simple act of selection. The transformation in the value of the object had to be publicly marked:

> There was a correct way of riding. You stuck your feet out at an angle of forty-five degrees and the guy on the pillion seat held his hands behind his back and leaned back . . . [49]

Sometimes the object was physically transformed. According to Richard Barnes,[50] Eddie Grimstead, who owned two scooter shops in London during the mid-1960s, specialised in customising scooters for the mods. The machines were resprayed (Lambretta later adopted some of Grimstead's colour schemes) and fitted with accessories: foxtails, pennants, mascots, chromium, horns, extra lights and mirrors, whip aeriels, fur trim, and leopard-skin seats. Such features extended the original design concept organically.

Although the scooter imposed no constraints on the rider's dress (this, after all, was what had originally made the scooter "suit-able" for the fashion-conscious mods), a style became fixed around the vehicle—a uniform of olive green (parka) anoraks, levi jeans and hush puppies. Sometimes French berets were worn to stress the affiliation with the Continent and to further distinguish the "scooter boys" from the rockers whose own ensemble of leather jackets, flying boots and cowboy hats signalled an alternative defection to America, an immersion in the myth of the frontier.

The innovative drive within Mod, the compulsion to create ever newer, more distinctive looks was eventually to lead to another customising trend, one which, once again, seems to contradict the logic of the scooter's appeal. As the banks of lights and lamps began to multiply, a reaction set in amongst the hard core of stylists—scooters were stripped: side panels, front mudguards, sometimes even the footboards, were removed and the remaining body-work painted in muted colors with a matte finish.[51] These were the last, irreverent transformations. By this time Mod had surfaced as a set of newspaper photographs and Bank Holiday headlines. Fixed in the public gaze, Mod turned, finally, against itself. After baroque, minimalism: the image of the scooter was deconstructed, the object "re-materialised" . . .

THE AESTHETICISATION OF EVERYDAY LIFE

It'll be a great day when cutlery and furniture swing like the Supremes.
MICHAEL WOLFF WRITING IN THE SIA JOURNAL, IN 1964

However, Mod's significance (and influence) stretched beyond the confines of the subcultural milieu. It was largely through Mod that the demand for more "sophisticated" and autonomous forms of teenaged leisure was expressed. And provision expanded accordingly. By 1964, the coffee bars, "Shirt-stores and bra-stores" of MacInnes's *Absolute Beginners* had given way to discotheques and boutiques. There was now a Mod television programme, *Ready, Steady, Go* (opening sequence: Mod on scooter at traffic lights/voice-over: "The Weekend Starts Here . . ."). There was a thriving teenaged fashion industry in London based on Carnaby Street and the Kings Road. There were bowling alleys, Wimpey bars and no less than six weekly magazines aimed directly at the Mod market.[52]

At a more general level, Mod highlighted the emergence of a new consumer sensibility, what Raymond Williams might call a "structure of feeling," a more discriminating "consumer awareness." It was, after all, during the late 1950s when the term "modernist" first came into use, that the Coldstream Council recommended the expansion of Design within Higher Education, that Design Departments were set up in all the major art schools, that royal patronage was formally extended to industrial design,[53] that the Design Centre itself opened in the Haymarket, that magazines like *Which?, Shopper's Guide, Home* and *House Beautiful* began publicising the ideas of "consumer satisfaction" and "tasteful home improvement." And it was in 1964 when "mod" became a household word, that Terence Conran opened the first of the Habitat shops which, according to the advertising copy, offered "a pre-selected shopping programme . . . instant good taste . . . for switched-on people."[54]

The mirrors and the chromium of the "classic" Mod scooter reflected not only the group aspirations of the mods but a whole historical Imaginary, the Imaginary of affluence. The perfection of surfaces within Mod was part of the general "aestheticisation" of everyday life achieved through the intervention of the Image, through the conflation of the "public" and the "personal," consumption and display. In 1966, a Wolverhampton reader of a national newspaper felt concerned enough about a "decorating problem" to write in for advice:

> I have painted walls and woodwork white and covered the floors with Olive Sullivan's "Bachelor's Button" carpet in burnt oak orange chestnut. Upholstery is Donald Bros unbleached linen mullein cloth. Curtains are orange and in a bright Sekers fabric and I am relying upon pictures, books, cushions, and rug for bright contrasting accessories. I have found a winner in London Transport's poster "Greenwich Observatory" which I think looks marvellous against the white walls.[55]

The separation of a room into its parts (each part labelled, placed), of a suit into its "features" (each button counted, sited on a map) spring from a common impulse. Together they delineate a new disposition. The reader's room in Wolverhampton, the Dean's suit in Soho—both are "integrated structures," designed environments. Both are held in high regard. They are subjected to the same anxious and discriminating gaze. This is the other side of affluence: a rapacious specularity: the coming of the greedy I.

BRIGHTON REVISITED REVISITED

In 1964, on the stately promenades of the South Coast resorts, a battle was enacted between two groups of adolescents representing different tastes and tendencies. The seaside riots provided a spectacle which was circulated as an "event" first as news, later, as history (the film *Quadrophenia* appeared in 1979). The spectacle "just happened" to be watched (". . . one local paper carried a photo of a man amongst a crowd of boys swinging deck-chairs holding his child above his head to get a better view . . ."[56]).

According to a survey conducted at Margate, the mods tended to come from London, were from lower-middle- or upper-working-class backgrounds and worked in skilled or semi-skilled trades or in the service industries. (Jimmy, the hero of *Quadrophenia*, is presented as a typical mod, he works as an office boy in a London advertising agency. . . .) The rockers were more likely to do manual jobs and to live locally.[57] Most observers agree that mods far out-numbered rockers at the coast. When interviewed, the mods used the words "dirty" and "ignorant" to typify the rockers. The rockers referred to the mods as "pansy" and "soft."

The clash of opinion between design and motorcycling interests, between service and productive sectors, "adaptive" and "outmoded" elements was translated at Brighton and Margate into images of actual violence. The rocker/mod polarity cannot be so neatly transposed into options on gender (i.e., sexist/counter-sexist). Apparently, girls occupied equally subordinate positions within both subcultures. Male mods sometimes referred to girlfriends as "pillion fodder." There were proportionately fewer girls driving scooters within the mod subculture than outside it in the "respectable" scootering community . . .

THE MOD REVIVAL

The scooter fanatic of eighteen to twenty really doesn't know what it is about. It isn't impossible to be Mod [in 1980], they just go about it the wrong way—a scooter was a means of transport. You didn't worship it . . .

ORIGINAL MOD QUOTED IN OBSERVER MAGAZINE, 1979

The disappearance of the service stations, the recession, small Japanese motorcycles, compulsory crash helmets, Scooters India, the Red Brigades: the original "network of relations" transformed over time, and with it the object, and the relationship of the user to the object.

The scooter is "undressed": all new mods are amateur mechanics. The shortage of spare parts and the collapse of the support structure of garages mean that more scooterists are forced to service and maintain their own machines.

CONCLUSION

In the *Evening Standard* (24 February, 1977), a Mr Derek Taylor, "one of these new fashionable middle-management people," explained why he had sold his car and bought a secondhand Lambretta:

. . . with road tax at £4 a year, insurance £12 and petrol consumption of nearly 100mpg, I reckon I'm on to a good buy . . . I still enjoy my comfort and want to get to work in a clean and presentable condition . . .

Fashion remains a significant vector but its significance resides in the fact that it can be turned in on itself: ". . . fashion takes a back-seat, but the practical scooter man has all the accessories on board (monsoon-proof mac . . . RAF long johns) . . ." (ibid.)

The fashion paradigm is punctured by the practical scooter-man. The fuel crisis and the plight of the *Evening Standard*'s "neglected" middle-management have redefined the object (some traces linger . . . "comfort . . . clean . . . presentable"). The image falls off into irony.

On the London Underground, a new poster advertising the "more attractive angular look"[58] of the "New Line" P range Vespa takes its place alongside the Suzuki and the Mini Metro ads, the images of Adonis briefs, the Elliott twins and the "This Insults Women" stickers. The Italian scooter cycle kicks off again in slightly higher gear . . .

ENDNOTES

1. Roland Barthes, "Introduction," *Mythologies*, Paladin, 1972(a).

2. Roland Barthes, quoted in J. Bird, *The Politics of Representation, Block 2*, 1980.

3. Roland Barthes, "Ecrivains et ecrivants," in *Critical Essays*, Evanston, 1972(b).

4. Roland Barthes, "The New Citroen," in Barthes, op. cit., 1972(a).

5. Roland Barthes, op. cit., 1972(b).

6. Roland Barthes, "The New Citroen": "The bodywork, the lines of union are touched, the upholstery palpated, the seats tried, the doors caressed, the cushions fondled; . . . The object here is totally prostituted, appropriated: originating from the heaven of *Metropolis*, the Goddess is in a quarter of an hour mediatized, actualizing through this exorcism the very essence of petit-bourgeois advancement."

7. Lisa Tickner, "Women and Trousers: unisex clothing and sex-role changes in the 20th Century," in *Leisure in the 20th Century*, Design Council, 1977.

8. Paul Willis, "The Motor Cycle Within the Subcultural Group," in *Working Papers in Cultural Studies* (2), University of Birmingham.

9. Roland Barthes, op. cit., 1972(a).

10. Vance Packard, *The Wastemakers*, Penguin, 1963.

11. Ibid.

12. T. Adorno, quoted in Colin MacCabe, *Godard: Sound Image: politics*, BFI Publications, 1981.

13. Louis Althusser, "Contradiction and Overdetermination," in *For Marx*, Allen Lane, 1969.

14. Jan Stevens, *Scootering*, Penguin, 1966.

15. Mike Karslake, *Jet-Set*, Lambretta Club of Great Britain, December, 1974.

16. Paul Sweezey, "On the Theory of Monopoly Capitalism," in *Modern Capitalism and Other Essays*, Monthly Review Press, 1972. Peter Donaldson in *Economics of the Real World*, Penguin, 1973, provides some interesting statistics here on the transfer of capital in Britain during the post-war period. He writes: "Spending on take-overs during the first half of the 1960s was something like ten times that of the 1950s . . . One estimate is that the mergers movement during the 1960s must have involved the transfer of some twenty per cent of the total net assets of manufacturing industry . . ."

17. See Vance Packard, *The Status-Seekers*, Penguin, 1961.

18. Stuart Ewen, "Advertising as Social Production," in *Communication and Class Struggle*, Vol. 1, IG/IMMRC, 1979. Also Stuart Ewen, *Captains of Consciousness: Advertising and the Social Roots of the Consumer Culture*, McGraw-Hill, 1977.

19. Quoted ibid.

20. J. K. Galbraith, *The Affluent Society*, Penguin, 1970.

21. Richard Hamilton in S. Bayley (ed.), *In Good Shape: Style in Industrial Products 1900–1960*, Design Council, 1979.

22. Ann Ferebee, *A History of Design from the Victorian Era*, Van Nos. Reinhold, 1970.

23. "This exquisite social appliance," a line from *We Carry On*, Innocenti promotion film, 1966.

24. R. Barthes, 1972(a).

25. Henry Lefebvre, *Everyday Life in the Modern World*, Allen Lane, 1971.

26. Vance Packard, op. cit., 1963.

27. "A New Race of Girls," in *Picture Post*, 5 September, 1954.

28. From an advertising jingle used on Australian radio during 1962, sung by the Bee Gees.

29. S. Bayley, op. cit., 1979.

30. Jack Woods, "Is the Scooter Making a Comeback?," in *Motorcycle Sport*, November, 1979.

31. Ibid.

32. Reyner Banham, "Mediated Environments," in *Superculture: American Popular Culture and Europe*, Paul Elek, 1975, (ed.) C. W. E. Bigsby.

33. F. K. Henrion, "Italian Journey," in *Design*, January 1949.

34. Ibid.

35. Ibid.

36. Ann Ferebee, op. cit., 1970.

37. John Heskett, *Industrial Design*, Thames & Hudson, 1980.

38. Mike Karslake, op. cit., 1974.

39. Ibid.

40. Personal recollection from Mike Karslake.

41. Jack Woods, op. cit., 1979.

42. From an article entitled "The Buzzing Wasp" which appeared in *On Two Wheels*. The series also carried an article on Lambrettas called "The Alternative Society."

43. Colin MacInnes, *Absolute Beginners*, reissued by Allison & Busby, 1980.

44. Ibid.

45. See R. Barnes, *Mods!*, Eel Pie Publishing, 1980, on which I drew heavily for the mod sections in this paper; *Generation X* (eds.) Hamblett & Deverson, Tandem, 1964; Gary Herman, *The Who*, Studio Vista, 1971; S. Cohen, *Folk Devils and Moral Panics*. Paladin, 1972. See also D. Hebdige, "The Style of the Mods," in S. Hall et. al. (eds.), *Resistance Through Rituals*, Hutchinson, 1976.

46. Baron Isherwood and Mary Douglas, *The World of Goods: Towards an Anthropology of Consumption*, Penguin, 1980. Isherwood and Douglas define consumption as a "ritual process whose primary function is to make sense of the inchoate flux of events. . . . rituals are conventions that set up visible public definitions." Luxury goods are particularly useful as "weapons of exclusion." This idea compares interestingly with Bourdieu's definition of "taste": "Tastes (i.e., manifested preferences) are the practical affirmation of an inevitable difference . . . asserted purely negatively by the refusal of other tastes . . ."

47. R. Barnes, op. cit., 1980.

48. Ibid.

49. Ibid.

50. Ibid.

51. Ibid.

52. S. Cohen, op. cit., 1972.

53. See Fiona MacCarthy, *A History of British Design 1830–1970*, Allen & Unwin, 1979. The Design Centre opened in 1956. The Duke of Edinburgh's Prize for Elegant Design was first awarded three years later; also *The Practical Idealists*, J. & A. Blake, Lund Humphries, 1969.

54. Ibid.

55. Quoted in F. MacCarthy, *All Things Bright and Beautiful*, Allen & Unwin, 1972.

56. S. Cohen, op. cit., 1972.

57. P. Barker and A. Little, in T. Raison (ed.), *Youth in New Society*, Hart-Davis, 1966. Peter Willmott gives some interesting figures on patterns of scooter and motorcycle ownership in a working-class London borough in *Adolescent Boys in East London*, Penguin, 1966, during the mod-rocker period. Of his sample of 264 boys, one in ten over sixteen owned scooters (mainly in the sixteen- to seventeen-year range) whilst only one in twenty over sixteen owned a motor bike (they tended to be slightly older, seventeen to eighteen).

58. This comes from a review of the new Vespa P200 in "The Buzzing Wasp," in *On Two Wheels*.

Thanks to Mary Rose Young and thanks especially to Mike Karslake, president of the Lambretta Preservation Society, for giving me so much of his time and allowing me access to his collection of Innocenti publicity material and memorabilia.

9
Thomas C. O'Guinn
"TOUCHING GREATNESS: THE CENTRAL MIDWEST BARRY MANILOW FAN CLUB"[1]
(1991)

MODERN CELEBRITY

Christianity will go. We're more popular than Jesus now.

—JOHN LENNON (1966)

It seemed to me then, as it does now, that one of the undeniable hallmarks of American consumer culture is a fascination with celebrity. Each week approximately 3.3 million Americans read *People* (Simmons Market Research Bureau 1990). Anyone who reads newspapers or magazines or watches television, will have no doubt noted that a great deal of air time and print space is devoted to covering celebrities. This interest and attention is not restricted to a certain social class; all have their celebrities, although each class tends to think the other misguided or too unsophisticated to appreciate the truly great. Some read of their admired ones in tabloids, others in the chic magazine of the "intelligentsia."

At the center of all this attention is a great deal of consumption. At least one million Americans belong to a fan club (Dornay 1989). Approximately five million tourists have visited Graceland since being opened to the public in 1982, 60,000 alone during "Elvis Week"[2] marking the tenth anniversary of Mr. Presley's death. Tourists throng to celebrity graveyards in Los Angeles; the most famous of them, Forest Lawn is often referred to as the Disneyland of cemeteries. Others take drive-by bus tours of the homes of the stars. "Meet-a-Celebrity" tie-ins and other promotions are becoming routine. The production and marketing of celebrity could reasonably be called one of America's largest industries.

Yet, the question of why remains. Why do we devote so much attention to celebrities? Why do "we live in a society bound together by the talk of fame" (Braudy 1986, p. vii)? Why do celebrities matter so much to us; and from the perspective of consumer research, why do they sit at the center of so much buying and consuming?

Apparently no one is really even sure how long the celebrity has been with us.[3] Braudy (1986) traces the notion back to Homeric legends and early concepts of gods. Another frequently applied model is the traditional hero within the context of myth, probably best described by Campbell in his classic, *Hero With a Thousand Faces* (1949). Heros and their associated myths help us make sense of our lives, better understand our connections to each other and our culture. There is also something special about heros in a techno-science culture where the concept of god is so fundamentally threatened. The need for magic may be at its greatest in such a world. This is the modern "crisis of heroism" put forth by Becker (1973) in *The Denial of Death*. When heros and gods are reasoned away, a vacuum of anxiety remains. Amplifying Becker (1973), Rollin (1983; 38) says:

> the therapy for the Age of Anxiety is apotheosis, the transformation of a human being into a heavenly being, a star, a hero, a god, a symbol of human potential realized.

Others (i.e., Klapp 1969; Lowenthal 1961) have argued that celebrities exist to give the individual identity in a modern mass culture. In this notion's most recent incarnation, Reeves (1988) presents an intriguing thesis on stardom, casting it as a cultural agent of personality development and social identification. Even though his specific focus is television stardom, the idea that stardom is a "cultural ritual of typification and individuation" extends well beyond that particular medium. Drawing on the work of Carey (1975), Geertz (1973), Bakhtin (1981) and Dyer (1979), Reeves (p. 150) argues that television stars help the individual connect who he or she is with "appropriate modes of being in American culture," or cultural "types," while at the same time providing just enough quirks against type to believe that we, like the stars, are actually unique individuals.

One of the more influential thoughts in conceptualizations of celebrity is Max Weber's (1968, v. 1. 241) concept of "charisma":

> to be endowed with powers and properties which are supernatural and superhuman, or at least exceptional even where accessible to others; or again as sent by God, or as if adorned with exemplary value and thus worthy to be a leader.

However, as impactful as this concept has been, few suggest a wholesale application of the "charismatic leader" (Weber 1968) concept to modern celebrity. The reasons are generally because the sociologist-cum-economist Weber's formulation requires a purposeful leader, a stable social system, and a clearly discernable power relationship. Two of these almost never exist in the case of modern celebrity, and the other, a stable social system, is a matter of some debate and interpretation (see Dyer

1979 and Alberoni 1972). Edward Shils (1965) also takes Weber to task for his narrow institutional conceptualization of charisma, and offers a much broader view of the concept. Still, it is Italian sociologist Francesco Alberoni who proposes a purely apolitical and modern model of celebrity.

Alberoni (1972) argues that the modern "star" does not and cannot possess generalized "charisma" in the true Weberian sense. Modern societies are too specialized to allow stars the kind of institutionalized power that Weber's charismatic leader demands. However, he does believe that they are perceived by their adoring masses as possessing some demi-divine characteristics that make them "elite" rather than charismatic. They are seen as spiritually special, but lacking any type of political power. Alberoni thus terms stars the "powerless elite."

In fact, it could be that ritual is the central element in the Touching Greatness phenomenon. Rituals linger well beyond their substance. They can still be comforting even though their spiritual basis is long gone. Prayers said to a god not truly believed in may still benefit the supplicant. So too may be visiting the place of rituals, the church—even though the gods have gone away. Touching greatness may be a form that is substantially vestigial. The practice satisfies even though it is absent of much contemporary meaning. This could help explain why we seem to have such a need for celebrities which Boorstin (1962) saw as nothing more than "human pseudo-events," and people famous for being famous.

TOUCHING GREATNESS

The Touching Greatness project began at Mann's Theater in Los Angeles. We (Belk, O'Guinn, Sherry, Wallendorf) interviewed several people engaged in what seemed a particularly interesting form of consumer behavior. People spent from a few minutes to a few hours milling about looking at the hand and foot prints of movie stars. Some, such as the individual in Figure 10, chose to bend down, often while being photographed by a family member or friend, and place their own hands or feet in the impressions left by the stars. Some bought Hollywood and celebrity related souvenirs, signed up for tours of the stars' homes, and otherwise participated in the celebrity centered consumption experience. Interviews then and during a return trip by Belk and O'Guinn two years later revealed that to many it was merely something to do, just situationally normative behavior and curiosity. For others, it meant something more: a chance to remember and pay homage, to explain to their children who these men and women were and why they were important in their lives. Touching Greatness is more about the latter, or "true fans," but is not wholly without connection to the former appreciative

FIGURE 10

masses. It remains an interesting and legitimate question why behaviors such as those observed at Mann's Theater are norms within our culture, and why such popular shrines exist at all.

The Central Midwest Barry Manilow Fan Club (CMBMFC) data are offered here as a case within the larger phenomenon and not as complete ethnography. These data will not allow the reader the depth necessary to fully appreciate the unique character of this particular club, for they were not collected for that purpose. Rather, they illustrate some of the themes observed across locales and fans.

CENTRAL MIDWEST BARRY MANILOW FAN CLUB

Barry Manilow[4] is a celebrity. I talked to some of his fans. At the time the data were collected several themes had emerged from work at other Touching Greatness sites. The data collected here and at subsequent locales were used to expand upon what had already been learned, and to test the evolving model with new data. What follows are some of these findings, along with illustrative text and photos.

The findings being reported here are based on thirty hours of interviews with eighteen members of the CMBMFC. The informants were all women. Most were in their mid-thirties to mid-forties. Socioeconomic-status varied, but was typically observed to be lower middle class. We saw no men, but were told that there were a few male members.[5] Interviews were conducted in three places: a small restaurant, the home of the CMBMFC president, Bobbie, six hours prior to a Barry Manilow concert, and in a backstage press area secured exclusively for our use before and after the show. Besides the author, five graduate assistants, three men and two women, participated in the fieldwork.

THEMATIC FINDINGS

The Touching Greatness phenomenon has a broad cultural foundation. Apart from aspects of religion, I observed evidence of the fan club as surrogate family, and what could reasonably be viewed as a socialization outcome of life in a society in which the average family watches over seven hours of television a day (Condry 1989). Yet, the single best organizing structure is the first of these: religion. Perhaps it is because it is such a primal structure. Humans have been using it as a conceptual framework for explaining their existence, plight, and just about everything else for centuries. It is a very convenient and familiar source for interpretation and attribution. Religion has so many points of contact with so many aspects of believers' lives, that it is sometimes hard to see where it starts and stops. With this caveat in mind, a discussion of some of the uncovered themes follows. They are not exclusively religious, but are not inconsistent with a religious interpretation.

BARRY IS EVERYTHING

"He's a husband, he's a lover, he's a friend, he's everything."

Barry Manilow pervades the lives of the members of the CMBMFC. In a very real sense, he is "everything." Evidence of this comes in several forms. First, there is the more concrete, such as the expenditure of time and money. It is not uncommon for the members to attend five shows a year, often traveling considerable distances. There is also the purchase and creation of Barry Manilow paraphernalia. These include hundreds of photographs, extensive album and video collections, clipping files and other memorabilia. Large phone bills from calling other Barry Manilow members are common. Vacations are scheduled around tour dates. Life revolves around Barry. In terms of time and money, Barry is a primary beneficiary of these typically scarce resources.

Invoking Barry's name and spirit also makes important rituals and life events even more special, or sacred (Belk, Sherry and Wallendorf 1991). A particularly palpable example was when Bobbie and her husband were married. The couple had a number of Barry's songs played at the wedding, and the sheet music to a particular song, "Who Needs to Dream," was superimposed over the couple's wedding photograph (Figure 11). Many religions place a god or other important personage (i.e., saint, martyr, prophet, etc.) at the center of celebrations and rituals marking important life events, such as weddings, which thereby come to be regarded as sacred institutions.

Barry's pervasiveness in the lives of the CMBMFC members was also apparent in that they often referred to him in terms of a significant other, most typically as lover, husband or friend. This love was, however, rarely sexual. It was rather more spiritual love, though often with an idealized romantic pallor. For example, one woman who describes herself as a very faithful wife, says she takes off her wedding ring on only one occasion: to attend Barry Manilow concerts. She does this although she and Barry Manilow have no personal relationship in any traditional sense; yet, she sees important symbolism in the act. This is an important thing for her to do. It would, after all, be wrong to be married to two men at once. Extending the religious metaphor, some nuns wear wedding bands to symbolize their marriage to Christ.

Perhaps most significantly, informants explain that Barry is able to provide the emotional support and understanding they need like no one else in their lives. I was told that he "never lets them down." CMBMFC members frequently describe him as "all" of these important roles or personages "rolled into one," someone who can be all, provide all.

> I believe in God, and I kind of think God sent Barry to help me. I think a lot of people feel that way, he's got a special gift and he kind of reaches out to a lot of people.

Barry's specialness occasionally borders on the miraculous. Bobbie tells of a time when a group of CMBMFC members were camping out for tickets in cold and wet weather. They had been out all night in rain and cold when sandwiches and coffee arrived "from nowhere." Bobbie was amazed that what initially seemed like a meager amount of food had "fed everyone." We also spoke to a woman who told us that Barry had "somehow" heard of her child who had cancer, picked him up in his limousine and visited with he and his mother at their home. On another occasion, the CMBMFC members were waiting for Barry's plane to land. The weather was bad, but when Barry's plane approached, the sky cleared and it was able to land. When he was safely inside the terminal, it started raining again.

FIGURE 11

BARRY'S WORK

Like most religions, this church has a mission; there is work to be done. Among the important duties are taking care of Barry, protecting him from bad fans, recruiting new followers, and always being there for him. These are all seen as important functions for members of the CMBMFC.

Perhaps chief among them is the idea of providing emotional support to Barry and otherwise taking care of him. Sometimes, we think of gods taking care of their followers, and not vice versa. But in fact, in many religions that is precisely the purpose of human existence, to serve god. Christians, for example, are told that the path to heaven and happiness is through serving the Lord, doing His work. Sometimes "His work" is in the form of altruism, serving god by serving others. Such behavior is very consistent with that observed among CMBMFC members. They are quick to point out that Barry and his fans do a great deal of charity work.

It is here that the role of wife/mother becomes most intermingled with that of religious follower. The women of the CMBMFC seem to derive a very important benefit from taking care of Barry, giving of themselves. They believe he needs and appreciates this effort, his appreciation being very significant. In preparation for the show we attended, four different fan clubs competed to decorate Barry's dressing room. The members of the CMBMFC explained that decorations let Barry know they care, and are "there for him." They also wanted to make him as "comfortable as possible."

Some members have very personal ideas and aspirations about serving Barry. The president of the CMBMFC, herself a professional secretary, says that if she could be anything at all in relation to Barry she would be his secretary:

> I would like to just spend a day following him around with my little clipboard or whatever saying "you've gotta be here, you've gotta be here, you've got a meeting with so and so" and just do that for a day. That's all I want.

Serving Barry even extends to cleaning for Barry. After one show a group of CMBMFC members waited for Barry to leave his dressing room. When he did, he looked at the arena and commented on how dirty it was. They then explained that this was true except for the rows in which they had sat. Those were clean:

> He [Barry] said something like "what went on here today, looks like they had a circus, popcorn all over the floor" and I said "yes, but the first three rows are clean." He turns to Mark and he says "you're right, where they sat, those rows are clean."

Churches must be kept clean. True believers respect the sacred space, whereas infidels defile it. Members of the CMBMFC are true believers.

Still, after telling the researchers so much about what they did for Barry, the opposite question was posed.

> Researcher: And what does he give you?
> Bobbie: Just knowing that he's there and he cares, you know, like I told

her (my friend) tonight going to the mall. I said "this man, the fact that he does realize what he puts us through."

Appreciation, particularly from a male, seemed very important. Further, it doesn't seem entirely coincidental that when asked to explain what makes Barry so good, informants very frequently mention that Barry is very good to his mother. Here is where the devoted religious follower and the role of the long suffering and nurturing woman intertwine. The fan's object of devotion is a person to whom they ascribe the attributes of specialness, extending to religious proportions. They serve him, and are happy in their work. It is not, however, insignificant that this minor deity or religiously imbued person is male. It is also important that this paradoxical relationship to suffering and pleasure seems so central to the gratifications derived by these women. It is also entirely consistent with the happy sufferer paradox of many religious experiences.

SUFFERING FOR BARRY

"Our day will come."

"Mostly they just sit and shake their heads at us."

"I mean he cares for us too. In fact, he even told us . . . ; "I know you put up with a lot of grief and I've heard every name in the book just like you've heard every name in the book and you put up with a lot," and he said "I want you to know I'm here," and he did everything he could do to make sure it doesn't happen but it's always gonna happen and he feels terrible about it because we're considered his ladies and he takes care of us . . ."

"He realizes what he puts you through."

The members of the CMBMFC speak of the ridicule and oppression they must face for their beliefs. Their families, particularly their husbands, do not understand their devotion and love for Barry. People make fun of them. Yet, it is suffering not entirely without reward; there is a bit of martyrdom related satisfaction apparent in some informants.

SHRINES AND RELICS

Many fans have collections of Barry Manilow things. Some have special "Barry Rooms" set aside for the display of their collections. Others have only parts of rooms, some just closets. Almost all attribute lack of room for Barry to unsympathetic husbands. Consistent with other research on collections (Belk, Wallendorf and Sherry 1989), the job is never done, collections are never complete. There's always more Barry stuff. Few would sell even a single piece of their collections, and they rank their contents as their most prized and meaningful possessions.

I'd kill just about anybody if they just go in the room and try to walk out of the room with a poster, a record, just a clipping out of a newspaper,

FIGURE 12

scraps of tickets, you name it. A lot of us have rooms devoted to just that, in fact, few of us have understanding husbands. I'm about one of the only ones in the entire Central Midwest Club that lets me do all of that.

Bobbie's room is featured in two photographs (Figures 12 and 13). She devotes one of the bedrooms of her house to this pursuit. The room is covered in posters, photographs, clippings, letters, autographs, etc. These things have a great deal of meaning for Bobbie. These are special because they involve Barry, and form an important emotional conduit to networks of friends, memories and an important sense of self.

The highest status things in the collections are the things actually touched by Barry. This somehow proves that Barry exists for them, through this person-to-object-to-person connection (McCracken 1986). It is physical evidence of a personal relationship. A good example was a Perrier bottle from which Barry had drunk. This bottle occupies a prominent place on Bobbie's shelf. The smaller bottles belong to members of Barry's entourage.

This collecting of things actually touched by the admired one is a particularly interesting aspect of the Touching Greatness phenomenon. It was observed consistently across venues and celebrities, and is very consistent with a liturgical interpretation, going as far as the levels of sacredness assigned to religious relics (Geary 1986) depending on how "near" they were once to the sacred being. It also draws us back full circle to the behavior observed at Mann's Theater, of wanting to actu-

FIGURE 13

ally touch the concrete images left by the stars. It wouldn't be the same consumption experience if Plexiglas covered the concrete impressions.

Yet another important distinction concerning collections should be noted. Apparently, "real fans" don't sell Barry things at a profit. This helps distinguish the infidel from the true believer. One of the most common behaviors at a Manilow concert is taking photographs of Barry, lots of them. Bobbie, for example, will take four to eight 24 exposure rolls per show, and see several shows per year. The photos taken of Barry are sold at cost or traded with other fans, but "it would be wrong" to sell them.

> The only thing I ever charge is if they want copies and they send me just for the print. Barry doesn't like when you make a profit.

This is very reminiscent of the parable of Christ driving the merchants from the temple. Apparently, putting a price on something that is seen as without price would seem profane or vulgar and would move something sacred into the secular domain, and thus cheapen it (Belk, Sherry and Wallendorf 1989).

FELLOWSHIP

Fellowship seemed to be the greatest of all the benefits of CMBMFC membership. Respondents talked at length of how much getting together with one another meant to them. Many said that relationships started via membership have become some of the most important in their lives. The behavior we observed supports this assertion. The members of the CMBMFC seemed very close and legitimately interested in each others' well-being. The greatest thing they have in common is the love for and devotion to Barry Manilow. They get together and talk and reminisce, and share one another's joys and sorrows. There was a clear bond between them. This may be the strongest evidence for a Church of Barry interpretation, the centrality of fellowship. They gather in his name, but for each other.

Touching Greatness also provides other social benefits. When at Mann's Theater it seemed that the concrete shrines facilitated communication among visitors, much of it inter-generational. Why Jimmy Stewart or Marilyn Monroe were important to father was explained to son. For others, the stars were known-in-common referents. Their films marked time, set events in context, and seemed to provide meaning in a non-trivial way. There was something important underneath this, a connection to culture and the individual within it, with consumption being an important part of the link. Buying, giving and collecting things within the touching greatness phenomenological frame is common and important to those involved. It concertizes the experiences and facilitates social interaction.

DISCUSSION

Religion is one of the oldest of culture's creations. Yet, "dead are all the gods" (Nietzsche 1893). Science and the ascendancy of the individual has either killed them or made of them vestigial forms which only vaguely resemble their ancestors. As the traditional social structures are challenged, evolve or succumb, contemporary cultures recast old into new. What were god-centered religions may be easily converted into social structures for celebrity worship. Even though few if any CMBMFC members actually believe Barry Manilow to be a god, they do attribute the qualities of the religiously blessed to him. They certainly believe him to be closer to god than they are. Clouds part when his plane lands; he supplies food in mysterious ways; and he possesses a special sense of knowing about his followers' lives that is clearly beyond mortal. This is a religious system. By any standards Barry Manilow is worshipped by his fans. He is someone more than a priest and someone less than the son of God in a traditional Protestant Christian model. In contrast, data from Elvis Presley fan clubs show his fans as seeing him closer to truly divine; whereas data from Johnny Cash fan clubs show a very fallible mortal, but still spiritually special.

The Touching Greatness data provide support for the thesis that celebrities perform some of the functions of gods, or god-sent beings. Yet, also clear is support for the idea that the fan club serves some of the social function churches once did. There, people who share a deep devotion or admiration for a special individual, meet and form important bonds, and fulfill important social needs once facilitated by the church. Maybe these fan clubs have taken on such a liturgical feel because the religious form was simply the most familiar, the most easily borrowed and transformed. The church is replaced in form, if not substance because it has the best, most familiar and most comfortable bundle of social uses, gratifications and shared meanings. We may miss God less than we miss each other.

While it is sometimes argued that extreme or marginal forms of behavior such as fanaticism are both qualitatively and quantitatively distinct from their more "normal" expression, it seems difficult to explain one without the other. The very fact that Graceland and Mann's Theater exist and flourish means something apart from fanaticism. Likewise, the significance of the Touching Greatness phenomenon exists beyond the dispositional properties of individuals. It says something about the stage of a society's development (Alberoni 1972), our collective needs, motivations and values, and how these are expressed through consumption.

There's a great deal of consumption in the Touching Greatness phenomenon. Yet as a field we have chosen not to give this and other aspects of popular culture much attention. Perhaps that is precisely the reason; it is too popular. Academics can be the worst snobs of all in their refusal to consider the popular (see Lewis 1988; Bellah et al. 1985). This seems odd, since by definition, it is where so much of life occurs.

ENDNOTES

1. The author would like to thank Mark Michicich, L. J. Shrum, Lisa Kay Slabon, Lisa Braddock, Ian Malbon, and Connie O'Guinn, who participated in this research. Further thanks go to Bill Wallendorf, Molly Ziske, Kim Rotzoll, Russell Belk, and the staff of the Overland Café, Los Angeles.

2. An Elvis week consists of nine days.

3. While there are many reasonable definitions of celebrity, and related terms such as "fame," "star," and "renown," I choose to simply define a celebrity as one who is known by many, but knows far fewer, and the object of considerable attention.

4. Barry Manilow is a popular contemporary song stylist.

5. Most males mentioned were Barry impersonators.

REFERENCES

Alberoni, Francesco (1972). "The Powerless Elite: Theory and Sociological Research on the Phenomenon of Stars," in D. McQuail (ed.) *Sociology of Mass Communication*, Baltimore: Penguin, 75–98.

Bakhtin, M. M. (1981), *The Dialogic Imagination: Four Essays*, M. Holquist (ed.), C. Emerson and M. Holquist (trans.), Austin: University of Texas Press.

Becker, Ernest (1973), *The Denial of Death*, New York: The Free Press.

Belk, Russell W., Melanie Wallendorf and John F. Sherry, Jr. (1989). "The Sacred and the Profane in Consumer Behavior: Theodicy on the Odyssey," *Journal of Consumer Research*, (16:1), 1–38.

Belk, Russell W., Melanie Wallendorf, John Sherry, Jr. and Morris B. Hol-
brook (1991), "Collecting in a Consumer Culture," in Russell W. Belk (ed.),
*Highways and Buyways: Naturalistic Research from the Consumer Behavior
Odyssey*, Provo, UT: Association for Consumer Research.

Bellah, Robert N., Richard Madsen, William M. Sullivan, Ann Swindle, and
Steven M. Tipton (1985), *Habits of the Heart: Individualism and Commitment in American Life*, Berkeley: University of California Press.

Boorstin, Daniel (1962), *The Image: Or What Happened to the American
Dream*, New York: Atheneum.

Braudy, Leo (1986), *The Frenzy of Renown: Fame and Its History*, New York:
Oxford University Press.

Campbell, Joseph (1949), *The Hero With a Thousand Faces*, New York: Pantheon.

Carey, James (1975), "A Cultural Approach to Communication," *Communication*, 2, 1–22.

Condry, John (1989), *The Psychology of Television*, Hillsdale, New Jersey:
Lawrence Erlbaum.

Darnay, Brigitte T. (ed.) (1989), *Encyclopedia of Associations 1990*, vl. pt. 2,
sections 7–18, Detroit: Gale Research.

Dyer, R. (1979), *Stars*, London: British Film Institute.

Geertz, Clifford (1973), *The Interpretation of Cultures*, New York: Basic
Books.

Geary, Patrick (1986), "Sacred Commodities: The Circulation of Medieval Relics," in Arjun Appadurai (ed.), *The Social Life of Things: Commodities in
Cultural Perspective*, New York: Cambridge University Press, 169–191.

Klapp, Orrin E. (1969), *Collective Search for Identity*, New York: Holt, Rine-
hart and Winston.

Lennon, John (1966), *New York Times*, "Comment on Jesus Spurs a Radio
Ban," Aug 5, 1966, page 20, column 3.

Lewis, George H. (1988), "Dramatic Conversations: The Relationship Between
Sociology and Popular Culture," in Ray B. Browne and Marshall W. Fish-
wick (eds.), *Symbiosis: Popular Culture and Other Fields*, Bowling Green,
Ohio: Bowling Green State University Popular Press, 70–84.

Lincoln, Yvonna S. and Egon G. Guba (1985), *Naturalistic Inquiry*, Beverly
Hills, CA: Sage.

Lowenthal, Lowel (1961), "The Triumph of Mass Idols," in Lowel Lowenthal
(ed.), *Literature, Popular Culture and Society*, Englewood Cliffs, NJ: Pren-
tice Hall, pp. 109–140.

McCracken Grant (1986), "Culture and Consumption: A Theoretical Account
of the Structure and Movement of the Cultural Meaning of Consumer
Goods," *Journal of Consumer Research*, 13:1 (June), 71–84.

Nietzsche, Friedrich (1893), *Also Sprach Zarathustra*, Leipzig: C. G. Nau-
mann.

Reeves, Jimmy L. (1988), "Television Stardom: A Ritual of Social Typification," in James W. Carey (ed.), *Media, Myths and Narratives: Television
and the Press*, Newbury Park, CA: Sage, 146–160.

Rollin, Roger R. (1983), "The Lone Ranger and Lenny Skutnik: The Hero as
Popular Culture," in Ray B. Browne and Marshall W. Fishwick (eds.), *The
Hero in Transition*, Bowling Green, Ohio: Bowling Green University Popular
Press, 14–45.

Shills, Edward (1965), "Charisma, Order and Status," *American Sociological
Review*, 199–233.

Simmons Market Research Bureau (1990), "Study of Media and Markets,"
New York: Simmons Media Research Bureau.

Weber, Max (1968), *Economy and Society*, v-13, New York: Bedminster.

10

Janice A. Radway
"The Act of Reading the Romance: Escape and Instruction"
(1984)

By the end of my first full day with Dorothy Evans and her customers, I had come to realize that although the Smithton women are not accustomed to thinking about what it is in the romance that gives them so much pleasure, they know perfectly well why they like to read. I understood this only when their remarkably consistent comments forced me to relinquish my inadvertent but continuing preoccupation with the text. Because the women always responded to my query about their reasons for reading with comments about the pleasures of the act itself rather than about their liking for the particulars of the romantic plot, I soon realized I would have to give up my obsession with textual features and narrative details if I wanted to understand their view of romance reading. Once I recognized this it became clear that romance reading was important to the Smithton women first because the simple event of picking up a book enabled them to deal with the particular pressures and tensions encountered in their daily round of activities. Although I learned later that certain aspects of the romance's story do help to make this event especially meaningful, the early interviews were interesting because they focused so resolutely on the significance of the *act of romance reading* rather than on the meaning of the romance.

The extent of the connection between romance reading and my informants' understanding of their roles as wives and mothers was impressed upon me first by Dot herself during our first two-hour interview which took place before I had seen her customers' responses to the pilot questionnaire. In posing the question, "What do romances do better than other novels today?," I expected her to concern herself in her answer with the characteristics of the plot and the manner in which the story evolved. To my surprise, Dot took my query about "doing" as a transitive question about the *effects* of romances on the people who read them. She responded to my question with a long and puzzling answer that I found difficult to interpret at this early stage of our discussions. It seems wise to let Dot speak for herself here because her response introduced a number of themes that appeared again and again in my subsequent talks with other readers. My question prompted the following careful meditation:

> It's an innocuous thing. If it had to be . . . pills or drinks, this is harmful. They're very aware of this. Most of the women are mothers. And they're aware of that kind of thing. And reading is something they would like to generate in their children also. Seeing the parents reading is . . . just something that I feel they think the children should see them doing. . . . I've got a woman with teenage boys here who says "you've got books like . . . you've just got oodles of da . . . da . . . da . . . [counting an imaginary stack of books]." She says, "Now when you ask Mother to buy you something, you don't stop and think how many things you have. So this is Mother's and it is my money." Very, almost defensive. But I think they get that from their fathers. I think they heard their fathers sometime or other saying, "Hey, you're spending an awful lot of money on books aren't you?" You know for a long time, my ladies hid 'em. They would hide their books; literally hide their books. And they'd say, "Oh, if my husband [we have distinctive blue sacks], if my husband sees this blue sack coming in the house. . . ." And you know, I'd say, "Well really, you're a big girl. Do you really feel like you have to be very defensive?" A while ago, I would not have thought that way. I would have thought, "Oh, Dan is going to hit the ceiling." For a while Dan was not thrilled that I was reading a lot. Because I think men do feel threatened. They want their wife to be in the room with them. And I think my body is in the room but the rest of me is not (when I am reading).[1]

Only when Dot arrived at her last observation about reading and its ability to transport her out of her living room did I begin to understand that the real answer to my question, which she never mentioned and which was the link between reading, pills, and drinks, was actually the single word, "escape," a word that would later appear on so many of the questionnaires. She subsequently explained that romance novels provide escape just as Darvon and alcohol do for other women. Whereas the latter are harmful to both women and their families, Dot believes romance reading is "an innocuous thing." As she commented to me in another interview, romance reading is a habit that is not very different from "an addiction."

Although some of the other Smithton women expressed uneasiness about the suitability of the addiction analogy, as did Dot in another interview, nearly all of the original sixteen who participated in lengthy conversations agreed that one of their principal goals in reading was their desire to do something *different* from their daily routine. That claim was borne out by their answers to the open-ended question about the functions of romance reading. At this point, it seems worth quoting a few of those fourteen replies that expressly volunteered the ideas of escape and release. The Smithton readers explained the power of the romance in the following way:

They are light reading—escape literature—I can put down and pick up effortlessly.

Everyone is always under so much pressure. They like books that let them escape.

Escapism.

I guess I feel there is enough "reality" in the world and reading is a means of escape for me.

Because it is an Escape [sic], and we can dream and pretend that it is our life.

I'm able to escape the harsh world for a few hours a day.

They always seem an escape and they usually turn out the way you wish life really was.

The response of the Smithton women is apparently not an unusual one. Indeed, the advertising campaigns of three of the houses that have conducted extensive market-research studies all emphasize the themes of relaxation and escape. Potential readers of Coventry Romances, for example, have been told in coupon ads that "month after month Coventry Romances offer you a beautiful new escape route into historical times when love and honor ruled the heart and mind."[2] Similarly, the Silhouette television advertisements featuring Ricardo Montalban asserted that "the beautiful ending makes you feel so good" and that romances "soothe away the tensions of the day." Montalban also touted the value of "escaping" into faraway places and exotic locales. Harlequin once mounted a travel sweepstakes campaign offering as prizes "escape vacations" to romantic places. In addition, they included within the books themselves an advertising page that described Harlequins as "the books that let you escape into the wonderful world of romance! Trips to exotic places . . . interesting places . . . meeting memorable people . . . the excitement of love. . . . These are integral parts of Harlequin Romances—the heartwarming novels read by women everywhere."[3] Fawcett, too, seems to have discovered the escape function of romance fiction, for Daisy Maryles has reported that the company found in in-depth interviewing that "romances were read for relaxation and to enable [women] to better cope with the routine aspects of life."[4]

Reading to escape the present is neither a new behavior nor one peculiar to women who read romances. In fact, as Richard Hoggart demonstrated in 1957, English working-class people have long "regarded art as escape, as something enjoyed but not assumed to have much connection with the matter of daily life."[5] Within this sort of aesthetic, he continues, art is conceived as "marginal, as 'fun,' " as something "for you to *use*." In further elaborating on this notion of fictional escape, D. W. Harding has made the related observation that the word is most often used in criticism as a term of disparagement to refer to an activity that the evaluator believes has no merit in and of itself. "If its intrinsic appeal is high," he remarks, "in relation to its compensatory appeal or the mere relief it promises, then the term escape is not generally used."[6] Harding argues, moreover, on the basis of studies conducted in the 1930s, that "the compensatory appeal predominates mainly in states of depression or irritation, whether they arise from work or other causes."[7] It is interesting to note that the explanations employed by Dot and her women to interpret their romance reading for themselves are thus representative in a general way of a form of behavior common in an industrialized society where work is clearly distinguished from and more highly valued than leisure despite the fact that individual labor is often routinized, regimented, and minimally challenging.[8] It is equally essential to add, however, that although the women will use the word "escape" to explain their reading behavior, if given another comparable choice that does not carry the connotations of disparagement, they will choose the more favorable sounding explanation. To understand why, it will be helpful to follow Dot's comments more closely.

In returning to her definition of the appeal of romance fiction—a definition that is a highly condensed version of a commonly experienced process of explanation, doubt, and defensive justification—it becomes clear that romance novels perform this compensatory function for women because they use them to diversify the pace and character of their habitual existence. Dot makes it clear, however, that the women are also troubled about the propriety of indulging in such an obviously pleasurable activity. Their doubts are often cultivated into a full-grown feeling of guilt by husbands and children who object to this activity because it draws the women's attention away from the immediate family circle. As Dot later noted, although some women can explain to their families that a desire for a new toy or gadget is no different from a desire to read a new romantic novel, a far greater number of them have found it necessary to hide the evidence of their self-indulgence. In an effort to combat both the resentment of others and their own feelings of shame about their "hedonist" behavior, the women have worked out a complex rationalization for romance reading that not only asserts their equal right to pleasure but also legitimates the books by linking them with values more widely approved within American culture. Before turning to the pattern, however, I want to elaborate on the concept of escape itself and the reasons for its ability to produce such resentment and guilt in the first place.

Both the escape response and the relaxation response on the second questionnaire immediately raise other questions. Relaxation implies a reduction in the state of tension produced by prior conditions, whereas escape obviously suggests flight from one state of being to another more desirable one.[9] To understand the sense of the romance experience, then, as it is enjoyed by those who consider it a welcome change in their day-to-day existence, it becomes necessary to situate it within a larger temporal context and to specify precisely how the act of reading manages to create that feeling of change and differentiation so highly valued by these readers.

In attending to the women's comments about the worth of romance reading, I was particularly struck by the fact that they tended to use the word escape in two distinct ways. On the one hand, they used the term literally to describe the act of denying the present, which they believe they accomplish each time they begin to read a book and are drawn into its story. On the other hand, they used the word in a more figurative fashion to give substance to the somewhat vague but nonetheless intense sense of relief they experience by identifying with a heroine whose life does not resemble their own in certain crucial aspects. I think it important to reproduce this subtle distinction as accurately as possible because it indicates that romance reading releases women from their present pressing concerns in two different but related ways.

Dot, for example, went on to elaborate more fully in the conversation quoted above about why so many husbands seem to feel threatened by their wives' reading activities. After declaring with delight that when she reads her body is in the room but she herself is not, she said, "I think this is the case with the other women." She continued, "I think men cannot do that unless they themselves are readers. I don't think men are *ever* a part of anything even if it's television." "They are never really out of their body either," she added. "I don't care if it's a football game; I think they are always consciously aware of where they are." Her triumphant conclusion, "but I think a woman in a book isn't," indicates that Dot is aware that reading not only demands a high level of attention but also draws the individual *into* the book because it requires her participation. Although she is not sure what it is about the book that prompts this absorption, she is quite sure that television viewing and film watching are different. In adding immediately that "for some reason, a lot of men feel threatened by this, very, very much threatened," Dot suggested that the men's resentment has little to do with the kinds of books their wives are reading and more to do with the simple fact of the activity itself and its capacity to absorb the participants' entire attention.

These tentative observations were later corroborated in the conversations I had with other readers. Ellen, for instance, a former airline stewardess, now married and taking care of her home, indicated that she also reads for "entertainment and escape." However, she added, her husband sometimes objects to her reading because he wants her to watch the same television show he has selected. She "hates" this, she said, because she does not like the kinds of programs on television today. She is delighted when he gets a business call in the evening because her husband's preoccupation with his caller permits her to go back to her book.

Penny, another housewife in her middle thirties, also indicated that her husband "resents it" if she reads too much. "He feels shut out," she explained, "but there is nothing on TV I enjoy." Like Ellen's husband, Penny's spouse also wants her to watch television with him. Susan, a woman in her fifties, also "read[s] to escape" and related with almost no bitterness that her husband will not permit her to continue reading when he is ready to go to sleep. She seems to regret rather than resent this only because it limits the amount of time she can spend in an activity she finds enjoyable. Indeed, she went on in our conversation to explain that she occasionally gives herself "a very special treat" when she is "tired of housework." "I take the whole day off," she said, "to read."

This theme of romance reading as a special gift a woman gives herself dominated most of the interviews. The Smithton women stressed the privacy of the act and the fact that it enables them to focus their attention on a single object that can provide pleasure for themselves alone. Interestingly enough, Robert Escarpit has noted in related fashion that reading is at once "social and asocial" because "it temporarily suppresses the individual's relations with his [sic] universe to construct new ones with the universe of the work."[10] Unlike television viewing, which is a very social activity undertaken in the presence of others and which permits simultaneous conversation and personal interaction, silent reading requires the reader to block out the surrounding world and to give consideration to other people and to another time. It might be said, then, that the characters and events of romance fiction populate the woman's consciousness even as she withdraws from the familiar social scene of her daily ministrations.

I use the word ministrations deliberately here because the Smithton women explained to me that they are not trying to escape their husbands and children "per se" when they read. Rather, what reading takes them away from, they believe, is the psychologically demanding and emotionally draining task of attending to the physical and affective needs of their families, a task that is solely and peculiarly theirs. In other words, these women, who have been educated to believe that females are especially and naturally attuned to the emotional requirements of others and who are very proud of their abilities to communicate with and to serve the members of their families, value reading precisely because it is an intensely private act. Not only is the activity private, however, but it also enables them to suspend temporarily those familial relationships and to throw up a screen between themselves and the arena where they are required to do most of their relating to others.

It was Dot who first advised me about this phenomenon. Her lengthy commentary, transcribed below, enabled me to listen carefully to the other readers' discussions of escape and to hear the distinction nearly all of them made between escape from their families, which they believe they do *not* do, and escape from the heavy responsibilities and duties of the roles of wife and mother, which they admit they do out of emotional need and necessity. Dot explained their activity, for instance, by paraphrasing the thought process she believes goes on in her customers' minds. "Hey," they say, "this is what I want to do and I'm gonna do it. This is for me. I'm doin' for you all the time. Now leave me, just leave me alone. Let me have my time, my space. Let me do what I want to do. This isn't hurting you. I'm not poaching on you in any way." She then went onto elaborate about her own duties as a mother and wife:

> As a mother, I have run 'em to the orthodontist. I have run 'em to the swimming pool. I have run 'em to baton twirling lessons. I have run up to school because they forgot their lunch. You know, I mean, really! And you do it. And it isn't that you begrudge it. That isn't it. Then my husband would walk in the door and he'd say, "Well, what did you do today?" You know, it was like, "Well, tell me how you spent the last eight hours, because I've been out working." And I finally got to the point where I would say, "Well, I read four books, and I did all the wash and got the meal on the table and the beds are all made, and the house is tidy." And I would get defensive like, "So what do you call all this? Why should I have to tell you because I certainly don't ask you what you did for eight hours, step by step."—But their husbands do do that. We've compared notes. They hit the house and it's like "Well all right, I've been out earning a living. Now what have you been doin' with your time?" And you begin to be feeling, "Now really, why is he questioning me?"

Romance reading, it would seem, at least for Dot and many of her customers, is a strategy with a double purpose. As an activity, it so engages their attention that it enables them to deny their physical presence in an environment associated with responsibilities that are acutely felt and occasionally experienced as too onerous to bear. Reading, in this sense, connotes a free space where they feel liberated from the need to perform duties that they otherwise willingly accept as their own. At the same time, by carefully choosing stories that make them feel particularly happy, they escape figuratively into a fairy tale where a heroine's similar needs are adequately met. As a result, they vicariously attend to their own requirements as independent individuals who require emotional sustenance and solicitude.

Angie's account of her favorite reading time graphically represents the significance of romance reading as a tool to help insure a woman's sense of emotional well-being. "I like it," she says, "when my husband—he's an insurance salesman—goes out in the evening on house calls. Because then I have two hours just to totally relax." She continued, "I love to settle in a hot bath with a good book. That's really great." We might conclude, then, that reading a romance is a regressive experience for these women in the sense that for the duration of the time devoted to it they feel gratified and content. This feeling of pleasure seems to derive from their identification with a heroine whom they believe is deeply appreciated and tenderly cared for by another. Somewhat paradoxically, however, they also seem to value the sense of self-sufficiency they experience as a consequence of the knowledge that they are capable of making themselves feel good.

Nancy Chodorow's observations about the social structure of the American family in the twentieth century help to illuminate the context that creates both the feminine need for emotional support and validation and the varied strategies that have evolved to meet it. As Chodorow points out, most recent studies of the family agree that women traditionally reproduce people, as she says, "physically in their housework and child care, psychologically in their emotional support of husbands and their maternal relation to sons and daughters."[11] This state of affairs occurs, these studies maintain, because women alone are held responsible for home maintenance and early child care. Ann Oakley's 1971 study of forty London housewives, for instance, led her to the following conclusion: "In the housekeeping role the servicing function is far more central than the productive or creative one. In the roles of wife and mother, also, the image of women as services of men's and children's needs is prominent: women 'service' the labor force by catering to the physical needs of men (workers) and by raising children (the next generation of workers) so that the men are free *from* child-socialization and free *to* work outside the home."[12] This social fact, documented also by Mirra Komarovsky, Helena Lopata, and others, is reinforced ideologically by the widespread belief that females are *naturally* nurturant and generous, more selfless than men, and, therefore, cheerfully self-abnegating. A good wife and mother, it is assumed, will have no difficulty meeting the challenge of providing all of the labor necessary to maintain a family's physical existence including the cleaning of its quarters, the acquisition and preparation of its food, and the purchase, repair, and upkeep of its clothes, even while she masterfully discerns and supplies individual members' psychological needs.[13] A woman's interests, this version of "the female mystique" maintains, are exactly congruent with those of her husband and children. In serving them, she also serves herself.[14]

As Chodorow notes, not only are the women expected to perform this extraordinarily demanding task, but they are also supposed to be capable of executing it without being formally "reproduced" and supported themselves. "What is . . . often hidden, in generalizations about the family as an emotional refuge," she cautions, "is that in the family as it is currently constituted no one supports and reconstitutes women affectively and emotionally—either women working in the home or women working in the paid labor force."[15] Although she admits, of course, that the accident of individual marriage occasionally provides a woman with an unusually nurturant and "domestic" husband, her principal argument is that as a social institution the contemporary family contains no role whose principal task is the reproduction and emotional support of the wife and mother. "There is a fundamental asymmetry in daily reproduction," Chodorow concludes, "men are socially and psychologically reproduced by women, but women are reproduced (or not) largely by themselves."[16]

That this lack of emotional nurturance combined with the high costs of lavishing constant attention on others is the primary motivation behind the desire to lose the self in a book was made especially clear to me in a group conversation that occurred late in my stay in Smithton. The discussion involved Dot, one of her customers, Ann, who is married and in her thirties, and Dot's unmarried, twenty-three-year-old daughter, Kit. In response to my question, "Can you tell me what you escape from?", Dot and Ann together explained that reading keeps them from being overwhelmed by expectations and limitations. It seems advisable to include their entire conversation here, for it specifies rather precisely the source of those felt demands:

DOT: All right, there are pressures. Meeting your bills, meeting whatever standards or requirements your husband has for you or whatever your children have for you.

ANN: Or that you feel you should have. Like doing the housework just so.

DOT: And they do come to you with problems. Maybe they don't want you to—let's see—maybe they don't want you to solve it, but they certainly want to unload on you. You know. Or they say, "Hey, I've got this problem."

ANN: Those pressures build up.

DOT: Yeah, it's pressures.

ANN: You should be able to go to one of those good old—like the MGM musicals and just . . .

DOT: True.

ANN: Or one of those romantic stories and cry a little bit and relieve the pressure and—a legitimate excuse to cry and relieve some of the pressure build-up and not be laughed at.

DOT: That's true.

ANN: And you don't find that much anymore. I've had to go to books for it.

DOT: This is better than psychiatry.

ANN: Because I cry over books. I get wrapped up in them.

DOT: I do too. I sob in books! Oh yes. I think that's escape. Now I'm not gonna say I've got to escape my husband by reading. No.

ANN: No.

DOT: Or that I'm gonna escape my kids by getting my nose in a book. It isn't any one of those things. It's just—it's pressures that evolve from being what you are.

KIT: In this society.

DOT: And people do pressure you. Inadvertently, maybe.

ANN: Yes, it's being more and more restrictive. You can't do this and you can't do that.[17]

This conversation revealed that these women believe romance reading enables them to relieve tensions, to diffuse resentment, and to indulge in a fantasy that provides them with good feelings that seem to endure after they return to their roles as wives and mothers. Romance fiction, as they experience it, is, therefore, *compensatory literature*. It supplies them with an important emotional release that is proscribed in daily life because the social role with which they identify themselves leaves little room for guiltless, self-interested pursuit of individual pleasure. Indeed, the search for emotional gratification was the one theme common to all of the women's observations about the function of romance reading. Maureen, for instance, a young mother of two intellectually gifted children, volunteered, "I especially like to read when I'm depressed." When asked what usually caused her depression, she commented that it could be all kinds of things. Later she added that romances were comforting after her children had been especially demanding and she felt she needed time to herself.

In further discussing the lack of institutionalized emotional support suffered by contemporary American women, Chodorow has observed that in many preindustrial societies women formed their own social networks through which they supported and reconstituted one another.[18] Many of these networks found secondary institutional support in the local church while others simply operated as informal neighborhood societies. In either case, the networks provided individual women with the opportunity to abandon temporarily their stance as the family's self-sufficient emotional provider. They could then adopt a more passive role through which they received the attention, sympathy, and encouragement of other women. With the increasing suburbanization of women, however, and the concomitant secularization of the culture at large, these communities became exceedingly difficult to maintain. The principal effect was the even more resolute isolation of women within their domestic environment. Indeed, both Oakley in Great Britain and Lopata in the United States have discovered that one of the features housewives dislike most about their role is its isolation and resulting loneliness.[19]

I introduce Chodorow's observations here in order to suggest that through romance reading the Smithton women are providing themselves with another kind of female community capable of rendering the so desperately needed affective support. This community seems not to operate on an immediate local level although there are signs, both in Smithton and nationally, that romance readers are learning the pleasures of regular discussions of books with other women.[20] Nonetheless, during the early group discussions with Dot and her readers I was surprised to discover that very few of her customers knew each other. In fact, most of them had never been formally introduced although they recognized one another as customers of Dot. I soon learned that the women rarely, if ever, discussed romances with more than one or two individuals. Although many commented that they talked about the books with a sister, neighbor, or with their mothers, very few did so on a regular or extended basis. Indeed, the most striking feature of the interview sessions was the delight with which they discovered common experiences, preferences, and distastes. As one woman exclaimed in the middle of a discussion, "We were never stimulated before into thinking why we like [the novels]. Your asking makes us think why we do this. I had no idea other people had the same ideas I do."

The romance community, then, is not an actual group functioning at the local level. Rather, it is a huge, ill-defined network composed of readers on the one hand and authors on the other. Although it performs some of the same functions carried out by older neighborhood groups, this female community is mediated by the distances of modern mass publishing. Despite the distance, the Smithton women feel personally connected to their favorite authors because they are convinced that these writers know how to make them happy. Many volunteered information about favorite authors even before they would discuss specific books or heroines. All expressed admiration for their favorite writers and indicated that they were especially curious about their private lives. Three-fourths of the group of sixteen had made special trips to autographing sessions to see and express their gratitude to the women who had given them so much pleasure. The authors reciprocate this feeling of gratitude and seem genuinely interested in pleasing their readers. Many are themselves romance readers and, as a consequence, they, too, often have definite opinions about the particular writers who know how to make the reading experience truly enjoyable.[21]

It seems highly probable that in repetitively reading and writing romances, these women are participating in a collectively elaborated female fantasy that unfailingly ends at the precise moment when the heroine is gathered into the arms of the hero who declares his intention to protect her forever because of his desperate love and need for her. These women are telling themselves a story whose central vision is one of total surrender where all danger has been expunged, thus permitting the heroine to relinquish self-control. Passivity *is* at the heart of the romance experience in the sense that the final goal of each narrative is the creation of that perfect union where the ideal male, who is masculine and strong yet nurturant too, finally recognizes the intrinsic worth of the heroine. Thereafter, she is required to do nothing more than *exist* as the center of this paragon's attention. Romantic escape is, therefore, a temporary but literal denial of the demands women recognize as an integral part of their roles as nurturing wives and mothers. It is also a figurative journey to a utopian state of total receptiveness where the reader, as a result of her identification with the heroine, feels herself the *object* of someone else's attention and solicitude. Ultimately, the romance permits its reader the experience of feeling cared for and the sense of having been reconstituted affectively, even if both are lived only vicariously.

Dot's readers openly admit that parts of the romantic universe little resemble the world as they know it. When asked by the questionnaire how closely the fictional characters resemble the people they meet in real life, twenty-two answered "they are not at all similar," eighteen checked "they are somewhat similar," and two asserted that "they are very similar." None of Dot's customers believed that romantic characters are "almost identical" to those they meet daily.[22] In a related set of responses, twenty-three revealed that they consider the events in romances to be "not at all similar" to those occurring in real life. An additional eighteen said that the two sets of events are "somewhat similar," while only one checked "very similar."

It is interesting to note, however, that when the questionnaire asked them to compare the heroine's reactions and feelings with their own, only thirteen saw no resemblance whatsoever, while twenty-two believed that the heroine's feelings "are somewhat like mine." Five women did not answer the question. The general shift from perceptions of no similarity to detection of some resemblance suggests that Dot's readers believe that the heroine is more realistically portrayed than other characters. At the very least, they recognize something of themselves in her feelings and responses. Thus while the lack of similarity between events in the fantasy realm and those in the real world seems to guarantee a reading experience that is "escapist," emotional identification with the central character also insures that the experience will be an affectively significant one for the reader.

These conclusions are supported by comments about the nature of escape reading culled from the interviews. Jill, a very young mother of two, who had also begun to write her own romance, commented, for example, that "we read books so we won't cry." When asked to elaborate, she responded only that romances portray the world as "I would like it to be, not as it really is." In discussing why she preferred historicals to contemporary romances, Susan explained that "the characters shouldn't be like now because then you couldn't read to escape." "I don't want to read about people who have all the problems of today's world," she added. Her sentiments were echoed by Joy who mentioned in her discussion of "bad romances" that while "perfection's not the main thing," she still hates to see an author "dwelling on handicaps or disfigurements." "I find that distasteful and depressing," she explained. This sort of desire to encounter only idealized images is carried over even into meetings with romance authors. Several told of their disappointment at meeting a favorite writer at an autograph session who was neither pretty nor attractively dressed. All agreed, however, that Kathleen Woodiwiss is the ideal romance author because she is pretty, petite, feminine, and always elegantly turned out.

When I pursued this unwillingness to read about ugliness, despair, or serious human problems with Dot, she indignantly responded, "Why should we read depressing stuff when we have so much responsibility?" Ann made a similar remark, mentioning that she particularly dislikes books that attribute the hero's "nastiness" toward the heroine to a bad love affair that soured him on other women. When I asked her for her reasons, she said, "because *we've* been through it, we've been ditched, and it didn't sour us!" This comment led immediately to the further observation, "Optimistic! That's what I like in a book. An optimistic plot. I get sick of pessimism all the time."

Her distinction between optimistic and pessimistic stories recurred during several of the interviews, especially during discussions of the difference between romances and other books. At least four of the women mentioned Colleen McCullough's best-selling novel, *The Thorn Birds*, as a good example of a tale that technically qualified as a romance but that all dislike because it was too "depressing." When urged to specify what made the story pessimistic, none cited specific events in the plot or the death of the hero. Rather, they referred to the general tenor of the story and to the fact that the characters were poor. "Too much suffering," one reader concluded. In similarly discussing a writer whose books she never enjoys, Dot also mentioned the problem of the depressing romance and elaborated on her usual response to such a story. She described her typical argument with herself as follows:

"Well, Dorothy, you were absolutely, physically exhausted, mentally exhausted because everything was down—it was depressing." And I'd get through it and it was excellently written but everyone worked in the coal mines. They were poor as church mice. They couldn't make ends meet.

Somebody was raped, an illegitimate kid. By the time I got through, I said, "What am I reading this for? This is dumb." So I quit.

Dot's sentiments were echoed by Ann when she volunteered the information that she dislikes historical romances set in Ireland, "because they always mention the potato famine" and "I tend to get depressed about that."

In a related discussion, Dot's daughter, Kit, observed that an unhappy ending is the most depressing thing that can happen in a romance. She believes, in fact, as does nearly everyone else, that an unhappy ending excludes a novel that is otherwise a romantic love story from the romance category. Kit is only one of the many who insist on reading the endings of the stories *before* they buy them to insure that they will not be saddened by emotionally investing in the tale of a heroine only to discover that events do not resolve themselves as they should. Although this latter kind of intolerance for ambiguity and unhappiness is particularly extreme, it is indicative of a tendency among Dot's customers to avoid any kind of reading matter that does not conform to their rigid requirements for "optimism" and escapist stories. Romances are valuable to them in proportion to their lack of resemblance to the real world. They choose their romances carefully in an attempt to assure themselves of a reading experience that will make them feel happy and hold out the promise of utopian bliss, a state they willingly acknowledge to be rare in the real world but one, nevertheless, that they do not want to relinquish as a conceptual possibility.

ENDNOTES

1. See chap. 2, n. 5, of *Reading the Romance* for the method of citing spoken quotations in this chapter and elsewhere in the text.

2. These coupon ads appeared sporadically in national newspapers throughout the spring and summer of 1980.

3. Neels, Betty. *Cruise to a Wedding*. Toronto: Harlequin Books, Harlequin Salutes Edition, 1980, p. 190.

4. Maryles, Daisy. "Fawcett Launches Romance Imprint with Brand Marketing Techniques." *Publishers Weekly*, 3 September 1979, p. 70.

5. Hoggart, Richard. *The Uses of Literacy: Changing Patterns in English Mass Culture*. Fair Lawn, N.J.: Essential Books, 1957, p. 196.

6. Harding, D. W. "The Notion of 'Escape' in Fiction and Entertainment." *Oxford Review* 4 (Hilary 1967), p. 24.

7. Ibid., p. 25.

8. For discussions of the growth of the reading public and the popular press, see Williams, Raymond, *The Long Revolution*, New York: Columbia University Press, 1961, pp. 156–213, and Altick, Richard, *The English Common Reader: A Social History of the Mass Reading Public, 1800–1900*. Chicago: University of Chicago Press, 1957, passim.

9. As Robert Escarpit has observed, "there are a thousand ways to escape and it is essential to know from what and toward what we are escaping." *The Sociology of Literature*. Translated by Ernest Pick. Painesville, Ohio: Lake Erie College Press, 1965, p. 91.

10. Escarpit, ibid., p. 88. Although Dot's observations are not couched in academic language, they are really no different from Escarpit's similar observation that "reading is the supreme solitary occupation." He continues that "the man [sic] who reads does not speak, does not act, cuts himself away from society, isolates himself from the world which surrounds him . . . reading allows the senses no margin of liberty. It absorbs the entire conscious mind, making the reader powerless to act" (p. 88). For a detailed discussion of the different demands made upon an individual by reading and radio listening, see Lazarsfeld, Paul F., *Radio and the Printed Page: An Introduction to the Study of Radio and Its Role in the Communication of Ideas.* New York: Duell, Sloan and Pearce, 1940, pp. 170–79.

11. Chodorow, Nancy. *The Reproduction of Mothering: Psychoanalysis and the Sociology of Gender.* Berkeley: University of California Press, 1978, p. 36.

12. Oakley, Ann. *The Sociology of Housework.* New York: Pantheon Books, 1974, p. 179. See also Oakley, Ann, *Woman's Work: The Housewife, Past and Present.* New York: Vintage Books, 1976, pp. 60–155; McDonough, Roisin, and Rachael Harrison, "Patriarchy and Relations of Production," In *Feminism and Materialism: Women and Modes of Production,* edited by Annette Kuhn and AnnMarie Wolpe, London: Routledge and Kegan Paul, 1978, pp. 11–41; Kuhn, Annette, "Structures of Patriarchy and Capitalism in the Family." In *Feminism and Materialism: Women and Modes of Production,* edited by Annette Kuhn and AnnMarie Wolpe, London: Routledge and Kegan Paul, 1978, pp. 42–67; Sacks, Karen, "Engels Revisited: Women, the Organization of Production, and Private Property." In *Women, Culture and Society,* edited by Michelle Zimbalist Rosaldo and Louise Lamphere, Stanford: Stanford University Press, 1974, pp. 207–22; and Lopata, Helena Znaniecki, *Occupation: Housewife.* New York: Oxford University Press, 1971, passim.

13. In addition to Lopata, see Komarovsky, Mirra. *Blue-Collar Marriage.* 1962. Reprint. New York: Random House, 1964; Myrdal, Alva and Viola Klein. *Women's Two Roles: Home and Work.* 2d ed. London: Routledge and Kegan Paul, 1968; Friedan, Betty, *The Feminine Mystique.* New York: W. W. Norton and Co., 1963; Mitchell, Juliet. *Woman's Estate.* New York: Pantheon Books, 1971; and Steinmann, Ann, "A Study of the Concept of the Feminine Role of 51 Middle-Class American Families." *Genetic Psychology Monographs* 67 (1963): 275–352.

14. With respect to this view of woman as a *natural* wife and mother, Dorothy Dinnerstein has observed that women are treated as "natural resources to be mined, reaped, used up without concern for their future fate." *The Mermaid and the Minotaur: Sexual Arrangements and Human Malaise.* New York: Harper and Row, 1976, p. 101.

15. Chodorow, *The Reproduction of Mothering,* p. 36.

16. Ibid.

17. It is worth remarking here that the feeling that housework ought to be done according to some abstract standard is apparently common to many women who work in the home. For a discussion of these standards, their origins in the generally unsupervised nature of housework, and the guilt they produce in the women who invariably feel they seldom "measure up," see Oakley, *The Sociology of Housework,* pp. 100–112.

18. Chodorow, *The Reproduction of Mothering,* p. 36. For studies of contemporary working-class versions of these networks, see Stack, Carol, *All Our Kin: Strategies for Survival in a Black Community.* New York: Harper and Row, 1974; Young, Michael and Peter Willmott. *Family and Kinship in East London.* London: Penguin Books, 1966; and Lamphere, Louise, "Strategies, Cooperation, and Conflict among Women in Domestic Groups." In *Women, Culture, and Society,* edited by Michelle Zimbalist Rosaldo and Louise Lamphere, pp. 97–112. Stanford: Stanford University Press, 1974.

19. Oakley, *The Sociology of Housework,* pp. 52–54, 75, 88–92; Oakley, *Woman's Work,* pp. 101–2; Lopata, *Occupation Housewife,* pp. 36, 244–45.

20. A few months before I arrived in Smithton, several of Dot's customers expressed an interest in getting together with other romance readers. Accord-

ingly, Dot arranged an informal gathering in her home at which five to ten women socialized and discussed romances. Although the women claimed they enjoyed themselves, they have not yet met again.

21. There is ample evidence to indicate that writers' and readers' perceptions of romances are remarkably similar. This holds true not only for the subject of the story itself but also for conceptions of the romance's function. For comments very similar to Dot's, see Van Slyke, Helen. " 'Old-Fashioned' and 'Up-to-the-Minute,' " *Writer* 88 (November 1975), pp. 14–16.

22. It is important to point out here that certain behaviors of the Smithton readers indicate that they actually hold contradictory attitudes about the realism of the romance. Although they admit the stories are unreal they also claim that they learn about history and geography from their reading.

PART FOUR

Consumption and Social Inequality

Thorstein Veblen
"Conspicuous Consumption"
(1899)

In what has been said of the evolution of the vicarious leisure class and its differentiation from the general body of the working classes, reference has been made to a further division of labor,—that between different servant classes. One portion of the servant class, chiefly those persons whose occupation is vicarious leisure, come to undertake a new, subsidiary range of duties—the vicarious consumption of goods. The most obvious form in which this consumption occurs is seen in the wearing of liveries and the occupation of spacious servants' quarters. Another, scarcely less obtrusive or less effective form of vicarious consumption, and a much more widely prevalent one, is the consumption of food, clothing, dwelling, and furniture by the lady and the rest of the domestic establishment.

But already at a point in economic evolution far antedating the emergence of the lady, specialised consumption of goods as an evidence of pecuniary strength had begun to work out in a more or less elaborate system. The beginning of a differentiation in consumption even antedates the appearance of anything that can fairly be called pecuniary strength. It is traceable back to the initial phase of predatory culture, and there is even a suggestion that an incipient differentiation in this respect lies back of the beginnings of the predatory life. This most primitive differentiation in the consumption of goods is like the later differentiation with which we are all so intimately familiar, in that it is largely of a ceremonial character, but unlike the latter it does not rest on a difference in accumulated wealth. The utility of consumption as an evidence of wealth is to be classed as a derivative growth. It is an adaptation to a new end, by a selective process, of a distinction previously existing and well established in men's habits of thought.

In the earlier phases of the predatory culture the only economic differentiation is a broad distinction between an honourable superior class made up of the able-bodied men on the one side, and a base inferior class of labouring women on the other. According to the ideal scheme of life in force at that time it is the office of the men to consume what the women produce. Such consumption as falls to the women is merely incidental to their work; it is a means to their continued labour, and not a consumption directed to their own comfort and fulness of life. Unproductive consumption of goods is honourable, primarily as a mark of prowess and a perquisite of human dignity; secondarily it becomes substantially honourable in itself, especially the consumption of the more desirable things. The consumption of choice articles of food, and frequently also of rare articles of adornment, becomes tabu to the women and children; and if there is a base (servile) class of men, the tabu holds also for them. With a further advance in culture this tabu may change into simple custom of a more or less rigorous character; but whatever be the theoretical basis of the distinction which is maintained, whether it be a tabu or a larger conventionality, the features of the conventional scheme of consumption do not change easily. When the quasi-peaceable stage of industry is reached, with its fundamental institution of chattel slavery, the general principle, more or less rigorously applied, is that the base, industrious class should consume only what may be necessary to their subsistence. In the nature of things, luxuries and the comforts of life belong to the leisure class. Under the tabu, certain victuals, and more particularly certain beverages, are strictly reserved for the use of the superior class.

The ceremonial differentiation of the dietary is best seen in the use of intoxicating beverages and narcotics. If these articles of consumption are costly, they are felt to be noble and honorific. Therefore the base classes, primarily the women, practice an enforced continence with respect to these stimulants, except in countries where they are obtainable at a very low cost. From archaic times down through all the length of the patriarchal régime it has been the office of the women to prepare and administer these luxuries, and it has been the perquisite of the men of gentle birth and breeding to consume them. Drunkenness and the other pathological consequences of the free use of stimulants therefore tend in their turn to become honorific, as being a mark, at the second remove, of the superior status of those who are able to afford the indulgence. Infirmities induced by over-indulgence are among some peoples freely recognised as manly attributes. It has even happened that the name for certain diseased conditions of the body arising from such an origin has passed into everyday speech as a synonym for "noble" or "gentle." It is only at a relatively early stage of culture that the symptoms of expensive vice are conventionally accepted as marks of a superior status, and so tend to become virtues and command the deference of the community; but the reputability that attaches to certain expensive vices long retains so much of its force as to appreciably lessen the disapprobation visited upon the men of the wealthy or noble class for any excessive indulgence. The same invidious distinction adds force to the current disapproval of any indulgence of this kind on the part of women, minors, and inferiors. This invidious traditional distinction has not lost its force even among the more advanced peoples of to-day. Where the example set by the leisure class retains its imperative force in the regulation of the conventionalities, it is observable that the women still in great measure practice the same traditional continence with regard to stimulants.

This characterisation of the greater continence in the use of stimulants practiced by the women of the reputable classes may seem an excessive refinement of logic at the expense of common sense. But facts within easy reach of any one who cares to know them go to say that the greater abstinence of women is in some part due to an imperative conventionality; and this conventionality is, in a general way, strongest where the patriarchal tradition—the tradition that the woman is a chattel—has retained its hold in greatest vigour. In a sense which has been greatly qualified in scope and rigour, but which has by no means lost its meaning even yet; this tradition says that the woman, being a chattel, should consume only what is necessary to her sustenance,—except so far as her further consumption contributes to the comfort or the good repute of her master. The consumption of luxuries, in the true sense, is a consumption directed to the comfort of the consumer himself, and is, therefore, a mark of the master. Any such consumption by others can take place only on a basis of sufferance. In communities where the popular habits of thought have been profoundly shaped by the patriarchal tradition we may accordingly look for survivals of the tabu on luxuries at least to the extent of a conventional deprecation of their use by the unfree and dependent class. This is more particularly true as regards certain luxuries, the use of which by the dependent class would detract sensibly from the comfort or pleasure of their masters, or which are held to be of doubtful legitimacy on other grounds. In the apprehension of the great conservative middle class of Western civilisation the use of these various stimulants is obnoxious to at least one, if not both, of these objections; and it is a fact too significant to be passed over that it is precisely among these middle classes of the Germanic culture, with their strong surviving sense of the patriarchal proprieties, that the women are to the greatest extent subject to a qualified tabu on narcotics and alcoholic beverages. With many qualifications—with more qualifications as the patriarchal tradition has gradually weakened—the general rule is felt to be right and binding that women should consume only for the benefit of their masters. The objection of course presents itself that expenditure on women's dress and household paraphernalia is an obvious exception to this rule; but it will appear in the sequel that this exception is much more obvious than substantial.

During the earlier stages of economic development, consumption of goods without stint, especially consumption of the better grades of goods,—ideally all consumption in excess of the subsistence minimum,—

pertains normally to the leisure class. This restriction tends to disappear, at least formally, after the later peaceable stage has been reached, with private ownership of goods and an industrial system based on wage labor or on the petty household economy. But during the earlier quasi-peaceable stage, when so many of the traditions through which the institution of a leisure class has affected the economic life of later times were taking form and consistency, this principle has had the force of a conventional law. It has served as the norm to which consumption has tended to conform, and any appreciable departure from it is to be regarded as an aberrant form, sure to be eliminated sooner or later in the further course of development.

The quasi-peaceable gentleman of leisure, then, not only consumes of the staff of life beyond the minimum required for subsistence and physical efficiency, but his consumption also undergoes a specialisation as regards the quality of the goods consumed. He consumes freely and of the best, in food, drink, narcotics, shelter, services, ornaments, apparel, weapons and accoutrements, amusements, amulets, and idols or divinities. In the process of gradual amelioration which takes place in the articles of his consumption, the motive principle and the proximate aim of innovation is no doubt the higher efficiency of the improved and more elaborate products for personal comfort and well-being. But that does not remain the sole purpose of their consumption. The canon of reputability is at hand and seizes upon such innovations as are, according to its standard, fit to survive. Since the consumption of these more excellent goods is an evidence of wealth, it becomes honorific; and conversely, the failure to consume in due quantity and quality becomes a mark of inferiority and demerit.

This growth of punctilious discrimination as to qualitative excellence in eating, drinking, etc., presently affects not only the manner of life, but also the training and intellectual activity of the gentleman of leisure. He is no longer simply the successful, aggressive male,—the man of strength, resource, and intrepidity. In order to avoid stultification he must also cultivate his tastes, for it now becomes incumbent on him to discriminate with some nicety between the noble and the ignoble in consumable goods. He becomes a connoisseur in creditable viands of various degrees of merit, in manly beverages and trinkets, in seemly apparel and architecture, in weapons, games, dancers, and the narcotics. This cultivation of the aesthetic faculty requires time and application, and the demands made upon the gentleman in this direction therefore tend to change his life of leisure into a more or less arduous application to the business of learning how to live a life of ostensible leisure in a becoming way. Closely related to the requirement that the gentleman must consume freely and of the right kind of goods, there is the requirement that he must know how to consume them in a seemly manner. His life of leisure must be conducted in due form. Hence arise good manners in the way pointed out in an earlier chapter. High-bred manners and ways of living are items of conformity to the norm of conspicuous leisure and conspicuous consumption.

Conspicuous consumption of valuable goods is a means of reputability to the gentleman of leisure. As wealth accumulates on his hands, his own unaided effort will not avail to sufficiently put his opulence in evidence by this method. The aid of friends and competitors is therefore brought in by resorting to the giving of valuable presents and expensive feasts and entertainments. Presents and feasts had probably another origin than that of naïve ostentation, but they acquired their utility for this purpose very early, and they have retained that character to the present; so that their utility in this respect has now long been the substantial ground on which these usages rest. Costly entertainments, such as the potlatch or the ball, are peculiarly adapted to serve this end. The competitor with whom the entertainer wishes to institute a comparison is, by this method, made to serve as a means to the end. He consumes vicariously for his host at the same time that he is a witness to the consumption of that excess of good things which his host is unable to dispose of single-handed, and he is also made to witness his host's facility in etiquette.

In the giving of costly entertainments other motives, of a more genial kind, are of course also present. The custom of festive gatherings probably originated in motives of conviviality and religion; these motives are also present in the later development, but they do not continue to be the sole motives. The latter-day leisure-class festivities and entertainments may continue in some slight degree to serve the religious need and in a higher degree the needs of recreation and conviviality, but they also serve an invidious purpose; and they serve it none the less effectually for having a colourable non-invidious ground in these more avowable motives. But the economic effect of these social amenities is not therefore lessened, either in the vicarious consumption of goods or in the exhibition of difficult and costly achievements in etiquette.

As wealth accumulates, the leisure class develops further in function and structure, and there arises a differentiation within the class. There is a more or less elaborate system of rank and grades. This differentiation is furthered by the inheritance of wealth and the consequent inheritance of gentility. With the inheritance of gentility goes the inheritance of obligatory leisure; and gentility of a sufficient potency to entail a life of leisure may be inherited without the complement of wealth required to maintain a dignified leisure. Gentle blood may be transmitted without goods enough to afford a reputably free consumption at one's ease. Hence results a class of impecunious gentlemen of leisure, incidentally referred to already. These half-caste gentlemen of leisure fall into a system of hierarchical gradations. Those who stand near the higher and the highest grades of the wealthy leisure class, in point of birth, or in point of wealth, or both, outrank the remoter-born and the pecuniarily weaker. These lower grades, especially the impecunious, or marginal, gentlemen of leisure, affiliate themselves by a system of dependence or fealty to the great ones; by so doing they gain an increment of repute, or of the means with which to lead a life of leisure, from their patron. They become his courtiers or retainers, servants; and being fed and countenanced by their patron they are indices of his rank and vicarious consumers of his superfluous wealth. Many of these affiliated gentlemen of leisure are at the same time lesser men of substance in their own right; so that some of them are scarcely at all, others only partially, to be rated as vicarious consumers. So many of them, however, as make up the retainers and hangers-on of the patron may be classed as vicarious consumers without qualification. Many of these again, and also many of the other aristocracy of less degree, have in turn attached to their persons a more or less comprehensive group of vicarious consumers in the persons of their wives and children, their servants, retainers, etc.

Throughout this graduated scheme of vicarious leisure and vicarious consumption the rule holds that these offices must be performed in some such manner, or under some such circumstance or insignia, as shall point plainly to the master to whom this leisure or consumption pertains, and to whom therefore the resulting increment of good repute of right inures. The consumption and leisure executed by these persons for their master or patron represents an investment on his part with a view to an increase of good fame. As regards feasts and largesses this is obvious enough, and the imputation of repute to the host or patron here takes place immediately, on the ground of common notoriety. Where leisure and consumption is performed vicariously by henchmen and retainers, imputation of the resulting repute to the patron is effected by their residing near his person so that it may be plain to all men from what source they draw. As the group whose good esteem is to be secured in this way grows larger, more patent means are required to indicate the imputation of merit for the leisure performed, and to this end uniforms, badges, and liveries come into vogue. The wearing of uniforms or liveries implies a considerable degree of dependence, and may even be said to be a mark of servitude, real or ostensible. The wearers of uniforms and liveries may be roughly divided into two classes—the free and the servile, or the noble and the ignoble. The services performed by them are likewise divisible into noble and ignoble. Of course the distinction is not observed with strict consistency in practice; the less debasing of the base services and the less honorific of the noble functions are not infrequently merged in the same person. But the general distinction is not on that account to be overlooked. What may add some perplexity is the fact that this fundamental distinction between noble and ignoble, which rests on the nature of the ostensible service performed, is traversed by a secondary distinction into honorific and humiliating, resting on the rank of the person for whom the service is performed or whose livery is worn. So, those offices which are by right the proper employment of the leisure class are noble; such are government, fighting, hunting, the care of arms and accoutrements, and the like,—in short, those which may be classed as ostensibly predatory employments. On the other hand, those employments which properly fall to the industrious class are ignoble; such as handicraft or other productive labour, menial services, and the like. But a base service performed for a person of very high degree may become a very honorific office; as for instance the office of a Maid of Honour or of a Lady in Waiting to the Queen, or the King's Master of the Horse or his Keeper of the Hounds. The two offices last named suggest a principle of some general bearing. Whenever, as in these cases, the menial service in question has to do directly with the primary leisure employments of fighting and hunting, it easily acquires a reflected honorific character. In this way great honour may come to attach to an employment which in its own nature belongs to the baser sort.

In the later development of peaceable industry, the usage of employing an idle corps of uniformed men-at-arms gradually lapses. Vicarious consumption by dependents bearing the insignia of their patron or master narrows down to a corps of liveried menials. In a heightened degree, therefore, the livery comes to be a badge of servitude, or rather of servility. Something of a honorific character always attached to the livery of the armed retainer, but this honorific character disappears when the livery becomes the exclusive badge of the menial. The livery becomes obnoxious to nearly all who are required to wear it. We are yet so little removed from a state of effective slavery as still to be fully sensitive to the sting of any imputation of servility. This antipathy asserts itself even in the case of the liveries or uniforms which some corporations prescribe as the distinctive dress of their employees. In this country the aversion even goes the length of discrediting—in a mild and uncertain way— those government employments, military and civil, which require the wearing of a livery or uniform.

With the disappearance of servitude, the number of vicarious consumers attached to any one gentleman tends, on the whole, to decrease. The like is of course true, and perhaps in a still higher degree, of the number of dependents who perform vicarious leisure for him. In a general way, though not wholly nor consistently, these two groups coincide. The dependent who was first delegated for these duties was the wife, or the chief wife; and, as would be expected, in the later development of the institution, when the number of persons by whom these duties are customarily performed gradually narrows, the wife remains the last. In the higher grades of society a large volume of both these kinds of service is required; and here the wife is of course still assisted in the work by a more or less numerous corps of menials. But as we descend the social scale, the point is presently reached where the duties of vicarious leisure and consumption devolve upon the wife alone. In the communities of the Western culture, this point is at present found among the lower middle class.

And here occurs a curious inversion. It is a fact of common observation that in this lower middle class there is no pretence of leisure on the part of the head of the household. Through force of circumstances it has fallen into disuse. But the middle-class wife still carries on the business of vicarious leisure, for the good name of the household and its master. In descending the social scale in any modern industrial community, the primary fact—the conspicuous leisure of the master of the household—disappears at a relatively high point. The head of the middle-class household has been reduced by economic circumstances to turn his hand to gaining a livelihood by occupations which often partake largely of the character of industry, as in the case of the ordinary business man of to-day. But the derivative fact—the vicarious leisure and consumption rendered by the wife, and the auxiliary vicarious performance of leisure by menials—remains in vogue as a conventionality which the demands of reputability will not suffer to be slighted. It is by no means an uncommon spectacle to find a man applying himself to work with the utmost assiduity, in order that his wife may in due form render for him that degree of vicarious leisure which the common sense of the time demands.

The leisure rendered by the wife in such cases is, of course, not a simple manifestation of idleness or indolence. It almost invariably occurs disguised under some form of work or household duties or social amenities, which prove on analysis to serve little or no ulterior end beyond showing that she does not and need not occupy herself with anything that is gainful or that is of substantial use. As has already been noticed under the head of manners, the greater part of the customary round of domestic cares to which the middle-class housewife gives her time and effort is of this character. Not that the results of her attention to household matters, of a decorative and mundificatory character, are not pleasing to the sense of men trained in middle-class proprieties; but the taste to which these effects of household adornment and tidiness appeal is a taste which has been formed under the selective guidance of a canon of propriety that demands just these evidences of wasted effort. The effects are pleasing to us chiefly because we have been taught to find them pleasing. There goes into these domestic duties much solicitude for a proper combination of form and colour, and for other ends that are to be classed as aesthetic in the proper sense of the term; and it is not denied that effects having some substantial aesthetic value are sometimes attained. Pretty much all that is here insisted on is that, as regards these amenities of life, the housewife's efforts are under the guidance of traditions that have been shaped by the law of conspicuously wasteful expenditure of time and substance. If beauty or comfort is achieved,— and it is a more or less fortuitous circumstance if they are,—they must be achieved by means and methods that commend themselves to the great economic law of wasted effort. The more reputable, "presentable" portion of middle-class household paraphernalia are, on the one hand, items of conspicuous consumption, and on the other hand, apparatus for putting in evidence the vicarious leisure rendered by the housewife.

The requirement of vicarious consumption at the hands of the wife continues in force even at a lower point in the pecuniary scale than the requirement of vicarious leisure. At a point below which little if any pretence of wasted effort, in ceremonial cleanness and the like, is observable, and where there is assuredly no conscious attempt at ostensible leisure, decency still requires the wife to consume some goods conspicuously for the reputability of the household and its head. So that, as the latter-day outcome of this evolution of an archaic institution, the wife, who was at the outset the drudge and chattel of the man, both in fact and in theory,—the producer of goods for him to consume,—has become the ceremonial consumer of goods which he produces. But she still quite unmistakably remains his chattel in theory; for the habitual rendering of vicarious leisure and consumption is the abiding mark of the unfree servant.

This vicarious consumption practiced by the household of the middle and lower classes can not be counted as a direct expression of the leisure-class scheme of life, since the household of this pecuniary grade does not belong within the leisure class. It is rather that the leisure-class scheme of life here comes to an expression at the second remove. The leisure class stands at the head of the social structure in point of reputability; and its manner of life and its standards of worth therefore afford the norm of reputability for the community. The observance of these standards, in some degree of approximation, becomes incumbent upon all classes lower in the scale. In modern civilised communities the lines of demarcation between social classes have grown vague and transient, and wherever this happens the norm of reputability imposed by the upper class extends its coercive influence with but slight hindrance down through the social structure to the lowest strata. The result is that the members of each stratum accept as their ideal of decency the scheme of life in vogue in the next higher stratum, and bend their energies to live up to that ideal. On pain of forfeiting their good name and their self-respect in case of failure, they must conform to the accepted code, at least in appearance.

The basis on which good repute in any highly organised industrial community ultimately rests is pecuniary strength; and the means of showing pecuniary strength, and so of gaining or retaining a good name, are leisure and a conspicuous consumption of goods. Accordingly, both of these methods are in vogue as far down the scale as it remains possible; and in the lower strata in which the two methods are employed, both offices are in great part delegated to the wife and children of the household. Lower still, where any degree of leisure, even ostensible, has become impracticable for the wife, the conspicuous consumption of goods remains and is carried on by the wife and children. The man of the household also can do something in this direction, and, indeed, he commonly does; but with a still lower descent into the levels of indigence—along the margin of the slums—the man, and presently also the children, virtually cease to consume valuable goods for appearances, and the woman remains virtually the sole exponent of the household's pecuniary decency. No class of society, not even the most abjectly poor, forgoes all customary conspicuous consumption. The last items of this category of consumption are not given up except under stress of the direct necessity. Very much of squalor and discomfort will be endured before the last trinket or the last pretence of pecuniary decency is put away. There is no class and no country that has yielded so abjectly before the pressure of physical want as to deny themselves all gratification of this higher or spiritual need.

From the foregoing survey of the growth of conspicuous leisure and consumption, it appears that the utility of both alike for the purposes of reputability lies in the element of waste that is common to both. In the one case it is a waste of time and effort, in the other it is a waste of goods. Both are methods of demonstrating the possession of wealth, and the two are conventionally accepted as equivalents. The choice between them is a question of advertising expediency simply, except so far as it may be affected by other standards of propriety, springing from a different source. On grounds of expediency the preference may be given to the one or the other at different stages of the economic development. The question is, which of the two methods will most effectively reach the persons whose convictions it is desired to affect. Usage has answered this question in different ways under different circumstances.

So long as the community or social group is small enough and compact enough to be effectually reached by common notoriety alone,— that is to say, so long as the human environment to which the individual is required to adapt himself in respect of reputability is comprised within his sphere of personal acquaintance and neighbourhood gossip,—so long the one method is about as effective as the other. Each will therefore serve about equally well during the earlier stages of social growth. But when the differentiation has gone farther and it becomes necessary to reach a wider human environment, consumption begins to hold over leisure as an ordinary means of decency. This is especially true during the later, peaceable economic stage. The means of communication and the mobility of the population now expose the individual to the observation of many persons who have no other means of judging of his reputability than the display of goods (and perhaps of breeding) which he is able to make while he is under their direct observation.

The modern organisation of industry works in the same direction also by another line. The exigencies of the modern industrial system frequently place individuals and households in juxtaposition between whom there is little contact in any other sense than that of juxtaposition. One's neighbours, mechanically speaking, often are socially not one's neighbours, or even acquaintances; and still their transient good opinion has a high degree of utility. The only practicable means of impressing one's pecuniary ability on these unsympathetic observers of one's everyday life is an unremitting demonstration of ability to pay. In the modern community there is also a more frequent attendance at large gatherings of people to whom one's everyday life is unknown; in such places as churches, theatres, ballrooms, hotels, parks, shops, and the like. In order to impress these transient observers, and to retain one's self-complacency under their observation, the signature of one's pecuniary strength should be written in characters which he who runs may read. It is evident, therefore, that the present trend of the development is in the direction of heightening the utility of conspicuous consumption as compared with leisure.

It is also noticeable that the serviceability of consumption as a means of repute, as well as the insistence on it as an element of decency, is at its best in those portions of the community where the human contact of the individual is widest and the mobility of the population is greatest. Conspicuous consumption claims a relatively larger portion of the income of the urban than the rural population, and the claim is also more imperative. The result is that, in order to keep up a decent appearance, the former habitually live hand-to-mouth to a greater extent than the latter. So it comes, for instance, that the American farmer and his wife and daughters are notoriously less modish in their dress, as well as less urbane in their manners, than the city artisan's family with an equal income. It is not that the city population is by nature much more eager for the peculiar complacency that comes of a conspicuous consumption, nor has the rural population less regard for pecuniary decency. But the provocation to this line of evidence, as well as its transient effectiveness, are more decided in the city. This method is therefore more readily resorted to, and in the struggle to outdo one another the city population push their normal standard of conspicuous consumption to a higher point, with the result that a relatively greater expenditure in this direction is required to indicate a given degree of pecuniary decency in the city. The requirement of conformity to this higher conventional standard becomes mandatory. The standard of decency is higher, class for class, and this requirement of decent appearance must be lived up to on pain of losing caste.

Consumption becomes a larger element in the standard of living in the city than in the country. Among the country population its place is to some extent taken by savings and home comforts known through the medium of neighbourhood gossip sufficiently to serve the like general purpose of pecuniary repute. These home comforts and the leisure indulged in—where the indulgence is found—are of course also in great part to be classed as items of conspicuous consumption; and much the same is to be said of the savings. The smaller amount of the savings laid by by the artisan class is no doubt due, in some measure, to the fact that in the case of the artisan the savings are a less effective means of advertisement, relative to the environment in which he is placed, than are the savings of the people living on farms and in the small villages. Among the latter, everybody's affairs, especially everybody's pecuniary status, are known to everybody else. Considered by itself simply—taken in the first degree—this added provocation to which the artisan and the urban labouring classes are exposed may not very seriously decrease the amount of savings; but in its cumulative action, through raising the standard of decent expenditure, its deterrent effect on the tendency to save cannot but be very great.

A felicitous illustration of the manner in which this canon of reputability works out its results is seen in the practice of dram-drinking, "treating," and smoking in public places, which is customary among the labourers and handicraftsmen of the towns, and among the lower middle class of the urban population generally. Journeymen printers may be named as a class among whom this form of conspicuous consumption has a great vogue, and among whom it carries with it certain well-marked consequences that are often deprecated. The peculiar habits of the class in this respect are commonly set down to some kind of an ill-defined moral deficiency with which this class is credited, or to a morally deleterious influence which their occupation is supposed to exert, in some unascertainable way, upon the men employed in it. The state of the case for the men who work in the composition and press rooms of the common run of printing-houses may be summed up as follows. Skill acquired in any printing-house or any city is easily turned to account in almost any other house or city; that is to say, the inertia due to special training is slight. Also, this occupation requires more than the average of intelligence and general information, and the men employed in it are therefore ordinarily more ready than many others to take advantage of any slight variation in the demand for their labour from one place to another. The inertia due to the home feeling is consequently also slight. At the same time the wages in the trade are high enough to make movement from place to place relatively easy. The result is a great mobility of the labour employed in printing; perhaps greater than in any other equally well-defined and considerable body of workmen. These men are constantly thrown in contact with new groups of acquaintances, with whom the relations established are transient or ephemeral, but whose good opinion is valued none the less for the time being. The human proclivity to ostentation, reenforced by sentiments of goodfellowship, leads them to spend freely in those directions which will best serve these needs. Here as elsewhere prescription seizes upon the custom as soon as it gains a vogue, and incorporates it in the accredited standard of decency. The next step is to make this standard of decency the point of departure for a new move in advance in the same direction,—for there is no merit in simple spiritless conformity to a standard of dissipation that is lived up to as a matter of course by every one in the trade.

The greater prevalence of dissipation among printers than among the average of workmen is accordingly attributable, at least in some measure, to the greater ease of movement and the more transient character of acquaintance and human contact in this trade. But the substantial ground of this high requirement in dissipation is in the last analysis no other than that same propensity for a manifestation of dominance and pecuniary decency which makes the French peasant-proprietor parsimonious and frugal, and induces the American millionaire to found colleges, hospitals and museums. If the canon of conspicuous consumption were not offset to a considerable extent by other features of human nature, alien to it, any saving should logically be impossible for a population situated as the artisan and labouring classes of the cities are at present, however high their wages or their income might be.

But there are other standards of repute and other, more or less imperative, canons of conduct, besides wealth and its manifestation, and some of these come in to accentuate or to qualify the broad, fundamental canon of conspicuous waste. Under the simple test of effectiveness for advertising, we should expect to find leisure and the conspicuous consumption of goods dividing the field of pecuniary emulation pretty evenly between them at the outset. Leisure might then be expected gradually to yield ground and tend to obsolescence as the economic development goes forward, and the community increases in size; while the conspicuous consumption of goods should gradually gain in importance, both absolutely and relatively, until it had absorbed all the available product, leaving nothing over beyond a bare livelihood. But the actual course of development has been somewhat different from this ideal scheme. Leisure held the first place at the start, and came to hold a rank very much above wasteful consumption of goods, both as a direct exponent of wealth and as an element in the standard of decency, during the quasi-peaceable culture. From that point onward, consumption has gained ground, until, at present, it unquestionably holds the primacy, though it is still far from absorbing the entire margin of production above the subsistence minimum.

The early ascendency of leisure as a means of reputability is traceable to the archaic distinction between noble and ignoble employments. Leisure is honourable and becomes imperative partly because it shows exemption from ignoble labour. The archaic differentiation into noble and ignoble classes is based on an invidious distinction between employments as honorific or debasing; and this traditional distinction grows into an imperative canon of decency during the early quasi-peaceable stage. Its ascendency is furthered by the fact that leisure is still fully as effective an evidence of wealth as consumption. Indeed, so effective is it in the relatively small and stable human environment to which the individual is exposed at that cultural stage, that, with the aid of the archaic tradition which deprecates all productive labour, it gives rise to a large impecunious leisure class, and it even tends to limit the production of the community's industry to the subsistence minimum. This extreme inhibition of industry is avoided because slave labour, working under a compulsion more rigorous than that of reputability, is forced to turn out a product in excess of the subsistence minimum of the working class. The subsequent relative decline in the use of conspicuous leisure as a basis of repute is due partly to an increasing relative effectiveness of consumption as an evidence of wealth; but in part it is traceable to another force, alien, and in some degree antagonistic, to the usage of conspicuous waste.

This alien factor is the instinct of workmanship. Other circumstances permitting, that instinct disposes men to look with favour upon productive efficiency and on whatever is of human use. It disposes them to deprecate waste of substance or effort. The instinct of workmanship is present in all men, and asserts itself even under very adverse circumstances. So that however wasteful a given expenditure may be in reality, it must at least have some colourable excuse in the way of an ostensible purpose. The manner in which, under special circumstances, the instinct eventuates in a taste for exploit and an invidious discrimination between noble and ignoble classes has been indicated in an earlier chapter. In so far as it comes into conflict with the law of conspicuous waste, the instinct of workmanship expresses itself not so much in insistence on substantial usefulness as in an abiding sense of the odiousness and aesthetic impossibility of what is obviously futile. Being of the nature of an instinctive affection, its guidance touches chiefly and immediately the obvious and apparent violations of its requirements. It is only less promptly and with less constraining force that it reaches such substantial violations of its requirements as are appreciated only upon reflection.

So long as all labour continues to be performed exclusively or usually by slaves, the baseness of all productive effort is too constantly and deterrently present in the mind of men to allow the instinct of workmanship seriously to take effect in the direction of industrial usefulness; but when the quasi-peaceable stage (with slavery and status) passes into the peaceable stage of industry (with wage labour and cash payment), the instinct comes more effectively into play. It then begins aggressively to shape men's views of what is meritorious, and asserts itself at least as an auxiliary canon of self-complacency. All extraneous considerations apart, those persons (adults) are but a vanishing minority today who harbour no inclination to the accomplishment of some end, or who are not impelled of their own motion to shape some object or fact or relation for human use. The propensity may in large measure be overborne by the more immediately constraining incentive to a reputable leisure and an avoidance of indecorous usefulness, and it may therefore work itself out in make-believe only; as for instance in "social duties," and in quasi-artistic or quasi-scholarly accomplishments, in the care and decoration of the house, in sewing-circle activity or dress reform, in proficiency at dress, cards, yachting, golf, and various sports. But the fact that it may under stress of circumstances eventuate in inanities no more disproves the presence of the instinct than the reality of the brooding instinct is disproved by inducing a hen to sit on a nestful of china eggs.

This latter-day uneasy reaching-out for some form of purposeful activity that shall at the same time not be indecorously productive of either individual or collective gain marks a difference of attitude between the modern leisure class and that of the quasi-peaceable stage. At the earlier stage, as was said above, the all-dominating institution of slavery and status acted resistlessly to discountenance exertion directed to other than naïvely predatory ends. It was still possible to find some habitual employment for the inclination to action in the way of forcible aggression or repression directed against hostile groups or against the subject classes within the group; and this served to relieve the pressure and draw off the energy of the leisure class without a resort to actually useful, or even ostensibly useful employments. The practice of hunting also served the same purpose in some degree. When the community developed into a peaceful industrial organisation, and when fuller occupation of the land had reduced the opportunities for the hunt to an inconsiderable residue, the pressure of energy seeking purposeful employment was left to find an outlet in some other direction. The ignominy which attaches to useful effort also entered upon a less acute phase with the disappearance of compulsory labour; and the instinct of workmanship then came to assert itself with more persistence and consistency.

The line of least resistance has changed in some measure, and the energy which formerly found a vent in predatory activity, now in part takes the direction of some ostensibly useful end. Ostensibly purposeless leisure has come to be deprecated, especially among that large portion of the leisure class whose plebeian origin acts to set them at variance with the tradition of the *otium cum dignitate*. But that canon of reputability which discountenances all employment that is of the nature of productive effort is still at hand, and will permit nothing beyond the most transient vogue to any employment that is substantially useful or productive. The consequence is that a change has been wrought in the conspicuous leisure practiced by the leisure class; not so much in substance as in form. A reconciliation between the two conflicting requirements is effected by a resort to make-believe. Many and intricate polite observances and social duties of a ceremonial nature are developed; many organisations are founded, with some specious object of amelioration embodied in their official style and title; there is much coming and going, and a deal of talk, to the end that the talkers may not have occasion to reflect on what is the effectual economic value of their traffic. And along with the make-believe of purposeful employment, and woven inextricably into its texture, there is commonly, if not invariably, a more or less appreciable element of purposeful effort directed to some serious end.

In the narrower sphere of vicarious leisure a similar change has gone forward. Instead of simply passing her time in visible idleness, as in the best days of the patriarchal régime, the housewife of the advanced peaceable stage applies herself assiduously to household cares. The salient features of this development of domestic service have already been indicated.

Throughout the entire evolution of conspicuous expenditure, whether of goods or of services or human life, runs the obvious implication that in order to effectually mend the consumer's good fame it must be an expenditure of superfluities. In order to be reputable it must be wasteful. No merit would accrue from the consumption of the bare necessaries of life, except by comparison with the abjectly poor who fall short even of the subsistence minimum; and no standard of expenditure could result from such a comparison, except the most prosaic and unattractive level of decency. A standard of life would still be possible which should admit of invidious comparison in other respects than that of opulence; as, for instance, a comparison in various directions in the manifestation of moral, physical, intellectual, or aesthetic force. Comparison in all these directions is in vogue to-day; and the comparison made in these respects is commonly so inextricably bound up with the pecuniary comparison as to be scarcely distinguishable from the latter. This is especially true as regards the current rating of expressions of intellectual and aesthetic force or proficiency; so that we frequently interpret as aesthetic or intellectual a difference which in substance is pecuniary only.

The use of the term "waste" is in one respect an unfortunate one. As used in the speech of everyday life the word carries an undertone of deprecation. It is here used for want of a better term that will adequately describe the same range of motives and of phenomena, and it is not to be taken in an odious sense, as implying an illegitimate expenditure of human products or of human life. In the view of economic theory the expenditure in question is no more and no less legitimate than any other expenditure. It is here called "waste" because this expenditure does not serve human life or human well-being on the whole, not because it is waste or misdirection of effort or expenditure as viewed from the standpoint of the individual consumer who chooses it. If he chooses it, that disposes of the question of its relative utility to him, as compared with other forms of consumption that would not be deprecated on account of their wastefulness. Whatever form of expenditure the consumer chooses, or whatever end he seeks in making his choice, has utility to him by virtue of his preference. As seen from the point of view of the individual consumer, the question of wastefulness does not arise within the scope of economic theory proper. The use of the word "waste" as a technical term, therefore, implies no deprecation of the motives or of the ends sought by the consumer under this canon of conspicuous waste.

But it is, on other grounds, worth nothing that the term "waste" in the language of everyday life implies deprecation of what is characterised as wasteful. This common-sense implication is itself an outcropping of the instinct of workmanship. The popular reprobation of waste goes to say that in order to be at peace with himself the common man must be able to see in any and all human effort and human enjoyment an enhancement of life and well-being on the whole. In order to meet with unqualified approval, any economic fact must approve itself under the test of impersonal usefulness—usefulness as seen from the point of view of the generically human. Relative or competitive advantage of one individual in comparison with another does not satisfy the economic conscience, and therefore competitive expenditure has not the approval of this conscience.

In strict accuracy nothing should be included under the head of conspicuous waste but such expenditure as is incurred on the ground of an invidious pecuniary comparison. But in order to bring any given item or element in under this head it is not necessary that it should be recognised as waste in this sense by the person incurring the expenditure. It frequently happens that an element of the standard of living which set out with being primarily wasteful, ends with becoming, in the apprehension of the consumer, a necessary of life; and it may in this way become as indispensable as any other item of the consumer's habitual expenditure. As items which sometimes fall under this head, and are therefore available as illustrations of the manner in which this principle applies, may be cited carpets and tapestries, silver table service, waiter's services, silk hats, starched linen, many articles of jewelry and of dress. The indispensability of these things after the habit and the convention have been formed, however, has little to say in the classification of expenditure as waste or not waste in the technical meaning of the word. The test to which all expenditure must be brought in an attempt to decide that point is the question whether it serves directly to enhance human life on the whole—whether it furthers the life process taken impersonally. For this is the basis of award of the instinct of workmanship, and that instinct is the court of final appeal in any question of economic truth or adequacy. It is a question as to the award rendered by a dispassionate common sense. The question is, therefore, not whether, under the existing circumstances of individual habit and social custom, a given expenditure conduces to the particular consumer's gratification or peace of mind; but whether, aside from acquired tastes and from the canons of usage and conventional decency, its result is a net gain in comfort or in the fulness of life. Customary expenditure must be classed under the head of waste in so far as the custom on which it rests is traceable to the habit of making an invidious pecuniary comparison—in so far as it is conceived that it could not have become customary and prescriptive without the backing of this principle of pecuniary reputability or relative economic success.

It is obviously not necessary that a given object of expenditure should be exclusively wasteful in order to come in under the category of conspicuous waste. An article may be useful and wasteful both, and its utility to the consumer may be made up of use and waste in the most varying proportions. Consumable goods, and even productive goods, generally show the two elements in combination, as constituents of their utility; although, in a general way, the element of waste tends to predominate in articles of consumption, while the contrary is true of articles designed for productive use. Even in articles which appear at first glance to serve for pure ostentation only, it is always possible to detect the presence of some, at least ostensible, useful purpose; and on the other hand, even in special machinery and tools contrived for some particular industrial process, as well as in the rudest appliances of human industry, the traces of conspicuous waste, or at least of the habit of ostentation, usually become evident on a close scrutiny. It would be hazardous to assert that a useful purpose is ever absent from the utility of any article or of any service, however obviously its prime purpose and chief element is conspicuous waste; and it would be only less hazardous to assert of any primarily useful product that the element of waste is in no way concerned in its value, immediately or remotely.

12
Pierre Bourdieu
"THE AESTHETIC SENSE AS THE SENSE OF DISTINCTION"
(1979; translation 1984)

The aesthetic disposition is one dimension of a distant, self-assured relation to the world and to others which presupposes objective assurance and distance. It is one manifestation of the system of dispositions produced by the social conditionings associated with a particular class of conditions of existence when they take the paradoxical form of the greatest freedom conceivable, at a given moment, with respect to the constraints of economic necessity. But it is also a distinctive expression of a privileged position in social space whose distinctive value is objectively established in its relationship to expressions generated from different conditions. Like every sort of taste, it unites and separates. Being the product of the conditionings associated with a particular class of conditions of existence, it unites all those who are the product of similar conditions while distinguishing them from all others. And it distinguishes in an essential way, since taste is the basis of all that one has—people and things—and all that one is for others, whereby one classifies oneself and is classified by others.

Tastes (i.e., manifested preferences) are the practical affirmation of an inevitable difference. It is no accident that, when they have to be justified, they are asserted purely negatively, by the refusal of other tastes.[1] In matters of taste, more than anywhere else, all determination is negation;[2] and tastes are perhaps first and foremost distastes, disgust provoked by horror or visceral intolerance ("sick-making") of the tastes of others. "De gustibus non est disputandum": not because "tous les goûts sont dans la nature," but because each taste feels itself to be natural—and so it almost is, being a habitus—which amounts to rejecting others as unnatural and therefore vicious. Aesthetic intolerance can be terribly violent. Aversion to different life-styles is perhaps one of the strongest barriers between the classes; class endogamy is evidence of this. The most intolerable thing for those who regard themselves as the possessors of legitimate culture is the sacrilegious reuniting of tastes which taste dictates shall be separated. This means that the games of artists and aesthetes and their struggles for the monopoly of artistic legitimacy are less innocent than they seem. At stake in every struggle over art there is also the imposition of an art of living, that is, the transmutation of an arbitrary way of living into the legitimate way of life which casts every other way of living into arbitrariness.[3] The artist's life-style is always a challenge thrown at the bourgeois life-style, which it seeks to condemn as unreal and even absurd, by a sort of practical demonstration of the emptiness of the values and powers it pursues. The neutralizing relation to the world which defines the aesthetic disposition potentially implies a subversion of the spirit of seriousness required by bourgeois investments. Like the visibly ethical judgments of those who lack the means to make art the basis of their art of living, to see the world and other people through literary reminiscences and pictorial references, the "pure" and purely aesthetic judgments of the artist and the aesthete spring from the dispositions of an ethos;[4] but because of the legitimacy which they command so long as their relationship to the dispositions and interests of a group defined by strong cultural capital and weak economic capital remains unrecognized, they provide a sort of absolute reference point in the necessarily endless play of mutually self-relativizing tastes. By a paradoxical reversal, they thereby help to legitimate the bourgeois claim to "natural distinction" as difference made absolute.

Objectively and subjectively aesthetic stances adopted in matters like cosmetics, clothing or home decoration are opportunities to experience or assert one's position in social space, as a rank to be upheld or a distance to be kept. It goes without saying that the social classes are not equally inclined and prepared to enter this game of refusal and counterrefusal; and that the strategies aimed at transforming the basic dispositions of a life-style into a system of aesthetic principles, objective differences into elective distinctions, passive options (constituted externally by the logic of the distinctive relationships) into conscious, elective choices are in fact reserved for members of the dominant class, indeed the very top bourgeoisie, and for artists, who as the inventors and professionals of the "stylization of life" are alone able to make their art of living one of the fine arts. By contrast, the entry of the petite bourgeoisie into the game of distinction is marked, inter alia, by the anxiety of exposing oneself to classification by offering to the taste of others such infallible indices of personal taste as clothes or furniture, even a simple pair of armchairs, as in one of Nathalie Sarraute's novels. As for the working classes, perhaps their sole function in the system of aesthetic positions is to serve as a foil, a negative reference point, in relation to which all aesthetics define themselves, by successive negations.[5] Ignoring or ignorant of manner and style, the "aesthetic" (in itself) of the working classes and culturally most deprived fractions of the middle classes defines as "nice," "pretty," "lovely" (rather than "beautiful") things that are already defined as such in the "aesthetic" of calendars and postcards:

a sunset, a little girl playing with a cat, a folk dance, an old master, a first communion, a children's procession. The striving toward distinction comes in with petit-bourgeois aestheticism, which delights in all the cheap substitutes for chic objects and practices—driftwood and painted pebbles, cane and raffia, "art" handicrafts and art photography.

This aestheticism defines itself against the "aesthetic" of the working classes, refusing their favorite subjects, the themes of "views," such as mountain landscapes, sunsets and woods, or souvenir photos, such as the first communion, the monument or the old master (see diagram 1). In photography, this taste prefers objects that are close to those of the popular aesthetic but semi-neutralized by more or less explicit reference to a pictorial tradition or by a visible stylistic intention combining the human picturesque (weaver at his loom, tramps quarreling, folk dance) with gratuitous form (pebbles, rope, tree bark).

It is significant that this middle-brow art par excellence finds one of its preferred subjects in one of the spectacles most characteristic of middle-brow culture (along with the circus, light opera and bull-fights), the folk dance (which is particularly appreciated by skilled workers and foremen, junior executives, clerical and commercial employees) (C.S. VII). Like the photographic recording of the social picturesque, whose populist objectivism distances the lower classes by constituting them as an object of contemplation or even commiseration or indignation, the spectacle of the "people" making a spectacle of itself, as in folk dancing, is an opportunity to experience the relationship of distant proximity, in the form of the idealized vision purveyed by aesthetic realism and populist nostalgia, which is a basic element in the relationship of the petite bourgeoisie to the working or peasant classes and their traditions. But this middle-brow aestheticism in turn serves as a foil to the most alert members of the new middle-class fractions, who reject its favored subjects, and to the secondary teachers whose aestheticism (the aestheticism of consumers, since they are relatively infrequent practitioners of photography and the other arts) purports to be able to treat any object aesthetically, with the exception of those so constituted by the middle-brow art of the petite bourgeoisie (such as the weaver and the folk dance, which are deemed merely "interesting").[6] These would-be aesthetes demonstrate by their distinctive refusals that they possess the practical mastery of the relationships between objects and groups which is the basis of all judgments of the type "Ça fait" ("It looks . . .") ("Ça fait petit-bourgeois," "Ça fait nouveau riche," etc.), without being able to go so far as to ascribe beauty to the most marked objects of the popular aesthetic (first communion) or the petit-bourgeois aesthetic (mother and child, folk dance) which the relations of structural proximity spontaneously lead them to detest.

Explicit aesthetic choices are in fact often constituted in opposition to the choices of the groups closest in social space, with whom the

Diagram 1 The aesthetic disposition in the petite bourgeoisie (the various objects are ranked for each class fraction according to the percentage saying they would make a beautiful photo).

Most choices	Independent crafts- men, shopkeepers	Clerical, junior admin. executives	Technicians	Primary teachers	New petite bourgeoisie
	sunset	sunset	sunset	sunset	sunset
	landscape	landscape	landscape	woman breast-feeding	landscape
	folk dance	folk dance	girl with cat	girl with cat	woman breast-feeding
	girl with cat	girl with cat	woman breast-feeding	landscape	girl with cat
	woman breast-feeding	woman breast-feeding	weaver	bark	bark
	weaver	old master	folk dance	weaver	weaver
	first communion	still life	still life	folk dance	still life
	old master	first communion	bark	snake	folk dance
	famous monument	bark	snake	pregnant woman	rope
	still life	monument	first communion	monument	snake
	bark of tree	weaver	monument	still life	old master
	pregnant woman	snake	metal structure	metal structure	cabbages
	metal structure	metal structure	old master	rope	pregnant woman
	snake	pregnant woman	scrap-yard	old master	metal structure
	tramps' quarrel	cabbages	rope	scrap-yard	tramps' quarrel
	wounded man	tramps' quarrel	pregnant woman	tramps' quarrel	monument
	scrap-yard	rope	cabbages	cabbages	first communion
	rope	butcher's stall	tramps' quarrel	butcher's stall	scrap-yard
	cabbages	scrap-yard	wounded man	wounded man	butcher's stall
	butcher's stall	wounded man	butcher's stall	first communion	wounded man
Fewest	car crash	car crash	car crash	car crash	car crash

competition is most direct and most immediate, and more precisely, no doubt, in relation to those choices most clearly marked by the intention (perceived as pretension) of marking distinction vis-à-vis lower groups, such as, for intellectuals, the primary teachers' Brassens, Jean Ferrat or Ferré. Thus the song, as a cultural property which (like photography) is almost universally accessible and genuinely common (since hardly anyone is not exposed at one moment or another to the "successes" of the day), calls for particular vigilance from those who intend to mark their difference. The intellectuals, artists and higher-education teachers seem to hesitate between systematic refusal of what can only be, at best, a middle-brow art, and a selective acceptance which manifests the universality of their culture and their aesthetic disposition.[7] For their part, the employers and professionals, who have little interest in the "intellectual" song, indicate their distance from ordinary songs by rejecting with disgust the most popular and most "vulgar" singers, such as Les Compagnons de la Chanson, Mireille Mathieu, Adamo or Sheila, and making an exception for the oldest and most consecrated singers (like Edith Piaf or Charles Trénet) or those closest to operetta and bel canto. But it is the middle classes who find in song (as in photography) an opportunity to manifest their artistic pretension by refusing the favorite singers of the working classes, such as Mireille Mathieu, Adamo, Charles Aznavour or Tino Rossi, and declaring their preference for the singers who endeavour to dignify this "minor" genre. That is why the primary teachers distinguish themselves most clearly from the other fractions of the petite bourgeoisie in this area, where, more easily than in the domain of legitimate art, they can invest their academic dispositions and assert their own taste in the choice of singers who offer populist poetry in the primary-school tradition, such as Jacques Douai or Brassens (who was on the syllabus of the Saint-Cloud entrance examination a few years ago).[8]

It may also be assumed that the affirmation of the omnipotence of the aesthetic gaze found among higher-education teachers, the group most inclined to say that all the objects mentioned could make a beautiful photograph and to profess their recognition of modern art or of the artistic status of the photograph, stems much more from a self-distinguishing intention than from a true aesthetic universalism. This has not escaped the most knowing avant-garde producers, who carry sufficient authority to challenge, if need be, the very dogma of the omnipotence of art,[9] and are in a position to recognize this faith as a defensive maneuver to avoid self-exposure by reckless refusals: "Who would say this: 'When I look at a picture, I'm not interested in what it represents'? Nowadays, the sort of people who don't know much about art. Saying that is typical of someone who hasn't any idea about art. Twenty years ago, I'm not even sure that twenty years ago the abstract painters would have said that; I don't think so. It's exactly what a guy says when he hasn't a clue: 'I'm not one of these old fogies, I know what counts is whether it's pretty' " (avant-garde painter, age 35). They alone, at all events, can afford the audacious imposture of refusing all refusals by recuperating, in parody or sublimation, the very objects refused by the lower-degree aestheticism. The "rehabilitation" of "vulgar" objects is more risky, but also more "profitable," the smaller the distance in social space or time, and the "horrors" of popular kitsch are easier to "recuperate" than those of petit-bourgeois imitation, just as the "abominations" of bourgeois taste can begin to be found "amusing" when they are sufficiently dated to cease to be "compromising."

The artist agrees with the "bourgeois" in one respect: he prefers naivety to "pretentiousness." The essential merit of the "common people" is that they have none of the pretensions to art (or power) which inspire the ambitions of the "petit bourgeois." Their indifference tacitly acknowledges the monopoly. That is why, in the mythology of artists and intellectuals, whose outflanking and double-negating strategies sometimes lead them back to "popular" tastes and opinions, the "people" so often play a role not unlike that of the peasantry in the conservative ideologies of the declining aristocracy.

ENDNOTES

1. Two examples, chosen from among hundreds, but paradigmatic, of explicit use of the scheme "something other than": "*La Fiancée du pirate* is one of those very true French films that are *really* satirical, *really* funny, because it does not resort to the carefully defused, prudently inoffensive comedy one finds in *La Grande Vadreuille* and *le Petit Baigneur*. . . . In short, it is *something other than* the dreary hackwork of boulevard farce" (J. L. Bory, *Le Nouvel Observateur*, 8 December 1969: italics mine). "Through distance, or at least, through difference, to endeavour to present a text on pictorial modernity *other than* the hackneyed banalities of *a certain style of art criticism*. *Between* verbose aphasia, the textual transcription of pictures, endamations of recognition, *and* the works of specialized aesthetics, perhaps *marking* some-of the ways in which conceptual, theoretical work gets to grips with contemporary plastic production" (G. Gassiot-Talabot et al., *Figurations 1960–1973* [Paris, Union générale des éditions, 1973], p. 7; italics mine).

2. This essential negativity, which is part of the very logic of the constitution of taste and its change, explains why, as Gombrich points out, "the terminology of art history was so largely built on words denoting some principle of exclusion. Most movements in art erect some new taboo, some new negative principle, such as the banishing from painting by the impressionists of all 'anecdotal' elements. The positive slogans and shibboleths which we read in artists' or critics' manifestos past or present are usually much less well defined" (E. H. Gombrich, *News and Form: Studies in the Art of the Renaissance* [London, New York, Phaidon Press, 1966], p. 89).

3. This is seen clearly in the case of the theater, which touches more directly and more overtly on the implicit or explicit principles of the art of living. Especially in the case of comedy, it presupposes common values or interests or, more precisely, a complicity and connivance based on immediate assent to the same self-evident propositions, those of the *doxa*, the totality of opinions accepted at the level of pre-reflective belief. (This explains why the institutions supplying the products, and the products themselves, are more sharply differentiated in the theater than in any other art.)

4. For an analysis of "art for art's sake" as the expression of the artistic life-style, see P. Bourdieu, "L'invention de la vie d'artiste," *Actes*, 2 (1975), 67–93.

5. This is true despite the apparent exception in which some artists return to certain popular preferences, which had a totally different meaning in a cultural configuration dominated by choices which for them would be quite improbable or even impossible. These returns to the "popular" style, which often pass for a return to the "people," are determined not by any genuine relationship to the working classes, who are generally spurned—even in idealization, which is a form of refusal—but by the internal relations of the field of artistic production or the field of the dominant class. (This point has a general validity, and one would need to examine what the writings of intellectuals on the working classes owe to the specific interests of intellectuals in struggles in which what is at stake, if not the people, is the legitimacy conferred, in certain conditions, by appearing as the spokesman for popular interests.)

6. It is in these two categories that we encounter the most marked refusal of souvenir photos ("Souvenir photos are stupid and banal"; "The main point of a photo is to preserve the images of those one loves"), of realism in painting ("A beautiful picture should reproduce what is beautiful in nature") or in photography ("For a photograph to be good, you just have to be able to recognize what it shows"), and the most resolute assertion of faith in modern painting (in refusal of the opinion: "Modern painting is just slapped on anyhow . . .").

7. One of the major limitations imposed by the list of pre-formed choices is that it does not bring out these "conflicts" and the strategies aimed at getting around them. A respondent who has, "against the grain," chosen Georges Brassens or Jacques Douai might have been able to indicate his refusal of song, while showing his "open-mindedness," by citing (with an implicit redefinition) something by Kurt Weill or an old Neapolitan song. (The France-Musique radio program of "personal selections," "Le concert égoiste," is very revealing in this respect.)

8. Saint-Cloud: second to ENS rue d'Ulm in the hierarchy of the Ecoles normales supérieures (translator).

9. This dogma is still recognized and professed in less advanced sectors of the field of artistic production, as this typical declaration shows: "However, I will say that these paintings by Gaston Planet are totally incomprehensible: I will say that I like them to be so. Not enigmatic. But entirely mute. Without points of reference. Without distractions" (Paul Rossi, Gaston Planet catalogue).

13
Douglas B. Holt
"DOES CULTURAL CAPITAL STRUCTURE AMERICAN CONSUMPTION?" (1998)*

Although consumption has, throughout history, served as a conse-quential site for the reproduction of social class boundaries, the particular characteristics of consumption that are socially consecrated and, hence, used to demarcate these boundaries have been configured in myriad ways. For example, elite lifestyles have been characterized by a rigid, formal interactional style and understated simplicity (the gentry of the eighteenth century), extravagant, fashion-conscious public socia-bility (high society in "the Gilded Age" of the late nineteenth century), informal social clubbiness (the new upper-middle class of the early twen-tieth century), and cultural refinement (the highbrow taste of urban elites in the twentieth century; see Collins 1975, pp. 187–211). But, many academics and critics now claim that in postmodern consumer societies, the United States in particular, consumption patterns no longer act to structure social classes. The massive proliferation of cultural meanings and the fragmentation of unitary identities, two primary traits of postmodern culture, have shattered straightforward correspondences between social categories and consumption patterns. So we find conser-vative, individualist arguments typical of marketing and economics (e.g., Schouten and McAlexander 1995), liberal sociological arguments (e.g., Halle 1993), and radical postmodern arguments (Baudrillard 1981), all inveighing that consumption patterns are no longer consequential to class reproduction. In such societies, critical analysis of the reproduction of social class through consumption has become an increasingly treach-erous interpretive exercise. Analyses that seek out such patterns are of-ten dismissed as essentialist or worse. But is it true that social class is no longer produced through distinctive patterns of consumption? Or, alternatively, is this relationship occluded when old theorizing is used to analyze a new social formation?

Pierre Bourdieu's (1984) theory of cultural capital and taste offers the most comprehensive and influential attempt to develop a theoretical frame-

---

* Edited for this volume.

work to plumb the social patterning of consumption in an increasingly mystified social world. Yet this theory has received a chilly reception in the United States, routinely subject to both theoretical critique and empirical refutation. This study is motivated by the premise that these criticisms have misconstrued Bourdieu's research and so have not explored fully the potential usefulness of the theory for disentangling the relationship between class and consumption in contemporary postmodern societies.

DISTINGUISHING BOURDIEU

Max Weber (1978) coined the term "social class" to capture the idea that, in addition to the economic resources described by Marx, hierarchical social strata are also expressed and reproduced through "styles of life" that vary in their honorific value. Societies segregate into different reputational groupings based not only on economic position, but also on noneconomic criteria such as morals, culture, and lifestyle that are sustained because people tend to interact with their social peers. American social class strata were first analyzed in Veblen's ([1899] 1970) bombastic essays about the leisure class, Simmel's ([1904] 1957) theory of trickle-down status imitation, and in the Lynds' studies of "Middletown," but it is the approach developed by W. Lloyd Warner and his associates in a series of widely publicized studies of the stratification of small American cities following World War II that has dominated consumer research for more than 30 years (Coleman 1983; Coleman and Rainwater 1978; Rainwater, Coleman, and Handel 1959; Warner, Meeker, and Eells 1949). Notwithstanding a variety of incisive critiques, the Warnerian approach offers an important formulation of the relationship between social class and lifestyle that is foundational for the advances made by Bourdieu. Yet the advantages of Bourdieu's theory relative to Warner have never been foregrounded, likely because Warner's social Darwinist presuppositions are directly at odds with Bourdieu's (1984) critical view of consumption patterns as a consequential site of class reproduction.

WARNER'S ANTHROPOLOGICAL APPROACH

The Warnerian approach to social class describes the primary social strata within a community by mapping the relative amount of respect and deference accorded to each group. The primary Warnerian method, evaluated participation, requires ethnographic interviews with a stratified random sample of the population of a town or small city. The interview is structured to allow informants to express specific criteria used to judge the reputation of fellow townspeople. This approach yielded a multidimensional conception of status: reputation is influenced by a wide range of moral, aesthetic, intellectual, educational, religious, ethnic, and personal behaviors for which hierarchical judgments can be formed. Like Veblen, Simmel, and the Lynds before him, Warner finds that consumer behaviors (e.g., "the 'right' kind of house, the 'right' neighborhood, the 'right' furniture"), are among the most important expressions of particular status positions in a community (Warner et al. 1949, p. 23). In addition, institutional affiliations (churches, clubs, political organizations) and neighborhoods are used to make judgments. These data are interpreted relationally to build the status hierarchy operating in each town. Because ethnographic studies using evaluated participation are prohibitively expensive to administer, Warnerian status studies since the 1950s have relied instead on surrogate measures such as the Index of Status Characteristics (Warner et al. 1949), the Index of Social Position (Hollingshead and Redlich 1959), or the Computerized Status Index (Coleman 1983), which are derived from survey measures of occupation, income, neighborhood, and house type.

There is still much to value in Warner's conception of status. In particular, its structuralist emphasis on relational differences in collective understandings of social position is an important but largely unacknowledged precursor to recent American sociological studies of the symbolic boundaries that sustain social hierarchies (e.g., Lamont 1992). However, in sociology, the Warnerian approach was long ago discredited owing to its narrow functionalist presuppositions that deny the interplay between cultural, economic, and political resources in the construction of social classes (Bendix and Lipset 1951; Gordon 1963; Pfautz and Duncan 1950). Beyond this metatheoretic problem, two specific conceptual lacunae become evident when Warner's approach is compared with Bourdieu's theory.

Conflating Dimensions of Social Class.

Warner's community studies provide extensive empirical support for Weber's multidimensional conception of social class: collective understandings of reputation are formed on the basis of criteria such as consumption patterns, economic position, morals, and educational attainment.[1] Yet, Warnerian research never isolates and investigates the relationships between these dimensions. Without so doing, it is impossible to understand the distinctive contributions of consumption to social class. Instead, consumption is an untheorized covariate. Warner argues that each status group develops, like a society in microcosm, a unique way of life; the consumer goods and activities that classes adopt are arbitrary. Any good or activity can be used as a means of maintaining in-group solidarity and excluding status inferiors. So he does not offer a coherent theory describing the conditions leading to status group formation, how these differences structure tastes, and why they are relatively durable over time. This lack of specification decreases the usefulness of Warner's approach since it offers no explanation for the elective affinities between particular groups and particular consumption patterns. One example of this theoretical black box is the debate in marketing concerning the relative explanatory power of income and social class in predicting consumption patterns (see Schaninger [1981] for a review). Consistent findings that social class measures capture more variance than income alone never broach the central theoretical question underlying demonstrations of covariation: If factors other than income influence stratified consumption patterns, what are they and how do they work?

Object Signification.

For Warner, American social classes are organized in a manner analogous to the social structure of small, isolated, preindustrial societies of classic anthropological ethnographies—"*Gemeinshaft*" communities bound by affiliative ties within strong, interpenetrating social networks. Thus, his method emphasizes descriptions of peoples' networks of friends, acquaintances, and organizational affiliations. This view of social organization motivates Warner's incipient theory of status-based consumption patterns. Similar to Veblen, Simmel, and the Lynds, Warner views consumption objects as positional markers reinforcing status boundaries. In this emulationist model, elites are engaged in a continual game with those below in which elite consumption patterns are universally valorized, and thus lower-class groups attempt to emulate them, leading elites to defend the distinctiveness of their consumption through pecuniary symbolism (Veblen), stylistic innovation (Simmel), and activities bounded by closed social networks (Warner).

This view of social class is an anachronism built upon a Rockwellian image of small town life that represents a minuscule and declining fraction of the contemporary United States (in contradistinction to Warner's famous aphorism, "To study Jonesville is to study America"). Although status judgments based on the goods one owns and the activities in which one participates have merit for describing small, isolated, relatively immobile populations, they are of little value for most of the population in an era of transnational consumer capitalism. Status construction now must contend with the tremendous geographic mobility of American professionals and managers, the privatization of social life, the proliferation of media and travel, and the anonymity of urban environments, all of which have impersonalized the "other" whom one views as social references (Collins 1981; DiMaggio 1987; DiMaggio and Mohr 1985; Meyrowitz 1985). With interactional groups multiplying and in constant flux, it becomes exceedingly difficult to develop stable consensus goods that represent the group.

In addition, Warner's object signification approach implies a highly strategized conception of consumption: people learn about, acquire, and experience consumption objects as status markers. Yet cultural consumer research has demonstrated repeatedly that consumption patterns can never be explained primarily by recourse to theories based on a view

of consumption as instrumental or strategic action. Consuming is significantly an autotelic activity in which tastes are formed around the
desires for and pleasures gained from particular goods and activities
relative to others; so, to be empirically compelling, a theory describing
differences in consumption across groups must explain these differences
in terms of tastes, pleasures, and desires rather than strategic action.

BOURDIEU'S THEORY OF TASTES

Across a diverse range of substantive studies, Pierre Bourdieu has synthesized Weberian, Marxist, Durkheimian, and phenomenological
traditions to argue for a model of social organization, the generative
mechanism for which is competition for various types of capital within
social fields. In *Distinction* (Bourdieu 1984), arguably the most important application of this grand theoretical project, Bourdieu describes
how these various capitals operate in the social fields of consumption.
I first review briefly Bourdieu's key concepts and then discuss how the
theory addresses the limitations of Warnerian social class research.[2]

Bourdieu argues that social life can be conceived as a multidimensional status game in which people draw on three different types of
resources (what he terms economic, cultural, and social capital) to compete for status (what he terms "symbolic capital"). Distinct from economic capital (financial resources) and social capital (relationships,
organizational affiliations, networks), cultural capital consists of a set
of socially rare and distinctive tastes, skills, knowledge, and practices.
Cultural capital entails what Gouldner (1979) has called a "culture of
critical discourse": a set of decontextualized understandings, developed
through a reflexive, problematizing, expansionist orientation to meaning
in the world, that are readily recontextualized across new settings (as
opposed to knowledge of specific facts; see Hannerz 1990). Cultural
capital exists in three primary forms: embodied as implicit practical
knowledges, skills, and dispositions; objectified in cultural objects; and
institutionalized in official degrees and diplomas that certify the existence of the embodied form. Cultural capital is fostered in an overdetermined manner in the social milieu of cultural elites: upbringing in
families with well-educated parents whose occupations require cultural
skills, interaction with peers from similar families, high levels of formal
education at institutions that attract other cultural elites studying areas
that emphasize critical abstract thinking and communication over the
acquisition of particularized trade skills and knowledges, and then refinement and reinforcement in occupations that emphasize symbolic production. These innumerable, diverse, yet redundant, experiences
particular to cultural elites become subjectively embodied as ways of
feeling, thinking, and acting through the generative social psychological
structure that Bourdieu terms the "habitus." The habitus is an abstracted, transposable system of schema that both classifies the world

and structures action. Bourdieu emphasizes that the contents of the habitus are largely presuppositional rather than discursive and that the habitus structures actions through a process of creative typification to particular situations. In its subjective embodied form, cultural capital is a key element of the habitus.

Like other capital resources, cultural capital exists only as it is articulated in particular institutional domains. According to Bourdieu (as well as many other theorists of modernity), the social world consists of many distinctive, relatively autonomous, but similarly structured (i.e., "homologous") fields such as politics, the arts, religion, education, and business. Fields are the key arenas in which actors compete for placement in the social hierarchy through acquisition of the statuses distinctive to the field. Thus, cultural capital takes on a distinctive form in each field: for example, in the academic field, cultural capital takes the form of intellectual brilliance, research competence, and detailed expertise that is embodied in presentations, teaching, and informal interactions, objectified in journal articles and books, and institutionalized in prestigious university degrees and society fellowships. In *Distinction*, Bourdieu documents how cultural capital is enacted in fields of consumption, not only the arts but also food, interior decor, clothing, popular culture, hobbies, and sport. Although cultural capital is articulated in all social fields as an important status resource, it operates in consumption fields through a particular conversion into tastes and consumption practices.

Unlike economic theories of markets in which people are conceived as strategic actors, in Bourdieu's theory, resources that are valued in fields of consumption are naturalized and mystified in the habitus as tastes and consumption practices. The habitus organizes how one classifies the universe of consumption objects to which one is exposed, constructing desire toward consecrated objects and disgust toward objects that are not valued in the field. The manifestation of the structuring capabilities of the habitus as tastes and consumption practices across many categories of goods and activities results in the construction of a distinctive set of consumption patterns, a lifestyle ("manifested preferences") that both expresses and serves to reproduce the habitus. Within the field of consumption, tastes and their expression as lifestyles are stratified on the basis of the objective social conditions that structure the habitus. Thus, the field of consumption is stratified so that there exist different lifestyles organized by class position. (To continue the academic field example, the same stratified patterns can be discerned in the desired qualities for faculty members at elite "research" schools, "balanced" schools, "teaching" schools, and community colleges.)

Isolating Cultural Capital, Tastes, and Consumption Fields.

Bourdieu argues that it is critical to distinguish between the different types of statuses that accrue in different fields: consumption is a particular status game that must be analyzed in isolation rather than lumped together with work, religion, education, and politics as Warner does. In addition, compared with Warner's conflation of the different bases of social class, a key contribution of Bourdieu's theory is that it effectively disaggregates the key dimensions of taste and explains their unique contribution to social reproduction. Economic capital is inscribed in consumption fields as tastes and consumption practices organized around the exchange value of consumption objects. Like Veblen's pecuniary distinctions, consumption objects can symbolize differences in economic resources of the consumer. But, whereas economic capital is expressed through consuming goods and activities of material scarcity and inputed luxury, cultural capital is expressed through consuming via aesthetic and interactional styles that fit with cultural elite sensibilities and that are socially scarce.

Taste as Practice.

Warner and Bourdieu both argue that status is expressed and reproduced through implicit evaluations in everyday social interactions. However, for Warner, these interactions occur within heavily sedimented social networks and formal organizations such as leisure and service clubs and religious groups. This allowed him to assume, like Veblen, the Lynds, and Simmel before him, that elites evolve a distinctive constellation of consumption objects that express their status position. Public signaling of these consensus goods affirms one's social position.

Significantly, Bourdieu offers a theory of social class consonant with social relations in advanced capitalist societies. Downplaying public displays of status symbols, Bourdieu emphasizes that status is continually reproduced as an unintended consequence of social interaction because all interactions necessarily are classifying practices; that is, micropolitical acts of status claiming in which individuals constantly negotiate their reputational positions (see also Collins 1981; Goffman 1967). Crucial to this process is the expression of cultural capital embodied in consumer actions. Rather than accruing distinction from pecuniary rarity or from elite consensus, Bourdieu argues that cultural capital secures the respect of others through the consumption of objects that are ideationally difficult and so can only be consumed by those few who have acquired the ability to do so. To take an example that Bourdieu might use were he to study the contemporary United States, when someone details Milos Forman's directorial prowess in *The People vs. Larry Flynt* to a friend over dinner (or, conversely, offers a damning harangue of Forman as an unrepentant proselytizer of the dominant gender ideology), this discussion not only recreates the experiential delight that the movie provided but also serves as a claim to particular resources (here, knowledge of directorial styles in movies and the ability to carefully analyze these characteristics) that act as reputational currency. Such actions are perceived not as explicit class markers but as bases for whom one is attracted to and admires, whom one finds uninteresting or does not understand, or whom one finds unimpressive and so seeks to avoid. Thus, status boundaries are reproduced simply through expressing one's tastes.

In addition to this embodied form, Bourdieu argues that cultural capital also becomes objectified in consumption objects. At first blush, this idea appears to parallel the object signification approach since consumption objects serve as signals of status in both. However, with objectified cultural capital, the stratificatory power of cultural objects results not from group consensus or economic scarcity but from the inferred cultural aptitude of the consumers of the object. In other words, cultural objects such as the high arts that require significant cultural capital to understand and appreciate properly imply that their consumers apply distinctive practices and so serve as surrogate representations of these practices. A foundational premise of Bourdieu's theory, then, is that categories of cultural goods and activities vary in the level of cultural capital required to consume them successfully (i.e., to fully enjoy the act of consuming).

RECOVERING BOURDIEU'S THEORY OF TASTES FROM ITS CRITICS

Cultural sociologists have vigorously debated the applicability of Bourdieu's theory to the contemporary United States for over a decade. Although early research offered modest support, influential recent studies have challenged its usefulness for explaining how social reproduction works in the contemporary United States (Erikson 1996; Gartman 1991; Halle 1992; Lamont 1992). I argue that two crucial flaws in operationalizing tastes limit the credibility of these refutations (see Holt [1997a] for a more detailed version of this argument):

Forms of Taste.

Quantitative empirical studies of Bourdieu's theory routinely operationalize tastes only in their objectified form—preferences for particular categories, genres, or types of cultural objects. Exemplary studies of this type such as those conducted by Paul DiMaggio (1987; DiMaggio and Mohr 1985; DiMaggio and Ostrower 1990; DiMaggio and Useem 1978) and Richard Peterson (Hughes and Peterson 1983; Peterson and DiMaggio 1975; Peterson and Simkus 1992) use large-scale surveys that are analyzed through regression and factor analyzes. The obvious advantage to measuring only objectified tastes is that there are large databases available and this type of data is compatible with sophisticated statistical analysis.

But operationalizing Bourdieu's theory in terms of preferences for cultural objects has become problematic, regardless of whether these objects are conceived as Warnerian consensus goods or as Bourdieuian objectified cultural capital. The utility of goods as consensus class markers has weakened substantially owing to a variety of widely noted historical shifts. Technological advances have led to the wide accessibility of goods, travel, and media by all but the poor (Bell 1976). Innovative styles and designs now diffuse rapidly between haute and mass markets, and between core and periphery states, thus dissolving lags that once allowed for stylistic leadership. From a different vantage point, theorists of postmodernity such as Jean Baudrillard, Jean-Francois Lyotard, and Fredric Jameson have argued that a defining characteristic of advanced capitalist societies is the massive overproduction of commodity signs. This proliferation of signs leads to an anarchic welter of consumer symbols that are not readily assimilated by social groups in any coherent way. This argument is supported by sociological research demonstrating a high degree of overlap in consumer preferences across social categories (e.g., Bourdieu 1984; Peterson and Simkus 1992). In postmodern cultures, it is increasingly difficult to infer status directly from consumption objects, as the object signification approach requires.

Historical changes are also draining the symbolic potency of objectified cultural capital. The postmodern condition is characterized by the breakdown of the hierarchy distinguishing legitimate (or high) culture from mass (or low) culture (Foster 1985; Frow 1995; Huyssen 1986; Jameson 1991). Many of the distinguishing traits of mass culture, such as seriality and mass reproduction, have now become central concerns of the art world, and many popular cultural forms from comic books to rock music to celebrities to television programs are produced and consumed using increasingly complex and esoteric formal lexicons that parallel modern art (Gamson 1994; Jenkins 1992). The objectified form of cultural capital becomes less effective in such a world since it depends on cultural categories and genres for which necessary levels of cultural competence are immanent and vary significantly. Objectified cultural capital can operate effectively only within a stable cultural hierarchy. Thus, as cultural hierarchies have dramatically blurred in advanced capitalist societies, objectified cultural capital has become a relatively weak mechanism for exclusionary class boundaries.

I suggest, then, that the cultural capital requirements necessary to consume successfully particular consumption objects today pose few constraints. Objects no longer serve as accurate representations of consumer practices; rather, they allow a wide variety of consumption styles. But this increasing semiotic malleability does not imply that cultural capital differences in consumption no longer signify. Rather, class differences in American consumption have gone underground; no longer easily identified with the goods consumed, distinction is becoming more and more a matter of practice. As popular goods become aestheticized and as elite goods become "massified" (Peterson and DiMaggio 1975) the objectified form of cultural capital has in large part been supplanted by the embodied form. Given the deteriorating classificatory power of objectified tastes, cultural elites in advanced capitalist societies now attempt to secure distinction by adapting their consumption practices to accentuate the embodied form.

Emphasizing embodied tastes leads to a different style of consuming than in previous eras. In fields organized by a hierarchy of objectified tastes, consumption practices emphasize knowing about and consuming the appropriate goods (e.g., Bourdieu uses Mondrian paintings and Bach concertos as measures). However, for fields in which there is great overlap in the objects consumed, to consume in a rare, distinguished manner requires that one consume the same categories in a manner inaccessible to those with less cultural capital (see Bourdieu's [1984, p. 282] description of the lifestyles of cultural producers). In other words, to express distinction through embodied tastes leads cultural elites to emphasize the distinctiveness of consumption practices themselves, apart from the cultural contents to which they are applied.

Contents of Taste.

Although not always clear in *Distinction*, it appears that Bourdieu, his supporters, and his critics all now agree that the particular cultural objects in which cultural capital is invested are conventions that are differentially configured across sociohistorical settings (Calhoun, LiPuma, and Postone 1993; Joppke 1986; Lamont 1992; Lamont and Lareau 1988).[3] It is unlikely, then, that the cultural objects Bourdieu describes as resources for the expression of exclusionary tastes in 1960s Parisian society will operate similarly in other sociohistorical settings. Rather than a nomothetic theory, Bourdieu's theory is a set of sensitizing propositions concerning the relations between social conditions, taste, fields of consumption, and social reproduction that must be specified in each application to account for their particular configuration.

American refutations of Bourdieu's theory (Erikson [1996]; Hall [1992]; Halle [1992]; and Lamont [1992] are the most significant) have, with few exceptions, operationalized elite taste using the same variables as Bourdieu. These studies evaluate whether the particular articulation of cultural capital in Parisian society of the 1960s, objectified primarily in the legitimate arts and embodied in formal aesthetic appreciation, applies to the contemporary United States. These critics echo a claim that is well documented in historical, demographic, and humanist writings (see, e.g., Huyssen 1986), that the fine arts are much less popular among cultural elites in the United States. Only a small fraction of the American population, cultural producers and a small coterie of insiders from the urban upper class, are knowledgeable fine arts consumers of the type Bourdieu describes as predominant in middle-class circles in France. Art history is not currently a regular part of academic training or informal family socialization in the United States, Bourdieu's two primary channels for cultural capital accumulation. And, as sociological studies of genre preferences report, those with high cultural capital are the most ardent consumers of mass culture (DiMaggio and Useem 1978; Peterson and Simkus 1992). Thus, critics conclude that since the high arts play only a peripheral role in the lives of cultural elites, Bourdieu's theory has little explanatory value in the contemporary United States (Erikson 1996; Halle 1992; Lamont 1992).

The flaw in this argument is that the arts constitute only a small fraction of the universe of consumption fields that can be leveraged for social reproduction. By focusing exclusively on art, these studies give short shrift to the activities that American cultural elites expend the vast majority of their nonwork energies pursuing, such as food, interior decor, vacations, fashion, sports, reading, hobbies, and socializing. These fields should be central to empirical studies of Bourdieu's theory in the contemporary United States since tastes serve as a resource for social reproduction only in fields in which cultural elites have invested the requisite time and psychic energy to convert their generic cultural capital assets to particular field-specific cultural capitals.

METHODS

I used this reformulation of Bourdieu, specified to account for the sociohistorical context of the contemporary United States by emphasizing mass consumption practices, to guide the design of an interpretive study. The goal of the study is to explore whether variation in cultural capital resources leads to systematic differences in tastes and consumption practices for mass cultural categories. In so doing, I respond to Lamont's call for a detailed mapping of how cultural capital currently operates in the United States (Lamont 1992; Lamont and Lareau 1988). I began with a sample of 50 informants from the vicinity of State College, a small city in rural central Pennsylvania dominated by Penn State University, who were randomly selected from the phone book (about 20 percent response rate). From this group, I compare 10 informants in the top quintile of cultural capital resources (whom I will refer to as "HCCs") to 10 informants whose cultural capital resources are in the lowest quintile (hereafter "LCCs").[4] I view this comparison as a conservative evaluation of Bourdieu's theory since the most significant class differences in cultural-capital-structured taste are found in large urban areas, where the new class (Gouldner 1979) of symbolic manipulators is larger and more cosmopolitan (Lamont 1992) and where there exist many urban subcultures of cultural producers that are more distinctive than the new class populations of suburban, ex-urban, and rural locations (Crane 1992). While LCCs are all from the local area and so express certain regional particularities in their tastes, the HCCs have lived across the country and the world, so their upbringing and education is similar to other HCCs in the United States.

Informants, all adult permanent residents of the county, were randomly selected from the local phone book, contacted by phone, and offered $20 to participate in an in-home interview. Although more women than men agreed to be interviewed, I compared the male and female informants and did not find any differences on the dimensions of taste reported below (DiMaggio and Mohr [1985] report similar findings). Following prior research (Halle 1992; Lamont 1992; Rainwater et al. 1959; Warner et al. 1949), in-home ethnographic interviews were used to collect data. The interviews lasted an average of one hour and forty minutes, and ranged from one to three hours. The interviews were transcribed into about 950 single-spaced pages of text. In addition to these transcripts, the data examined in the analysis also included details observed in the homes and a demographic questionnaire.

The two groups were constructed on the basis of cultural capital resources. According to Bourdieu and his American interlocutors, cultural capital resources are accumulated in three primary sites of acculturation: family upbringing, formal education, and occupational culture (Bourdieu 1984; DiMaggio and Unseem 1978; Lamont 1992; Peterson and Simkus 1992). The cultural capital rating scheme for this study uses all three of these antecedents, equally weighted. Family upbringing is measured in terms of father's education and occupation, because the father's status dominated family status when these informants were young. Five categories were created for each dimension (5 = high resources for cultural capital accumulation, 1 = low resources for cultural capital accumulation), guided by previous work that has calibrated differences in American education and occupation with differences in cultural capital (see Lamont 1992; Peterson and Simkus 1992). The 10 HCC informants are roughly equivalent to Gouldner's (1979) "New Class": all have at least bachelor's degrees and work in professional, technical, and managerial jobs. Most come from families in which the parents are college educated. In contrast, the 10 LCC informants are from a working-class background: they have at most a high school education, do manual labor or service/clerical work if they have jobs, and come from families where the father has at most a high school education (usually less) and did manual labor.[5]

The goal of the data collection was to elicit detailed descriptions of people's tastes and consumption practices across a variety of popular cultural categories prevalent in the contemporary United States—food, clothing, home decor and furnishings, music, television, movies, reading, socializing, vacations, sports, and hobbies. I developed an interview guide to elicit people's understandings and evaluations of different consumption objects, and the ways in which they consume their choices. Within each category, questions probed for detailed preferences and recountings of particular episodes across a variety of situations and time periods (e.g., for eating: breakfast, lunch, dinner, and snacks; at home vs. take-out, or eat-in restaurants; with family vs. alone; weeknights vs. weekends; before vs. after having children; special meals) to elicit as much detail as possible. Follow-up questions probed key emic terms that emerged in these descriptions.

In the next section, I describe six systematic differences in tastes and consumption practices between HCCs and LCCs that are structured by differences in social conditions. Like all social patterns, these dimensions are significant tendencies rather than orthogonal characteristics of the two groups.

MATERIALITY AND TASTE

A central contention in *Distinction* is that tastes are structured through continuities in interactions with material culture. The LCCs are accul- turated in a social milieu in which they engage continually the material rigors of everyday life (e.g., paying monthly utility bills, keeping the car running, saving money to visit relatives) and so the ability to manage these material constraints becomes a primary value. The tastes of LCCs are organized to appreciate that which is functional or practical—the taste of necessity (Bourdieu 1984, p. 177). Goods and activities are val- ued for their embodiment of the practical: virtuoso skills that achieve utilitarian ends evoke praise, cultural texts that realistically capture per- sonal experiences are appreciated, corporeal pleasures take precedence.

In contrast, HCCs are acculturated in a social milieu in which they seldom encounter material difficulties and in which their education em- phasizes abstracted discussion of ideas and pleasures removed from the material world. For HCCs, the material value of cultural objects is taken for granted: instead taste becomes a realm of self-expression, a means of constructing subjectivity. The tastes of HCCs express this distance from necessity, a distanced, formal gaze and a playful attitude that often takes the material value of cultural objects for granted.

This fundamental distinction in relationship to material culture un- derlies three important dimensions of taste and consumption practice that distinguish LCC and HCC informants across many of the categories discussed in the interviews: material versus formal aesthetics, referential versus critical appreciation, and materialism versus idealism.

MATERIAL VERSUS FORMAL AESTHETICS

For categories that are an important and a routine part of everyday life such as furniture, food, and clothing, LCC tastes are organized by a desire for pragmatic solutions to basic requirements. The LCC inform- ants express concern for the utilitarian characteristics of their house and its furnishings; they must be comfortable, functional, durable, and easy to care for:

INTERVIEWER: What kind of decor do you like in your house?

KATIE (LCC): I like comfort. And things that people don't have to be afraid of when they come in the house, that they have to take off their shoes. Like the dark carpet that you don't have to worry about. I used to have a dark carpet, but the lighter carpet is easier to clean than the dark carpet. The dark carpet shows every little lint and this can go for a week without having to vacuum. I think we go for comfort more than anything else. We each have our own couch, as you see. Now if I had a larger room, I'd have more rocking chairs or another chair. . . . And if I had another house I'd build a larger kitchen. I'd have a rocking chair in the kitchen and I would have it more comfortable in the kitchen.

INTERVIEWER: When you're setting up your house, what kinds of things do you like?

BETSY (LCC): Well, wood. We both like . . . well, we have a lot of wood.

INTERVIEWER: When you say you like wood, what about it? Just any furniture that's made with wood you prefer?

BETSY (LCC): Yes, that's basically what we do. When we go for a piece of furniture, like when we were looking for a recliner, because I knew it was going to be used a lot, I said I want wood and he agreed because you get kids or company or whatever and they're always going to go for the recliner and, of course, they're not always going to have their arms clean or whatever. I said that's basically what always wore out on mom's furniture because of all the kids. You know, it's just one of those things. I mean you wear out the arms of the furniture. I said, "I want wood." So we basically always go for wood because it's more durable and you just polish it and you know it's going to last. I mean it's not like cloth.

Although material characteristics dominate LCC tastes for interior and furniture, three informants do mention particular styles: two favor a country look, which uses colonial furniture, calico prints, and handmade crafts decorating walls and tables, while one is redecorating her house in Victorian antiques and decor. However, unlike HCCs, LCCs do not invoke a discourse of style to talk about these decorative preferences. Instead, they describe their tastes in terms of the traditions in which they have been raised, which makes their choices comfortable and reassuring.

The HCCs often share LCC material requirements for home interiors; comfort and durability are still important. But rather than dominant dimensions of their taste, material characteristics are baseline criteria; choices between materially satisfactory options are based on formal aesthetic qualities. The HCCs view their homes as canvases upon which they express their aesthetic sensibilities. Interiors need to be visually appealing, to provide the appropriate experiential properties. Decorating is a highly personalized and personalizing activity that is an aesthetic expression of the cultivated sensibilities of the decorator:

KATHRYN (HCC): I like choosing things and fitting things together, and bringing a few things from my old life into the new one, and putting them there as a reminder of where you came from. . . . Houses should be a background and they shouldn't interrupt. They shouldn't make people look at them rather than the people in them. . . . [when decorating] The main thing is not to draw attention to what we're going to do. . . . That's my philosophy, and anything that's glaring or ostentatious or says it's important is out the window to me. I don't like something that is built to impress.

INTERVIEWER: Tell me about the changes you've made to the house.

JOHN (HCC): Well, this house was a disaster. I hadn't done anything to it in almost 30 years. It's almost a shrink question. I decided to get my life in order. And part of getting my life in order, now that I have the intellectual energy to do so after [he had recently taken early retirement]. . . . You know, when I'm not working it's amazing how much intellectual energy you have and it's all for you. I realized that my surroundings had to be harmonious and sympathetic and supportive and all of that.

Similarly, preferred clothes of LCC informants are durable, comfortable, reasonably priced, well fitted, and, for clothes that will be seen by others, conforming to role norms (i.e., they are appropriate "work clothes" or "church clothes"). A common reference point that illuminates this materialist idea of desirable clothing is that many of the LCC women but none of the HCC women raise (with no prompting) the option of making clothes as a relevant baseline to evaluate store-bought clothing:

INTERVIEWER: What kind of clothes do you like?

HEATHER (LCC): Stuff that will last. I don't really like to go with what's fashionable, necessarily, just for the sake of being fashionable. I like to be comfortable.

INTERVIEWER: What kinds of clothes are comfortable?

HEATHER (LCC): Knits, something, you know, that's comfortable. To work, I wear sneakers and knit pants and t-shirts, you know, that type of stuff 'cause you didn't know when you were going to have to have to be holding somebody on the floor or whatever [she's a teacher's assistant]. For church and stuff, I wear skirts and sweaters or a blouse or whatever, or if we're going somewhere, I like to dress, not necessarily overdress, but to be dressed nice and be comfortable. . . . I'm just as happy getting something at K-Mart or Wal-Mart or even T J Maxx or something like that, but to go to Hesses or Brooks or, you know, some place really expensive, what I consider is really expensive. I find it difficult to spend thirtysome dollars on a shirt, or, you know, $50 or $60 on a skirt when I could go out and buy the material if I have the time to make it for a lot less.

In contrast, HCCs express tastes similar to those applied to decor; they expect material quality as a given and so tastes are structured by particular ideas of what is fashionable:

KATHRYN (HCC): I do not like clothes that draw attention to themselves. . . . But, I'm wearing more bright-colored clothes than I used to, because my first husband didn't like me to draw attention to myself so I was dressed in very pale colors. But now, I think partly in reaction to that, I will buy clothes that are more brightly colored if I like them. . . . I don't like clothes that are covered with—I call them "suburban clothes"—they are made of very synthetic fabrics and they have lots of gold on them, and buttons that shine a lot. They look kind of as if they're shouting.

When HCCs do talk of economical choices, these are couched as less desirable outcomes forced by budgetary constraints (i.e., driven by economic capital) rather than as acculturated desires:

INTERVIEWER: How about clothing, what types of clothes do you like?

DENISE (HCC): What kind of clothes do I like—it's different from what kind of clothes I can afford. I like well-made, well-tailored clothes that have absolutely luxurious fabrics. However, I have been buying a lot of stuff from L. L. Bean because it's durable and I like gorgeous colors and all those kind of things.

INTERVIEWER: When you say tailored. . . . What kind of styles?

DENISE (HCC:) I don't like really trendy looking clothes that you're not going to be able to wear next week. I'm trying to think of a look, you know Chanel?

Some HCCs prefer "functional" clothing, but this term has a very different meaning for HCCs than for LCCs. Functional, for HCCs, is a distinctive aesthetic based on parsimonious design and utilitarian construction similar to the functionalism of high modern architecture and design. "Function," rather than a pragmatic solution to everyday needs, is inverted by HCCs into form through an aesthetic opposition to the frivolity of "fashion."

JOHN (HCC): Today I'm buying practical clothes. That is to say they're mostly cotton. They're all washable. Mostly they don't require ironing because I got tired of ironing. . . . I look for—now when I'm buying clothing—I really don't care what the current style is anymore. You know, if it has good design it will always be in style. And I also tend to look for things which probably are more expensive but which I know will be more durable.

INTERVIEWER: Are there any particular clothing styles that you like?

JOHN: Yeah, I guess the best way to say it would be styles that are functional and designed to be worn by human bodies as they are; as opposed to designed to be worn only standing up at cocktail parties or the races or, you know, as soon as you sit down you know it was a mistake.

CRITICAL VERSUS REFERENTIAL RECEPTION OF CULTURAL TEXTS

Habitus-structured orientations toward material culture also organize distinctive styles of consuming mass cultural texts such as books, television, film, and music. Applying a formal interpretive lens, HCCs read popular entertainment as entertaining fictions that are potentially edifying but that do not reflect directly the empirical world (i.e., what Liebes and Katz [1990] term "critical" interpretations).

INTERVIEWER: Why did you like *Rain Man* so much? Why is that on your list?

SHARON (HCC): Partly because I thought the dynamic between Dustin Hoffman and Tom Cruise was really entertaining and because Dustin Hoffman did such a good job in the role.

INTERVIEWER: When you say just that Dustin Hoffman was really good, what do you mean by that?

SHARON: I found it amazing. . . . When you watch a string of movies— like I've seen most of the Tom Cruise movies—to me most of his roles it's Tom Cruise, not the character that he becomes, even though he does a really pretty decent job, more decent than a lot of actors do. But you're still very aware of who the actor is and in him I see a lot of the same very subtle mannerisms that he brings to every role probably without even realizing it. And I've seen Dustin Hoffman in other things and to me in that movie he became the person he was portraying where your mind. . . . you didn't even think of the fact that you'd seen him in how many other shows or movies because you were into the character. I like it when an actor and actress can do that. I think it's rare.

The LCCs, in contrast, tend to interpret cultural texts from a referential perspective: they read these texts as more or less realistic depictions of the world that are potentially relevant to their own lives (see Press 1991). Because LCCs apply the classificatory system used in everyday life to cultural texts, they are attracted to programs and movies they feel are "real" and to music that speaks directly to their life situation.

INTERVIEWER: What did you like about *Sleepless in Seattle?*

DAVID (LCC): It has a good ending and it's realistic. Yeah, in a way, realistic. In a way it's kind of far out because, you know, there's a tremendous amount of money spent in phone calls and transportation back and forth and that bothered me all during the movie, you know, who can afford that? You know, maybe these people in their positions can. I'm never going to be in that position where I can afford that kind of . . . but, you know, if I could, I would probably get involved with somebody with that. If I had the money to do it, you know.

The LCCs' referential interpretations lead them to dislike programs, movies, and music whose characters, plots, and lyrics conflict with their worldview or remind them of disturbing past experiences:

INTERVIEWER: Do you like Steven Spielberg movies?

BETSY (LCC): We liked *E.T.* I haven't seen the one [*Schindler's List*]. Because I'm not in . . . I know it's all real, as far as what happened to the people, but I can't get into these . . . even when they have them on A&E like when they're showing how the concentration camps were and things like that. But this movie, everyone I've talked to at work said the same thing as even what the critics are saying that he really did a good job showing exactly what happened to these people for real. I talked to a couple of people that seen the movie: "You have to see the movie." Well, I can't watch that kind of movie. I know it's real and I know this happened to these people, but I can't get into those kind of movies.

INTERVIEWER: What kind of movies do you like?

LYNN (LCC): I like the more romantic ones. I try to steer away from the ones that people die of anything, like any diseases or anything like that. . . . Because my mom died of cancer in 1981 so I usually try to stay away from those.

Some HCCs also dislike and actively avoid scenes with graphic violence, but they see a tension between the use of violence in a fictional art form and their visceral reactions to it and so do not reject disturbing scenes categorically. For example, like Betsy above, Sue (HCC) has avoided seeing *Schindler's List* because of its graphic depiction of genocide, but her rationale for doing so is quite different. Betsy wouldn't think of seeing *Schindler's List* because the horrific scenes of concentration camps are an extremely disturbing reality—she calls it "too real"—one that is too painful to voluntarily expose oneself to. Sue, in contrast, knows that she also will have an intense emotional response to *Schindler's List* but is conflicted about seeing it because she perceives the movie as an artistic statement about an important event rather than just "reality."

MATERIALISM VERSUS IDEALISM

Because LCCs are acculturated in materially constrained environments, the good life is often cast in terms of having an abundance of things one likes and having things that are popularly understood as luxurious (Bourdieu 1984, p. 177). These materialist tastes are particularly influential in preferences for housing, food, and vacations. The LCC informants grew up and currently live in relatively small living spaces—apartments, trailers, and bungalows. So these informants value uniformly a large living space and large yards and have pursued these goals to the limits of their financial resources.

HEATHER (LCC): Well it's kinda weird how we settled on this house. We weren't looking to buy a house 'cause we had the house in [town near college], but it was really, really small. Really small. I mean, our bedroom, you walked sideways around the bed. It was small. . . . [Seeing the new house for the first time] First word out—"Wow!" And we walked in and "Whoa!" 'cause it's really big.

I asked Heather if their old house was a Victorian since the town has a large Victorian housing stock. She nods and continues to talk about the advantages of the floor plan in the new house. In contrast, HCCs Anna and Rebecca do not evaluate old versus new houses in terms of size. Instead they emphasize the charm and character of historic houses that new houses lack. Other LCC informants who have the money to do so (Ruth, Betsy, Susan) have also moved to larger houses on bigger pieces of property away from neighbors, while others without the necessary income dream of doing so ("any house out of town where I have some space").

The LCCs with higher incomes consistently express preferences for consumption objects that are indicative of luxury and material abundance: Ruth and her husband own one Mercedes coupe and are shopping for more of these, they have recently acquired numerous antiques, and they enjoy dining regularly at the most expensive restaurant in the county. She tells a story about a birthday party she threw for her husband at this restaurant where they paid for dinner for a large group of friends. Similarly, Lisa and her husband recently dined at an expensive French restaurant, and she professes a desire to own a BMW someday, while Susan and her husband took up yachting on Cheseapeake Bay four years ago and have recently upgraded to a sailboat that can sleep seven people comfortably.

Desirable vacation destinations also reveal a yearning for abundance and luxury. For three of the LCCs an ocean cruise is the ideal vacation, and they speak excitedly about the cruises they have taken, describing the cornucopia of dining and social activities (Nancy: "If you're bored on a cruise, it's your own fault"). Cruises are an ideal expression of LCC materialist tastes because they are popularly constructed as luxurious and they promote an abundance of activities, food, and drink. Another LCC informant spoke in similar terms about her vacations to Poconos resorts:

LISA (LCC): [Poconos resorts] have all kinds of activities. . . . The next year we went to a different place and got the room with the pool in your own room and that place had horseback riding and carriage rides and it had a shooting range. . . . You pay like $400 a night and it's most of your meals and entertainment, mostly all the activities they had.

Many LCC informants cannot afford these objects of luxury and abundance, yet they too express a yearning for abundance and luxury within the universe of consumption objects that is economically feasible. Among LCCs, restaurants that serve buffet style are consensus favorites—the contemporary American equivalent of the French working-class meals characterized by "plenty" and "freedom" (Bourdieu 1984, p. 194):

DAVID (LCC): Well, generally when I go out to eat, I'm sitting there thinking, "If I was at home I could fix this, a bigger portion for a whole lot less money than what I'm paying here." It destroys the whole thing, because I'm thinking so much about how much . . . they're making a bloody fortune off me for, you know. . . . where a buffet, you know, I'm in the driver's seat kind of you know. I know up front how much it's going to cost me and I can eat as much as I want. If I go away hungry it's my fault, you know.

KATE (LCC): Of late, we've been going over to Milroy for seafood. Every Friday night they have a buffet. . . . They have crab legs, shrimp, all kinds of fish deep fried, with clams that are deep fried. Along with ham, chicken, beef. You have your beverage and delicious homemade dessert and soft ice cream for $6.95. . . . I wish you could see people eat those crab legs. They bring them out on trays and the minute they bring them to the salad bar, everyone rushes to get them.

RUTH (LCC): At the Hotel Edison—it's a family-style that has chicken, turkey, or ham that you can pick; there's filling, and there's lettuce with that, Jell-O salad, dessert, and coffee, all for like $10, you get all this food, as much as you want, they keep bringing it out, plus waffles. That's why it's his favorite thing to eat is to go there and have waffles.

In contrast, through informal and formal humanistic education, HCCs learn to emphasize and value metaphysical aspects of life. They emphasize the subjective production of experience through creative, contemplative, aestheticized, abstracted engagement with the world rather than brute encounters with an empirical reality. Material abundance and luxury are crass forms of consumption because they are antithetical to the ethereal life of the mind. Since HCCs have been raised with few material constraints, they experience material deprivation differently than LCCs. Material paucity is often aestheticized, similar to functionalist design, into an ascetic style by HCCs (cf. Bourdieu 1984, p. 196). This said, it should also be noted that HCCs are at least as willing to make material acquisitions, often spending large amounts of money in so doing, provided that the good or activity supplies (or, at least, can be rationalized or imagined to supply) desired metaphysical experiences.

Materialism and idealism, then, refer to the cultural understandings that are inscribed in consumption practices rather than the quantities and physical characteristics of consumption objects. The HCCs are able to consume luxurious and scarce goods while at the same time negating connotations of waste, ostentation, and extravagance through tastes that assign value based on the ability of the good to facilitate metaphysical experience. In contrast, LCCs value abundance and luxury because these objects, with material and symbolic attributes far beyond what they understand as appropriate "use value," signify a seldom-experienced distance from material needs. For example, although HCCs tend to have higher incomes, they live in smaller houses than the economically secure LCCs, have smaller yards, and place little value on house size. Charles, whose yearly income is over $100,000, lives in a small ramshackle bungalow in a middle-class town; John lives in a tiny row house in the historic district of another nearby town; Kathryn, whose family income is nearly $100,000, lives in a nondescript townhouse with well-worn furniture. Sue and Margaret have both recently purchased smaller houses that are more manageable and livable than previous ones. This sense of material frugality is evinced throughout the day-to-day lives of this group. For example, Kathryn emphasizes several times that, because she was brought up in England during the war, she is very careful about her spending and is incensed when food is wasted. Though designer clothes very much appeal to her, she would never buy these items at full price, nor would she buy something that requires dry cleaning. Charles is a vegetarian whose standard lunch is some type of cooked grain (corn, wheat, barley, or oats) or soybeans with dried fruit and skim milk, and then some fruit or Jell-O for dessert. For dinner, he has rice, either plain or with some tomatoes or vegetables. Later in the evening, he eats raw vegetables; and he eats apples throughout the course of the day. He carries a briefcase and wears a leather jacket that he has owned for over 40 years.

Unlike the higher-income LCCs, HCCs never emphasize the extravagance of restaurants as a quality influencing their favorite places to dine. Rather, they use extravagance to contrast with their own tastes, which favor cuisines from other countries, often the peasant variety, eclecticism (interesting foods), artisanry, and casual atmospherics rather than the pretense associated with status-oriented restaurants. Since State College offers little in the way of such restaurants, HCCs expressed little interest in local dining. For example, Margaret denies the material symbolism of expensive restaurants connoting luxury and elegance and instead judges them on their ability to deliver experientially. Since none of the restaurants in the area deliver to her expectations, she occasionally dines at family-style restaurants but usually cooks at home. Similarly, Denise and her family usually go out for pizza and would only go to one of the expensive French restaurants "if one of my sons graduates from medical school or something." Kathryn occasionally takes out-of-town visitors to this restaurant but prefers a local salad bar because she is always watching her figure. Anna and her husband tried a "nice" restaurant near their home, found the food atrocious, and, so, they prefer going out for "bar food" instead.

WORK AND TASTE

Another central premise of cultural capital theory is that class reproduction occurs through acculturation in particular skills and dispositions required for occupational success (Willis 1978). These cultural capital assets not only allow for occupational success but also become valorized as ends in themselves and so serve as a currency to accrue status in the parallel symbolic economy of consumption (Bourdieu 1984; Collins 1975; DiMaggio 1987).

HCC careers are characterized by an emphasis on symbolic analysis, the necessity to synthesize and manipulate information, to understand and respond to new situations, to innovate rather than follow rote instructions. Structured by an ideology of meritocracy and entrepreneurialism, these knowledge-driven occupations place a premium on professional autonomy, peer competition, and the pursuit of an ever-changing knowledge base needed to maintain leverage in the labor market. Further, in the contemporary United States, HCC employment is characterized by a highly mobile national labor market for professional positions that requires frequent integration into new social networks with heterogeneous interests and values (DiMaggio 1987), structuring a cosmopolitan sensibility among HCCs (Hannerz 1990; Merton 1957). In sum, the labor market conditions experienced by contemporary American HCCs structures their tastes, through the habitus, to emphasize cosmopolitanism, individuality, and self-actualization.

In contrast, LCCs participate in a local labor market for highly routinized jobs (Leidner 1993). Work is a job, rarely a career. While many LCC informants like their jobs, particularly because of the social outlet they provide, and express pride in what they do, they also describe the tasks they are asked to perform as mundane, providing little intellectual or creative challenge. Instead, working-class jobs are characterized by rote application of technique, high levels of surveillance, and a low emphasis on creativity and problem solving. Consumption by LCCs, then, is often constructed in opposition to rather than contiguous with work, pursuing experiences more exciting and fulfilling than work provides (Halle 1984; Rubin 1976). This orientation results in consumption practices that have a more autotelic cast compared with the instrumental, achievement orientation of HCCs. There is little sense of a competitive job market in which improving skills is critical in maintaining labor market leverage. Rather than individual achievement, working-class positions emphasize local communal mores (such as found in collective workplace practices to resist managerial control; see Burawoy 1979). The work of LCCs, then, structures tastes that emphasize the local, the autotelic, and the collective (cf. Rainwater et al. 1959).

Cosmopolitan versus Local

The HCCs understand their social world to be much more expansive than do the LCCs. All of the HCC informants have lived in other states and five in other countries. They travel routinely throughout the United States and overseas to visit friends and family, for business, and for vacations. In contrast, only two of the LCC informants have lived outside the state in which they currently reside, they rarely travel outside of the mideastern states, and rarely mention friends or family outside the immediate vicinity:

Lynn (LCC): I like State College because you're within an hour of everything here, or two hours if you want to go to Harrisburg, a mall, or something like that.

Interviewer: Do you take vacations?

Lynn: Usually, I'll go to my grandparents [in the county] and cook dinner and go out to eat. During the school year usually the days I take off there is something going on at her school—chaperoned a field trip. I don't take a whole lot of days off.

INTERVIEWER: Any other places?

LYNN: Yeah, a little bit, especially during the summer we usually go out to all the little carnivals [around the county].

The HCCs talk frequently about the trade-offs of moving to a rural college town, comparing the physical beauty and peaceful way of life to the lack of cultural resources and demographic diversity. Some feel that the balance attained by a university town is just right, but many feel that they have made a significant lifestyle sacrifice because of the paucity of cultural resources. Because HCCs construct their reference groups on a national and even international basis, a common issue is how to maintain these relationships while living in a small isolated community. For example, Kathryn regularly invites out-of-town friends from Washington, Philadelphia, and New York to stay "out in the country," and these friends reciprocate by putting her up in the city in order to get needed exposure to city life. Charles spends several months of the year visiting friends in Europe and the western United States. Margaret chose weaving as an avocation because it did not require her to become too invested in the local community: it had to "be moveable, to be portable, because I knew that it was likely that we'd be moving around a lot. And I needed something that I could take with me, that I wouldn't feel resentful because I had to pick up and leave something there I had invested time and energy in."

Tastes for news offer another informative example since what one considers relevant news depends on the breadth of the perceived social world in which one lives. The LCCs strongly favor the local newspaper because it covers the nexus that concerns them: they read the local section, obituaries, and local sports. The HCCs view the local newspaper as a poorly written and parochial substitute for big-city papers. For example, Anna uses hunting articles featured in the local newspaper as a synecdoche standing for the parochial LCC mores that she disdains:

INTERVIEWER: Why do you choose to subscribe to the [New York] *Times* as opposed to local newspapers?

ANNA (HCC): Well, we subscribed to the local newspaper and we stopped our subscription for I guess two major reasons. One is we were sick of seeing the dead animals that hunters have caught on the front page during hunting season. In color, yeah, the bears. And two is we were . . . we felt that a lot of the editorials were really very . . . I just think very conservative and I just wasn't . . . when they withheld "Doonesbury" . . . that was kind of the final blow.

Exoticism.

The most powerful expression of the cosmopolitan-local opposition in the realm of tastes is through perceptions of and desires for the exotic—consumption objects far removed conceptually from what is considered to be normative within a category. Both HCCs and LCCs enjoy variety in their consumption to a greater or lesser extent, but they differ in their subjective understandings of what constitutes variety. What is exotic for LCCs is mundane for HCCs, and what is exotic for HCCs is unfathomable or repugnant for LCCs. And, while LCCs find comfort in objects that are familiar, HCCs seek out and desire exotic consumption objects.

Discussing food, LCCs offer conventional choices as their favorites for both home-cooked meals and restaurant meals, voicing uncertainty about or disdain toward more exotic choices. For example, while many HCCs eat Chinese food as a regular part of their diet and so do not use this cuisine as a signifier of exoticism, LCCs understand Chinese cuisine as exotic and so tend to avoid it. They rarely cook Chinese at home, they order Chinese dishes conservatively at restaurants by always choosing the same dish or often choosing dishes most similar to American food such as sweet-and-sour pork, and some avoid it completely: "I'll walk past a Chinese restaurant in State College and the smell of walking past it about gags me" (David).

The HCCs, however, frequently emphasize preferences for what they consider to be exotic foods. For example, Ronald asserts his distinctive tastes by describing a business trip to France where he enjoyed dishes that Americans generally consider inedible:

INTERVIEWER: Were there any dishes that you really liked when you were [in France]?

RONALD (HCC): I guess the morel mushrooms were the part that I remember the most because they had them on practically everything and they're really great. I also had some very good horsemeat of all things. . . . It was a specialty of the house. It was a tenderloin where they . . . one of these thick French sauces on it. It was really great. . . . I've also been known to eat brains. If those are done properly by a French chef, they can be very good.

Similar differences were evident in entertainment choices as well. For whites who live outside of urban areas, one of the most culturally distant populations imaginable is the predominantly African-American ghetto. How informants position their tastes in regard to urban African-American cultural forms such as rap music, then, is revealing. The LCCs either adamantly dislike or express bewilderment about rap:

INTERVIEWER: How about rap?

LISA (LCC): No, that's one thing I don't like.

INTERVIEWER: Why don't you like it?

LISA: I don't know, I just never did. I just think it's silly, these people are talking or whatever you call it, rapping, I call it weird. Any fool can do that, that's my opinion of it when it came out.

SUSAN (LCC): I like all kinds of music. Classical . . . rap I hate. I shouldn't say I like all, because I do not like rap.

INTERVIEWER: What don't you like about rap?

SUSAN: I can't understand it half the time. It's too noisy. Too confusing. I just don't like it. The beat. . . . I don't like the talking all the time.

Among HCCs, however, showing respect for and interest in rap expresses cosmopolitan tastes—the tastes of a person whose social world is not only geographically but also racially and economically inclusive:

INTERVIEWER: What do you think of rap music?

SUE (HCC): What little I know about it, is that I think it's the kind of music that's really kind of neat. I like the beat of it. It's very unique culturally. But some of the rap music that is on the radio, I don't care for some of it. But I don't want to denounce all of rap music because of the actions of a few. I think there is a place for it.

INTERVIEWER: So you just heard a little of it here?

SUE: Yeah. Even like some of Sister Souljah and some of those things. I've seen some on MTV. Every so often I'll turn it on. And, as I said, I think it's . . . it seems to have a lot of potential. I know it's very popular among African-Americans and expresses their culture. But I don't like the violence of some of it. And what appalls me about some of the rap music is that it's done by African-Americans but it really degrades, particularly African-American women.

INTERVIEWER: When you say you think it has a lot of potential, what . . . ?

SUE: Well, it's . . . because I think it expresses emotion. I think the rhythm of it and the rhyming to it, is that you can get a lot of . . . what am I trying to say? The music kind of expresses what the words are trying to say. Because of that staccato beat to it. And that's what I find attractive about it. But it's what some of the words are saying that I don't like.

CONSUMER SUBJECTIVITY AS INDIVIDUALITY
VERSUS LOCAL IDENTITY

Cultural historians and critics argue persuasively that the pursuit of individuality through consumption is a central characteristic of advanced capitalist (often "consumer") societies, the United States in particular (Baudrillard 1981; Ewen and Ewen [1982] 1992; Jameson 1991). This characterization aptly describes HCCs, but is inaccurate for LCCs. Daniel Miller's (1987) conception of the relationship between consumption and subjectivity provides a framework that can be used to explain this difference. The process of consumption allows people to reappropriate meanings that have become objectified in consumption objects through mass production. In highly differentiated, monetized societies dominated by the proliferation and fragmentation of objectified culture (i.e., meanings inscribed in objects found in the public world such as material goods, services, places, media, architecture, etc.), this process of appropriation becomes increasingly problematic. So practical strategies evolve to allow for the construction of subjectivity through consumption.

Although consumer subjectivity is problematic for both HCCs and LCCs, they pursue different strategies to overcome this tension. Consumption practices always simultaneously express the contradictory tendencies of individual distinction and social affiliation, but HCCs and LCCs differentially inflect this dialectic. For LCCs, consumer subjectivity is produced through passionate and routinized participation in particular consumption activities. In most cases these subjectivities are explicitly collective, positioning one within an idioculture of other participants in the locality.

In contrast, given their cosmopolitan social milieu and their equation of subjectivity with individuality, consumer subjectivity for HCCs requires constructing what is perceived to be a unique, original style through consumption objects. The HCCs experience the potential for homogenization of commodity goods to a far greater extent than do LCCs and, thus, are far more energetic in their attempts to individuate their consumption. To express an individualistic sense of subjectivity through consumption is inherently contradictory in an era in which most goods are mass produced and experiences are mass consumed (see Clarke 1993; Holt 1995; Miller 1987), yet HCCs attempt to produce individual subjectivity through authenticity and connoisseurship.

Authenticity.

The HCCs locate subjectivity in what they perceive to be authentic goods, artisanal rather than mass produced, and auratic experiences that are perceived as removed from, and so minimally contaminated by, the commodity form. The HCCs tend to disavow mass culture even when mass-produced goods are of high quality, and they camouflage their use of mass-produced goods when using them is unavoidable. John expresses this perspective explicitly in describing a particular plate that has captured his imagination:

INTERVIEWER: What really interests you about this type of pottery right now?

JOHN (HCC): Well, it's very beautiful. It has . . . first of all, I guess good art pottery is probably part of the arts and crafts movement. It's not mass produced. Most of it is not machine made. It has individuality. There isn't very much of it, relative to something like say to Roseville or some of the later potteries where they stamped out millions of them, you know . . . I think that our culture is to homogenize people. Homogenize their taste. And I think that, you know, you have subdivisions that are full of houses that all have vinyl siding and if you look at it in the right light, they all have a bulge in where they didn't do it right. They'll never be any different color. It will never weather. There's the sameness that I find really—I don't know—it's suffocating. I mean you go into shopping malls, you go into one shopping mall and it seems like every other shopping mall.

Similarly, Kathryn decorates her home with one-of-a-kind artisanal objects, which she views as personally meaningful, rather than mass-produced goods, which express exchange value:

KATHRYN (HCC): Things that matter to me are things that remind me of things, rather than things that have their own intrinsic value. In other words, I'd rather put something on the wall that was painted by a friend . . . than something an interior designer had just written up. . . . So I'd never hire an interior designer because I can't imagine living in someone else's stage set, you know.

She approaches her clothing in the same way, hunting through Washington, D.C., thrift stores, out-of-town friends' hand-me-downs, even deceased people's clothing, in order to find articles that are unique and so more personalizable in relation to mass-merchandised fashion. Decommodified authenticity is taken to the extreme by Charles, who completely dismisses all of mass culture and, hence, professes complete ignorance of it. When asked about his favorite movies, he has a hard time recalling the last time he's seen one and, out of desperation, dredges up *Casablanca* as his favorite. He never watches television so he does not know of *Roseanne*, and he has barely heard of Madonna or Michael Jackson. Rather, he repeatedly redirects my questions to discussions of his own creations and those of his friends (such as the pieces of art he has scattered about his living room).

The desires of HCCs for decommodified authenticity are also prevalent in vacation preferences. Those LCCs who can afford to take a vacation uniformly favor popular destinations such as Disney World, Sea World, Atlantic City, and the beaches of New Jersey and Delaware. They also tend to prefer trips where the activities are planned by others and are highly routinized (ocean cruises, "all-in-one" bus and plane tours, theme parks). In contrast, HCCs dislike and so tend to avoid what they perceive to be mass-produced (and, so, artificial) tourist activities and, instead, wherever they are, engage in a tourist style that seeks the "authentic" experience that is found through exploration and happenstance rather than routinized and popular activities (cf. MacCannell 1976). The authentic is achieved when one actually enters the "world" of a different social milieu, rather than gazing at it from outside:

KATHRYN (HCC): When traveling, I go to see friends who know their way around. Two of my friends were artists from down in Manhattan, so we go and see them and eat with them. And it's sort of weird vegetarian restaurants in SoHo you know. . . . So we look for those things. Or we go and see another friend who's in theater and we eat at a Chinese restaurant he knows. We go and see people who know their way around. . . . If we go to Philadelphia, we stay with my sister and we go with them to their lives, which is kind of rather "Mainline." You know, sort of snooty, the Ivy League type. And that's fun for a change, too. And so we see friends and family and go with them into their lives.

The HCCs on occasion "do" popular tourist destinations such as Fisherman's Wharf in San Francisco. But their understanding of these activities—they defensively admit to doing so and suggest that these activities are frivolous compared with other more interesting experiences on the trip—expresses their interests in authentic, decommodified experiences in contrast with LCCs who view these same activities as highlights.

Country music provides another site for invoking tastes for decommodified authentic cultural objects versus the popular. Country music is sharply divided into "traditional" and "contemporary" genres (see Peterson 1978). The most popular radio station in the area plays contemporary country, while the traditional variant (which is usually understood to include bluegrass, swing, and Appalachian "old time" music as well as the "hard" country music of the 1950s–1970s exemplified by Hank Williams, Merle Haggard, and George Jones) is much less popular, played occasionally on the local National Public Radio (NPR) station and in live performances at some clubs in the area. For LCCs, traditional country music is the music they grew up with, a style that, except for the eldest informants, they now view as old-fashioned and backward. All but one who likes country, then, invokes the distinction between this style of country—often describing it as "twangy" and critically stereotyping the lyrical content (Heather: "The guy talks about his dog dying")—and "new" or "contemporary" country. The LCCs strongly prefer the latter because it is has a modern sensibility with lyrics that aptly express their self-understandings. The three HCCs who express a preference for country, however, have little interest in contemporary country. Instead they favor bluegrass and other much less popular traditional styles that are described as original, unique varieties of American music, rather than a music genre that speaks to their lives. (These different tastes for country also provide another example of LCC's referential vs. HCC's critical interpretations of cultural texts described above.)

Connoisseurship.

While authenticity involves avoiding contact with mass culture, connoisseurship involves reconfiguring mass cultural objects. Applying a highly nuanced, often idiosyncratic approach to understand, evaluate, and appreciate consumption objects, connoisseurs accentuate aspects of the consumption object that are ignored by other consumers. Thus, personal style is expressed through consumption practice even if the object itself is widely consumed. This stylistic practice necessitates the development of finely grained vocabularies to tease out ever more detailed nuances within a category, the expression of opinionated and often eclectic evaluations of alternatives, and the ability to engage in passionate appreciation of consumption objects meeting one's calculus of "quality" within a category.

All HCCs have at least one category for which they have developed the requisite knowledge and interest of a connoisseur and many have several such categories. John, a quintessential connoisseur, expresses such tastes for virtually every topic in the interview. We spend about 20 minutes talking about oriental rugs, touring his house to admire and evaluate the dozen or so rugs spread throughout. He waxes enthusiastically about their qualities, such as the use of vegetable dye, that make a rug beautiful rather than ordinary.

JOHN (HCC): By the way, these are all vegetable dyes as opposed to aniline dye, which is another level of sophistication that I've worked my way up to. I've reached the point where when I see something that's done with aniline dyes, I don't like it anymore. . . . I mean this is a new Turkish carpet (points to a rug), but they're once again using vegetable dyes. Well . . . I know we're running out of time but I want to show you something. Now is that (points to another rug) bad color or is that bad color?

INTERVIEWER: It's different.

JOHN: This is a very nice rug. But this is aniline dye and that's vegetable dye. And it says it all right there.

Similarly, Sue approaches going out to eat as a connoisseur. She purposely accumulates specialized knowledge about cuisines and restaurants that she uses to construct a distinctive style, leveraged as an important interactional resource to interact with her HCC friends.

SUE (HCC): I really like going out to a good meal and having a glass of wine and making an event out of eating. And that's true when I travel, too. I'm one of these people. . . . I research restaurants when I travel and I pick out restaurants in various areas where I'm going if they have good reputations because when I travel I think food is as important as the sights I see. You know, I can skimp on a hotel, but I don't want to skimp on good food. And maybe it's because my lifestyle is so hectic that I enjoy being waited on. But that's something that I really do enjoy doing.

INTERVIEWER: When you say it's like an event for you, what do you mean by that?

SUE: Well, it's something I look forward to. It's something I find relaxing. I have . . . I love eating. I mean talk to my friends at work. I mean, you know, I have a reputation for loving to eat. And I do, I love to try new and different foods. With the exception of insects and octopus, there's very few things I don't like to eat. So . . . I tell you, to me that's a very important recreational activity.

In addition to the application of detailed knowledge and the accompanying enthusiasm these minutiae bring forth, eclecticism is, in addition to an expression of cosmopolitanism, an important dimension of connoisseurship. Eclecticism allows connoisseurs to construct distinctive tastes in categories in which the use of conventional goods is difficult to avoid because choices are largely constrained to a limited range of mass-produced goods. In categories such as interior decor, clothing, and food, in which consuming often requires combinations of goods (e.g., furniture and decorative items are combined to set up a living room or a bedroom, clothes are combined into an outfit, foods are combined into a meal), eclecticism can take the form of combinatorial inventiveness. For example, while LCCs always offer normative combinations when asked about what they prepare for "special meals" (e.g., turkey dinner "with all the fixings" such as stuffing, potatoes, a green vegetable, gravy, and cranberry sauce), HCC connoisseurs break down these conventions. For example, Kathryn's special meal is an intercontinental pastiche bearing no resemblance to normative combinations (all the more individualized due to the exotic components):

INTERVIEWER: What would you prepare for a special meal?

KATHRYN (HCC): Start with a cold soup like vichyssoise or gazpacho, my husband makes a spicy Jamaican chicken with rice, or maybe trout sauced with red wine base with Cointreau, and make a big salad with bitter greens, and a different dessert such as a great big souffle or something like that. We have wine with meals and my husband makes planter's punch.

The same pattern is also evident in discussion of interior decor. Whereas the LCCs who express design preferences favor conventional styles of "country" or "Victorian," HCCs explicitly disavow following a style that is widely adhered to and, instead, talk about how they mix and match to create their own personal look.

For reception-oriented categories such as reading, television and movies and music, people cannot actively combine different consumption objects, so eclecticism takes a different form: instead of eclectic combinations, connoisseurs express eclectic tastes by crossing or subverting institutionalized genre boundaries. The LCCs typically identify their movie tastes (e.g., "drama" or "action/adventure"), their reading choices (e.g., "historical romance"), and music tastes ("contemporary country") using a popularly constructed genre distinction. Compare this to John, who describes his music tastes as beginning in high school with chamber music (for which he continues to prefer to listen to particular recordings on record rather than compact disc), moving on to the Statler Brothers, George Harrison, folk music by artists such as Pete Seeger and the Weavers, Gilbert and Sullivan, the Beach Boys, and "lots of Vivaldi; lots and lots and lots and lots and lots and lots of Vivaldi."

The HCCs' regard for connoisseurship is also evident when they discuss those categories in which they have not invested the resources to develop fine-grained tastes. For these, they evaluate their actions against a connoisseur standard and discuss, apologetically or defensively, their relative neglect:

INTERVIEWER: What are some of your favorite meals generally?

REBECCA (HCC): Okay. Well, this will be a real short section of your interview. I'm not a person who is picky about food. I'm not a person who can tell you necessarily what the ingredients in something are. I'm not a cook. I'm able to cook when I have to. But it's not a priority for me. I can eat the same thing every day, you know.

In contrast, because LCC subjectivity is local and collective, consumer subjectivity depends on community acknowledgment of particular tastes and practices. Rather than seek out authentic decommodified goods and apply idiosyncratic tastes to mass goods, LCC subjectivity parallels the role of insider core members of consumer subcultures (Schouten and McAlexander 1995): they develop the requisite knowledge, skills, and social capital within a particular activity that then become key resources for the construction of subjectivity by self and others. For example, Nancy and her husband started a folk dancing club and spend most of

their free time organizing events, going to dance practices, and socializing with some of the members who have become very close friends.
From the interview, it is clear that she thinks of herself, first and foremost, as a folk dancer; it is through this avocation that she attains much
of her subjective sense of self. Yet, she does not claim this as a distinctive
identity. Instead, her sense of self vested in this avocation is a communal
one, located in sharing great enthusiasm and development of skills with
like-minded others. This is a particularly powerful source of identity for
Nancy, not because she has carved out a qualitatively distinctive style,
but because, through her devotion, she is located at the nucleus of this
local group. Likewise, Katie and her husband have played cards with
the same group of six or eight friends two or three times per week for
many years. Card playing has become a central constitutive element of
Katie's identity, one that exists only to the extent that it is jointly constructed with local others.

Because for LCCs subjectivity does not require asserting individuality
in relation to mass culture or normative local tastes, there is no contradiction between subjectivity, mass consumer goods, and the conventions
of mass culture. In fact, mass goods and conventions often provide useful resources from which a local identity is constructed. For example,
Heather prides herself on wearing clothes with a nautical theme, which
she will buy whenever she comes across such clothing at a local department store. Even when describing individuated consumption objects, LCCs rarely camouflage their use of mass-produced objects:

INTERVIEWER: What are some of your favorite meals for dinner?

LYNN (LCC): I like my chicken broccoli casserole.

INTERVIEWER: How do you make that?

LYNN: You just put everything in a casserole pan, cut up your cooked
    chicken and your cooked vegetables and you can use mixed vegetables
    and potatoes, and you have a thing of broccoli soup and one thing
    of broccoli and one broccoli cheese and just throw that in with milk
    and put it in the oven for 15 minutes and cut out biscuits that come
    in a round metal can, cut them up and put them on the top and then
    throw it back in until it's brown. It's pretty good and it's real easy.

Since LCCs do not participate in social worlds in which subjectivity
is constructed through individuated consumption, they seldom use the
connoisseur's vocabulary of expertise and passion to talk about their
preferences. Interview questions that HCCs use as opportunities to express fine-grained sensibilities provoke terse responses from LCCs, who
understand these questions to ask for trivial expressions of preference
rather than as an invitation for a consumerist performance. For example, Joseph has an impressive collection of 19 rifles hanging on his living

room wall. When I inquire about the guns, Joseph makes clear that he is not so much interested in talking about different models and styles of guns to express connoisseur tastes (he would add "almost anything" for the right price) as he is in telling stories about acquiring and using the guns, such as trading with a friend for a gun, hunting deer and wild turkey with friends, and teaching his sons how to hunt, which invest the guns with particularized local meanings.

Ruth's description of her antiques is particularly poignant in this regard. Through much determination and sacrifice over the last 20 years, Ruth and her husband have raised their income to the upper strata of the State College area. Now that they have reached this position, they are engaged in a project to evolve their lifestyle to match their economic position. Yet, even though Ruth lives in a nice neighborhood, has acquired a large collection of antiques, and entertains expensively, she does not convey an HCC style because she has not acquired the performative means to do so. Although most of her free time over the past five years has been devoted to antiquing, she has not developed the vocabulary of appreciation and evaluation to convey this interest as does an HCC connoisseur such as John:

INTERVIEWER: How did you get into [antiques]?

RUTH (LCC): I always liked antiques, but I never had them. I would go to garage sales. I mean, like 10 years ago, when I was buying stuff at auctions and putting it in the garage, and after the children went and I said "We're gonna re-do the house." And so I started getting, I decided I was gonna do it. And I like Victorian and country and . . . so I went to the garage and started pulling these things out and then it just, I would buy more. (laughs)

INTERVIEWER: You just got more, more involved in it?

RUTH: Yeah.

INTERVIEWER: And so how'd you find out about where all this stuff is, and which pieces you wanted?

RUTH: Oh, just. . . . If I like it, I buy it. I mean, I, I look. Every weekend I look. (laughs) I made some purchases last weekend. In State College at a garage sale that picture for $35.

INTERVIEWER: What, what do you like about the picture?

RUTH: Oh, I just like . . . It just has personality. Something like a . . . different than new things. (laughs) . . . Plus if it gives you a little more . . . a homey feeling, I think. I don't know, maybe it's my age. (both laugh) This sofa here, I paid $22 for it. But I ended up reupholstering it. It costs me like $700 to refinish it, so, still in all $722. Where can you get a sofa like that?

INTERVIEWER: Are there certain types of things you're looking for?

RUTH: I like Victorian things. [pause] I have country things in my kitchen. [pause] But, I just keep looking. [pause] If it appeals to me, we buy it.

Instead of describing her antiques in connoisseur terms, she reverts to pragmatic evaluations (e.g., good prices). Throughout the interview, she is uncomfortable making any strong and specific evaluative claims about the qualities of her antiques compared to others; she just likes them. The interview was uncomfortable for both parties because we both understood that some of my questions encouraged her to express connoisseur tastes and that she was not able to respond as an HCC person might. She quickly became conscious of this inability and felt uncomfortable; likewise, I understood that my questions put her in an uncomfortable position because she had trouble responding as she wanted to, which made me feel uncomfortable.

By comparison, for HCCs, evaluating consumption objects is a primary, sometimes even dominant aspect of consuming. Thus, in many HCC interviews the mention of even the most mundane of consumption objects (e.g., water!) led, with little prompting, to lengthy soliloquies elaborating in great detail the prized and disliked qualities within a category. In these interviews, I was often left with the impression that a primary attraction of many consumption objects is that they serve as resources for very detailed and opinionated conversations about the relative merits of different goods within a category. For HCCs, the interview itself was clearly an enjoyable experience since it closely paralleled this style of consuming.

DISCUSSION

Contemporary American ideology holds that tastes are individualized and disinterested. "Be your own dog!" the Red Dog Beer ad shouts. But tastes are never innocent of social consequences. To be "cultured" is a potent social advantage in American society, providing access to desirable education, occupations, social networks, and spouses. Conversely, to grow up in conditions that deny the accumulation of cultural capital leads to exclusion from these privileged social circles and condescension and demands of deference from elites—a form of "symbolic violence" (Bourdieu 1984) that is rarely acknowledged because tastes are understood as idiosyncratic choices.

One of the most important questions in the consumer society debate concerns materialism: the extent to which "things" (typically consumer goods) are linked to human happiness, and the unintended social and environmental consequences that result. My findings suggest that it is important to conceive of materialism sociologically as a class practice.

A defining characteristic of modern capitalist societies is that human relationships are transmogrified into the symbolic qualities of goods produced for sale—what Marx called commodity fetishism. The competitive dynamics of advanced capitalism have led to the ever expanding colonization by marketplace symbolism of experiences that have historically been enacted in social domains other than commodified material culture (e.g., consider religion, health, family relationships, sexuality). The experiences of social life that create and sustain human subjectivity—love, prestige, security, fear, happiness, joy, anticipation—are increasingly reconstituted as "benefits" in the world of commodities. Rather than material mediators of culture (as Grant McCracken [1986] would have it), consumer goods now sit at the cultural epicenter. Postmodern consumer society, then, is the logical culmination of this migration of meanings and values from relationships with people to relationships with market goods and spectacles. (While the Beatles may not have been more popular than Jesus Christ, Michael Jordan no doubt is.)

Materialism is one important mode in which social identities are constructed through interaction with the marketplace. To understand materialism requires understanding who consumes in a materialist style, who uses the term "materialist" to characterize whom, and the social consequences that result from these practices. Reflecting their workplace ethos and relative advantage in the status marketplace, people whose capital volume is strongly weighted toward economic rather than cultural capital tend to consume using a materialist style of consumption. For economic elites, this means pursuing the newest fashions, the latest technologies, the most luxurious, pampering products and services. For the ever increasing majority with relatively small and declining incomes, living in a society that so emphasizes material satisfactions constructs relative material deprivation as an intense lack and, thus, their tastes are structured around attaining glimpses (or simulacra) of elite comforts. But, with materialism as the dominant status game, how are cultural elites to distinguish themselves? The only option, structurally speaking, is to develop a set of tastes in opposition to materialism: consuming which emphasizes the metaphysical over the material—idealism—is prestigious currency in the cultural sphere. Hence, HCCs have constructed "materialist" as a pejorative term—synonymous with "showy," "ostentatious," "gaudy," "unrefined"—used to denigrate the tastes of people whose tastes are formed by economic capital.

It is a misnomer, then, to equate materialism with status seeking. Materialists are no more (or less) interested in prestige than HCC idealists. Instead, they seek to acquire prestige in a particular status game (materialism) structured around particular practices (acquiring goods and participating in activities that are inscribed with economic symbolism: luxury, leisure, pampering, extravagance). From the perspective of

HCCs, those who participate in this mode of status consumption seem particularly desperate to win prestige from their consumption. But, as I demonstrate in this study, cultural elites have their own set of exclusionary practices in which they invert materialism to affirm their societal position. Thus, materialism scales that isolate materialism as a vulgar form of status-claiming, while leaving uninterred the status claims embodied in the practices of cultural elites, serves to reinforce rather than challenge the exclusionary class boundaries erected by HCC consumption. Idealists are also inveterate status-seekers who are just as capable of selfishness as materialists.

But what about the societal and environmental consequences of materialism? It is important to disentangle the socially beneficial aspects of idealism from its use as a pernicious symbolic boundary. To do so, we need to recognize that cultural elites are in a privileged position to pursue alternatives to materialism both because they typically are socialized in environments free of material scarcity and also because they reap prestige from idealist practices. Psychometric scales can be useful in weeding the negative social consequences of idealist consumption from its enormous positive possibilities, but they need to be informed by a social reflexivity that acknowledges that values, and social effects, are built into these measures. For example, to understand and ameliorate environmental degradation rather than perpetuate class boundaries, materialism research needs to examine the relationship between materialist and idealist consumption practices and the amount of material resources expended and pollution generated. I'm not convinced that idealist consumption is necessarily more environment-friendly than materialist consumption. One can abhor the idea that happiness and identity can be derived through objects and still mail order an abundance of experience-facilitating goods that overload dumps with packaging materials. And, alternatively, one can be extremely materialistic as measured by psychometric scales yet consume many fewer material resources than those who profess to be idealist, as the status condensed in a single pair of Nikes worn by a poor African-American urban teen attests.

REFERENCES

Baudrillard, Jean (1981), *Towards a Critique of the Political Economy of the Sign*, St. Louis, MO: Telos.
Belk, Russell (1985), "Materialism: Trait Aspects of Living in the Material World," *Journal of Consumer Research*, 12 (December), 265–280.
———, Melanie Wallendorf, and John F. Sherry, Jr. (1989), "The Sacred and Profane in Consumer Behavior: Theodicy on the Odyssey," *Journal of Consumer Research*, 16 (June), 1–38.
Bell, Daniel (1976), *The Cultural Contradictions of Capitalism*, New York: Basic.
Bendix, Reinhard and Seymour Martin Lipset (1951), "Social Status and Social Structure: A Reexamination of Data and Interpretations," *British Journal of Sociology*, 2 (June), 150–168; (September), 230–254.

Bourdieu, Pierre (1977), *Outline of a Theory of Practice*, Cambridge: Cambridge University Press.

—— (1984), *Distinction: A Social Critique of the Judgment of Taste*, Cambridge, MA: Harvard University Press.

—— and Loic Wacquant (1992), *An Invitation to Reflexive Sociology*, Chicago: University of Chicago Press.

Burawoy, Michael (1979), *Manufacturing Consent: Changes in the Labor Process under Monopoly Capitalism*, Chicago: University of Chicago Press.

Calhoun, Craig (1993), "Habitus, Field, and Capital: The Question of Historical Specificity," in *Bourdieu: Critical Perspectives*, ed. Craig Calhoun et al., Chicago: University of Chicago Press, 61–88.

——, Edward LiPuma, and Moishe Postone, eds. (1993), *Bourdieu: Critical Perspectives*, Chicago: University of Chicago Press.

Clarke, John (1993), *New Times and Old Enemies: Essays on Cultural Studies and America*, London: HarperCollins Academic.

Coleman, Richard P. (1983), "The Continuing Significance of Social Class to Marketing," *Journal of Consumer Research*, 10 (December), 265–280.

—— and Lee Rainwater (1978), *Social Standing in America*, New York: Basic.

Collins, Randall (1975), *Conflict Sociology*, New York: Academic Press.

—— (1981), "On the Microfoundations of Macrosociology," *American Journal of Sociology*, 86 (5), 984–1014.

Crane, Diane (1992), *The Production of Culture: Media and the Urban Arts*, Newbury Park, CA: Sage.

DiMaggio, Paul (1987), "Classification in Art," *American Sociological Review*, 52 (August), 440–455.

—— and John Mohr (1985), "Cultural Capital, Educational Attainment, and Marital Selection," *American Journal of Sociology*, 90 (May), 1231–1261.

—— and Francie Ostrower (1990), "Participation in the Arts by Black and White Americans," *Social Forces*, 68 (March), 753–778.

—— and Michael Useem (1978), "Social Class and Arts Consumption: The Origins and Consequences of Class Differences in Exposure to the Arts in America," *Theory and Society*, 5 (March), 141–161.

Erikson, Bonnie H. (1996), "Culture, Class, and Connections," *American Journal of Sociology*, 102(1): 217–251.

Ewen, Stuart and Elizabeth Ewen ([1982] 1992), *Channels of Desire: Mass Images and the Shaping of American Consciousness*, Minneapolis: University of Minnesota Press.

Featherstone, Mike (1991), *Consumer Culture and Postmodernism*, Newbury Park, CA: Sage.

Foster, Hal, ed. (1985), *The Anti-Aesthetic*, Port Townsend, WA: Bay.

Frow, John (1995), *Cultural Studies and Cultural Value*, New York: Oxford University Press.

Gamson, Joshua (1994), *Claims to Fame: Celebrity in Contemporary America*, Berkeley and Los Angeles: University of California Press.

Gartman, David (1991), "Culture as Class Socialization or Mass Reification: A Critique of Bourdieu's *Distinction*," *American Journal of Sociology*, 97 (September), 421–447.

Goffman, Erving (1967), *Interaction Ritual: Essays on Face-to-Face Behavior*, New York: Pantheon.

Gordon, Milton (1963), *Social Class in American Sociology*, New York: McGraw-Hill.

Gouldner, Alvin (1979), *The Future of the Intellectuals and the Rise of the New Class*, London: Macmillan.

Hall, John R. (1992), "The Capital(s) of Cultures: A Nonholistic Approach to Status Situations, Class, Gender, and Ethnicity," in *Cultivating Differences: Symbolic Boundaries and the Making of Inequality*, ed. Michele Lamont and Marcel Fournier, Chicago: University of Chicago Press, 257–285.

Halle, David (1984), *America's Working Man*, Chicago: University of Chicago Press.

—— (1993), *Inside Culture: Art and Class in the American Home*, Chicago: University of Chicago Press.

Hannerz, Ulf (1990), "Cosmopolitans and Locals in World Culture," *Theory, Culture, and Society*, 7, 237–251.

Hollingshead, A. B. and F. Redlick (1959), *Social Class and Mental Illness*, New York: Wiley.

Holt, Douglas B. (1995), "How Consumers Consume: A Typology of Consumption Practices," *Journal of Consumer Research*, 22 (June), 1–16.

———— (1997a), "Distinction in America? Recovering Bourdieu's Theory of Tastes from Its Critics," *Poetics*, 25, 93–120.

———— (1997b), "Poststructuralist Lifestyle Analysis: Conceptualizing the Social Patterning of Consumption in Postmodernity," *Journal of Consumer Research*, 23 (March), 326–350.

Horkheimer, Max and Theodor Adorno ([1944] 1972), *Dialectic of Enlightenment*, New York: Herder & Herder.

Hughes, Michael and Richard Peterson (1983), "Isolating Cultural Choice Patterns in the U.S. Population," *American Behavioral Scientist*, 26, 459–478.

Huyssen, Andreas (1986), *After the Great Divide: Modernism, Mass Culture, Postmodernism*, Bloomington: Indiana University Press.

Jameson, Fredric (1991), *Postmodernism, or The Cultural Logic of Late Capitalism*, Durham, NC: Duke University Press.

Jenkins, Henry (1992), *Textural Poachers: Television Fans and Participatory Culture*, New York: Routledge.

Joppke, Christian (1986), "The Cultural Dimension of Class Formation and Class Struggle: On the Social Theory of Pierre Bourdieu," *Berkeley Journal of Sociology*, 31, 53–78.

Kellner, Douglas (1989), *Jean Baudrillard: From Marxism to Postmodernism and Beyond*, Stanford, CA: Stanford University Press.

Lamont, Michele (1992), *Money, Morals, and Manners: The Culture of the French and American Upper-Middle Class*, Chicago: University of Chicago Press.

———— and Annette Lareau (1988), "Cultural Capital: Allusions, Gaps, and Glissandos in Recent Theoretical Developments," *Sociological Theory*, 6, (2), 153–168.

Leidner, Robin (1993), *Fast Food, Fast Talk: Service Work and the Routinization of Everyday Life*, Berkeley and Los Angeles: University of California Press.

Levy, Sidney (1966), "Social Class and Consumer Behavior," in *On Knowing the Consumer*, ed. Joseph Newman, New York: Wiley, 146–160.

———— (1996), "Stalking the Amphisbaena," *Journal of Consumer Research*, 23 (December), 163–176.

Liebes, Tamar and Elihu Katz (1990), *The Export of Meaning: Cross-Cultural Readings of "Dallas,"* New York: Oxford University Press.

Lynd, Robert and Helen Lynd ([1929] 1956), *Middletown: A Study in Modern American Culture*, New York: Harvest.

Lyotard, Jean-Francois (1984), *The Postmodern Condition*, Minneapolis: University of Minnesota Press.

MacCannell, Dean (1976), *The Tourist: A New Theory of the Leisure Class*, New York: Schocken.

McCracken, Grant (1986), "Culture and Consumption: A Theoretical Account of the Structure and Movement of the Cultural Meaning of Consumer Goods," *Journal of Consumer Research*, 13 (June), 71–84.

Merton, Robert (1957), *Social Theory and Social Structure*, Glencoe, IL: Free Press.

Meyrowitz, Joshua (1985), *No Sense of Place: The Impact of Electronic Media on Social Behavior*, New York: Oxford University Press.

Miller, Daniel (1987), *Material Culture and Mass Consumption*, New York: Basil Blackwell.

Myers, James and Jonathan Gutman (1974), "Life Style: The Essence of Social Class," in *Life Style and Psychographics*, ed. William Wells, Chicago: American Marketing Association, 235–256.

Peterson, Richard (1978), "The Production of Cultural Change: The Case of Contemporary Country Music," *Social Research*, 45, 292–314.

———— and Paul DiMaggio (1975), "From Region to Class, the Changing Locus of Country Music: A Test of the Massification Hypothesis," *Social Forces*, 53, 497–506.

———— and Albert Simkus (1992), "How Musical Tastes Mark Occupational

Status Groups," in *Cultivating Differences*, ed. Michele Lamont and Marcel Fournier, Chicago: University of Chicago Press, 152–186.

Pfautz, Harold and Otis Dudley Duncan (1950), "A Critical Evaluation of Warner's Work in Community Stratification," *American Sociological Review*, 15 (April), 205–215.

Press, Andrea (1991), *Women Watching Television: Gender, Class, and Generation in the American Television Experience*, Philadelphia: University of Pennsylvania Press.

Rainwater, Lee, Richard Coleman, and Gerald Handel (1959), *Workingman's Wife: Her Personality, World, and Lifestyle*, New York: Oceana.

Richins, Marsha and Scott Dawson (1992), "A Consumer Values Orientation for Materialism and Its Measurement: Scale Development and Validation," *Journal of Consumer Research*, 19 (December), 303–316.

Rubin, Lillian Breslow (1976), *Worlds of Pain*, New York: Basic.

Schaninger, Charles (1981), "Social Class versus Income Revisited: An Empirical Investigation," *Journal of Marketing Research*, 18 (May), 192–208.

Schouten, John W. and James H. McAlexander (1995), "Subcultures of Consumption: An Ethnography of the New Bikers," *Journal of Consumer Research*, 22 (June), 43–61.

Simmel, Georg ([1904] 1957), "Fashion," *American Journal of Sociology*, 62 (May), 541–558.

Thompson, Craig J. (1996), "Caring Consumers: Gendered Consumption Meanings and the Juggling Lifestyle," *Journal of Consumer Research*, 22 (March), 388–407.

Tobin, Joseph J., ed. (1992), *Re-Made in Japan: Everyday Life and Consumer Taste in a Changing Society*, New Haven, CT: Yale University Press.

Veblen, Thorstein ([1899] 1970), *The Theory of the Leisure Class*, London: Unwin.

Wallendorf, Melanie and Eric Arnould (1991), "We Gather Together: Consumption Rituals of Thanksgiving Day," *Journal of Consumer Research*, 18 (June), 13–31.

Warner, W. Lloyd, Marsha Meeker, and Kenneth Eells (1949), *Social Class in America: The Evaluation of Status*, New York: Harper Torchbooks.

Weber, Max (1978), *Economy and Society*, Berkeley: University of California Press.

Wilensky, Harold (1964), "Mass Society and Mass Culture," *American Sociological Review*, 29 (2), 173–197.

Willis, Paul (1977), *Learning to Labor: How Working Class Kids Get Working Class Jobs*, New York: Columbia University Press.

ENDNOTES

1. Compare Warner's findings to imperialist interpretations in consumer research asserting that lifestyle and social class are synonomous (Levy 1966; Myers and Gutman 1974).

2. It is impossible to do justice to Bourdieu's theory, complexly articulated over many dozens of studies over more than 30 years, in a short review. Instead I briefly summarize the key concepts that pertain specifically to Bourdieu's work on social reproduction linking cultural capital to the field of consumption, and then highlight those aspects of the theory that distinguish it from Warner. Interested readers are encouraged to read *Distinction* and supporting theoretical statements that outline Bourdieu's project, such as Bourdieu and Wacquant (1992) and Bourdieu (1977).

3. Bourdieu's broad theoretical statements support the contemporary interpretation, yet he often makes ahistorical generalizations about the superordinate status of the high arts as a locus for high cultural capital consumption. In *Distinction*, Bourdieu encourages the latter reading because, in his intensive effort to isolate and describe synchronic differences in formal qualities of taste that vary with cultural capital, he does not execute a fully cultural analysis in which social differences in meanings of those objects consumed, and their sociohistorical genesis, also become a focus of investigation (Calhoun 1993; Gartman 1991).

4. I selected the terms "HCC" and "LCC" to connote a hierarchy of tastes and, thus, of social and moral value. The terms are not intended to denigrate LCCs. Just the opposite: by illuminating hierarchies that are smoothed over in everyday life, I hope to defuse their exclusionary power.

5. Empirical assessments of Bourdieu's theory typically compare two or more social class groupings as I do here. However, many studies use measures of social class to group informants that conflict directly with Bourdieu's formulation. For example, Halle (1992) uses Warnerian measures of income and and neighborhood measures that necessarily conflate economic and social capital with cultural capital, while Erikson (1996) uses Erik Olin Wright's class measures, which are primarily measures of economic capital. I follow Bourdieu's theory more carefully in distinguishing the three socialization agents that are considered central in developing cultural capital resources (for a detailed discussion, see Holt [1997a]). Most studies do not measure all three sources of cultural capital acculturation. The occupation scale is adapted from Peterson and Simkus (1992), and arguments relating occupation and cultural capital are found in Collins (1975). The education scale is adapted from Bourdieu (1984) and Lamont (1992), calibrating the scale downward for parents given the tremendous status inflation in education over the past several decades (Bourdieu 1984). Although the two resulting groups of informants approximately resemble the upper-middle "New Class" of symbolic manipulators, who derive labor market leverage primarily from cultural capital assets, and the working class, whose social conditions rarely facilitate cultural capital formation, they are not identical. A significant percentage of the middle class with upwardly mobile trajectories out of the working class, particularly those who have entered managerial and entrepreneurial occupations that emphasize economic capital, will still have low cultural capital resources. Similarly, newly minted New Class members whose parents were working class and who were the first in their families to attend college do not typically have the highest level of cultural capital resources. Alternatively, a growing number of HCCs (though none in this sample), such as urban artists, have working-class jobs.

14
Alex Kotlowitz
"FALSE CONNECTIONS"
(1999)

A drive down Chicago's Madison Street, moving west from the lake, is a short lesson in America's fault lines of race and class. The first mile runs through the city's downtown—or the Loop, as it's called locally—past high-rises that house banks and law firms, advertising agencies and investment funds. The second mile, once lined by flophouses and greasy diners, has hitched onto its neighbor to the east, becoming a mecca for artists and new, hip restaurants, a more affordable appendage to the Loop. And west from there, past the United Center, home to the Chicago Bulls, the boulevard descends into the abyssal lows of neighborhoods where work has disappeared. Buildings lean like punchdrunk boxers. Makers of plywood do big business here, patching those same buildings' open wounds. At dusk, the gangs claim ownership to the corners and hawk their wares, whatever is the craze of the moment, crack or smack or reefer. It's all for sale. Along one stretch, young women, their long, bare legs shimmering under the lamplight, smile and beckon and mumble short, pithy descriptions of the pleasures they promise to deliver.

Such is urban decay. Such are the remains of the seemingly intractable, distinctly American version of poverty, a poverty not only "of the pocket" but also, as Mother Teresa said when she visited this section of the city, "of the spirit."

What is most striking about this drive down Madison, though, is that so few whites make it. Chicago's West Side, like other central-city neighborhoods, sits apart from everything and everyone else. Its inhabitants have become geographically and spiritually isolated from all that surrounds them, islands unto themselves. Even the violence—which, myth has it, threatens us all—is contained within its borders. Drug dealers shoot drug dealers. Gang members maul gang members. And the innocents, the passersby who get caught in the crossfire, are their neighbors and friends. It was that isolation which so struck me when I first began to spend time at the Henry Horner Homes, a Chicago public housing complex that sits along that Madison Street corridor. Lafeyette and Pharoah, the two boys I wrote about in my book *There Are No Children Here*, had never been to the Loop, one mile away. They'd never walked the halls of the Art Institute of Chicago or felt the spray from the Buckingham Fountain. They'd never ogled the sharks at the John G. Shedd Aquarium or stood in the shadow of the stuffed pachyderms at the Field Museum. They'd never been to the suburbs. They'd never been to the countryside. In fact, until we stayed at a hotel one summer on their first fishing trip, they'd never felt the steady stream of a shower. (Henry Horner's apartments had only bathtubs.) At one point, the boys, so certain that their way of life was the only way of life, insisted that my neighborhood, a gentrified community on the city's North Side, had to be controlled by gangs. They knew nothing different.

And yet children like Lafeyette and Pharoah do have a connection to the American mainstream: it is as consumers that inner-city children, otherwise so disconnected from the world around them, identify themselves not as ghetto kids or project kids but as Americans or just plain kids. And they are as much consumers as they are the consumed; that is, they mimic white America while white America mimics them. "Inner-city kids will embrace a fashion item as their own that shows they have a connection, and then you'll see the prep school kids reinvent it, trying to look hip-hop," says Sarah Young, a consultant to businesses interested in tapping the urban market. "It's a cycle."[1] A friend, a black nineteen-year-old from the city's West Side, suggests that this dynamic occurs because the inner-city poor equate classiness with suburban whites while those same suburban whites equate hipness with the inner-city poor. If he's right, it suggests that commercialism may be our most powerful link, one that in the end only accentuates and prolongs the myths we have built up about each other.

Along Madison Street, halfway between the Loop and the city's boundary, sits an old, worn-out shopping strip containing small, transient stores. They open and close almost seasonally—balloons mark the openings; "Close-Out Sale" banners mark the closings—as the African American and Middle Eastern immigrant owners ride the ebb and flow of unpredictable fashion tastes. GQ Sports. Dress to Impress. Best Fit. Chic Classics. Dream Team. On weekend afternoons, the makeshift mall is thronged with customers blithely unaware that store ownership and names may have changed since their last visit. Young mothers guiding their children by the shoulders and older women seeking a specific purchase pick their way through packs of teenagers who laugh and clown, pulling and pushing one another into the stores. Their whimsical tastes are the subject of intense curiosity, longing, and marketing surveys on the part of store owners and corporate planners.

On a recent spring afternoon, as I made my way down Madison Street toward Tops and Bottoms, one of the area's more popular shops, I detected the unmistakable sweet odor of marijuana. Along the building's side, two teenage boys toked away at cigar-sized joints, called blunts. The store is long and narrow; its walls are lined with shoes and caps and its center is packed with shirts, jeans, and leather jackets. The owner of the store, a Palestinian immigrant, recognized me from my previous visits there with Lafeyette and Pharoah. "You're a probation officer, right?" he asked. I told him what my connection was with the boys. He completed a sale of a black Starter skullcap and then beckoned me toward the back of the store, where we could talk without distraction.

Behind him, an array of nearly 200 assorted shoes and sneakers lined the wall from floor to ceiling. There were the predictable brands: Nike, Fila, and Reebok, the shoes that have come to define (and nearly bankrupt) a generation. There were the heavy boots by Timberland and Lugz that have become popular among urban teens. But it was the arrangement of shoes directly in front of me that the proprietor pointed to, a collection of Hush Puppies. "See that?" he asked. "It's totally whitebread." Indeed, Hush Puppies, once of earth tones and worn by preppies, have caught on among urban black teens—and the company has responded in kind, producing the shoes in outrageous, gotta-look-at-me colors such as crayon orange and fire-engine red. I remember the first time Pharoah appeared in a pair of lime green Hush Puppies loafers— I was dumbfounded. But then I thought of his other passions: Tommy Hilfiger shirts, Coach wallets, Guess? jeans. They were the fashions of the economically well heeled, templates of those who had "made it." Pharoah, who is now off at college, ultimately found his path. But for those who are left behind, these fashions are their "in." They give them cachet. They link them to a more secure, more prosperous world, a world in which they have not been able to participate—except as consumers.

Sarah Young, whose clients include the company that manufactures Hush Puppies, suggests that "for a lot of these kids, what they wear is who they are because that's all they have to connect them to the rest of the larger community. It marks their status because there's not a lot else."[2]

It's a false status, of course. They hold on to the idea that to "make it" means to consume at will, to buy a $100 Coach wallet or an $80 Tommy Hilfiger shirt. And these brand-name companies, knowing they have a good thing going, capitalize on their popularity among the urban poor, a group that despite its economic difficulties represents a surprisingly lucrative market. The companies gear their advertising to this market segment. People such as Sarah Young nurture relationships with rap artists, who they lure into wearing certain clothing items. When the company that makes Hush Puppies was looking to increase their presence in the urban market, Young helped persuade Wyclef Jean, a singer with the Fugees, to wear powder blue Bridgeport chukkas, which bear a sneaking resemblance to the Wallabee shoes familiar to members of my generation. In a recent issue of *Vibe*, a magazine aimed at the hip-hop market, rappers Beenie Man and Bounty Killer are pictured posing in Ralph Lauren hats and Armani sweaters, sandwiched between photographs of other rappers decked out in Calvin Klein sunglasses and Kenneth Cole shoes. The first three full-page advertisements in that same issue are for Hilfiger's athletic line, Coach handbags (with jazz singer Cassandra Wilson joyfully walking along with her Coach bag slung over her shoulder), and Perry Ellis casual wear (with a black man and three young boys lounging on the beach). This, as Pharoah told me, represents class—and, as Young suggested, the one connection that children growing up amid the ruins of the inner city have to a more prosperous, more secure world. It is as consumers that they claim citizenship. And yet that Coach handbag or that Tommy Hilfiger or Perry Ellis shirt changes nothing of the cruel realities of growing up poor and black. It reminds me of the murals painted on abandoned buildings in the South Bronx: pictures of flowers, window shades, and curtains, and the interiors of tidy rooms. As Jonathan Kozol observes in his book *Amazing Grace*, "the pictures have been done so well that when you look, the first time, you imagine that you're seeing into people's homes—pleasant-looking homes, in fact, that have a distinctly middle-class appearance."[3]

But the urban poor are more than just consumers. They help drive fashions as well. The Tommy Hilfiger clothing line, aimed initially at preppies, became hot in the inner city, pushed in large part by rap artists who took to the clothing maker's stylish, colorful vestments. A 1997 article in *Forbes* magazine suggests that Hilfiger's 47 percent rise in earnings over the first nine months of its fiscal year 1996–1997 had much to do with the clothing line's popularity among the kinds of kids who shop Chicago's Madison Street.[4] Suddenly, Tommy Hilfiger became cool, not only among the urban teens but also among their counterparts in the suburbs. "That gives them a sense of pride, that they're bringing a style to a new height," Sarah Young suggests.[5] Thus, those who don't have much control over other aspects of their life find comfort in having at least some control over something—style.

There's another facet to this as well: the romanticization of urban poverty by some white teens. In St. Joseph, Michigan, a nearly all-white town of 9,000 in the state's southwestern corner, a group of teens mimicked the mannerisms and fashions of their neighbors across the river in Benton Harbor, Michigan, a nearly all-black town that has been economically devastated by the closing of the local factories and foundries. This cadre of kids called themselves "wiggers." A few white boys identified themselves with one of the Benton Harbor gangs, and one small band was caught carrying out holdups with a BB gun. A local police detective laughingly called them "wannabes." At St. Joseph High School, the wiggers greeted one another in the hallways with a high five or a twitch of the head. "Hey, Nigger, wha's up?" they'd inquire. "Man, just chillin'."

But it was through fashions—as consumers—that they most clearly identified themselves with their peers across the way. They dressed in the hip-hop fashion made popular by M.C. Hammer and other rap artists, wearing blue jeans big enough for two, the crotch down at their knees. (The beltless, pants-falling-off-hips style originated, many believe, in prison, where inmates must forgo belts.) The guys wore Starter jackets and hats, the style at the time. The girls hung braided gold necklaces around their necks and styled their hair in finger waves or braids. For these teens, the life of ghetto kids is edgy, gutsy, risky—all that adolescents crave. But do they know how edgy, how gusty, how risky? They have never had to comfort a dying friend, bleeding from the head because he was on the wrong turf. They have never sat in a classroom where the desks are arranged so that no student will be hit by falling plaster. They have never had to say "Yes, Sir" and "No, Sir," as a police officer, dripping with sarcasm, asks, "Nigger, where'd you get the money for such a nice car?" From a safe distance—as consumers—they can believe they are hip, hip being defined as what they see in their urban counterparts. With their jeans sagging off their boxer shorts, with their baseball caps worn to the side, with their high-tops unlaced, they find some connection, though in the end it is a false bond.

It is as consumers that poor black children claim membership to the larger community. It is as purchasers of the talismans of success that they can believe they've transcended their otherwise miserable situation. In the late 1980s, as the drug trade began to flourish in neighborhoods such as Chicago's West Side, the vehicle of choice for these big-time entrepreneurs was the Chevrolet Blazer, an icon of suburban stability. As their communities were unraveling, in part because of their trade, they sought a connection to an otherwise stable life. And they sought it in the only way they knew how, the only way available to them: as consumers. Inner-city teens are eager to participate in society; they want to belong.

And for the white teens like those in St. Joseph, who, like all adolescents, want to feel that they're on the edge, what better way than to build some connection—however manufactured—to their contemporaries across the river who must negotiate that vertical drop every day? By purchasing, in complete safety, all the accoutrements associated with skirting that fall, they can believe that they've been there, that they've experienced the horrors and pains of growing up black and poor. Nothing, of course, could be further from the truth. They know nothing of the struggles their neighbors endure.

On the other hand, fashions in the end are just that—fashions. Sometimes kids yearn for baggy jeans or a Tommy Hilfiger shirt not because of what it represents but because it is the style of their peers. Those "wiggers," for example, may equate the sagging pants with their neighbors across the river, but kids a few years younger are mimicking them as much as their black counterparts. Fashions grow long limbs that, in the end, are only distantly connected to their roots.

Take that excursion down Madison Street—and the fault lines will become abundantly clear. One can't help but marvel at the spiritual distance between those shopping at Tops and Bottoms on the blighted West Side and those browsing the pricey department stores in the robust downtown. And yet many of the children have one eye trained down Madison Street, those on each side watching their counterparts and thinking they know the others' lives. Their style of dress mimics that of the others. But they're being cheated. They don't know. They have no idea. Those checking out the array of Hush Puppies at Tops and Bottoms think they have the key to making it, to becoming full members of this prosperous nation. And those trying on the jeans wide enough for two think they know what it means to be hip, to live on the edge. And so, in lieu of building real connections—by providing opportunities or rebuilding communities—we have found some common ground as purchasers of each other's trademarks. At best, that link is tenuous; at worst, it's false. It lets us believe that we are connected when the distance, in fact, is much farther than anyone cares to admit.

ENDNOTES

1. Sarah Young, telephone interview with the author, January 1998.

2. Ibid.

3. Jonathan Kozol, *Amazing Grace: The Lives of Children and the Conscience of a Nation* (New York: HarperPerennial, 1996).

4. Joshua Levine, "Baad Sells," *Forbes* 159, no. 8 (April 21, 1997): 142.

5. Sarah Young, telephone interview with the author, January 1998.

15

Ann DuCille
"TOY THEORY: BLACK BARBIE AND THE DEEP PLAY OF DIFFERENCE" (1996)

This is my doll story (because every black journalist who writes about race gets around to it sometime). Back when I started playing with Barbie, there were no Christies (Barbie's black friend, born in 1968) or black Barbies (born in 1980, brown plastic poured into blond Barbie's mold). I had two blonds, which I bought with Christmas money from girls at school. I cut off their hair and dressed them in African-print fabric ... After an "incident" at school (where all of the girls looked like Barbie and none of them looked like me), I galloped down our stairs with one Barbie, her blond head hitting each spoke of the banister ... until her head popped off, lost to the grave-yard behind the stairwell. Then I tore off each limb, and sat on the stairs for a long time twirling the torso like a baton.

—LISA JONES, *VILLAGE VOICE*

BASIC TRAINING

More than simple instruments of pleasure and amusement, toys and games play crucial roles in helping children to determine what is valuable in and around them. As elements of the rites and rituals of childhood, dolls, games, storybooks, fairytales, and comics assist children in the process of becoming, in the task of defining themselves in relation to the world around them. As marketed by Mattel, Inc., Barbie dolls in particular invite children to imagine themselves in the dolls' image, to transport themselves into a realm of beauty, glamour, fun, success, and conspicuous consumption. "Imagine appearing on magazine covers, starring in fashion shows, and going to Hollywood parties," one ad reads, "as you, Shani, Asha and Nichelle [black Barbie dolls] live your dreams of beauty and success, loving every marvelous minute!"

Person, persona, and personality, Barbie is marketed not simply as a doll, a toy, but as "a role model for girls."[1] In fact, one concept behind the doll was the notion that its adult female form would help to teach little girls how to become beautiful, feminine women—"just like Barbie," a simile that still appears in advertising copy. Early Barbie dolls came with accessories such as bras, petticoats, girdles, and garters, which would guide little girls in negotiating these then-essential accouterments of womanhood and fashion.[2] In the words of Billy Boy, a British fashion designer and Barbie doll aficionado, Barbie's undergarment sets of the fifties and early sixties symbolized adulthood for most girls. As such, they "allowed young women to anticipate the structured and difficult-to-wear undergarments of the era."[3]

Today, at a time when Madonna has transformed underwear into outerwear, Barbie also takes to the streets in such underclothes as see-through bustiers and spandex leggings. Whether for day or night, lingerie has made a comeback as popular accessories for Barbie dolls, which are generally sold without undergarments. (In 1995 Teacher Barbie's lack of underwear triggered consumer complaints that the doll seemed to be teaching something other than reading, writing, and arithmetic.) A line of lingerie introduced in 1991 as Barbie's "Fancy Frills" presents little girls—"5 and over"—with four sets of accessories in which to dress their dolls, including lacy, see-through teddies and satin bras and panties. Other lingerie sets on the market include a "Wedding Day" ensemble, blue satin panties and camisole with a matching bed jacket and high-heel pumps. The label on the package may say "Wedding Day," but the garments inside more readily suggest the wedding night.

While these ensembles are sold separately as accessories, some of the dolls come prepackaged with alternative nighttime wear. For example, Madison Avenue Barbie, a special F.A.O. Schwarz limited-edition doll introduced in 1991, is dressed to the nines in a fashionable pink suit and stylish green trapeze coat, but what she's shopping for—what she carries in her Schwarz rocking-horse-emblazoned shopping bag—is no teddy bear but a hot-pink teddy, a sexy undergarment of the Victoria's Secret variety.

The contradiction of the toystore tote bag and the hot-pink teddy suggests the same blurring of the lines between innocent child's play and adult sexual fantasy that the Barbie doll itself suggests. The hot-pink teddy and similar garments not only teach little girls how to be grown up; they also prepare them for their role as adult consumers. But the messages that Barbie and her garments send are mixed and not just for or about little girls who would be women and shoppers. The elaborate lingerie ensembles, day-glow bustiers, lace panties, and Lycra tights of the nineties teach more than dress, deportment, and consumption; they spell out the ABCs of sex and seduction.

Moreover, the narrative of sensuality underneath the doll's wardrobe is intertwined with the narrative of beauty and success that is the enabling script for Barbie's personal romance and commercial empire. As would-be toys for girls, then, Barbie and her intimate trappings

represent a seemingly innocent space for the displacement of adult ambivalence about sexuality. Like any good fetish, Barbie at once absorbs
our sins and absolves us of them. She transforms the unclean thoughts
of grown-ups into the immaculate conceptions of children. Figured as
mere child's play, Victoria's Secret is let out of the brown paper bag, as
it were, and placed rocking-horse pure in the presexual space of the
little girl's playroom.

There is still more to the story. The original (or, as it turns out, not
so original) 1959 Barbie was modeled after a sexy, adult-bodied,
German-made doll called "Bild Lilli." The Lilli doll, itself taken from a
gold-digging comic-strip character, became a kind of sex toy, which
reportedly was sold primarily to men in tobacco shops and other male
haunts. Barbie's taste in clothes—or, rather, Mattel's—betrays the doll's
European origins as erotica. In their U.S. incarnations, Barbie and her
wardrobe reflect the American ideal of continental decadence and the
degree to which that decadence—a "No, No, Nanette" naughtiness—is
located in the female form.

Probing deeper, a Freudian interpretation might even uncover both
repressed sexual desire and a kind of Paris envy. In Paris and throughout
Europe, lingerie resonates with a certain *je-ne-sais-quoi*, which Americans have envied but never gotten quite right. In the European underwear world, distinctions are finely drawn between the decadent and the
delicate. Barbie's intimate apparel, however, "blurs the boundary between the bordello and the boudoir,"[4] transporting into toyland a perhaps uniquely American confusion about sex, sin, and the body.

For Mattel, of course, any relationship between sex and the text of
Barbie—especially the charge that sex sells Barbie—is a figment of the
imaginations of dirty-minded adults, who project their own sexual preoccupations and perversions onto innocent toys intended for children.
Whether a fashion model, a flight attendant, or an astronaut, Barbie,
according to her manufacturer, has always been a fine, upstanding career girl (as opposed to the "working girl" her wardrobe may suggest).
But the company's own marketing strategies and advertising copy would
seem to contradict this plea of innocence, since the prose and pictures
used to sell Barbie often sexualize the doll and position it as an object
of both desire and emulation. An ad for a Barbie T-shirt, for example,
shows a truncated (head and torso only) version of the doll—arms bent
back and chest thrust forward—floating above a caption that reads:
"Your Barbie doll will look hot in this cool T-shirt." In such ads—
which replicate the calendar-girl and sex-kitten poses of adult models—
both the graphics and the words invite an erotic gaze. Mattel also markets a line of "cool" career fashions for its Barbie dolls, but most of
Barbie's wardrobe has more to do with the bedroom and the ballroom
than with the boardroom. If Barbie is indeed a role model for girls, just

what role is she modeling? Linked as they are to a master narrative of beauty, boys, and fun, fun, fun, these lingerie sets may teach little girls more about taking their clothes off than about putting them on.

This lesson is reinforced through hundreds of other components of Barbie culture—from video and board games, puzzles, and comic books to an exercise tape and a line of girls' clothing called Barbie for Girls. Board games such as "Barbie Dress Up," "Barbie Dream Date," and "Barbie Queen of the Prom," along with a new line of video games for Sega Genesis and Super Nintendo, all invite players to join Barbie in the happiness of her favorite pursuits: shopping, dressing up, dating, and having fun. "Barbie Fashion Designer," a CD-ROM computer game introduced in 1996, allows players to design Barbie clothes on the computer and print them on a light fabric that works in any printer. In "Barbie Magic Fairy Tales," another computer game still in the planning stage, Barbie as Rapunzel reportedly gets to rescue Prince Charming Ken from the spell of a wicked witch. The would-be heroic twist to this plot does not disguise the fact that in all of these games, winning or succeeding is synonymous with having the right looks, the right hair, the right clothes, and the right boyfriend.

The same messages are imparted by *Barbie, the Magazine for Girls*, a bimonthly fanzine aimed at girls roughly between the ages of four and twelve. Like the Miss America pageant, which bills itself as a scholarship program rather than a beauty contest, the Barbie magazine presents itself as educational rather than commercial. Any given issue might include a recipe for frozen fruit pops, a feature on outstanding American girls, or a math lesson that asks readers to use their arithmetic skills to assist Barbie on a shopping spree. ("Barbie is shopping for a new party dress. Read the clues below to figure out which dress she is going to buy.") What the magazine actually does, however, is sell Barbie. Child models—often striking adult poses replete with grown-up hairdos—are used to sell the doll and a variety of Barbie-related products. Ingeborg Majer O'Sickey argues in fact that the publication uses child-women models to sell highly particularized notions of beauty and femininity. Both the images and the editorial beauty guides function as a kind of "basic training" designed to lure little girls into the adult world of clothes, cosmetics, and consumption.[5]

It is exactly this indoctrination into a particular, fixed notion of femininity that concerns me: the role-model persona Barbie projects, along with the like-me correlative that Mattel uses to sell black versions of the doll. It is surely significant that these dolls, which once came only in white, are now mass-produced and mass-marketed to "look like" the racial other; to resemble the "like me" missing from my own childhood play; to represent the vast array of colors, races, ethnicities, and nationalities that make up the real world.

· · ·

Like Madonna, Barbie has developed both a posse of devoted fans and a gang of hostile critics. For millions of children and adults in the United States and around the world, she is the most popular, most enduring of all toys—the doll that children and collectors most love to consume. For others—wary parents and feminist scholars in particular—Barbie is a dangerous weapon against womankind—the icon of idealized femininity they most love to hate or at least interrogate, deconstruct if not destruct. The doll's exaggerated proportions and the standard set by her morbidly thin form have been at the center of controversy. (If life-size, her measurements would be something like 36-18-33, depending on who's calculating, and she wouldn't have enough body fat to menstruate regularly.) Indeed, read by many as a metaphor for young women often described pathologically as empty-headed, self-absorbed, anorexic material girls, Barbie has long attracted the ire of feminists, who revile her as yet another manifestation of the damaging myths of female beauty and the feminine body that patriarchy thrusts upon girls and women.

But while Anna Quindlen and other feminists may want to drive a silver lamé stake through her plastic heart, Barbie has her feminist fans too, some of whom see her as a revolutionary doll whose professional roles have run ahead of the prevailing images of women as housewives, secretaries, and nurses.[6] "Barbie was an astronaut years before Sally Ride," one of the doll's defenders points out.[7] And though she toys with Ken, she is not dependent on him or any other man. In fact, Ken is little more than another accessory—like Barbie's lingerie or her condo or her Porsche. Not just an empty-headed, materialistic bimbo who finds math class tough,[8] Barbie is for some a feminist heroine who has been first in war (Desert Storm Barbie saw active duty in the Gulf), first in peace (Ambassador Barbie held her own summit in 1990), and always in the hearts of her people (Americans buy her at the rate of one doll every second).

TO MARKET, TO MARKET

As the queenpin of a billion-dollar industry, Barbie reigns supreme at the intersection of gender and capitalism. Moreover, the tremendous boost in sales that accompanied Mattel's marketing of ethnic Barbie dolls may suggest a critical link between consumerism and multiculturalism. Though it seems clear that black consumers buy black Barbie dolls, it is also clear that others buy them too. Doll collecting is big business, and Mattel's ethnic dolls—particularly those in its Dolls of the World series—are designed and marketed at least as much with adult collectors in mind as with little girls. Donna Gibbs told me that the national dolls are intended more for adults, "although appropriate for children." She explained that Mattel cultivates a competitive market for these "premium value" dolls by producing them in limited quantities, issuing them strategically (two or three different nations or cultures each year), and retiring a given national doll after only a year or two on the market.[9]

Doll catalogues, buyers' guides, and classified ads in *Barbie Bazaar* suggest precisely how premium this value currently is. According to the *Collectors Encyclopedia of Barbie Dolls*, Colored Francie is now one of the most sought-after dolls ever produced by Mattel.[10] It may have been a flop when it appeared in 1967, but today, in mint condition, Colored Francie is worth between $700 and $900.[11] Finding this now premium-value vintage doll—especially finding it NRFB (never-removed-from-box)—is the dream of serious collectors. "With the quality of the ethnic dolls," writes Westenhauser, "Mattel has created a successful market of variety with Barbie that represents the racially diverse world in which we live." Saying perhaps more than she intends about difference as decoration, Westenhauser adds that "such a large variety of Barbie dolls turns any home into a museum."[12]

Questions about the ties between multiculturalism and capitalism are by all means larger than Barbie. But given the doll's status as an American icon, interrogating Barbie may facilitate an analysis of the commodity culture of which she is both part and product. What makes such an interrogation difficult, however, is the fact that Barbie simultaneously performs several disparate, often contradictory operations. On the one hand, ethnic Barbie dolls seem to color in the whitewashed spaces of my childhood. They give little colored girls toys to play with that look like them. On the other hand, this seeming act of racializing the dolls is accomplished by a contrapuntal action of erasure. In other words, Mattel is only able to racialize its dolls by blurring the sharp edges of the very difference that the corporation produces and profits from. It is able to make and market ethnicity by ignoring not only the body politics of the real people its dolls are meant to represent, but by ignoring the body politic as well—by eliding the material conditions of the masses it dolls up.

Here and elsewhere in commodity culture, this concurrent racing and erasing occurs precisely because big business both adores and abhors difference. It thrives on a heterogeneity that is cheaply reducible to its lowest common denominator—an assembly-line or off-the-rack difference that is actually sameness mass-reproduced in a variety of colors, flavors, fabrics, and other interchangeable options. For the most part, the corporate body is far less fond of more complex, less easily commodified distinctions—differences whose modes of production require constant retooling and fine-tuning. The exceptions here, of course, are the big-ticket specialty items—the handmade, one-of-a-kind originals and limited editions—which are intended not to be consumed rapidly by hordes who pay a little but to be acquired with deliberation by a few who pay a lot.

In today's toy world, race and ethnicity have fallen into the category of precious ready-to-ware difference. To be profitable, racial and cultural diversity—global heterogeneity—must be reducible to such common, reproducible denominators as color and costume. Race and racial differences—whatever that might mean in the grander social order—must be reducible to skin color or, more correctly, to the tint of the plastic poured into each Barbie mold. Each doll is marketed as representing something or someone in the real world, even as the political, social, and economic particulars of that world are not only erased but, in a curious way, made the same. Black Jamaican Barbie—outfitted as a peasant or a maid—stands alongside white English Barbie, who is dressed in the fancy riding habit of a lady of leisure. On the toystore shelf or in the collector's curio cabinet, maid and aristocrat enjoy an odd equality (they even sell for the same price), but this seeming sameness denies the historical relation they bear to each other as the colonized and the colonizer.

If we could line up the ninety or so different colors, cultures, and other incarnations in which Barbie currently exists, the physical facts of her unrelenting sameness (or at least similarity) would become immediately apparent. Even two dolls might do the trick: white Western Fun Barbie and black Western Fun Barbie, for example. Except for their dye jobs, the dolls are identical: the same body, size, shape, and apparel. Or perhaps I should say *nearly* identical because in some instances—with black and Asian dolls in particular—coloring and other subtle changes (slanted eyes in the Asian dolls, thicker lips in the black dolls) suggest differently coded facial features.

In other instances, when Barbie moves across cultural as opposed to racial lines, it is costume rather than color that distinguishes one ethnic group or nation from another. Nigeria and Jamaica, for instance, are represented by the same basic brown body and face mold, dolled up in different native garbs, or Mattel's interpretation thereof.[13] With other costume changes, this generic black body and face can be Marine Barbie or Army Barbie or even Presidential Candidate Barbie. Much the same is true of the generic Asian doll—sometimes called Kira—who reappears in a variety of different dress-defined ethnicities. In other words, where Barbie is concerned, clothes not only make the woman, they mark the racial and/or cultural difference.

Such difference is marked as well by the miniature cultural history and language lessons that accompany each doll in Mattel's international collection. The back of Jamaican Barbie's box tells us: "*How-you-du* (Hello) from the land of Jamaica, a tropical paradise known for its exotic fruit, sugar cane, breathtaking beaches, and reggae beat!" In an odd rendering of cause and effect, the box goes onto explain that "most Jamaicans have ancestors from Africa, so even though our official language is English, we speak patois, a kind of '*Jamaica Talk*,' filled with

English and African words.[14] For example, when I'm filled with *boon-oonoonoos*, I'm filled with much happiness!" So written, Jamaica becomes an exotic tropical isle where happy, dark-skinned, English-speaking peasants don't really speak English.

Presented as if out of the mouths of native informants, the cultural captions on the boxes help to sell the impression that what we see isn't all we get with these dolls. The use of first-person narration lends a stamp of approval and a voice of authority to the object, confirming that the consumer has purchased not only a toy or a collector's item to display but access to another culture, inside knowledge of an exotic, foreign other. The invariably cheerful greetings and the warm, chatty tone affirm that all's well with the small world. As a marketing strategy, these captions contribute to the museum of culture effect, but as points of information, such reductive ethnographies only enhance the extent to which these would-be multicultural dolls make race and ethnicity collectors' items, contributing more to the stock exchange than to cultural exchange.

SHANI AND THE POLITICS OF PLASTIC

Not entirely immune to criticism of its identity politics, Mattel sought advice from black parents and specialists in early childhood development in the making and marketing of a new assortment of black Barbie dolls—the Shani line. Chief among the expert witnesses was the clinical psychologist Darlene Powell Hopson, who coauthored with her husband Derek Hopson a study of racism and child development, *Different and Wonderful: Raising Black Children in a Race-Conscious Society* (1990). As part of their research and clinical work, the Hopsons repeated a groundbreaking study conducted by the black psychologists Kenneth and Mamie Clark in the 1940s.

The Clarks used dolls to demonstrate the negative effects of racism and segregation on black children. When given a choice between a white doll and a black doll, nearly 70 percent of the black children in the study chose the white doll. The Clarks' findings became an important factor in *Brown v. Board of Education* in 1954. More recently, scholars have called into question both the Clarks' methodology and the meaning ascribed to their findings: the assumption that a black child's choosing a white doll necessarily reflects a negative self-concept.[15] William Cross has argued, for example, that the Clarks confounded two different issues: attitude toward race in general and attitude toward the self in particular. How one feels about race or what one knows of societal attitudes toward the racially marked is not always an index of one's own self-esteem; or, as Harriette Pipes McAdoo suggests, perhaps black children "are able to compartmentalize their view of themselves from their view of their racial group."[16]

Such qualifications—coupled with the evidence of my own experience (my dreaming through the white male persona of Glenn Evans as a child did not mean that I hated my black female self)—have also led me to question the Clark studies. For Darlene and Derek Hopson, however, the research remains compelling. In 1985 they repeated the Clarks' doll test and found that 65 percent of the black children in their sample chose a white doll over a black one. Moreover, 76 percent of the children interviewed said that the black dolls looked "bad" to them. Based on their own doll tests and their clinical work with children, the Hopsons concluded that black children, "in great numbers," continue to identify with white images—even when black images are made available. "Our empirical results confirmed the messages Black children were sending us every day in our practice," the Hopsons explain. "We're not as good, as pretty, or as nice as Whites . . . We don't like being Black. We wish we could be like *them*."[17]

The Hopson findings sent shock waves across the country and around the world. The interest their results generated among social scientists, parents, and the popular press prompted the Hopsons to write *Different and Wonderful*, a guidebook in which they use their experience as psychologists and as parents to suggest ways of counteracting negative racialized imagery. Several of their interventional strategies involve "doll play," and here again the ubiquitous Barbie has a featured role.

"If your daughter likes 'Barbie' dolls, by all means get her Barbie," the Hopsons advise black parents. "*But also* choose Black characters from the Barbie world."[18] Admittedly, I know more about word usage than about child psychology, but it seems to me that the Hopsons' own phrasing may speak to at least one problem with their positive play methodology and the role of Barbie in it. "Barbie," unmodified in the preceding statement, apparently means *white* Barbie, suggesting that the Hopsons also take white Barbie dolls as the norm. Black Barbie is toyland's "but also," just as black people are society's "but also."

The problem here is not simply semantic. Barbie has a clearly established persona and a thoroughly pervasive presence as a white living doll. The signature Barbies, the dolls featured on billboards, on boxes, in video and board games, on clothing, and in the Barbie exercise tape (as well as the actresses who play Barbie on Broadway and the models who make special appearances as Barbie at Disneyland and elsewhere) are always blond, blue-eyed, and white. Colorizing Barbie, selling her in black-face, does not necessarily make her over into a positive black image.

"My daughter wants to know why she can't have a white Barbie doll," one African American mother told me. "She's been playing happily with black Barbie dolls since she was two, but lately she wants to know why she can't have a white doll; why she can't have a *real Barbie*." The four-year-old's words, like the Hopsons' "but also," speak to the larger color biases of imagery, texts, and toys that persist more than fifty years after the Clark study. If black children continue to identify with white images, it may be because even the would-be positive black images around them—including black Barbie dolls—serve to reinforce their second-class citizenship.[19]

But there may be other problems with the well-meaning advice offered black parents in *Different and Wonderful*. The Hopsons suggest that parents should not only provide their children with ethnic dolls but that they also should get involved in the doll play. "Help them dress and groom the dolls while you compliment them both," they advise, offering this routine: "This is a beautiful doll. It looks just like you. Look at her hair. It's just like yours. Did you know your nose is as pretty as your doll's?" They further recommend that parents use "complimentary words such as *lovely, pretty,* or *nice* so that [the] child will learn to associate them with his or her own image."[20]

Certainly it is important to help black children feel good about them-selves, which includes helping them to be comfortable with their own bodies. One might argue, however, that these suggestions run the risk of transmitting to the black child a colorized version of the same old white beauty myth. Like Barbie dolls themselves, these techniques for positive play not only make beauty a desirable fixed physical fact—a matter of characteristics rather than character—they make this embod-ied beauty synonymous with self-worth. A better strategy might be to use the doll to show children how *unlike* any real woman Barbie is. In spite of their own good intentions, the Hopsons in effect have endorsed the same bill of goods Mattel has made the basis of its ethnically ori-ented marketing campaign—a campaign launched perhaps not entirely coincidentally in the fall of 1991, the year after the Hopsons' book *Different and Wonderful* appeared.

Though one can only speculate about a link between the publication of *Different and Wonderful* and Mattel's going ethnic in its advertising, it is clear that the Hopsons' strategies for using dolls to instill ethnic pride caught the company's attention.[21] In 1990 Darlene Hopson was asked to consult with Mattel's product manager Deborah Mitchell and designer Kitty Black Perkins—both African Americans—in the devel-opment of a new line of "realistically sculpted" black fashion dolls. Hopson agreed, and about a year later Shani and her friends Asha and Nichelle became the newest members of Barbie's entourage.

According to the doll's package:

Shani means marvelous in the Swahili language . . . and marvelous she is! With her friends Asha and Nichelle, Shani brings to life the special style and beauty of the African American woman. Each one is beautiful in her own way, with her own lovely skin shade and unique facial features. Each has a different hair color and texture, perfect for braiding, twisting and creating fabulous hair styles! Their clothes, too, reflect the vivid colors and ethnic accents that showcase their exotic looks and fashion flair![22]

These words attempt to convey a message of black pride—after the fashion of the Hopsons' recommendations for positive play—but that message is clearly tied to bountiful hair, lavish and exotic clothes, and other external signs of beauty, wealth, and success.

Mattel gave Shani a coming-out party at the International Toy Fair in February 1991. Also making their debuts were Shani's friends Asha and Nichelle, notable for the different hues in which their black plastic skin comes—an innovation due in part to Darlene Hopson. Shani, the signature doll of the line, is what some would call brown-skinned; Asha is honey-colored; and Nichelle is deep mahogany. Their male friend Jamal, added in 1992, completes the collection.

The three-to-one ratio of the Shani quartet—three black females to one black male—may be the most realistic thing about these dolls. In the eyes of Mattel, however, Shani and her friends are the most authentic black dolls yet produced in the mainstream toy market. Billed as "Tomorrow's African American woman," Shani has broader hips, fuller lips, and a broader nose, according to Deborah Mitchell. Kitty Black Perkins, who has dressed black Barbies since their birth in 1980, adds that the Shani dolls are also distinguished by their unique, culturally specific clothes in "spice tones, [and] ethnic fabrics," rather than "fantasy colors like pink or lavender"[23]—evidently the colors of the faint of skin.

The notion that fuller lips, broader noses, wider hips, and higher derrieres make the Shani dolls more realistically African American again raises many difficult questions about difference, authenticity, and the problematic categories of the real and the symbolic, the typical and the stereotypical. Again we have to ask what authentic blackness looks like. Even if we knew, how could this ethnic or racial authenticity ever be achieved in a doll? Also, where capital is concerned, the profit motive must always intersect with all other incentives.

The Shani doll is an apt illustration of this point. On the one hand, Mattel was concerned enough about producing a more "ethnically correct" black doll to seek the advice of black image specialists in the development and marketing of the Shani line. On the other hand, the company was not willing to follow the advice of such experts where doing so would entail a retooling that would cost the corporation more than the price of additional dyes and fabrics.

For example, Darlene Hopson argued not just for gradations in skin tones in the Shani dolls but also for variations in body type and hair styles. But, while Mattel acknowledged both the legitimacy and the ubiquity of such arguments, the ever-present profit incentive militated against breaking the mold, even for the sake of the illusion of realism. "To be truly realistic, one [Shani doll] should have shorter hair," Deborah Mitchell has admitted. "But little girls of all races love hair play. We added more texture. But we can't change the fact that long, combable hair is still a key seller."

In fact, there have been a number of times when Mattel has changed the length and style of its dolls' hair. Christie, the black doll that replaced Colored Francie in 1968, had a short Afro, which was more in keeping with what was perhaps the signature black hairstyle of the sixties. Other shorter styles have appeared as the fashions of the moment dictated. In the early sixties, Barbie sported a bubble cut like Jacqueline Kennedy's.[24] Today, though, Mattel seems less willing to crop Barbie's hair in accord with fashion. Donna Gibbs told me that the long hair of Mattel's dolls is the result of research into play patterns. "Combing, cutting, and styling hair is basic to the play patterns of girls of all ethnicities," she said. All of the products are test-marketed first with both children and adults, and the designs are based on such research.[25]

Hair play is no doubt a favorite pastime with little girls. But Mattel, I would argue, doesn't simply respond to the desire among girls for dolls with long hair to comb; it helps to produce those desires. Most Barbie dolls come with a little comb or brush, and ads frequently show girls brushing, combing, and braiding their dolls' long hair. In recent years Mattel has taken its invitation to hair play to new extremes with its mass production of Totally Hair Barbie, Hollywood Hair Barbie, and Cut and Style Barbie—dolls whose Rapunzel-like hair lets down in seemingly endless locks. (Cut and Style Barbie comes with "functional sharp edge" scissors and an extra wad of attachable hair. Hair refill packs are sold separately.) But what does the transference of flowing fairy-princess hair onto black dolls mean for the black children for whom these dolls are supposed to inspire self-esteem?

In the process of my own archival research—poking around in the dusty aisles of Toys R Us—I encountered a black teenage girl in search of the latest black Barbie. During the impromptu interview that ensued, my subject confessed to me in graphic detail the many Barbie murders and mutilations she had committed over the years. "It's the hair," she said emphatically several times. "The hair, that hair; I want it. I want it!" Her words recalled my own torturous childhood struggles with the straightening combs, curling irons, and chemical relaxers that biweekly transformed my woolly "just like a sponge" kinks into what the white kids at school marveled at as my "Cleopatra [straight] hair."

Many African American women and quite a few African American men have similar tales about dealing with their hair or with the hair of daughters or sisters or mothers. In "Life with Daughters," the black essayist Gerald Early recounts the difficulties that arose when Linnet, the elder of his two daughters, decided that she wanted hair that would "blow in the wind," while at the same time neither she nor her mother wanted her to have her hair straightened. "I do not think Linnet wanted to change her hair to be beautiful," Early writes; "she wanted to be like everyone else. But perhaps this is simply wishful thinking here or playing with words, because Linnet must have felt her difference as being a kind of ugliness."[26]

Indeed, "colored hair," like dark skin, has been both culturally and commercially constructed as ugly, nappy, wild, and woolly, in constant need of taming, straightening, cropping, and cultivating.[27] In the face of such historically charged constructions, it is difficult for black children not to read their hair as different and that difference as ugly. Stories and pictures abound of little black girls putting towels on their heads and pretending that the towels are long hair that can blow in the wind or be tossed over the shoulder. But ambivalence about or antipathy toward the hair on our heads is hardly limited to the young. Adult African Americans spend millions each year on a variety of products that promise to straighten, relax, or otherwise make more manageable kinky black hair.[28] And who can forget the painful scene—made hilarious by Spike Lee and Denzel Washington in *Malcolm X*—in which his friend Shorty gives the young Malcolm Little his first conk?

Mattel may have a point. It may be that part of Shani's and black Barbie's attraction for little black girls—as for all children and perhaps even for adults—is the dolls' fairy-princess good looks, the crowning touch of glory of which is long, straight hair, combable locks that cascade down the dolls' backs. Even though it is not as easy to comb as Mattel maintains, for black girls the simulated hair on the heads of Shani and black Barbie may suggest more than simple hair play; it may represent a fanciful alternative to what society presents as their own less attractive, short, kinky, hurts-to-comb hair.

As difficult as this prospect is to consider, its ancillary implications are even more jarring. If Colored Francie failed in 1967 partly because of her "Caucasian features" and her long, straight hair, is Shani such a success in the 1990s because of those same features? Is the popularity of these thin-bodied, straight-haired dolls a sign that black is most beautiful when readable in traditional white terms? Have blacks, too, bought the dominant ideals of beauty inscribed in Barbie's svelte figure and flowing locks?

It would be difficult to answer these questions, I suppose, without making the kinds of reductive value judgments about the politics of black hair that Kobena Mercer has warned us against: the assumption that "hair styles which avoid artifice and look 'natural,' such as the Afro or Dreadlocks, are the more authentically black hair-styles and thus more ideologically 'right-on.' "[29] Suffice it to say that Barbie's svelte figure—like her long hair—became Shani's body type as well, even as Mattel claims to have done the impossible, even as they profess to have captured in this new doll the "unique facial features" and the "special style and beauty of the African American people." This claim seems to be based on subtle changes in the doll that apparently are meant to signify Shani's black difference. Chief among these changes—especially in Soul Train Shani, a scantily clad hiphop edition of the series released in 1993—is the *illusion* of broader hips and an elevated buttocks.

This illusion is achieved by a technological sleight of design that no doubt costs the company far less than all the talk about Shani's broader hips and higher derriere would suggest. No matter what Mattel spokespersons say, Shani—who has to be able to wear Barbie's clothes—is not larger or broader across the hips and behind than other Barbie dolls. In fact, according to the anthropologists Jacqueline Urla and Alan Swedlund, who have studied the anthropometry (body measurements) of Barbie, Shani's seemingly wider hips are if anything a fraction smaller in both circumference and breadth than those of other Barbie dolls. The effect of a higher buttocks is achieved by a change in the angle of the doll's back.[30]

On closer examination, one finds that not only is Shani's back arched, but her legs are also bent in and backward. When laid face down, other Barbie dolls lie flat, but the legs of Soul Train Shani rise slightly upward. This barely noticeable backward thrust of the legs also enhances the impression of protruding buttocks, the technical term for which is "steatopygia," defined as an excessive accumulation of fat on the buttocks. (The same technique was used in nineteenth-century art and photography in an attempt to make subjects look more primitive.) Shani's buttocks may appear to protrude, but actually the doll has no posterior deposits of plastic fat and is not dimensionally larger or broader than all the other eleven-and-a-half-inch fashion dolls sold by Mattel. One might say that reports of Shani's butt enhancement have been greatly exaggerated. Her signifying black difference is really just more (or less) of the same.

There is a far more important point to be made, however. Illusion or not, Shani's buttocks can pass for uniquely black only if we accept the stereotypical notion of what black looks like. Social scientists, historians, literary scholars, and cultural theorists have long argued that race is socially constructed rather than biologically determined. Yet, however coded, notions of race remain finely connected to the biological, the phenotypical, and the physiological in discussions about the racially marked body, not to mention the racially marketed body.

No matter how much scholars attempt to intellectualize it otherwise, "race" generally means "nonwhite," and "black" is still related to skin color, hair texture, facial features, body type, and other outward signifiers of difference. A less neutral term for such signifiers is, of course, stereotypes. In playing the game of difference with its ethnic dolls, Mattel either defies or deploys these stereotypes, depending on cost and convenience. "Black hair" might be easy enough to simulate (as in Kenyan Barbie's astro-turf Afro), but—if we buy what Mattel says about its market research—anything other than long straight hair could cost the company some of its young consumers. Mechanical manipulation of Shani's plastic body, on the other hand, represents a facile deployment of stereotype in the service of capital. A *trompe l'oeil* derriere and a dye job transform the already stereotypical white archetype into the black stereotype—into what one might call the Hottentot Venus of toyland.

Indeed, in identifying buttocks as the signifier of black female difference, Mattel may unwittingly be taking us back to the eugenics and scientific racism of earlier centuries. One of the most notorious manifestations of this racism was the use and abuse of so-called Hottentot women such as Sarah Bartmann, whom science and medicine identified as the essence of black female sexuality. Presented to European audiences as the "Hottentot Venus," Saartjie or Sarah Bartmann was a young African woman whose large buttocks (common among the people of southern Africa whom Dutch explorers called Hottentots or Bushmen) made her an object of sexual curiosity for white westerners traveling in Africa. According to Sander Gilman, for Victorians the protruding buttocks of these African women pointed to "the other, hidden sexual signs, both physical and temperamental, of the black female." "Female sexuality is linked to the image of the buttocks," Gilman writes, "and the quintessential buttocks are those of the Hottentot."[31]

Transformed from individual to icon, Bartmann was taken from Cape Town in the early 1900s and widely exhibited before paying audiences in Paris and London between 1910 and her death in 1915 at age twenty-five. According to some accounts, she was made to appear on stage in a manner that confirmed her as the primitive beast she and her people were believed to be. Bartmann's body, which had been such a curiosity during her life, was dissected after her death, her genitals removed, preserved under a bell jar, and placed on display at the Musée de l'Homme in Paris.[32] But as Anne Fausto-Sterling has argued so persuasively, even attempting to tell the known details of the exploitation of this woman, whose given African name is not known, only extends her victimization in the service of intellectual inquiry. The case of Sarah Bartmann, Fausto-Sterling points out, can tell us nothing about the woman herself; it can only give us insight into the minds and methodologies of the scientists who made her their subject.[33]

Given this history, it is ironic that Shani's would-be protruding buttocks (even as a false bottom) should be identified as the site and signifier of black female alterity—of "butt also" difference, if I may be pardoned the pun. Georges Cuvier, one of several nineteenth-century scientists to dissect and to write about Bartmann, maintained that the black female "looks different"; her physiognomy, her skin color, and her genitalia mark her as "inherently different."[34] Long since recognized as morbidly racist, the language of Cuvier's "diagnosis" nevertheless resembles the terms in which racial difference is still written today. The problems that underpin Mattel's deep play with Shani's buttocks, then, are the very problems that reside within the grammar of difference in contemporary critical and cultural theory.

FROM BELL JAR TO BELL CURVE

With Shani and its other black Barbie dolls, Mattel has made blackness simultaneously visible and invisible, at once different and the same. What Mattel has done with Barbie is not at all unlike what society has done with the facts and fictions of difference over the course of several centuries. In theoretical terms, what's at stake in studying Barbie is much more than just fun and games. In fact, in its play with racial and ethnic alterity, Mattel may well have given us a prism through which to see in living color the degree to which difference is an impossible space—antimatter located not only beyond the grasp of low culture but also beyond the reach of high theory.

Just as Barbie reigns ubiquitously white, blond, and blue-eyed over a rainbow coalition of colored optical illusions, human social relations remain in hierarchical bondage, one to the other, the dominant to the different. Difference is always relational and value-laden. We are not just *different*; we are always *different from*. All theories of difference—from Saussure and Derrida to Fanon and Foucault—are bound by this problematic of relativity. More significantly, all notions of human diversity necessarily constitute difference as oppositional. From the prurient nineteenth-century racism that placed Sarah Bartmann's genitals under a bell jar, to the contemporary IQ-based social Darwinism that places blacks at the bottom of a bell curve, difference is always stacked up against a (superior) center. This is the irony of deconstruction and its failure: things fall apart, but the center holds remarkably firm. It holds precisely because the very act of theorizing difference affirms that there is a center, a standard, or—as in the case of Barbie—a mold.

Yet, however deep its fissures, deconstruction—rather than destruction—may be the closest we can come to a solution to the problem for which Barbie is but one name. Barbie, like racism (if not race), is indestructible. Not even Anna Quindlen's silver-lamé stake through the doll's plastic heart would rid us of this immovable object, which is destined to outlive even its most tenacious critics. (This is literally true, since Barbie dolls are not biodegradable. Remembering the revenge the faithful took on Nietzsche—" 'God is dead,' signed Nietzsche" / " 'Nietzsche is dead,' signed God"—I can see my obituary in *Barbie Bazaar:* " 'duCille is dead,' signed Barbie.") But if, as Wordsworth wrote, we murder to dissect, deconstructing Barbie may be our only release from the doll's impenetrable plastic jaws, just as deconstructing race and gender may be the only way out of the deep space or muddy waters of difference.

The particulars of black Barbie illustrate the difficulties and dangers of treating race and gender differences as biological stigmata that can be fixed in plastic and mass-reproduced. But if difference is indeed an impossible space—a kind of black hole, if you will—it is antimatter that continues to matter tremendously, especially for those whose bodies bear its visible markings and carry its material consequences.

The answer, then, to the problematic of difference cannot be, as some have argued, that gender does not exist or that race is an empty category. Such arguments throw the body out with the murky bath water. But, as black Barbie and Shani also demonstrate, the body will not be so easily disposed of. If we pull the plug on gender, if we drain race of any meaning, we are still left with the material facts and fictions of the body—with the different ifs, ands, and butts of different bodies. It is easy enough to theorize difference in the abstract, to posit "the body" in one discourse or another. But in the face of real bodies, ease quickly expands into complexity. To put the question in disquietingly personal terms: from the ivory towers of the academy I can criticize the racist fictions inscribed in Shani's false bottom from now until retirement, but shopping for jeans in Filene's Basement, how am I to escape the physical fact of my own steatopygic hips? Do the facts of my own body leave me hoisted not on my own petard, perhaps, but on my own haunches?

We need to theorize race and gender not as meaning*less* but as meaning*ful*—as sites of difference, filled with constructed meanings that are in need of constant decoding and interrogation. Such analysis may not finally free us of the ubiquitous body-biology bind or release us from the quagmire of racism and sexism, but it may be at once the most and the least we can do to reclaim difference from the molds of mass production and the casts of dominant culture.

Yet, if the process of deconstruction also constructs, tearing Barbie down runs the risk of building Barbie up—of reifying difference in much the same way that commodity culture does. Rather than representing a critical kiss of death, readings that treat Barbie as a real threat to womankind—a harbinger of eating and shopping disorders—actually breathe life into the doll's plastic form. This is not to say that Barbie can simply be reduced to a piece of plastic. It is to say that hazard lies less in buying Barbie than in buying into Barbie, internalizing the larger mythologies of gender and race that make possible both the "like me" of Barbie and its critique. So, if this is a cautionary tale, the final watchword for consumers and critics alike must be not only *caveat emptor* but also *caveat lector*: let the buyer and the reader beware.

ENDNOTES

1. Ruth Handler, who came up with the idea for the doll and thinks of herself as Barbie's mother, has had much to say about the Barbie doll as a role model. This particular quotation is taken from a booklet that comes with

35th Anniversary Barbie, an "authentic reproduction" of the first Barbie dolls sold in 1959. Handler, by the way, named Barbie after her daughter Barbara and Ken after her son.

2. In her biography of Barbie, Lord maintains that the original dolls were given undergarments because Charlotte Johnson, Barbie's first dress designer, insisted that a fashion doll couldn't wear haute-couture ensembles without the proper foundations. *Forever Barbie*, p. 34.

3. See Billy Boy, *Barbie: Her Life and Times* (New York: Crown, 1987), p. 22. Barbie herself would seem to agree with BillyBoy. In *Barbie: What a Doll!* "by Barbie, as told to Laura Jacobs" (New York: Abbeville Press, 1994), the putative author informs her readers: "In the early 1960s, when fashions required more elaborate foundations like girdles and garters (before pantyhose had come along), my repertoire of intimate apparel was a bit more various. But as feminism and fashion together moved women away from a standardized ideal of perfection and toward a more embracing acceptance of fitness and its many different physiques, we no longer needed undergarments that would shape everyone the same way . . . A figure was now akin to a fingerprint; no two bodies wore the same dress the same way" (p. 75).

4. Greta Slobin, personal conversation, December 14, 1994.

5. Ingeborg Majer O'Sickey, "*Barbie Magazine* and the Aesthetic Commodification of Girls' Bodies," in Shari Benstock and Suzanne Ferriss, eds., *On Fashion* (New Brunswick: Rutgers University Press, 1994), pp. 21–40, esp. p. 23.

6. Anna Quindlen, "Barbie at 35," *New York Times*, September 10, 1994, p. 19.

7. Helen Cordes, "What a Doll! Barbie: Materialistic Bimbo or Feminist Trailblazer?," *Utne Reader*, March–April 1992, p. 50.

8. Among the 270 phrases programmed into the computer chip of some editions of Teen Talk Barbie in 1992 was "Math class is tough." This drew protests from a variety of sources, including formal complaints from the National Council of Teachers of Mathematics, the Association for Women in Mathematics, and the American Association of University Women. Mattel, not wanting to convey "anything but the most inspirational of messages," promptly removed the offending phrase from Barbie's microchip. See Tony Kornheiser, "Shut Up, Barbie," *Washington Post*, October 4, 1992, p. F1. See also Constance Holden, "Mathematicians Talk Tough to New Barbie," *Science* 258 (1992), 396; and "No More Math Phobia for Barbie," *New York Times*, October 2, 1994, p. 28.

9. Phone conversation with Gibbs, September 9, 1994.

10. Sibyl DeWein and Joan Ashabraner, *The Collectors Encyclopedia of Barbie Dolls and Collectibles* (Paducah: Collector Books, 1994), p. 35.

11. This is the price range listed in the 11th edition of Jan Foulke's *Blue Book: Dolls and Values* (Grantsville, Md.: Hobby House Press, 1993), p. 83. Many of what are called vintage dolls—early or otherwise special-edition Barbie dolls—have the "premium value" described by Donna Gibbs. For example, according to the *Blue Book* a first-edition 1959 Barbie never removed from its box would be worth between $3,200 and $3,700. A Barbie infomercial airing in 1994–95 placed the value as high as $4,500. The same doll sold in 1959 for $2.99.

12. Westenhauser, *The Story of Barbie* (Paducah: Collector Books, 1994), pp. 138, 119. Serious Barbie collectors often purchase duplicates of a given doll: one to keep in mint condition in its box and one to display. Or, as we used to say of the two handkerchiefs we carried to Sunday school: one for show and one for blow. For an intriguing psychosocial analysis of the art of collecting, see Jean Baudrillard, "The System of Collecting," in John Elsner and Roger Cardinal, eds., *The Cultures of Collecting* (Cambridge, Mass.: Harvard University Press, 1994), pp. 7–24.

13. After many calls to the Jamaican embassy in Washington and to various cultural organizations in Jamaica, I have concluded that Jamaican Barbie's cos-

tume—a floor-length granny dress with apron and head-rag—bears some resemblance to what is considered the island's traditional folk costume. But it was also made clear to me that these costumes have more to do with tourism than with local traditions. According to Gibbs at Mattel, decisions about costuming are made by the design and marketing teams in consultation with other senior staffers. The attempt, Gibbs informed me, "is to determine and roughly approximate" the national costume of each country in the collection (conversation, September 9, 1994). I still wonder, though, about the politics of these design decisions: why the doll representing Jamaica is figured as a maid, while the doll representing Great Britain is presented as a lady—a blond, blue-eyed Barbie doll dressed in a fancy riding habit with boots and hat.

14. Actually, Jamaican *patois* is spelled differently: *potwah*, I believe.

15. See e.g. Morris Rosenberg, *Conceiving the Self* (New York: Basic Books, 1979) and *Society and the Adolescent Self-Image* (Hanover: University Press of New England, 1989), and William E. Cross, *Shades of Black: Diversity in African American Identity* (Philadelphia: Temple University Press, 1991), which challenge the Clarks' findings. The psychologist Na'im Akbar argues that just as the Moynihan Report pathologized the black family, the Clark doll studies pathologized the black community by the implied assumption that it was "psychologically unhealthy for 'colored' children to go to school only with one another," since "the outcome is likely to be self-hatred, lowered motivation, and so on." According to Akbar, this problematic assumption gave rise to a racist logical fallacy embedded in the1954 Supreme Court decision: that it was "psychologically healthy for Black children to attend school with white children," since "such an opportunity is likely to improve the African-American child's self-concept, intellectual achievement, and overall social and psychological adjustment." Akbar, "Our Destiny: Authors of a Scientific Revolution," in Harriette Pipes McAdoo and John Lewis McAdoo, eds., *Black Children: Social, Educational, and Parental Environments* (Beverly Hills: Sage Publications, 1985), pp. 24–25. Akbar's analysis seems to miss the point that what concerned black parents in the 1950s (as well as before and since) was the material effects of Jim Crow education: separate was not equal.

16. Harriette Pipes McAdoo, "Racial Attitudes and Self Concept of Young Black Children over Time," in *Black Children: Social, Educational and Parental Enviorments* (Beverly Hills: Sage, 1985), p. 214.

17. Darlene Powell Hopson and Derek S. Hopson, *Different and Wonderful: Raising Black Children in a Race-Conscious Society* (New York: Simon and Schuster, 1990), pp. xix–xx.

18. Ibid., p. 127; my emphasis. "*You do not want your child to grow up thinking that only White dolls, and by extension White people, are attractive and nice*," the Hopsons go on to explain (emphasis in the original).

19. The cover of the November–December 1993 issue of *Barbie* offers a good illustration of my point. It is dominated by a full-page image of white Happy Holiday Barbie. Tucked away in a tiny insert in the upper-left corner is the face of a black Barbie doll, presumably stuck in to let us know that Happy Holiday Barbie also comes in black. Black Barbie was the cover story in *Barbie Bazaar*, May–June 1996.

20. Hopson and Hopson, *Different and Wonderful*, pp. 119, 124.

21. It is also clear that other factors influenced Mattel's decision to go ethnic, including a marketing survey done in the late 1980s, which reportedly identified the top fourteen cities with the highest concentrations of black residents. According to the doll dealer and appraiser A. Glenn Mandeville, Mattel used this information and the complaints and suggestions of consumers to help develop its Shani line. In his words, "Mattel has indeed gone out in the 1990s to make sure they capture all markets." *Doll Fashion Anthology and Price Guide*, 3rd ed. (Cumberland: Hobby House Press, 1992), p. 174.

22. Asha is a variant of the Swahili and Arabic name Aisha or Ayisha, meaning "life" or "alive." It is also the name of Muhammad's chief wife. As a minor

point of interest, "Nichelle" is the first name of the black actress (Nichelle Nichols) who played Lieutenant Uhura on the original *Star Trek* TV series (1966–1969).

23. Quoted in Lisa Jones, "A Doll Is Born," *Village Voice*, March 26, 1991, p. 36.

24. Kenyan Barbie, introduced in 1994, has the most closely cropped hair of any Barbie doll to date. I asked Donna Gibbs if Mattel was concerned that the doll's severely cropped hair (little more than peach fuzz, or what a colleague described as "Afro turf") would hamper sales. She told me that the company expected Kenyan Barbie to sell as well as all the other national dolls, which are intended more for adult collectors. Kenyan Barbie received a "short-cropped Afro in an attempt to make her look more authentic," Gibbs informed me. "She represents a more authentic-looking doll." (The doll also has bare feet and wears Mattel's interpretation of the native dress of the Masai woman; the first-person narrative on the back of the box tells us that most Kenyan people wear modern dress and that spears are banned in the city.)

25. Gibbs, conversation, September 9, 1994.

26. See Gerald Early, "Life with Daughters: Watching the Miss America Pageant," in his *The Culture of Bruising: Essays on Prizefighting, Literature, and Modern American Culture* (Hopewell: Ecco Press, 1994), p. 268.

27. Among many texts on the politics of black people's hair, see Cheryl Clarke's poem "Hair: A Narrative," in her *Narratives: Poems in the Tradition of Black Women* (New York: Kitchen Table/Women of Color Press, 1982); Kobena Mercer, "Black Hair/Style Politics," in Ferguson, Gever, Minh-ha, and West, eds., *Out There*, pp. 247–264; and Ayoka Chinzera, director, *Hairpiece: A Film for Nappy-Headed People*, 1982. In fiction see Toni Morrison's *The Bluest Eye*.

28. I intend no value judgment in making this observation about what we do with our hair. Though Afros, braids, and dreadlocks may be seen by some as more "authentically black" or more Afrocentrically political than straightened or chemically processed hair, I am inclined to agree with Kobena Mercer that all black hairstyles are political as a historical, ethnic signifier (p. 251). It is history that has made black hair "*mean.*"

29. Mercer, "Black Hair/Style Politics," pp. 247–248.

30. Jacqueline Urla and Alan Swedlund, "The Anthropometry of Barbie: Unsettling Ideas of the Feminine in Popular Culture," in Jennifer Terry and Jacqueline Urla, eds., *Deviant Bodies: Critical Perspectives on Difference in Science and Popular Culture* (Bloomington: Indiana University Press, 1995).

31. Sander L. Gilman, "Black Bodies, White Bodies: Toward an Iconography of Female Sexuality in Late Nineteenth-Century Art, Medicine, and Literature," in Henry Louis Gates Jr., ed., *"Race," Writing, and Difference* (Chicago: University of Chicago Press, 1985), p. 238.

32. See Stephen Jay Gould, "The Hottentot Venus," *Natural History* 91 (1982), 20–27. For a poetic interpretation of Sarah Bartmann's story, see the title poem in Elizabeth Alexander's *The Venus Hottentot* (Charlottesville: University of Virginia Press, 1990), pp. 3–7.

33. Anne Fausto-Sterling, "Gender, Race, and Nation: The Comparative Anatomy of 'Hottentot' Women in Europe: 1815–1817," in Terry and Urla, eds., *Deviant Bodies*, pp. 19–48.

34. Gilman, "Black Bodies, White Bodies," p. 232.

PART FIVE

The Liberatory Dimensions of Consumer Society

16

James Twitchell
"Two Cheers for Materialism"
(1999)

Of all the strange beasts that have come slouching into the 20th century, none has been more misunderstood, more criticized, and more important than materialism. Who but fools, toadies, hacks, and occasional loopy libertarians have ever risen to its defense? Yet the fact remains that while materialism may be the most shallow of the 20th century's various -isms, it has been the one that has ultimately triumphed. The world of commodities appears so antithetical to the world of ideas that it seems almost heresy to point out the obvious: most of the world most of the time spends most of its energy producing and consuming more and more stuff. The really interesting question may be not why we are so materialistic, but why we are so unwilling to acknowledge and explore what seems the central characteristic of modern life.

When the French wished to disparage the English in the 19th century, they called them a nation of shopkeepers. When the rest of the world now wishes to disparage Americans, they call us a nation of consumers. And they are right. We are developing and rapidly exporting a new material culture, a mallcondo culture. To the rest of the world we do indeed seem not just born to shop, but alive to shop. Americans spend more time tooling around the mallcondo—three to four times as many hours as our European counterparts—and we have more stuff to show for it. According to some estimates, we have about four times as many things as Middle Europeans, and who knows how much more than people in the less developed parts of the world. The quantity and disparity are increasing daily, even though, as we see in Russia and China, the "emerging nations" are playing a frantic game of catch-up.

This burst of mallcondo commercialism has happened recently—in my lifetime—and it is spreading around the world at the speed of television. The average American consumes twice as many goods and services as in 1950; in fact, the poorest fifth of the current population buys more than the average fifth did in 1955. Little wonder that the average new home of today is twice as large as the average house built in the early years after World War II. We have to put that stuff somewhere—quick!—before it turns to junk.

Sooner or later we are going to have to acknowledge the uncomfortable fact that this amoral consumerama has proved potent because human beings *love* things. In fact, to a considerable degree we live for things. In all cultures we buy things, steal things, exchange things, and horde things. From time to time, some of us collect vast amounts of things, from tulip bulbs to paint drippings on canvases to matchbook covers. Often these objects have no observable use.

We live through things. We create ourselves through things. And we change ourselves by changing our things. In the West, we have even developed the elaborate algebra of commercial law to decide how things are exchanged, divested, and recaptured. Remember, we call these things "goods," as in "goods and services." We don't—unless we are academic critics—call them "bads." This sounds simplistic, but it is crucial to understanding the powerful allure of materialism.

Our commercial culture has been blamed for the rise of eating disorders, the spread of "affluenza," the epidemic of depression, the despoliation of cultural icons, the corruption of politics, the carnivalization of holy times like Christmas, and the gnat-life attention span of our youth. All of this is true. Commercialism contributes. But it is by no means the whole truth. Commercialism is more a mirror than a lamp. In demonizing it, in seeing ourselves as helpless and innocent victims of its overpowering force, in making it the scapegoat du jour, we reveal far more about our own eagerness to be passive in the face of complexity than about the thing itself.

Anthropologists tell us that consumption habits are gender-specific. Men seem to want stuff in the latent and post-midlife years. That's when the male collecting impulse seems to be felt. Boys amass playing marbles first, Elgin marbles later. Women seem to gain potency as consumers after childbirth, almost as if getting and spending is part of a nesting impulse.

Historians, however, tell us to be careful about such stereotyping. Although women are the primary consumers of commercial objects today, they have enjoyed this status only since the Industrial Revolution. Certainly in the pre-industrial world men were the chief hunter-gatherers. If we can trust works of art to accurately portray how booty was split (and cultural historians such as John Berger and Simon Schama think we can), then males were the prime consumers of fine clothes, heavily decorated furniture, gold and silver articles, and of course, paintings in which they could be shown displaying their stuff.

Once a surplus was created, in the 19th century, women joined the fray in earnest. They were not duped. The hegemonic phallocentric patriarchy did not brainwash them into thinking goods mattered. The Industrial Revolution produced more and more things not simply because it had the machines to do so, and not because nasty producers twisted their handlebar mustaches and whispered, "We can talk women into buying anything," but because both sexes are powerfully attracted to the world of things.

Karl Marx understood the magnetism of things better than anyone else. In *The Communist Manifesto* (1848), he wrote:

> The bourgeoisie, by the rapid improvement of all instruments of production, by the immensely facilitated means of communication, draws all, even the most barbarian nations into civilization. The cheap prices of its commodities are the heavy artillery with which it batters down all Chinese walls ... It compels all nations, on pain of extinction, to adopt the bourgeois mode of production; it compels them to introduce what it calls civilization into their midst, i.e. to become bourgeois themselves. In one word, it creates a world after its own image.

Marx used this insight to motivate the heroic struggle against capitalism. But the struggle should not be to deter capitalism and its mad consumptive ways, but to appreciate how it works so its furious energy may be understood and exploited.

Don't turn to today's middle-aged academic critic for any help on that score. Driving about in his totemic Volvo (unattractive and built to stay that way), he can certainly criticize the bourgeois afflictions of others, but he is unable to provide much actual insight into their consumption practices, much less his own. Ask him to explain the difference between "Hilfiger" inscribed on an oversize shirt hanging nearly to the knees and his rear-window university decal (My child goes to Yale, sorry about yours), and you will be met with a blank stare. If you were then to suggest that what that decal and automotive nameplate represent is as overpriced as Calvin Klein's initials on a plain white T-shirt, he would pout that you can't compare apples and whatever. If you were to say next that aspiration and affiliation are at the heart of both displays, he would say that you just don't get it, just don't get it at all.

If you want to understand the potency of American consumer culture, ask any group of teenagers what democracy means to them. You will hear an extraordinary response. Democracy is the right to buy anything you want. Freedom's just another word for lots of things to buy. Appalling perhaps, but there is something to their answer. Being able to buy what you want when and where you want it was, after all, the right that made 1989 a watershed year in Eastern Europe.

Recall as well that freedom to shop was another way to describe the right to be served in a restaurant that provided one focus for the early civil rights movement. Go back further. It was the right to consume

freely which sparked the fires of separation of this country from England. The freedom to buy what you want (even if you can't pay for it)
is what most foreigners immediately spot as what they like about our
culture, even though in the next breath they will understandably criticize
it.

The pressure to commercialize—to turn things into commodities and
then market them as charms—has always been particularly Western. As
Max Weber first argued in *The Protestant Ethic and the Spirit of Capitalism* (1905), much of the Protestant Reformation was geared toward
denying the holiness of many things that the Catholic church had endowed with meanings. From the inviolable priesthood to the sacrificial
holy water, this deconstructive movement systematically unloaded
meaning. Soon the marketplace would capture this off-loaded meaning
and apply it to secular things. Buy this, you'll be saved. You deserve a
break today. You, you're the one. We are the company that cares about
you. You're worth it. You are in good hands. We care. Trust in us. We
are here for you.

Materialism, it's important to note, does not crowd out spiritualism;
spiritualism is more likely a substitute when objects are scarce. When
we have few things we make the next world holy. When we have plenty
we enchant the objects around us. The hereafter becomes the here and
now.

We have not grown weaker but stronger by accepting the self-
evidently ridiculous myths that sacramentalize mass-produced objects;
we have not wasted away but have proved inordinately powerful; have
not devolved and been rebarbarized, but seem to have marginally improved. Dreaded affluenza notwithstanding, commercialism has lessened
pain. Most of us have more pleasure and less discomfort in our lives
than most of the people most of the time in all of history.

As Stanley Lebergott, an economist at Wesleyan University, argues in
Pursuing Happiness (1993), most Americans have "spent their way to
happiness." Lest this sound overly Panglossian, what Lebergott means
is that while consumption by the rich has remained relatively steady,
the rest of us—the intractable poor (about four percent of the population) are the exception—have now had a go of it. If the rich really are
different, as F. Scott Fitzgerald said, and the difference is that they have
longer shopping lists and are happier for it, then we have, in the last
two generations, substantially caught up.

The most interesting part of the book is the second half. Here Lebergott
unloads reams of government statistics and calculations to chart the
path that American consumption has taken in a wide range of products
and services: food, tobacco, clothing, fuel, domestic service, and medicine—to name only a few. Two themes emerge strongly from these data.

The first, not surprisingly, is that Americans were far better off by 1990 than they were in 1900. And the second is that academic critics—from Robert Heilbroner, Tibor Scitovsky, Robert and Helen Lynd, and Christopher Lasch to Juliet Schor, Robert Frank, and legions of others—who've censured the waste and tastelessness of much of American consumerism have simply missed the point. Okay, okay, money can't buy happiness, but you stand a better chance than with penury.

The cultural pessimists counter that it may be true that materialism offers a temporary palliative against the anxiety of emptiness, but we still must burst joy's grape. Consumption will turn sour because so much of it is based on the chimera of debt. Easy credit=overbuying= disappointment=increased anxiety.

This is not just patronizing, it is wrongheaded. As another economist, Lendol Calder, has argued in *Financing the American Dream* (1999), debt has been an important part of families' financial planning since the time of Washington and Jefferson. And although consumer debt has consistently risen in recent times, the default rate has remained remarkably stable. More than 95.5 percent of consumer debt gets paid, usually on time. In fact, the increased availability of credit to a growing share of the population, particularly to lower-income individuals and families, has allowed many more "have nots" to enter the economic mainstream.

There is, in fact, a special crippling quality to poverty in the modern Western world. For the penalty of intractable, transgenerational destitution is not just the absence of things; it is also the absence of meaning, the exclusion from participating in the essential socializing events of modern life. When you hear that some ghetto kid has killed one of his peers for a pair of branded sneakers or a monogrammed athletic jacket you realize that chronically unemployed poor youths are indeed living the absurdist life proclaimed by existentialists. The poor are truly the self-less ones in commercial culture.

Clearly what the poor are after is what we all want: association, affiliation, inclusion, magical purpose. While they are bombarded, as we all are, by the commercial imprecations of being cool, of experimenting with various presentations of disposable self, they lack the wherewithal to even enter the loop.

The grandfather of today's academic scolds is Thorstein Veblen (1857–1929), the eccentric Minnesotan who coined the phrase "conspicuous consumption" and has become almost a cult figure among critics of consumption. All of his books (save for his translation of the *Lexdaela Saga*) are still in print. His most famous, *The Theory of the Leisure Class*, has never been out of print since it was first published in 1899.

Veblen claimed that the leisure class set the standards for conspicuous consumption. Without sumptuary laws to protect their markers of distinction, the rest of us could soon make their styles into our own—the Industrial Revolution saw to that. But since objects lose their status distinctions when consumed by the hoi polloi, the leisure class must eternally be finding newer and more wasteful markers. Waste is not just inevitable, it is always increasing as the foolish hounds chase the wily fox.

Veblen lumped conspicuous consumption with sports and games, "devout observances," and aesthetic display. They were all reducible, he insisted, to "pecuniary emulation," his characteristically inflated term for getting in with the in-crowd. Veblen fancied himself a socialist looking forward to the day when "the discipline of the machine" would be turned around to promote stringent rationality among the entire population instead of wasted dispersion. If only we had fewer choices we would be happier, there would be less waste, and we would accept each other as equals.

The key to Veblen's argumentative power is that like Hercules cleaning the Augean stables, he felt no responsibility to explain what happens next. True, if we all purchased the same toothpaste things would be more efficient and less wasteful. Logically we should all read *Consumer Reports*, find out the best brand, and then all be happy using the same product. But we aren't. Procter & Gamble markets 36 sizes and shapes of Crest. There are 41 versions of Tylenol. Is this because we are dolts afflicted with "pecuniary emulation," obsessed with making invidious distinctions, or is the answer more complex? Veblen never considered that consumers might have other reasons for exercising choice in the marketplace. He never considered, for example, that along with "keeping up with the Joneses" runs "keeping away from the Joneses."

Remember in *King Lear* when the two nasty daughters want to strip Lear of his last remaining trappings of majesty? He has moved in with them, and they don't think he needs so many expensive guards. They whittle away at his retinue until only one is left. "What needs one?" they say. Rather like governments attempting to redistribute wealth or like academics criticizing consumption, they conclude that Lear's needs are excessive. They are false needs. Lear, however, knows otherwise. Terrified and suddenly bereft of purpose, he bellows from his innermost soul, "Reason not the need."

Lear knows that possessions are definitions—superficial meanings, perhaps, but meanings nonetheless. And unlike Veblen, he knows those meanings are worth having. Without soldiers he is no king. Without a BMW there can be no yuppie, without tattoos no adolescent rebel, without big hair no Southwestern glamor-puss, without Volvos no academic intellectual, and, well, you know the rest. Meaning is what we are after, what we need, especially when we are young.

What kind of meaning? In the standard academic view, growing out of the work of the Frankfurt school theorists of the 1950s and '60s (such as Antonio Gramsci, Theodor Adorno, and Max Horkheimer) and later those of the Center for Contemporary Cultural Studies at the University of Birmingham, it is meaning supplied by capitalist manipulators. What we see in popular culture, in this view, is the result of the manipulation of the many for the profit of the few.

For an analogy, take watching television. In academic circles, we assume that youngsters are being reified (to borrow a bit of the vast lexicon of jargon that accompanies this view) by passively consuming pixels in the dark. Meaning supposedly resides in the shows and is transferred to the sponge-like viewers. So boys, for example, see flickering scenes of violence, internalize these scenes, and willy-nilly are soon out jimmying open your car. This is the famous Twinkie interpretation of human behavior—consuming too much sugar leads to violent actions. Would listening to Barry Manilow five hours a day make adolescents into loving, caring people?

Watch kids watching television and you see something quite different from what is seen by the critics. Most consumption, whether it be of entertainment or in the grocery store, is active. We are engaged. Here is how I watch television. I almost never turn the set on to see a particular show. I am near the machine and think I'll see what's happening. I know all the channels; any eight-year-old does. I am not a passive viewer. I use the remote control to pass through various programs, not searching for a final destination but making up a shopping basket, as it were, of entertainment.

But the academic critic doesn't see this. He sees a passive observer who sits quietly in front of the set letting the phosphorescent glow of mindless infotainment pour over his consciousness. In the hypodermic analogy beloved by critics, the potent dope of desire is pumped into the bleary dupe. This paradigm of passive observer and active supplier, a receptive moron and smart manipulator, is easily transported to the marketplace. One can see why such a system would appeal to the critic. After all, since the critic is not being duped, he should be empowered to protect the young, the female, the foreign, the uneducated, and the helpless from the onslaught of dreck.

In the last decade or so, however, a number of scholars in the humanities and social sciences have been challenging many of the academy's assumptions.* What distinguishes the newer thinking is that scholars have

---

* This reconsideration of consumption is an especially strong current in anthropology, where the central text is *The World of Goods: Towards an Anthropology of Consumption* (1979), by Mary Douglas and Baron Isherwood. It can also be seen in the work of scholars such as William Leiss in communication studies; Dick Hebdige in sociology; Jackson Lears in history; David Morley in cultural studies; Michael Schud-

left the office to actually observe and question their subjects. Just one example: Mihaly Csikszentmihalyi, a psychology professor at the University of Chicago, interviewed 315 Chicagoans from 82 families, asking them what objects in the home they cherished most. The adult members of the five happiest families picked things that reminded them of other people and good times they'd had together. They mentioned a memento (such as an old toy) from their childhood 30 percent of the time. Adults in the five most dissatisfied families cited such objects only six percent of the time.

In explaining why they liked something, happy family members often described, for example, the times their family had spent on a favorite couch, rather than its style or color. Their gloomier counterparts tended to focus on the merely physical qualities of things. What was clear was that both happy and unhappy families derived great meaning from the consumption and interchange of manufactured things. The thesis, reflected in the title of his co-authored 1981 book, *The Meaning of Things: Domestic Symbols and the Self*, is that most of the "work" of consumption occurs after the act of purchase. Things do not come complete, they are forever being assembled.

Twentieth-century French sociologists have taken the argument even further. Two of the most important are Pierre Bourdieu, author of *Distinction: A Social Critique of the Judgement of Taste* (1984), and Jean Baudrillard, whose books include *The Mirror of Production* (1983) and *Simulacra and Simulation* (1994). In the spirit of reader-response theory in literary criticism, they see meaning not as a single thing that producers affix to consumer goods, but as something created by the user, who jumbles various interpretations simultaneously. Essentially, beneath the jargon, this means that the Budweiser you drink is not the same as the one I drink. The meaning tastes different. The fashion you consider stylish, I think is ugly. If we buy the package not the contents, it is because the package means more.

The process of consumption is creative and even emancipating. In an open market, we consume the real and the imaginary meanings, fusing objects, symbols, and images together to end up with "a little world made cunningly." Rather than lives, individuals since midcentury have had *lifestyles*. For better or worse, lifestyles are secular religions, coherent patterns of valued things. Your lifestyle is not related to what you do for a living but to what you buy. One of the chief aims of the way

---

son in the study of advertising; Sidney Levy in consumer research; Tyler Cowan in economics; Grant McCracken in fashion; and Simon Schama in art history. There are many other signs of change. One of the more interesting recent shows at the Museum of Modern Art, "Objects of Desire: The Modern Still Life," actually focused on the salutary influence of consumer culture on high culture.

we live now is the enjoyment of affiliating with those who share the same clusters of objects as we do.

Mallcondo culture is so powerful in part because it frees us from the strictures of social class. The outcome of material life is no longer pre-ordained by coat of arms, pew seat, or trust fund. Instead, it evolves from a never-ending shifting of individual choice. No one wants to be middle class, for instance. You want to be cool, hip, with it, with the "in" crowd, instead.

One of the reasons terms like Yuppie, Baby Boomer, and GenX have elbowed aside such older designations as "upper middle class" is that we no longer understand social class as well as we do lifestyle, or what marketing firms call "consumption communities." Observing stuff is the way we understand each other. Even if no one knows exactly how much money it takes to be a yuppie, or how young you have to be, or how upwardly aspiring, everybody knows where yuppies gather, how they dress, what they play, what they drive, what they eat, and why they hate to be called yuppies.

For better or worse, American culture is well on its way to becoming world culture. The Soviets have fallen. Only quixotic French intellec-tuals and anxious Islamic fundamentalists are trying to stand up to it. By no means am I sanguine about such a material culture. It has many problems that I have glossed over. Consumerism is wasteful, it is devoid of otherworldly concerns, it lives for today and celebrates the body, and it overindulges and spoils the young with impossible promises.

"Getting and spending" has eclipsed family, ethnicity, even religion as a defining matrix. That doesn't mean that those other defining sys-tems have disappeared, but that an increasing number of young people around the world will give more of their loyalty to Nike than to creeds of blood, race, or belief. This is not entirely a bad thing, since a lust for upscale branding isn't likely to drive many people to war, but it is, to say the least, far from inspiring.

It would be nice to think that materialism could be heroic, self-abnegating, and redemptive. It would be nice to think that greater ma-terial comforts will release us from racism, sexism, and ethnocentrism, and that the apocalypse will come as it did at the end of romanticism in Shelley's *Prometheus Unbound*, leaving us "Scepterless, free, uncir-cumscribed . . . Equal, unclassed, tribeless, and nationless."

But it is more likely that the globalization of capitalism will result in the banalities of an ever-increasing worldwide consumerist culture. The French don't stand a chance. The untranscendent, repetitive, sensational, democratic, immediate, tribalizing and unifying force of what Irving Kristol calls the American Imperium need not necessarily result in a Bronze Age of culture. But it certainly will not produce what Shelley had in mind.

We have not been led into this world of material closeness against our better judgment. For many of us, especially when young, consumerism *is* our better judgment. We have not just asked to go this way, we have demanded. Now most of the world is lining up, pushing and shoving, eager to elbow into the mall. Getting and spending has become the most passionate, and often the most imaginative, endeavor of modern life. While this is dreary and depressing to some, as doubtless it should be, it is liberating and democratic to many more.

17
Elizabeth Wilson
"FEMINISM AND FASHION"
(1985)

Proust knew how much the fleeting expression of fashion . . .
can reflect something beyond its limited time, something that
whispers of the nostalgia of human impermanence and mirrors
man's . . . destiny.

—CECIL BEATON, *THE GLASS OF FASHION*

One dimension to the history of fashion is the history of the individuals who created this world in which reality and fantasy mingle and become confused, a world in which we go adorned in our dreams. It is a world of microcosmic detail and of the grand gesture, of long term obsessions and love at first sight, of hysterical excitement and abject despair.

For everyone clothes are compulsory. This produces two kinds of individual at each extreme of the spectrum: those who hate it all, who, were it not for social pressure, would not bother with the aesthetics of their appearance and who experience fashion as a form of bondage; and those who live it as compulsion, the fashion freaks for whom dress is a source of passionate interest, who are its addicts; "fashion victims," junkies of the art of self adornment.

Many addicts made a career from their obsession. In the London of the 1870s, Mary Eliza Haweis was the wife of a fashionable but impecunious clergyman. She supplemented the ever-failing family purse by writing articles and books on style, dress and interior decoration, some of which were best sellers. She loved fashion, and understood the horror of a faulty ensemble: "After I had made myself killing," she wrote in her diary before her marriage, "all my roses and silver were in vain, I had forgotten my white shoes and had to creak about and dance in my walking Oxfords! Awful." She regarded persons of taste and sensitivity as a persecuted minority:

Those whose taste has been cultivated by having beautiful things always about them are incredibly sensitive to awkward forms and inappropriate colors in inharmonious combinations. To such persons [these] . . . cause not only the mere feeling of disapprobation but even a kind of physical pain.[1]

Today, the Italian fashion journalist, Anna Piaggi, has taken the addiction to even further extremes. As reported in the *Observer* (1 May 1983):

> She is a fashion phenomenon. The most dedicated follower of fashion pales into insignificance beside a woman who has spent months traveling by train because the exaggerated crinolines she was affecting at the time would not fit through the door of an airplane.

Many men as well as women have made not simply a career but a life work out of being fashion addicts. The supreme example was perhaps Beau Brummell, for whom perfection in dress was a symbolic philosophy. There was Paul Poiret, a great impresario of fashion. There was a whole coterie of artists and designers in Paris in the 1930s and 1940s: Christian Bérard, Jean Cocteau, Christian Dior.

Many of these men and women paid dearly for their addiction, gave their lives, in a sense, to "that most difficult of all causes—to make oneself a work of art."[2] Poiret died in the poorhouse, as did Beau Brummell. Many of the beauties died young, mysteriously of rare illnesses, tragically of drink or drugs, or both. Some became the walking epitome of their epoch, and could not move on when times changed. There sometimes seems something almost mad about these women and men who dedicated their lives to the "tragic game" of being chic.

Secrecy—addiction—obsession: these words gesture toward our feeling that a love of fashion is not quite respectable. Halfway between hobby and ritual it is indulged in the "privacy of the home," yet flaunted in the public world, is stigmatized by its uncertain status as not quite art, yet certainly not really life.

Caught between the addicts and the puritans, however, many, perhaps most, individuals experience above all an intense ambivalence about fashion and a love of fine dressing. This ambivalence has reproduced itself within contemporary feminism in a specific way.

It is difficult to discuss fashion in relation to the feminism of today, because the ideologies about dress that have circulated within the women's movement seem never to have been made explicit. This may be one reason for the intense irritation and confusion that the subject provoked from the beginning of the women's liberation movement in 1970, and still provokes.

One cause for irritation has been that from the earliest days of contemporary feminism the mass media promoted a caricature of feminists—the bra-burning "women's libbers" who hated men but dressed just like them; a caricature virtually unchanged from nineteenth-century *Punch*. It seems that bra-burning was an invention of the media. There were, however, many demonstrations, both in England and in America, against sexism in the media, against the way in which stereotyped ideals of beauty were forced on women, and against the way in which women were seen only as sexual objects, not as people.[3] This was an important theme in the early years of the contemporary women's movement but the mass media consistently and willfully confused anti-sexism with being anti-sex.

Meanwhile, two different ways of understanding culture emerged within feminism. The first of these was a wholehearted condemnation of every aspect of culture that reproduced sexist ideas and images of women and femininity, all of which came to seem in some sense "violent" and "pornographic"; the other, by contrast, was a populist liberalism which argued that it would be élitist to criticize any popular pastime which the majority of women enjoyed, whether it were reading pulp romances or dressing in smart clothes, an approach that was an offshoot of a general intellectual interest in popular culture.

Underlying these two approaches were hidden discourses rooted in the history of culture. On the one hand there was the continuing effect of the nineteenth-century cult of the natural sciences, which I discussed in relation to utopias; yet simultaneously feminists were influenced by the beliefs of nineteenth-century liberalism and its twentieth-century reinterpretations, although these contradict the more authoritarian "Fabian utilitarianism." These two views are mutually inconsistent, although no debate within feminism has fully brought this out. They possibly reflect a deeper division, which, it has been suggested, underlies many current political debates—a division between

on the one hand, those committed to "cultures of identity" and the achievement of true self and expression. On the other hand, those who act on the basis that human interaction depends on dissimulation, who insist on the central value of the city, its unpredictability, the fluidity of its codes and the subversive play with them.[4]

This division between the "authentic" and the "modernist" can be applied to many of the fashions I have discussed, and especially to contemporary counter-cultural fashions. The hippie, for example, would be "authentic," the punk, as I suggested, "modernist." The nineteenth-century dress reformers were "authentic," but the dandies, like the courtesans of the French Second Empire, were "modernists"—preoccupied with the creation of an image, not the discovery of the "true" self. The division suggests two radically divergent ways of seeing the world—and fashion—and two radically different kinds of politics. Is fashionable dress part of the oppression of women, or is it a form of adult play? Is it part of the empty consumerism, or is it a site of struggle symbolized in dress codes? Does it muffle the self, or create it?

An unresolved tension between "authenticity" and "modernism" haunts contemporary feminism. The recurring theme of women's relationship to nature, of women's utopias, and of the vision of a wholly other world in which "women's values" hold sway suggests a longing for a more "authentic" world, closely bound to "nature," in which we will find our true selves. Engagement in the political battle, the use of avant-garde art, the appropriation of jazz and rock by women's bands and of an anarchic tradition of humor by women comics, and the belief in the social construction of the gendered self represent the "modernist" approach. (Sometimes the two converge, as at Greenham.)

This unresolved tension marks a number of feminist debates, for example the debate about heterosexual love, the controversies over pornography and romantic fiction, and the debate about dress and feminist attitudes to personal adornment. Some feminists, for example, have defined men—men at least in so-called "patriarchal society"—as the oppressors of women, and the construction of female sexuality as the core of female subordination; since they have also acknowledged that most women, including most feminists, do wish to relate sexually and emotionally to men, they have set up an insoluble problem. Thesis and antithesis can never dissolve into a synthesis; the dialectic simply leaves a wound. Others, of course, have argued that it is fine for women to pursue their desires in whatever direction they lead; lesbian sadomasochism has been the practice most frequently justified, but the arguments apply equally to heterosexuality in any form.[5]

In the sphere of literature, while some feminists have argued that pornography constitutes actual violence toward women, others have asserted our right to look, and, indeed, to be turned on by it. In discussions about pulp fiction there is a similar dispute between the moralists who denounce it as promoting false values and as being a form of ideological subordination of women, and the hedonists who emphasize its fantasy and erotic potential.

Similarly with dress: the thesis is that fashion is oppressive, the antithesis that we find it pleasurable; again no synthesis is possible. In all these arguments the alternatives posed are between moralism and hedonism; either doing your own thing is okay, or else it convicts you of false consciousness. Either the products of popular culture are the supports of a monolithic male ideology, or they are there to be enjoyed and justified.

A slightly different version of these arguments acknowledges that desires for the "unworthier" artifacts of the consumer society have been somehow implanted in us, and that we must try to resolve the resulting guilt by steering some moderate middle way. To care about dress and our appearance *is* oppressive, this argument goes, and our love of clothes *is* a form of false consciousness—yet, since we *do* love them we are locked in a contradiction. The best we can then do, according to this scenario, is to try to find some form of reasonably attractive dress that will avoid the worst pitfalls of extravagance, self-objectification and snobbery, while avoiding also becoming "platform women in dingy black."

Susan Brownmiller's *Femininity* exemplifies this false logic. She defines the erotically appealing as being in direct conflict with the serious and the functional, and offers feminists only the choice between the two:

> Why do I persist in not wearing skirts? Because I don't like this artificial gender distinction. Because I don't wish to start shaving my legs again. Because I don't want to return to the expense and aggravation of nylons. Because I will not reacquaint myself with the discomfort of feminine shoes ... Because the nature of feminine dressing is superficial in essence.[6]

Yet she finds unshaven legs unappealing, and low-heeled shoes unerotic (although they were certainly *fashionable* in 1984, the year the book was published) and longs for the gracefulness and pretty colors of her discarded gowns.

Neither a puritanical moralism, nor a hedonism that supports *any* practice in the name of "freedom" is an adequate politics of popular culture. The body of theory, or ideology, that I have called "utilitarianism" contributed to the construction of this impasse with the unacknowledged, and unrecognized, influence of its machine philosophy, its glorification of the work ethic and its inability to grant pleasure a proper place in human culture—the influence of Veblen. Later nineteenth-century feminism was marked by this Fabian spirit which posed use against beauty; the same utilitarianism marks it today. The logic of this view is ultimately that the only justification for clothing is function—utility.

The emphasis on function leads to an image of what is "natural" which is inseparably locked into this debate. The belief that nature is superior to culture was enshrined within the Romantic reaction to the industrial revolution. Janet Radcliffe Richards, one of the few writers to have examined feminist attitudes to dress, suggests that underlying feminist contempt for fashion and cosmetics is a "muddle" about "the natural person being the real thing."[7] She argues that feminists share what is actually a conservative view: that to try to "make the most of oneself" is to create a *false* impression, somehow to deceive the world.

Human beings, however, are not natural. They do not live primarily by instinct. They live in socially constructed cultures. To suggest, therefore, as Professor Jaegar did, that we would do better to dress as much as possible like sheep, since we, like sheep, are mammals, is to make a fundamental mistake about what human existence is.

To set up the "natural" as superior to the "artificial" (as if the very concept of human culture were not artificial) is a view also influenced by some of the non-conformist, puritan versions of Christianity, which confused the natural with simplicity, and so the uncorrupt. These, like Fabianism, have influenced British and American non-Marxist socialism. Since contemporary feminism, in Britain at least, has been greatly influenced by the socialist tradition, it is hardly surprising that the feminist debate about dress has been marked by this counter-liberatory ideology. One side of the stifled debate about dress has been simply a re-run in very different circumstances of the whole nineteenth-century dress reform project: to *get out of* fashion.

It would be wrong to deny the rational aspects of this view: the dreadful exploitation of garment workers throughout the world is a reality, and feminists should support campaigns against it. In the United States, for example, there is a label in clothes made by properly unionized labor stating that fact. Ultimately only progressive economic policies can end this exploitation, and in that sense the clothes we wear are part of a wider struggle that doesn't necessarily imply a rejection of finery as such. There is also the issue of the way in which certain styles of female dress are held to signal sexuality in a way that invites sexual harassment, makes women vulnerable (when they wear high heels, for example, so that they can't run away from a rapist, or to catch a bus) and also punishes them by making them uncomfortable.

Yet these arguments are often used not rationally, but as rationalizations. Exploitation in the electronics industry does not lead feminists to reject the use of videos and word-processors; the horrors of the agri-industry in no way restrict their enjoyment of gourmet food.[8] Those who can afford foreign holidays usually take them, notwithstanding the despoliation that international tourism inflicts on the third world. The quite special rage reserved for fashionable dressing tells us that dress speaks the irrational-unconscious in a special way.

This relates also to an attitude of persistent hostility to the fine arts that has been evident in certain veins of progressive thought. A "progressive" condemnation of fashion can extend to a general denigration of "bourgeois art." Aesthetes are then equated with the degenerate upper classes, and their preoccupations become suspect. To care or know about traditional art, classical music or "high culture" generally is often to be convicted of pretentiousness and a damaging involvement with the norms of bourgeois culture. The ultimate example of such an attitude is the radical feminist who dismisses Tintoretto and Rubens as "all tits and bums" or as "pornography."[9]

The self-righteousness of such attitudes surfaces whenever, as happened several times in recent years, "serious" British newspapers carried articles about feminism and fashion. One correspondent (a man) wrote to the *Guardian* in response to such a piece:[10]

> The strength of the feminist movement lies in the fact that they do not need to rely on such superficiality—they gain their sisterhood through

being women in a patriarchal environment. They are fighting the oppression of society—a fight they will never win if they feel obliged to conform to the fashions that society imposes on them.

while a woman responded:

I can't be the only woman who reaches for the first t-shirt and skirt/trousers that come to hand in the morning, adding a jumper (knitted by Mum from age-old patterns) when it looks chilly . . . I'm wearing the same summer frocks that I've worn for the past two years. Well, they're not worn out, are they? I have absolutely no idea what is going on in the distant, nonsensical world of fashion. And oddly enough I don't think I'm the one out of touch.

More recently the same issue surfaced in the pages of *Spare Rib*, a feminist magazine. One woman wrote to the letters page (*Spare Rib* no. 139, November 1983):

Recently I have been the target of a lot of criticism from women . . . because they do not like the way that I dress and wear my hair (i.e. Mohican, Bondage, etc.). They tell me that I am ignoring its racist and sexist overtones, that it is not "feminist," and that I am allowing myself to be exploited by the fashion market . . .

Do you criticize your sisters because they don't wear dungarees and Kickers? Is a woman any less emancipated because she "chooses" to wear make-up and stilettos?

Is not the whole point of feminism to help a woman to realize her right to control her own life and make decisions for herself?

If so, why are we as feminists oppressing women with a new set of rules . . . Would anyone with any individuality call that liberation?

Other readers wrote in to agree with her.

This letter shows how, coexisting with a tradition of puritanism (a word not used as a term of abuse, but to indicate a specific historical tradition) is a wholly other ideology of individualism and free choice. While feminists with one voice condemn the consumerist poison of fashion, with another they praise the individualism made possible by dress. "I thought that the feminist ideal was to dress according to personal preference and choice, and not according to a set of rules," wrote a correspondent to the *Sunday Times* (29 August 1982) in response to an article (*Sunday Times*, 22 August 1982) in which Adrianne Blue had tried to *describe* feminist styles of dress. Although she made no attempt to tell anyone what to wear, the writers of several letters published appeared to object to the very attempt even to classify "feminist" ways of dressing, perhaps partly because it seemed to confirm stereotypes, but also, I suspect, because it subtly undermined the "free choice" ideology.

Liberated dress, according to this ideology, means "doing your own thing." The idea of free choice has contributed significantly to contemporary feminism. Perhaps feminists should have questioned it more than they have. Perhaps feminists haven't dared to, because the idea of free choice is so powerful in western societies. Yet "free choice" is really a myth, and is inconsistent with the belief, to which all feminists pay at least lip service, that human beings are "socially constructed." The concept of social construction is based on the view that at birth a baby has the potential to develop in a variety of ways, limited to some extent by genetic heritage, but equally, or more importantly, dependent on the environmental influences that shape its experience and provide a comparatively favorable or unfavorable soil for growth. Many of the most important aspects of this development occur in early childhood. By the time we become adults, therefore, our capacity to choose freely is greatly restricted by the way in which our personality has developed. It is also equally restricted by external circumstances such as class, wealth, gender, age, and where we live.

Despite their apparent acceptance of this "social construction" model, many feminists continue to discuss moral choice as though we were all free agents, as if they had never heard of the well-worn but sensible aphorism: "men make their history, but they do so in circumstances that are not of their own choosing." In the realm of aesthetics the very idea of "free choice" is inappropriate; styles of dress are not dictated simply by economics or sexist ideology but are, as I have argued, intrinsically related to contemporary art styles.

In so far as feminists have dressed differently from other women (and most have not) their style of dress has still borne a close relationship to currently circulating styles. The initial "look" of movement women was the counter-cultural look of the student movement at the end of the 1960s when mini-skirts and Egyptian wig hairstyles (by then slightly out of date) coexisted with hippie robes and curls. Feminists wore floor length dresses in dusty tints, and long, pre-Raphaelite hair. Soon, to cut off your hair curtains became a symbol of liberation, and make-up was seldom worn—but then naturalism was fashionable in the mainstream.

If liberated dress meant doing your own thing, no one ever commented on how strange it was that everyone wanted to do the *same* thing. In the early seventies alternative lifestyle gear varied only within a narrow and predictable range of ethnic blouses, cheesecloth skirts, Biba sleeves, Laura Ashley smocks, bell-bottomed denims and cords and woolly sweaters with that special matted jumble sale finish. (Fifteen years later a different set of aesthetic conventions dictated trousers that are either much baggier or much tighter, bold colors and black and gray instead of Biba greenery-yallery, and hair that is dyed in flashes instead of being hennaed.)

In pioneering thrift-shop styles and retro-chic, feminism was innovative rather than anti-fashion. The hacking jacket worn with a flower skirt (1977), the trilby hat (1979) and the old-fashioned handmade sweaters were fashions that feminism initiated and the mainstream copied.

Some feminists did disdain skirts and high heels, and the popular public stereotype of the feminist was of a stalwart woman in dungarees or boiler suit and Dr. Martens boots. Some feminists did wear such clothes, perhaps partly in order to avoid sexual harassment. Some lesbians had always worn boyish or "butch" styles, and lesbian feminists sometimes took over these styles as a way of proudly proclaiming their sexuality.

Even feminists who never wore a skirt or make-up went crazy about Kickers, or wore beautifully hand-painted boots in rainbow colors; they adorned themselves with rings and long, bright earrings made of feathers, beads or metal—drawing attention with all these, and with their brightly flashed hair, away from the body and toward its periphery. Fashion, banished from clothing, reappeared surreptitiously in forms of adornment that were less obviously feminine or sexualized.

Dungarees and boiler suits can in any case—and have been—redefined as "fashionable" and "sexy." Yet the very idea of them has sometimes seemed to send men into a frenzy of agitation. In the spring of 1979 a debate was staged in London between Arthur Scargill, later President of the National Union of Miners, and Anna Coote, a feminist journalist, following an article in the *Morning Star* which had attacked the *Yorkshire Miner*, the newspaper of the most militant section of the National Union of Miners, for its policy of having "page three" pinups. Maurice Jones, then editor of the *Yorkshire Miner*, who was also on the platform, at one stage in the proceedings worked himself up into an incoherent frenzy at the outrage of women in dungarees (of whom there were none in an audience consisting in large part of feminists). Such irrational rage could only indicate some deep seated fear, presumably because "dungarees" when associated with "feminists" has become shorthand for rejection of men, for the most menacing (to men) aspect of lesbianism.[11]

The rage of men such as Maurice Jones suggests that it may well be important for women to challenge norms of feminine dress, and even if there is nothing especially political about wearing "whatever you like," women (and men) should be able to choose not to dress fashionably in so far as this is possible—I have argued that it is not really possible. Nevertheless it is mistaken to set up something called "alternative fashion" as a morally superior ideal, as another series of correspondents in the *Guardian* (25 October 1983) tried to do:

I'm sick of being patronized by . . . subtle propaganda . . . It's no news to me and millions of other women who wear bright, cheap clothes, that overalls per se are not revolutionary. What matters is dressing to please ourselves and to say what we want. Men may like "impossible heels"— we want to walk and run, not deform our spines . . . Let's hear about who runs the fashion industry and why it's there at all.

So wrote one London woman. Another, from Yorkshire, bewailed the absence of alternative fashion in the north of England:

High street chic is the ultimate fashion goal for young women. The linched waist, dolman sleeve and three-quarter length leather boot is more eagerly sought than any amount of [alternative fashion].

Why is it . . . that despite dwindling incomes and few jobs people want conformist fashion instead of cheaper, imaginative and experimental apparel? Can alternative fashion only exist if it is under-written by well established sub-cultures? Or do people prefer to display the badges of achievement and status in mainstream society, no matter how precarious their own position is?

Some pertinent questions are asked; but the writers seem not to doubt that their own mode of dressing is both freely chosen and rationally superior. They thus manage to collapse together the two opposed traditions of liberal free choice and utilitarianism. This doesn't resolve the contradiction, the ambivalence; it merely expunges it with the false claim that there exists some form of "alternative dress" that *is* both these things.

To the extent that a feminist style does exist, it has to be understood as a sub-theme of the general fashion discourse. Boiler suits and dungarees are after all fashion garments, not just a feminist uniform. They are commercially marketed items of casual chic; and the contortions necessary in the lavatory, and the discomfort in cold weather of having to undress completely in order to relieve oneself, should prove conclusively that this form of dress is worn not to promote rational apparel, but to announce the wearer's feminism in public. In urban society, clothes are the poster for one's act. In the pre-industrial world clothes were the badge of rank, profession or trade. As classes fragment we revert to a state in which our clothes once more informally define us. Feminism, in evolving a style among these styles, joins the discourse rather than breaking with it, capitulates rather than transcends—which it could in any case never do.

Feminist style relates to a wider social structure. It is the style of dress adopted by intellectuals and white-collar workers of a certain status, what might be called polytechnic dressing (if "polytechnic" wasn't used as a term of abuse along with "feminist"). Anita Brookner again mistakes this form of dressing for an expression of freedom:

A five-minute survey of my immediate community reveals a preponderance of blue jeans, dungarees, pullovers, tennis shoes, boots, shawls, odd waistcoats, long skirts, plaid blouses . . . To be sure academic gatherings are

not noted for their elegance, but . . . there are several messages to be read
here . . .

The first is that all degrees of seniority are obliterated in the desire to
look as young, as carefree, as natural as possible. The second is that these
unreconstructed dressers, although brought together for purposes of work
. . . are dressed for play . . . The rules have disappeared . . . there does not
seem to be the slightest awareness of the purpose of dressing: there is no
disguise, no self-consciousness—and certainly no shame. (*London Review
of Books*, 15 April–5 May 1982)

Yet, in the environment described, this form of dress is virtually compulsory, and does conform to a set of unspoken rules, of which one is
the pseudo-democracy of 1960s liberal views on education: that it is
possible to abolish the hierarchic distinctions between teachers and
taught. In reality, the differences in status and power have changed little
since the student rebellions; it is simply that now the informal dress of
teachers gestures rather placatingly toward some alternative ideal. Angela Carter is nearer the mark when she suggests that "Jeans have lost
their outlaw chic since the class of '68 took them into the senior common room by a natural progression. They are now . . . a sign of grumpy
middle age" (*New Society*, 13 January 1983).

The casual dress described by Anita Brookner, far from being the
inspiration of free spirits, is the latter-day version of the Fabian style,
of the vegetarians and socialists in sandals and hairy knickerbockers
whom George Orwell used to refer to as "gruff lesbians," "sandals
wearers," "orange juice drinkers," "pansies" and other "cranks" unfortunately attracted to socialism. Orwell's caricatures are offensive;
moreover these "cranks" *had* been innovative. For example, it *was* liberating when Edward Carpenter wore open sandals. Then he broke a
taboo; now casual dress may surely be optional. The idea that casual
dress must be both freely chosen and somehow "better" is mixed up
with another ideology from the 1960s: that formality is always repressive. We confuse opposition to the repressive rituals of our society with
opposition to all ritual.

In relation to dress, some feminists, mostly American, have tried to
retrieve fashion as one among other traditional female skills. They
would argue that women's creativity in the art of dress has been un-
derrated, as have most feminine skills. Lois Banner uses a slightly different argument in suggesting that "the pursuit of beauty and of its
attendant features, fashion and dress, has more than any other factor
bound together women of different classes, regions and ethnic groups,
and constituted a key element in women's separate experience of life."[12]
She offers no evidence for this, and it would be as easy to argue that
dress, beauty and fashion have promoted competitiveness and envy
among women.

I have suggested that more typical of feminist discourse on dress has been its tendency to set up a kind of syllogism that cannot be resolved. It attempts to address and to resolve the ambivalence that is such a widespread response to fashion; yet the terms of the debate inevitably perpetuate that very ambivalence.

I have argued that to understand all "uncomfortable" dress as merely one aspect of the oppression of women, is fatally to over-simplify; that dress is never primarily functional, and that it is certainly not natural. I have argued, against those who see fashion as one form of capitalist "consumerism," that these critics fail to understand that women and men may use the "unworthiest" items of capitalist culture to criticize and transcend that culture. The disaffected use bizarre dress to thumb the nose at consumerism and to create jeering cartoons of society's most cherished conventions. But the fashionably dressed and the more traditionally glamorous are not therefore to be dismissed as necessarily the slaves of consumerism. Socially determined we may be, yet we consistently search for the crevices in culture that open to us moments of freedom. Precisely because fashion is at one level a game (although it is not *just* a game), it can be played for pleasure.

This perspective on fashion is diametrically opposed to that of those radicals who make a root and branch attack on "consumerism." Many radicals do advocate a return to "use values." We should struggle for a world, they argue, in which we would respect craft-made objects and lovingly *use* them. The beauty of pottery, fabrics and furniture—and of course clothes—resides in their simplicity and functionalism. Such critics contrast this sturdy "use" with modern culture in which we "consume," that is, "use up." Consumerism then comes to have destructive and voracious implications. Theodor Adorno and other cultural critics of the "Frankfurt School" developed a deeply pessimistic view of consumer culture, seeing its very diversity, hedonism and inventiveness as a hidden form of uniformity—as I discussed earlier. But the political implication of this was "repressive tolerance" and the idea that *every* aspect of consumer culture duped and doped the masses: consumer culture was a form of "false consciousness." These critics used psychoanalysis—a theory of the *unconscious*, to try to explain the way in which this false consciousness takes over the individual. Consumerism becomes a compulsive form of behavior, over which we have little conscious control. According to this puritanical view, we are squeezed between the imperatives of the market and the urges of an unconscious whose desires are warped and invalidated by the culture in which we live. Fashionable dressing and our pleasure in it then becomes one example of a mass outbreak of authenticity.

I believe that, on the contrary, fashion is one among many forms of aesthetic creativity which make possible the exploration of alternatives. For after all, fashion is more than a game; it is an art form and a symbolic social system:

Once literacy and a rich vocabulary of visual, aural and dramatic expressions exist, then society has a permanently available . . . resource in which all the tabooed, fantastic, possible and impossible dreams of humanity can be explored in blueprint.[13]

This is a far more democratic view than the élitism of the radicals—whether these are the Frankfurt School, Christopher Lasch, Stuart and Elizabeth Ewen or some feminists—who see consumer culture as nothing more than "false consciousness." Apart from anything else, it is clear that while the modern educational system, based ultimately on élitist principles, has failed many of its pupils, these same young men and women have managed to develop what is often an extremely knowing and sophisticated visual taste and a capacity to use images and the adorned person to make complex—if often cynical and nihilist—commentaries on contemporary life.

The pointlessness of fashion, what Veblen hated, is precisely what makes it valuable. It is in this marginalized area of the contingent, the decorative, the futile, that not simply a new aesthetic but a new cultural order may seed itself. Out of the cracks in the pavements of cities grow the weeds that begin to rot the fabric.

In the sense, therefore, that we can use and play with fashion, we should reject feminist ambivalence as an inappropriate if understandable response. Yet there is another sense in which fashion elicits an ambivalent response, and that has to do with an ambivalence that runs deeper and is more tightly embedded in fashion itself.

Fashion acts as a vehicle for fantasy. The utopias both of right and left, which were themselves fantasies, implied an end to fantasy in the perfect world of the future. There will, however, never be a human world without fantasy, which expresses the unconscious unfulfillable. All art draws on unconscious fantasy; the performance that is fashion is one road from the inner to the outer world. Hence its compulsiveness, hence our ambivalence, hence the immense psychological (and material) *work* that goes into the production of the social self, of which clothes are an indispensable part.

In this sense, ambivalence *is* an appropriate response to dress; and in this sense "modernism" is a more adequate response than the "cult of the authentic," since the latter allows for no ambivalence:

Take the example of nudity as it is presented in . . . the mass media's discovery of the body and sex. This nudity claims to be rational, progressive: it claims to rediscover the truth of the body, its natural reason, beyond clothing, taboos and fashion. In fact, it is too rationalistic, and bypasses the body . . . and the true path of desire, which is always ambivalent, love and death simultaneously.[14]

This ambivalence is that of contradictory and irreconcilable desires, inscribed in the human psyche by that very "social construction" that decrees such a long period of cultural development for the human ego. Fashion—a performance art—acts as vehicle for this ambivalence; the daring of fashion speaks dread as well as desire; the shell of chic, the aura of glamour, always hide a wound.

Fashion reflects also the ambivalence of the fissured culture of modernity, is only like all modern art in expressing a flawed culture. The dilemma of fashion is the dilemma of all modern art: what is its purpose and how is it to be used in the world of "mechanical reproduction"? Where fashion differs from some forms of art is that whereas in some fields high art and popular culture have veered further and further apart, in dress the opposite has happened. High fashion has become to some extent demotic. All chic is now gutter chic.

Like all art, it has a troubled relationship with morality, is almost always in danger of being denounced as immoral. Yet also, like all art, it is likely to become most "immoral" when it comes closest to the truth. Utilitarian dress, like conventional "good" clothes and academic art, expresses conservatism. The progressive project is not to search for some aesthetically pleasing form of utilitarian dress, for that would be to abandon the medium; rather we should use dress to express and explore our more daring aspirations, while respecting those who use it to disguise personal inadequacies, real or imagined, or to make themselves feel confident or important.

Art is always seeking new ways to illuminate our dilemmas; dress, however tainted a medium—from its association with the body and with daily life and behavior—nevertheless does this too. Fashion is ambivalent—for when we dress we wear inscribed upon our bodies the often obscure relationship of art, personal psychology and the social order. And that is why we remain endlessly troubled by fashion—drawn to it, yet repelled by a fear of what we might find hidden within its purposes, masked by the enigma of its Mona Lisa smile.

ENDNOTES

1. Haweis, Mary Eliza (1818), "Pre-Raphaelite Dress," quoted in Newton, Stella Mary (1974), *Health, Art and Reason: Dress Reformers of the Nineteenth Century*, London: John Murray, p. 9. The diary quotation comes from Howe, Bea (1967), *Arbiter of Elegance*, London: The Harvill Press, p. 69.

2. Beaton, Cecil, (1954), *The Glass of Fashion*, London: Weidenfeld and Nicolson.

3. I thought I remembered reading of a demonstration that was staged on Wall Street, New York City, at which bras were symbolically burned. An account of a demonstration against the Miss America Contest, which took place in Atlantic City in August 1968, is accompanied by a note from the editor of the anthology in which it appears saying "Bras were never burned"; however, one feature of the demonstration was "a huge Freedom Trash Can (into which we will throw bras, girdles, curlers, false eyelashes, wigs, and representative issues of *Cosmopolitan, Ladies' Home Journal, Family Circle,* etc. Bring any such woman-garbage you have around the house)." See Morgan, Robin (ed.) (1970), *Sisterhood Is Powerful: An Anthology of Writings from the Women's Liberation Movement*, New York: Random House,

p. 521. See also O'Sullivan, Sue (1982), "Passionate Beginnings: Ideological Politics 1969–82," *Feminist Review*, no. 11, for an account of the English demonstration against the Miss World Contest at the Albert Hall, London, in November 1970.

4. Chalmers, Martin (1983), "Politics of Crisis," in *City Limits*, 19–25 August.

5. See Snitow, Ann, Stansell, Christine and Thompson, Sharon (1984), *Desire: The Politics of Sexuality*, London: Virago, for a discussion of some of these issues.

6. Brownmiller, Susan (1984), *Femininity*, New York: Linden Press, Simon and Schuster. I am indebted for the information about Susan Brownmiller's book to Chapkis, Wendy (1984), "The Gender Divide: A Discussion of *Femininity* by Susan Brownmiller." Unpublished paper.

7. Radcliffe Richards, Janet (1980), *The Sceptical Feminist*, London: Routledge and Kegan Paul.

8. I have avoided the discussion of vegetarianism here. There is, of course, a whole series of preoccupations surrounding food, some of which are, supposedly at any rate, concerned with health, some with the exploitation of animals, some with conditions in the developing countries. The point still seems to me to stand—that western radical culture is far less ascetic about food—or drink—than it is about dress.

9. I have myself heard women refer to all nude paintings in the National Gallery, London, as pornography. Bel Mooney tells a similar anecdote in the *Sunday Times* (March 1984). Obviously this is a generalization on the basis of anecdote and open to criticism on that score; but such views do flavor parts of the radical scene.

10. The original article was Wilson, Elizabeth (1982), "If You're so Sure You're a Feminist, Why do you read the Fashion Page?," *Guardian*, 26 July. The letters appeared on 2 August 1982.

11. For a description of this event, see Wilson, Elizabeth (1982), *What Is to Be Done about Violence Toward Women?*, Harmondsowrth: Penguin.

12. Banner, Lois (1983), *American Beauty*, New York: Alfred Knopf.

13. Martin, Bernice (1981), *A Sociology of Contemporary Cultural Change*, Oxford: Basil Blackwell, p. 51.

14. Baudrillard, Jean (1981), *For a Critique of the Political Economy of the Sign*, St. Louis, Mo.: Telos Press, p. 97.

18
John Fiske
"Shopping for Pleasure: Malls, Power, and Resistance" (1989)

Shopping malls are cathedrals of consumption—a glib phrase that I regret the instant it slides off my pen. The metaphor of consumerism as a religion, in which commodities become the icons of worship and the rituals of exchanging money for goods become a secular equivalent of holy communion, is simply too glib to be helpful, and too attractive to those whose intentions, whether they be moral or political, are to expose the evils and limitations of bourgeois materialism. And yet the metaphor *is* both attractive and common precisely because it does convey and construct *a* knowledge of consumerism; it does point to one set of "truths," however carefully selected a set.

Truths compete in a political arena, and the truths that the consumerism-as-contemporary-religion strives to suppress are those that deny the difference between the tenor and vehicle of the metaphor. Metaphor always works within that tense area within which the forces of similarity and difference collide, and aligns itself with those of similarity. Metaphor constructs similarity out of difference, and when a metaphor becomes a cliché, as the shopping mall–cathedral one has, then a resisting reading must align itself with the differences rather than the similarities, for clichés become clichés only because of their centrality to common sense: the cliché helps to construct the commonality of common sense.

So, the differences: the religious congregation is powerless, led like sheep through the rituals and meanings, forced to "buy" the truth on offer, all the truth, not selective bits of it. Where the interests of the Authority on High differ from those of the Congregation down Low, the congregation has no power to negotiate, to discriminate: all accommodations are made by the powerless, subjugated to the great truth. In the U.S. marketplace, 90 percent of new products fail to find sufficient buyers to survive (Schudson 1984), despite advertising, promotions, and all the persuasive techniques of the priests of consumption. In Australia, Sinclair (1987) puts the new product failure rate at 80 percent—such statistics are obviously best-guesstimates: what matters is that the failure rate is high. The power of consumer discrimination evidenced here has no equivalent in the congregation: no religion could tolerate a rejection rate of 80 or 90 percent of what it has to offer.

Religion may act as a helpful metaphor when our aim is to investigate the power of consumerism; when, however, our focus shifts to the power of the consumer, it is counterproductive. Shopping malls and the cultural practices, the variety of shoppings that take place within them, are key arenas of struggle, at both economic and ideological levels between those with the power of ideological practice (Althusser), hegemony (Gramsci), or strategy (de Certeau) and those whose construction as subjects in ideology is never complete, whose resistances mean that hegemony can never finally relax in victory, and whose tactics inflict a running series of wounds upon the strategic power. Shopping is the crisis of consumerism: it is where the art and tricks of the weak can inflict most damage on, and exert most power over, the strategic interests of the powerful. The shopping mall that is seen as the terrain of guerrilla warfare looks quite different from the one constructed by the metaphor of religion.

Pressdee (1986), in his study of unemployed youth in the South Australian town of Elizabeth, paints a clear picture of both sides in this war. The ideological practices that serve the interests of the powerful are exposed in his analysis of the local mall's promotional slogan, which appears in the form of a free ticket: "Your ticket to a better shopping world: ADMITS EVERYONE." He comments:

> The words "your" and "everyone" are working to socially level out class distinction and, in doing so, overlook the city's two working class groups, those who have work and those who do not. The word "admits" with a connotation of having to have or be someone to gain admittance is cancelled out by the word "everyone"—there are no conditions of admittance; everyone is equal and can come in. (p. 10)

This pseudoticket to consumerism denies the basic function of a ticket—to discriminate between those who possess one and those who do not—in a precise moment of the ideological work of bourgeois capitalism with its denial of class difference, and therefore of the inevitability of class struggle. The equality of "everyone" is, of course, an equality attainable only by those with purchasing power: those without are defined out of existence, as working-class interests (derived from class *difference*) are defined out of existence by bourgeois ideology. "The ticket to a better shopping world does not say 'Admits everyone with at least some money to spend' . . . ; money and the problems associated with getting it conveniently disappear in the official discourse" (Pressdee 1986: 10–11).

Pressdee then uses a variation of the religious metaphor to sum up the "official" messages of the mall:

The images presented in the personal invitation to all in Elizabeth is then that of the cargo cult. Before us a lightshaft beams down from space, which contains the signs of the "future"; "Target," "Venture"—gifts wrapped; a table set for two. But beamed down from space they may as well be, because . . . this imagery can be viewed as reinforcing denial of the production process—goods are merely beamed to earth. The politics of their production and consumption disappear. (p. 12)

Yet his study showed that 80 percent of unemployed young people visited the mall at least once a week, and nearly 100 percent of young unemployed women were regular visitors. He comments on these uninvited guests:

For young people, especially the unemployed, there has been a congregating within these cathedrals of capitalism, where desires are created and fulfilled and the production of commodities, the very activity that they are barred from, is itself celebrated on the alter of consumerism. Young people, cut off from normal consumer power are invading the space of those with consumer power. (p. 13)

Pressdee's shift from the religious metaphor to one of warfare signals his shift of focus from the powerful to the disempowered.

Thursday nights, which in Australia are the only ones on which stores stay open late, have become the high points of shopping, when the malls are at their most crowded and the cash registers ring up their profits most busily, and it is on Thursday nights that the youth "invasion" of consumer territory is most aggressive. Pressdee (1986) describes this invasion vividly:

Thursday nights vibrate with youth, eager to show themselves—it belongs to them, they have possessed it. This cultural response is neither spectacular nor based upon consumerism itself. Nor does it revolve around artifacts or dress, but rather around the possession of space, or to be more precise the possession of consumer space where their very presence challenges, offends and resists.

Hundreds of young people pour into the center every Thursday night, with three or four hundred being present at any one time. They parade for several hours, not buying, but presenting, visually, all the contradictions of employment and unemployment, taking up their natural public space that brings both life and yet confronts the market place. Security men patrol all night aided by several police patrols, hip guns visible and radios in use, bringing a new understanding to law and order.

Groups of young people are continually evicted from this opulent and warm environment, fights appear, drugs seem plentiful, alcohol is brought in, in various guises and packages. The police close in on a group of young women, their drink is tested. Satisfied that it is only coca-cola they are moved on and out. Not wanted. Shopkeepers and shoppers complain. The security guards become agitated and begin to question all those seen drinking out of cans or bottles who are under 20, in the belief that they *must* contain alcohol. They appear frightened, totally outnumbered by young people as they continue their job in keeping the tills ringing and the passage to the altar both free and safe. (p. 14)

Pressdee coins the term "proletarian shopping" (p. 16) to describe this window shopping with no intention to buy. The youths consumed images and space instead of commodities, a kind of sensuous consumption that did not create profits. The positive pleasure of parading up and down, of offending "real" consumers and the agents of law and order, of asserting their difference within, and different use of, the cathedral of consumerism became an oppositional cultural practice.

The youths were "tricksters" in de Certeau's terms—they pleasurably exploited their knowledge of the official "rules of the game" in order to identify where these rules could be mocked, inverted, and thus used to free those they were designed to discipline. De Certeau (1984) points to the central importance of the "trickster" and the "guileful ruse" throughout peasant and folk cultures. Tricks and ruses are the art of the weak that enables them to exploit their understanding of the rules of the system, and to turn it to their advantage. They are a refusal to be subjugated:

The actual order of things is precisely what "popular" tactics turn to their own ends, without any illusion that it will change any time soon. Though elsewhere it is exploited by a dominant power . . . here order is *tricked* by an art. (de Certeau 1984: 26)

This trickery is evidence of "an ethics of *tenacity* (countless ways of refusing to accord the established order the status of a law, a meaning or a fatality)" (p. 26).

Shopping malls are open invitations to trickery and tenacity. The youths who turn them into their meeting places, or who trick the security guards by putting alcohol into some, but only some, soda cans, are not actually behaving any differently from lunch hour window shoppers who browse through the stores, trying on goods, consuming and playing with images, with no intention to buy. In extreme weather people exploit the controlled climate of the malls for their own pleasure—mothers take children to play in their air-conditioned comfort in hot summers, and in winter older people use their concourses for daily walks. Indeed, some malls now have notices welcoming "mall walkers," and a few have even provided exercise areas set up with equipment and instructions so that the walkers can exercise more than their legs.

Of course, the mall owners are not entirely disinterested or altruistic here—they hope that some of the "tricky" users of the mall will become real economic consumers, but they have no control over who will, how many will, how often, or how profitably. One boutique owner told me that she estimated that 1 in 30 browsers actually bought something.

Shopping malls are where the strategy of the powerful is most vulnerable to the tactical raids of the weak. And women are particularly adept guerrillas.

CONSUMING WOMEN

Bowlby (1987) takes as a premise "Women shop." Within this condensed truism, she finds a number of problems to do with the socially produced definitions of both women and shopping and with the connections between the two. While pondering some of these problems, I was browsing through a shop (where else?) selling cards and gifts. Three items took my eye. One was a bumper sticker proclaiming "When the going gets tough, the tough go shopping"; the second was a birthday card that said, "Happy Birthday to a guy who's sensitive, intelligent and fun to be with—if you liked to shop you'd be perfect"; the third was a card designed for no specific occasion whose front cover showed a stylish, modern young woman and the words "Work to Live, Live to Love, and Love to Shop, so you see . . ." the dots led to the inside and the words "if I can buy enough things I'll never have to work at love again."

These slogans are all commodities to be bought, and while from one perspective they may be yet more evidence of the power of consumerism to invade and take over our most personal lives in that they are seducing us to abrogate our ability to make our own utterances to a commercially motivated producer—the ultimate incorporation—we must recognize that these are not only commodities in the financial economy but also texts in the cultural economy. The meanings that are exchanged are in no way determined by the exchange of money at the cash register. Culturally all three are operating, with different emphases, in two semantic areas—those of gender difference and work versus leisure—and are questioning the distribution of power and values within them.

Each slogan is a feminine utterance, and each utterance depends for its effect upon its foregrounded difference from patriarchal norms. The bumper sticker sets its user apart as different from the "normal" (i.e., masculine) user of the saying's normal form—"When the going gets tough, the tough get going"—so as to distance her from its competitive masculinity (it is used typically to motivate sportsmen, soldiers, and, by extension, businessmen). In so doing, it manages simultaneously to mock such masculine power and to transfer it to a female practice, so that success in shopping becomes as much a source of power as success in sport, war, or business. Shopping entails achievement against a powerful oppositional force (that of capital) and the successful shopper is properly "tough." The user of such a slogan would pronounce "Women shop" in a quite different tone of voice from that used by, for instance, a dismissive patriarch. Shopping is seen as an oppositional, competitive act, and as such as a source of achievement, self-esteem, and power.

The uses of the message's masculine original deny the difference between work and leisure: masculinity is appropriately and equally achieved in sport, war, and work, and conflates these into the single category of the public domain, which it colonizes for the masculine, implicitly leaving the domestic or private for the feminine. Its feminine appropriation, then, speaks against the confinement of femininity to the domains of nonwork, nonpublic, and the "meaning" of the household, the meaning of the domestic, as the place of leisure, relaxation, and privacy—all of which are patriarchal meanings in that they deny the social, economic, and political meanings of the unwaged labor of women in the house.

Opposite the card shop was one selling kitchen equipment; hanging prominently in the window was an apron (the sign of women's domestic slavery) bearing the slogan "Woman's place is in the mall." Of course, one reading of this positions women as mere consumers in patriarchal capitalism, but the slogan also opposes "mall" to "home," and offers up oppositional meanings—if "home" means for women domestic slavery and the site of subordination of women to the demands of patriarchal capitalism exerted through the structure of the nuclear family, then the mall becomes the site of all the opposite, liberational meanings. The mall is where women can be public, empowered, and free, and can occupy roles other than those demanded by the nuclear family. Later on in this essay I will summarize Bowlby's arguments that the department store was the first public space that could legitimately be occupied by respectable women on their own, and Williamson's that buying can bear meanings of empowerment. Both of these arguments are clearly relevant to understanding the contradictory meanings of this apron and its slogan.

But my attention has wandered from the greeting cards. Both of the cards described above link shopping and romantic love as practices in which women excel and men are deficient. Even the "sensitive, intelligent" (i.e., nonjock) male recipient of the birthday card is incapable of understanding shopping. And for the other card, shopping has become, defiantly, the way to solve the problems faced by women in both work and love in a culture that patriarchally attempts to organize both in the interests of men. The conclusion, "If I can buy enough things I'll never have to work at love again," is nonsensical; it deliberately uses the logic of patriarchal capitalism to come to a nonsensical conclusion, the pleasure of which lies in exposing the nonsense for women of the dominant (i.e., patriarchal, capitalist) senses of commodities, work, and love.

The connection made by the two cards between shopping and romantic love may, at first sight, seem odd. But as capitalism developed throughout the nineteenth century it produced and naturalized first the nuclear family as the foundation social unit, and second a new and specific role for women within this unit and thus within the social formation at large. The woman became the domestic manager of both the economic and emotional resources of the family. The romance genre developed as a form of emotional training of women for their wifely role within the capitalist nuclear family. The development of the feminine as the sensitive, emotional, romantic gender was a direct product of the capitalist economy, so there are clear historical reasons for the interlinking of the romantic and the economic within the definition of the feminine that we have inherited from the nineteenth century.

The popular TV game show *The New Price Is Right* shares many characteristics with the slogans on the cards and bumper sticker. Most obviously it takes women's skills as household managers, their knowledge of commodity prices, and their ability to assess relative values, and gives to them the power and public visibility that patriarchy more normally reserves for the masculine. These skills and knowledges are taken out of the devalued feminine sphere of the domestic, and displayed, like masculine skills, in public, on a studio set before an enthusiastic studio audience and millions of TV viewers. In "normal" life, deploying these skills meets with little acclaim or self-esteem—the woman is expected to be a good household manager and all too frequently her role is noticed only when she is deemed to have failed in it. On *The New Price Is Right*, however, her skills and successes are not just acclaimed, but receive excessive applause and approbation from the excited studio audience. The excess provides a carnivalesque inversion of the more normal silence with which such skills are met in everyday life. Such silence is, of course, a means of subjugation, a form of discipline exerted by patriarchy over the feminine; their excessively noisy recognition is thus a moment of licensed liberation from the normal oppression, and women's pleasure in it derives from a recognition that such skills and knowledges can produce positive values despite their devaluation in the patriarchal everyday. *The New Price Is Right* and "When the going gets tough, the tough go shopping" are both cultural resources that can be used to speak and assert the feminine within and against a patriarchal "normality." Similarly, the inadequacy of the sensitive, intelligent birthday boy when it comes to shopping would debar him from success on *The New Price Is Right*.

Successful contestants on the show receive expensive commodities or cash as their prizes. In another carnivalesque and therefore political inversion, the women's skills are rewarded not by spending less of the family money (i.e., that earned by the man), but by money or goods for *her*. Feminine skills do not just *husband* (sic) masculine earnings and thus benefit the family, but actually produce rewards for the women. Similarly, in the "live" versions of this and other games sometimes played in shopping malls, the entry "ticket" is typically a receipt from one of the shops in the mall. The proof of having spent opens up the chance of winning. The receipt as money is a carnivalesque inversion of economic subjugation.

The deep structure of values that underlies patriarchal capitalism now needs to be extended to include earning as typically masculine, and, therefore, spending as typically feminine. So it is not surprising that such a society addresses women as consumers and men as producers. We may summarize the value structure like this:

THE MASCULINE	THE FEMININE
PUBLIC	PRIVATE (DOMESTIC AND SUBJECTIVE)
WORK	LEISURE
EARNING	SPENDING
PRODUCTION	CONSUMPTION
EMPOWERED	DISEMPOWERED
FREEDOM	SLAVERY

Bowlby (1987) makes some interesting points about how shopping enables women to cross the boundary between the public and the private. In her history of the Paris store Bon Marché and its origins at the end of the last century, Bowlby notes that the "diaries" the store gave to its customers as a form of promotion contained detailed information about how to reach the store by public transport:

> That this should have been practically available to the bourgeois lady marks a significant break with the past: department stores were in fact the first public places—other than churches or cathedrals—which were considered respectable for her to visit without a male companion. But this also signified, at another level, a stepping out from domestic bounds. (p. 189)

The value to women of a public space to which they had legitimate and safe access is not confined to the late nineteenth century. Ferrier (1987) makes a similar point about contemporary malls:

> For women there may be a sense of empowerment from their competency in shopping operations, their familiarity with the terrain and with what they can get out of it. The space is designed to facilitate their shopping practices, and in our built environment there are few places designed for women. The shoppingtown offers public conveniences, free buses, parking, toilets, entertainment, free samples, competitions. In the shoppingtown, women have access to public space without the stigma or threat of the street. (p. 1)

She goes on to associate the freedom malls offer women to reject the gendered opposition of public versus domestic with the equal opportunities to reject the gendered opposition between work and leisure, and the economic one of for sale (i.e., public) versus bought (i.e., private):

The shoppingtown, with its carnival atmosphere, seems set to collapse the distinction between work and leisure. . . . The consumer is allowed to wander in and out of private space to look at, handle and try out products that she does not own. In a department store it is possible to wander through privately owned space, holding or wearing someone else's property as if it were your own, without asking to do so, often without even having to go through the usual social intercourse appropriate to being a guest in someone's place. Boundaries between public and private become ambiguous. (p. 2)

Women can find sources of empowerment both in "their" side of the structured values that patriarchy has provided for them (see above) and in their ability to escape the structure itself. Similarly, Bowlby (1985) finds evidence that spending the "man's" money can be a resisting act within the politics of marriage. She quotes a typical piece of advice given to a congressman's wife by Elizabeth Cady Stanton in her lectures in the 1850s:

Go out and buy a new stove! Buy what you need! Buy while he's in Washington! When he returns and flies into a rage, you sit in a corner and weep. That will soften him! Then, when he tastes his food from the new stove, he will know you did the wise thing. When he sees you so much fresher, happier in your new kitchen, he will be delighted and the bills will be paid. I repeat—GO OUT AND BUY!

Bowlby comments:

Significantly, the injunction to buy comes from woman to woman, not from a man, and involves first bypassing and then mollifying a male authority. To "go out" and buy invokes a relative emancipation in women's active role as consumers. (p. 22)

This is an example of de Certeau's (1984) dictum that subordinated people "make do with what they have," and if the only economic power accorded to women is that of spending, then being a woman in patriarchy necessarily will involve feminine "tricks" that turn the system back on itself, that enables the weak to use the resources provided by the strong in their own interests, and to oppose the interests of those who provided the resources in the first place.

In the same way that language need not be used to maintain the social relations that produced it, so too commodities need not be used solely to support the economic system of capitalism, nor need the resources provided by patriarchy go solely to the support of the system. The conditions of production of any cultural system are not the same as, and do not predetermine, the conditions of its use or consumption.

The gendered structure of values given above constitutes not only a way of constructing the social meanings of gender and of inserting those meanings into social domains, but also a means of discipline through knowledge. The "knowledge" that, for instance, femininity finds its meanings in the domestic, in consumption, in leisure, in the disempowered, is a means of disciplining women into the roles and values that patriarchy has inscribed for them. Yet shopping, while apparently addressing women precisely as disempowered domestic consumers, may actually offer opportunities to break free not just from these meanings, but from the structure of binary oppositions that produces them. So Ferrier (1987) can argue:

> It seems that the successful consumer system must have ambiguous boundaries; between leisure and work, public and private space, inside and out, desire and satisfaction, to attract consumers and to make shopping pleasurable. The shoppingtown is in some ways an extension of the consumer's domestic space, and at the same time a totally separate "new world." As Hartley (1983) points out, power resides in the interface between individuals in ambiguous boundaries. In the ambiguous boundaries of the shoppingtown, there is space for fantasy, for inversions, for pleasure. The pleasure and power are linked with the acts of transgression that are sanctioned. (p. 4)

COMMODITIES AND WOMEN

Judith Williamson (1986a) incisively analyzes the problems that left-wing cultural critics face when grappling with what she calls "the politics of consumption." She argues that in our society the conditions of production are ones over which people have no control, no choice about if or where to work, or about the conditions under which to work; consumption, however, offers some means of coping with the frustrations of capitalist conditions of production. It thus serves both the economic interests of the producers and the cultural interests of the consumers while not completely separating the two. The cultural interests of the consumers are essentially, Williamson argues, ones of control. Mainly this is a sense of control over meanings: "The conscious chosen meaning in most people's lives comes much more from what they consume than what they produce" (p. 230). Consumption, then, offers a sense of control over communal meanings of oneself and social relations, it offers a means of controlling to some extent the context of everyday life. The widespread use of VCRs is a case in point. In Morley's 1986 study of lower-middle- and working-class families' use of TV, he found that every household, even those with no wage earners, owned a VCR, which was used both to time-shift TV programs and to play rented films: in the first case the VCR allowed control over scheduling, in the second it allowed control over programming.

Williamson (1986a) argues that in a capitalist society buying and ownership not only offer a sense of control, but form the main, if not the only, means of achieving this:

Ownership is at present the *only* form of control legitimized in our culture. Any serious attempts at controlling products from the other side—as with the miners' demand to control the future of *their* product, coal (or the printing unions' attempts to control their product, newspaper articles, etc.) are not endorsed. Some parts of the left find these struggles less riveting than the struggles over meanings in street style. Yet underlying *both* struggles is the need for people to control their environment and produce their own communal identity; it is just that the former, if won, could actually fulfill that need while the latter ultimately never will. (p. 231)

It is also worth noting not only that the pleasures of control are found in the ownership of commodities through which people can create or modify the context of everyday life and thus many of the meanings it bears, but also that the consumer's moment of choice is an empowered moment. If money is power in capitalism, then buying, particularly if the act is voluntary, is an empowering moment for those whom the economic system otherwise subordinates. And any one single act of buying necessarily involves multiple acts of rejection—many commodities are rejected for every one chosen, and rejecting the offerings of the system constitutes adopting a controlling relationship to it. The following anecdote related to me by a woman shopper is both typical and significant:

> When I was a girl my mother would sometimes take me to the shopping town to go shopping for shoes. She'd spend hours in the shoe shop trying on dozens of pairs, having the assistant running backwards and forwards nonstop. Eventually she'd choose one pair to take home, but I knew she wouldn't buy them, she'd always return them next day saying they didn't fit or weren't right or something.

My informant's apparent embarrassment at the "exploitation" of the shop assistant indicates that she understood the relations between her mother and the assistant at the personal level; her mother, however, was operating on the level of the system, the relationships were those between consumer and producer/distributor, and her pleasure was caused by her empowered position in this relationship. These shopping expeditions were "tactical raids" (de Certeau 1984) upon the system, or a highly developed form of "proletarian shopping" (Pressdee 1986).

But there is another dimension of meaning to this anecdote that can also be traced in Williamson's comparison of the context of production with that of consumption, and that is one of class meanings. The woman telling me the anecdote also characterized her mother as traditionally middle-class, so part of her lack of embarrassment over her treatment of the shop assistant can be explained in terms of mistress-servant class relations, and thus appears less politically acceptable than when it is seen as a tactical raid upon the system.

This raises the suggestion that production may be essentially proletarian and consumption bourgeois. The attempt to control the context of production poses a radical threat to capitalism because it positions proletarian interests in direct, naked, uncompromising conflict with bourgeois interests; it thus invites (and receives) the full weight of the bourgeois ideological and repressive state apparatuses to control and ultimately squash it. The social allegiances formed when aligning oneself with those subordinated by the conditions of production are with those most severely subordinated by capitalism, and therefore those whose struggles are least likely to succeed.

Consumption, however, is more a bourgeois act; it appears to support, rather than threaten, bourgeois values, and by forging these social allegiances, the weak do not invite the repressive attentions of the strong, but can catch them "off guard," as it were. Guerrilla tactics are often most successful when the guerrillas do not wear the uniform of "the enemy." Shopping can never be a radical, subversive act; it can never change the system of a capitalist-consumerist economy. Equally, however, it cannot be adequately explained as a mere capitulation to the system. Williamson's (1986a) key point here is that commodities are furnished by market capitalism, and in themselves cannot be radical; but, she argues, traces of radicalism are to be found in the way they are consumed and the needs that underlie their consumption: "What are potentially radical are the needs that underlie their use: needs both sharpened and denied by the economic system that makes them" (p. 232).

Stedman-Jones (1982), in his study of the culture of the London working classes in the nineteenth and early twentieth centuries, gives us further evidence of this use of commodities not to express radicalism itself, but to meet a need that is potentially radical:

> More generally, evidence about patterns of spending among the London poor suggests that a concern to demonstrate self-respect was infinitely more important than any forms of saving based upon calculations of utility. When money was available which did not have to be spent on necessities, it was used to purchase articles for display rather than articles of use. (p. 101)

The need for "display" is a need for self-esteem and respect that is denied by the conditions of production, but that may be met by the conditions of consumption. This display may involve the purchase of "middle-class" commodities, and thus give the appearance of buying into middle-class values and the social system that advantages them, but Stedman-Jones takes pains to point out that this is not so:

> For the poor, this effort to keep up appearances, to demonstrate "respectability" entailed as careful a management of the weekly family budget as any charity organizer could have envisaged. But its priorities were quite different. "Respectability" did not mean church attendance, teetotalism or

the possession of a post office savings account. It meant the possession of a presentable Sunday suit, and the ability to be seen wearing it. . . .

It is clear from these and other accounts that the priorities of expenditure among the poor bore little relation to the ambitions set before them by advocates of thrift and self-help. (p. 102)

The meanings of a respectable suit for the poor are quite different from those for the affluent, even though the appearance of the poor man's suit may derive many features from that worn by his "social betters." The point is that the meanings of commodities do not lie in themselves as objects, and are not determined by their conditions of production or distribution, but are produced finally by the way they are consumed. The ways and the whys of consumption are where cultural meanings are made and circulated; the system of production and distribution provides the signifiers only.

In his ethnographic study of Bostonian Italians in the West End, Gans (1962) found similar patterns of consumption. He found that display of self through clothes was as common among West Enders as among other working-class groups, and that they were adept at making their own fashions out of what the fashion system provided:

At the time of the study, for example, the "Ivy League" style was beginning to be seen among the young men of the West End. Their version of this style, however, bore little resemblance to that worn on the Harvard campus: flannel colors were darker, shirts and ties were much brighter, and the belt in the back of the pants was more significant in size if not in function. (p. 185)

Gans's description of this style as "informal and jaunty" points to its "display." It would seem that self-display is, for those denied social power, a performance of their ability to be different, of their power to construct their meanings from the resources of the system. It has within it elements of defiance and of pride in self- and subcultural identities, and it is pleasurable insofar as it is a means of controlling social relations and one's cultural environment. There is a sense of freedom underlying display, and it is this that frequently attracts the disapproval of the middle classes, who are prone to label such performance as vulgar or tasteless. Gans finds that the car contains all these cultural meanings and pleasures for the West Enders:

The automobile, for example, serves as an important mode of self-expression to the male West Ender—as it does to many other working-class Americans: it displays his strength and his taste. When the man has the money—and the freedom to spend it—he thus will buy the most powerful automobile he can afford, and will decorate it with as many accessories as possible. The size of the car and the power of its motor express his toughness; the accessories, the carefully preserved finish, and chrome are an extension of the self he displays to the peer group. (p. 184)

The complexity and subtlety of the roles played by commodities in our culture are all too easily dismissed by the concept of a "consumer society." In one sense all societies are consumer societies, for all societies value goods for cultural meanings that extend far beyond their usefulness. In this context, Marx's distinction between use-value and exchange-value is less than helpful, for it suggests a difference between a "real" value, that of the material and human labor in goods, and a "false" value that society gives to commodities as it exchanges them.

Baudrillard (1981) claims that the ultimate effect of capitalism, certainly of its late variant in which we currently live, is to confuse the relationship of use-value and exchange-value, and, in fact, to turn a system of use-values into one of exchange-values. Exchange-values are culturally useful: "Through objects, each individual and each group searches out his-her place in an order" (p. 83). The function of commodities, then, is not just to meet individual needs, but also to relate the individual to the social order. Consumption is not just the end-point of the economic chain that began with production, but a system of exchange, a language in which commodities are goods to think with in a semiotic system that precedes the individual, as does any language. For Baudrillard there is no self-contained individual, there are only ways of using social systems, particularly those of language, goods, and kinship, to relate people differently to the social order and thus to construct the sense of the individual.

Sinclair (1987) points out that Baudrillard's poststructuralist account of the meaning of commodities differs from the more structuralist and Marxist ones of Williamson in an earlier work (1978) and Leiss (1978), both of whom conceive

> of a system of persons on one hand made to correspond to a system of goods on the other, with individual subjects finding it increasingly difficult to maintain a coherent sense of unified identity as the satisfaction of their needs becomes ever more fragmented by greater product differentiation. (Sinclair 1987:55)

Williamson's later work reserves this emphasis, and traces ways in which people can make meanings out of the commodity system, rather than, as here, having their meanings of themselves made for them by that system.

The semiotic function of goods is stressed even more strongly by Douglas and Isherwood (1979), who argue that "consumption is the very arena in which culture is fought over and licked into shape" (p. 57), and that goods "are needed for making visible and stable the categories of culture" (p. 59). They conclude:

> Enjoyment of physical consumption is only part of the service yielded by goods; the other part is the enjoyment of sharing names. . . . Physical consumption involves proving, testing or demonstrating that the experience

in question is feasible. But the anthropological argument insists that by far the greater part of utility is yielded not at proving but in sharing names that have been learned and graded. This is culture. (pp. 75–76; quoted in Sinclair 1987:56)

The important point made by Douglas and Isherwood is that people constantly strive not just to gain access to cultural meaning systems, but rather to exert control over the meanings such systems can produce. Consumption then becomes a way of using the commodity system that gives the consumer some degree of control over the meanings it makes possible. Commodities are not just objects of economic exchange; they are goods to think with, goods to speak with.

Every society has some kind of map, a grid of the terms available to think in at any given time. In ours, consumer goods are just some of the chief landmarks which define the "natural" categories we are accustomed to. (Williamson 1986a:227)

Speech and thought, of course, are finally social practices, ways of relating to the social order. Products therefore "map out the social world, defining, not what we do, but the ways in which we can conceive of doing things" (Williamson 1986a:226). The crucial point that Williamson makes is that

the world of consumerism is the one we live in—it is too late to opt out: but there are two important questions—one, what we say in the language available, the other, what that language itself means.

For the meanings and uses of products cannot be entirely controlled; they can be appropriated and turned around on the society which produces them. (p. 226)

The active semiotic use of commodities blurs the distinction between use-value and exchange-value, and that between materially based and socially produced values, for all values are arbitrary. The values of commodities can be transformed by the practices of their users, as can those of language, for as language can have no fixed reference point in a universal reality, neither can commodities have final values fixed in their materiality. The practices of the users of a system not only can exploit its potential, but can modify the system itself. In the practices of consumption the commodity system is exposed to the power of the consumer, for the power of the system is not just top-down, or center-outward, but always two-way, always a flux of conflicting powers and resistances.

Consumption is not necessarily evidence of the desire for ownership of commodities for its own sake (that is the dominant ideological meaning of ownership), but is rather a symptom of the need for control, for cultural autonomy and for security that the economic system denies subordinated peoples. While agreeing strongly with Williamson that the problem facing the left is not how to turn people away from consumerism, but how to devise new ways in which the legitimate, and admirable, needs and desires appropriated by consumer goods can be met, we must also recognize that, until (if) the revolution comes, the left does not help its cause by devaluing, denigrating, or ignoring the "art of making do," the everyday practices by which people in subordinated social formations win tricks against the system. Nor can we adequately or productively explain such tricks through the inoculation model (Barthes 1973), by which the system takes controlled doses of the disease of radicalism into itself in order finally to strengthen its resistance to it. At the very least such tricks are tactical victories that maintain the morale of the subordinate, and may well produce real gains in their cultural and social experience.

The desire to investigate the practices of making do, wherein can be found the cunning, the creativity, and the power of the subordinate, has been part of a shift in academia that has transformed much of academic theory and research over the past few years. In this shift some feminist scholarship and popular cultural theory come together to partake in a general academic shift of emphasis away from the "grand narrative" toward the particular, away from the text to the reading, away from the speech system toward the utterance, away from ideology and hegemony to the everyday practices of the subordinate. This shift may be summed up as the movement of interest from structures to practices, "from the totalizing structures and mechanisms of power to the heterogeneous practices of everyday life" (Ferrier 1987:2).

Feminist scholarship has been particularly acute in exposing both the broad structures of patriarchy and the minutiae within which they are embodied. Similarly, Marxian scholarship has exposed the structures and practices of ideology and hegemony, and structuralism and psychoanalysis have done equally important work on the structures of language and subjectivity. As our understanding of these totalizing structures has become more sophisticated and more satisfying, so the realization is growing that this knowledge tells us only half the story, and of itself it can induce only a pessimistic elitism. It requires an often contradictory, sometimes complementary, knowledge of the everyday practices by which subordinated groups negotiate these structures, oppose and challenge them, evade their control, exploit their weaknesses, trick them, turn them against themselves and their producers.

Women, despite the wide variety of social formations to which they belong, all share the experience of subordination under patriarchy and have evolved a variety of tactical responses that enable them to deal with it on a day-to-day level. So, too, other subordinated groups, however defined—by class, race, age, religion, or whatever—have evolved everyday practices that enable them to live within and against the forces that subordinate them. Scholarship that neglects or devalues these practices seems to me to be guilty of a disrespect for the weak that is polit-ically reprehensible. This is particularly the case in certain strands of Marxian or feminist scholarship that end up in the position of despis-ing—or, at least, looking down on—those for whom they attempt to speak, and those whose sociopolitical interests they claim to promote. Similarly, studies of popular culture that are optimistic and positive, rather than pessimistic and negative, frequently celebrate the ritual func-tions of popular texts and thus deny or ignore the ability of disempow-ered groups to make their popular culture, often by oppositional practices, out of industrially provided and distributed cultural resources. Such work has traditionally drawn upon anthropological models (those of Turner or Lévi-Strauss) or rhetorical ones (e.g., Burke) to reveal and explain the ritualistic structures of popular culture. In this approach the shift of emphasis from structures to practices has resulted in the move from structural anthropology to cultural ethnography.

CONSPICUOUS CONSUMPTION

One of the commonest practices of the consumer is window shopping, a consumption of images, an imaginative if imaginary use of the lan-guage of commodities that may or may not turn into the purchase of actual commodities. This "proletarian shopping" is closely bound up with the power of looking. As Madonna controls her "look," that is, how she looks to others and therefore how they look upon her, so the window shopper searches a visual vocabulary from which to make state-ments about herself and her social relations. Looking is as much a means of exerting social control as speaking. Elsewhere, I have argued that shopping malls are a visual feast, a plethora of potential meanings, pal-aces of pleasures offered particularly to women (Fiske et al. 1987). The connections among femininity, women's subordination in patriarchy, and looking have been well theorized, particularly in regard to film and advertising. In patriarchy, the woman has been constructed as the object of the masculine voyeuristic look, which places him in a position of power over her and gives him possession of her, or at least of her image. Women's narcissistic pleasure, then, lies in seeing themselves as idealized objects of the male gaze; a woman is always the bearer of her own image, sees herself through the eyes of the other. While there is much evidence, particularly in cinema, to support this theory of the gender politics of looking, its ability to explain the pleasures of shopping, of the use of commodities to construct images of self, is more limited.

Despite the fact that the language of fashion shows strong patriarchal characteristics as it swings its focus around the female body—now em-phasizing the bust, now the buttocks, now the legs or the waist, but always guiding the eye toward the eroticized areas—the meaning of fashion for women cannot be reduced to such political simplicity, nor can the pleasures offered to women by their own bodies be adequately explained by the giving of pleasure to the masculine other. The pleasure of the look is not just the pleasure of looking good for the male, but rather of controlling how one looks and therefore of controlling the look of others upon oneself. Looking makes meanings; it is therefore a means of entering social relations, of inserting oneself into the social order in general, and of controlling one's immediate social relations in particular. Commodities are the resources of the woman (or man) who is exercising some control over her look, her social relations, and her relation to the social order. The Madonna "wanna-bes" who buy fingerless lacey gloves are not buying the meanings these items would have, for instance, at a Buckingham Palace garden party—they are buying a cultural resource out of which to make their own meanings, to make a statement about their own subcultural identity and thus about their relationship to the social order. It is unhelpful to denigrate such a visual speech act by saying that it is pseudospeech or severely limited speech, in that the language of commodities only allows all the fans to say the same thing.

A number of points need raising in response to this criticism. The first is that if commodities speak class identities rather than individual identities, this does not mean that they are necessarily an inferior language system; such a criticism derives from the ideology of individualism and denies, first, the extent to which individual inflections of class meanings can be made within the commodity system (see the discussion on taste and style below), and, second, the extent to which class meanings are spoken by verbal language, however "creatively" or "originally" it may be used. All language systems relate the user to the social order and thus to others who share that or a similar relationship, at the same time they allow concrete and specific differences in their use by each person. The pleasures of linguistic control traverse the realms of the personal and the social. The pleasures and meanings offered by the plenitude of goods in shopping malls are multiple, and bear the dominant ideology while offering considerable scope for cultural maneuver within and against it. On the economic level such glittering excess provides a daily demonstration that the capitalist system works, and on the ideological level that individualism can flourish within it. A wide consumer choice is not an economic requirement, but a requirement of the ideology of individualism. But exercising choice is not just "buying into" the system: choice also enhances the power of the subordinate to make their cultural uses of it.

Two people wearing the same clothes, or furnishing their houses in the same way, are embarrassed to the extent that they feel that their similarity of taste has denied their individual differences, for the centrality of individualism in our ideology gives priority to these meanings rather than to ones of social or class allegiance. It is not surprising, then, that one of our commonest ways of marking the difference between capitalist and communist societies is by the commodity system and consumer choice. Westerners typically mythologize communist societies as providing very limited consumer choice, and, therefore, of producing a gray, undifferentiated mass of people, instead of the vibrant individuals of the West. The "sheeplike" nature of such people, which leads them to accept such a totalitarian social system, is mapped out inconically in their monotonous grayness, resulting from the lack of consumer choice. Because style and taste have, according to this capitalist myth, no role in a communist system that denies its people the language of commodities as it denies them individual "freedom," then the people in such a system have no control over their social relations, no way of varying or determining their points of entry into the social order.

It is therefore essential for capitalist shopping centers to emphasize the plenitude of commodities—goods tumble over each other in a never-ending plethora of objects, a huge cultural resource bank. Of course, such a plenitude of differences can exist only within an overall similarity—all the goods are, after all, produced at the same historical moment by the same capitalist society—but any sense of individuality is constructed, as are all meanings, upon the play of similarity and difference. Similarity is the means of entry into the social order; difference negotiates the space of the individual within that order.

The difference between style and taste is never easy to define, but style tends to be centered on the social, and taste upon the individual. Style then works along axes of similarity to identify group membership, to relate to the social order; taste works within style to differentiate and construct the individual. Style speaks about social factors such as class, age, and other more flexible, less definable social formations; taste talks of the individual inflection of the social.

Such an interplay of style and taste is given spatial representation in Sydney's Centrepoint. Its three levels are class determined, but within each level is a huge variety of commodities. Individuality is a construction of the social, of language, of gendered experience, of family, education, and so on; commodities are used to bear the already constructed sense of individual difference. They are no truer and no falser than our idiolect, our accent, our ways of behaving toward others in the family, and so on. All such markers of individual difference are social, commodities no more and no less than any other. So the class-differential levels of Centrepoint are used by people whose identity already, necessarily, contains class meanings, and riding the escalators through them becomes a concrete metaphor for class mobility. In late capitalist societies blue-collar workers can earn as much, if not more, than white- or pink-collar workers, so style and taste displace economics as markers of class identity and difference. And insofar as style/taste is symbolic and clearly arbitrary, with little of the material base of the economic, it becomes less determined, more open to negotiation: class identities based on economics offer little scope for negotiation; those based on style are not only more flexible, but also offer the consumer greater control in their construction.

In an earlier study, my colleagues and I argued that in Centrepoint class markers are found in the location of shops within the overall structure and in their design, both of which are spatial metaphors for social relations (see Fiske et al. 1987). The most "democratic" shops—those with low-priced goods that appeal to everyone, such as news agents, card shops, and pharmacies—are on the lowest level and tend not to have windows, but open fronts so the boundaries between their territory and the public concourse are leaky; their goods spill over into the pedestrian areas, minimizing the distinction between the public-democratic and the private-exclusive. On the "middle-class" level—that of the medium-priced, trendy fashion shops selling clothes, shoes, bags, and accessories—the shops mark their boundaries a little more clearly, but not exclusively. They have windows, but racks of shoes or T-shirts often push out onto the concourse. And the windows are packed full of goods, tastefully arranged according to color and style, but bursting with them. They offer a plenitude of differences, a bottomless cup of resources for individual tastes to draw upon. These windows, too, reveal the shop: the multitude of goods in the windows never obscures the even greater number of goods within the shop itself. The lighting of both the shop and the windows is bright and cleverly designed to give an identity to the shop that differentiates it from others and from the concourse. As different individuals construct their images within the similarity of fashion, so different shops construct their identity, frequently by the use of lighting and color, within the overall stylistic unity of the shopping center. Window shopping involves a seemingly casual, but actually purposeful, wandering from shop to shop, which means wandering from potential identity to potential identity until a shop identity is found that matches the individual identity, or, rather, that offers the means to construct that identity. The windows and lighting of these middle-range shops create an identity for them that differentiates them from each other and from the public areas, but then opens them up; their brightness invites the gaze, invites the browser inside.

The "democratic" shops do not stress their own identity, do not differentiate themselves so clearly either from each other or from the public areas. The "middle-class" shops identify themselves as different, but as available to all who have the taste to want the identity they offer. The importance of individual differences increases as we ride the elevators up the class structure. So the "upper-class" shops are individualistic to the point of exclusivity. Their windows have fewer goods in them, signaling the opposite of mass availability; their lighting is more subdued, with highlights on the individual commodity, and the shop behind the window is much less easily seen—sometimes, indeed, it is invisible. The contrast in lighting styles between the middle- and upper-class windows is a contrast in class taste and social identity. The highlight on the exclusive commodity, a fur coat or a haute-couture dress, suggests that the wearer will be in the spotlight, picked out from the others. The overall bright lighting in the middle-class windows suggests that the wearers of the commodities within them will be members of the group that shares that style and taste. In theatrical terms, it is the difference between lighting the star and lighting the chorus line. The windows of these upscale shops exclude the mass viewer and signal the limited availability of their commodities, and thus of the identities they offer.

Centrepoint uses vertical differentiation to materialize class difference, a typical instance of the bourgeois ideological practice of conceptualizing classes as though they existed in a spatial, rather than a social, relationship to each other. So the upper-class shops are "naturally" on the highest floor, the "democratic" ones "naturally" on the lowest. This is a good example of how language constructs rather than reflects social reality, for there is no logical reason, if we wish to conceptualize the relationships among classes in spatial terms, that we should not use, for example, *right, center*, and *left*. There may not be a logical reason for our culture's selection of the metaphor here, but there is, of course, an ideological one. Using right, center, and left as a metaphor would suggest both the arbitrary nature of class differences and their political dimension, whereas using upper, middle, and lower grounds these differences in material reality and makes them appear natural. It also gives them a natural value system—as Lakoff and Johnson (1980) have shown, *up* in our culture is good (it is, after all, where God is) and *down* is bad. The spatial up-down metaphor that we commonly use to express moral and social values has been (literally) made concrete by Centrepoint's system of levels.

PROGRESS AND THE NEW

A key feature of the styles on offer is newness, and shopping malls emphasize newness over almost any other characteristic. The plethora of shiny surfaces, the bright lights, the pervasive use of glass and mirrors all serve to make both the commodities and the center itself appear brand new, as though minted yesterday. In Centrepoint (Sydney) and Carillon (Perth) everything is squeaky clean, never a smear or finger mark on the acres of plate glass, never a dull patch on the shiny walls or ceiling. It all adds up to an overwhelming image of newness, a space with no place for the old, the shabby, the worn—no place for the past, only an invitation to the future. So the publicity for Centrepoint and Carillon is dotted with words like *trend, new, fashion, now, today*; newness and "nowness" mark the threshold of the future, not the culmination of the past.

Newness, of course, is central to the economic and ideological interests of capitalism: the desire for the new keeps the production processes turning and the money flowing toward the producers and distributors. The fashion industry has been frequently and accurately criticized for creating artificial newness and therefore artificial obsolescence to further its own economic interests, and, implicitly, to work against the interests of its consumers. Such a criticism, accurate as far as it goes, does not go far enough, for it fails to question why consumers, largely women, continue to want the new, if this desire is totally against their own interests. The "cultural dope" theory would have to work enormously, not to say impossibly, hard to offer a finally convincing explanation of this.

The desire to be up to date, and there is plenty of evidence that it is a common desire, cannot be created entirely by slick publicity, for advertising can only harness and shape socially created desires, it cannot create them from scratch. At the ideological level, the origins of the desire for the new can be traced back to the ideology of progress that has pervaded the economic, political, and moral domains of post-Renaissance Christian capitalist democracies. Such Western societies see time as linear, forward moving and inevitably productive of change. The forward movement of time and the changes it brings are then made social sense of by the concept of progress, improvement, and development. Other societies in which time is seen as circular rather than linear give a quite different value to the relationships among the past, the present, and the future, and make a quite different sense of newness.

But, of course, ideologies do not suit all groups in a society equally well; indeed, it is their function not to do so. The sense of pleasure or satisfaction occasioned by progress achieved is not equally available to all; rather, it is most "naturally" accessible to the mature, white, middle-class male, and becomes progressively less available as social groups are distanced from the ideological norm. The life opportunities available to, for instance, a young, black, working-class female offer limited chances of experiencing the pleasures of progress achieved, yet people of such a group experience the same ideology of progress as do the "successful."

There is, I suggest, an inverse relationship between the possession of a job that offers the pleasures of progress achieved and the seeking of alternative inflections of these pleasures in trendy fashions and the desire to be up to date. Chodorow (1978), for instance, has argued that men's jobs in patriarchy have tended to be goal-oriented and to offer a sense of achievement, of a job done. Women's jobs, on the other hand, tend to be repetitious and circular, of which domestic labor is the prime example and secretarial labor the commercial equivalent. Chodorow's emphasis on gender difference, however, leads her to neglect class, age, and race differences within men (and women)—so it is the mature, white, middle-class male who is most likely to have the sort of job that

Chodorow characterizes as men's. It is also likely that such a man will have conservative tastes in fashion, and will not find pleasure in up-to-dateness; indeed, he will often avoid it. For women, on the other hand, who are likely to have the nonprogressive, nonachieving job of wife-mother, or, if in the workforce, are likely to be in more routine, more repetitive jobs, it may be that participation in fashion is their prime, if not their only, means of participating in the ideology of progress. And because progress and the new have been masculinized, the pleasures they offer can receive public acclaim and validation. The stereotype of the dowdy housewife who has "let herself go" is encumbered with negative values partly because she is seen to have missed out on both the progressive and the public.

For a woman in patriarchy, commodities that enable her to be "in fashion" enable her to relate to the social order in a way that grants her access to the progressive and the public. Such a move may not be radical in that it does not challenge the right of patriarchy to offer these pleasures to men more readily than women, but it can be seen as both progressive and empowering insofar as it opens up masculine pleasures to women. Just as the department store was the first public space legitimately available to women, so the fashionable commodities it offers provide a legitimated public identity and a means of participating in the ideology of progress.

Similarly, many youth subcultures, for both genders, are characterized by a strong desire for up-to-date tastes, in dress and music particularly. Those whose position in the social system denies them the sort of goal achievements of middle-class jobs frequently turn to style and fashion both as a source of pleasure and as a means of establishing themselves in a controlling rather than dependent relationship to the social order. By the imaginative use of commodities, young people can and do make themselves into icons of street art (Chambers 1986). Commodities provided by an industrialized culture can be used for subcultural, resisting purposes (Hebdige 1979).

So the greeting cards discussed earlier in this chapter are not merely silly. In "Work to Live, Live to Love, and Love to Shop," the female speaker recognizes that working, loving, and shopping are all ways of forming social relations; the utterance inside the card—"If I can buy enough things I'll never have to work at love again"—recognizes that patriarchy's grip on working and love is tighter than its grip on shopping. Thus it is that buying commodities offers a sense of freedom, however irrational, from the work involved in working and loving under patriarchy: working and loving are conflated as chores from which shopping offers an escape.

PART SIX

The Tendency of Capitalism to Commodify

19

Karl Marx
"THE FETISHISM OF THE COMMODITY AND ITS SECRET" (1867)*

THE FETISHISM OF THE COMMODITY AND ITS SECRET

A commodity appears at first sight an extremely obvious, trivial thing. But its analysis brings out that it is a very strange thing, abounding in metaphysical subtleties and theological niceties. So far as it is a use-value, there is nothing mysterious about it, whether we consider it from the point of view that by its properties it satisfies human needs, or that it first takes on these properties as the product of human labor. It is absolutely clear that, by his activity, man changes the forms of the materials of nature in such a way as to make them useful to him. The form of wood, for instance, is altered if a table is made out of it. Nevertheless the table continues to be wood, an ordinary, sensuous thing. But as soon as it emerges as a commodity, it changes into a thing which transcends sensuousness. It not only stands with its feet on the ground, but, in relation to all other commodities, it stands on its head, and evolves out of its wooden brain grotesque ideas, far more wonderful than if it were to begin dancing of its own free will.[1]

The mystical character of the commodity does not therefore arise from its use-value. Just as little does it proceed from the nature of the determinants of value. For in the first place, however varied the useful kinds of labor, or productive activities, it is a physiological fact that they are functions of the human organism, and that each such function, whatever may be its nature or its form, is essentially the expenditure of human brain, nerves, muscles and sense organs. Secondly, with regard to the foundation of the quantitative determination of value, namely the duration of that expenditure or the quantity of labor, this is quite palpably different from its quality. In all situations, the labor-time it costs to produce the means of subsistence must necessarily concern mankind,

---

* From Karl Marx, *Capital: A Critique of Political Economy*, Vol. 1, translated by Ben Fowkes, Vintage Books, 1976.

although not to the same degree at different stages of development.[2] And finally, as soon as men start to work for each other in any way, their labor also assumes a social form.

Whence, then, arises the enigmatic character of the product of labor, as soon as it assumes the form of a commodity? Clearly, it arises from this form itself. The equality of the kinds of human labor takes on a physical form in the equal objectivity of the products of labor as values; the measure of the expenditure of human labor-power by its duration takes on the form of the magnitude of the value of the products of labor; and finally the relationships between the producers, within which the social characteristics of their labors are manifested, take on the form of a social relation between the products of labor.

The mysterious character of the commodity-form consists therefore simply in the fact that the commodity reflects the social characteristics of men's own labor as objective characteristics of the products of labor themselves, as the socio-natural properties of these things. Hence it also reflects the social relation of the producers to the sum total of labor as a social relation between objects, a relation which exists apart from and outside the producers. Through this substitution, the products of labor become commodities, sensuous things which are at the same time suprasensible or social. In the same way, the impression made by a thing on the optic nerve is perceived not as a subjective excitation of that nerve but as the objective form of a thing outside the eye. In the act of seeing, of course, light is really transmitted from one thing, the external object, to another thing, the eye. It is a physical relation between physical things. As against this, the commodity-form, and the value-relation of the products of labor within which it appears, have absolutely no connection with the physical nature of the commodity and the material [dinglich] relations arising out of this. It is nothing but the definite social relation between men themselves which assumes here, for them, the fantastic form of a relation between things. In order, therefore, to find an analogy we must take flight into the misty realm of religion. There the products of the human brain appear as autonomous figures endowed with a life of their own, which enter into relations both with each other and with the human race. So it is in the world of commodities with the products of men's hands. I call this the fetishism which attaches itself to the products of labor as soon as they are produced as commodities, and is therefore inseparable from the production of commodities.

As the foregoing analysis has already demonstrated, this fetishism of the world of commodities arises from the peculiar social character of the labor which produces them.

Objects of utility become commodities only because they are the products of the labor of private individuals who work independently of each other. The sum total of the labor of all these private individuals forms the aggregate labor of society. Since the producers do not come into social contact until they exchange the products of their labor, the specific social characteristics of their private labors appear only within this exchange. In other words, the labor of the private individual manifests itself as an element of the total labor of society only through the relations which the act of exchange establishes between the products, and, through their mediation, between the producers. To the producers, therefore, the social relations between their private labors appear as what they are, i.e., they do not appear as direct social relations between persons in their work, but rather as material [*dinglich*] relations between persons and social relations between things.

It is only by being exchanged that the products of labor acquire a socially uniform objectivity as values, which is distinct from their sensuously varied objectivity as articles of utility. This division of the product of labor into a useful thing and a thing possessing value appears in practice only when exchange has already acquired a sufficient extension and importance to allow useful things to be produced for the purpose of being exchanged, so that their character as values has already to be taken into consideration during production. From this moment on, the labor of the individual producer acquires a twofold social character. On the one hand, it must, as a definite useful kind of labor, satisfy a definite social need, and thus maintain its position as an element of the total labor, as a branch of the social division of labor, which originally sprang up spontaneously. On the other hand, it can satisfy the manifold needs of the individual producer himself only in so far as every particular kind of useful private labor can be exchanged with, i.e., counts as the equal of, every other kind of useful private labor. Equality in the full sense between different kinds of labor can be arrived at only if we abstract from their real inequality, if we reduce them to the characteristic they have in common, that of being the expenditure of human labor-power, of human labor in the abstract. The private producer's brain reflects this twofold social character of his labor only in the forms which appear in practical intercourse, in the exchange of products. Hence the socially useful character of his private labor is reflected in the form that the product of labor has to be useful to others, and the social character of the equality of the various kinds of labor is reflected in the form of the common character, as values, possessed by these materially different things, the products of labor.

Men do not therefore bring the products of their labor into relation with each other as values because they see these objects merely as the material integuments of homogeneous human labor. The reverse is true: by equating their different products to each other in exchange as values, they equate their different kinds of labor as human labor. They do this without being aware of it.[3] Value, therefore, does not have its description branded on its forehead; it rather transforms every product of labor into a social hieroglyphic. Later on, men try to decipher the hieroglyphic, to get behind the secret of their own social product: for the characteristic which objects of utility have of being values is as much men's social product as is their language. The belated scientific discovery that the products of labor, in so far as they are values, are merely the material expressions of the human labor expended to produce them, marks an epoch in the history of mankind's development, but by no means banishes the semblance of objectivity possessed by the social characteristics of labor. Something which is only valid for this particular form of production, the production of commodities, namely the fact that the specific social character of private labors carried on independently of each other consists in their equality as human labor, and, in the product, assumes the form of the existence of value, appears to those caught up in the relations of commodity production (and this is true both before and after the abovementioned scientific discovery) to be just as ultimately valid as the fact that the scientific dissection of the air into its component parts left the atmosphere itself unaltered in its physical configuration.

What initially concerns producers in practice when they make an exchange is how much of some other product they get for their own; in what proportions can the products be exchanged? As soon as these proportions have attained a certain customary stability, they appear to result from the nature of the products, so that, for instance, one ton of iron and two ounces of gold appear to be equal in value, in the same way as a pound of gold and a pound of iron are equal in weight, despite their different physical and chemical properties. The value character of the products of labor becomes firmly established only when they act as magnitudes of value. These magnitudes vary continually, independently of the will, foreknowledge and actions of the exchangers. Their own movement within society has for them the form of a movement made by things, and these things, far from being under their control, in fact control them. The production of commodities must be fully developed before the scientific conviction emerges, from experience itself, that all the different kinds of private labor (which are carried on independently of each other, and yet, as spontaneously developed branches of the social division of labor, are in a situation of all-round dependence on each other) are continually being reduced to the quantitative proportions in which society requires them. The reason for this reduction is that in the midst of the accidental and ever-fluctuating exchange relations between the products, the labor-time socially necessary to produce them asserts itself as a regulative law of nature. In the same way, the law of gravity asserts itself when a person's house collapses on top of him. The determination of the magnitude of value by labor-time is therefore a secret hidden under the apparent movements in the relative values of commodities. Its discovery destroys the semblance of the merely accidental determination of the magnitude of the value of the products of labor, but by no means abolishes that determination's material form.

Reflection on the forms of human life, hence also scientific analysis of those forms, takes a course directly opposite to their real development. Reflection begins *post festum*,* and therefore with the results of the process of development ready to hand. The forms which stamp products as commodities and which are therefore the preliminary requirements for the circulation of commodities, already possess the fixed quality of natural forms of social life before man seeks to give an account, not of their historical character, for in his eyes they are immutable, but of their content and meaning. Consequently, it was solely the analysis of the prices of commodities which led to the determination of the magnitude of value, and solely the common expression of all commodities in money which led to the establishment of their character as values. It is however precisely this finished form of the world of commodities—the money form—which conceals the social character of private labor and the social relations between the individual workers, by making those relations appear as relations between material objects, instead of revealing them plainly. If I state that coats or boots stand in a relation to linen because the latter is the universal incarnation of abstract human labor, the absurdity of the statement is self-evident. Nevertheless, when the producers of coats and boots bring these commodities into a relation with linen, or with gold or silver (and this makes no difference here), as the universal equivalent, the relation between their own private labor and the collective labor of society appears to them in exactly this absurd form.

The categories of bourgeois economics consist precisely of forms of this kind. They are forms of thought which are socially valid, and therefore objective, for the relations of production belonging to this historically determined mode of social production, i.e., commodity production. The whole mystery of commodities, all the magic and necromancy that surrounds the products of labor on the basis of commodity production, vanishes therefore as soon as we come to other forms of production.

As political economists are fond of Robinson Crusoe stories,[4] let us first look at Robinson on his island. Undemanding though he is by nature, he still has needs to satisfy, and must therefore perform useful labors of various kinds: he must make tools, knock together furniture, tame llamas, fish, hunt and so on. Of his prayers and the like, we take no account here, since our friend takes pleasure in them and sees them as recreation. Despite the diversity of his productive functions, he knows that they are only different forms of activity of one and the same Robinson, hence only different forms of human labor. Necessity itself compels him to divide his time with precision between his different functions. Whether one function occupies a greater space in his total activity than another depends on the magnitude of the difficulties to be overcome in attaining the useful effect aimed at. Our friend Robinson

---

* "After the feast," i.e., after the events reflected on have taken place.

Crusoe learns this by experience, and having saved a watch, ledger, ink and pen from the shipwreck, he soon begins, like a good Englishman, to keep a set of books. His stock-book contains a catalog of the useful objects he possesses, of the various operations necessary for their production, and finally of the labor-time that specific quantities of these products have on average cost him. All the relations between Robinson and these objects that form his self-created wealth are here so simple and transparent that even Mr. Sedley Taylor* could understand them. And yet those relations contain all the essential determinants of value.

Let us now transport ourselves from Robinson's island, bathed in light, to medieval Europe, shrouded in darkness. Here, instead of the independent man, we find everyone dependent—serfs and lords, vassals and suzerains, laymen and clerics. Personal dependence characterizes the social relations of material production as much as it does the other spheres of life based on that production. But precisely because relations of personal dependence form the given social foundation, there is no need for labor and its products to assume a fantastic form different from their reality. They take the shape, in the transactions of society, of services in kind and payments in kind. The natural form of labor, its particularity—and not, as in a society based on commodity production, its universality—is here its immediate social form. The *corvée* can be measured by time just as well as the labor which produces commodities, but every serf knows that what he expends in the service of his lord is a specific quantity of his own personal labor-power. The tithe owed to the priest is more clearly apparent than his blessing. Whatever we may think, then, of the different roles in which men confront each other in such a society, the social relations between individuals in the performance of their labor appear at all events as their own personal relations, and are not disguised as social relations between things, between the products of labor.

For an example of labor in common, i.e., directly associated labor, we do not need to go back to the spontaneously developed form which we find at the threshold of the history of all civilized peoples.[5] We have one nearer to hand in the patriarchal rural industry of a peasant family which produces corn, cattle, yarn, linen and clothing for its own use. These things confront the family as so many products of its collective labor, but they do not confront each other as commodities. The different kinds of labor which create these products—such as tilling the fields, tending the cattle, spinning, weaving and making clothes—are already in their natural form social functions; for they are functions of the fam-

---

* The original German has here "Herr M. Wirth," chosen by Marx as a run-of-the-mill vulgar economist and propagandist familiar to German readers. Engels introduced "Mr. Sedley Taylor," a Cambridge don against whom he polemicized in his preface to the fourth German edition.

ily, which, just as much as a society based on commodity production, possesses its own spontaneously developed division of labor. The distribution of labor within the family and the labor-time expended by the individual members of the family, are regulated by differences of sex and age as well as by seasonal variations in the natural conditions of labor. The fact that the expenditure of the individual labor-powers is measured by duration appears here, by its very nature, as a social characteristic of labor itself, because the individual labor-powers, by their very nature, act only as instruments of the joint labor-power of the family.

Let us finally imagine, for a change, an association of free men, working with the means of production held in common, and expending their many different forms of labor-power in full self-awareness as one single social labor force. All the characteristics of Robinson's labor are repeated here, but with the difference that they are social instead of individual. All Robinson's products were exclusively the result of his own personal labor and they were therefore directly objects of utility for him personally. The total product of our imagined association is a social product. One part of this product serves as fresh means of production and remains social. But another part is consumed by the members of the association as means of subsistence. This part must therefore be divided among them. The way this division is made will vary with the particular kind of social organization of production and the corresponding level of social development attained by the producers. We shall assume, but only for the sake of a parallel with the production of commodities, that the share of each individual producer in the means of subsistence is determined by his labor-time. Labor-time would in that case play a double part. Its apportionment in accordance with a definite social plan maintains the correct proportion between the different functions of labor and the various needs of the associations. On the other hand, labor-time also serves as a measure of the part taken by each individual in the common labor, and of his share in the part of the total product destined for individual consumption. The social relations of the individual producers, both toward their labor and the products of their labor, are here transparent in their simplicity, in production as well as in distribution.

For a society of commodity producers, whose general social relation of production consists in the fact that they treat their products as commodities, hence as values, and in this material [*sachlich*] form bring their individual, private labors into relation with each other as homogeneous human labor, Christianity with its religious cult of man in the abstract, more particularly in its bourgeois development, i.e., in Protestantism, Deism, etc., is the most fitting form of religion. In the ancient Asiatic, Classical-antique, and other such modes of production, the transformation of the product into a commodity, and therefore men's existence as producers of commodities, plays a subordinate role, which however increases in importance as these communities approach nearer and nearer to the stage of their dissolution. Trading nations, properly so called, exist only in the interstices of the ancient world, like the gods of Epicurus in the *intermundia*,* or Jews in the pores of Polish society. Those ancient social organisms of production are much more simple and transparent than those of bourgeois society. But they are founded either on the immaturity of man as an individual, when he has not yet torn himself loose from the umbilical cord of his natural species-connection with other men, or on direct relations of dominance and servitude. They are conditioned by a low stage of development of the productive powers of labor and correspondingly limited relations between men within the process of creating and reproducing their material life, hence also limited relations between man and nature. These real limitations are reflected in the ancient worship of nature, and in other elements of tribal religions. The religious reflections of the real world can, in any case, vanish only when the practical relations of everyday life between man and man, and man and nature, generally present themselves to him in a transparent and rational form. The veil is not removed from the countenance of the social life-process, i.e., the process of material production, until it becomes production by freely associated men, and stands under their conscious and planned control. This, however, requires that society possess a material foundation, or a series of material conditions of existence, which in their turn are the natural and spontaneous product of a long and tormented historical development.

Political economy has indeed analyzed value and its magnitude, however incompletely,[6] and has uncovered the content concealed within these forms. But it has never once asked the question why this content has assumed that particular form, that is to say, why labor is expressed in value, and why the measurement of labor by its duration is expressed in the magnitude of the value of the product.[7] These formulas, which bear the unmistakable stamp of belonging to a social formation in which the process of production has mastery over man, instead of the opposite, appear to the political economists' bourgeois consciousness to be as much a self-evident and nature-imposed necessity as productive labor itself. Hence the pre-bourgeois forms of the social organization of production are treated by political economy in much the same way as the Fathers of the Church treated pre-Christian religions.[8]

The degree to which some economists are misled by the fetishism attached to the world of commodities, or by the objective appearance

---

* According to the Greek philosopher Epicurus (c. 341–c. 270 B.C.), the gods existed only in the *intermundia*, or spaces between different worlds, and had no influence on the course of human affairs. Very few of the writings of Epicurus have been preserved in the original Greek, and this particular idea survived only by being included in Cicero, *De natura deorum*, Book I, Section 18.

of the social characteristics of labor, is shown, among other things, by the dull and tedious dispute over the part played by nature in the formation of exchange-value. Since exchange-value is a definite social manner of expressing the labor bestowed on a thing, it can have no more natural content than has, for example, the rate of exchange.

As the commodity-form is the most general and the most undeveloped form of bourgeois production, it makes its appearance at an early date, though not in the same predominant and therefore characteristic manner as nowadays. Hence its fetish character is still relatively easy to penetrate. But when we come to more concrete forms, even this appearance of simplicity vanishes. Where did the illusions of the Monetary System come from? The adherents of the Monetary System did not see gold and silver as representing money as a social relation of production, but in the form of natural objects with peculiar social properties. And what of modern political economy, which looks down so disdainfully on the Monetary System? Does not its fetishism become quite palpable when it deals with capital? How long is it since the disappearance of the Physiocratic illusion that ground rent grows out of the soil, not out of society?

But, to avoid anticipating, we will content ourselves here with one more example relating to the commodity-form itself. If commodities could speak, they would say this: our use-value may interest men, but it does not belong to us as objects. What does belong to us as objects, however, is our value. Our own intercourse as commodities proves it. We relate to each other merely as exchange-values. Now listen how those commodities speak through the mouth of the economist:

"Value (i.e., exchange-value) is a property of things, riches (i.e., use-value) of man. Value, in this sense, necessarily implies exchanges, riches do not."[9]

"Riches (use-value) are the attribute of man, value is the attribute of commodities. A man or a community is rich, a pearl or a diamond is valuable . . . A pearl or a diamond is valuable as a pearl or diamond."[10]

So far no chemist has ever discovered exchange-value either in a pearl or a diamond. The economists who have discovered this chemical substance, and who lay special claim to critical acumen, nevertheless find that the use-value of material objects belongs to them independently of their material properties, while their value, on the other hand, forms a part of them as objects. What confirms them in this view is the peculiar circumstance that the use-value of a thing is realized without exchange, i.e., in the direct relation between the thing and man, while, inversely, its value is realized only in exchange, i.e., in a social process. Who would not call to mind at this point the advice given by the good Dogberry to the night-watchman Seacoal?*

---

* Shakespeare's comedy *Much Ado About Nothing*, Act 3, Scene 3.

"To be a well-favored man is the gift of fortune; but reading and writing comes by nature."[11]

ENDNOTES

1. One may recall that China and the tables began to dance when the rest of the world appeared to be standing still—*pour encourage les autres.* "To encourage the others." This is a reference to the simultaneous emergence in the 1850s of the Taiping revolt in China and the craze for spiritualism which swept over upper-class German society. The rest of the world was "standing still" in the period of reaction immediately after the defeat of the 1848 Revolutions.

2. Among the ancient Germans the size of a piece of land was measured according to the labor of a day; hence the acre was called *Tagwerk, Tagwanne (jurnale, or terra jurnalis, or diornalis), Mannswerk, Mannskraft, Mannsmaad, Mannshauet,* etc. See Georg Ludwig von Maurer, *Einleitung zur Geschichte der Mark-, Hof-, usw. Verfassung,* Munich, 1854, p. 129 ff.

3. Therefore, when Galiani said: Value is a relation between persons (*"La Ricchezza é una ragione tra due persone"*) he ought to have added: a relation concealed beneath a material shell. (Galiani, *Della Moneta,* p. 221, Vol. 3 of Custodi's collection entitled *Scrittori classici italiani di economia politica, Parte moderna,* Milan, 1803.)

4. Even Ricardo has his Robinson Crusoe stories. "Ricardo makes his primitive fisherman and primitive hunter into owners of commodities who immediately exchange their fish and game in proportion to the labor-time which is materialized in these exchange-values. On this occasion he slips into the anachronism of allowing the primitive fisherman and hunter to calculate the value of their implements in accordance with the annuity tables used on the London Stock Exchange in 1817. Apart from bourgeois society, the 'parallelograms of Mr Owen' seem to have been the only form of society Ricardo was acquainted with" (Karl Marx, *Zur Kritik etc.,* pp. 38–9) [English translation, p. 60].

   The "parallelograms" were the utopian socialist Robert Owen's suggestion for the most appropriate layout for a workers' settlement, made in *A New View of Society* (1813) and immediately seized on by his critics. Ricardo's reference to them is from his *On Protection of Agriculture,* London, 1822, p. 21.

5. "A ridiculous notion has spread abroad recently that communal property in its natural, spontaneous form is specifically Slav, indeed exclusively Russian. In fact, it is the primitive form that we can prove to have existed among Romans, Teutons and Celts, and which indeed still exists to this day in India, in a whole range of diverse patterns, albeit sometimes only as remnants. A more exact study of the Asiatic, and specifically of the Indian form of communal property would indicate the way in which different forms of spontaneous, primitive communal property give rise to different forms of its dissolution. Thus the different original types of Roman and Germanic private property can be deduced from the different forms of Indian communal property" (Karl Marx, *Zur Kritik, etc.,* p. 10) [English translation, p. 33].

6. The insufficiency of Ricardo's analysis of the magnitude of value—and his analysis is by far the best—will appear from the third and fourth books of this work. [These are the books that appeared, respectively, as Volume 3 of *Capital,* and *Theories of Surplus-Value* (3 volumes).] As regards value in general, classical political economy in fact nowhere distinguishes explicitly and with a clear awareness between labor as it appears in the value of a product, and the same labor as it appears in the product's use-value. Of course the distinction is made in practice, since labor is treated sometimes from its quantitative aspect, and at other times qualitatively. But it does not occur to the economists that a purely quantitative distinction between the kinds of labor presupposes their qualitative unity or equality, and therefore their reduction to abstract human labor. For instance, Ricardo declares that he agrees with Destutt de Tracy when the latter says: "As it is certain that

our physical and moral faculties are alone our original riches, the employment of those faculties, labor of some kind, is our original treasure, and it is
always from this employment that all those things are created which we call
riches . . . It is certain too, that all those things only represent the labor
which has created them, and if they have a value, or even two distinct values, they can only derive them from that" (the value) "of the labor from
which they emanate" (Ricardo, *The Principles of Political Economy*, 3rd
edn, London, 1821, p. 334 and Destutt de Tracy, *Elémens d'idéologie*, Parts
4 and 5, Paris, 1826, pp. 35–6). We would here only point out that Ricardo
imposes his own more profound interpretation on the words of Destutt. Admittedly Destutt does say that all things which constitute wealth "represent
the labor which has created them," but, on the other hand, he also says that
they acquire their "two different values" (use-value and exchange-value)
from "the value of labor." He thus falls into the commonplace error of the
vulgar economists, who assume the value of one commodity (here labor) in
order in turn to use it to determine the values of other commodities. But Ricardo reads him as if he had said that labor (not the value of labor) is represented both in use-value and in exchange-value. Nevertheless, Ricardo
himself makes so little of the dual character of the labor represented in this
twofold way that he is forced to spend the whole of his chapter "Value and
Riches, their Distinctive Properties" on a laborious examination of the trivi-
alities of a J. B. Say. And at the end he is therefore quite astonished to find
that while Destutt agrees with him that labor is the source of value, he nevertheless also agrees with Say about the concept of value. ["I am sorry to be
obliged to add that M. de Tracy supports, by his authority, the definitions
which M. Say has given of the words 'value,' 'riches,' and 'utility' " (Ricardo, op. cit., p. 334).]

7. It is one of the chief failings of classical political economy that it has never
succeeded, by means of its analysis of commodities, and in particular of their
value, in discovering the form of value which in fact turns value into
exchange-value. Even its best representatives, Adam Smith and Ricardo, treat
the form of value as something of indifference, something external to the nature of the commodity itself. The explanation for this is not simply that their
attention is entirely absorbed by the analysis of the magnitude of value. It
lies deeper. The value-form of the product of labor is the most abstract, but
also the most universal form of the bourgeois mode of production; by that
fact it stamps the bourgeois mode of production as a particular kind of social production of a historical and transitory character. If then we make the
mistake of treating it as the eternal natural form of social production, we
necessarily overlook the specificity of the value-form, and consequently of
the commodity-form together with its further developments, the money form,
the capital form, etc. We therefore find that economists who are entirely
agreed that labor-time is the measure of the magnitude of value, have the
strangest and most contradictory ideas about money, that is, about the universal equivalent in its finished form. This emerges sharply when they deal
with banking, where the commonplace definitions of money will no longer
hold water. Hence there has arisen in opposition to the classical economists
a restored Mercantilist System (Ganilh etc.), which sees in value only the social form, or rather its insubstantial semblance. Let me point out once and
for all that by classical political economy I mean all the economists who,
since the time of W. Petty, have investigated the real internal framework
[*Zusammenhang*] of bourgeois relations of production, as opposed to the
vulgar economists who only flounder around within the apparent framework
of those relations, ceaselessly ruminate on the materials long since provided
by scientific political economy, and seek there plausible explanations of the
crudest phenomena for the domestic purposes of the bourgeoisie. Apart from
this, the vulgar economists confine themselves to systematizing in a pedantic
way, and proclaiming for everlasting truths, the banal and complacent notions held by the bourgeois agents of production about their own world,
which is to them the best possible one.

8. "The economists have a singular way of proceeding. For them, there are
only two kinds of institutions, artificial and natural. The institutions of feu-
dalism are artificial institutions, those of the bourgeoisie are natural institutions. In this they resemble the theologians, who likewise establish two kinds

of religion. Every religion which is not heirs is an invention of men, while their own is an emanation of God . . . Thus there has been history, but there is no longer any" (Karl Marx, *Misère de la philosophie. Résponse à la philosophie de la misére de M. Proudhon*, 1847, p. 113; English translation: Karl Marx, *The Poverty of Philosophy*, London, 1966, p. 105). Truly comical is M. Bastiat, who imagines that the ancient Greeks and Romans lived by plunder alone. For if people live by plunder for centuries there must, after all, always be something there to plunder; in other words, the objects of plunder must be continually reproduced. It seems, therefore, that even the Greeks and the Romans had a process of production, hence an economy, which constituted the material basis of their world as much as the bourgeois economy constitutes that of the present-day world. Or perhaps Bastiat means that a mode of production based on the labor of slaves is based on a system of plunder? In that case he is on dangerous ground. If a giant thinker like Aristotle could err in his evaluation of slave-labor, why should a dwarf economist like Bastiat be right in his evaluation of wage-labor? I seize this opportunity of briefly refuting an objection made by a German-American publication to my work *Zur Kritik der Politischen Ökonomie*, 1859. My view is that each particular mode of production, and the relations of production corresponding to it at each given moment, in short "the economic structure of society," is "the real foundation, on which arises a legal and political superstructure and to which correspond definite forms of social consciousness," and that "the mode of production of material life conditions the general process of social, political and intellectual life." [These passages are taken from the Preface to *A Contribution to the Critique of Political Economy*, written in January 1859 (English translation, pp. 20–21).]

In the opinion of the German-American publication this is all very true for our own times, in which material interests are preponderant, but not for the Middle Ages, dominated by Catholicism, nor for Athens and Rome, dominated by politics. In the first place, it strikes us as odd that anyone should suppose that these well-worn phrases about the Middle Ages and the ancient world were unknown to anyone else. One thing is clear: the Middle Ages could not live on Catholicism, nor could the ancient world on politics. On the contrary, it is the manner in which they gained their livelihood which explains why in one case politics, in the other case Catholicism, played the chief part. For the rest, one needs no more than a slight acquaintance with, for example, the history of the Roman Republic, to be aware that its secret history is the history of landed property. And then there is Don Quixote, who long ago paid the penalty for wrongly imagining that knight errantry was compatible with all economic forms of society.

9. *Observations on Some Verbal Disputes in Pol. Econ., Particularly Relating to Value, and to Supply and Demand*, London, 1821, p. 16.

10. Bailey, Samual, *A Critical Dissertation on the Nature, Measures, and Causes of Values: Chiefly in Reference to the Writings of Mr. Ricardo and His Followers*. By the Author of Essays on the Formation and Publication of Opinions, London 1825.

11. Both the author of *Observations etc.*, and S. Bailey accuse Ricardo of converting exchange-value from something relative into something absolute. The reverse is true. He has reduced the apparent relativity which these things (diamonds, pearls, etc.) possess to the true relation hidden behind the appearance, namely their relativity as mere expressions of human labor. If the followers of Ricardo answer Bailey somewhat rudely, but by no means convincingly, this is because they are unable to find in Ricardo's own works any elucidation of the inner connection between value and the form of value, or exchange-value.

bell hooks
"EATING THE OTHER: DESIRE AND RESISTANCE"
(1992)

This is theory's acute dilemma: that desire expresses itself most fully where only those absorbed in its delights and torments are present, that it triumphs most completely over other human preoccupations in places sheltered from view. Thus it is paradoxically in hiding that the secrets of desire come to light, that hegemonic impositions and their reversals, evasions, and subversions are at their most honest and active, and that the identities and disjunctures between felt passion and established culture place themselves on most vivid display.

—JOAN COCKS
THE OPPOSITIONAL IMAGINATION

Within current debates about race and difference, mass culture is the contemporary location that both publicly declares and perpetuates the idea that there is pleasure to be found in the acknowledgment and enjoyment of racial difference. The commodification of Otherness has been so successful because it is offered as a new delight, more intense, more satisfying than normal ways of doing and feeling. Within commodity culture, ethnicity becomes spice, seasoning that can liven up the dull dish that is mainstream white culture. Cultural taboos around sexuality and desire are transgressed and made explicit as the media bombards folks with a message of difference no longer based on the white supremacist assumption that "blondes have more fun." The "real fun" is to be had by bringing to the surface all those "nasty" unconscious fantasies and longings about contact with the Other embedded in the secret (not so secret) deep structure of white supremacy. In many ways it is a contemporary revival of interest in the "primitive," with a distinctly postmodern slant. As Marianna Torgovnick argues in *Gone Primitive: Savage Intellects, Modern Lives*:

What is clear now is that the West's fascination with the primitive has to do with its own crises in identity, with its own need to clearly demarcate subject and object even while flirting with other ways of experiencing the universe.

Certainly from the standpoint of white supremacist capitalist patriarchy, the hope is that desires for the "primitive" or fantasies about the Other can be continually exploited, and that such exploitation will occur in a manner that reinscribes and maintains the *status quo*. Whether or not desire for contact with the Other, for connection rooted in the longing for pleasure, can act as a critical intervention challenging and subverting racist domination, inviting and enabling critical resistance, is an un-realized political possibility. Exploring how desire for the Other is ex-pressed, manipulated, and transformed by encounters with difference and the different is a critical terrain that can indicate whether these potentially revolutionary longings are ever fulfilled.

Contemporary working-class British slang playfully converges the dis-course of desire, sexuality, and the Other, evoking the phrase getting "a bit of the Other" as a way to speak about sexual encounter. Fucking is the Other. Displacing the notion of Otherness from race, ethnicity, skin-color, the body emerges as a site of contestation where sexuality is the metaphoric Other that threatens to take over, consume, transform *via* the experience of pleasure. Desired and sought after, sexual pleasure alters the consenting subject, deconstructing notions of will, control, coercive domination. Commodity culture in the United States exploits conventional thinking about race, gender, and sexual desire by "work-ing" both the idea that racial difference marks one as Other and the assumption that sexual agency expressed within the context of racialized sexual encounter is a conversion experience that alters one's place and participation in contemporary cultural politics. The seductive promise of this encounter is that it will counter the terrorizing force of the *status quo* that makes identity fixed, static, a condition of containment and death. And that it is this willingness to transgress racial boundaries within the realm of the sexual that eradicates the fear that one must always conform to the norm to remain "safe." Difference can seduce precisely because the mainstream imposition of sameness is a provoca-tion that terrorizes. And as Jean Baudrillard suggests in *Fatal Strategies*:

> Provocation—unlike seduction, which allows things to come into play and appear in secret, dual and ambiguous—does not leave you free to be; it calls on you to reveal yourself as you are. It is always blackmail by identity (and thus a symbolic murder, since you are never that, except precisely by being condemned to it).

To make one's self vulnerable to the seduction of difference, to seek an encounter with the Other, does not require that one relinquish for-ever one's mainstream positionality. When race and ethnicity become commodified as resources for pleasure, the culture of specific groups, as well as the bodies of individuals, can be seen as constituting an alternative playground where members of dominating races, genders, sexual practices affirm their power-over in intimate relations with the Other. While teaching at Yale, I walked one bright spring day in the downtown area of New Haven, which is close to campus and invariably brings one into contact with many of the poor black people who live nearby, and found myself walking behind a group of very blond, very white, jock type boys. (The downtown area was often talked about as an arena where racist domination of blacks by whites was contested on the sidewalks, as white people, usually male, often jocks, used their bodies to force black people off the sidewalk, to push our bodies aside, without ever looking at us or acknowledging our presence.) Seemingly unaware of my presence, these young men talked about their plans to fuck as many girls from other racial/ethnic groups as they could "catch" before graduation. They "ran" it down. Black girls were high on the list, Native American girls hard to find, Asian girls (all lumped into the same category), deemed easier to entice, were considered "prime targets." Talking about this overheard conversation with my students, I found that it was commonly accepted that one "shopped" for sexual partners in the same way one "shopped" for courses at Yale, and that race and ethnicity was a serious category on which selections were based.

To these young males and their buddies, fucking was a way to confront the Other, as well as a way to make themselves over, to leave behind white "innocence" and enter the world of "experience." As is often the case in this society, they were confident that non-white people had more life experience, were more worldly, sensual, and sexual because they were different. Getting a bit of the Other, in this case engaging in sexual encounters with non-white females, was considered a ritual of transcendence, a movement out into a world of difference that would transform, an acceptable rite of passage. The direct objective was not simply to sexually possess the Other; it was to be changed in some way by the encounter. "Naturally," the presence of the Other, the body of the Other, was seen as existing to serve the ends of white male desires. Writing about the way difference is recouped in the West in "The 'Primitive' Unconscious of Modern Art, or White Skin, Black Masks," Hal Foster reminds readers that Picasso regarded the tribal objects he had acquired as "witnesses" rather than as "models." Foster critiques this positioning of the Other, emphasizing that this recognition was "contingent upon instrumentality": "In this way, through affinity and use, the primitive is sent up into the service of the Western tradition (which is then seen to have partly produced it)." A similar critique can be made of contemporary trends in inter-racial sexual desire and contact initiated by white males. They claim the body of the colored Other instrumentally, as unexplored terrain, a symbolic frontier that will be fertile ground for their reconstruction of the masculine norm, for asserting themselves as transgressive desiring subjects. They call upon the Other to be both witness and participant in this transformation.

For white boys to openly discuss their desire for colored girls (or boys) publicly announces their break with a white supremacist past that would have such desire articulated only as taboo, as secret, as shame. They see their willingness to openly name their desire for the Other as affirmation of cultural plurality (its impact on sexual preference and choice). Unlike racist white men who historically violated the bodies of black women/women of color to assert their position as colonizer/conqueror, these young men see themselves as non-racists, who choose to transgress racial boundaries within the sexual realm not to dominate the Other, but rather so that they can be acted upon, so that they can be changed utterly. Not at all attuned to those aspects of their sexual fantasies that irrevocably link them to collective white racist domination, they believe their desire for contact represents a progressive change in white attitudes toward non-whites. They do not see themselves as perpetuating racism. To them the most potent indication of that change is the frank expression of longing, the open declaration of desire, the need to be intimate with dark Others. The point is to be changed by this convergence of pleasure and Otherness. One dares—acts—on the assumption that the exploration into the world of difference, into the body of the Other, will provide a greater, more intense pleasure than any that exists in the ordinary world of one's familiar racial group. And even though the conviction is that the familiar world will remain intact even as one ventures outside it, the hope is that they will reenter that world no longer the same.

The current wave of "imperialist nostalgia" (defined by Renato Rosaldo in *Culture and Truth* as "nostalgia, often found under imperialism, where people mourn the passing of what they themselves have transformed" or as "a process of yearning for what one has destroyed that is a form of mystification") often obscures contemporary cultural strategies deployed not to mourn but to celebrate the sense of a continuum of "primitivism." In mass culture, imperialist nostalgia takes the form of reenacting and reritualizing in different ways the imperialist, colonizing journey as narrative fantasy of power and desire, of seduction by the Other. This longing is rooted in the atavistic belief that the spirit of the "primitive" resides in the bodies of dark Others whose cultures, traditions, and lifestyles may indeed be irrevocably changed by imperialism, colonization, and racist domination. The desire to make contact with those bodies deemed Other, with no apparent will to dominate, assuages the guilt of the past, even takes the form of a defiant gesture where one denies accountability and historical connection. Most importantly, it establishes a contemporary narrative where the suffering imposed by structures of domination on those designated Other is deflected by an emphasis on seduction and longing where the desire is not to make the Other over in one's image but to become the Other.

Whereas mournful imperialist nostalgia constitutes the betrayed and abandoned world of the Other as an accumulation of lack and loss, contemporary longing for the "primitive" is expressed by the projection onto the Other of a sense of plenty, bounty, a field of dreams. Commenting on this strategy in "Readings in Cultural Resistance," Hal Foster contends, "Difference is thus used productively; indeed, in a social order which seems to know no outside (and which must contrive its own trangressions to redefine its limits), difference is often fabricated in the interests of social control as well as of commodity innovation."

Masses of young people dissatisfied by U.S. imperialism, unemployment, lack of economic opportunity, afflicted by the postmodern malaise of alienation, no sense of grounding, no redemptive identity, can be manipulated by cultural strategies that offer Otherness as appeasement, particularly through commodification. The contemporary crises of identity in the west, especially as experienced by white youth, are eased when the "primitive" is recouped *via* a focus on diversity and pluralism which suggests the Other can provide life-sustaining alternatives. Concurrently, diverse ethnic/racial groups can also embrace this sense of specialness, that histories and experience once seen as worthy only of disdain can be looked upon with awe.

Cultural appropriation of the Other assuages feelings of deprivation and lack that assault the psyches of radical white youth who choose to be disloyal to western civilization. Concurrently, marginalized groups, deemed Other, who have been ignored, rendered invisible, can be seduced by the emphasis on Otherness, by its commodification, because it offers the promise of recognition and reconciliation. When the dominant culture demands that the Other be offered as a sign that progressive political change is taking place, that the American Dream can indeed be inclusive of difference, it invites a resurgence of essentialist cultural nationalism. The acknowledged Other must assume recognizable forms. Hence, it is not African American culture formed in resistance to contemporary situations that surfaces, but nostalgic evocation of a "glorious" past. And even though the focus is often on the ways that this past was "superior" to the present, this cultural narrative relies on stereotypes of the "primitive," even as it eschews the term, to evoke a world where black people were in harmony with nature and with one another. This narrative is linked to white western conceptions of the dark Other, not to a radical questioning of those representations.

Should youth of any other color not know how to move closer to the Other, or how to get in touch with the "primitive," consumer culture promises to show the way. It is within the commercial realm of advertising that the drama of Otherness finds expression. Encounters with

Otherness are clearly marked as more exciting, more intense, and more threatening. The lure is the combination of pleasure and danger. In the cultural marketplace the Other is coded as having the capacity to be more alive, as holding the secret that will allow those who venture and dare to break with the cultural anhedonia (defined in Sam Keen's *The Passionate Life* as "the insensitivity to pleasure, the incapacity for experiencing happiness") and experience sensual and spiritual renewal. Before his untimely death, Michel Foucault, the quintessential transgressive thinker in the west, confessed that he had real difficulties experiencing pleasure:

> I think that pleasure is a very difficult behavior. It's not as simple as that to enjoy one's self. And I must say that's my dream. I would like and hope I die of an overdose of pleasure of any kind. Because I think it's really difficult and I always have the feeling that I do not feel *the* pleasure, the complete total pleasure and, for me, it's related to death. Because I think that the kind of pleasure I would consider as *the* real pleasure, would be so deep, so intense, so overwhelming that I couldn't survive it. I would die.

Though speaking from the standpoint of his individual experience, Foucault voices a dilemma felt by many in the west. It is precisely that longing for *the* pleasure that has led the white west to sustain a romantic fantasy of the "primitive" and the concrete search for a real primitive paradise, whether that location be a country or a body, a dark continent or dark flesh, perceived as the perfect embodiment of that possibility.

Within this fantasy of Otherness, the longing for pleasure is projected as a force that can disrupt and subvert the will to dominate. It acts to both mediate and challenge. In Lorraine Hansberry's play *Les Blancs*, it is the desire to experience closeness and community that leads the white American journalist Charles to make contact and attempt to establish a friendship with Tshembe, the black revolutionary. Charles struggles to divest himself of white supremacist privilege, eschews the role of colonizer, and refuses racist exoticization of blacks. Yet he continues to assume that he alone can decide the nature of his relationship to a black person. Evoking the idea of a universal transcendent subject, he appeals to Tshembe by repudiating the role of oppressor, declaring, "I am a man who feels like talking." When Tshembe refuses to accept the familiar relationship offered him, refuses to satisfy Charles' longing for camaraderie and contact, he is accused of hating white men. Calling attention to situations where white people have oppressed other white people, Tshembe challenges Charles, declaring that "race is a device— no more, no less," that "it explains nothing at all." Pleased with this disavowal of the importance of race, Charles agrees, stating "race hasn't a thing to do with it." Tshembe then deconstructs the category "race" without minimizing or ignoring the impact of racism, telling him:

I believe in the recognition of devices as *devices*—but I also believe in the reality of those devices. In one century men choose to hide their conquests under religion, in another under race. So you and I may recognize the fraudulence of the device in both cases, but the fact remains that a man who has a sword run through him because he will not become a Moslem or a Christian—or who is lynched in Mississippi or Zatembe because he is black—is suffering the utter reality of that device of conquest. And it is pointless to pretend that it doesn't *exist*—merely because it is a lie . . .

Again and again Tshembe must make it clear to Charles that subject to subject contact between white and black which signals the absence of domination, of an oppressor/oppressed relationship, must emerge through mutual choice and negotiation. That simply by expressing their desire for "intimate" contact with black people, white people do not eradicate the politics of racial domination as they are made manifest in personal interaction.

Mutual recognition of racism, its impact both on those who are dominated and those who dominate, is the only standpoint that makes possible an encounter between races that is not based on denial and fantasy. For it is the ever present reality of racist domination, of white supremacy, that renders problematic the desire of white people to have contact with the Other. Often it is this reality that is most masked when representations of contact between white and non-white, white and black, appear in mass culture. One area where the politics of diversity and its concomitant insistence on inclusive representation have had serious impact is advertising. Now that sophisticated market surveys reveal the extent to which poor and materially underprivileged people of all races/ethnicities consume products, sometimes in a quantity disproportionate to income, it has become more evident that these markets can be appealed to with advertising. Market surveys revealed that black people buy more Pepsi than other soft drinks and suddenly we see more Pepsi commercials with black people in them.

The world of fashion has also come to understand that selling products is heightened by the exploitation of Otherness. The success of Benneton ads, which with their racially diverse images have become a model for various advertising strategies, epitomize this trend. Many ads that focus on Otherness make no explicit comments, or rely solely on visual messages, but the recent fall *Tweeds* catalogue provides an excellent example of the way contemporary culture exploits notions of Otherness with both visual images and text. The catalog cover shows a map of Egypt. Inserted into the heart of the country, so to speak, is a photo of a white male (an *Out of Africa* type) holding an Egyptian child in his arms. Behind them is not the scenery of Egypt as modern city, but rather shadowy silhouettes resembling huts and palm trees. Inside, the copy quotes Gustave Flaubert's comments from *Flaubert in Egypt*. For seventy-five pages Egypt becomes a landscape of dreams, and its darker-skinned people background, scenery to highlight whiteness, and the longing of whites to inhabit, if only for a time, the world of the Other. The front page copy declares:

> We did not want our journey to be filled with snapshots of an antique land. Instead, we wanted to rediscover our clothing in the context of a different culture. Was it possible, we wondered, to express our style in an unaccustomed way, surrounded by Egyptian colors, Egyptian textures, even bathed in an ancient Egyptian light?

Is this not imperialist nostalgia at its best—potent expression of longing for the "primitive"? One desires "a bit of the Other" to enhance the blank landscape of whiteness. Nothing is said in the text about Egyptian people, yet their images are spread throughout its pages. Often their faces are blurred by the camera, a strategy which ensures that readers will not become more enthralled by the images of Otherness than those of whiteness. The point of this photographic attempt at defamiliarization is to distance us from whiteness, so that we will return to it more intently.

In most of the "snapshots," all carefully selected and posed, there is no mutual looking. One desires contact with the Other even as one wishes boundaries to remain intact. When bodies contact one another, touch, it almost always a white hand doing the touching, white hands that rest on the bodies of colored people, unless the Other is a child. One snapshot of "intimate" contact shows two women with their arms linked, the way close friends might link arms. One is an Egyptian woman identified by a caption that reads "with her husband and baby, Ahmedio A'bass, 22, leads a gypsy's life"; the second woman is a white-skinned model. The linked hands suggest that these two women share something, have a basis of contact and indeed they do, they resemble one another, look more alike than different. The message again is that "primitivism," though more apparent in the Other, also resides in the white self. It is not the world of Egypt, of "gypsy" life, that is affirmed by this snapshot, but the ability of white people to roam the world, making contact. Wearing pants while standing next to her dark "sister" who wears a traditional skirt, the white woman appears to be cross-dressing (an ongoing theme in *Tweeds*). Visually the image suggests that she and First World white women like her are liberated, have greater freedom to roam than darker women who live peripatetic lifestyles.

Significantly, the catalog that followed this one focused on Norway. There the people of Norway are not represented, only the scenery. Are we to assume that white folks from this country are as at "home" in Norway as they are here so there is no need for captions and explanations? In this visual text, whiteness is the unifying feature—not culture. Of course, for *Tweeds* to exploit Otherness to dramatize "whiteness" while in Egypt, it cannot include darker-skinned models since the play on contrasts that is meant to highlight "whiteness" could not happen nor could the exploitation that urges consumption of the Other whet the appetite in quite the same way; just as inclusion of darker-skinned models in the Norway issue might suggest that the west is not as unified by whiteness as this visual text suggests. Essentially speaking, both catalogues evoke a sense that white people are homogeneous and share "white bread culture."

Those progressive white intellectuals who are particularly critical of "essentialist" notions of identity when writing about mass culture, race, and gender have not focused their critiques on white identity and the way essentialism informs representations of whiteness. It is always the non-white, or in some cases the non-heterosexual Other, who is guilty of essentialism. Few white intellectuals call attention to the way in which the contemporary obsession with white consumption of the dark Other has served as a catalyst for the resurgence of essentialist based racial and ethnic nationalism. Black nationalism, with its emphasis on black separatism, is resurging as a response to the assumption that white cultural imperialism and white yearning to possess the Other are invading black life, appropriating and violating black culture. As a survival strategy, black nationalism surfaces most strongly when white cultural appropriation of black culture threatens to decontextualize and thereby erase knowledge of the specific historical and social context of black experience from which cultural productions and distinct black styles emerge. Yet most white intellectuals writing critically about black culture do not see these constructive dimensions of black nationalism and tend to see it instead as naive essentialism, rooted in notions of ethnic purity that resemble white racist assumptions.

In the essay "Hip, and the Long Front of Color," white critic Andrew Ross interprets Langston Hughes' declaration ("You've taken my blues and gone—You sing 'em on Broadway—And you sing 'em in Hollywood Bowl—And you mixed 'em up with symphonies—And you fixed 'em—So they don't sound like me. Yep, you done taken my blues and gone.") as a "complaint" that "celebrates . . . folk purism." Yet Hughes' declaration can be heard as a critical comment on appropriation (not a complaint). A distinction must be made between the longing for ongoing cultural recognition of the creative source of particular African American cultural productions that emerge from distinct black experience, and essentialist investments in notions of ethnic purity that undergird crude versions of black nationalism.

Currently, the commodification of difference promotes paradigms of consumption wherein whatever difference the Other inhabits is eradicated, *via* exchange, by a consumer cannibalism that not only displaces the Other but denies the significance of that Other's history through a process of decontextualization. Like the "primitivism" Hal Foster maintains "absorbs the primitive, in part *via* the concept of affinity" contemporary notions of "crossover" expand the parameters of cultural production to enable the voice of the non-white Other to be heard by a larger audience even as it denies the specificity of that voice, or as it recoups it for its own use.

This scenario is played out in the film *Heart Condition* when Mooney, a white racist cop, has a heart transplant and receives a heart from Stone, a black man he has been trying to destroy because Stone has seduced Chris, the white call girl that Mooney loves. Transformed by his new "black heart," Mooney learns how to be more seductive, changes his attitudes toward race, and, in perfect Hollywood style, wins the girl in the end. Unabashedly dramatizing a process of "eating the Other" (in ancient religious practices among so called "primitive" people, the heart of a person may be ripped out and eaten so that one can embody that person's spirit or special characteristics), a film like *Heart Condition* addresses the fantasies of a white audience. At the end of the film, Mooney, reunited with Chris through marriage and surrounded by Stone's caring black kin, has become the "father" of Chris and Stone's bi-racial baby who is dark-skinned, the color of his father. Stone, whose ghost has haunted Mooney, is suddenly "history"—gone. Interestingly, this mainstream film suggests that patriarchal struggle over "ownership" (i.e., sexual possession of white women's bodies) is the linchpin of racism. Once Mooney can accept and bond with Stone on the phallocentric basis of their mutual possession and "desire" for Chris, their homosocial bonding makes brotherhood possible and eradicates the racism that has kept them apart. Significantly, patriarchal bonding mediates and becomes the basis for the eradication of racism.

In part, this film offers a version of racial pluralism that challenges racism by suggesting that the white male's life will be richer, more pleasurable, if he accepts diversity. Yet it also offers a model of change that still leaves a white supremacist capitalist patriarchy intact, though no longer based on coercive domination of black people. It insists that white male desire must be sustained by the "labor" (in this case the heart) of a dark Other. The fantasy, of course, is that this labor will no longer be exacted *via* domination, but will be given willingly. Not surprisingly, most black folks talked about this film as "racist." The young desirable handsome intelligent black male (who we are told *via* his own self-portrait is "hung like a shetland pony") must die so that the aging white male can both restore his potency (he awakens from the transplant to find a replica of a huge black penis standing between his legs) and be more sensitive and loving. Torgovnick reminds readers in *Gone Primitive* that a central element in the western fascination with primitivism is its focus on "overcoming alienation from the body, restoring the body, and hence the self, to a relation of full and easy harmony with nature or the cosmos." It is this conceptualization of the "primitive" and the black male as quintessential representative that is dramatized in

Heart Condition. One weakness in Torgovnick's work is her refusal to recognize how deeply the idea of the "primitive" is entrenched in the psyches of everyday people, shaping contemporary racist stereotypes, perpetuating racism. When she suggests, "our own culture by and large rejects the association of blackness with rampant sexuality and irrationality, with decadence and corruption, with disease and death," one can only wonder what culture she is claiming as her own.

Films like *Heart Condition* make black culture and black life backdrop, scenery for narratives that essentially focus on white people. Nationalist black voices critique this cultural crossover, its decentering of black experience as it relates to black people, and its insistence that it is acceptable for whites to explore blackness as long as their ultimate agenda is appropriation. Politically "on the case" when they critique white cultural appropriation of black experience that reinscribes it within a "cool" narrative of white supremacy, these voices can not be dismissed as naive. They are misguided when they suggest that white cultural imperialism is best critiqued and resisted by black separatism, or when they evoke outmoded notions of ethnic purity that deny the way in which black people exist in the west, are western, and are at times positively influenced by aspects of white culture.

Steve Perry's essay "The Politics of Crossover" deconstructs notions of racial purity by outlining the diverse inter-cultural exchanges between black and white musicians, yet he seems unable to acknowledge that this reality does not alter the fact that white cultural imperialist appropriation of black culture maintains white supremacy and is a constant threat to black liberation. Even though Perry can admit that successful black crossover artists, such as Prince, carry the "cross-over impulse" to the point where it "begins to be a denial of blackness," he is unable to see this as threatening to black people who are daily resisting racism, advocating ongoing decolonization, and in need of an effective black liberation struggle.

Underlying Perry's condescension, and at times contemptuous attitude toward all expressions of black nationalism, is a traditional leftist insistence on the primacy of class over race. This standpoint inhibits his capacity to understand the specific political needs of black people that are addressed, however inadequately, by essentialist-based black separatism. As Howard Winant clarifies in "Postmodern Racial Politics in the United States: Difference and Inequality," one must understand race to understand class because "in the postmodern political framework of the contemporary United States, hegemony is determined by the articulation of race and class." And most importantly it is the "ability of the right to represent class issues in racial terms" that is "central to the current pattern of conservative hegemony." Certainly an essentialist-based black nationalism imbued with and perpetuating many racial stereotypes is an inadequate and ineffective response to the urgent demand that there be renewed and viable revolutionary black liberation struggle that would take radical politicization of black people, strategies of de-colonization, critiques of capitalism, and ongoing resistance to racist domination as its central goals.

Resurgence of black nationalism as an expression of black people's desire to guard against white cultural appropriation indicates the extent to which the commodification of blackness (including the nationalist agenda) has been reinscribed and marketed with an atavistic narrative, a fantasy of Otherness that reduces protest to spectacle and stimulates even greater longing for the "primitive." Given this cultural context, black nationalism is more a gesture of powerlessness than a sign of critical resistance. Who can take seriously Public Enemy's insistence that the dominated and their allies "fight the power" when that declaration is in no way linked to a collective organized struggle. When young black people mouth 1960s' black nationalist rhetoric, don Kente cloth, gold medallions, dread their hair, and diss the white folks they hang out with, they expose the way meaningless commodification strips these signs of political integrity and meaning, denying the possibility that they can serve as a catalyst for concrete political action. As signs, their power to ignite critical consciousness is diffused when they are commodified. Communities of resistance are replaced by communities of consumption. As Stuart and Elizabeth Ewen emphasize in *Channels of Desire*:

> The politics of consumption must be understood as something more than what to buy, or even what to boycott. Consumption is a social relation-ship, the dominant relationship in our society—one that makes it harder and harder for people to hold together, to create community. At a time when for many of us the possibility of meaningful change seems to elude our grasp, it is a question of immense social and political proportions. To establish popular initiative, consumerism must be transcended—a difficult but central task facing all people who still seek a better way of life.

Work by black artists that is overtly political and radical is rarely linked to an oppositional political culture. When commodified it is easy for consumers to ignore political messages. And even though a product like rap articulates narratives of coming to critical political conscious-ness, it also exploits stereotypes and essentialist notions of blackness (like black people have natural rhythm and are more sexual). The tele-vision show *In Living Color* is introduced by lyrics that tell listeners "do what you wanna do." Positively, this show advocates transgression, yet it negatively promotes racist stereotypes, sexism, and homophobia. Black youth culture comes to stand for the outer limits of "outness." The commercial nexus exploits the culture's desire (expressed by whites and blacks) to inscribe blackness as "primitive" sign, as wildness, and with it the suggestion that black people have secret access to intense pleasure, particularly pleasures of the body. It is the young black male body that is seen as epitomizing this promise of wildness, of unlimited physical prowess and unbridled eroticism. It was this black body that was most "desired" for its labor in slavery, and it is this body that is most represented in contemporary popular culture as the body to be watched, imitated, desired, possessed. Rather than a sign of pleasure in daily life outside the realm of consumption, the young black male body is represented most graphically as the body in pain.

Regarded fetishisticly in the psycho-sexual racial imagination of youth culture, the real bodies of young black men are daily viciously assaulted by white racist violence, black on black violence, the violence of over-work, and the violence of addiction and disease. In her introduction to *The Body in Pain*, Elaine Scarry states that "there is ordinarily no language for pain," that "physical pain is difficult to express; and that this inexpressibility has political consequences." This is certainly true of black male pain. Black males are unable to fully articulate and acknowledge the pain in their lives. They do not have a public discourse or audience within racist society that enables them to give their pain a hearing. Sadly, black men often evoke racist rhetoric that identifies the black male as animal, speaking of themselves as "endangered species," as "primitive," in their bid to gain recognition of their suffering.

When young black men acquire a powerful public voice and presence *via* cultural production, as has happened with the explosion of rap music, it does not mean that they have a vehicle that will enable them to articulate that pain. Providing narratives that are mainly about power and pleasure, that advocate resistance to racism yet support phallocentrism, rap denies this pain. True, it was conditions of suffering and survival, of poverty, deprivation, and lack that characterized the marginal locations from which breakdancing and rap emerged. Described as "rituals" by participants in the poor urban non-white communities where they first took place, these practices offered individuals a means to gain public recognition and voice. Much of the psychic pain that black people experience daily in a white supremacist context is caused by dehumanizing oppressive forces, forces that render us invisible and deny us recognition. Michael H. (commenting on style in Stuart Ewen's book *All Consuming Images*) also talks about this desire for attention, stating that breakdancing and rap are a way to say "listen to my story, about myself, life, and romance." Rap music provides a public voice for young black men who are usually silenced and overlooked. It emerged in the streets—outside the confines of a domesticity shaped and informed by poverty, outside enclosed spaces where young males body had to be contained and controlled.

In its earliest stages, rap was "a male thing." Young black and brown males could not breakdance and rap in cramped living spaces. Male creativity, expressed in rap and dancing, required wide-open spaces, symbolic frontiers where the body could do its thing, expand, grow, and move, surrounded by a watching crowd. Domestic space, equated with repression and containment, as well as with the "feminine" was resisted and rejected so that an assertive patriarchal paradigm of competitive masculinity and its concomitant emphasis on physical prowess could emerge. As a result, much rap music is riddled with sexism and misogyny. The public story of black male lives narrated by rap music speaks directly to and against white racist domination, but only indirectly hints at the enormity of black male pain. Constructing the black male body as site of pleasure and power, rap and the dances associated with it suggest vibrancy, intensity, and an unsurpassed joy in living. It may very well be that living on the edge, so close to the possibility of being "exterminated" (which is how many young black males feel) heightens one's ability to risk and make one's pleasure more intense. It is this charge, generated by the tension between pleasure and danger, death and desire, that Foucault evokes when he speaks of that *complete total pleasure* that is related to death. Though Foucault is speaking as an individual, his words resonate in a culture affected by anhedonia—the inability to feel pleasure. In the United States, where our senses are daily assaulted and bombarded to such an extent that an emotional numbness sets in, it may take being "on the edge" for individuals to feel intensely. Hence the overall tendency in the culture is to see young black men as both dangerous and desirable.

Certainly the relationship between the experience of Otherness, of pleasure and death, is explored in the film *The Cook, the Thief, His Wife and Her Lover*, which critiques white male imperialist domination even though this dimension of the movie was rarely mentioned when it was discussed in this country. Reviewers of the film did not talk about the representation of black characters; one would have assumed from such writing that the cast was all white and British. Yet black males are a part of the community of subordinates who are dominated by one controlling white man. After he has killed her lover, his blond white wife speaks to the dark-skinned cook, who clearly represents non-white immigrants, about the links between death and pleasure. It is he who explains to her the way blackness is viewed in the white imagination. The cook tells her that black foods are desired because they remind those who eat them of death, and that this is why they cost so much. When they are eaten (in the film, always and only by white people), the cook as native informant tells us it is a way to flirt with death, to flaunt one's power. He says that to eat black food is a way to say "death, I am eating you," thereby conquering fear and acknowledging power. White racism, imperialism, and sexist domination prevail by courageous consumption. It is by eating the Other (in this case, death) that one asserts power and privilege.

A similar confrontation may be taking place within popular culture in this society as young white people seek contact with dark Others.

They may long to conquer their fear of darkness and death. On the reactionary right, white youth may be simply seeking to affirm "white power" when they flirt with having contact with the Other. Yet there are many white youths who desire to move beyond whiteness. Critical of white imperialism and "into" difference, they desire cultural spaces where boundaries can be transgressed, where new and alternative relations can be formed. These desires are dramatized by two contemporary films, John Waters' *Hairspray* and the more recent film by Jim Jarmusch, *Mystery Train*. In *Hairspray*, the "cool" white people, working-class Traci and her middle-class boyfriend, transgress class and race boundaries to dance with black folks. She says to him as they stand in a rat-infested alley with winos walking about, "I wish I was dark-skinned." And he replies, "Traci, our souls are black even though our skin is white." Blackness—the culture, the music, the people—is once again associated with pleasure as well as death and decay. Yet their recognition of the particular pleasures and sorrows black folks experience does not lead to cultural appropriation but to an appreciation that extends into the realm of the political—Traci dares to support racial integration. In this film, the longing and desire whites express for contact with black culture is coupled with the recognition of the culture's value. One does not transgress boundaries to stay the same, to reassert white domination. *Hairspray* is nearly unique in its attempt to construct a fictive universe where white working class "undesirables" are in solidarity with black people. When Traci says she wants to be black, blackness becomes a metaphor for freedom, an end to boundaries. Blackness is vital not because it represents the "primitive" but because it invites engagement in a revolutionary ethos that dares to challenge and disrupt the *status quo*. Like white rappers MC Search and Prime Minister Pete Nice who state that they "want to bring forth some sort of positive message to black people, that there are white people out there who understand what this is all about, who understand we have to get past all the hatred," Traci shifts her positionality to stand in solidarity with black people. She is concerned about her freedom and sees her liberation linked to black liberation and an effort to end racist domination.

Expressing a similar solidarity with the agenda of "liberation," which includes freedom to transgress, Sandra Bernhard, in her new film *Without You I'm Nothing*, also associates blackness with this struggle. In the March issue of *Interview* she says that the movie has "this whole black theme, which is like a personal metaphor for being on the outside." This statement shows that Bernhard's sense of blackness is both problematic and complex. The film opens with her pretending she is black. Dressed in African clothing, she renders problematic the question of race and identity, for this representation suggests that racial identity can be socially constructed even as it implies that cultural appropriation falls short because it is always imitation, fake. Conversely, she contrasts her attempt to be a black woman in drag with the black female's attempt to imitate a white female look. Bernhard's film suggests that alternative white culture derives its standpoint, its impetus from black culture. Identifying herself with marginalized Others, Bernhard's Jewish heritage as well as her sexually ambiguous erotic practices are experiences that already place her outside the mainstream. Yet the film does not clarify the nature of her identification with black culture. Throughout the film, she places herself in a relationship of comparison and competition with black women, seemingly exposing white female envy of black women and their desire to "be" imitation black women; yet she also pokes fun at black females. The unidentified black woman who appears in the film, like a phantom, looking at herself in the mirror has no name and no voice. Yet her image is always contrasted with that of Bernhard. Is she the fantasy Other Bernhard desires to become? Is she the fantasy Other Bernhard desires? The last scene of the film seems to confirm that black womanhood is the yardstick Bernhard uses to measure herself. Though she playfully suggests in the film that the work of black women singers like Nina Simone and Diana Ross is derivative, "stolen" from her work, this inversion of reality ironically calls attention to the way white women have "borrowed" from black women without acknowledging the debt they owe. In many ways, the film critiques white cultural appropriation of "blackness" that leaves no trace. Indeed, Bernhard identifies that she had her artistic beginnings working in black clubs, among black people. Though acknowledging where she is coming from, the film shows Bernhard clearly defining an artistic performance space that only she as a white woman can inhabit. Black women have no public, paying audience for our funny imitations of white girls. Indeed, it is difficult to imagine any setting other than an all black space where black women could use comedy to critique and ridicule white womanhood in the way Bernhard mocks black womanhood.

 Closing the scene shrouded in a cloak that resembles an American flag, Bernhard unveils her nearly nude body. The film ends with the figure of the black woman, who has heretofore only been in the background, foregrounded as the only remaining audience watching this seductive performance. As though she is seeking acknowledgment of her identity, her power, Bernhard stares at the black woman, who returns her look with a contemptuous gaze. As if this look of disinterest and dismissal is not enough to convey her indifference, she removes a tube of red lipstick from her purse and writes on the table "fuck Sandra Bernhard." Her message seems to be: "you may need black culture since without us you are nothing, but black women have no need of you." In the film, all the white women strip, flaunt their sexuality, and appear to be directing their attention to a black male gaze. It is this standpoint that the film suggests may lead them to ignore black women and only notice what black women think of them when we are "right up in their face."

Bernhard's film walks a critical tightrope. On one hand it mocks white appropriation of black culture, white desire for black (as in the scene where Bernhard with a blond white girl persona is seen being "boned" by a black man whom we later find is mainly concerned about his hair— i.e., his own image) even as the film works as spectacle largely because of the clever ways Bernhard "uses" black culture and standard racial stereotypes. Since so many of the representations of blackness in the film are stereotypes it does not really go against the Hollywood cinematic grain. And like the *Tweeds* catalogue on Egypt, ultimately black people are reduced, as Bernhard declares in *Interview*, to "a personal metaphor." Blackness is the backdrop of Otherness she uses to insist on and clarify her status as Other, as cool, hip, and transgressive. Even though she lets audiences know that as an entertainment "rookie" she had her start working in close association with black people, the point is to name where she begins to highlight how far she has come. When Bernhard "arrives," able to exploit Otherness in a big time way, she arrives alone, not in the company of black associates. They are scenery, backdrop, background. Yet the end of the film problematizes this leave-taking. Is Bernhard leaving black folks or has she been rejected and dismissed? Maybe it's mutual. Like her entertainment cohort Madonna, Bernhard leaves her encounters with the Other richer than she was at the onset. We have no idea how the Other leaves her.

When I began thinking and doing research for this piece, I talked to folks from various locations about whether they thought the focus on race, Otherness, and difference in mass culture was challenging racism. There was overall agreement that the message that acknowledgment and exploration of racial difference can be pleasurable represents a breakthrough, a challenge to white supremacy, to various systems of domination. The over-riding fear is that cultural, ethnic, and racial differences will be continually commodified and offered up as new dishes to enhance the white palate—that the Other will be eaten, consumed, and forgotten. After weeks of debating with one another about the distinction between cultural appropriation and cultural appreciation, students in my introductory course on black literature were convinced that something radical was happening, that these issues were "coming out in the open." Within a context where desire for contact with those who are different or deemed Other is not considered bad, politically incorrect, or wrong-minded, we can begin to conceptualize and identify ways that desire informs our political choices and affiliations. Acknowledging ways the desire for pleasure, and that includes erotic longings, informs our politics, our understanding of difference, we may know better how desire disrupts, subverts, and makes resistance possible. We cannot, however, accept these new images uncritically.

21

Malcolm Gladwell
"THE COOLHUNT"
(1997)

Baysie Wightman met DeeDee Gordon, appropriately enough, on a coolhunt. It was 1992. Baysie was a big shot for Converse, and DeeDee, who was barely twenty-one, was running a very cool boutique called Placid Planet, on Newbury Street in Boston. Baysie came in with a camera crew—one she often used when she was coolhunting—and said, "I've been watching your store, I've seen you, I've heard you know what's up," because it was Baysie's job at Converse to find people who knew what was up and she thought DeeDee was one of those people. DeeDee says that she responded with reserve—that "I was like, 'Whatever' "—but Baysie said that if DeeDee ever wanted to come and work at Converse she should just call, and nine months later DeeDee called. This was about the time the cool kids had decided they didn't want the hundred-and-twenty-five-dollar basketball sneaker with seventeen different kinds of high-technology materials and colors and air-cushioned heels anymore. They wanted simplicity and authenticity, and Baysie picked up on that. She brought back the Converse One Star, which was a vulcanized, suède, low-top classic old-school sneaker from the nineteen-seventies, and, sure enough, the One Star quickly became the signature shoe of the retro era. Remember what Kurt Cobain was wearing in the famous picture of him lying dead on the ground after committing suicide? Black Converse One Stars. DeeDee's big score was calling the sandal craze. She had been out in Los Angeles and had kept seeing the white teen-age girls dressing up like cholos, Mexican gangsters, in tight white tank tops known as "wife beaters," with a bra strap hanging out, and long shorts and tube socks and shower sandals. DeeDee recalls, "I'm like, 'I'm telling you, Baysie, this is going to hit. There are just too many people wearing it. We have to make a shower sandal.' " So Baysie, DeeDee, and a designer came up with the idea of making a retro sneaker-sandal, cutting the back off the One Star and putting a thick outsole on it. It was huge, and, amazingly, it's still huge.

Today, Baysie works for Reebok as general-merchandise manager—

part of the team trying to return Reebok to the position it enjoyed in the mid-nineteen-eighties as the country's hottest sneaker company. DeeDee works for an advertising agency in Del Mar called Lambesis, where she puts out a quarterly tip sheet called the L Report on what the cool kids in major American cities are thinking and doing and buying. Baysie and DeeDee are best friends. They talk on the phone all the time. They get together whenever Baysie is in L.A. (DeeDee: "It's, like, how many times can you drive past O. J. Simpson's house?"), and between them they can talk for hours about the art of the coolhunt. They're the Lewis and Clark of cool.

What they have is what everybody seems to want these days, which is a window on the world of the street. Once, when fashion trends were set by the big couture houses—when cool was trickle-down—that wasn't important. But sometime in the past few decades things got turned over, and fashion became trickle-up. It's now about chase and flight—designers and retailers and the mass consumer giving chase to the elusive prey of street cool—and the rise of coolhunting as a profession shows how serious the chase has become. The sneakers of Nike and Reebok used to come out yearly. Now a new style comes out every season. Apparel designers used to have an eighteen-month lead time between concept and sale. Now they're reducing that to a year, or even six months, in order to react faster to new ideas from the street. The paradox, of course, is that the better coolhunters become at bringing the mainstream close to the cutting edge, the more elusive the cutting edge becomes. This is the first rule of the cool: The quicker the chase, the quicker the flight. The act of discovering what's cool is what causes cool to move on, which explains the triumphant circularity of coolhunting: because we have coolhunters like DeeDee and Baysie, cool changes more quickly, and because cool changes more quickly, we need coolhunters like DeeDee and Baysie.

DeeDee is tall and glamorous, with short hair she has dyed so often that she claims to have forgotten her real color. She drives a yellow 1977 Trans Am with a burgundy stripe down the center and a 1973 Mercedes 450 SL, and lives in a spare, Japanese-style cabin in Laurel Canyon. She uses words like "rad" and "totally," and offers non-stop, deadpan pronouncements on pop culture, as in "It's all about Pee-wee Herman." She sounds at first like a teen, like the same teens who, at Lambesis, it is her job to follow. But teen speech—particularly girl-teen speech, with its fixation on reported speech ("so she goes," "and I'm like," "and he goes") and its stock vocabulary of accompanying grimaces and gestures—is about using language less to communicate than to fit in. DeeDee uses teen speech to set herself apart, and the result is, for lack of a better word, really cool. She doesn't do the teen thing of climbing half an octave at the end of every sentence. Instead, she drags out her vowels for emphasis, so that if she mildly disagreed with something I'd said she would say "Maalcolm" and if she strongly disagreed with what I'd said she would say "Maaalcolm."

Baysie is older, just past forty (although you would never guess that), and went to Exeter and Middlebury and had two grandfathers who went to Harvard (although you wouldn't guess that, either). She has curly brown hair and big green eyes and long legs and so much energy that it is hard to imagine her asleep, or resting, or even standing still for longer than thirty seconds. The hunt for cool is an obsession with her, and DeeDee is the same way. DeeDee used to sit on the corner of West Broadway and Prince in SoHo—back when SoHo was cool—and take pictures of everyone who walked by for an entire hour. Baysie can tell you precisely where she goes on her Reebok coolhunts to find the really cool alternative white kids ("I'd maybe go to Portland and hang out where the skateboarders hang out near that bridge") or which snowboarding mountain has cooler kids—Stratton, in Vermont, or Summit County, in Colorado. (Summit, definitely.) DeeDee can tell you on the basis of the L Report's research exactly how far Dallas is behind New York in coolness (from six to eight months). Baysie is convinced that Los Angeles is not happening right now: "In the early nineteen-nineties a lot more was coming from L.A. They had a big trend with the whole Melrose Avenue look—the stupid goatees, the shorter hair. It was cleaned-up aftergrunge. There were a lot of places you could go to buy vinyl records. It was a strong place to go for looks. Then it went back to being horrible." DeeDee is convinced that Japan is happening: "I linked onto this future-technology thing two years ago. Now look at it, it's huge. It's the whole resurgence of Nike—Nike being larger than life. I went to Japan and saw the kids just bailing the most technologically advanced Nikes with their little dresses and little outfits and I'm like, 'Whoa, this is trippy!' It's performance mixed with fashion. It's really superheavy." Baysie has a theory that Liverpool is cool right now because it's the birthplace of the whole "lad" look, which involves soccer blokes in the pubs going superdressy and wearing Dolce & Gabbana and Polo Sport and Reebok Classics on their feet. But when I asked DeeDee about that, she just rolled her eyes: "Sometimes Baysie goes off on these tangents. Man, I love that woman!"

I used to think that if I talked to Baysie and DeeDee long enough I could write a coolhunting manual, an encyclopedia of cool. But then I realized that the manual would have so many footnotes and caveats that it would be unreadable. Coolhunting is not about the articulation of a coherent philosophy of cool. It's just a collection of spontaneous observations and predictions that differ from one moment to the next and from one coolhunter to the next. Ask a coolhunter where the baggy-jeans look came from, for example, and you might get any number of answers: urban black kids mimicking the jailhouse look, skateboarders looking for room to move, snowboarders trying not to look like skiers, or, alternatively, all three at once, in some grand concordance.

Or take the question of exactly how Tommy Hilfiger—a forty-five-year-old white guy from Greenwich, Connecticut, doing all-American preppy clothes—came to be the designer of choice for urban black America. Some say it was all about the early and visible endorsement given Hilfiger by the hip-hop auteur Grand Puba, who wore a dark-green-and-blue Tommy jacket over a white Tommy T-shirt as he leaned on his black Lamborghini on the cover of the hugely influential "Grand Puba 2000" CD, and whose love for Hilfiger soon spread to other rappers. (Who could forget the rhymes of Mobb Deep? "Tommy was my nigga/And couldn't figure/How me and Hilfiger/used to move through with vigor.") Then I had lunch with one of Hilfiger's designers, a twenty-six-year-old named Ulrich (Ubi) Simpson, who has a Puerto Rican mother and a Dutch-Venezuelan father, plays lacrosse, snowboards, surfs the long board, goes to hip-hop concerts, listens to Jungle, Edith Piaf, opera, rap, and Metallica, and has working with him on his design team a twenty-seven-year-old black guy from Montclair with dreadlocks, a twenty-two-year-old Asian-American who lives on the Lower East Side, a twenty-five-year-old South Asian guy from Fiji, and a twenty-one-year-old white graffiti artist from Queens. That's when it occurred to me that maybe the reason Tommy Hilfiger can make white culture cool to black culture is that he has people working for him who are cool in both cultures simultaneously. Then again, maybe it was all Grand Puba. Who knows?

One day last month, Baysie took me on a coolhunt to the Bronx and Harlem, lugging a big black canvas bag with twenty-four different shoes that Reebok is about to bring out, and as we drove down Fordham Road, she had her head out the window like a little kid, checking out what everyone on the street was wearing. We went to Dr. Jay's, which is the cool place to buy sneakers in the Bronx, and Baysie crouched down on the floor and started pulling the shoes out of her bag one by one, soliciting opinions from customers who gathered around and asking one question after another, in rapid sequence. One guy she listened closely to was maybe eighteen or nineteen, with a diamond stud in his ear and a thin beard. He was wearing a Polo baseball cap, a brown leather jacket, and the big, oversized leather boots that are everywhere uptown right now. Baysie would hand him a shoe and he would hold it, look at the top, and move it up and down and flip it over. The first one he didn't like: "Oh-kay." The second one he hated: he made a growling sound in his throat even before Baysie could give it to him, as if to say, "Put it back in the bag—now!" But when she handed him a new DMX RXT—a low-cut run/walk shoe in white and blue and mesh with a translucent "ice" sole, which retails for a hundred and ten dollars—he looked at it long and hard and shook his head in pure admiration and just said two words, dragging each of them out: "No doubt."

Baysie was interested in what he was saying, because the DMX RXT she had was a girls' shoe that actually hadn't been doing all that well. Later, she explained to me that the fact that the boys loved the shoe was critical news, because it suggested that Reebok had a potential hit if it just switched the shoe to the men's section. How she managed to distill this piece of information from the crowd of teenagers around her, how she made any sense of the two dozen shoes in her bag, most of which (to my eyes, anyway) looked pretty much the same, and how she knew which of the teens to really focus on was a mystery. Baysie is a Wasp from New England, and she crouched on the floor in Dr. Jay's for almost an hour, talking and joking with the homeboys without a trace of condescension or self-consciousness.

Near the end of her visit, a young boy walked up and sat down on the bench next to her. He was wearing a black woollen cap with white stripes pulled low, a blue North Face pleated down jacket, a pair of baggy Guess jeans, and, on his feet, Nike Air Jordans. He couldn't have been more than thirteen. But when he started talking you could see Baysie's eyes light up, because somehow she knew the kid was the real thing.

"How many pairs of shoes do you buy a month?" Baysie asked.

"Two," the kid answered. "And if at the end I find one more I like I get to buy that, too."

Baysie was on to him. "Does your mother spoil you?"

The kid blushed, but a friend next to him was laughing. "Whatever he wants, he gets."

Baysie laughed, too. She had the DMX RXT in his size. He tried them on. He rocked back and forth, testing them. He looked back at Baysie. He was dead serious now: "Make sure these come out."

Baysie handed him the new "Rush" Emmitt Smith shoe due out in the fall. One of the boys had already pronounced it "phat," and another had looked through the marbleized-foam cradle in the heel and cried out in delight, "This is bug!" But this kid was the acid test, because this kid knew cool. He paused. He looked at it hard. "Reebok," he said, soberly and carefully, "is trying to get butter."

In the car on the way back to Manhattan, Baysie repeated it twice. "Not better. Butter! That kid could totally tell you what he thinks." Baysie had spent an hour coolhunting in a shoe store and found out that Reebok's efforts were winning the highest of hip-hop praise. "He was so fucking smart."

If you want to understand how trends work, and why coolhunters like Baysie and DeeDee have become so important, a good place to start is with what's known as diffusion research, which is the study of how ideas and innovations spread. Diffusion researchers do things like spending five years studying the adoption of irrigation techniques in a Colombian mountain village, or developing complex matrices to map the spread of new math in the Pittsburgh school system. What they do may seem like a far cry from, say, how the Tommy Hilfiger thing spread from Harlem to every suburban mall in the country, but it really isn't: both are about how new ideas spread from one person to the next.

One of the most famous diffusion studies is Bruce Ryan and Neal Gross's analysis of the spread of hybrid seed corn in Greene County, Iowa, in the nineteen-thirties. The new seed corn was introduced there in about 1928, and it was superior in every respect to the seed that had been used by farmers for decades. But it wasn't adopted all at once. Of two hundred and fifty-nine farmers studied by Ryan and Gross, only a handful had started planting the new seed by 1933. In 1934, sixteen took the plunge. In 1935, twenty-one more followed; the next year, there were thirty-six, and the year after that a whopping sixty-one. The succeeding figures were then forty-six, thirty-six, fourteen, and three, until, by 1941, all but two of the two hundred and fifty-nine farmers studied were using the new seed. In the language of diffusion research, the handful of farmers who started trying hybrid seed corn at the very beginning of the thirties were the "innovators," the adventurous ones. The slightly larger group that followed them was the "early adopters." They were the opinion leaders in the community, the respected, thoughtful people who watched and analyzed what those wild innovators were doing and then did it themselves. Then came the big bulge of farmers in 1936, 1937, and 1938—the "early majority" and the "late majority," which is to say the deliberate and the skeptical masses, who would never try anything until the most respected farmers had tried it. Only after they had been converted did the "laggards," the most traditional of all, follow suit. The critical thing about this sequence is that it is almost entirely interpersonal. According to Ryan and Gross, only the innovators relied to any great extent on radio advertising and farm journals and seed salesmen in making their decision to switch to the hybrid. Everyone else made his decision overwhelmingly because of the example and the opinions of his neighbors and peers.

Isn't this just how fashion works? A few years ago, the classic brushed-suède Hush Puppies with the lightweight crêpe sole—the moc-toe oxford known as the Duke and the slip-on with the golden buckle known as the Columbia—were selling barely sixty-five thousand pairs a year. The company was trying to walk away from the whole suède casual look entirely. It wanted to do "aspirational" shoes: "active casuals" in smooth leather, like the Mall Walker, with a Comfort Curve technology outsole and a heel stabilizer—the kind of shoes you see in Kinney's for $39.95. But then something strange started happening. Two Hush Puppies executives—Owen Baxter and Jeff Lewis—were doing a fashion shoot for their Mall Walkers and ran into a creative consultant from Manhattan named Jeffrey Miller, who informed them that the Dukes and the Columbias weren't dead, they were dead chic. "We were being told," Baxter recalls, "that there were areas in the Village, in SoHo, where the shoes were selling—in resale shops—and that people were wearing the old Hush Puppies. They were going to the ma-and-pa stores, the little stores that still carried them, and there was this authenticity of being able to say, 'I am wearing an original pair of Hush Puppies.' "

Baxter and Lewis—tall, solid, fair-haired Midwestern guys with thick, shiny wedding bands—are shoe men, first and foremost. Baxter was working the cash register at his father's shoe store in Mount Prospect, Illinois, at the age of thirteen. Lewis was doing inventory in his father's shoe store in Pontiac, Michigan, at the age of seven. Baxter was in the National Guard during the 1968 Democratic Convention, in Chicago, and was stationed across the street from the Conrad Hilton downtown, right in the middle of things. Today, the two men work out of Rockford, Michigan (population thirty-eight hundred), where Hush Puppies has been making the Dukes and the Columbias in an old factory down by the Rogue River for almost forty years. They took me to the plant when I was in Rockford. In a crowded, noisy, low-slung building, factory workers stand in long rows, gluing, stapling, and sewing together shoes in dozens of bright colors, and the two executives stopped at each production station and described it in detail. Lewis and Baxter know shoes. But they would be the first to admit that they don't know cool. "Miller was saying that there is something going on with the shoes—that Isaac Mizrahi was wearing the shoes for his personal use," Lewis told me. We were seated around the conference table in the Hush Puppies headquarters in Rockford, with the snow and the trees outside and a big water tower behind us. "I think it's fair to say that at the time we had no idea who Isaac Mizrahi was."

By late 1994, things had begun to happen in a rush. First, the designer John Bartlett called. He wanted to use Hush Puppies as accessories in his spring collection. Then Anna Sui called. Miller, the man from Manhattan, flew out to Michigan to give advice on a new line ("Of course, packing my own food and thinking about *Fargo* in the corner of my mind"). A few months later, in Los Angeles, the designer Joel Fitzpatrick put a twenty-five-foot inflatable basset hound on the roof of his store on La Brea Avenue and gutted his adjoining art gallery to turn it into a Hush Puppies department, and even before he opened—while he was still painting and putting up shelves—Pee-wee Herman walked in and asked for a couple of pairs. Pee-wee Herman! "It was total word of mouth. I didn't even have a sign back then," Fitzpatrick recalls. In 1995, the company sold four hundred and thirty thousand pairs of the classic Hush Puppies. In 1996, it sold a million six hundred thousand, and that was only scratching the surface, because in Europe and the rest of the world, where Hush Puppies have a huge following—where they might outsell the American market four to one—the revival was just beginning.

The cool kids who started wearing old Dukes and Columbias from thrift shops were the innovators. Pee-wee Herman, wandering in off the street, was an early adopter. The million six hundred thousand people who bought Hush Puppies last year are the early majority, jumping in because the really cool people have already blazed the trail. Hush Puppies are moving through the country just the way hybrid seed corn moved through Greene County—all of which illustrates what coolhunters can and cannot do. If Jeffrey Miller had been wrong—if cool people hadn't been digging through the thrift shops for Hush Puppies—and he had arbitrarily decided that Baxter and Lewis should try to convince non-cool people that the shoes were cool, it wouldn't have worked. You can't convince the late majority that Hush Puppies are cool, because the late majority makes its coolness decisions on the basis of what the early majority is doing, and you can't convince the early majority, because the early majority is looking at the early adopters, and you can't convince the early adopters, because they take their cues from the innovators. The innovators do get their cool ideas from people other than their peers, but the fact is that they are the last people who can be convinced by a marketing campaign that a pair of suède shoes is cool. These are, after all, the people who spent hours sifting through thrift-store bins. And why did they do that? Because their definition of cool is doing something that nobody else is doing. A company can intervene in the cool cycle. It can put its shoes on really cool celebrities and on fashion runways and on MTV. It can accelerate the transition from the innovator to the early adopter and on to the early majority. But it can't just manufacture cool out of thin air, and that's the second rule of cool.

At the peak of the Hush Puppies craziness last year, Hush Puppies won the prize for best accessory at the Council of Fashion Designers' awards dinner, at Lincoln Center. The award was accepted by the Hush Puppies president, Louis Dubrow, who came out wearing a pair of custom-made black patent-leather Hush Puppies and stood there blinking and looking at the assembled crowd as if it were the last scene of *Close Encounters of the Third Kind*. It was a strange moment. There was the president of the Hush Puppies company, of Rockford, Michigan, population thirty-eight hundred, sharing a stage with Calvin Klein and Donna Karan and Isaac Mizrahi—and all because some kids in the East Village began combing through thrift shops for old Dukes. Fashion was at the mercy of those kids, whoever they were, and it was a wonderful thing if the kids picked you, but a scary thing, too, because it meant that cool was something you could not control. You needed someone to find cool and tell you what it was.

• • •

When Baysie Wightman went to Dr. Jay's, she was looking for customer response to the new shoes Reebok had planned for the fourth quarter of 1997 and the first quarter of 1998. This kind of customer testing is critical at Reebok, because the last decade has not been kind to the company. In 1987, it had a third of the American athletic-shoe market, well ahead of Nike. Last year, it had sixteen per cent. "The kid in the store would say, 'I'd like this shoe if your logo wasn't on it,' " E. Scott Morris, who's a senior designer for Reebok, told me. "That's kind of a punch in the mouth. But we've all seen it. You go into a shoe store. The kid picks up the shoe and says, 'Ah, man, this is nice.' He turns the shoe around and around. He looks at it underneath. He looks at the side and he goes, 'Ah, this is Reebok,' and says, 'I ain't buying this,' and puts the shoe down and walks out. And you go, 'You was just digging it a minute ago. What happened?' " Somewhere along the way, the company lost its cool, and Reebok now faces the task not only of rebuilding its image but of making the shoes so cool that the kids in the store can't put them down.

Every few months, then, the company's coolhunters go out into the field with prototypes of the upcoming shoes to find out what kids really like, and come back to recommend the necessary changes. The prototype of one recent Emmitt Smith shoe, for example, had a piece of molded rubber on the end of the tongue as a design element; it was supposed to give the shoe a certain "richness," but the kids said they thought it looked overbuilt. Then Reebok gave the shoes to the Boston College football team for wear-testing, and when they got the shoes back they found out that all the football players had cut out the rubber component with scissors. As messages go, this was hard to miss. The tongue piece wasn't cool, and on the final version of the shoe it was gone. The rule of thumb at Reebok is that if the kids in Chicago, New York, and Detroit all like a shoe, it's a guaranteed hit. More than likely, though, the coolhunt is going to turn up subtle differences from city to city, so that once the coolhunters come back the designers have to find out some way to synthesize what was heard, and pick out just those things that all the kids seemed to agree on. In New York, for example, kids in Harlem are more sophisticated and fashion-forward than kids in the Bronx, who like things a little more colorful and glitzy. Brooklyn, meanwhile, is conservative and preppy, more like Washington, D.C. For reasons no one really knows, Reeboks are coolest in Philadelphia. In Philly, in fact, the Reebok Classics are so huge they are known simply as National Anthems, as in "I'll have a pair of blue Anthems in nine and a half." Philadelphia is Reebok's innovator town. From there trends move along the East Coast, trickling all the way to Charlotte, North Carolina.

Reebok has its headquarters in Stoughton, Massachusetts, outside Boston—in a modern corporate park right off Route 24. There are basketball and tennis courts next to the building, and a health club on the ground floor that you can look directly into from the parking lot. The front lobby is adorned with shrines for all of Reebok's most prominent athletes—shrines complete with dramatic action photographs, their sports jerseys, and a pair of their signature shoes—and the halls are filled with so many young, determinedly athletic people that when I visited Reebok headquarters I suddenly wished I'd packed my gym clothes in case someone challenged me to wind sprints. At Stoughton, I met with a handful of the company's top designers and marketing executives in a long conference room on the third floor. In the course of two hours, they put one pair of shoes after another on the table in front of me, talking excitedly about each sneaker's prospects, because the feeling at Reebok is that things are finally turning around. The basketball shoe that Reebok brought out last winter for Allen Iverson, the star rookie guard for the Philadelphia 76ers, for example, is one of the hottest shoes in the country. Dr. Jay's sold out of Iversons in two days, compared with the week it took the store to sell out of Nike's new Air Jordans. Iverson himself is brash and charismatic and faster from foul line to foul line than anyone else in the league. He's the equivalent of those kids in the East Village who began wearing Hush Puppies way back when. He's an innovator, and the hope at Reebok is that if he gets big enough the whole company can ride back to coolness on his coattails, the way Nike rode to coolness on the coattails of Michael Jordan. That's why Baysie was so excited when the kid said Reebok was trying to get butter when he looked at the Rush and the DMX RXT: it was a sign, albeit a small one, that the indefinable, abstract thing called cool was coming back.

When Baysie comes back from a coolhunt, she sits down with marketing experts and sales representatives and designers, and reconnects them to the street, making sure they have the right shoes going to the right places at the right price. When she got back from the Bronx, for example, the first thing she did was tell all these people they had to get a new men's DMX RXT out, fast, because the kids on the street loved the women's version. "It's hotter than we realized," she told them. The coolhunter's job in this instance is very specific. What DeeDee does, on the other hand, is a little more ambitious. With the L Report, she tries to construct a kind of grand matrix of cool, comprising not just shoes but everything kids like, and not just kids of certain East Coast urban markets but kids all over. DeeDee and her staff put it out four times a year, in six different versions—for New York, Los Angeles, San Francisco, Austin-Dallas, Seattle, and Chicago—and then sell it to manufacturers, retailers, and ad agencies (among others) for twenty thousand dollars a year. They go to each city and find the coolest bars and clubs, and ask the coolest kids to fill out questionnaires. The information is then divided into six categories—You Saw It Here First, Entertainment and Leisure, Clothing and Accessories, Personal and Individual, Aspirations, and Food and Beverages—which are, in turn, broken up into dozens of subcategories, so that Personal and Individual, for example, includes Cool Date, Cool Evening, Free Time, Favorite Possession, and on and on. The information in those subcategories is subdivided again by sex and by age bracket (14–18, 19–24, 25–30), and then, as a control, the L Report gives you the corresponding set of preferences for "mainstream kids."

Few coolhunters bother to analyze trends with this degree of specificity. DeeDee's biggest competitor, for example, is something called the Hot Sheet, out of Manhattan. It uses a panel of three thousand kids a year from across the country and divides up their answers by sex and age, but it doesn't distinguish between regions, or between trendsetting and mainstream respondents. So what you're really getting is what all kids think is cool—not what cool kids think is cool, which is a considerably different piece of information. Janine Misdom and Joanne De-Luca, who run the Sputnik coolhunting group out of the garment district in Manhattan, meanwhile, favor an entirely impressionistic approach, sending out coolhunters with video cameras to talk to kids on the ground that it's too difficult to get cool kids to fill out questionnaires. Once, when I was visiting the Sputnik girls—as Misdom and DeLuca are known on the street, because they look alike and their first names are so similar and both have the same awesome New York accents— they showed me a video of the girl they believe was the patient zero of the whole eighties revival going on right now. It was back in September of 1993. Joanne and Janine were on Seventh Avenue, outside the Fashion Institute of Technology, doing random street interviews for a major jeans company, and, quite by accident, they ran into this nineteen-year-old raver. She had close-cropped hair, which was green at the top, and at the temples was shaved even closer and dyed pink. She had rings and studs all over her face, and a thick collection of silver tribal jewelry around her neck, and vintage jeans. She looked into the camera and said, "The sixties came in and then the seventies came in and I think it's ready to come back to the eighties. It's totally eighties: the eye makeup, the clothes. It's totally going back to that." Immediately, Joanne and Janine started asking around. "We talked to a few kids on the Lower East Side who said they were feeling the need to start breaking out their old Michael Jackson jackets," Joanne said. "They were joking about it. They weren't doing it yet. But they were going to, you know? They were saying, 'We're getting the urge to break out our Members Only jackets.' " That was right when Joanne and Janine were just starting up; calling the eighties revival was their first big break, and now they put out a full-blown videotaped report twice a year which is a collection of clips of interviews with extremely progressive people.

What DeeDee argues, though, is that cool is too subtle and too variegated to be captured with these kind of broad strokes. Cool is a set of dialects, not a language. The L Report can tell you, for example, that nineteen-to-twenty-four-year-old male trendsetters in Seattle would most like to meet, among others, King Solomon and Dr. Seuss, and that nineteen-to-twenty-four-year-old female trendsetters in San Francisco have turned their backs on Calvin Klein, Nintendo Gameboy, and sex. What's cool right now? Among male New York trendsetters: North Face jackets, rubber and latex, khakis, and the rock band Kiss. Among female trendsetters: ska music, old-lady clothing, and cyber tech. In Chicago, snowboarding is huge among trendsetters of both sexes and all ages. Women over nineteen are into short hair, while those in their teens have embraced mod culture, rock climbing, tag watches, and bootleg pants. In Austin-Dallas, meanwhile, twenty-five-to-thirty-year-old women trendsetters are into hats, heroin, computers, cigars, Adidas, and velvet, while men in their twenties are into video games and hemp. In all, the typical L Report runs over one hundred pages. But with that flood of data comes an obsolescence disclaimer: "The fluctuating nature of the trendsetting market makes keeping up with trends a difficult task." By the spring, in other words, everything may have changed.

The key to coolhunting, then, is to look for cool people first and cool things later, and not the other way around. Since cool things are always changing, you can't look for them, because the very fact they are cool means you have no idea what to look for. What you would be doing is thinking back on what was cool before and extrapolating, which is about as useful as presuming that because the Dow rose ten points yesterday it will rise another ten points today. Cool people, on the other hand, are a constant.

When I was in California, I met Salvador Barbier, who had been described to me by a coolhunter as "the Michael Jordan of skateboarding." He was tall and lean and languid, with a cowboy's insouciance, and we drove through the streets of Long Beach at fifteen miles an hour in a white late-model Ford Mustang, a car he had bought as a kind of ironic status gesture ("It would look good if I had a Polo jacket or maybe Nautica," he said) to go with his '62 Econoline van and his '64 T-bird. Sal told me that he and his friends, who are all in their mid-twenties, recently took to dressing up as if they were in eighth grade again and gathering together—having a "rally"—on old BMX bicycles in front of their local 7-Eleven. "I'd wear muscle shirts, like Def Leppard or Foghat or some old heavy-metal band, and tight, tight tapered Levi's, and Vans on my feet—big, like, checkered Vans or striped Vans or camouflage Vans—and then wristbands and gloves with the fingers cut off. It was total eighties fashion. You had to look like that to participate in the rally. We had those denim jackets with patches on the back and combs that hung out the back pocket. We went without I.D.s, because we'd have to have someone else buy us beers." At this point, Sal laughed. He was driving really slowly and staring straight ahead and talking in a low drawl—the coolhunter's dream. "We'd ride to this bar and I'd have to carry my bike inside, because we have really expensive bikes, and when we got inside people would freak out. They'd say, 'Omigod,' and I was asking them if they wanted to go for a ride on the handlebars. They were like, 'What is wrong with you. My boyfriend used to dress like that in the eighth grade!' And I was like, 'He was probably a lot cooler then, too.' "

This is just the kind of person DeeDee wants. "I'm looking for somebody who is an individual, who has definitely set himself apart from everybody else, who doesn't look like his peers. I've run into trendsetters who look completely Joe Regular Guy. I can see Joe Regular Guy at a club listening to some totally hardcore band playing, and I say to myself 'Omigod, what's that guy doing here?' and that totally intrigues me, and I have to walk up to him and say, 'Hey, you're really into this band. What's up?' You know what I mean? I look at everything. If I see Joe Regular Guy sitting in a coffee shop and everyone around him has blue hair, I'm going to gravitate toward him, because, hey, what's Joe Regular Guy doing in a coffee shop with people with blue hair?"

We were sitting outside the Fred Segal store in West Hollywood. I was wearing a very conservative white Brooks Brothers button-down and a pair of Levi's, and DeeDee looked first at my shirt and then my pants and dissolved into laughter: "I mean, I might even go up to you in a cool place."

Picking the right person is harder than it sounds, though. Piney Kahn, who works for DeeDee, says, "There are a lot of people in the gray area. You've got these kids who dress ultra funky and have their own style. Then you realize they're just running after their friends." The trick is not just to be able to tell who is different but to be able to tell when that difference represents something truly cool. It's a gut thing. You have to somehow just know. DeeDee hired Piney because Piney clearly knows: she is twenty-four and used to work with the Beastie Boys and has the formidable self-possession of someone who is not only cool herself but whose parents were cool. "I mean," she says, "they named me after a tree."

Piney and DeeDee said that they once tried to hire someone as a coolhunter who was not, himself, cool, and it was a disaster.

"You can give them the boundaries," Piney explained. "You can say that if people shop at Banana Republic and listen to Alanis Morissette they're probably not trendsetters. But then they might go out and assume that everyone who does that is not a trendsetter, and not look at the other things."

"I mean, I myself might go into Banana Republic and buy a T-shirt," DeeDee chimed in.

Their non-cool coolhunter just didn't have that certain instinct, that sense that told him when it was O.K. to deviate from the manual. Because he wasn't cool, he didn't know cool, and that's the essence of the third rule of cool: you have to be one to know one. That's why Baysie is still on top of this business at forty-one. "It's easier for me to tell you what kid is cool than to tell you what things are cool," she says. But that's all she needs to know. In this sense, the third rule of cool fits perfectly into the second: the second rule says that cool cannot be manufactured, only observed, and the third says that it can only be observed by those who are themselves cool. And, of course, the first rule says that it cannot accurately be observed at all, because the act of discovering cool causes cool to take flight, so if you add all three together they describe a closed loop, the hermeneutic circle of coolhunting, a phenomenon whereby not only can the uncool not see cool but cool cannot even be adequately described to them. Baysie says that she can see a coat on one of her friends and think it's not cool but then see the same coat on DeeDee and think that it is cool. It is not possible to be cool, in other words, unless you are—in some larger sense—already cool, and so the phenomenon that the uncool cannot see and cannot have described to them is also something that they cannot even attain, because if they did it would no longer be cool. Coolhunting represents the ascendancy, in the marketplace, of high school.

Once, I was visiting DeeDee at her house in Laurel Canyon when one of her L Report assistants, Jonas Vail, walked in. He'd just come back from Niketown on Wilshire Boulevard, where he'd bought seven hundred dollars' worth of the latest sneakers to go with the three hundred dollars' worth of skateboard shoes he'd bought earlier in the afternoon. Jonas is tall and expressionless, with a peacoat, dark jeans, and short-cropped black hair. "Jonas is good," DeeDee says. "He works with me on everything. That guy knows more pop culture. You know: What was the name of the store Mrs. Garrett owned on *The Facts of Life*? He knows all the names of the extras from eighties sitcoms. I can't believe someone like him exists. He's fucking unbelievable. Jonas can spot a cool person a mile away."

Jonas takes the boxes of shoes and starts unpacking them on the couch next to DeeDee. He picks up a pair of the new Nike ACG hiking boots, and says, "All the Japanese in Niketown were really into these." He hands the shoes to DeeDee.

"Of *course* they were!" she says. "The Japanese are all into the tech-looking shit. Look how exaggerated it is, how bulbous." DeeDee has very ambivalent feelings about Nike, because she thinks its marketing has got out of hand. When she was in the New York Niketown with a girlfriend recently, she says, she started getting light-headed and freaked out. "It's cult, cult, cult. It was like, 'Hello, are we all drinking the Kool-Aid here?' " But this shoe she loves. It's Dr. Jay's in the Bronx all over again. DeeDee turns the shoe around and around in the air, tapping the big clear-blue plastic bubble on the side—the visible Air-Sole unit—with one finger. "It's so fucking rad. It looks like a platypus!" In front of me, there is a pair of Nike's new shoes for the basketball player Jason Kidd.

I pick it up. "This looks . . . cool," I venture uncertainly.

DeeDee is on the couch, where she's surrounded by shoeboxes and sneakers and white tissue paper, and she looks up reprovingly because, of course, I don't get it. I can't get it. "Beyooond cool, Malcolm. Beyooond cool."

22

Thomas C. Frank
"Advertising as Cultural Criticism: Bill Bernbach versus the Mass Society"
(1997)

HOW TO DO IT DIFFERENT

The towering figure of the advertising world of the 1960s—and a man of immense cultural significance generally—was Bill Bernbach, the guiding spirit of the Doyle Dane Bernbach agency (DDB). DDB altered the look, language, and tone of American advertising with its long-running campaign for Volkswagen and dozens of other brands; it altered the managerial style of Madison Avenue when its competitors, stunned by the power of DDB's ads, rushed to replicate its less ordered corporate structure and its roster of creative talent. Advertising writer Larry Dobrow does not exaggerate when he insists that "among advertising professionals then and now, there is unanimous—often reverent—belief that the Doyle Dane Bernbach agency was the unchallenged leader of the creative revolution of the sixties."[1] Nor does Randall Rothenberg when, discussing the agency's landmark campaign for Volkswagen, he writes simply that it "changed the culture of advertising."[2] Bernbach was at once a hardheaded adman and one of postwar consumerism's most trenchant critics, Madison Avenue's answer to Vance Packard. The ads his agency produced had an uncanny ability to cut through the overblown advertising rhetoric of the 1950s, to speak to readers' and viewers' skepticism of advertising, to replace obvious puffery with what appeared to be straight talk. Bernbach was the first adman to embrace the mass society critique, to appeal directly to the powerful but unmentionable public fears of conformity, of manipulation, of fraud, and of powerlessness, and to sell products by so doing. He invented what we might call anti-advertising: a style which harnessed public mistrust of consumerism—perhaps the most powerful cultural tendency of the age—to consumerism itself.

Doyle Dane Bernbach, the agency which he founded in the decidedly unrevolutionary year of 1949, was dedicated to what proved to be a unique but sound advertising principle. As the industry's preeminent leaders and theorists were amassing mountains of research and formulating scientific rules for effective advertising, Bernbach was declaring that rules were to be scrupulously ignored. The advertising business was fundamentally a matter of creating convincing advertisements, he believed, and no amount of formulas could replace the talented creative individual who performed this function. Bernbach's impulses ran in direct contradiction to the larger trends of the fifties. While writers from Norman Mailer to Theodore Roszak assumed (as many still assume) that the business "establishment" required a rigid, repressive system of order, Bernbach's philosophy of advertising, which would reign triumphant in the 1960s amid a seemingly endless series of successful and celebrated DDB campaigns, was exactly the opposite—a hostility to rules of any kind; a sort of commercial antinomianism.[3]

Bill Bernbach was an enemy of technocracy long before the counterculture raised its own voice in protest of conformity and the Organization Man. In 1947, he wrote a letter to the owners of the Grey agency, where he was then employed, which spelled out his opposition to the features of business organization that the mass society theorists would soon identify and attack. "I'm worried that we're going to fall into the trap of bigness," he wrote, "that we're going to worship techniques instead of substance. . . ." The crucial problem, Bernbach insisted, was the dominance of rules and science, the priority of statistics and routines, the methods that would soon be heralded by Reeves and others as the hallmarks of an era of certainty.

> There are a lot of great technicians in advertising. And unfortunately they talk the best game. They know all the rules. They can tell you that [pictures of] people in an ad will get you greater readership. They can tell you that a sentence should be this short or that long. They can tell you that body copy should be broken up for easier and more inviting reading. They can give you fact after fact after fact. They are the scientists of advertising. But there's one little rub. Advertising is fundamentally persuasion and persuasion happens to be not a science, but an art.[4]

Bernbach was an ideologue of disorder, an untiring propagandist for the business value of the principles of modern art. He repeated his mantra in a variety of forms for years: advertising was an art; art could not be produced by a rigid scientific system. A booklet of his memorable sayings compiled by DDB begins with this aphorism: "Rules are what the artist breaks; the memorable never emerged from a formula." "Imitation can be commercial suicide," runs another. "Research inevitably leads to conformity," he announced in 1967. "For creative people rules can be prisons," he said elsewhere.[5] Not only were rules deleterious to the creation of good advertising, but the very idea of established techniques had to be resisted. "Even among the scientists, men who are regarded as worshippers of facts," he wrote in a pamphlet called "Facts Are Not

Enough," intuition is critical to discovery: "the real giants have always been poets, men who jumped from facts into the realm of imagination and ideas."[6] Sometimes Bernbach's hostility to rules even took on a Consciousness III sort of aversion to reason generally. "Logic and over-analysis can immobilize and sterilize an idea," he said. "It's like love—the more you analyze it the faster it disappears."[7]

In his 1957 account *Madison Avenue, U.S.A.*, Martin Mayer treats DDB as a peculiar anomaly among the large agencies he studies since it "deliberately rejects most of the tenets of modern agency operation," including research along with rules.[8] Instead, Bernbach maximized the freedom of creative workers and eliminated much of the hierarchy and bureaucracy that was customary at large agencies in the 1950s, aiming several years before the publication of Douglas McGregor's book on Theory X and Theory Y to create a less inhibited environment where creative inspiration could be translated more directly into finished advertising. Pointing out in a 1969 interview that excessive supervision was "part and parcel of the big agency curse," DDB copywriter Bob Levenson noted that the agency "isn't highly disciplined, supervised, committeed, raked over, mulled over."[9] Bernbach's second great organization innovation was to rationalize the creative operation. Artist and writer would work together on a project rather than somewhere down a chain from top executives. DDB represented a shift in management style that would have vast consequences for the way ads were made, for the way ads appeared, and, ultimately, for the way American capitalism understood itself: Theory X hierarchy came to an end here, and Theory Y management arrived with great financial success.[10] So great was the contrast between the organizational style of corporate agencies and that of DDB that, in her early days at the agency, star copywriter Phyllis Robinson told a Japanese publication that "we just felt very free, as if we had broken our shackles, had gotten out of jail, and were free to work the way we wanted to work."[11] In 1968, Robinson recalled how DDB's less hierarchical organization proceeded to revolutionize the industry:

> In the early days of DDB, everybody on the outside was very hot to know how it was on the inside. How did we do it? So we told them. Bill told them. And told them. And told them.
>
> So then they knew. And what happened? Whole agencies introduced their copywriters to their art directors. They'd never met before. The way I understand it, the writers used to put the copy in those pneumatic tubes they used to use in department stores, and it would scoot over to the art director to be "laid out." So—the agencies introduced them, and left them Alone Together. And they gave them Freedom. They said, make, do, create! Break rules! And you know what? A lot of very fine stuff started to come out. Some not so fine. But a lot that was.[12]

For Bernbach's anti-organization to work, though, he had to dramatically alter the traditional relationship between agency and clients in order to convince those who paid for advertising that, even though art had dethroned science in the offices of DDB, his assortment of scribblers was every bit as expert as the "scientists" of Rosser Reeves, and their opinions must be respected. Admen—even of the creative sort—were advertising specialists, he argued. DDB would produce no campaigns like Wakeman's repetitive "Love That Soap" because it refused to accede to clients' tastes, however strong-willed they were. As Bernbach told Martin Mayer, "I feel that if the agency makes an ad and the client doesn't like it, the client ought to run it anyway." "Factual error and a violation of corporate policy are the only reasons we'll accept for correction," added DDB account executive Joe Daly.[13] Charlie Moss, who began his advertising career at DDB before moving on to Wells, Rich, Greene, one of the era's "hottest" and most successful creative agencies (he ultimately became WRG's president), tells this story about the seriousness of Bernbach's attitude toward a client:

> Doyle Dane had a major client, a big advertiser. They had been used to having their own way of advertising for years and years, very specialized product category. They had a brand from this client, and they had been trying to come up with a campaign the client would accept for months and months, and they kept getting rejected. Every time they'd go to the client, marketing people, advertising people, they'd say, "no, we don't like that, we want to do it this way, and this and that." And Doyle Dane, the people were outraged, because this was not the normal for Doyle Dane, they were normally used to getting their way. So they went to Bill Bernbach, and they said, "Look, you've got to come to this next meeting, we're going to have it with the chairman of the client company, . . . you've got to convince the chairman to tell his people to let us have our way, we know what we're doing." So . . . they all went, they're sitting across the table in this big board room. Bernbach says to this guy, "you know, we're working with your people for six months now, we can't get anything through, you have to tell them that we are advertising experts, we know what we're doing, and we demand some respect in this area." And the chairman says to Bernbach, "Well, I'm sorry, Mr. Bernbach, but we've been selling our products for years and years and years, and we've been extremely successful as you know, we think we know something about how to market them. And I'm sorry, but our people will have to have final say over what the advertising's going to be." At which point Bernbach, who was prepared for this, turned to him and said, "well, then in that case, Doyle Dane Bernbach will have to resign your business." And the chairman of the client company looked at his marketing director and said, "Are they allowed to do that?"[14]

Even as it was overturning the pseudo-science of Reeves and Ogilvy in favor of the intangibles of aesthetic inspiration, the Creative Revolution greatly advanced those men's efforts to professionalize advertising. In Wakeman's day, admen had been glorified "hucksters," cringing yes-men without independent will or access to any knowledge at all that might contradict the client's authority, but in the age of Bernbach they were to be creative geniuses, in touch with a spirit of commerce that resided beyond the mundane world of hierarchy and order. The limitations Bernbach placed on his clients' authority also led directly to the rapidly escalating willingness to violate the conventions of commercial speech that characterized his agency's—and the coming decade's—advertising. A number of DDB's most famous campaigns, like the Volkswagen ads that played on the car's ugliness and the Avis ads that proclaimed "We're Number Two," were extremely distasteful to clients and would surely have been nixed had they not already agreed to defer to the agency's decision.[15] Charlie Moss believes that "because it operated that way," DDB vastly increased the latitude within which creative people could operate.

> For those talented people, it really gave them the strength of their convictions. It said, "Hey, look, if I really believe this, if I really think this is going to work for that client, I can push it, really, to the point of almost resigning the business." And what happened was, there were big ideas that would have normally been thrown right out, which prevailed. The Avis campaign was a very good example. It tested terribly, they hated the idea when they first saw it. Everything would have dictated these days that campaign would have been history.[16]

The reign of "groupthink" began to end, at least in the advertising industry, in the early 1960s. Freed to do what the agency thought best, DDB's creative teams would proceed to smash the advertising conventions built up throughout the age of organization.

ALIENATED BY THE CONFORMITY
AND HYPOCRISY OF MASS SOCIETY?
HAVE WE GOT A CAR FOR YOU!

Bernbach's innovations in agency organization contradicted the prevailing management theories of the 1950s. But if his management style seems to have been designed to avoid the quagmire of "groupthought" and bureaucracy, his approach to advertising itself took mass society on directly, discarding the visual and verbal cliches of Madison Avenue, U.S.A., and saying the unsayable: consumerism has given us a civilization of plastic and conformity, of deceit and shoddiness. Bernbach's style wasn't so much promotion as it was cultural criticism, foreshadowing the postmodern meta-advertising of the 1990s discussed by Randall Rothenberg and James B. Twitchell.[17] And while DDB's less-hierarchical structure was copied in office towers across Manhattan, its characteristic advertising style was, by the end of the decade, pervasive across the sponsored surfaces of American public space.

The advertising that DDB began making for Volkswagen in 1959 is one of the most analyzed, discussed, and admired campaigns in the industry's history, studied in introductory marketing classes and included in advertising retrospectives of all kinds. Not only did it excite critics and incite commentary from every branch of the media, but it is widely believed to have made Volkswagen a competitive brand in America. The campaign's power derived from its blatant transgression of nearly every convention of auto advertising. And its success validated overnight the Bernbach creative philosophy, set a thousand corporations off in search of similar ads for themselves, and precipitated a revolution in ad-making. Within a few years, it had become a revered classic for an age at war with reverence and classicism. Randall Rothenberg enumerates the varieties of transgression that the campaign would unleash:

> It changed the rules. Agencies were now no longer punished but *rewarded* for arguing with clients, for breaking the guidelines of art direction, for clowning around in the copy, for using ethnic locutions and academic references and a myriad of other once-forbidden formulae. Seemingly overnight, a great wave of originality engulfed the advertising profession, transforming agencies and agency-client relationships and, in turn, the impressions made on millions of Americans.[18]

The history of consumer society is largely the history of the automobile, of the prosperity it brought to blue-collar workers, of the mobility and sexual freedom it permitted, and of the myriad consumer fantasies with which it was associated in the years after World War II. In the 1950s, the advertising of the three big Detroit automakers (which are always among the ten largest advertisers in the country) was the stuff of technocratic fantasy. Cars were designed and advertised to resemble the exciting hardware of the Cold War: streamlined, finned like airplanes, fitted with elaborate-looking controls, decorated with flashing chrome and abstract representations of rockets or airplanes. In ads, cars were posed next to jet fighters and radar dishes; Buick put holes in the side of its hoods to resemble airplane exhausts and named one model "B-58"; Oldsmobile offered "rocket action," built both an "F-85" and a "Starfire" (the actual name for the Air Force F-94); a 1958 Dodge advertisement invited readers to "take off" in a new model and declared that "the new Swept-Wing look for '59 is set off by thrusting Jet-Trail Tail Lamps."[19] Cars were markers of managerial efficiency in the worst Organization Man way. While the 1958 Edsel merely "says you're going places," ads for the 1961 Buick marked a pinnacle of other-directed boorishness:

What a wonderful sense of well-being just being seen behind its wheel. No showing off. Just that Clean Look of Action which unmistakably tells your success.[20]

Auto advertising of the 1950s redounded with empty phrases and meaningless neologisms, announcing cars with "radical new Turbo-Thrust" engines, "Quadra-Power Roadability," and "Finger-tip TorqueFlite."[21] The cars so trumpeted were always populated with idealized white nuclear families, manly husbands, fawning wives, and playful children. In television commercials, cars were objects of worship mounted on rotating platforms and, in one famous 1963 Chevrolet commercial, perched atop an insurmountable mesa and photographed from an orbiting airplane.[22] And every year cars' designs would change, the new models trumpeted in advertising ("All new all over again!" exclaimed those for the 1959 Chevrolet[23]) as the epitome of modernity, the old models and all their fine adjectives forgotten and discarded as surely as the cars themselves would be by the time they traveled 100,000 miles.

And each of these aspects of the car culture was, by the early 1960s, a point of considerable popular annoyance and even disaffection. Cars and their advertising, which brought together so many objectionable features of the era, were the aspect of the mass society most vulnerable to criticism, pounded with particular effectiveness in popular books by Vance Packard, John Kenneth Galbraith, and John Keats (*The Insolent Chariots*). Americans learned that the big three automakers changed styles every year in order to intentionally obsolete their earlier products and that their cars were designed to break down and fall apart after a certain amount of time. The car culture—and perhaps consumer culture in general—was a gigantic fraud. In his 1964 book *One Dimensional Man*, Herbert Marcuse describes the conflicted thinking of American car buyers of those years:

I ride in a new automobile. I experience its beauty, shininess, power, convenience—but then I become aware of the fact that in a relatively short time it will deteriorate and need repair; that its beauty and surface are cheap, its power unnecessary, its size idiotic; and that I will not find a parking place. I come to think of *my* car as a product of one of the Big Three automobile corporations. The latter determine the appearance of my car and make its beauty as well as its cheapness, its power as well as its shakiness, its working as well as its obsolescence. In a way, I feel cheated. I believe that the car is not what it could be, that better cars could be made for less money. But the other guy has to live, too. Wages and taxes are too high; turnover is necessary; we have it much better than before. The tension between appearance and reality melts away and both merge in one rather pleasant feeling.[24]

With the exception of the final three sentences, Marcuse might well have been writing copy for a Volkswagen ad. Although Volkswagen, no doubt, wanted consumers to experience a "rather pleasant feeling," their ads aimed to *push* the "tension between appearance and reality" to the point of breaking the bond between Americans and the Big Three, steering consumers toward what they repeatedly described as a "better car . . . made for less money."

Doyle Dane Bernbach's debunking campaign for Volkswagen began in 1959, puncturing the mythos of the American automobile in the very year of maximum tailfins on the GM cars. The ads, as a veritable army of advertising writers has noted over the years, defied the auto-advertising conventions of the 1950s in just about every way they could. While the American automakers used photographic tricks to elongate cars,[25] DDB photographically foreshortened the Volkswagen. The early ads were in black and white and were startlingly minimalist: the cars appeared on a featureless background without people or passengers; copy was confined to three small columns on the bottom of the page. The ads were always organized around a pun or joke, an extremely rare thing at the time, especially since the pun or joke usually seemed to mock the car's distinctive shape or its no-tailfin, little-chrome ugliness. Instead of boasting with Technicolor glare, the artwork for the Volkswagen campaign committed such bizarre heresies as including only a tiny picture in the upper lefthand corner of an almost blank page, depicting the car floating in water, drawn onto an egg, drawn onto a graph, dented in an accident, crossed out, crushed by a car-scrapping machine, or absent altogether except for a pair of tracks in the snow.

Aside from the Volkswagen ads' graphic distinctiveness, the "honesty" of their copy is their most often-remarked feature, and it is certainly the most striking characteristic when viewed in context, alongside conventional advertising from the 1950s. Gone is the empty claptrap Americans had learned to associate with advertising; gone are the usual buzzwords, the heavily retouched photographs, the idealized drawings. In their place is a new tone of plain talk, of unadorned simplicity without fancy color pictures and beautiful typefaces.[26] But what really distinguishes the Volkswagen ads is their attitude toward the reader. The advertising style of the 1950s had been profoundly contemptuous of the consumer's intelligence, and consumers knew it: in the wake of *The Hucksters*, *The Hidden Persuaders*, the quiz show scandals, and the various FTC lawsuits against fraudulent advertisers, consumer skepticism toward advertising was at an all-time high. The genius of the Volkswagen campaign—and many of DDB's other campaigns—is that they took this skepticism into account and made it part of their ads' discursive apparatus. They spoke to consumers as canny beings capable of seeing through the great heaps of puffery cranked out by Madison Avenue. As Jerry Della Femina admiringly observed, the Volkswagen campaign was "the first time the advertiser ever talked to the consumer as though he was a grownup instead of a baby."[27]

What made the Volkswagen ads seem "honest" are the curious admissions of (what appear to be) errors with which the ads are peppered. The sedan is "ugly" and "looks like a beetle"; the Volkswagen station wagon is "a monster" that "looked like a shoe box" with "a flat face and square shape"; an experimental model that never saw production was "something awful. Take our word for it." To make such admissions, even counterbalanced as they were with humor ("Could it be that ours aren't the funny looking cars, after all?") was a violation of fundamental principles of salesmanship. So were the campaign's occasional admissions that Volkswagen was, like everyone else, a profit-driven corporation: "since we have this burning desire to stay in business," etc.[28] This species of commercial "honesty" was a strategy DDB used to great effect in a number of other campaigns as well: Avis forthrightly declaring itself the "Number Two" auto-renter, Lowrey Piano confessing in 1965 that 1923 was "The year to be in the piano business," or Utica Beer admitting that "Our beer is 50 years behind the times." Within a few years, the technique was copied widely: creative superstars Wells, Rich, Greene's Benson & Hedges advertising focused on "The Disadvantages" of long cigarettes; J. Walter Thompson's ads for Listerine admitted the product's terrible flavor, exclaiming "I Hate It, But I Love It."[29]

But by far the most powerful feature of the Volkswagen ads—and a feature which one can find throughout DDB's oeuvre—is their awareness of and deep sympathy with the mass society critique. Not only do the authors of these ads seem to have been reading *The Hidden Persuaders, The Waste Makers* and *The Insolent Chariots*, they are actively contributing to the discourse, composing cutting jibes against the chrome-plated monsters from Detroit and proffering up Volkswagens as badges of alienation from the ways of a society whose most prominent emblems were the tailfin and the tract home with a two-car garage.

The foolishness of planned obsolescence was a particular target of DDB's Volkswagen campaign. Ads from the early sixties emphasized the car's lack of highly visible change and mocked Detroit's annual restyling sprees. Below one picture of the car, spotlighted as if at an auto show (a favorite Volkswagen target), runs the caption "The '51 '52 '53 '54 '55 '56 '57 '58 '59 '60 '61 Volkswagen." In another, headlined "How to tell the year of a Volkswagen," close-up photographs point out the minute changes the manufacturer has in fact made over the years (the picture for 1957 is blank: "No visible change"), each of them done not "to make it look different" but "only to make it work better." The ads appealed, as did the works of popular criticism which informed them, to a preconsumerist thriftiness and a suspicion of ornament and fashion. The Volkswagen boasted "no fancy gadgets, run by push buttons"; instead, ads spoke of the car's reliability, its solid construction, its ease of repair, and its efficiency.[30]

Later ads extended the attack to other aspects of the car culture. A 1964 ad took on the questionable and tasteless practices of car dealers, dressing up the anti-car in ludicrous sale decorations, wondering "why they run clearance sales on brand new cars," and faux-confessing, "Maybe it's because we don't quite understand the system." A 1966 ad assailed the vanity of cars as status symbols, comparing the efficiency of the "ugly little bug" to the fleeting looks of "a big beautiful chariot, drawn by 300 horses!" and quietly reversing the old Edsel slogan: "If you want to show you've gotten somewhere, get a big beautiful chariot. But if you simply want to get somewhere, get a bug." Another 1966 ad heaped scorn on "frivolous" automotive faddishness by asking, "Has the Volkswagen fad died out?" and confessing that, since it is so "completely sensible," "as a fad, the car was a flop."[31]

On occasion, DDB even encouraged readers to demystify the techniques of admaking. Volkswagen advertisements called attention to themselves as advertisements, and to the admaking philosophy that informed them. As one from 1964 put it rather disingenuously, "Just because we sell cars doesn't put selling at the top of our agenda." Another asked, "How much longer can we hand you this line?" (the "line" being the car's peculiar sihouette). So similar in format were the various Volkswagen print ads, and so familiar to readers, that in 1963 the company ran an ad with no picture, no headline, three blank columns, and instructions on "How to do a Volkswagen ad." But the ad's Volkswagen message was overshadowed by its pitch for DDB and the new style of advertising that acknowledged the audience's intelligence:

> 4. Call a spade a spade. And a suspension a suspension. Not something like "orbital cushioning."
>
> 5. Speak to the reader. Don't shout. He can hear you. Especially if you talk sense.[32]

The ad knocks Detroit's standard puffery in a way that Detroit could not possibly refute given its standard admaking style of the 1950s. In pretending to teach the reader to read ads critically, it naturally overlooks the new style invented by DDB: advertisers are liars, except, of course, this one. Conventional ad campaigns were incapable of responding in kind, since their appeal rested not on empowered readers but the fraudulent appeal of retouched photographs, dream-world imagery, and empty celebrity testimonials. For one of the Big Three's ads to admit to its ad-ness would be to undermine the various tricks that gave them whatever appeal they still had.

The Volkswagen critique was easily extended to the other objectionable features of consumer society. Even though it varied only little over the years, DDB cast it as a car for people who thought for themselves and were worried about conformity. A 1965 print ad confronts the issue directly, incorporating one of the standard icons of postwar order: a suburban street lined with look-alike houses, no trees, and tiny shrubs. But parked in the driveway of each house is a Volkswagen station wagon. "If the world looked like this, and you wanted to buy a car that sticks out a little," the copy advised,

> you probably wouldn't buy a Volkswagen Station Wagon.
> But in case you haven't noticed, the world doesn't look like this.
> So if you've wanted to buy a car that sticks out a little, you know just what to do.[33]

Volkswagen's television commercials went out of their way to lampoon various sacred rituals of the consumer culture. A 1967 spot mocks game shows, the glittering dream factories of daytime television whose charm has been undermined by a congressional investigation ten years before. "Gino Milano," a "little shoemaker" in awkward-looking glasses and bushy hair, answers questions about cars on a parody program called "The Big Plateau" while an audience of dowdy-looking women in pearls and cats-eye glasses watches anxiously. This quintessential middle American is eventually "done in by [questions about] the 1968 Volkswagen," failing to appreciate the nuances of the company's anti-obsolescence policy.[34]

Volkswagen's most incisive critique of American consumer frivolity came in a 1969 television commercial that lampooned the "1949 Auto Show," one of the great promotional fairs held in the year Volkswagen was introduced to America. Filmed in black and white to establish the setting, the spot focuses on the elaborate displays and misguided decorative designs of several defunct automakers. The Hudson display features three women singing, in the style of the Andrews Sisters, a little ditty that features the line, "Longer, lower, wider." A spokeswoman for Studebaker compares her car's peculiar styling to "Long skirts," which she assured her audience to "be the next look on the fashion scene." A DeSoto dazzles from a revolving platform. And a man in a white smock gestures toward his model (a Buick, although its brand name is not given) with a pointer and says, "So there's no doubt about it. Next year, every car in America will have [pause] holes in its side." Meanwhile, in an unadorned corner, without benefit of microphone, revolving pedestal, or audience, the Volkswagen spokesman delivers his simple talk about "constantly . . . changing, improving, and refining this car. Not necessarily to keep it in style with the times, but to make a better car." Not only is the industry's puffery transparently ridiculous in retrospect, but a number of its practitioners have actually gone out of business.

"1949 Auto Show" was a celebration of victory in two distinct ways. First, it trumpeted Volkswagen's spectacular sales success since 1949, the year in which, according to a 1960 ad, it had sold only two cars in America. Second, it signaled the victory of the Creative Revolution, of the DDB techniques over the empty puffery of the recent past. As the camera pans over the "1949 Auto Show," many of the standard postwar advertising cliches are represented: the glamorous singing girls, the Reevesian authority figure in spectacles and white smock, the handsome pitchman with a microphone, the car on the revolving platform. As a result of DDB's campaigns for Volkswagen, which first brought national attention to the new creativity, all of these selling methods are as obsolete as the tailfins, chrome, and portholes for which they were once employed. By 1969, none of the major automakers would dare to use such techniques: in just a few years, the DDB approach had made them stilted and old-fashioned, awkward emblems of a laughably outmoded past, so ancient that they had to be filmed in black and white to be properly distanced from the present.[35]

FROM NAZI CAR TO LOVE BUG

The Volkswagen campaign also marks a strange episode in the history of co-optation. Accounts of the counterculture generally agree on the Volkswagen (either "bug" or "microbus") as the auto of choice among the dropped-out. For many countercultural participants, the Volkswagen seemed an antithesis to the tailfinned monsters from Detroit, a symbolic rebuke of the product that had become a symbol both of the mass society's triumph and of its grotesque excesses. The Volkswagen was the anti-car, the automotive signifier of the uprising against the cultural establishment.

But "anti-car" was hardly a natural or normal signifier for the brand. In fact, at one time Volkswagen bore the ugly stigma of the mass society to an extent that American cars could never touch: in the fifties, the Volkswagen was known as nothing less than a Nazi product. George Lois, who worked on the Volkswagen account when it first went to Doyle Dane Bernbach in 1959, recalled some years later that

> It was hard to forget that Hitler himself was directly involved in designing the Volkswagen. Even though the Fuehrer was helped along by the Austrian car engineer Dr. Ferdinand Porsche, the cute Volkswagen in 1959 reminded lots of people about the ovens. Julian [Koenig, who wrote the first around of copy for the campaign] was Jewish and wouldn't forget it.[36]

Bernbach himself was Jewish as well, and it is one of the great ironies of the decade that his agency, which also produced celebrated advertising for El Al airlines and Levy's Jewish Rye Bread, was responsible for humanizing what Lois calls "the Nazi car."

That by the end of the decade the Volkswagen had acquired an image that was more hip than Nazi must be regarded as one of the great triumphs of American marketing. The irony that several of the creators of this image were Jewish was trumped by the irony implicit in that Volkswagen's hipness was a product of advertising, the institution of mass society against which hip had declared itself most vehemently at odds. The Volkswagen story, in other words, is the co-optation theory turned upside down, a clear and simple example of a product marketed as an emblem of good-humored alienation and largely accepted as such by the alienated.

DDB's ads for Volkswagen simultaneously attacked obsolescence in the world of automobiles and contributed to it mightily in the world of advertising, rendering ancient overnight the Madison Avenue dreams of the fifties. As a form of anti-advertising that worked by distancing a product from consumerism, the Volkswagen ads introduced Americans to a new aesthetic of consuming. No longer would advertising labor to construct an idealized but self-evidently false vision of consumer perfection: instead it would offer itself as an antidote to the patent absurdities of affluence. This, then, was the great innovation of the Creative Revolution, the principle to which Bernbach referred when he spoke so enthusiastically of "difference": the magic cultural formula by which the life of consumerism could be extended indefinitely, running forever on the discontent that it itself had produced. Hip was indeed the solution to the problems of the mass society, although not in the way its ideologues had intended. What distinguishes the advertising of the Creative Revolution is that, following Volkswagen's lead, it takes into account—and offers to solve—the problems that consumerism had created. In the hands of a newly enlightened man in gray flannel, hip would become the dynamic principle of the 1960s, a cultural perpetual motion machine transforming disgust with consumerism into fuel for the ever-accelerating consumer society.[37]

Thanks to the agency's signature visual style (simple photographs, minimalist layout, large, clever headlines), DDB advertising of the early sixties is generally easy to distinguish from the other ads in the glossy magazines where it appeared. Even more remarkable, though, is the consistency with which the agency referred to the mass society critique. Remarks about the fraudulence of consumerism and expressions of disgust with the system's masters run as a sort of guiding theme through virtually everything DDB did. Disgust with the consumer society was both the agency's aesthetic forte and its best product pitch, applicable to virtually anything: Buy this to escape consumerism.

The DDB critique is visible in such out-of-the-way places as a 1961 ad for "The remarkable Parker 61" fountain pen, which declares that "In this age of mass production and slickness (and sometimes, shoddiness), it's good to look upon a truly fine thing."[38] Or it can be seen, more openly, in a 1967 ad for El Al that cast the Israeli airline as a place free of the affected manners of the technocracy. Above a rather alarming photograph of a stewardess with a clownlike smile painted on her face is the declaration, "Maybe You Don't Want to Look at a Painted-on Smile All the Way to Europe." People are not robots or laboratory animals, and El Al knows it: "we feel our engines should turn on and off with a flick of a switch; not our stewardesses."[39]

Ads for American Tourister mocked, in typically self-effacing DDB style, virtually any aspect of the consumer culture that could be brought into contact with suitcases. Since the point was to demonstrate the product's resistance to clumsiness, accidents, and malicious misbehavior, the campaign provided ample opportunity for more "realistic" renderings of consumer life. People foolishly run over American Touristers in cars; they drop American Touristers from airplanes. American Touristers (like Volkswagens) are too durable to serve as status symbols: "The trouble with an American Tourister is nobody knows you've been around," a 1968 ad faux-confessed.[40] Even the jolly menials of the consumer world who were always romanticized in older advertising (the admiring butler, the compliant porter, the beloved Philip Morris bellboy) are lampooned in one 1970 American Tourister television commercial: a suitcase is tossed into a zoo cage, snatched up by a particularly violent ape who snorts and growls and smashes it about. Meanwhile, a placid announcer speaks of "savage baggagemasters," "clumsy bellboys," "brutal cab drivers," and "all butter-fingered luggage handlers all over the world." While in earlier spots such humble figures would have been rendered in friendly terms, here they are compared to apes.[41]

The most mockable institution of the consumer society was, of course, the deeply mistrusted practice of the advertising industry, and DDB took to the task with gusto. Many of their ads commented on previous advertising and knocked the deceptive legs out from under the older style. DDB played on the reader's cognizance of clutter, his boredom and disgust with advertising discourse. Before the 1960s, most ads approached the reader as a neutral element of the "editorial" text that surrounds it: its intent to sell is rarely mentioned openly, the assumptions and processes by which it is created remain concealed. But the works of DDB would occasionally admit themselves to be and even discuss themselves as ads, aware of the medium by which they are presented and of the discourse into which they have been inserted. A 1964 ad for Chivas Regal whiskey typifies the agency's pseudo-hostility toward advertising: under the headline, "Don't bother to read this ad," the full page of copy below is crossed out.[42]

The agency's ads for Calvert Whiskey, which it dubbed "The Soft Whiskey," made a point of mocking more conventional whiskey advertising. After having come up with what may well be the most slickly meaningless product claim for a whiskey of all time ("soft" whiskey was supposed to be somehow "easier to swallow," a double-entendre of which the ads made much), the agency proceeded to denounce liquor advertising in general for its slick meaninglessness. "Is it just another slogan?" asked one of the campaign's 1966 headlines. Of course not: It required far more than "some sharp talk on Madison Avenue" to make the brand so popular.[43]

DDB's Calvert ads contained a streak of consumer populism as profound as those for Volkswagen. "It just so happens, you can't fool all the people all the time," one insisted, in the course of explaining why the advertising industry's tricks would be insufficient to sell the stuff. "One sip and you can write your own Soft Whiskey ad," proclaimed another, over a layout of product photos and blank lines. One 1964 installment actually depicted a consumer defacing one of the brand's special Christmas decanters by removing its label under running water, encouraging this anti-consumer practice on the grounds that "The people who drink it will know it's Soft Whiskey anyhow."[44]

Sometimes the DDB strategy of identifying products with public suspicion of advertising was more overt than others. As a 1966 print ad in the Avis rent-a-car campaign put it,

> People in this country don't believe anything they read in ads anymore.
>   And with good reason.
>   Most advertising these days is long on the big promise—a promise that the product doesn't always deliver.[45]

As a rule, advertising never acknowledges authorship or any other factors which would make clear its status as artifice; yet an Avis ad from 1965 openly proclaims itself to have been fabricated by a professional adman. "I write Avis ads for a living," the copy maintains. "But that doesn't make me a paid liar." The writer goes on to complain about an Avis car he rented which did not meet one of Avis's minor promises. Again the sponsor admits to a minor shortcoming, and again the end result is not the destruction of Avis's reputation, but its burnishing. Avis confesses—it's human, too—and its credibility is thus increased, as it is when the company forthrightly admits itself to be "Number Two." The anonymous ad writer even declares his professional reputation (that quality mocked by Victor Norman in *The Hucksters*) to have been threatened so severely by Avis's tiny oversight that it must never be allowed to happen again: "So if I'm going to continue writing these ads, Avis had better live up to them. Or they can get themselves a new boy." The ad concludes with a trick that seems to "prove" Avis's honesty by challenging them to "confess" their wrongdoing, "They'll probably never run this ad." And yet there it is, being run![46]

The familiar spokesman models of the fifties, in their suits or lab coats, were a particular target of the DDB critique. In the Rosser Reeves era, the product pitchman had been a pretty predictable figure: a deep-voiced male whose authority was often augmented by spectacles and books, smiling when appropriate and always speaking earnestly and glibly of the product in question. Boring and respectable, he was a stock image of postwar order, an obvious symptom of the corporate world's problems with creativity and bureaucracy. And he was the target of several humiliating Doyle Dane Bernbach commercials. In a 1965 television spot for Campbell's Pork and Beans, the product's flavorfulness is demonstrated by a male spokesman, accompanied by his female assistant, who tastes the product while seated in a convertible with the top down and headed into a car wash. The spokesman carries on gamely through the soap and brushes, talking up the beans even as he is thoroughly soaked; his assistant insists, in the best product-demonstrator fashion, that despite the deluge "You can still taste the sauce!" At the spot's conclusion the car is filled to the brim with water, and the discomfited male is now unable to start the motor. "D'you think it's flooded?" asks his assistant, laughing uncontrollably. A famous 1968 commercial demonstrated the nonsagging qualities of Burlington Mid-Length Socks by showing them in action on the legs of a balding businessman in horn-rimmed glasses, white shirt, and narrow tie sitting in a minimalist modern chair. Everything about him is respectable, even distinguished-looking, except for the fact that he wears no trousers, only underwear and one of the socks in question. "We've asked you to put on a short sock the length most men wear," an announcer says, "and Burlington's new mid-length sock." The man is challenged to "make it fall down," and accordingly he begins to leap about the set, gritting his teeth, whirling around and waving his arms. Naturally, all his activity is for nought, the sock refuses to sag, and he abandons the struggle in exhaustion. The pant-less patriarch's humiliation is complete.[47]

Then there is the DDB commercial that won all the prizes—and still does, whenever a trade group or publication decides to designate the "top ads of all time." It is a 1970 spot for Alka-Seltzer that dramatizes the product by depicting, of all things, the making of a television commercial in which an actor is required to eat from a plate of spaghetti and exclaim, "Mama mia! That's a spicy meatball!" Unfortunately, the actor fumbles his lines again and again, and we hear a director's voice saying things like "cut" and "take fifty-nine." The viewer suffers through each attempt with short clips that appear to be actual outtakes from a filming session. The commercial was a masterpiece of the agency's long effort to turn public skepticism into brand loyalty: it recognizes advertising as artifice, and as a particularly ridiculous—and transparent—form of artifice as well. The actor is plugging an absurd product, a brand of ready-made meatballs that come in an enormous jar; he is filmed on an absurdly contrived set, with a smiling Italian mother type standing over him as he essays the dish; and when delivering his lines he adopts a grotesque Italian accent, which, of course, he drops when pleading with the director. Advertising itself—especially the prerevolutionary variety with its stock figures, its stereotypes, its contrivances, its fakery—is ridiculous stuff. Only Alka-Seltzer, which intervenes to rescue the long-suffering actor's tormented digestion, stands above the mockery. Consumerism, like Alka-Seltzer, now promised to relieve Americans from their consuming excesses.[48]

But the agency's best-remembered achievement was its 1964 election-year effort to sell none other than President Johnson as a symbol of opposition to mass society's greatest horror—the specter of nuclear war. Without giving Barry Goldwater's name, the commercial managed to portray the 1964 contest as a choice between automated holocaust and preconsumer innocence: a child playing with a daisy fades into a mechanical-sounding adult voice counting down to a nuclear explosion. Over the years, the commercial has been criticized as an unfair portrayal of Goldwater's views, and it is certainly true that Goldwater was not, strictly speaking, in favor of nuclear destruction. But the commercial's power has nothing to do with Goldwater, or with Johnson, for that matter. It aimed, rather, to case the election as an expression of the archetypal cultural conflict of the age. Its stark division of the world into flower-child and technocratic death-count couldn't have caught the mood of the nation more accurately or more presciently. And although it was run only a limited number of times (and DDB never did political advertising again), it summarizes the aesthetics and faiths of the consumer revolution more concisely and convincingly than almost any other document of the decade.[49]

ENDNOTES

1. Dobrow, Larry. *When Advertising Tried Harder. The Sixties: The Golden Age of Advertising* (New York: Friendly Press, 1984) p. 12.

2. Rothenberg, Randall. *Where the Suckers Moon: The Life and Death of an Advertising Campaign* (New York: Vintage, 1995), p. 66.

3. In *The Cultural Contradictions of Capitalism*, Daniel Bell argues that a certain species of cultural and philosophical "antinomianism"—"an antinomian attitude to moral norms and even to the idea of cultural judgment itself"—has become the central doctrine of postmodernity. Aesthetic modernism's assault on "orthodoxy" has become a commonplace of bourgeois life, he asserts, and transgression has become an act of routine: "The paradox is that 'heterodoxy' itself has become conformist in liberal circles, and exercises that conformity under the banner of an antinomian flag" (Bell, *The Cultural Contradictions of Capitalism* [New York: Basic Books, 1978], pp. xxii, xxvii).

4. Bob Levenson, *Bill Bernbach's Book* (New York: Villard, 1978), pp. xvi, xvii. This work is a compilation of Bernbach's aphorisms, writings, and DDB's best-remembered ads.

5. *Bill Bernbach Said . . .*, pamphlet, n.d., n.p, in the library of the DDB-Needham [Doyle Dane Bernbach], New York; *Advertising Age*, July 3, 1967, p. 8. Levenson, *Bill Bernbach's Book*, p. ix.

6. Bill Bernbach, "Facts Are Not Enough," pamphlet reprinting a speech given at the 1980 meeting of the AAAA, p. 9. In the library of DDB-Needham, New York.

7. *Bill Bernbach Said*, n.p.

8. Mayer, Martin. *Madison Avenue, U.S.A.* (New York: Harper & Brothers, 1958), pp. 67–68.

9. Bob Levenson and Len Sirowitz, interview by Henry Lee, *Madison Avenue*, June 1969, p. 28.

10. George Lois recalls the significance of the resulting change in the way advertising was produced: "Up to that time, basically, most creative work was written by writers who maybe met with clients, but basically took their information from marketing people, and then they handed what they wanted to do to the art director, and the art director laid it out. They were called 'layout men.' And it all changed with Bernbach saying no, putting these two talented people in there with the marketing people, getting all the information, and let them create something mind-bogglingly fresh and different." George Lois, interviewed by Thomas Frank, May 13, 1992. Jerry Della Femina offers a similar picture of the prerevolutionary creative process: "To the establishment agencies, an art director is a guy who draws. 'He's our drawing guy.' So they go in to their drawing guy with a headline that says 'Fights Headaches Three Ways.' Maybe the copywriter has got a little scribble of how the ad should look. . . . The copywriter comes in and says, 'Okay, here's what we did. We want to say "Fights Headaches Three Ways" and I think we should show a big pill.' The art director says, 'Terrific.' " See Jerry Della Femina, *From Those Wonderful Folks Who Gave You Pearl Harbor: Front Line Dispatches from the Advertising War*, edited by Charles Sopkin (New York: Simon and Schuster, 1970), p. 153.

11. Interview with Phyllis Robinson in Tadahisa Nishio, *Great American Copywriters*, Vol. 2 (Tokyo: Seibundo-Shinkosha Publishing Co., 1971), p. 238.

12. Phyllis Robinson, acceptance speech upon being elected to the Copywriters Hall of Fame, as printed in DDB's house journal, *DDB News*, July 1968, p. 2.

13. As quoted in Mayer, *Madison Avenue, U.S.A.*, p. 67.

14. Charlie Moss, interviewed by Thomas Frank, at Wells, Rich, Greene, New York, June 2, 1992.

15. Victor Navasky, "Advertising Is a Science? An Art? A Business?" *New York Times Magazine*, November 20, 1966, pp. 170, 169.

16. Charlie Moss, June 2, 1992, interview with author.

17. Rothenberg refers to one of these, an ad done by Wieden & Kennedy and featuring Lou Reed, "art that explicated, through irony, camp, iconic reference or self-reference, the commercial itself and the consumer culture of which it was a part" (*Where the Suckers Moon*, p. 211). Twitchell calls these "The jig is up" advertising, and notes their prevalence in appealing to "Generation X." See Twitchell, *Adcult USA* (New York: Columbia University Press, 1966), pp. 238–42.

18. Rothenberg, *Where the Suckers Moon*, p. 66.

19. Advertisement for the 1959 Dodge, *Life*, October 20, 1958.

20. Advertisement for the 1958 Edsel, *Life*, April 14, 1958; Advertisement for the 1961 Buick, *Life*, March 17, 1961.

21. These were features discussed in advertising for, respectively, the 1958 Chevrolet, the 1958 Pontiac, and the 1959 Dodge. "Quadra-Power Roadability" was apparently a suspension system. "Finger-tip TorqueFlite" referred to the 1959 Dodge's push-button transmission controls. See *Life*, February 3, 1958; January 13, 1958; October 20, 1958.

22. 1955 Cadillac and 1963 Chevrolet commercials in collections of Museum of Television & Radio (MT&R), New York.

23. Advertisement for the 1959 Chevrolet, *Life*, October 20, 1958.

24. Herbert Marcuse, *One Dimensional Man* (Boston: Beacon Press, 1964), p. 226.

25. In 1959, art director Wallace W. Elton noted that, "Every car artist had his own pet system for 'stretching' cars," involving "wide-angle lenses and print manipulation" in order to "keep pace in the trend toward exaggeration." See *Advertising Directions*, edited by Edward M. Gottschall and Arthur Hawkins (New York: Art Directions Book Company, 1959), p. 90.

26. Navasky, "Advertising Is a Science?" p. 169; Dobrow on buzzwords and photo-retouching, *When Advertising Tried Harder*, p. 9.

27. Della Femina, *From Those Wonderful Folks Who Gave You Pearl Harbor*, p. 27.

28. Volkswagen advertisements, *Life*, November 5, 1965; June 9, 1961; November 2, 1962; October 8, 1965; February 5, 1965.

29. Lowrey: 1965 *Annual*. Utica; 1963 *Annual*. Benson & Hedges: WRG agency reel. Listerine: JWT collection, Duke University library.

30. Volkswagen advertisements, *Life*, February 10, 1961; November 10, 1961; July 15, 1966.

31. Volkswagen advertisements, *Life*, April 17, 1964; September 16, 1966; February 4, 1966. This last ad contained this immortal line: "When you drive the latest fad to a party, and find 2 more fads there ahead of you, it catches you off your avant-garde."

32. Volkswagen ads, reproduced in 1964, 1963 *Annuals*.

33. Volkswagen advertisement, 1965 *Annual*.

34. Volkswagen commercial, Museum of Television & Radio (MT&R).

35. Volkswagen commercial, 1969, MT&R. Print ad from 1960 reproduced in Dobrow, *When Advertising Tried Harder*, p. 85.

36. George Lois with Bill Pitts, *George, Be Careful: A Greek Florists's Kid in the Roughhouse World of Advertising* (New York: Saturday Review Press, 1972), p. 57. The irony that the creative revolution originated in the collaboration of a largely Jewish agency and a German company manufacturing the Nazi car has since become a standard part of advertising lore. See Robert Glatzer, *The New Advertising* (New York: Citadel Press, 1970), p. 19; Rothenberg, *Where the Suckers Moon*, pp. 63–64; Charles Goodrum and Helen Dalrymple, *Advertising in America* (New York: Harry N. Abrams, 1990), p. 244.

37. Larry Dobrow writes that the Volkswagen campaign is "considered by most experts to be the best in the history of advertising" (Dobrow, *When Advertising Tried Harder*, p. 9). In *Advertising in America: The First 200 Years*, Charles Goodrum and Helen Dalrymple write that "the innovative Doyle Dane Bernbach campaign had a major part" in Volkswagen's expanding export business. Furthermore, "people stopped at the ads and read every word and were able to recall the illustration and the point months after the publication . . ." ([New York: Harry N. Abrams, 1990] p. 244).

38. Advertisement for Parker pens, *Life*, November 10, 1961.

39. Advertisement for El Al airline, *Life*, January 20, 1967.

40. Ad for American Tourister luggage, *Life*, December 6, 1968.

41. Commercial for American Tourister, MT&R. Here, as in the Volkswagen commercial mocking the game show, one can discern a certain ugly undercurrent of contempt for consumerism's suckers.

42. Advertisement for Chivas Regal, reprinted in the 1964 *Art Directors' Annual*, n.p.

43. Advertisements for Calvert Whiskey, *Life*, June 19, 1964; September 9, 1966.

44. Advertisements for Calvert Whiskey, *Life*, October 7, 1966; December 18, 1964.

45. This ad reproduced in *Madison Avenue*, September, 1966.

46. Advertisement for Avis, reproduced in 1965 *Annual*. The Avis campaign was one of DDB's most spectacular successes. In 1967, *Editor & Publisher* quoted Winston Morrow, president of Avis, as saying: "Since 1963, when DDB launched us on the We Try Harder road 'because we're only No. 2,' the results of this campaign have been the best that ever happened to Avis and indeed to the whole rent-a-car industry."

"Trying harder, via the now famous DDB theme," the magazine continued, "has seen Avis business climb from $20 million to $100 million in a four-year period. And as more people slammed Avis doors, the ad budget— split roughly between print and electronic media—grew accordingly from $1.2 million to $6 million" (Tony Brenna, "A Cause for Client—Agency Contentment," *Editor & Publisher*, December 9, 1967, p. 18).

47. Commercials for Campbell's Pork and Beans, n.d. [1965], MT&R; Burlington socks, 1966, MT&R.

48. Alka-Seltzer television commercial, 1970, MT&R. This commercial is discussed in almost every book on the advertising of the 1960s. Nonetheless, it was not a successful ad in the most tangible of ways for DDB: soon after it appeared, DDB lost the Alka-Seltzer account (although the reasons for this are, of course, hotly disputed).

49. Commercial for Johnson for President, 1964, DDB reel, MT&R.

PART SEVEN

New Critiques of Consumer Society

23
Duane Elgin
"Voluntary Simplicity and the New Global Challenge"
(1993)

At the heart of the simple life is an emphasis on harmonious and purposeful living. Richard Gregg was a student of Gandhi's teaching and, in 1936, he wrote the following about a life of "voluntary simplicity":

> Voluntary simplicity involves both inner and outer condition. It means singleness of purpose, sincerity and honesty within, as well as avoidance of exterior clutter, of many possessions irrelevant to the chief purpose of life. It means an ordering and guiding of our energy and our desires, a partial restraint in some directions in order to secure greater abundance of life in other directions. It involves a deliberate organization of life for a purpose. Of course, as different people have different purposes in life, what is relevant to the purpose of one person might not be relevant to the purpose of another. . . . The degree of simplification is a matter for each individual to settle for himself.[1]

There is no special virtue to the phrase *voluntary simplicity*—it is merely a label, and a somewhat awkward label at that. Still, it does acknowledge explicitly that simpler living integrates both inner and outer aspects of life into an organic and purposeful whole.

To live more *voluntarily* is to live more deliberately, intentionally, and purposefully—in short, it is to live more consciously. We cannot be deliberate when we are distracted from life. We cannot be intentional when we are not paying attention. We cannot be purposeful when we are not being present. Therefore, to act in a voluntary manner is to be aware of ourselves as we move through life. This requires that we not only pay attention to the actions we take in the outer world, but also that we pay attention to ourselves acting—our inner world. To the extent that we do not notice both inner and outer aspects of our passage through life, then our capacity for voluntary, deliberate, and purposeful action is commensurately diminished.

To live more simply is to live more purposefully and with a minimum of needless distraction. The particular expression of *simplicity* is a per-

sonal matter. We each know where our lives are unnecessarily complicated. We are all painfully aware of the clutter and pretense that weigh
upon us and make our passage through the world more cumbersome
and awkward. To live more simply is to unburden ourselves—to live
more lightly, cleanly, aerodynamically. It is to establish a more direct,
unpretentious, and unencumbered relationship with all aspects of our
lives: the things that we consume, the work that we do, our relationships
with others, our connections with nature and the cosmos, and more.
Simplicity of living means meeting life face-to-face. It means confronting
life clearly, without unnecessary distractions. It means being direct and
honest in relationships of all kinds. It means taking life as it is—straight
and unadulterated.

When we combine these two ideas for integrating the inner and outer
aspects of our lives, we can describe *voluntary simplicity* as a manner
of living that is outwardly more simple and inwardly more rich, a way
of being in which our most authentic and alive self is brought into direct
and conscious contact with living. This way of life is not a static condition to be achieved, but an ever-changing balance that must be continuously and consciously made real. Simplicity in this sense is not
simple. To maintain a skillful balance between the inner and outer aspects of our lives is an enormously challenging and continuously changing process. The objective is not dogmatically to live with less, but is a
more demanding intention of living with balance in order to find a life
of greater purpose, fulfillment, and satisfaction.

MISCONCEPTIONS ABOUT THE SIMPLE LIFE

Some people tend to equate ecological living with a life characterized
by poverty, antagonism to progress, rural living, and the denial of
beauty. It is important to acknowledge these misconceptions so that we
can move beyond them.

IMPOVERISHED LIVING

Although some spiritual traditions have advocated a life of extreme renunciation, it is inaccurate to equate simplicity with poverty. My awakening to the harsh reality of poverty began on my father's farm in Idaho,
where I worked with people who lived on the edge of subsistence. I
remember one fall harvest when I was about ten years old in the early
1950s. We were harvesting a forty-acre field of lettuce, and a crew of
twenty or so migrant laborers arrived to go to work. I still recall a family
of three—a father, mother, and a daughter about my age—that drove
their old Mercury sedan down the dusty road into our farm. They
parked in the field and, with solemn faces, worked through the day
doing piece labor—getting paid for the number of crates of lettuce they
filled. At the end of the day they received their few dollars of wages as

a family, earning roughly sixty-five cents an hour. That evening I returned to the fields with my father to check on the storage of the crates of lettuce and found the family parked at the edge of the field, sitting against the side of their car, and eating an evening meal that consisted of a loaf of white bread, a few slices of lunch meat, and a small jar of mayonnaise. I wondered how they managed to work all day on such a limited meal but asked no questions. When I arrived for work the following morning, they got out of their car where they had slept the night and began working another day. After they had repeated this cycle for three days, the harvest was finished and they left. This was just one of innumerable personal encounters with poverty. Over the next fifteen years I worked in the fields each summer and gradually came to realize that most of these people did not know whether, in another week or month, their needs for food and shelter would be met by their meager salary.

As I worked side by side with these fine people, I saw that poverty has a very human face—one that is very different from "simplicity." Poverty is involuntary and debilitating, whereas simplicity is voluntary and enabling. Poverty is mean and degrading to the human spirit, whereas a life of conscious simplicity can have both a beauty and a functional integrity that elevates the human spirit. Involuntary poverty generates a sense of helplessness, passivity, and despair, whereas purposeful simplicity fosters a sense of personal empowerment, creative engagement, and opportunity. Historically those choosing a simpler life have sought the golden mean—a creative and aesthetic balance between poverty and excess. Instead of placing primary emphasis on material riches, they have sought to develop, with balance, the invisible wealth of experiential riches.

If the human family sets a goal for itself of achieving a moderate standard of living for everyone, computer projections suggest that the world could reach a sustainable level of economic activity that is roughly "equivalent in material comforts to the average level in Europe in 1990."[2] If we do not delay but act with decision and determination, then humanity need not face a future of poverty and sacrifice. The earth can sustain a moderate and satisfying material standard of living for the entire human family.

TURNING AWAY FROM PROGRESS

Ecological living does not imply turning away from economic progress; rather it seeks to discover which technologies are most appropriate and helpful in moving toward a sustainable future. Ecological living is not a path of "no growth" but a path of "new growth" that includes both material and spiritual dimensions of life. A simpler way of life is not a retreat from progress; in fact it is essential to the advance of civilizations. After a lifetime of study of the rise and fall of the world's civilizations, historian Arnold Toynbee concluded that the measure of a civilization's growth was not to be found in the conquest of other people or in the possession of land. Rather he described the essence of growth in what he called the *Law of Progressive Simplification*.[3] True growth, he said, is the ability of a society to transfer increasing amounts of energy and attention from the material side of life to the nonmaterial side and thereby to advance its culture, capacity for compassion, sense of community, and strength of democracy. We are now being pushed by necessity to discover freshly the meaning of "true growth" by progressively simplifying the material side of our lives and enriching the nonmaterial side.

RURAL LIVING

In the popular imagination there is a tendency to equate the simple life with Thoreau's cabin in the woods by Walden Pond and to assume that people must live an isolated and rural existence. Interestingly, Thoreau was not a hermit during his stay at Walden Pond. His famous cabin was roughly a mile from the town of Concord, and every day or two he would walk into town. His cabin was so close to a nearby highway that he could smell the pipe smoke of passing travelers. Thoreau wrote that he had "more visitors while I lived in the woods than any other period of my life."[4]

The romanticized image of rural living does not fit the modern reality, as a majority of persons choosing a life of conscious simplicity do not live in the backwoods or rural settings; they live in cities and suburbs. While ecological living brings with it a reverence for nature, this does not require moving to a rural setting. Instead of a "back to the land" movement, it is more accurate to describe this as a "make the most of wherever you are" movement.

DENIAL OF BEAUTY

The simple life is sometimes viewed as a primitive approach to living that advocates a barren plainness and denies the value of beauty and aesthetics. While the Puritans, for example, were suspicious of the arts, many other advocates of simplicity have seen it as essential for revealing the natural beauty of things. Many who adopt a simpler life would surely agree with Pablo Picasso, who said that "art is the elimination of the unnecessary." The influential architect Frank Lloyd Wright was an advocate of an "organic simplicity" that integrates function with beauty and eliminates the superfluous. In his architecture a building's interior and exterior blend into an organic whole, and the building, in turn, blends harmoniously with the natural environment.[5] Rather than involving a denial of beauty, simplicity liberates the aesthetic sense by freeing things from artificial encumbrances. From a transcendental perspective, simplicity removes the obscuring clutter and discloses the spirit that infuses all things.

It is important to acknowledge these misleading stereotypes because they suggest a life of regress instead of progress. These misconceptions make a simpler life seem impractical and unapproachable and thereby reinforce the feeling that nothing can be done to respond to our critical world situation. To move from denial to action, we need an accurate understanding of the nature of simpler living and its relevance for the modern era.

COMMON EXPRESSIONS OF ECOLOGICAL WAYS OF LIVING

There is no cookbook for defining a life of conscious simplicity. Richard Gregg, for example, was insistent that "simplicity is a relative matter depending on climate, customs, culture, and the character of the individual."[6] Henry David Thoreau was also clear that no simple formula could define the worldly expression of a simpler life. He said, "I would not have anyone adopt my mode of living on my account. . . . I would have each one be very careful to find out and pursue his own way."[7] Nor did Mahatma Gandhi advocate a blind denial of the material side of life. He said, "As long as you derive inner help and comfort from anything, you should keep it. If you were to give it up in a mood of self-sacrifice or out of a stern sense of duty, you would continue to want it back, and that unsatisfied want would make trouble for you. Only give up a thing when you want some other condition so much that the thing no longer has any attraction for you."[8] Because simplicity has as much to do with each person's purpose in living as it does with his or her standard of living, it follows that there is no single, "right and true" way to live more ecologically and compassionately.

Although there is no dogmatic formula for simpler living, there is a general pattern of behaviors and attitudes that is often associated with this approach to living. Those choosing a simpler life:

- Tend to invest the time and energy freed up by simpler living in activities with their partner, children, and friends (walking, making music together, sharing a meal, camping, etc.), or volunteering to help others, or getting involved in civic affairs to improve the life of the community.

- Tend to work on developing the full spectrum of their potentials: physical (running, biking, hiking, etc.), emotional (learning the skills of intimacy and sharing feelings in important relationships), mental (engaging in lifelong learning by reading, taking classes, etc.), and spiritual (learning to move through life with a quiet mind and compassionate heart).

- Tend to feel an intimate connection with the earth and a reverential concern for nature. In knowing that the ecology of the earth is a part of our extended "body," people tend to act in ways that express great care for its well-being.

- Tend to feel a compassionate concern for the world's poor; a simpler life fosters a sense of kinship with people around the world and thus a concern for social justice and equity in the use of the world's resources.

- Tend to lower their overall level of personal consumption—buy less clothing (with more attention to what is functional, durable, aesthetic, and less concern with passing fads, fashions, and seasonal styles), buy less jewelry and other forms of personal ornamentation, buy fewer cosmetic products and observe holidays in a less commercialized manner.

- Tend to alter their patterns of consumption in favor of products that are durable, easy to repair, nonpolluting in their manufacture and use, energy-efficient, functional, and aesthetic.

- Tend to shift their diet away from highly processed foods, meat, and sugar toward foods that are more natural, healthy, simple, and appropriate for sustaining the inhabitants of a small planet.

- Tend to reduce undue clutter and complexity in their personal lives by giving away or selling those possessions that are seldom used and could be used productively by others (clothing, books, furniture, appliances, tools, etc.).

- Tend to use their consumption politically by boycotting goods and services of companies whose actions or policies they consider unethical.

- Tend to recycle metal, glass, and paper and to cut back on consumption of items that are wasteful of nonrenewable resources.

- Tend to pursue a livelihood that directly contributes to the well-being of the world and enables a person to use more fully his or her creative capacities in ways that are fulfilling.

- Tend to develop personal skills that contribute to greater self-reliance and reduce dependence upon experts to handle life's ordinary demands (for example, basic carpentry, plumbing, appliance repair, gardening, crafts, etc.).

- Tend to prefer smaller-scale, more human-sized living and working environments that foster a sense of community, face-to-face contact, and mutual caring.

- Tend to alter male-female roles in favor of nonsexist patterns of relationship.

- Tend to appreciate the simplicity of nonverbal forms of communication—the eloquence of silence, hugging and touching, the language of the eyes.

- Tend to participate in holistic health-care practices that emphasize preventive medicine and the healing powers of the body when assisted by the mind.

- Tend to involve themselves with compassionate causes, such as protecting rain forests and saving animals from extinction, and tend to use nonviolent means in their efforts.

- Tend to change transportation modes in favor of public transit, car pooling, smaller and more fuel-efficient autos, living closer to work, riding a bike, and walking.

Because there is a tendency to emphasize the external changes that characterize simpler living, it is important to reiterate that this approach to life is intended to integrate both inner and outer aspects of existence into a satisfying and purposeful whole.

MAINTAINING OURSELVES AND SURPASSING OURSELVES

An ecological approach to living invites us to continuously balance two aspects of life—maintaining ourselves (creating a workable existence) and surpassing ourselves (creating a meaningful existence). A statement by the philosopher and feminist Simone de Beauvoir helps clarify this: "Life is occupied in both perpetuating itself and in surpassing itself; if all it does is maintain itself, then living is only not dying." On the one hand, if we seek *only* to maintain ourselves, then no matter how grand our style of living might be, we are doing little more than "only not dying." On the other hand, if we strive *only* for a meaningful existence without securing the material foundation that supports our lives, then our physical existence is in jeopardy and the opportunity to surpass ourselves becomes little more than a utopian dream. Although many of the expressions of a simple life listed above emphasize actions that promote a more sustainable existence, this should not distract us from the importance of the surpassing or inner dimensions of a life of conscious simplicity.

The many expressions of simpler living, both inner and outer, indicate that this is much more than a superficial change in the *style* of life. A "style" change refers generally to an exterior change, such as a new fad or fashion. Simplicity goes far deeper and involves a change in our *way* of life. Ecological living is a sophisticated response to the demands of deteriorating industrial civilizations. Table 1 shows the contrast between the worldview of the industrial era and that of the emerging ecological era. Simpler ways of living in the ecological era will result in changes as great as the transition from the agrarian era to the industrial era. In an interdependent, ecologically conscious world every aspect of life will

Contrasts in Worldview Between the Industrial Era and the Ecological Era

Industrial-Era View	Ecological-Era View
The goal in life is material progress.	The goal in life is to co-evolve both the material and spiritual aspects with harmony and balance.
Emphasis on conspicuous consumption—the "good life" is dependent upon having enough money to buy access to life's pleasures and to avoid life's discomforts.	Emphasis on conservation and frugality—using only as much as is needed; a satisfying life emerges with balanced development in cooperation with others.
Identity is defined by material possessions and social position.	Identity is revealed through our loving and creative participation in life.
The individual is defined by his or her body and is ultimately separate and alone.	The individual is both unique and an inseparable part of the larger universe; identity is not limited to our physical existence.
The universe is viewed as material and largely lifeless; it is natural that we who are living exploit the lifeless universe for our ends.	The universe is a living organism that is infused with a subtle life-force; it is important to act in ways that honor the preciousness and dignity of all life.
Emphasis on self-serving behavior (get as much for myself as I can while giving no more than is required in return).	Emphasis on life-serving behavior (give as much of myself to life as I am able and ask in return no more than I require).
Cutthroat competition prevails; compete against others and strive to "make a killing."	Fair competition prevails; cooperate with others and work to earn a living.
The mass media are dominated by commercial interests and are used aggressively to promote a high-consumption culture.	The mass media are used to promote a balanced diet of information and messages, including the importance of ecological approaches to living.
Nations adopt a "lifeboat ethic" in global relations.	Nations adopt a "spaceship Earth ethic" in global relations.
The welfare of the whole is left to the workings of the free market and/or government bureaucracies.	Each person takes responsibility for the well-being of the world.
Emphasis on personal autonomy and mobility.	Emphasis on connectedness and community.

be touched and changed: consumption levels and patterns, living and working environments, political attitudes and processes, international ethics and relations, the uses of mass media, education, and many more.

THE PUSH OF NECESSITY AND THE PULL OF OPPORTUNITY

Two compelling reasons exist for choosing more ecological approaches to living: the push of necessity and the pull of opportunity. The combined impact of the various *pushes of necessity* are staggering to contemplate. Here is an overview of our predicament:

- In 1930 the world had 2 billion people, in 1975 roughly 4 billion people, by the year 2000 the population is expected to exceed 6 billion people, and in 2025 the world's population will approach 9 billion people. The vast majority of the increase in human numbers is occurring in the less-developed nations. Because the world's ecosystem is already under great stress, as these new billions of persons seek a decent standard of living, the global ecology could easily be strained beyond the breaking point, producing a calamity of unprecedented proportions.

- The gap between rich and poor nations is already a chasm and is growing wider rapidly. The average person in the richest one-fifth of the world's countries earned $15,000 in 1990, whereas the average person in the poorest one-fifth of the world's countries earned $250. This sixty-fold differential between the rich and poor is double what it was in 1960.[9]

- More than a thousand million people (1.2 billion) now live in absolute poverty—"a condition of life so limited by malnutrition, illiteracy, disease, squalid surroundings, high infant mortality and low life expectancy as to be beneath any reasonable definition of human decency."[10]

- Global warming will likely alter patterns of rainfall and disrupt food production, flood enormous areas of low-lying lands, displace millions of people, destroy fragile ecosystems, and alter patterns of disease in unpredictable ways.[11]

- Tropical rain forests are being cut down at an alarming rate, contributing to global warming and destroying precious ecosystems that required millions of years to evolve (and that contain a treasury of undiscovered pharmaceuticals).

- Cheaply available supplies of oil are being depleted rapidly and, within a generation, the world will be deprived of an energy source basic to our current form of high-intensity agriculture.

- Toxic wastes are being poured into the environment, and pollution-induced outbreaks of cancer and genetic damage may reach massive proportions.

- Overfishing and pollution of the world's oceans have led to a leveling off in annual fish catch at the same time that the demand for food from the world's oceans is increasing.

- The ozone layer is thinning over populated regions of both the Southern and the Northern Hemispheres and threatens to cause skin cancer and cataracts in humans and unknown damage to the rest of the food chain.

- Thousands of plant and animal species are becoming extinct each year, representing the greatest loss of life on the planet since the massive extinction of dinosaurs and other animal and plant life roughly 65 million years ago.

- Acid rains from coal burning and sulfur-producing industrial processes are damaging forests, farmland, and freshwater streams.

These are not isolated problems; instead they comprise a tightly intertwined system of problems that require us to develop new approaches to living if we are to live sustainably. To live *sustainably*, we must live efficiently—not misdirecting or squandering the earth's precious resources. To live *efficiently*, we must live peacefully, for military expenditures represent an enormous diversion of resources from meeting basic human needs. To live *peacefully*, we must live with a reasonable degree of *equity*, or fairness, for it is unrealistic to think that, in a communications-rich world, a billion or more persons will accept living in absolute poverty while another billion live in conspicuous excess. Only with greater fairness in the consumption of the world's resources can we live peacefully, and thereby live sustainably, as a human family. Without a revolution in fairness, the world will find itself in chronic conflict over dwindling resources, and this in turn will make it impossible to achieve the level of cooperation necessary to solve problems such as pollution and overpopulation.

The United Nations *Human Development Report* of 1992 said, "In a world of 5 billion people, we discovered that the top billion people hold 83 percent of the world's wealth, while the bottom billion have only 1.4 percent."[12] We cannot expect to live in a peaceful world with such enormous disparities between the rich and the poor. The prosperity of the technologically interdependent, wealthy nations is vulnerable to disruption by terrorism by those who have nothing left to lose and no hope for the future. *Only with greater equity can we expect to live peacefully, and only with greater harmony can we expect to live sustainably.*

If the world is profoundly divided materially, there is very little hope that it can be united socially, psychologically, and spiritually. Therefore if we intend to live together peacefully as members of a single, human family, then each individual has a right to a reasonable share of the world's resources. Each person has a right to expect a fair share of the world's wealth sufficient to support a "decent" standard of living—one that provides enough food, shelter, education, and health care to enable people to realize their potentials as productive and respected members of the family of humanity. This does not mean that the world should adopt a single manner and standard of living; rather, it means that each person needs to feel part of the global family and, within a reasonable range of differences, valued and supported in realizing his or her unique human potentials.

With sustainability we can expand our experiential riches of culture, compassion, community, and self-determination. With a growing abundance of experiential riches the entire process of living will be encouraged, and a self-reinforcing spiral of development will unfold. Therefore, reinforcing the powerful push of necessity is the *pull of opportunity*— the potential of the simple life to yield a more satisfying and soulful existence. Many persons in developed nations find life to be psychologically and spiritually hollow—living in massive urban environments of alienating scale and complexity, divorced from the natural environment, and working in jobs that are unsatisfying. Many yearn for a more authentic approach to living, one that provides a fulfilling relationship with oneself, with others, with the earth, and with the universe. *Time* magazine and CNN television conducted a survey of Americans for *Time*'s April 8, 1991, cover story entitled "The Simple Life." The results are striking:

- Sixty-nine percent of the people surveyed said they would like to "slow down and live a more relaxed life," in contrast to only 19 percent who said they would like to "live a more exciting, faster-paced life."

- Sixty-one percent agreed that "earning a living today requires so much effort that it's difficult to find time to enjoy life."

- When asked about their priorities, 89 percent said it was more important these days to spend time with their families.

- Only 13 percent saw importance in keeping up with fashion trends, and just 7 percent thought it was worth bothering to shop for status-symbol products.

Another survey reported in a 1989 article in *Fortune* magazine entitled "Is Greed Dead?" found that 75 percent of working Americans between the ages of twenty-five and forty-nine would like "to see our country return to a simpler lifestyle, with less emphasis on material success."[13] Only 10 percent of those polled thought that "earning a lot of money" was an indicator of success. These polls reveal that a large fraction of the American public has experienced the limited rewards from the material riches of a consumer society and is looking for the experiential riches that can be found, for example, in satisfying relationships, living in harmony with nature, and being of service to the world.

The combination of the push of necessity and the pull of opportunity creates an entirely new situation for humanity. On the one hand, a life of creative simplicity frees energy for the soulful work of spiritual discovery and loving service—tasks that all of the world's wisdom traditions say we should give our highest priority. On the other hand, a simpler way of life also responds to the urgent needs for moderating our use of the world's nonrenewable resources and minimizing the damaging impact of environmental pollution. Working in concert, these pushes and pulls are creating an immensely powerful dynamic for transforming our ways of living, working, relating, and thinking.

HISTORICAL ROOTS OF SIMPLICITY

While simpler living has unprecedented relevance for coping with the current ecological crisis, it has deep roots in human experience. Although these historical roots are far too extensive to examine in depth, a brief review helps to reveal the breadth and richness of this approach to living.[14]

CHRISTIAN VIEWS

Jesus embodied a life of compassionate simplicity. He taught by work and example that we should not make the acquisition of material possessions our primary aim; instead we should develop our capacity for loving participation in life. The Bible speaks frequently about the need to find a balance between the material and the spiritual side of life; for example:

- "Give me neither poverty nor wealth." (Proverbs 30: 8)

- "Do not store up for yourselves treasure on earth, where it grows rusty and moth-eaten, and thieves break in to steal it. Store up treasure in heaven. . . . For wherever your treasure is, there will your heart be also." (Matthew 6:19–21)

- "Therefore I tell you, do not be anxious about your life, what you shall eat or what you shall drink, nor about your body, what you shall put on. Is not life more than food, and the body more than clothing?" (Matthew 6:25)

- "If a man has enough to live on, and yet when he sees his brother in need shuts up his heart against him, how can it be said that the divine love dwells in him?" (John 3:17)

A common basis for living simply can be found in all the world's spiritual traditions and is expressed in the "golden rule"—the compassionate admonition that we should treat others as we would want ourselves to be treated. The theme of sharing and economic justice seems particularly strong in the Christian tradition. Basil the Great, bishop of

Caesarea, stated around A.D. 365: "When someone steals a man's clothes we call him a thief. Should we not give the same name to one who could clothe the naked and does not? The bread in your cupboard belongs to the hungry man; the coat hanging unused in your closet belongs to the man who needs it; the shoes rotting in your closet belong to the man who has not shoes; the money which you hoard up belongs to the poor."[15] In the modern era this implies that if people in developed nations consume more than their fair share of the world's resources, then they are taking food, clothing, and other essentials from those who are in great need.

A contemporary expression of simplicity in the Christian tradition is found in the "Shakertown Pledge," a statement developed in 1973 by a diverse group of Christians in an effort to describe a lifestyle appropriate to the new realities of the world.[16] Two key commitments give a feeling for this pledge: "I commit myself to lead an ecologically sound life," and "I commit myself to lead a life of creative simplicity and to share my personal wealth with the world's poor." These commitments are not meant to produce a pinched and miserly existence; instead they are intended to encourage an aesthetic simplicity that enhances personal freedom and fulfillment while promoting a just manner of living relative to the needs of the world.

EASTERN VIEWS

Eastern spiritual traditions such as Buddhism, Hinduism and Taoism have also encouraged a life of material moderation and spiritual abundance. From the Taoist tradition we have this saying from Lao-tzu: "He who knows he has enough is rich."[17] From the Hindu tradition we have these thoughts from Mahatma Gandhi, the spiritual and political leader who was instrumental in gaining India's independence: "Civilization, in the real sense of the term, consists not in the multiplication, but in the deliberate and voluntary reduction of wants. This alone promotes real happiness and contentment."[18] Gandhi felt the moderation of our wants increases our capacity to be of service to others and, in being of loving service to others, true civilization emerges.

Perhaps the most developed expression of a middle way between material excess and deprivation comes from the Buddhist tradition. While Buddhism recognizes that basic material needs must be met in order to realize our potentials, it does not consider our material welfare as an end in itself; rather, it is a means to the end of awakening to our deeper nature as spiritual beings. Self-control and a simple life are valued highly, as is the practice of charity and generosity without attachment to one's wealth or property.[19] A modern expression of this view is given by the monk Sulak Sivaraksa, who describes the necessity for a more compassionate and simple way of living: "We can only save ourselves when all humanity recognizes that every problem on earth is our own personal problem and our personal responsibility. . . . Unless the rich change their lifestyle considerably, there is no hope of solving [the problem of famine in the world]."[20]

E. F. Schumacher, author of the classic book *Small Is Beautiful*, described Buddhism as a middle path that emphasizes simplicity and nonviolence.[21] Applying the middle way to economics, Schumacher described a Buddhist economy as one that provides an adequate range of material goods and whose production processes are in harmony with both the environment and available resources. The middle way of Buddhist economics moves between mindless materialism, on the one hand, and needless poverty, on the other. The result is a balanced approach to living that harmonizes both inner and outer development.

EARLY GREEK VIEWS

Plato and Aristotle recognized the importance of the "golden mean" or a middle path through life characterized by neither excess nor deficit, but by sufficiency. Like many spiritual traditions, they did not view the material world as primary but as instrumental—as serving our learning about the more expansive world of thought and spirit. Plato's teacher, Socrates, also advocated a golden mean between wealth and poverty. Aristotle favored a balanced life that involved moderation on the material side and exertion on the intellectual side. He said that "temperance and courage" were destroyed by either excess or deficiency and could only be preserved by following the golden mean.[22]

PURITAN VIEWS

Paradoxically, although the United States is the world's most blatantly consumerist nation, the simple life has strong roots in American history. The early Puritan settlers brought to America their "puritan ethic," which stressed hard work, temperate living, participation in the life of the community, and a steadfast devotion to things spiritual. Puritans also stressed the golden mean by saying we should not desire more material things than we can use effectively. It is from the New England Puritans that we get the adage, Use it up, wear it out, make do, or do without. Although the Puritan tradition tended to be hierarchical, elitist, and authoritarian, it also had a compassionate side that encouraged people to use their excess wealth to help the deserving poor. Puritans were not opposed to prosperity itself, but to the greed and selfishness that seemed to accompany excessive abundance.

QUAKER VIEWS

The Quakers also had a strong influence on the American character, particularly with their belief that material simplicity was an important aid in evolving toward spiritual perfection. Unlike the Puritans, their strong sense of equality among people fostered religious tolerance. Quakers emphasized the virtues of hard work at one's calling, sobriety, and frugality. Although they thought it only natural for one to enjoy the fruits of their labor, they also recognized that our stay on earth is brief and that people should place much of their love and attention on things eternal.

TRANSCENDENTALIST VIEWS

Transcendentalist views flourished in the early to mid-1800s in America and are best exemplified by the lives and writing of Ralph Waldo Emerson and Henry David Thoreau. The Transcendentalists believed that a spiritual presence infuses the world and, by living simply, we can more easily encounter this miraculous and vital Life-force. For Emerson the Transcendental path began with self-discovery and then led to "an organic synthesis of that self with the natural world surrounding it."[23] The Transcendentalists had a reverential attitude toward nature and saw the natural world as the doorway to the divine. Nature was seen as the most fitting place for contemplation and receiving spiritual inspiration. By communing with nature, Emerson felt that people could become "part and parcel with God," thereby realizing the ultimate simplicity of oneness with the divine. Thoreau also viewed simplicity as a means to a higher end. Although he felt that a person "is rich in proportion to the number of things which he can afford to let alone," he was not particularly concerned with the specific manner in which someone lived a simpler life. Instead he was most interested in the rich inner life that could be gained through undistracted contemplation. For both Emerson and Thoreau, simplicity had more to do with one's intentions than with one's particular possessions.

This brief overview illustrates the long and rich tradition of simplicity of living in human experience. Historian of the simple life David Shi describes the common denominator among the various approaches to simpler living as the understanding that the making of money and the accumulation of things should not smother the purity of the soul, the life of the mind, the cohesion of the family, or the good of the society.[24] Clearly the simple life is not a new social invention—its value has long been recognized. What is new is the urgent need to respond to the radically changed material and ecological circumstances in which humanity finds itself in the modern world.

THE RESPONSIBILITY FOR CHANGE

Unless dramatic changes are made in the manner of living and consuming in industrialized nations, we will soon produce a world of monumental destruction, suffering, conflict, and despair. Within this generation we must begin a sweeping reinvention of our ways of living or invite the collapse of our biosphere and allow global civilization to veer off into a long detour and dark age.

Because we face a crisis in the interconnected global system, changes at every level are needed. At the personal level we need a magnified global awareness and simpler ways of living. At the neighborhood level we need new types of communities for sustainable living. At the national level we need to adopt new policies with regard to energy, environment, education, media, and many more. At the global level we need new partnerships among nations. Although changes are necessary at every level, the foundation upon which success can be built is the individual and the family. It is empowering to know that each person can make a difference by taking responsibility for changes in his or her immediate life.

Just as we tend to wait for our problems to solve themselves, so, too, do we tend to wait for our traditional institutions and leaders to provide us with guidance as to what we should do. Yet our leaders are bogged down, trying to cope with our faltering institutions. They are so enmeshed in crisis management that they have little time to exercise genuinely creative leadership. We may keep waiting for someone else, but a key message of this essay is that there is no one else. You are it. We are it. Each of us is responsible. It is we who, one by one, must take charge of our lives. It is we who, one by one, must act to restore the balance. We are the ones who are responsible for making it through this time of sweeping change as we work to build a sustainable future for the planet.

ENDNOTES

1. Richard Gregg, "Voluntary Simplicity," reprinted in *Co-Evolution Quarterly*, Sausalito, Calif., Summer 1977 (originally published in the Indian journal *Visva-Bharati Quarterly* in August 1936).

2. Donella H. Meadows et. al., *Beyond the Limits* (Post Mills, Vt.: Chelsea Green Publishing, 1992), p. 196.

3. Arnold Toynbee, *A Study of History*, Vol. 1 (New York: Oxford University Press, 1947), p. 198.

4. David Shi, *The Simple Life: Plain Living and High Thinking in American Culture* (New York: Oxford University Press, 1985), p. 145.

5. Ibid., p. 187.

6. Gregg, op. cit, p. 20.

7. Shi, op. cit, p. 149.

8. Quoted in Gregg, op. cit, p. 27.

9. Results from the 1992 *Human Development Report* (published by the United Nations) were reported in the *San Francisco Chronicle*, April 24, 1992, p. 20.

10. This definition of absolute poverty was taken from the "Address to the Board of Governors" of the World Bank by Robert McNamara, president, September 30, 1980, Washington, D.C.

11. See, for example, George Sanderson, "Climate Change: The Threat to Human Health," in *The Futurist*, Bethesda, Md., March–April 1992.

12. Ibid.

13. Survey done by *Research & Forecasts* for Chivas Regal, reported in the article by Ronald Henkoff, "Is Greed Dead," *Fortune*, August 14, 1989. Regional polls confirm these findings. A poll conducted in the San Francisco Bay area in 1986 found that when people were "given a choice between a simpler life with fewer material possessions and reaching a higher standard of living, they favored the simpler life by almost 3 to 1." Reported in the *San Francisco Chronicle*, October 2, 1986.

14. David Shi's book, *The Simple Life*, was invaluable in developing this historical overview.

15. Doris Janzen Longacre, *Living More with Less* (Scottdale, Pa.: Herald Press, 1980), p. 13.

16. Adam Finnerty, *No More Plastic Jesus* (New York: Orbis Books, 1977).

17. Quoted in Goldian VandenBroek, ed., *Less Is More* (New York: Harper Colophon Books, 1978), p. 116.

18. Ibid, p. 60.

19. Walpola Rahula, "The Social Teachings of the Buddha," in Fred Eppsteiner, ed., *The Path of Compassion*, 2nd ed. (Berkeley, Calif.: Parallax Press, 1988), pp. 103–110.

20. Sulak Sivaraksa, "Buddhism in a World of Change," Eppsteiner, op. cit., p. 17.

21. E. F. Schumacher, *Small Is Beautiful* (London: Blond & Briggs, 1973), p. 52.

22. Shi, op. cit, p. 4.

23. Ibid., p. 127.

24. Ibid., pp. 3–4.

24
Kalle Lasn
"Culture Jamming"
(1999)

THE REVOLUTIONARY IMPULSE

Most of the people in the world have never heard of "culture jamming." Yet it is not a new movement. We place ourselves on a revolutionary continuum that includes, moving backward in time, early punk rockers, the '60s hippie movement, a group of European intellectuals and conceptual artists called the Situationist International (born of the Lettrist International), the Surrealists, Dadaists, Anarchists, and a host of other social agitators down through the ages whose chief aim was to challenge the prevailing ethic in a way that was so primal and heartfelt it could only be true.

What we all have in common—besides a belligerent attitude toward authority—is a willingness to take big risks, and a commitment to the pursuit of small, spontaneous movements of truth. Opportunities to act boldly (which often means *not* the way you would normally, reflexively act) present themselves every day and maybe even every hour. Authentic acts tend to get noticed amidst the fakery and correctness on which postmodern culture thrives. "In a small room where people unanimously maintain a conspiracy of silence," said Nobel laureate Czeslaw Milosz, "one word of truth sounds like a pistol shot."

In his book *Lipstick Traces*, American cultural critic Greil Marcus fixes The Sex Pistols' Johnny Rotten squarely in the tradition of the rebel seer. Rotten was a gleeful anarchist who used the word "fuck" on television and sang like he meant to change the world—or at least explode the dreamy, Beatles-fueled optimism of the day, and stick a fork into classic rock. He somehow rose above the obvious joke of the Pistols— the naked commercialism and hype of a band without much talent— and created something vital.

It's not clear whether Rotten knew anything about the Situationist International. But the Sex Pistols and the SI were most definitely on the same page, philosophically. Their song "Anarchy in the U.K." espoused, in crudely poetic form, the philosophy of the movement. The Pistols wanted to live "not as an object but as a subject of the story," as Marcus put it. That's about as good a working definition of the culture jammers' ethos as you'll ever find.

Marcus recalls watching Johnny Rotten shouting madly over the band's guitars in front of the Berlin Wall and understanding that "his aim . . . was to take in all the rage, intelligence and strength in his being and then fling them back at the world; to make the world notice; to make the world doubt its most cherished and unexamined beliefs." I think culture jammers can learn a lot from the original punks. They were the first to feel the nihilism and to rail against a world that offered no future—and for a few years their rage shook the world.

The Punks, like the Hippies, Yippies, Beats, Anarchists, Dadaists, Surrealists, Automatistes, Fluxists and any number of other groups of disaffected visionaries, represented an age-old spirit of spontaneous defiance toward the established order. But it was the Situationists who first applied that spirit of anarchy to modern media culture. They were the first to understand how the media spectacle slowly corrodes the human psyche. They were, in a sense, the first postmodern revolutionaries.

The Situationists were originally just eight artists and writers, most of them European, who sat down one July day in 1957 in the little town of Cosio d'Arroscia, Italy, to have a little fun together over Gauloises and absinthe. Though reasonably short-lived (by the '70s, most everyone had forgotten about them), they generated an anarchic drive that a generation of students, artists and radicals recognized as the real thing.

The Situationists pronounced a commitment to "a life of permanent novelty." They were interested only in freedom, and just about any means to it were justified. The creativity of everyday people, which consumer capitalism and communism had weakened but not killed, desperately needed expressing. Down with the bureaucracies and hierarchies and ideologies that stifled spontaneity and free will. To the Situationists, you are—everyone is—a creator of situations, a performance artist, and the performance, of course, is your life, lived in your own way. Various stunts were concocted to foster spontaneous living. Situationist members suggested knocking down churches to make space for children to play, and putting switches on the street lamps so lighting would be under public control.

Many times a day, each of us comes to a little fork in the path, the Situationists believed. We can do one of two things: act the way we normally, reflexively act, or do something a little risky and wild, but genuine. We can choose to live our life as "a moral, poetic, erotic, and almost spiritual refusal" to cooperate with the demands of consumer culture.

The Situationists spoke often of the "spectacle" of modern life. The term encompassed everything from billboards to art exhibitions to soccer matches to radio and TV. Broadly speaking, it meant modern society's "spectacular" level of commodity consumption and hype. Everything human beings once experienced directly had been turned into a representation, a show put on by someone else. Real living had been replaced by pre-packaged experiences and media-created events. Immediacy was gone. Now there was only "mediacy"—life as mediated through other instruments, life as a media creation. The Situationists used the term "kidnapped": the spectacle had "kidnapped" our real lives, co-opting whatever authenticity we once had.

I think this helps explain the strong visceral reaction so many people had to Nike's use of the Beatles tune "Revolution," and later, to Apple's appropriation of Bob Dylan, and The Gap's (posthumous) mugging of Jack Kerouac. Nostalgic, griping yuppies may not have been able to perfectly articulate it, but they understood that some fundamental part of their lives had been stolen.

In the Richard Linklater film *Before Sunrise*, the young hero, played by Ethan Hawke, has an existential crisis: he suddenly grows sick to death of his own company. Every party he goes to, there he is. Every bus he rides, every class he attends, he runs into . . . himself. For him, even human identity had somehow become a spectacle. Here Linklater is staring into the Situationist abyss, and finding it a little terrifying. To paraphrase Situationist leader Guy Debord, where the self is by proxy, it is not. This may also explain why one of the juiciest consumer target groups is the man or woman known as the "emulator." Emulators look for products that make them feel like somebody else—somebody more important. Since no product can help you fully escape your old identity, frustration mounts, a credit card is produced and the cycle of alienation deepens. (Situationists might point to emulators as proof of a devolution in the state of living: from "being" to "having," and then from "having" to "appearing to have.")

Debord remains a largely unheralded visionary. Derided toward the end of his life, nearly canonized in France immediately following his suicide in 1967, and then gradually forgotten, Debord is only now enjoying a little posthumous fame—especially in France, where a group calling themselves the "Perpendiculaires" have positioned themselves as a spiritual progeny of the Situationists. They maintain that culture ought to be spread laterally (through salon-type discussions) rather than vertically (through TV and the Internet).

In some ways, Debord was even more of a pioneer of the mental environment than his high-profile coeval, Marshall McLuhan. Where McLuhan only described the mass-culture trance, Debord developed some effective ways to break out of it. One way was the *dérive*. Literally "the drift," the *dérive* was an idea borrowed from the Dadaists. The Situationists defined it as "locomotion without a goal." As a *dériviste*, you float through the city, open to whatever you come in contact with, thus exposing yourself to the whole spectrum of feelings you encounter by chance in everyday life. Openness is key. You embrace whatever you love, and in the process, you discover what it is you hate.

The Situationists believed the *dérive* could largely replace the old twin occupations of work and entertainment, and become a model for the "playful creation" of a new way of life. The *dériviste* is a drifter in the best possible sense, not someone down and out but up and beyond, living outside the stifling roles society prescribes for us. Living well, Debord said, involves "systematic questioning of all the diversions and works of a society, a total critique of its idea of happiness."

Another of the Situationist's favorite tropes was *détournement*, which Debord proposed as a way for people to take back the spectacle that had kidnapped their lives. Literally a "turning around," *détournement* involved rerouting spectacular images, environments, ambiances and events to reverse or subvert their meaning, thus reclaiming them. With its limitless supply of ideas, ranging from rewriting the speech balloons of comic-strip characters, to altering the width of streets and the heights of buildings and the colors and shapes of doors and windows, to radically reinterpreting world events such as the 1965 Watts riots in Los Angeles, the *Internationale Situationniste*—the journal the Situationists published between 1958 and 1969—was a sometimes profound, sometimes absurd laboratory of provocation and *détournement*. Once, Debord altered a famous drawing of Lenin by placing a bare-breasted woman on his forehead with the caption "The Universe Turns on the Tips of Tits." Debord had his book *Mémoires* bound in heavy sandpaper, so that when placed on the shelves of libraries, it would destroy other books. One famous *détournement* happened in the Notre Dame cathedral on Easter Sunday in 1950. With thousands of people watching, a Lettrist provocateur dressed as a Dominican monk slipped onto the altar and delivered a sermon accusing the Catholic Church of "the deadly diversion of the force of life in favor of an empty heaven," and then solemnly proclaimed that "God is dead." It was with this spirit of *détournement* that the Situationists invaded enemy territory and tried to "devalue the currency of the spectacle." And it was with this defiance that they intended to pull off a cultural revolution, "a gigantic turning around of the existing social world."

The Situationists had some fairly radical notions that, when you consider them deeply, make sense. They believed vacations, so cherished by the masses as a kind of sanity-saver, instead just enforce "the loop of alienation and domination" and symbolize "the false promises of modern life." (If you're living a full life, why would you want to "get away" from it?) A memorable Situationist slogan reads: "Club Med, a Cheap Holiday In Other People's Misery."

In *The Revolution of Everyday Life*, which apart from Debord's *The Society of Spectacle* is the seminal book to emerge from the Situationist movement, Raul Vaneigem argued that everyday life is ultimately the measure of all things, and the ground on which all revolutions must unfold. But, he argued, an unfortunate, alienating self-consciousness has recently crept into our lives. "Even the tiniest of gestures—opening a door, holding a teacup, a facial expression—and the most private and individual actions—coming home, making tea, arguing with a lover— have always already been represented and shown to us within the spectacle." Thus, our most intimate gestures have become stereotypes, and our lives clichéd. But Vaneigem passionately believed that the spectacle was fast approaching a saturation point, a crisis out of which "a new poetry of real experience and a reinvention of life are bound to spring."

Today, the stultifying passivity and alienation of the spectacle in our lives has increased to proportions Vaneigem and Debord could hardly have imagined. The great, insidious power of the spectacle lies in the fact that it is actually a form of mental slavery that we are free to resist, *only it never occurs to us to do so.* Our media saturated postmodern world, where all communication flows in one direction, from the powerful to the powerless, produces a population of lumpen spectators, "modern men and women, the citizens of the most advanced societies on earth, thrilled to watch whatever it is they're given to watch."

Greil Marcus calls this the "democracy of false desire." The spectacle is an instrument of social control, offering the illusion of unlimited choice, but in fact reducing the field of play to a choice of pre-selected experiences: adventure movies, nature shows, celebrity romances, political scandals, ball games, net surfing . . .

Boredom emerges in the Situationist literature as one of The Big Enemies. The Situationists saw a world crushed by wasted potential. Mass mechanization, for example, was supposed to create vast stretches of leisure time in which people could create free flowing, imaginative lives for themselves. Instead, people were allowing their leisure hours to be gobbled up by programmed entertainments. Increasingly, they weren't in control of their own fun anymore. The Situationist solution: *Take back the show.* Create your own atmospheres, ambiances and situations. Build something "provisional and lived." One might, to cite one Situationist example, take the predictable city and redesign it as a bunch of emotive neighborhoods—the "bizarre" quarter, the "sinister" quarter, the "tragic" quarter, the "happy" quarter, and the "useful" quarter— that people can drift in and out of.

Whatever else you might think of Guy Debord—that he was wildly idealistic and extreme in his views—he did walk the walk. He created a life free of spectacle (except right at the end, when sick and in pain, he carefully orchestrated his own spectacular suicide by a gunshot through the heart). He never had a job; he spent his time in taverns, arguing philosophy and drinking and writing. He consistently refused interviews with the press and wrote only six slim volumes. "I wrote much less than most people who write, but drank much more than most people who drink," he once remarked. For him, life really *was* an eternal festival. He believed passionately in his own destiny and that of his friends. "Our kind will be the first to blaze a trail into a new life," he boasted.

The heroes of the Situationists' era were unbridled and anarchical, pure vessels of poetic expression, living somehow out of time. They were the polar opposite of the kind of people often held up as examples in our age of workaholism—competitive, ambitious folks who, as Welsh historian L. T. C. Rolt put it in his classic book *High Horse Riderless*, "believe in faster trains and more traffic, who ravage the landscape while claiming to protect it, who disintegrate the family while assuring us it is their priority, who sanctify work while increasing unemployment. All this because they have jettisoned faith in the true spiritual nature of the human being and have not the courage to risk being real, but must always be striving to become superior to their competitors."

The cognitive psychologist Abraham Maslow spoke of the importance of peak experiences in the life of a fully functioning, or "self-actualized," human being. These experiences are so engrossing to the senses—in this instant, this act—that people actually feel they are living out of time. Other disciplines have other names for it. Zen Buddhists call peak experiences "satori." "Generations of poets, prophets, and revolutionaries, not to mention lovers, drug-takers, and all those who have somehow found the time to stand and stare," have craved this ecstatic feeling of oneness with the world. This is also why many culture jammers take daily leaps of faith, or of courage—acts that take them outside market-structured consciousness long enough to get a taste of real living. Living in the moment, pursuing the authentic gesture, living close to the edge—call it what you will—when it's genuine, it is the force that makes life worth living. It is also what consumer capitalism takes away from you every time it sells you brand name "cool" or this month's rebel attitude.

When I was shooting a film in Japan called *Satori in the Right Cortex*, I asked the head monk of a Zen monastery in Kamakura if I could take footage of his disciples meditating. Yes, he said, but first *you* must meditate. He wasn't talking about a quick namaste and a couple of mumbled koans: He meant sitting for two full days. So I took him up on his challenge. I sat on the floor meditating until my back stiffened, joints ached and muscles cramped. It was physical and psychological torture—a hell I will never forget. But by the end of the second day something really had changed. The monk had forced a painful interruption in my soft routine, and I emerged humbled, thankful and, for a few hours, euphoric. Maybe only when you're shoved into a new pattern of behavior and make the commitment not to back out—when your hand is held to the fire or you hold your own hand to the fire—do the real gains come. When the trance is interrupted, you catch a brief, tantalizing glimpse of the way life could be.

What does this have to do with revolution and culture jamming? Everything. Breaking the stupefyingly comfortable patterns we've fallen into isn't pleasant or easy. It's like crawling out of your warm bed in your dark room one December morning at five a.m. and plunging into a tub of ice water. It shocks the system. But sometimes shock is what a system needs. It's certainly what our bloated, self-absorbed consumer culture needs.

Culture jamming is, at root, just a metaphor for stopping the flow of spectacle long enough to adjust your set. Stopping the flow relies on an element of surprise. That's why a Zen master may suddenly throw you a wildly cryptic, inappropriate, even obscene answer to your harmless query. He might answer your question by removing his shoe and placing it on top of his head, or throwing it at you, or telling you that if you meet Buddha on the road you must kill him. The Zen master is trying to break your trance. He's showing you a new path to the waterfall. Debord called this kind of thing "breaking the old syntax," and replacing it with a new one. The new syntax carries the instructions for "a whole new way of being in the world."

What does the perceptual shift feel like when it comes? Imagine a desperately down-and-out soul who suddenly finds God. Now try to imagine the *opposite* of that process. This moment of reckoning is not so much like suddenly seeing heaven in a world you thought was hell as it is suddenly seeing hell in a world you thought was heaven. That world is the world of summer blockbusters and five-dollar lattes and Superbowls in which a 30-second ad slot sells for $1.5 million—the spectacular world of the American dream, a world you were raised to believe was the best of all worlds, but a world that collapses under scrutiny. If you stare at your reflection in the mirror long enough, your face becomes a monster's face, with enormous sunken gargoyle eyes.

In the 1998 film *The Truman Show*, a corporation adopts Truman Burbank at birth, then carefully scripts a whirl of product-placement and impression management into his life, which is televised live, 24 hours a day. The only time Truman upsets the managed order, when he catches a glimpse of the real world behind his scripted life, is when he does something spontaneous. Slowly, he comes to realize that only a chain of spontaneous acts will lead to salvation. The culture jammer is seized by a similar sense of urgency to do something, anything, to escape the consumerist script.

Buddhist mythology tells the tale of Buddha's enlightenment. In the beginning, Buddha is a plump, rich fellow living in an opulent palace. Occasionally, on his walks around the grounds, he spies, through fissures in the palace walls, the world of suffering, pain and disease. He is repulsed, but also mesmerized. Eventually he decides to leave the palace and live in that real world. There's a lesson here for jammers about how to snap the First World out of its media-consumer trance. Each time the flow of images and information is interrupted—by any spontaneous, individual act, or any act of mass media *détournement*—it's like the Buddha catching a glimpse through the palace wall. Over time— say five or ten years—the glimpses add up to a fairly detailed picture of life outside the palace.

If enough people saw the light and undertook spontaneous acts at once, the Situationists believed, the result would be a kind of mass awakening that would suddenly devalue the currency of the spectacle. "The détournement of the right sign, in the right place at the right time, could spark a mass reversal of perspective," Marcus said. Suddenly, the spectacle would be exposed in all its emptiness. Everyone would see through it.

This is how the spell is broken. This is how the revolution begins: a few people start slipping out of old patterns, daydreaming, questioning, rebelling. What happens naturally then, the Situationists believed, is a groundswell of support for this new way of being, with more and more people empowered to perform new gestures "unencumbered by history." The new generation, Guy Debord believed, "would leave nothing to chance."

These words still haunt us. The society of spectacle the Situationists rallied against has triumphed. The American dream has devolved into exactly the kind of vacant obliviousness they talked about—a have-a-nice-day kind of happiness that close examination tends to disturb. If you keep up appearances, keep yourself diverted with new acquisitions and constant entertainments, keep yourself pharmacologized and recoil the moment you feel real life seeping in between the cracks, you'll be all right.

Some dream.

If the old American dream was about prosperity, maybe the new one will be about spontaneity.

The Situationists maintained that ordinary people have all the tools they need for revolution. The only thing missing is a perceptual shift—a tantalizing glimpse of a new way of being—that suddenly brings everything into focus.

DEMARKETING LOOPS

Midtown Manhattan, 1999: In the boardroom of a famous lifestyle magazine, a young editor leans forward, removes his Gaulthier glasses and broaches a Big Idea.

"Two words: 'Demarketing Chic.' "

By the expressions of his colleagues, he can tell he's halfway there. They like it. They may love it.

"Here's the deal," he explains. "The world has gotten just unbelievably commercial, right? And people are starting to go a little crazy from it. They've completely bought into it, and it's been a hell of a ride, but now they're reaching a saturation point. They think maybe they're getting to the end of this business of glitz and hype and Ya Gotta Have It. So we say, in effect, Yeah. Your instincts are right. For the first time in forever, marketing isn't cool. Excess isn't cool."

He takes a slug of Pellegrino and continues.

"We do a trend piece—not a think piece but more of a package. Four or five spreads. Maybe we devote a whole issue to it. We really sell the idea hard."

"And we do that by . . ."

"By rounding up the least commercial people you can think of. People who stand in opposition to the whole idea of conspicuous consumerism. Anti-consumers. Icons of simplicity. We build the package around these people. We turn them into stars."

"Right . . ."

"So, for example, the Quaker on the side of the oatmeal box. We find the actual Quaker who posed for that picture and we do a Q-and-A thing."

"The actual Quaker?"

"Well, some actor who we say is the actual Quaker."

"Okay, good. Who else?"

"Sister Wendy."

"The art-critic nun?"

"Yeah. Very, very cool, in her way. We get her to hang out with Cy Twombly and Julian Schnabel. Just shoot the breeze with these guys. At Schnabel's place, by the pool."

"More."

"The Dalai Lama—a very funny guy, apparently—headlining on amateur night at The Comedy Store in L.A."

"More."

"Mother Teresa."

"Too late. More."

" 'Those Crafty Amish' " on The Learning Channel.

"More."

"Ralph Nader in a Martha Stewart–style shoot at Walden Pond, in front of Thoreau's cabin."

"Can we find Thoreau's old cabin?"

"Doesn't matter. We'll build another. No one will know."

Demarketing. The whole concept lends itself to satire, possibly because it seems so foreign to most of us. The world has a sinister ring to it. Whatever else demarketing is, it's certainly un-American.

Advertising and marketing are so deeply embedded in our culture now that it's hard to imagine a time when product placement and network logo "burns" and "bugs" weren't everywhere you looked, when our lifestyles and culture weren't predicated on consumption. But that pre-marketing era was not so long ago: only two generations. Demarketing is about restoring a little of the sanity we enjoyed back then. It's about uncooling our consumer culture, reclaiming the real, recovering some of what has been lost since consumerism became the First World's new religion.

The other day, in a moment of guy-to-guy candor, a friend challenged me on my demarketing philosophy and my whole outlook on life. "Kalle," he said, "you complain about advertising, you complain about the big, bad media, you bitch about how much we consume and how we govern ourselves and how corporations are ruining America. You say you want a radically different way of life—a revolution. But would you really want to live in the kind of world you're proposing?"

I asked him to be more specific.

"Isn't the live-fast, die-hard lifestyle you can't stand the very thing that makes it so much fun to be American? Living large is our inheritance. It's what we fought for and won. We have the highest standard of living in the world because we earned it. We did it by taking risks and being inventive and working our butts off. So now maybe I want to drive fast, and rattle the windows with my music, and have sex with my wife in our backyard swimming pool, and watch *Monday Night Football* while burgers grill on the barbecue. And I want to be able to do these things without having to listen to your sanctimonious objections."

My friend had just returned from New York, which he sees as an exciting microcosm of America. "Sure it has problems. It's big, it's loud, it's congested, you can step on a dirty needle in Central Park and the cab driver may be too scared to take you to Harlem. But I'll bet if you asked most New Yorkers they'd tell you they wouldn't want to live anywhere else. If you sanitized New York, it wouldn't be New York. It'd be Baltimore. And if you sanitized America, it wouldn't be America. It'd be Sweden or Canada. Life wouldn't be worth living."

"You don't get it at all," I told him. "I'm not trying to sanitize America. The world I'm proposing isn't some watered-down, politically correct place. It's wilder and more interesting than your world in every way. It's open TV airwaves where meme wars, not ratings wars, are fought every day. It's radical democracy—people telling governments and corporations what to do instead of the other way around. It's empowered citizens deciding for themselves what's 'cool'—not a society of consumer drones suckling at the corporate teat. It's living a life that's connected to the planet, knowing something about it, caring for it and handing it down to our children in some kind of decent shape.

"What I'm saying is that the American dream isn't working anymore, so let's face that reality and start building a new one."

I noticed my friend roll his eyes a couple of times as I spoke. In many ways he is the typical North American—ambitious, competitive, successful. If he could convince me that he really is happy and alive, I'd have to concede that his way, though it's not my way, is perfectly valid. But I just don't see it. The supersized American lifestyle generates at least a little guilt in every marginally thoughtful person who pursues it. There's a lot of dirty laundry in my friend's life that he can't ignore, no matter how far under the bed he shoves it. He sees me as a disgruntled lefty pissing on the American parade; I see him as a man in upper-income-bracket denial, getting what he can while the going is good even as his world is collapsing around him. Of one thing I am sure: his hyperconsumptive lifestyle just isn't cool anymore. The old American dream is dying. Change is coming.

One of the great secrets of demarketing the American dream is *détourning* it, in the public imagination, with a dream that's even more seductive. What's better than being rich? *Being spontaneous, authentic, alive.*

The new American dream is simply to approach life full-on, without undue fear or crippling self-censorship, pursuing joy and novelty as if tomorrow you'll be in the ground. The Situationists called this impulse "the will to playful creation," and they believed it should be extended "to all known forms of human relationships." There's no one more alive than the person who is openly, freely improvising—which is why the best stand-up comics love hecklers, and why the best hosts love wild-card dinner guests, and why the most electric political figures love deviating from their prepared scripts on live TV. There's no other way to discover what's at your core. This is what the new American dream is all about, and this is the kind of person the culture jammer aspires to be: someone who, to paraphrase Ray Bradbury, "jumps off cliffs and builds his wings on the way down."

UNCOOLING CONSUMPTION

On the most basic level, demarketing is simply about not buying. An anti-consumerist lifestyle flat-out repudiates the whole idea of marketing. When you don't buy, you don't buy in to consumer culture. When you don't buy in, corporations lose their hold on you.

One increasingly visible group of people has embraced this idea as a faith. They have looked hard at the way we do things in this country and decided it's no longer their way. Somewhere between the time Faith Popcorn coined the term "cashing out" and the time actor Sherry Stringfield walked away from the TV show *ER* (to rediscover the true meaning of life, a.k.a. leisure time and her partner), the downshifting movement took off. Thousands of Americans now call their lifestyle one of "voluntary simplicity" (after Duane Elgin's 1981 book of the same name). Some of these downshifters left high-powered jobs and took drastic pay cuts in order to make more time for family, friends, community, meaningful work. Others were wage slaves who simply decided to improve what Vicki Robin and Joe Dominguez (*Your Money or Your Life*) call their "joy-to-stuff ratio." Away with frantic living, they have declared. Away with the acquisitive, secular culture that causes even the most sensible souls to drift out of plumb. Too much work, too much clutter, too much distance between expectation and outcome, between investment and payoff, between head and heart, will spell the end of us. The downshifters concluded that a higher goal than to amass wealth is to concentrate on culture as Alexander Solzhenitsyn defined it: "the development, enrichment and improvement of non-material life." They understand intuitively what statistics bear out: that the aggregate level of American life fulfillment peaked in 1957, and with a couple of brief exceptions, it's been downhill from there.

We hear many dramatic downshifting stories: the eight-figure bond trader who, while getting his shoes shined, picks up a copy of *The Tightwad Gazette* or *Living Green* ("Live simply, that all may simply live"), has an epiphany, bails out of the modern contest and flees to the country to farm hogs or write murder mysteries. But this kind of downshifter is hardly the norm.

Many downshifters had no choice in the matter; they were canned, and that proved to be the best thing that ever happened to them. Alice Kline, whom Juliet Schor describes in *The Overspent American,* was a merchandising director for a high-fashion company. When she was wooed to return to lucrative full-time work after being laid off, Kline insisted on her own terms: chiefly, a four-day work week. Priceless to her was the freedom to pad around dreamily in her slippers on Friday mornings. Downshifters like Kline cling to the promise of three things: more time, less stress, and more balance. It's a fairly un-capitalistic brew, and to my knowledge only one advertiser has ever tried to sell it. In a network TV ad for the Mormon church some years ago, a little boy walks tentatively in to a board-meeting-in-progress, a tableful of men in suits. He shuffles over to the fellow at the end of the table, peers up and says, "Dad, is time really worth money?" The room falls silent. The boy has his father's attention. "Why yes, Jimmy, it is." Whereupon the kid plunks his piggy bank down on the table. "Well, I'd like to play ball after dinner."

Culture jammers are different from all of the downshifters thus far described. They aren't just trying to get themselves off the consumer treadmill and make more time for their kids. They dissent because they have a strong gut feeling that our culture has gone scandalously wrong and they just can't participate in it anymore. The old American dream of endless acquisition sickens them; it enervates them. For jammers, downshifting is not simply a way of adjusting our routines; it's adopting a lifestyle of defiance against a culture run amok, a revolutionary step toward a fundamental transformation of the American way of life.

In *Small Is Beautiful,* a key book in the downshifting canon, E. F. Schumacher sets up an exquisitely sensible template for living. The point of life, he says, is "to obtain the maximum of well-being with the minimum of consumption." This idea is so profoundly simple that it may well become the credo—the cool—of the 21st century. It applies in all areas of culture, from food to cars to fashion. "It would be the height of folly . . . to go in for complicated tailoring when a much more beautiful effect can be achieved by the skillful draping of uncut material," Schumacher writes. By this reasoning, it's cooler to ride a bike than cruise around in an air-conditioned BMW. Or to wear a plain white T-shirt than, say, a $125 Ashcroft Freddy Couples golf shirt. It's true, of course. And the truly cool have always known it.

UNCOOLING FAST FOOD

Buying and eating food is, like any act of consumption, political and even moral. "Every decision we make about food is a vote for the kind of world we want to live in," wrote Frances Lappe in his classic little book, *Diet for a Small Planet.* Every purchase of a can of Coke or a trucked-in Chilean nectarine initiates a multinational chain of responses that we simply can't afford to ignore.

Even when we don't ignore it—when we exercise some discretion, watching what we eat when we can, paying attention to whether we're buying Maxwell House coffee (a Philip Morris brand) or Nescafe or whole coffee beans from Sumatra—we can still be duped at the supermarket level. That's because we have allowed our eating habits to be shaped by transnational agribusiness. In the heavily concentrated food industry, the likes of Archer Daniels Midland ("supermarket to the world"), Cargill (the world's largest agribusiness) and Philip Morris (one of the world's largest food corporations)—are framing our choices.

Food corporations are formidable opponents because so much of what they do is invisible. One of the things they do is cut us off from the source of our food—a concept known as "distancing."

Distancing is a nasty bit of business, but it shouldn't surprise us. As Brewster Kneen, author of *Invisible Giant* puts it, we are "distanced" from our mother's breast the moment a baby bottle is inserted into our mouth. "From that moment on, corporate America gets involved, hawking processed 'junior' foods and baby foods that contain lots of salt, sugar and chemicals. Thus we become eager consumers of Kentucky Fried Chicken, Doritos, Pizza Hut and Pepsi (all the same company) later in life." Eventually, we find ourselves participating in the ultimate act of distancing: eating a genetically altered tomato whose mother plant does not even exist.

The average pound of food in America travels 1,300 miles before it reaches a kitchen table. That's inefficient and unsustainable. Demarketing food involves closing the gap between the source and the plate. It means turning away from fast foods and superstores and embracing farmers' markets and the family kitchen; away from hothouse tomatoes and toward your own local supplier, and, eventually perhaps, your own garden plot. These decisions will change your life, if you have the appetite for the journey.

The commitment involves cutting, bit by bit, the food megacorporations out of your life. This is not so different from weaning yourself off a destructive yet magnetic relationship with another human being. Every time you change your mind and don't slip into McDonald's for a quickie, every time you squirt some lemon into a glass of water instead of popping open a Coke, every time you decide to put that jar of Maxwell House coffee back on the shelf, you strike the gong of freedom.

When a groundswell of people train themselves to do all of these things, to demarket on a daily, personal level, we are applying the bottom jaw of the Strategic Pincer. The top jaw of the pincer is a series of radio and TV campaigns that ridicule the fast/junk food industry. Working from both ends—bottom up and the top down—the pincer will transform the way America, and the world, eats.

Junk food is one of the most frequently advertised products on TV; that makes it a big target. Today, food jammers take on the junk-food corporations the way anti-smoking activists locked horns with the tobacco industry in the '70s. They try to "contaminate" junk food in the public mind. Every time an anti-junk-food ad ("Fact: Over 50 percent of the calories in this Big Mac come from fat") airs, a replicating meme is planted. Every time an uncommercial appears on TV attacking those companies, their brands are a little bit uncooled.

Suppose one day a car full of teenage kids drives by the Golden Arches and everyone wants to stop for a bite. But one kid, inspired by a TV subvert he saw late last night, makes a crack about the McDonald's employee standing over the 900-degree french-fry boiler, wearing the funny hat, making minimum wage and saying, "Somebody remind me again why I'm not selling drugs?" His friends chuckle. And maybe they all still stop at McDonald's for that meal. But now they're thinking about McDonald's in a new way. The oppositional meme has been planted.

In the nutrition wars, change is afoot. People are rethinking their food and where it comes from. The idea that each of us should "have" a personal farmer, the way we now have a doctor, lawyer or dentist—a single individual we can trust to supply us with healthy, safe, flavorful produce—is catching on. So are farmers' markets where regional producers (and only regional producers) are invited to sell their fare. So are community "box schemes" where hampers of fresh fruit and vegetables—whatever's in season—are delivered direct from local farms to consumers' doors. Out with the *Wonder Bread* from megamarkets, in with community-supported agriculture, say the new food seers. Down with policies that encourage industrial, irradiated, bio-engineered food production to the detriment of everybody but agribusiness. Up with flavor! Up with nutrition! Up with local control!

UNCOOLING CALVIN

When fashion and cosmetics advertisers market our very physiognomy as a renewable, reinventable commodity, we are dehumanized. We are used up and discarded. In the semiotics of advertising, we are "cut." The young woman made to feel insecure about her sexuality stops behaving authentically. She either comes on like a virago, or, conversely, starts staying home Friday nights to compose sad poetry from her black heart. Likewise, a young man made to feel insecure about his sexuality, either withdraws, or grows angry and aggressive and starts taking what he wants.

As no other company in the last 15 years, Calvin Klein has modified sex, and in the process brutalized our notions of sexuality and self-worth. The man at the head of cK is a pioneer. He's credited with creating the ad strategy of moving fashion ads from magazines to outdoor billboards and bus cards, and of trumpeting the era of the commercial nude.

Most people remember his 1995 campaign in which young models were crudely filmed in cheesy wood-paneled basements as an adult voice called instructions from the wings. The ads reeked of chicken-hawk porn. *Advertising Age*'s Bob Garfield called it "the most profoundly disturbing campaign in TV history." The spots so offended public sensibility that they prompted an investigation by the U.S. justice department to see if the models were underage or child-porn laws were violated.

When I saw those ads I felt a kind of animal rage stirring inside me. This was an affront much worse than simple Skinner-box behaviorism. Calvin wasn't just trying to program young people's choice of jeans, he was down in the sub-basement of consciousness now, where the very rudiments of identity are formed.

I could imagine Mr. Klein wringing his hands with glee. Here he was exploiting one of our final taboos and milking the controversy that ensued for all it was worth. In marketing terms, he was in a win-win situation and the more controversy the better.

Imagine, for a moment, that the brand, cK, were the man, Calvin Klein. Would we feel any differently about the way he goes about his business? Calvin Klein is very interested in your teenage daughter. You see him flirting with her. He propositions her. He unzips her pants. He touches her. He sleeps with her. And later, he prostitutes her. He degrades her sexuality for his profit and then, when she has paid out—literally and figuratively—he dumps her.

If you discovered someone had done this to your daughter, you'd probably call up a couple of your big-armed friends and pay the sonofabitch a visit. Yet what's the difference, in the end, between Calvin's ads and imagery exploiting her and Calvin doing it himself? Psychically speaking, a hole is still a hole, whether it was made with an auger or a billion drops of water.

The first stage of demarketing our bodies involves realizing the true source of our self-esteem problems. It's important to understand that we ourselves are not to blame. Body-image distortions, eating disorders, dieting and exercise addictions—these are intensely personal issues, fought with therapy and lonely sessions of clandestine vomiting after dinner. They're our responsibility, *but they are not our fault:* The issue is primarily a cultural and a corporate one, and that's the level on which it must be tackled. We must learn to direct our anger, not inward at ourselves, but outward at the beauty industry.

Can the almighty fashion industry be uncooled? In some ways, its dependence on fads and trends makes it exceptionally vulnerable. Targetting one company, one man, is a good beginning. Cutting significantly into cK's sales will effectively launch the crusade to take back our bodies. Uncooling Calvin will send a shock wave through the whole industry; it will rattle the cosmetics companies, which now account for the largest individual product group (with the highest mark-ups) in most big department stores; and it will affect women's magazines, which have generated enormous profits by convincing women they are sexual machines. It will send a powerful message that the pageant is over, and that from now on beauty will no longer be defined by the likes of Mr. Klein—or any other Mr.

The jammer's best strategy is to plant anti-fashion memes on popular TV shows such as CNN's *Style With Elsa Klensch* and its Canadian knock-off, *Fashion File.* I sense fear in network executives' voices every time I try to buy airtime for our *Obsession Fetish* campaign on the big three networks or CNN. These executives practically do contortions trying to explain why they won't sell us the airtime; they know that Calvin Klein and indeed the whole fashion industry would significantly cut back on its TV advertising budgets as soon as our campaign started airing. The fashion industry is already held in disdain by many. The only thing that keeps their bubble aloft is their uncontested billion-dollar presence in women's magazines and on the airwaves. When we win the legal right to buy airtime and challenge them on TV, that bubble will burst. And then it will be Calvin's and the industries' turn to feel insecure.

UNCOOLING THE CAR

Jammers are now targeting automobiles as the next pariah industry. We want to sever the intimate connection between people and their cars, just as we cut the intimate connection between people and cigarettes. We want auto executives to feel just as squeezed and beleaguered as tobacco executives. We want them to have a hard time looking their kids in the eye and explaining exactly what they do for a living.

Resistance to private cars is already building. In San Francisco thousands of bicyclists roll out of the Embarcardaro district, snarling traffic; a few hold up a giant effigy of Willie Brown, the mayor who labeled cyclists "terrorists." In Portland, the city council experiments with an Amsterdam-style system of free commuter bicycles, which can be borrowed and returned at various points downtown. In Canada, jammers air anti-car ads, breaking the automobile industry's uncontested, uninterrupted 50-year run on TV.

Across the First World, pressure mounts for more bike lanes on urban streets. Several high-profile architects and planners weigh in with striking visions of the eco-friendly cities of the next era. Some big oil corporations, British Petroleum among them, finally accept some responsibility for global warming and pledge to sink money into R & D for cleaner petroleum products. Around the world, a half-dozen companies compete to produce commercially viable fuel cells that will power cars at highway speeds with fewer harmful byproducts. Seth Dunn of the Worldwatch Institute likens what's happening now to a full-circle return, one century later, to "engineless carriages."

But on a strategic level, much work remains undone.

More than any other product, the car stands as a symbol of the need for a true-cost marketplace, wherein the price you pay for a car reflects *all* the costs of production and operation. That doesn't just mean manufacturing cost plus markup, plus oil, gas and insurance. It means paying for the pollution, for building and maintaining the roads, for the medical costs of accidents and the noise and the aesthetic degradation caused by urban sprawl. It means paying for traffic policing and military protection of oil fields and supply lines.

The true cost of a car must also include the real but hard-to-estimate environmental cost to *future generations* of dealing with the oil and ozone depletion and climate change problems the car is creating today. If we added up the best available estimates, we'd come to a startling conclusion: the fossil-fuel-based automobile industry is being subsidized by unborn generations to the tune of hundreds of billions of dollars every year. Why should they have to pay to clean up our mess?

In the true-cost marketplace of the future, no one will prevent you from driving. You will simply have to pay the real cost of piloting your ton of metal, spewing a ton of carbon out of the tailpipe every year.

Your private automobile will cost you, by some estimates, around $100,000. And a tankful of gas, $250.

Moving over a ten-year period toward true-cost driving would force us to reinvent the way we get around. When the majority of people can no longer afford to drive, enormous public demand for monorails, bullet trains, subways and streetcars would emerge. Automakers would design eco-friendly alternatives: vehicles that recycle their own energy, human-and-fuel powered hybrids, lightweight solar vehicles. Citizens would demand more bike lanes, pedestrian paths and car-free downtowns. And a paradigm shift in urban planning would ensue.

Five or so years into the transition period, personal automobiles would become more trouble than they're worth. People would start enjoying their calmer lifestyles and the new psychogeography of their cities. The rich car owner who still cruises through town belching carbon would become the object of scorn and mockery.

In many ways the true-cost marketplace is the ultimate, all purpose demarketing device. Every purchase becomes a demarketing loop. Every transaction penalizes the "bad" products and rewards the "good." Jammers envision a global, true-cost marketplace in which the price of *every* product tells the ecological truth. The price of a pack of cigarettes would include the extra burden it places on the health care system; the price of an avocado would reflect the real cost of flying it over thousands of miles to your supermarket; the cost of nuclear energy (if indeed we can afford it) would include the estimated cost of storing the radioactive waste in the Earth's crust for up to tens of millions of years.

True-cost is a simple but potent way to redesign the global economy's basic incentives in a relatively uncharged political atmosphere. Conservatives like it because it's a logical extension of their free market philosophy. Progressives like it because it involves a radical restructuring of the status quo. Governments like it because it gives them a vital new function to fulfill: that of calculating the true-costs of products, levying eco-taxes and managing our bio-economic affairs for the long term. And environmentalists like it because it may be the only way to achieve sustainability in our lifetimes.

UNCOOLING THE SPECTACLE

Demarketing and the true-cost economy are the metamemes that bring the culture jammers' revolution together. It sounds ambitious, but the first steps are straightforward. A methodical, systematic social marketing campaign, we start at the personal level and grow in scope. We begin by demarketing our bodies, our minds, our children. Then we join with like-minded jammers to demarket whole systems. We go after our chief social and cultural rituals, now warped beyond recognition by commercial forces, and try to restore their original authenticity. Mother's

Day, Easter, Halloween, Thanksgiving, Christmas: all are ripe for de-marketing. All can be reclaimed.

Students insist on ad-free learning environments. Voters demand that election advertising be replaced with televised town-hall type meetings in which the candidates face the electorate directly. Sports players refuse to endorse unethical companies. Fans insist on naming stadiums after their heroes, not corporations. Reporters make sure that advertorials are not part of their job descriptions. Artists, writers and filmmakers work on product as well as social marketing campaigns. Families get food from their gardens, "therapy" from each other, from friends, neighbors and community.

We reverse the spin cycle. We demarket our news, our entertainments, our lifestyles and desires—and eventually, maybe even our dreams.

25
Angela McRobbie
"A NEW KIND OF RAG TRADE?"
(1997)

If we are to understand fashion as a vigorous cultural phenomenon, we must see it as a series of social processes involving mutual dependencies between each sector, from design and manufacture right through to magazines, advertising, and consumption. Likewise, if feminists want to escape the political paralysis that afflicts any vision of real change and improvement in the industry as a source of work and employment, we need an analysis which gathers together these constitutive parts and brings people involved at each stage into a dialogue. This has tended not to happen because it is assumed, especially among feminists, that there is an unbridgeable gap between, at one end of the spectrum, the women who make the clothes and, at the other end, those who eventually wear them. I will attempt here to describe those points at which political opportunities for dialogue and change do arise. This in turn should demonstrate why it is a mistake to view the fashion sector as the unmanageable thing it appears to be, discouraging close scrutiny of a fundamental area of human activity and employment.

Back in the 1970s, feminists drew attention to the exploitive conditions that prevailed in clothing manufacture and production on a global scale, and especially in the developing countries. Later, attention came to be focused on the realm of fashion representation, resulting in a barrage of assaults on fashion images of women in advertising and in magazines. Through the medium of clothes, it was argued, these images idealized forms of female beauty that are unattainable for most women and girls, giving rise to almost universal anxiety, self-hatred, and possibly eating disorders. This critique was then followed by a wholesale attack on consumer culture and the role fashion played in enslaving women to the imperative to buy. At this point in feminist thinking, fashion could only be seen as a bad thing. But then something happened, and by the mid-1980s fashion became, if not a good thing, at least not such a bad thing. What brought about this feminist revision?

By pushing to one side the difficult and seemingly unsolvable problems of sweatshop economies and child labor, feminist scholars began to reconsider those aspects of fashion that brought pleasure to women (and when they were able to admit it, to many of these feminists themselves). The guilt factor had hindered the feminist left, it was now suggested, by preventing an engagement with and understanding of the small, stubborn enjoyments of everyday life that are such a vital part of women's culture. Feminists ran the risk of political marginality and elitism by appearing to place themselves above ordinary women. It wasn't long before a flood of studies appeared which reclaimed commercial cultures of femininity as more open and disputatious than had previously been imagined. Fashion, romance, and even shopping could give rise to transgressive pleasures and defiant delights that were important to girls and women. There is a host of literature in this vein, including some of my own previous work on girls' and women's magazines.[1]

However, this reconceptualization of fashion often required silence on the question of the point of origin of clothes or the identity and working conditions of those who make them, since this would bring into view the suffering of "other" women. Alternately, knitting and home-dressmaking could be rediscovered as part of a tradition of female leisure culture (like quilting in the U.S.) as long as these activities were done for creative pleasure rather than for pay.[2] In fact, these remained part of the household economies in Britain until the late 1950s, and in some cases into the early '60s. If a mother couldn't knit or sew (and most women could do at least one of these), she would have to pay a local dressmaker or knitter, since ready-to-wear clothing and quality knitwear remained beyond the reach of most family budgets.

In effect, the emphasis on the social meaning of fashion in contemporary culture and in everyday life has often occurred at the expense of thinking seriously about the work that goes into making fashion consumption possible. But the analysis of consumption should not require neglect of the conditions of production. A new starting point for a feminist politics of fashion has to bridge this divide and encompass six major stages in the fashion cycle: manufacture and production; the practices of design; education and training; retailing and distribution; the magazine and image industry; and the practices of consumption. In the pages that follow, I will provide a brief account of the main dynamics of these sectors, drawing on some of the material from my own recent research on this subject. I will argue that fashion can be redefined as a feminist issue in a way that avoids both the deep pessimism of the approach to labor and production and the celebratory zeal of the more recent attention to women's pleasure in consumption. If the former envisages no light at the end of the tunnel, the latter runs the even greater risk of political complacency or indeed the flight from politics itself.

GARMENT MANUFACTURE AND PRODUCTION

There has been a good deal of interest in these areas within the socialist feminist tradition of scholarship in the U.K. Most recently, Sheila Rowbotham and Swasti Mitter have looked in depth at patterns of exploitation of women workers in the free trade zones and also at new forms of self-organization, while Jane Tate has developed further the extensive research on British women homeworkers. Annie Phizacklea's *Unpacking the Fashion Industry* offers the most useful account of recent developments in clothing production. In particular, she shows how new flexible units of production have sprung up in large cities, replacing the "sunset" factories of northern England which, for over a hundred years, produced textiles and clothing for both the home market and for export.[3] Some argue that if not for Marks and Spencers' commitment to use U.K. suppliers, most of these factories would have disappeared much sooner. However, Marks and Spencers has now joined the other large fashion chains, including C&A and the Hepworth Group (which together control an astounding 51 percent of the U.K. fashion and clothing market) in outsourcing up to 40 percent of their garments.

Phizacklea shows how, from the early 1980s, under the banner of Thatcher's new "enterprise culture," tiny units of production began to appear in London and the Midlands. Asian men, cashiered by the car factories and their subsidiaries, used their modest redundancy packages to establish themselves as small-scale garment entrepreneurs. This was possible because fashion remained a low-investment sector, requiring minimal space, a few sewing machines, an electronic cutter, and a press. Most important, these men had at their disposal a steady supply of cheap female labor within the immediate Asian community. Patriarchal family relations precluded work for these women outside the community, and financial need forced them to work long hours in tiny workshops or at home. Positioned on the wage floor of the labor market with all the forces of racial disadvantage weighing against them, these women continue to provide extraordinary cheap labor for the Cut, Make, and Trim chain of production.

In the U.K., then, it helps to see the "return of the sweatshop," ordinarily discussed as a *pure* result of globalization and/or import competition, in the context of Thatcher's own economic policies. Enterprise culture was as much a matter of avoiding unemployment and dependence on benefits as it was about setting up in business. And in the new business environment mandated by Thatcherism, there was no room for trade unionism, let alone any provision for sickness, holiday, or maternity pay. One of the results was the new flexible sweatshop—a potent example of the intensification of labor which has become almost the norm for those in employment in contemporary British society. For example, in my last home in North London, neighbors on either side participated in the Cut, Make, and Trim economy. On one side, an Asian grandmother worked as a child-minder during the day. All through the night we could hear the whirring of the sewing machine as she assembled fabric parts delivered by her sons and then returned to the wholesaler as finished goods the following morning. Likewise, on the other side, a Greek Cypriot woman received her garment pieces from a local Greek middleman, who would reappear the next day for the completed goods. Each of these women as a matter of course was expected to remain in or around the home rather than enter the world of "real work."

It is women like these who are now producing for the U.K. fashion industry. They manufacture for well-known fashion designers even though the doings and identities of each agent remains quite unknown to the other. The designers farm out their orders to wholesalers or merchandisers who place advertisements in local newsagents or in the trade press and who then subcontract out the various stages of the work through a long, anonymous chain of ethnic producers, each of whom takes a cut. For all the designers I interviewed (most of whom were themselves surviving on a shoestring budget), this was the only way to ensure that orders would be done in time, to cost, and to the standard required by the retailers or stockists. Having suppliers working locally rather than offshore also meant that mistakes could be rectified within the required time frame.

The privatized, nonunionized work carried out by these women, sometimes for less than £1 an hour, has made it difficult for feminists to see any way forward. Reformers and activists have suggested that the most feasible remedy is a revival of trade unionism on a global basis, focused on the self-organization of Third World women workers in the clothing industry and supported by First World consumers in the form of the boycott. But any such alliance has to be more inclusive. It is rarely suggested, for example, that other workers in the fashion sector be involved in these struggles, least of all designers, who are assumed to stand at the opposite end of the political spectrum, on the side of management. Nor is there any real attempt to engage with the politics of consumption outside the boycott (although in the last few months in the U.K. the charity Oxfam has launched a clothes code campaign, asking retailers to display a label indicating that basic human rights have not been violated in the production of their garments). But even the most successful boycott can quickly be forgotten when publicity wanes and when hard-pressed consumers return to the cheapest stores in disregard of their suppliers.

There is also an assumption that the women who make these clothes exist only as producers and never as consumers themselves. Some element of style and taste always enters into the small pleasures which the poorest garment workers also derive from items of consumption (TV sets, clothes, cosmetics, for example). If these are ignored, the effect is to "culturally deprive" these women and thus emphasize only their status as victims of capitalism, reducing every aspect of their lives to a matter of, as the title of Rowbotham and Mitter's book indicates, *Dignity and Daily Bread*. However, as Stuart Hall has argued, "everybody, including people in very poor societies whom we in the West frequently speak about as though they inhabit a world outside culture, knows that today's 'goods' double up as social signs and produce meanings as well as energy."[4]

I would like to suggest a less gloomy prognosis. In Britain at the present moment, it is not impossible to envisage higher degrees of self-organization and cooperation among low-paid clothing workers. This has already begun to happen with the appearance of homeworker associations. A New Labour government (committed also to introducing a minimum wage) could encourage local authorities to support such developments with fairly modest grants and funding. Skill levels and qualifications could also be improved by encouraging attendance at local community-based colleges, thus increasing the earning potential of these women. In the longer term, greater business confidence on the part of these women workers could lead to some elimination of the various middlemen who currently skim off most of the profits. This would bring ethnic women workers closer to the designers, who would also benefit from being able to see their work right through to the finished garments. It would give the designers better insight into a production process about which they remain surprisingly ignorant.

BRITISH FASHION DESIGNERS

The results of my recent study of art school–trained designers shows most of them setting up in business from within a culture of unemployment.[5] Every young designer I interviewed had been enrolled at some point in what was called the Enterprise Allowance Scheme (EAS). To be eligible, applicants technically had to be unemployed for at least three months. With £1,000 of capital (usually borrowed from relatives), they could receive payments of £40 or £50 a week, which could be retained alongside any profits made. The scheme was ended a couple of years ago, but during its existence provided the underpinning of the fashion design boom of the mid-1980s to early '90s. Despite all the publicity garnered by figures like Darlajane Gilroy, Pascal Smets, Pam Hogg, Sonnentag and Mulligan, Workers for Freedom, Pierce Fonda, and two sisters working under the English Eccentrics label, there have been many points in their career when they openly admit that they barely scraped a living. The cost of producing orders for well-known department stores in Britain and the U.S. while awaiting payment for sales from retailers has put too much stress on many of the small design companies. Cash-flow crises in what is a massively undercapitalized sector have made bankruptcies a very normal occurrence. For example, when I visited Sonnentag and Mulligan in 1993, I had high hopes they would survive. Their clothes were featured all across the fashion press, and the big clothing department stores on both sides of the Atlantic were placing regular orders. Even at this stage, however, they were living and working from the same studio space, employed only one machinist, were both on the EAS, and relied on a student intern to handle publicity. Despite their levelheaded approach and market savvy, they had to call in the receivers earlier this year.

What emerges as a career in fashion design is a mixed economy with designers surviving only if they free-lance for bigger, more commercial companies, while reserving time for their "own work" on a one/two-day a week basis. Sometimes they free-lance for up to three different companies, all the while harboring the dream of getting their own label off the ground. As one young woman put it:

> I was doing well and Madonna bought onxit, stitch for stitch, and then mass produce it. Bloomingdales didn't reorder, and with all the overhead, I went under. I was twenty-six, with over £20,000 of debts, so I gave up and went back on the dole.

In this context, it is not surprising that young designers are either silent or else embarrassed by discussions about how much they are able to pay their own in-house sample machinists, pattern cutters, etc.—never mind the women further down the chain who produce the orders. The designers I interviewed were, to some extent, willing victims of self-exploitation for the reason that they considered themselves artists first and entrepreneurs second. Even the most successful labels, like Ally Capellino, Helen Storey (which has since ceased trading), and Pam Hogg (likewise), on my estimate were working with an annual turnover in the range of £1 million to £2 million (figures that are borne out by the British Fashion Council survey of 150 companies in 1990). All fashion designers work a punitive round-the-clock schedule made more palatable by the knowledge that this is what creative people do.

While this might make it difficult to see designers lending support to machinists seeking union recognition and better working hours, it is not inconceivable that those who sketch might find they have quite a lot in common with those who sew. To do so, they would need to find a way of breaking down some of the social barriers that currently make it unlikely their paths ever cross. Nor should we assume that all fashion designers are the direct products of Thatcher's enterprise culture. Many have simply found ways of making enterprise fit with their artistic identities as creative designers. With so many of Britain's most successful designers coming from poor, working-class, or immigrant backgrounds, and with mothers who have worked in the rag trade, they are likely to be more than sympathetic to the idea of a better organized and better paid work force. My research certainly shows them to be angry and frustrated by Tory governments' refusal to take fashion design seriously as a matter for industrial policy. What is urgently needed is some strategic thinking about how these talented and highly trained young designers could, with small teams of well-paid and well-trained production workers, create an honest business culture that could survive in the face of global competition. This might well mean working periodically in partnership with the big fashion retailers who occupy such a powerful position in British fashion. But survival should not entail absorption by the big companies, a step that inevitably leads to the demise (or fatal compromise) of independent creative design.

EDUCATION AND TRAINING

Education and training should also play a role in this new survival strategy. British fashion education rightly has an international reputation for energetically encouraging young talent. It has expertise and knowledge in its academic staff, many of whom are prestigious figures on the international scene. Fashion academics also lobby hard on various official bodies. However, there are some points at which fashion education could play a more effective role in improving the performance of the design industry. At present, fashion design education is too committed to defending the fine art status of fashion to be interested in the messy business of manufacture and production. As a "feminine" field in the high-culture world of the art schools, and traditionally worried about being seen as merely teaching "dressmaking," educators in fashion have looked upwards to the fine arts for legitimacy and approval. The persona of the fashion designer is consequently modeled on that of the painter, sculptor, or auteur (noncommercial) filmmaker. The aura of creative genius provides a cultural framework for talking about, exhibiting, or "showing" the work.

While this attitude makes some sense both as a utopian strategy for personal reward in work and for psychological survival in a deindustrialized economy, it means that art students spurn and disavow the whole business of actually making clothes. Often it is a mark of professional pride not to know how to put in a zip. Fashion students never visit a factory throughout the course of their training. Perhaps it is convenient for them not to know about how orders are put into production and who makes them up, since this would raise unpleasant questions about pay and working conditions. As one fashion academic said to me, "It would take all the romance out of it." But ignorance of production can only be detrimental to this creative economy if the whole point of fashion design is to realize the original (or prototype) on a scale that reaches beyond the runway. Fashion educators would thus be doing their students a favor by overcoming the bias toward fine art and introducing core courses on fashion as a labor process. Apart from anything else, this would also make designers less vulnerable to exploitation by unscrupulous suppliers who ruthlessly overcharge on production costs while brutally underpaying their subcontracted labor force.

BRITISH FASHION RETAILING

There is no space here to enter into a full discussion of retailing save to explain that, despite the scale of this sector—estimated at £234 million in 1994, out of £7 billion for all clothing sales[6]—trade union representation has barely survived the Thatcher years. The Union of Shop Distributors and Allied Workers (USDAW) now reports an uphill struggle to hold on to a dwindling membership even in food retailing. There is no significant membership in fashion and clothing. What this means is that the early 1980s boom in retail culture (including new design-oriented chains like Next, the Gap, Jigsaw, Whistles, Hobbs, and in men's wear, Woodhouse and Paul Smith), complementing the ideologically driven consumer confidence championed by the Thatcher government, was entirely based on the employment of a nonunion work force. This is the reality that labor campaigners and policy makers now have to accept. One strategy is to work with more progressive retailers like Paul Smith to ensure better careers in fashion retail for the thousands of young people now employed in this sector, and at the same time to expose the atrocious working conditions that prevail in many other outlets in the hope that political attention and bad publicity might force employers to take action.

For example, in my conversations with a number of young women who had worked in these outlets, it became clear that in many down-market fashion shops in North and East London, owners paid their managers and assistants cash to avoid tax and insurance and on the "understanding" that staff could also claim unemployment benefits. Thus we see petty capital colluding to defraud the welfare state. By paying minimum wages of £3.50 an hour to single mothers as well as unqualified school-leavers, such employers oblige them to "fiddle" the social security. This raises a further political hot potato which no Labour or Tory politician can bear to confront, which is the pervasiveness of the hidden economy, itself the result of Britain's emergence as a low-pay and part-time workers economy. It seems quite absurd for New Labour to invest political energy in the aim of creating a "stakeholder society" based on the assumption that firms and companies will continue to employ hundreds of thousands of full-time workers. The reality could not be further from this vision. As even the biggest companies like British Telecom and the banks announce redundancies on a monthly basis, economic forecasts suggest that in the next ten years, by far the majority of British companies will be comprised of flexible units employing less than twelve people! Flexible here also means free-lance. In some respects, this puts the design industry at the forefront of the U.K.

economy. As an ideal type in the growing sector of cultural industries, there is more and more reason to take it seriously.

Of course, the scant prospect of a resurgence of trade unionism among shop workers does not mean that there are no possibilities for labor reform. I suspect this is more likely to happen if the work force who adorn the floor at Donna Karan can be brought into better contact with some newly constituted fashion industry forum or lobby group that would better represent the interests of shopfloor workers than other forms of labor organization. After all, they tend to see themselves as fashion people first and shop workers second. But what kind of job exactly is it to work for Paul Smith or for Whistles? Paul Smith is proud of his record of training up shop assistants to managerial positions in his now vast and highly successful company. But with a complete absence of research on this subject, it is impossible to say how the average shop assistant working in the local branch of Next or, for that matter, behind the counter at Calvin Klein, navigates a career in this field. What is clear is that part-time contracts are increasingly the norm and this in itself has consequences for sickness and maternity pay, pensions, and even holidays. Who knows what will happen when this currently youthful labor force needs maternity leave or days off to look after sick children. It may well be that workers in this sector will have recourse to the law to defend their rights rather than to the now largely defunct (and patriarchal) British trade union organizations.

THE FASHION MAGAZINES

Fashion magazines are astoundingly timid when it comes to any form of social criticism. As Roland Barthes pointed out many years ago, everything in their pages has to be therapeutic and reassuring so that nothing unpleasant intrudes on the wearing of fashionable clothes.[7] Nowadays, British fashion editors and their journalists play this card by professing "loyalty" to the U.K. fashion industry. They would not write about low pay and sweatshop conditions at home or abroad because their duty is to support the industry, an already fragile edifice as we have seen. But this could easily change with a few more adventurous editors or a little pressure from young journalists to run intelligent writing on the fashion industry, which would actually do justice to their increasingly well-educated and discerning female readership. In fact, such a strategy could push the magazines into a position of greater power and prominence. If they took the lead in cleaning up the fashion industry, they might be seen by policy makers and politicians as responsible players in this important field.

There is an additional incentive here. The women's magazine sector remains a low-status field of journalism. It is considered the trivial end of the commercial mass media and it is rare for a journalist (or indeed an editor) on a women's magazine to make the quantum leap into the national (even tabloid) press. Nor do the women who work on these magazines get many opportunities to move laterally into television except perhaps as a fashion commentator in a daytime magazine slot. The result is that there are limited jobs, and the great majority of these are free-lance. The turnover of writers is very high, since many become disillusioned and give up. These are sufficient reasons for the magazine industry to reconsider its role, function, and format. The current taste in fashion-oriented magazines like *Marie-Claire, Looks*, and *Company* for downmarket tabloid-style sleaze and sensationalism stands in contrast to their timidity when it comes to considering the option of speaking more intelligently to well-informed readers. The fear, of course, is that critical reportage on the fashion industry will lose advertising revenue (and top editorial jobs depend on keeping advertisers happy). But in an age when corporations are desperate to put an ethical gloss on their activities, these magazines should see the commercial incentive involved in supporting campaigns that would extend human rights to all garment workers. This dimension could also be understood as adding diversity to the rather formulaic menu of feminine commercial culture found in magazines rather than, as editors and journalists currently fear, putting themselves out of a job.

THE PRACTICES OF CONSUMPTION

The logic of conventional left and feminist thinking on issues of consumption is as follows. Having recognized how consumerism is the crucial means by which capitalism pulls us all into its unrelenting grip, we have to learn how to detach ourselves from its allure, break the spell of seduction, and become cautious, ethical, even parsimonious consumers. By the mid-1980s, this lofty, moralistic stance was coming under fire from feminists and those on what might be described as the cultural left. Suddenly, it was necessary to better understand our own and other people's participation in consumption and then to recognize the importance people attach to acts of consumption as markers or expressions of their own identity.

Now, in the mid-1990s, this endorsement of consumption (notably fashion consumption) by many feminists has gone too far. Celia Lury, Mica Nava, and others have suggested that consumption affords women a certain degree of power and authority to make choices.[8] But it is important to differentiate the power of boycott, for example, from the power or authority of the female consumer to treat the girl behind the counter as though she were a servant. The weakness of the new feminist consumer studies is that they tend to avoid questions about class relations in consumption. The general tendency is to narrowly focus on the activities of those who can afford to consume while neglecting to address the limits of consumption of those largely excluded from this realm. Lury and Nava each fail to recognize that for the vast majority of women, consumption, including fashion consumption, is an intensely frustrating economic activity.

The justification for this focus on what I would argue are affluent consumers is twofold. First, to counter the puritanism of the (now old) new left and feminist approaches, and second, to appear to be up-to-date in recognizing that with the decline in heavy industry, changes in class structure have produced a more aspiring, consumer-oriented working-class and lower-middle-class strata. Indeed, Lury seems to be suggesting that because production is now more or less out of sight, tucked away in the free trade zones, it is easier for consumers to participate unconstrained by a bad conscience or by the memory or direct experience of being a producer, since there is now a "relative independence of practices of consumption from those of production."[9]

It has to be acknowledged that most people, especially fashion-conscious youth, enjoy shopping for clothes and find it hard to reconcile their own pleasure in finding a bargain at Whistles or Agnes B with the political reality of the low wages and long hours involved in making these clothes. There is considerable psychological pressure to block out such thoughts; indeed, the pleasure of shopping depends on it. If this mindset is to change, then it cannot be left up to consumers alone. Garment companies would not be running scared of bad publicity if they did not take seriously the threat of consumer boycotts mobilized by exposés of superexploitation. But the rag trade has been associated with poverty wages for over a century, and this fact alone does not persuade people to make their clothing purchases with labor conditions in mind.

One of the problems of trying to develop a politics of consumption in relation to fashion is that so many people are involved at so many different locations that it is difficult to coordinate or think through such an analysis in an organized or manageable way. The only solution is to break down or disaggregate the practices of consumption to a more localized level, to contextualize particular forms of consumption in particular communities, cities, regions, or even neighborhoods. This then allows us at least to explore the social relations connecting producers with consumers. We can see signs of a closer dialogue between fashion producers and consumers where they each inhabit a shared cultural milieu, as they do for example in the club culture of Britain in the 1990s.

Currently, the latter is one of the few sectors of the small-scale design industry that is doing well. It comprises British designer/producers who share an involvement in the dance scene with their fellow dancers and with the musicians, DJs, producers, and promoters who in turn often put up the capital from club profits to set the designers up in business (usually with a store). The clothes are thus an integral part of the club circuit and can be bought from these new outlets or else from unit-type outlets across the country, including Hyper-Hyper, Covent Garden, and

Camden Market in London, and the Lace Market in Nottingham. Club designer labels like Sign of the Times, Sub Couture, and Wit and Wisdom all produce relatively cheap clothes for those young people for whom dancing has become a primary leisure activity. Sharing the same cultural values as the consumers gives the designer/producers (most of whom, with a couple of friends, design, sew, and sell themselves) a different kind of relationship with their market. Their services are more personal, and they function not unlike the corner store in the traditional working-class neighborhood, or indeed like the local dressmakers mentioned earlier. They survive by their ability to shape and anticipate what people want to be wearing inside and outside the clubs. Inevitably the big retail outlets pick up on these "innovators" and put copies of their styles into mass circulation, but that does not negate the cultural and economic significance of the original, nor can it replicate the active role of the original consumers who contribute directly to the vitality of the subculture. Where would punk have been if the customers hadn't come flooding into Westwood and Maclaren's Sex (then Seditionaries) shop on the Kings Road? This retail transaction was a crucial stage in the production of punk culture, just as the boutiques of Carnaby Street had been a crucible for pop in the 1960s.

What I have outlined above is an approach that insists on seeing fashion production and consumption in the economic context of leisure spaces. Club culture, in particular, has now become an important source of livelihood in what is arguably Britain's most profitable cultural sector. There is no doubt that some of the attraction of the club scene lies in its capacity to provide an economic as well as symbolic model for a more engaged sense of community than that offered by mainstream capitalist consumerism. But the dispersed, small-scale, survivalist economics of this model must be set alongside the dynamics of the global labor market and the toil it has exacted on the domestic work force. The situation of the garment industry in the U.K. raises the much larger question of the extension and penetration of low-wage economies in First World countries. In this respect, there is a smaller gap between the highly qualified designers and the low-skill producers than is commonly imagined. Neither group is well paid, and they survive on a casualized, free-lance, or semi-self-employed basis. Most are female, live in cities, find themselves disadvantaged in regard to health and welfare benefits, mortgage applications, maternity benefits, and even holiday pay. Although they are not well represented by the trade union, nor by any lobby or pressure group or trade organization, there is no good reason why designers and producers should not be allies in pursuit of common self-interest.

All it would take is a shared sense of frustration and the desire to utilize existing talents, skills, and expertise. It would be easy to establish some kind of fashion-forum pressure group with teeth (since such affinity groups remain one of the few real sources of political energy in Britain today). Government could then play its role. The Labour party would score points by supporting (even initiating) such a move, especially since most voters these days have a daughter, son, or relative who has some involvement in the vast culture industries. This would entail a commitment by Labour to find ways of helping fashion workers translate their skills and commitment as well as creative talent into a sustainable fashion design industry which can match international renown with living wages.

ENDNOTES

1. Angela McRobbie, *Feminism and Youth Culture: From Jackie to Just Seventeen* (London: Macmillan, 1991), and *Postmodernism and Popular Culture* (London: Routledge, 1994).

2. Rozsika Parker, *The Subversive Stitch: Embroidery and the Making of the Feminine* (London: Women's Press, 1984).

3. Sheila Rowbotham and Swasti Mitter, eds., *Dignity and Daily Bread: New Forms of Economic Organising among Poor Women in the Third World and the First* (London: Routledge, 1994); Jane Tate, "Homework in West Yorkshire," in ibid., Annie Phizacklea, *Unpacking the Fashion Industry: Gender, Racism, and Class in Production* (London: Routledge, 1990).

4. Stuart Hall, "The Meaning of New Times," in *New Times: The Changing Face of Politics in the 1990s,* ed. Stuart Hall and Martin Jacques (London: Lawrence & Wishart, 1989), p. 131.

5. Angela McRobbie, *Fashion and the Image Industries* (London: Routledge, 1997).

6. Government and Trade Association Statistics, KSA.

7. Roland Barthes, *The Fashion System* (New York: Hill and Wang, 1967).

8. Cella Lury, *Consumer Culture* (Oxford: Polity Press, 1996); Mica Nava, *Changing Cultures: Feminism, Youth, and Consumerism* (London: Sage, 1992).

9. Lury, *Consumer Culture,* p. 4.

26
Juliet B. Schor
"TOWARDS A NEW POLITICS
OF CONSUMPTION"
(1999)

In contemporary American culture, consuming is as authentic as it gets. Advertisements, getting a bargain, garage sales, and credit cards are firmly entrenched pillars of our way of life. We shop on our lunch hours, patronize outlet malls on vacation, and satisfy our latest desires with a late-night click of the mouse.

Yet for all its popularity, the shopping mania provokes considerable dis-ease: many Americans worry about our preoccupation with getting and spending. They fear we are losing touch with more worthwhile values and ways of living. But the discomfort rarely goes much further than that; it never coheres into a persuasive, well-articulated critique of consumerism. By contrast, in the 1960s and early '70s, a far-reaching critique of consumer culture was a part of our political discourse. Elements of the New Left, influenced by the Frankfurt School, as well as by John Kenneth Galbraith and others, put forward a scathing indictment. They argued that Americans had been manipulated into participating in a dumbed-down, artificial consumer culture, which yielded few true human satisfactions.

For reasons that are not hard to imagine, this particular approach was short-lived, even among critics of American society and culture. It seemed too patronizing to talk about manipulation or the "true needs" of average Americans. In its stead, critics adopted a more liberal point of view, and deferred to individuals on consumer issues. Social critics again emphasized the distribution of resources, with the more economistic goal of maximizing the incomes of working people. The good life, they suggested, could be achieved by attaining a comfortable, middle-class standard of living. This outlook was particularly prevalent in economics, where even radical economists have long believed that income is the key to well-being. While radical political economy, as it came to be called, retained a powerful critique of alienation in production and the distribution of property, it abandoned the nascent intellectual project of analyzing the consumer sphere. Few economists now think about how we consume, and whether it reproduces class inequality, alienation, or power. "Stuff" is the part of the equation that the system is thought to have gotten nearly right.

Of course, many Americans retained a critical stance toward consumer culture. They embody that stance in their daily lives—in the ways they live and raise their kids. But the rejection of consumerism, if you will, has taken place principally at an individual level. It is not associated with a widely accepted intellectual analysis, and a *accompanying critical politics of consumption.*

But such a politics has become an urgent need. The average American now finds it harder to achieve a satisfying standard of living than 25 years ago. Work requires longer hours, jobs are less secure, and pressures to spend more intense. Consumption-induced environmental damage remains pervasive, and we are in the midst of widespread failures of public provision. While the current economic boom has allayed consumers' fears for the moment, many Americans have long-term worries about their ability to meet basic needs, ensure a decent standard of living for their children, and keep up with an ever-escalating consumption norm.

In response to these developments, social critics continue to focus on income. In his impressive analysis of the problems of contemporary American capitalism, *Fat and Mean*, economist David Gordon emphasized income *adequacy.* The "vast majority of US households," he argues, "can barely make ends meet. . . . Meager livelihoods are a *typical* condition, an *average* circumstance." Meanwhile, the Economic Policy Institute emphasizes the distribution of income and wealth, arguing that the gains of the top 20 percent have jeopardized the well-being of the bottom 80 percent. Incomes have stagnated and the robust 3 percent growth rates of the 1950s and '60s are long gone. If we have a consumption problem, this view implicitly states, we can solve it by getting more income into more people's hands. The goals are redistribution and growth.

It is difficult to take exception to this view. It combines a deep respect for individual choice (the liberal part) with a commitment to justice and equality (the egalitarian part). I held it myself for many years. But I now believe that by failing to look deeper—to examine the very nature of consumption—it has become too limiting. In short, I do not think that the "income solution" addresses some of the most profound failures of the current consumption regime.

Why not? First, consuming is part of the problem. Income (the solution) leads to consumption practices that exacerbate and reproduce class and social inequalities, resulting in—and perhaps even worsening—an unequal distribution of income. Second, the system is structured such that an *adequate* income is an elusive goal. That is because adequacy is relative—defined by reference to the incomes of others. Without an anal-

ysis of consumer desire and need, and a different framework for understanding what is adequate, we are likely to find ourselves, twenty years
from now, arguing that a median income of $100,000—rather than half
that—is adequate. These arguments underscore the social context of
consumption: the ways in which our sense of social standing and belonging comes from what we consume. If true, they suggest that
attempts to achieve equality or adequacy of individual incomes without
changing consumption patterns will be self-defeating.

Finally, it is difficult to make an ethical argument that people in the
world's richest country need more, given that the global income gap is
so wide, the disparity in world resource use so enormous, and the possibility that we are already consuming beyond the earth's ecological
carrying capacity so likely. This third critique will get less attention in
this essay—because it is more familiar, not because it is less important—
but I will return to it in the conclusion.

I agree that justice requires a vastly more equal society, in terms of
income and wealth. The question is whether we should also aim for a
society in which our relationship to consuming changes, a society in
which we consume *differently*. I argue here for such a perspective: for
a critique of consumer culture and practices. We need voices for quality
of life, not just quantity of stuff. And to do so requires an approach
that does not trivialize consumption, but accords it the respect and centrality it deserves.

THE NEW CONSUMERISM

A new politics of consumption should begin with daily life, and recent
developments in the sphere of consumption. I describe these developments as "the new consumerism," by which I mean an upscaling of
lifestyle norms; the pervasiveness of conspicuous, status goods and of
competition for acquiring them; and the growing disconnect between
consumer desires and incomes.

Social comparison and its dynamic manifestation—the need to "keep
up"—have long been part of American culture. My term is "competitive
consumption," the idea that spending is in large part driven by a comparative or competitive process in which individuals try to keep up with
the norms of the social group with which they identify—a "reference
group." Although the term is new, the idea is not. Thorstein Veblen,
James Duesenberry, Fred Hirsch, and Robert Frank have all written
about the importance of relative position as a dominant spending motive. What's new is the definition of reference groups: today's comparisons are less likely to take place between or among households of
similar means. Instead, the lifestyles of the upper middle class and the
rich have become a more salient point of reference for people through-

out the income distribution. Luxury, rather than mere comfort, is a widespread aspiration.

One reason for the shift to "upscale emulation" is the decline of the neighborhood as a focus of comparison. Economically speaking, neighborhoods are relatively homogeneous groupings. In the 1950s and '60s, when Americans were keeping up with the Joneses down the street, they were comparing themselves to other households of similar incomes. Because of this focus on neighbors, the gap between aspirations and means tended to be moderate.

But as married women entered the workforce in large numbers—particularly in white collar jobs—they were exposed to a more economically diverse group of people, and became more likely to gaze upward. Neighborhood contacts correspondingly declined, and the workplace became a more prominent point of reference. Moreover, as people spent less time with neighbors and friends, and more time on the family room couch, television became more important as a source of consumer cues and information. Because television shows are so heavily skewed to the "lifestyles of the rich and and upper middle class," they inflate the viewer's perceptions of what others have, and by extension what is worth acquiring—what one must have in order to avoid being left behind.

Trends in inequality also helped to create the new consumerism. Since the 1970s, the distributions of income and wealth have shifted decisively in the direction of the top 20 percent. The share of after-tax family income going to the top 20 percent rose from 41.4 percent in 1979 to 46.8 percent in 1996. The share of wealth controlled by the top 20 percent rose from 81.3 percent in 1983 to 84.3 percent in 1997. This windfall resulted in a surge in conspicuous spending at the top. Remember the 1980s—the decade of greed and excess? Beginning with the super-rich, whose gains have been disproportionately higher, and trickling down to the merely affluent, visible status spending was the order of the day. Slowed down temporarily by the recession of the early 1990s, conspicuous luxury consumption has intensified during the current boom. Trophy homes, diamonds of a carat or more, granite countertops, and sport utility vehicles are the primary consumer symbols of the late-1990s. Television, as well as films, magazines, and newspapers ensure that the remaining 80 percent of the nation is aware of the status purchasing that has swept the upper echelons.

In the meantime, upscale emulation had become well-established. Researchers Susan Fournier and Michael Guiry found that 35 percent of their sample aspired to reach the top 6 percent of the income distribution, and another 49 percent aspired to the next 12 percent. Only 15 percent reported that they would be satisfied with "living a comfortable life"—that is, being middle class. But 85 percent of the population cannot earn the six-figure incomes necessary to support upper-middle-class lifestyles. The result is a growing aspirational gap: with desires persistently outrunning incomes, many consumers find themselves frustrated. One survey of US households found that the level of income needed to fulfill one's dreams doubled between 1986 and 1994, and is currently more than twice the median household income.

The rapid escalation of desire and need, relative to income, may also help to explain the precipitous decline in the savings rate—from roughly 8 percent in 1980, to 4 percent in the early 1990s, to the current level of zero. (The stock market boom may also be inducing households not to save; but financial assets are still highly concentrated, with half of all households at net worths of $10,000 or less, including the value of their homes.) About two-thirds of American households do not save in a typical year. Credit card debt has skyrocketed, with unpaid balances now averaging about $7,000 and the typical household paying $1,000 each year in interest and penalties. These are not just low-income households. Bankruptcy rates continue to set new records, rising from 200,000 a year in 1980 to 1.4 million in 1998.

The new consumerism, with its growing aspirational gap, has begun to jeopardize the quality of American life. Within the middle class—and even the upper middle class—many families experience an almost threatening pressure to keep up, both for themselves and their children. They are deeply concerned about the rigors of the global economy, and the need to have their children attend "good" schools. This means living in a community with relatively high housing costs. For some households this also means providing their children with advantages purchased on the private market (computers, lessons, extra-curriculars, private schooling). Keeping two adults in the labor market—as so many families do, to earn the incomes to stay middle class—is expensive, not only because of the second car, child-care costs, and career wardrobe. It also creates the need for time-saving, but costly, commodities and services, such as take-out food and dry cleaning, as well as stress-relieving experiences. Finally, the financial tightrope that so many households walk—high expenses, low savings—is a constant source of stress and worry. While precise estimates are difficult to come by, one can argue that somewhere between a quarter and half of all households live paycheck-to-paycheck.

These problems are magnified for low-income households. Their sources of income have become increasingly erratic and inadequate, on account of employment instability, the proliferation of part-time jobs, and restrictions on welfare payments. Yet most low-income households remain firmly integrated within consumerism. They are targets for credit card companies, who find them an easy mark. They watch more television, and are more exposed to its desire-creating properties. Low-income children are more likely to be exposed to commercials at school, as well as home. The growing prominence of the values of the market, materialism, and economic success make financial failure more consequential and painful.

These are the effects at the household level. The new consumerism has also set in motion another dynamic: it siphons off resources that could be used for alternatives to private consumption. Income is used in four basic ways: private consumption, public consumption, private savings, and leisure. When consumption standards can be met easily out of current income, there is greater willingness to support public goods, save privately, and cut back on time spent at work (in other words, to "buy leisure"). Conversely, when lifestyle norms are upscaled more rapidly than income, private consumption "crowds out" alternative uses of income. That is arguably what happened in the 1980s and 1990s: resources shifted into private consumption, and away from free time, the public sector, and saving. Hours of work have risen dramatically, saving rates have plummeted, public funds for education, recreation, and the arts have fallen in the wake of a grass-roots tax revolt. The timing suggests a strong coincidence between these developments and the intensification of competitive consumption—though I would have to do more systematic research before arguing causality. Indeed, this scenario makes good sense of an otherwise surprising finding: that indicators of "social health" or "genuine progress" (i.e., basic quality-of-life measures) began to diverge from GDP in the mid-1970s, after moving in tandem for decades. Can it be that consuming and prospering are no longer compatible states?

To be sure, other social critics have noted some of these trends. But they often draw radically different conclusions. For example, there is now a conservative jeremiad that points to the recent tremendous increases in consumption and concludes that Americans just don't realize how good they have it, that they have become overly entitled and spoiled. Reduced expectations, they say, will cure our discontents. A second, related perspective suggests that the solution lies in an act of psychological independence—individuals can just ignore the upward shift in consumption norms, remaining perfectly content to descend in the social hierarchy.

These perspectives miss the essence of consumption dynamics. Americans did not suddenly become greedy. The aspirational gap has been created by structural changes—such as the decline of community and social connection, the intensification of inequality, the growing role of mass media, and heightened penalties for failing in the labor market. Upscaling is mainly defensive, and has both psychological and practical dimensions.

Similarly, the profoundly social nature of consumption ensures that these issues cannot be resolved by pure acts of will. Our notions of what is adequate, necessary, or luxurious are shaped by the larger social context. Most of us are deeply tied into our particular class and other group identities, and our spending patterns help reproduce them.

Thus, a collective, not just an individual, response is necessary. Someone needs to address the larger question of the consumer culture itself. But doing so risks complaints about being intrusive, patronizing, or elitist. We need to understand better the ideas that fuel those complaints.

CONSUMER KNOWS BEST

The current consumer boom rests on growth in incomes, wealth, and credit. But it also rests on something more intangible: social attitudes toward consumer decision-making and choices. Ours is an ideology of non-interference—the view that one should be able to buy what one likes, where one likes, and as much as one likes, with nary a glance from the government, neighbors, ministers, or political parties. Consumption is perhaps the clearest example of an individual behavior which our society takes to be almost wholly personal, completely outside the purview of social concern and policy. The consumer is king. And queen.

This view has much to recommend it. After all, who would relish the idea of sumptuary legislation, rationing, or government controls on what can be produced or purchased? The liberal approach to consumption combines a deep respect for the consumer's ability to act in her own best interest and an emphasis on the efficiency gains of unregulated consumer markets: a commitment to liberty and the general welfare.

Cogent as it is, however, this view is vulnerable on a number of grounds. Structural biases and market failures in the operation of consumer markets undermine its general validity; consumer markets are neither so free nor so efficient as the conventional story suggests. The basis of a new consumer policy should be an understanding of the presence of structural distortions in consumers' choices, the importance of social inequalities and power in consumption practices, a more sophisticated understanding of consumer motivations, and serious analysis of the processes that form our preferences. To appreciate the force of these criticisms, we need a sharper statement of the position they reject.

THE CONVENTIONAL VIEW

The liberal view on markets for consumer goods has adherents in many disciplines, but its core analytic argument comes from standard economic theory, which begins from some well-known assumptions about consumers and the markets in which they operate.

1. *Consumers are rational.* They act to maximize their own well-being. They know what they prefer, and make decisions accordingly. Their "preferences" are taken as given, as relatively unchanging, and as un-

problematic in a normative sense. They do not act capriciously, impulsively, or self-destructively.

2. *Consumers are well-informed.* They have perfect information about the products offered in the market. They know about all relevant (to the consumer) characteristics pertaining to the production and use of the product.

3. *Consumer preferences are consistent (both at a point in time and over time).* Consistency at a point in time means transitivity: If A is preferred to B and B to C then A will be preferred to C. (In other words, if roast beef is preferred to hamburgers and hamburgers to hot-dogs, then roast beef is preferred to hot dogs.) Consistency over time can be thought of as a "no regrets" assumption. If the consumer is faced with a choice of a product that yields satisfaction in the present, but has adverse consequences in the future—eat chocolate today and feel great, but gain five unwanted pounds by next week—and the consumer chooses that product today, he or she will not regret the choice when the future arrives. (This does not mean the extra pounds are welcomed, only that the pleasure of the chocolate continues to outweigh the pain of the pounds.)

4. *Each consumer's preferences are independent of other consumers' preferences.* We are self-contained in a social sense. If I want a sport utility vehicle, it is because I like them, not because my neighbor does. The trendiness of a product does not affect my desire to have it, either positively or negatively.

5. *The production and consumption of goods have no "external" effects.* There are no consequences for the welfare of others that are unreflected in product prices. (A well-known example of external effects is pollution, which imposes costs on others that are not reflected in the price of the good that produces the pollution.)

6. *There are complete and competitive markets in alternatives to consumption.* Alternatives to consumption include savings, public goods, and the "purchase" of leisure. Unless these alternatives are available, the choice of consumption—over other uses of economic resources—may not be optimal.

Taken together, and combined with conditions of free entry and exit of firms providing consumer goods, these assumptions imply that no consumer policy is the best consumer policy. Individual consumers know best and will act in their own interest. Firms will provide what the consumers want; those that don't will not survive a competitive marketplace. Competition and rationality together ensure that consumers will be sovereign—that is, that their interests will "rule." And the results will be better than any we could achieve through government regulation or political action.

To be sure, conventional theory and policy have always admitted some deviations from these highly idealized conditions. In some areas interventionist policy has been long-standing. First, some consumers are not considered to be fully rational—for example, children or, in an earlier era, women. Because children are not thought to be capable of acting in their own interest, the state justifies protective policies, such as restricting advertising aimed at them. Second, the state has traditionally regulated highly addictive or harmful commodities, such as drugs, alcohol, and explosives. (As the debates surrounding the legalization of drugs make clear, the analytical basis for this policy is by no means universally accepted.) A third class of highly regulated commodities involve sex: pornography, contraceptives, sexual paraphernalia, and so forth. Here the rationale is more puritanical. American society has always been uncomfortable about sex and willing to override its bias against consumer regulation because of that. Finally, the government has for much of this century—though less forcefully since the Reagan administration—attempted to ensure minimum standards of product safety and quality.

These exceptions aside, the standard model holds strongly to the idea that unfettered markets yield optimal outcomes, a conclusion that follows logically and inexorably from the initial assumptions. Obviously, the assumptions of the standard model are extreme, and the real world deviates from them. On that everyone agrees. The question is by how much, how often, and under what conditions? Is the world sufficiently different from this model that its conclusions are misguided?

Serious empirical investigations suggest that these assumptions do not adequately describe a wide range of consumer behaviors. The simple rational-economic model is reasonable for predicting some fraction of choice behavior for some class of goods—apples versus oranges, milk versus orange juice—but it is inadequate when we are led to more consequential issues: consumption versus leisure, products with high symbolic content, fashion, consumer credit, and so on. In particular, it exaggerates how rational, informed, and consistent people are. It overstates their independence. And it fails to address the pressures that consumerism imposes on individuals with respect to available choices and the consequences of various consumption decisions. Understand those pressures, and you may well arrive at very different conclusions about politics and policy.

RATIONAL, DELIBERATIVE, AND IN CONTROL?

The economic model presents the typical consumer as deliberative and highly forward-looking, not subject to impulsive behavior. Shopping is seen as an information-gathering exercise in which the buyer looks for the best possible deal for product she has decided to purchase. Consumption choices represent optimizing within an environment of deliberation, control, and long-term planning.

Were such a picture accurate it would be news (and news of a very bad sort) to a whole industry of advertisers, marketers, and consultants whose research on consumer behavior tells a very different story. Indeed, their findings are difficult to reconcile with the picture of the consumer as highly deliberative and purposive.

Consider some of the stylized facts of modern marketing, for example, the "law of the invariant right": shoppers overwhelmingly turn right, rather than left, upon entering a store. This is only consistent with the rational search model if products are disproportionately to be found on the right side of the aisle. Or consider the fact that products placed in the so-called "decompression zone" at the entrance to a store are 30 percent less likely to be purchased than those placed beyond it. Or that the number of feet into a store the customer walks is correlated with the number of items purchased. It's far harder to square these findings with "rational" behavior than with an unplanned and contingent action. Finally, the standard model has a very hard time explaining the fact that if, while shopping, a woman is accidentally brushed from behind, her propensity to purchase falls precipitously.

Credit cards present another set of anomalies for the reigning assumptions. Surveys suggest that most people who acquire credit cards say that they do not intend to borrow on them; yet roughly two-thirds do. The use of credit cards leads to higher expenditures. Psychological research suggests that even the visual cue of a credit card logo spurs spending. Survey data shows that many people are in denial about the level of credit card debt that they hold, on average underestimating by a factor of two. And the explosion of personal bankruptcies, now running at roughly 1.4 million a year, can be taken as evidence of a lack of foresight, planning, and control for at least some consumers.

More generally, credit card habits are one example of what economists call "hyperbolic discounting," that is, an extreme tendency to discount the future. Such a perspective calls into question the idea of time consistency—the ability of individuals to plan spending optimally throughout their lifetimes, to save enough for the future, or to delay gratification. If people are constitutionally inclined to be hyperbolic discounters, as some are now arguing, then forced-saving programs such as Social Security and government-sponsored retirement accounts, restriction on access to credit, waiting periods for major purchases, and a variety of other approaches might improve well-being. Compulsive buying, as well as the milder and far more pervasive control problems that many consumers manifest, can also be incorporated into this framework.

The model of deliberative and informed rationality is also ill-adapted to account for the phenomenon of brand-preference, perhaps the backbone of the modern consumer market. As any beginning student of advertising knows, much of what advertising does is take functionally identical or similar goods and differentiate them on the basis of a variety of non-operational traits. The consumer is urged to buy Pepsi because it represents the future, or Reebok shoes because the company stands for strong women. The consumer develops a brand preference, and believes that his brand is superior in quality. The difficulty for the standard model arises because, absent the labels, consumers are often unable to distinguish among brands, or fail to choose their favorites. From the famous beer taste test of the 1960s (brand loyalists misidentified their beers), to cosmetics, garments, and other tests of more recent vintage, it seems that we love our brands, but we often can't tell which brands are which.

What can we conclude from consumers' inability to tell one washing powder, lipstick, sweater, or toothpaste from another? Not necessarily that they are foolishly paying a brand premium for goods. (Although there are some consumers who do fall into this category—they wouldn't pay the brand premium, as distinct from a true quality premium, if they knew it existed.) What is more generally true, I believe, is that many consumers do not understand why they prefer one brand over another, or desire particular products. This is because there is a significant dimension of consumer desire which operates at the non-rational level. Consumers *believe* their brand loyalties are driven by functional dimensions, but a whole host of other motivators are at work—for example, social meanings as constructed by advertisers; personal fantasies projected onto goods; competitive pressures. While this behavior is not properly termed "irrational," neither is it conscious, deliberative, and narrowly purposive. Consumers are not deluded, duped, or completely manipulated. But neither do they act like profit-maximizing entrepreneurs or scientific management experts. The realm of consumption, as a rich historical literature has taught us, has long been a "dream world," where fantasy, play, inner desire, escape, and emotion loom large. This is a significant part of what draws us to it.

CONSUMPTION IS SOCIAL

Within economics, the major alternative to the assumption that individuals' preferences are independent—that people do not want things because others want them—is the "relative" income, positional, or competitive consumption perspective noted above. In this model, a person's well-being depends on his or her relative consumption—how it compares to some selected group of others. Such positioning is one of the hallmarks of the new consumerism.

Of course, social comparison predates the 1980s. In 1984, French sociologist Pierre Bourdieu explored the social patterning of consumption and taste in *Distinction: A Social Critique of the Judgement of Taste*. Bourdieu found that family socialization processes and educational experiences are the primary determinants of taste for a wide range of cultural goods, including food, dress, and home decor. In contrast to the liberal approach, in which consumption choices are both personal and trivialized—that is, socially inconsequential—Bourdieu argues that class status is gained, lost, and reproduced in part through everyday acts of consumer behavior. Being dressed incorrectly or displaying "vulgar" manners can cost a person a management or professional job. Conversely, one can gain entry into social circles, or build lucrative business contacts, by revealing appropriate tastes, manners, and culture. Thus, consumption practices become important in maintaining the basic structures of power and inequality which characterize our world. Such a perspective helps to illuminate why we invest so much meaning in consumer goods—for the middle class its very existence is at stake. And it suggests that people who care about inequality should talk explicitly about the stratification of consumption practices.

If we accept that what we buy is deeply implicated in the structures of social inequality, then the idea that unregulated consumption promotes the general welfare collapses. When people care only about relative position, then general increases in income and consumption do not yield gains in well-being. If my ultimate consumer goal is to maintain parity with my sister, or my neighbor, or Frasier, and our consumption moves in tandem, my well-being is not improved. I am on a "positional treadmill." Indeed, because consuming has costs (in terms of time, effort, and natural resources), positional treadmills can have serious negative effects on well-being. The "working harder to stay in place" mantra of the early 1990s expresses some of this sentiment. In a pure reversal of the standard prescription, collective interventions which stabilize norms, through government policy or other mechanisms, *raise* rather than lower welfare. People should welcome initiatives that reduce the pressure to keep up with a rising standard.

FREE AND STRUCTURALLY UNBIASED?

The dynamic of positionally driven spending suggests that Americans are "overconsuming" at least those private goods that figure in our consumption comparisons. There is another reason we may be overconsuming, which has to do with the problems in markets for alternatives to status or positional goods. In particular, I am referring to non-positional private consumption, household savings, public goods, and leisure. Generally speaking, if the markets for these alternatives are incomplete, non-competitive, or do not fully account for social benefits and costs, then overconsumption with respect to *private consumption* may result. I do not believe this is the case with household savings:

financial markets are highly competitive and offer households a wide range of ways to save. (The deceptive and aggressive tactics of consumer credit companies might be reckoned a distortion in this market, but I'll leave that aside.) Similarly, I do not argue that the markets for private consumer goods which we tend not to compete about are terribly flawed. Still, there are two markets in which the standard assumptions do not apply: the market for public goods and the market for time. Here I believe the deviations from the assumptions are large, and extremely significant.

In the case of public goods there are at least two big problems. The first is the underproduction of a clean environment. Because environmental damage is typically not included in the price of the product which causes it (e.g., cars, toxic chemicals, pesticides), we overconsume environmentally damaging commodities. Indeed, because all production has an impact on the environment, we overconsume virtually all commodities. This means that we consume too much in *toto*, in comparison to non-environmentally damaging human activities.

The second problem arises from the fact that business interests—the interests of the producers of private goods—have privileged access to the government and disproportionately influence policy. Because they are typically opposed to public provision, the "market" for public goods is structurally biased against provision. In comparison to what a truly democratic state might provide, we find that a business-dominated government skews outcomes in the direction of private production. We don't get enough, or good enough, education, arts, recreation, mass transport, and other conventional public goods. We get too many cars, too many clothes, too many collectibles.

For those public goods that are complementary with private spending (roads and cars versus bicycle lanes and bicycles) this bias constrains the choices available to individuals. Without bicycle lanes or mass transport, private cars are unavoidable. Because so much of our consumption is linked to larger collective decisions, the individual consumer is always operating under particular constraints. Once we move to HDTV, our current televisions will become obsolete. As public telephone booths disappear, mobile phones become more necessary. Without adequate public libraries, I need to purchase more books.

We also underproduce "leisure." That's because employers make it difficult to choose free time, rather than long hours and higher incomes. To use the economist's jargon, the labor market offerings are incomplete with respect to trade-offs of time and money. Employers can exact severe penalties when individuals want to work part-time or forgo raises in favor of more vacations or days off. In some jobs the options are just not available; in others the sacrifices in terms of career mobility and benefits are disproportionate to any productivity costs to the employer.

This is not a minor point. The standard model assumes that employees are free to vary their hours, and that whatever combination of hours and income results represents the preferences of employees. But if employees lack the opportunity to vary their working hours, or to use improvements in productivity to reduce their worktime, then we can in no way assume that the trajectory of consumption reflects people's preferences. There may well be a path for the economy that involves less work and less stuff, and is preferred by people to the high-work/high-consumption track. But if that option is blocked, then the fact that we spend a lot can no longer be taken *ipso facto* as proof of our inherent consumer desires. We may merely be doing what is on offer. Because free time is now a strongly desired alternative to income for large numbers of employees, this argument is more than a theoretical possibility. It has become one of the most pressing failures of the current moment.

A POLITICS OF CONSUMPTION

The idea that consumption is private should not, then, be a conversation-stopper. But what should a politics of consumption look like? To start the discussion—not to provide final answers—I suggest seven basic elements:

1. *A right to a decent standard of living.* This familiar idea is especially important now because it points to a fundamental distinction between what people need and what they want. In the not very distant past, this dichotomy was not only well-understood, but the basis of data collection and social policy. Need was a social concept with real force. All that's left now is an economy of desire. This is reflected in polling data. Just over 40 percent of adults earning $50,000 to $100,000 a year, and 27 percent of those earning more than $100,000, agree that "I cannot afford to buy everything I really need." One third and 19 percent, respectively, agree that "I spend nearly all of my money on the basic necessities of life." I believe that our politics would profit from reviving a discourse of need, in which we talk about the material requirements for every person and household to participate fully in society. Of course, there are many ways in which such a right might be enforced: government income transfers or vouchers, direct-provision of basic needs, employment guarantees, and the like. For reasons of space, I leave that discussion aside; the main point is to revive the distinction between needs and desires.

2. *Quality of life rather than quantity of stuff.* Twenty-five years ago quality-of-life indicators began moving in an opposite direction from our measures of income, or Gross Domestic Product—a striking divergence from historic trends. Moreover, the accumulating evidence on well-being, at least its subjective measures (and to some extent objective measures, such as health), suggests that above the poverty line, income

is relatively unimportant in affecting well-being. This may be because what people care about is relative, not absolute income. Or it may be because increases in output undermine precisely those factors which *do* yield welfare. Here I have in mind the growing worktime requirements of the market economy, and the concomitant decline in family, leisure, and community time; the adverse impacts of growth on the natural environment; and the potential link between growth and social capital.

This argument that consumption is not the same as well-being has great potential to resonate with millions of Americans. Large majorities hold ambivalent views about consumerism. They struggle with ongoing conflicts between materialism and an alternative set of values stressing family, religion, community, social commitment, equity, and personal meaning. We should be articulating an alternative vision of a quality of life, rather than a quantity of stuff. That is a basis on which to argue for a re-structuring of the labor market to allow people to choose for time, or to penalize companies that require excessive hours for employees. It is also a basis for creating alternative indicators to the GNP, positive policies to encourage civic engagement, support for parents, and so forth.

3. *Ecologically sustainable consumption.* Current consumption patterns are wreaking havoc on the planetary ecology. Global warming is perhaps the best known, but many other consumption habits have major environmental impacts. Sport utility vehicles, air conditioning, and foreign travel are all energy-intensive, and contribute to global warming. Larger homes use more energy and building materials, destroy open space, and increase the use of toxic chemicals. Those granite countertops being installed in American kitchens were carved out of mountains around the world, leaving in their wake a blighted landscape. Our daily newspaper and coffee is contributing to deforestation and loss of species diversity. Something as simple as a T-shirt plays its part, since cotton cultivation accounts for a significant fraction of world pesticide use. Consumers know far less about the environmental impacts of their daily consumption habits than they should. And while the solution lies in greater part with corporate and governmental practices, people who are concerned about equality should be joining forces with environmentalists who are trying to educate, mobilize, and change practices at the neighborhood and household level.

4. *Democratize consumption practices.* One of the central arguments I have made is that consumption practices reflect and perpetuate structures of inequality and power. This is particularly true in the "new consumerism," with its emphasis on luxury, expensiveness, exclusivity, rarity, uniqueness, and distinction. These are the values which consumer markets are plying, to the middle and lower middle class. (That is what Martha Stewart is doing at K-Mart.)

But who needs to accept these values? Why not stand for consumption that is democratic, egalitarian, and available to all? How about making "access," rather than exclusivity, cool, by exposing the industries such as fashion, home decor, or tourism, which are pushing the upscaling of desire? This point speaks to the need for both cultural change, as well as policies which might facilitate it. Why not tax high-end "status" versions of products while allowing the low-end models to be sold tax-free?

5. *A politics of retailing and the "cultural environment."* The new consumerism has been associated with the homogenization of retail environments and a pervasive shift toward the commercialization of culture. The same mega-stores can be found everywhere, creating a blandness in the cultural environment. Advertising and marketing is also pervading hitherto relatively protected spaces, such as schools, doctors' offices, media programming (rather than commercial time), and so on. In my local mall, the main restaurant offers a book-like menu comprising advertisements for unrelated products. The daily paper looks more like a consumer's guide to food, wine, computer electronics, and tourism and less like a purveyor of news. We should be talking about these issues, and the ways in which corporations are re-making our public institutions and space. Do we value diversity in retailing? Do we want to preserve small retail outlets? How about ad-free zones? Commercial-free public education? Here too public policy can play a role by outlawing certain advertising in certain places and institutions, by financing publicly-controlled media, and enacting zoning regulations which take diversity as a positive value.

6. *Expose commodity "fetishism."* Everything we consume has been produced. So a new politics of consumption must take into account the labor, environmental, and other conditions under which products are made, and argue for high standards. This argument has been of great political importance in recent years, with public exposure of the so-called "global sweatshop" in the apparel, footwear, and fashion industries. Companies fear their public images, and consumers appear willing to pay a little more for products when they know they have been produced responsibly. There are fruitful and essential linkages between production, consumption, and the environment that we should be making.

7. *A consumer movement and governmental policy.* Much of what I have been arguing for could occur as a result of a consumer's movement. Indeed, the revitalization of the labor movement calls out for an analogous revitalization of long dormant consumers. We need independent organizations of consumers to pressure companies, influence the political agenda, provide objective product information, and articulate a vision of an appealing and humane consumer sphere. We also need a consumer movement to pressure the state to enact the kinds of policies that the foregoing analysis suggests are needed. These include taxes on luxury and status consumption, green taxes and subsidies, new policies

toward advertising, more sophisticated regulations on consumer credit, international labor and environmental standards, revamping of zoning regulations to favor retail diversity, and the preservation of open space. There is a vast consumer policy agenda which has been mainly off the table. It's time to put it back on.

27
Betsy Taylor and Dave Tilford
"WHY CONSUMPTION MATTERS"
(2000)

I. CONSUMER SOCIETY

Our enormously productive economy ... demands that we make consumption our way of life, that we convert the buying and use of goods into rituals, that we seek our spiritual satisfaction, our ego satisfaction, in consumption. ... We need things consumed, burned up, worn out, replaced, and discarded at an ever-increasing rate.[1]

—VICTOR LEBOW, 1950

Retail analyst Victor Lebow's statement might sound crass today, perhaps even a bit quaint in its unabashed promotion of materialism and waste. The words ring with a certain post–World War II naïveté—an unexamined faith in personal and spiritual fulfillment achieved via an endless stream of cheap and disposable consumer products.

If the words seem quaint, the message is not. The latter part of the twentieth century was spent largely following Victor Lebow's recipe for prosperity and fulfillment. Since 1950, the industrialized world has been on an unprecedented consumption binge, consuming more goods and services than the combined total of all humans who ever walked the planet before us.

From a certain limited perspective, Lebow was on target. By making conspicuous consumption our way of life, we have kept an "enormously productive economy" running full tilt. Unprecedented levels of consumption have powered unparalleled economic growth, with predictable material benefits. In industrial countries, the standard of living has risen so that items considered luxuries a few decades ago are common among the middle class today. Nonmaterial benefits have also accompanied this growth. Life expectancy is higher, and more people than ever before in the industrial world have adequate food, housing, clean water, warmth, electricity, and transportation, as well as many other comforts that make life easier.

From a broader, more farsighted perspective, the binge has been an ecological disaster. Latter twentieth-century consumption patterns (sparked initially by the industrial revolution of the late 1800s) have resulted in devastating levels of environmental deterioration, which threatens to eradicate the economic well-being that accompanied the growth. Lebow's vision of a better life through higher levels of consumption left out two very important parts of the equation: Where does all this stuff come from? Where does it go when we are done with it?

BORROWING FROM THE FUTURE

Every consumer product comes from the Earth and returns to it in one form or another. Soaring consumption of goods and services has been accomplished largely through increased resource extraction and waste production—at a grossly unsustainable level. In one sense, we have been "buying on credit" these past few decades: charging our current lifestyles on resources necessary for the well-being of future generations. From mining, refining, transport, manufacture, use, and disposal of goods, humans today—individually and collectively—are asking more of the planet than ever before. The impact, over the past half-century, has been overwhelming.

The United Nations' *Human Development Report 1998* (UNDP Report) stated that "Runaway growth in consumption in the past fifty years is putting strains on the environment never before seen." Forests are shrinking, fish stocks are declining, soil degradation and desertification are rising, and pollution and waste are being generated at a far greater rate than the Earth can absorb. Even our freshwater supply— perhaps our most precious commodity—is being pushed beyond the limit. Since 1950, withdrawals have nearly tripled, and many feel that water scarcity will be a major environmental issue of the twenty-first century.

The same year that the United Nations' *Human Development Report* cautioned that our consumption levels were straining environmental support systems, the World Wildlife Fund published its own *Living Planet Report*, an annual index of planetary resources. Examining a quarter-century of data, the report concluded that global ecosystems are in sharp decline: From 1970 to 1995, we lost more than 30 percent of the resources that sustain life on the planet. During that period, freshwater ecosystems declined by 50 percent, while marine ecosystems declined 30 percent and the world's forests declined 10 percent. Annually, the loss in natural forest cover amounted to an area the size of England and Wales combined.

The Living Planet Report is only the latest of a growing body of research linking excessive consumption to environmental degradation. The amount of vital resources being destroyed and degraded far exceed their rate of renewal. Overwhelming evidence—from a host of scientific sources—suggest that we are, in the language of the UNDP report, tearing "great holes on the web of life" while living beyond our ecological means. Some of the evidence of this degradation:

- Fifty-one percent of the freshwater animal species of the world are declining in number.[2]
- A recent survey found one in four vertebrate species to be in sharp decline or facing serious pressure from human activities.[3]
- One of every eight known plant species is threatened with extinction or is nearly extinct.[4]
- One in ten tree species are threatened with extinction.[5]
- The overall rate of extinction is at least fifty to one hundred times higher—and perhaps several thousand times higher—than the normal background rate. The last time such a mass extinction is believed to have occurred was 65 million years ago, when a dramatic shift in global climate patterns ended the age of the dinosaurs.[6]
- The year 1998 was the hottest on record. It replaced the previous hottest year on record, 1997, and followed a trend in which eight of the ten warmest years on record have occurred within the past decade. The dominant view among scientists is that a significant portion of this warming is the result of emissions of heat-trapping industrial waste gases such as carbon dioxide.[7]
- In September of 1998, the BBC, citing data from NASA, reported the hole in the ozone over Antarctica had reached record proportions: 10 million square miles, roughly three times the size of Australia.
- Global forest cover is shrinking by twenty-eight million acres a year. Causes include human-induced fires, agricultural expansion, logging, road-building, and exotic insect infestations.[8]
- Vast destruction of the world's forests is contributing to the spread of the world's deserts, increasing the loss of biodiversity and hampering the ability of the Earth's atmosphere to cleanse itself.[9]
- Massive erosion—related to intensive farming practices and deforestation—is causing a rapid loss in fertile soil and with it a potentially drastic drop in the ability to produce food for the world's people.[10]
- The United Nations Food and Agriculture Organization estimates that we have lost 75 percent of the genetic diversity of our crops since the beginning of the century.
- Fisheries are collapsing. About a quarter of stocks worldwide are currently depleted or in danger of depletion. Another 44 percent are being fished at their biological limit.[11]
- Some 58 percent of the world's coral reefs and one-third of all fish species may be at risk from human activities.[12]

In the introduction to the published edition of *Agenda 21*, a global action plan produced by the United Nations during the 1992 Earth Summit, editor Daniel Sitarz stated the case bluntly:

For the first time in history, humanity must face the risk of unintentionally destroying the foundations of life on Earth. The global scientific consensus is that if the current levels of environmental deterioration continue, the delicate life-sustaining qualities of this planet will collapse.

We are engaging in the ecological equivalent of running up a very substantial credit-card bill, hoping that tomorrow will take care of itself. It is misguided and dangerous, however, to spend beyond our means or to treat the natural world as a bank that does not have to be paid back.

II. POPULATION AND CONSUMPTION

Humankind's ecological impact depends on three primary factors: the size of the population, the average level of consumption by each individual, and the efficiency with which we convert raw materials into consumer goods and services. A simplified equation representing this relationship might read: I = PCT, or "ecological Impact equals Population × Consumption × Technological Efficiency."

In 1992, a joint report issued by the U.S. National Academy of Science and the Royal Society of London warned that "if current predictions of population growth prove accurate and patterns of human activity on the planet remain unchanged, science and technology may not be able to prevent either irreversible degradation of the environment or continued poverty for much of the world."[13] In other words, rapid growth in the first two components of the equation might swiftly nullify any gains made via technological innovations. Still, technology that results in less material consumption and waste is vital as we seek ways to check population growth and redirect personal consumption patterns.

POPULATION

The number of humans on the planet soared dramatically during the twentieth century. To understand current levels of growth, it is useful to review population figures for the past few hundred years. In the mid-seventeenth century, world population stood at one-half billion. By that time, however, a noticeable acceleration was taking place. Adding another half billion in less than a century, we passed the one billion mark in the early 1800s. By the mid-1920s, we had doubled our numbers to two billion. Over the next six decades, we had gained another three billion, bringing our total to five billion people by the mid-1980s. In late 1999, we passed the six-billion mark and were increasing in number at a rate of one billion every twelve years or so.

By simple principles of mathematics and physical space, this exponential population growth must cease. In 1974, a demographer calculated that at then-current growth rates, within seven centuries only one square foot of land would be available per person.[14] Indeed, the growth rate is already showing signs of moderating. However, the momentum of the past century and the vast numbers of those of child-bearing age will insure that population will continue to swell. (A slower rate of growth applied to a larger base population continues to add large numbers to the total population.) The United Nations predicts a world population of roughly 9.5 billion by 2050, a nineteenfold increase over the population of the mid-1700s.

Population growth in the industrialized world has slowed considerably. In the United States—the fastest-growing industrialized country—natural increase is about 0.6 percent a year (though total population growth, including immigration, is around 1.0 percent). Ninety percent of current population growth is occurring instead in the developing world,[15] where public health advances have contributed to lower death rates at all ages.[16] In these regions, population is increasing anywhere from 1.6 percent to 2.8 percent per year.[17]

In developing regions, where life exists closer to the margin, the pursuit of immediate sustenance as opposed to long-term sustainability is taking a huge toll on some the planet's richest centers of biodiversity. Tropical forests around the globe have fallen victim not only to extensive logging for wood products, but also to burning in order to clear land for subsistence farming. In 1997, satellite data showed a 50 percent increase over the previous year in the number of fires set by farmers to clear land for cultivation and pasture. About one-third of the fires are set in virgin forest areas, wiping out some of the world's richest and most important animal and plant habitats.[18]

Much of the food needs of a burgeoning population will be met through increased production on existing croplands—but at a price. Though global agriculture has made remarkable progress in keeping ahead of population growth,[19] progress has come at the expense of ecological systems. Erosion due to intensive farming practices leads to losses of 5 to 6 million hectares of topsoil a year. High-yield crop varieties require tremendous influxes of pesticides, herbicides, and nitrogen fertilizers. One dramatic casualty of this practice: In the Gulf of Mexico, a several thousand square mile oxygen-depleted "dead zone" appears every spring and summer at the mouth of the Mississippi River. This zone—within which marine life cannot survive—is caused by algal blooms traced to an influx of nitrogen from agricultural fertilizers. A large percentage of this comes from farms as far away as the Midwestern corn belt. In 1999, the dead zone reached record proportions: 7,700 square miles—roughly the size of New Jersey.

CONSUMPTION

Population growth is a serious problem that will continue to stress planetary resources well into the next century. The burden of population growth is magnified several-fold, however, by the fact that—on average—each individual today is consuming far more than an individual of fifty years ago. Worldwide, since the middle of the century, per capita consumption of timber, steel, copper, meat, and energy has doubled. Per capita aluminum consumption has increased sevenfold. Consumption of synthetic items drawn from natural resources has increased as well— per capita cement consumption has quadrupled, use of plastic quintupled.[20]

While population growth in developing areas endangers some of the last remaining wild areas of the planet, a different picture emerges when one compares consumption patterns among different segments of the population. The vast majority of consumption and subsequent ecological harm can be traced to consumer behavior not in the developing world, but in the industrial world.

To visualize world consumption patterns, it is helpful to divide human population into three distinct classes: the poor, the middle class, and the "consumer class." The poorest fifth of the world population—over one billion people—live in abject poverty, surviving on less than a dollar per day. The vast middle class—60 percent of world population—have most of their basic food, shelter, and water needs met, live in modest homes with lights, radios, and sometimes a refrigerator and a clothes washer, but own few material possessions and virtually no luxury items. Individuals in this group earn between $700 and $7,500 per person per year, very low by the standards of the industrial world.[21]

The remaining 20 percent are the "consumer class." Included in this class are most North Americans, West Europeans, Japanese, and Australians, and the oil sheikdoms of the Middle East, as well as smaller percentages of the population of other regions.[22] This 20 percent is responsible for the vast majority of ecological impacts associated with consumption.

The difference between consumption as practiced in the industrial world and consumption in the developing world is rather astounding: the one fifth of global population living in the highest-income countries account for 86 percent of private consumption expenditures. The poorest fifth account for a little over 1 percent.[23]

The average American consumes about fifty-three times more goods and services than someone from China. The United States contains 5 percent of the world's population but accounts for 22 percent of fossil-fuel consumption, 24 percent of carbon-dioxide emissions, and 33 percent of paper and plastic use. A child born in the United States will create thirteen times as much damage over the course of his or her lifetime than a child born in Brazil. He or she will cause as much damage as thirty-five natives of India.[24] In fact, given the statistics on actual resource use rather than sheer population numbers, some even suggest that the most overpopulated country on earth is—in terms of impact— the United States.

Overall, the environmental effects of increased consumer behavior among the world's richest 20 percent have been enormous:

The gaping divide in material consumption between the fortunate and unfortunate stands out starkly in their impacts on the natural world. . . . The consumer society's exploitation of resources threatens to exhaust, poison, or unalterably disfigure forests, soils, water, and air.[25]

III. CHASING THE DREAM

Meanwhile, to complicate matters, the world's "middle class"—the vast majority in the middle—understandably have their sights set on a higher standard of living. From afar, they are pursuing the American dream with gusto. All over the world, people watch American TV shows, read American magazines, and are exposed to American advertising. For these people, "development" means more than just electricity, telephones, and running water. It has come to mean having what Americans have: large living quarters, multiple cars, appliances, cable television, stereos:

- In Indonesia, reports the *Far Eastern Economic Review*, "construction crews work day and night to erect vast shopping malls, air-conditioned marble labyrinths where almost any local or imported luxury can be purchased—at a price."[26]
- In India, sales of consumer items are exploding—from automobiles to televisions to frozen dinners. The *Wall Street Journal* reports that "The traditional conservative Indian who believes in modesty and savings is gradually giving way to a new generation that thinks as freely as it spends."[27]
- In South Korea, *Fortune* magazine predicts "More of everything. More housing, and thus more telephones, appliances, TV sets, furniture, light bulbs and toilets and toilet cleaners."[28]
- From 1976 to 1996, China's total red meat consumption quintupled from less than 8 million tons to 42 million tons per year. If each Chinese consumed as much beef as the average American, the feedlots would need 343 million tons of grain—roughly the entire U.S. grain harvest.
- Since the mid-1980s, China's fleet of motor vehicles has grown by more than 10 percent a year. In 1996, more new cars were sold in Asia than in western Europe and North America combined. Government projections are for 22 million cars in China by 2010, and an even larger number of trucks and farm vehicles. Government planners in China have identified five "pillar" industries to receive special support in the country's drive for modernization: automobiles, housing construction, petrochemicals, machinery, and electronics.[29]

If China alone succeeds in becoming an American-class consumer nation, the environmental effects will be beyond reckoning. Though it is hypocritical to deny to others the luxuries (and basic necessities) we take for granted, the current ecological crisis will worsen dramatically as the "more is better" definition of the American dream spreads throughout the globe. According to a recent estimate by Mathis Wackernagel, coauthor of *Our Ecological Footprint*,[30] if everyone consumed at the level of the average North American, it would take four extra planets to provide the necessary resources to survive.[31] Globalization and the marketing of the American consumer lifestyle provokes millions of global consumers to suddenly "need" sport utility vehicles, big-screen TVs, and closets of stuff—something the already overburdened planet can ill-afford.

IV: SPENDING THE CAPITAL

The industrial revolution that gave rise to modern capitalism greatly expanded the possibilities for the material development of humankind. It continues to do so today, but at a severe price. Since the mid–eighteenth century, more of nature has been destroyed than in all prior history. While industrial systems have reached pinnacles of success, able to muster and accumulate human-made capital on vast levels, natural capital, on which civilization depends to create economic prosperity, is rapidly declining, and the rate of loss is increasing proportionate to gains in material well-being.[32]

A century ago, natural resources seemed unlimited. Cheap and plentiful, their ecological services little understood, it did not seem necessary to include such raw materials in the ledger sheet as they were extracted, degraded, or paved over to make way for human development.

Such practices became so entrenched that they still govern the market today. In the language and accounting of neo-classical economics, natural resources do not technically exist until they are removed and "put to use." Nature is treated as an externality. Unless someone can define its value (and find a buyer), the laws of commerce dictate that it be converted into something else—something tangible and useful in human terms.

The concept of limits is also downplayed in free-market economies, under the principle that resources are substitutable and the market will decide what is valuable. If the supply of coal, for example, nears exhaustion, prices will rise and consumers will be forced to seek out alternative fuels. Perhaps technological innovations—spurred by the market—will supply such fuels. Often, this process is viewed as a delicate and seamless series of solutions rising to meet problems—to the extent demanded by the market.

Unfortunately, the planet's ecosystems do not operate this way, or they do so on a scale well beyond the flexibility and response time of human economies. When resources produced over thousands or even millions of years are suddenly removed within the space of half a century, ecosystems may collapse. Nature, of course, does have its own draconian system of adjustments and substitutions—often involving the wholesale removal of species.

Furthermore, the value of some resources defy human comprehension. Focused on immediate and tangible needs and outcomes, we fail to account for the intricacies of biological systems or the long-term effects associated with destroying parts of the system. By the time we understand the value of some component of the natural world or begin to account for it in the marketplace, an irreversible downward spiral may have begun. At that point, no human attempt to place higher values on the object can reverse the trend or compensate for the loss. An economic system that ignores the unknown and unknowable aspects of nature is fated to fail in the end, dragging us down with it.

V. HIDDEN CONSUMPTION

Consumer goods come to us via a convoluted global resource network. Each day—each minute, practically—in the life of the modern consumer is filled with hidden interactions with portions of the planet beyond the horizon, hundreds and often thousands of miles away. Our cars, houses, hamburgers, televisions, sneakers, newspapers, and thousands upon thousands of other consumer items come to us via chains of production that stretch around the globe.[33] Along the length of this chain, we pull raw materials from the Earth in numbers that are too big even to conceptualize.

MOVING THE EARTH

Tremendous volumes of natural resources are displaced and ecosystems disrupted in the uncounted extraction processes that fuel modern human existence. Constructing highways or buildings, mining for gold, drilling for oil, harvesting crops and forest products all involve reshaping natural landscapes. Some of our activities involve minor changes to the landscape. Sometimes entire mountains are moved.

A study conducted by government and research institutes in the U.S., Germany, the Netherlands, and Japan examined just how much is uprooted in the process of creating consumer goods. For citizens of those four countries, the total volume of natural resources altered on a daily basis was enormous—45 to 85 metric tons per person per year. Converted to pounds, that means that each and every person is responsible for the displacement of between 271 and 512 pounds of the Earth and its resources *every day*.[34]

MANUFACTURING, PROCESSING

A portion of the resources displaced enters the industrial economy for further processing, as raw materials are distilled down or converted to the final products. The amount is still enormous. Most end up as waste discarded long before it is seen by the end consumer. The consumer, therefore, never sees most of what he or she consumes. Lacking feedback concerning true impacts, consumers are less motivated to "lighten their loads."

Americans, in particular, use and discard a lot of stuff. Since 1940, Americans alone have used up as large a share of the Earth's mineral resources as the combined total of every human being that ever existed on the planet before them.[35]

From 1900 until 1989, the U.S. population tripled while the use of raw materials multiplied 17 times.[36] With less than 5 percent of the world's population, the U.S. uses one-third of the world's paper, a quarter of the world's oil, 23 percent of the coal, 27 percent of the aluminum, and 19 percent of the copper.[37] Our per capita use of energy, metals, minerals, forest products, fish, grains, meat, and even freshwater dwarfs that of people living in the developing world.[38] In most consumer categories, we rank highest by a considerable margin even among other industrial nations. Our fossil-fuel consumption is double that of the average resident of Great Britain, two and a half times that of the average Japanese.[39] Our 5 percent of the population is also responsible for a full 50 percent of the world's solid waste.[40]

On a daily basis, the average American throws out four to five pounds of garbage. However, a National Academy of Sciences study found that, in 1990, the average American actually consumed about 124 pounds of materials per person, per day, excluding water.[41] Our daily 124-pound allotment consists of about 47 pounds of construction materials and energy fuels (i.e., coal, oil, gas), 6 pounds of industrial materials, 3 pounds of metals, 6 pounds of forest, and 15 pounds of agricultural materials. It is as if, each and every day, someone behind the scenes is throwing out thirty additional four-pound garbage bags for us.

UNEARTHING GOLD

Mining precious minerals is one of the most environmentally destructive activities in which humans participate. Mountains are moved in search of increasingly low-grade ore, creating permanent scars on the landscape. Separating the metal from the ore often involves toxic chemical processes—such as leaching with cyanide. Much of this process goes solely to support the production of luxury goods. One ton of ore is mined for every one karat diamond. For every ounce of silver, 5 tons are mined. To create a single tenth-of-an-ounce, fourteen karat gold ring, 2.8 tons of ore must be pulled from the earth.[42] Each year in the United States, roughly 350 metric tons (over 11 million troy ounces) of gold are produced.[43]

CONSUMING FORESTS

Americans use 27 percent of the wood commercially harvested worldwide. In the United States:

- Paper products make up roughly 39 percent of the municipal solid waste stream.[44]
- 14 million trees are used annually to make mail-order catalogs.
- Eleven percent of the total lumber cut in the United States—including two-fifths of hardwoods cut—goes into shipping crates and pallets, most of which are discarded after one use. At the close of the twentieth century, there were 1.5 billion pallets in the United States—six per person.[45]
- The average American office worker disposes of 100–200 pounds of office paper per year.[46]

HIDDEN COST OF BEEF

Ever wonder about the ingredients of a quarter-pound burger? One oft-overlooked ingredient is water. According to the authors of *Stuff: The Secret Lives of Everyday Things*,[47] over 700 gallons of water goes into the average "dressed" quarter-pound cheeseburger made in California:

a 4-ounce beef patty:	616 gallons
1-ounce of cheese:	56 gallons
a 2-ounce bun:	25 gallons
1-ounce of ketchup:	3.2 gallons
a 1-ounce slice of tomato:	1.8 gallons
1 ounce of lettuce:	1.3 gallons
Total:	703.3 gallons

Livestock also consume 70 percent of the U.S. grain harvest and are implicated in many forms of environmental destruction, including overgrazing, desertification, soil erosion, and deforestation. In Central and South America, millions of acres of rainforest have been cleared to make way for pastureland; one study estimated that for every quarter-pound burger produced, 165 pounds of living matter is destroyed.[48]

THE NOT-SO-SMALL IMPACT OF SHRIMP

Not so long ago, shrimp was considered an expensive delicacy. In the past two decades, shrimp prices have plummeted while production has skyrocketed. The two most common methods, trawling the ocean floor and creating "shrimp farms" along coastal areas, are enormously destructive.

- Trawlers drag the bottom of the ocean in search of shrimp with large, heavy bars attached to the nets. This is particularly disruptive to fragile reef systems. With every pound of shrimp caught by ocean trawlers, 5.2 pounds of marine life are dredged up as well, "bycatch" that is killed and thrown back to decompose, further disrupting ocean systems.

- Shrimp farming involves displacing natural landscapes with the farms. It is estimated that a quarter of the world's mangrove forests—which play a critical role in coastal ecosystems—have been destroyed by shrimp farming, according to the Food and Agriculture Organization of the United Nations (FAO). The farms also add to pollution by spilling antibiotics, pesticides, and nutrient-rich commercial feed into surrounding waterways.[49]

VI. RENEWABLES

Concern over resource shortages often focuses on non-renewables such as metals and fossil fuels. But using "renewables" at a rate faster than the earth can replenish them can be a bigger problem, especially when such renewables are part of the foundation of life on Earth. Once depleted, some are not easily replaced. According to the United Nations, "The world is facing a growing scarcity of renewable resources essential to sustain the ecosystem and for human survival—from deforestation, soil erosion, water, declining fish stocks, and lost biodiversity."[50]

FORESTS

The unprecedented scale and rate of deforestation and human-induced changes to forests is leading to the loss of immensely valuable ecosystem services. Soil conservation, flood control, provision of clean water, climate regulation, and maintenance of biodiversity are fundamental to human activity. Unlike goods and services traded in the market, they are assigned no monetary values, or none which are widely accepted. Yet those services cannot easily be substituted by human ingenuity and, even where substitution is possible, the economic costs are likely to prove prohibitive for many countries.[51]

Forests anchor terrestrial life on the planet. They serve as critical habitat, sheltering roughly two-thirds of the world's plant and animal species.[52] They protect and maintain healthy watersheds. When forests are cleared, erosion washes tons of soil into rivers and streams, making them unfit for human uses and aquatic life as well. Forests also play a vital role as "carbon sinks"—curbing human impacts on global climate by absorbing excess carbon dioxide released into the atmosphere.[53]

Human consumption, however, is causing the world's forests to shrink rapidly. Since 1850, more forests have been cleared than in all previous history, with the rate accelerating in the past few decades.[54] Every minute during the 1980s, 63 acres of forest disappeared from the planet.[55] Today, only one-fifth of global forest cover remains in intact ecosystems large enough to ensure the long-term survival of native species.[56] In the United States, only 3 percent remains.

In 1997, the world consumed 120 billion cubic feet of wood. Over half of that was burned for fuel, primarily in the developing world.

Sawn wood for industrial use and construction made up the second biggest category at 26 percent of total consumption. Processing woods for plywood and chipboard used 9 percent, and pulp for papermaking, 11 percent.

Forty years ago, most deforestation occurred in the industrial world. Today, deforestation is concentrated in the developing world.[57] Over the past decade, at least 380 million acres of tropical forest—an area three times the size of France—have been lost. Despite replanting in some areas, net annual deforestation continues at a rate of about 30 million acres a year.[58]

Both population growth and the advent of a global market have contributed to a rapid expansion of logging and conversion of forests to agriculture and human settlements. Though precise numbers are difficult to ascertain, the consensus now is that the primary cause of tropical deforestation worldwide is clearance for agriculture. However, logging remains the primary threat to ecologically intact old-growth forests. Often the two work in tandem: logging opens up roads into virgin forest areas, leading landless farmers to burn off more forestlands to create agricultural space on which to subsist.

Paper consumption, already a significant burden, is expected to rise in the coming century. In the past three decades, consumption of paper has more than tripled.[59] Though we live in an era of computers, in which documents can be created and passed on electronically, personal computers are actually responsible for a large part of the problem. They are estimated to consume over 115 billion sheets of paper annually.[60] In addition, the past few decades have seen a proliferation of copy machines and wasteful copying practices (especially in offices), paperboard containers for prepared foods, and incredible volumes of catalogs and junk mail. More than ever, forests are felled to produce excess packaging for consumer goods and other disposable products intended for one-time use.

In 1995, the average American consumed 751 pounds of paper, highest in the world. (The Japanese were second at 511 pounds each.)[61] In the United States, 14 million trees are felled annually to make mail-order catalogs. Each American gets 34 pounds of junk mail a year—a total of over 9 billion pounds in the U.S. alone. Newspapers and magazines are swelling because of advertising—Sunday papers in particular now contain a thin crust of news surrounding an ever expanding filling of advertising circulars and classifieds. The Sunday *New York Times* alone uses roughly 75,000 trees per edition.[62]

Though unable to keep up with demand, significant gains have been made in the recovery and recycling of paper. Worldwide, the amount of recovered paper used in paper production has increased from less than one quarter to over one third. In the late 1990s, over 45 percent of wastepaper in the United States was recycled, up from 29 percent a decade earlier. Germany recovers 67 percent of its wastepaper, South Korea 56 percent, and Japan 52 percent. More would be recycled in the United States were it not for the relatively low participation by offices and businesses, as well as uneven enforcement of laws mandating recycled content in new products.[63]

FISHERIES

Modern fishing techniques, both in capture fisheries and aquaculture, are disturbing many parts of an interlocking biological system that connects estuaries, coastal zones, continental shelves and banks, and the deep ocean. . . . Too many fish are being caught, or grown, in ways that are destroying natural habitats, wiping out key parts of the marine food chain, changing species balance, and degrading water quality. Coastal fishing activities also interact with other human stresses on the aquatic environment, notably pollution from sewage, industrial effluent, and agricultural runoff. . . . The consequent disruption of biological balance in aquatic ecosystems is critically impairing the natural ability of fish to survive and reproduce.[64]

About one billion people depend on seafood as their primary source of animal protein. In addition, fish serve as an important source of animal feed and oil. Since 1950, global fish harvest (including freshwater and aquaculture harvest) has risen from 21 million metric tons annually to 121 million tons in 1996, a nearly fivefold increase. Over the next decade, demand is expected to increase between 34 and 50 percent.[65]

The oceans may seem infinite and inexhaustible, but useful fishing areas are relatively confined—centered around coastal areas where both human and fish populations congregate. In recent decades, the strain of keeping up with human demands is stretching many fisheries to the breaking point.

Analysts are virtually unanimous in the opinion that our current levels of consumption cannot be met if production trends continue unchanged. The amount of fish available per capita has been shrinking since 1970. The global marine fish catch peaked in 1989 at 89 million metric tons and has hovered at around 85 million tons since then.[66] Decades of intensive fishing have already collapsed many northern hemisphere fisheries. Now, the same pressure is being applied to southern fisheries.[67] According to the FAO, eleven of the world's fifteen major fishing grounds are seriously depleted.[68] At current rates, the world's few remaining productive fishing grounds will be fished out in their turn, and total marine harvests will decline dramatically.[69]

There is also a growing consensus that the precipitous decline in so many of the world's fisheries is not just a response to human need, but the result of human disregard for the delicate complexities of aquatic ecosystems in our eagerness to exploit the resource.[70] Technological advances in the past few decades have enabled the world's fishing fleet to maximize its catch. Unfortunately, the focus has been on increasing volume at any cost, not on reducing waste or fostering a more sustainable relationship with the world's fisheries. Commercial fleets have increasingly invested in trawl nets and dredges that rake the ocean floor in a process more akin to mining than fishing, sweeping up unwanted flora and fauna along with the desired catch, obliterating seabed habitat in the process. Some overfished stocks can recover, but the devastation wreaked by deep-sea trawlers make this difficult.[71]

In 1994, over 27 million tons of non-target "bycatch" fish—one third of the total catch—were killed and tossed back, a tremendous waste of resources and a serious depletion of ocean ecosystems. Hundreds of thousands of birds, seals, dolphins, turtles, and other species are also killed as bycatch in an effort to maximize harvest.[72] The highest percentage of waste is found in the shrimp industry, which tosses back over 80 percent of the living matter brought up and killed in the process of dredging ocean floors and sensitive reef areas. In some tropical areas, in fact, bycatch exceeds the shrimp catch by a devastating 15 to 1 ratio.[73] Global taste for shrimp—once considered an expensive luxury item but now cheap and plentiful on world markets—is having an enormous effect on these ecosystems.

Aquaculture—fish farming—adds to production and will meet an increasing percentage of demand over the next decades, but at an extreme environmental price. Intensive fish farms produce high volumes of nutrients, pesticides, antibiotics, and other wastes, which are flushed out into surrounding waters. In tropical and semi-tropical regions, fish farms have displaced mangrove forests, which serve as essential buffers against coastal erosion, flooding, and drainage of river systems. Aquaculture also places a heavy burden on water supplies. Shrimp farms in particular require 29 to 35 thousand gallons of freshwater per pound of shrimp raised.[74]

Consumer demand for seafood, combined with destructive fishing techniques, are two primary factors in the collapse of fisheries. Pollution and habitat destruction—also connected to our consumption patterns— also reduce the productivity of many coastal zones, where some 90 percent of the world's fish harvest is caught. Development has destroyed about half the coastal wetlands on the planet. Eighty percent of marine pollution comes from land-based sources.[75]

VII. ENERGY USE

Eighty-five percent of the world's energy consumption consists of the burning of fossil fuels—oil, coal, and natural gas.[76] Though no immediate shortages of these resources exist,[77] they are finite and will not last forever. What took millions of years to produce, we are consuming in the space of a century or two. Every day, in fact, the worldwide economy burns an amount of energy the planet required 10,000 days to create.[78]

At current rates of consumption, some predict that oil production will peak in the early part of the twenty-first century, leading to much higher prices and—soon to follow—shortages. Other experts, however, point to the current glut of oil on the world market and remain confident that the market—through higher prices after supply becomes limited—will foster technological innovations and substitutions when it becomes necessary.

Placing confidence in our current supply or emphasizing exploitation of new reserves, however, clouds another, more pressing issue involved in the consumption of fossil fuels: the harmful effects we inflict on the planet through our prodigious use of these resources.[79] Whatever the benefits, our use of fossil fuels has an undeniable downside:

> In particular, the fossil fuels that power the consumer society are its most ruinous input. Wrestling coal, oil and natural gas from the earth permanently disrupts countless habitats; burning them causes an overwhelming share of the world's air pollution; and refining them generates huge quantities of toxic wastes.[80]

Increasingly, scientists are recognizing that the most significant and potentially most devastating impact from burning fossil fuels is its disruptive effect on global climate.

FALLING OFF THE WAGON

In 1973, oil producing nations imposed an embargo that drastically reduced the flow of oil to consumer nations. In the years that followed, higher costs and concern for the future of our oil supply fostered a wave of efficiency measures in the United States and elsewhere. From 1973 to 1983—even as population and the economy expanded—the United States reduced its overall energy consumption.[81] Automobiles were redesigned to travel farther on a gallon of gasoline. Homes and office buildings were fitted with insulation and energy-conserving features such as tighter windows. Factories began to drastically reduce consumption of fossil fuels. Industrial and commercial energy use in America fell 18 percent in the decade following the embargo.[82]

Today, that trend has reversed. American industry has long since given up the frugal ways of the 1970s: industrial energy use rose 37 percent from 1983 to 1997.[83] Individual Americans also have returned to and are moving beyond pre-1973 levels of consumption. Today, a much larger total population consumes at roughly the same per capita level as before the oil embargo. That level is expected to rise in coming years.

Though many of the efficiency technologies spawned by the crisis are still in place, a greater array of energy-hungry consumer products override the positive effects. Modern homes are filled with electronic devices absent from homes of thirty years ago. Central air-conditioning, security systems, extra televisions, VCRs, computers, microwave ovens, dishwashers, large refrigerators, and various other appliances have contributed to a 5 percent per year increase in energy use through the 1990s.[84]

The modern home itself is one of the biggest culprits—and a reflection of the new consumer ethic. Per square foot, homes built today are actually much more energy-efficient than homes in the 1970s. But they are also much bigger, and therefore use more total energy to operate. Since the early 1970s, the average household (in terms of occupants) has shrunk by one-sixth. The average new home, on the other hand, has grown in size by one-third.[85]

These big homes are also placed at greater distances from work, as suburban sprawl separates neighborhoods from town centers. This puts more miles on a growing number of less efficient vehicles parked in (much larger) garages. From 1983 to 1998, the average commuting distance jumped by one third while car-pooling and use of mass transit declined.[86] Meanwhile, sales of fuel-consuming sport utility vehicles (SUVs) and light trucks jumped. In November of 1998, for the first time ever, SUV and light truck sales surpassed those of passenger cars. The watershed year, however, was 1996: It marked the first time in history in which vehicles going to the junkyard got better gas mileage than vehicles rolling off the dealers' lots.[87]

Energy costs in the United States are far less than in other industrial nations, and this is reflected in the much lower level of energy efficiency of the American lifestyle. Waste is even encouraged by electric utilities, which have cut support in recent years for installation of more efficient heating, cooling, and lighting systems.[88] To drive our cars, fuel our appliances, and keep our homes comfortable, Americans use far and away the lion's share of the world's energy. With under 5 percent of world population, we use 25 percent of the world's oil and 23 percent of the world's coal. Coal supplies over half of U.S. electricity.[89]

Globally, energy use has risen almost 70 percent since 1971, and is expected to continue rising over the next several decades.[90] Adding to the slow, steady rise in consumption within the industrial world—where most energy use still takes place—is the more meteoric rise in consumption of the developing world. From 1990 to 1997, oil use increased 60 percent in China, 40 percent in Indonesia, and 25 percent in Brazil.[91] China, already the world's biggest coal user at 30 percent of the world's total, increased its usage 27 percent from 1990 to 1997. China's rise toward industrialization will almost certainly be fired by enormous amounts of coal, a cheaper though more polluting form of energy. In Beijing, coal supplies 80 percent of the energy for factories and homes,[92] contributing to epidemics of lung disease and ground-level air pollution.

HEALTH/ENVIRONMENTAL EFFECTS

Burning fossil fuels adds pollutants to the air, including carbon monoxide, sulfur dioxide, and nitrogen oxides, as well as fine particulate matter that causes respiratory ailments. Worldwide, estimates of mortality due to breathing polluted air range from 200,000 to 570,000 per year.[93] The European Environment Agency recently reported that roughly three quarters of the 105 European cities surveyed did not meet World Health Organization (WHO) air-quality standards.

In the United States, an estimated 80 million people live in areas that do not meet U.S. air-quality standards. In the developing world, air quality has become an enormous problem, as nations adopt the more polluting technologies of the industrial world without some of the safeguards. In cities such as Beijing, Delhi, Jakarta, and Mexico City, pollutant levels are three or more times the safety levels set by WHO.

Acid rain is caused by the emissions of nitrogen and sulfur oxides. In the United States, electric utility plants account for about 70 percent of sulfur dioxide emissions, and about 30 percent of nitrogen oxide emissions. Motor vehicles also contribute significantly to nitrogen oxide emissions. Overall, over 20 million tons of SO_2 and NO_x are emitted into the atmosphere each year.[94]

Acid rain can have devastating effects on ecosystems downwind from sources. It leads to acidification of lakes and streams in otherwise unpolluted areas, in some cases destroying aquatic life. The Canadian government estimates that, even with implementation of current acid rain programs in the U.S. and Canada, an area the size of France and Britain will continue to receive harmful levels of acid rain, and as many as 95,000 lakes will remain damaged. More than 500 lakes and ponds in New York's Adirondack Park alone are already too acidic to support native plant and aquatic wildlife.

Forests are also particularly hard hit by acid rain. In New Hampshire, hardwood forests have stopped growing. Through the front range of the Rockies, tree health is declining and evergreen forests are losing their needles downwind from power plants. In the Appalachians, spruce forests have been devastated—even in protected areas like Great Smoky Mountains National Park. The U.S. Forest Service estimates death rates for many Appalachian tree species to have doubled or tripled since the 1960s in areas that are dosed by sulfur- and nitrogen-based pollution.[95]

GLOBAL WARMING

The greatest threat to the long-term health of our planet, as the danger of nuclear war declines, is probably global climate

*change. For most climate scientists, it is no longer a question
of whether global warming will occur, but when.*[96]

—DR. JAMES HANSEN, DIRECTOR OF THE NASA
GODDARD INSTITUTE FOR SPACE STUDIES

One of the most significant gases emitted when fossil fuels are burned
is carbon dioxide, a gas that traps heat in the earth's atmosphere.
Though present in nature and essential to life on Earth, excess CO_2 is
disruptive to our planet's natural cycles and is expected to drastically
alter global ecosystems over the next century and beyond.

The Intergovernmental Panel on Climate Change, a global team of
over two thousand scientists, concluded in a 1995 report that the observed increase in global average temperature over the last century "is
unlikely to be entirely natural in origin" and that "the balance of evidence suggests that there is a discernible human influence on global
climate."[97] Since the mid-1800s, according to the EPA, our consumption
of fossil fuels has resulted in a nearly 30 percent increase in the amount
of carbon dioxide in our atmosphere. Energy burned to run cars and
trucks, heat homes and businesses, and power factories is responsible
for about 80 percent of society's carbon dioxide emissions.[98]

Though the effects of our carbon dioxide emissions will vary widely
across the globe, as wind and sea currents respond to the disruption,
one result predicted by climate scientists is a general increase in global
temperature. Already, this prediction is coming true: 1998 was the hottest year on record, and eight of the ten warmest years on record occurred within the past decade.

A continued warming trend could be devastating. In coastal areas,
sea-level rise due to the warming of the oceans and the melting of gla-
ciers may cause the ocean to flood coastal wetlands and river deltas—
as well as coastal cities and settlements where so much of human population resides. The disruption of normal weather patterns may result
in more extreme weather events. Some inland agricultural zones could
suffer an increase in the frequency of droughts.

THE UNSEEN COST OF AUTO USE

According to the EPA,[99] the average American car travels 12,500 miles
in the course of a year, at a rate of 22.7 miles per gallon, consuming
550 gallons of gasoline in the process. The average "light truck" (including sport utility vehicles and minivans) travels 14,000 miles at a
rate of 15.3 miles per gallon, and uses 915 gallons of gas.

The following table shows what each emits over the course of one
year:

Pollutant (Problem)	Emission per mile	Annual Emission
Hydrocarbons (smog, air toxins)	car: 2.9 grams truck: 3.7 grams	car: 80 pounds truck: 114 pounds
Carbon monoxide (poisonous gas)	car: 22 grams truck: 29 grams	car: 606 pounds truck: 894 pounds
Nitrogen oxides (smog, acid rain)	car: 1.5 grams truck: 1.9 grams	car: 41 pounds truck: 59 pounds
Carbon dioxide (global warming)	car: 0.8 pounds truck: 1.2 pounds	car: 10,000 pounds truck: 16,800 pounds

CONCLUSION: OUR ECOLOGICAL FOOTPRINT

One of the primary results—and one of the primary needs—of industrialism is the separation of people and places and products from their histories.[100]

—Wendell Berry

Consumer goods come to us via a convoluted global resource network. Each day—each minute, practically—the life of the modern consumer is filled with hidden interactions with portions of the planet beyond the horizon, hundreds and often thousands of miles away. In the modern electronic age, the global resource network has allowed humans to shift goods and services from where they originate to where they are desired at incredible speeds. That which is not within our grasp can be obtained—by land, sea, or air—in a matter of days, no matter the distance to the source.

A primary purpose of the network is to make us less beholden to our immediate surroundings. In shedding our dependence on the surrounding landscape, however, we lose our intimate relationship with it as well—without developing a corresponding level of knowledge and intimacy with the distant lands that supply our needs. Though the benefits of this network have been enormous, the tragic aspect is that it has allowed us to participate in environmental degradations of monumental proportions in a completely anonymous and unconscious fashion.

LIVING OFF THE LAND

How much of the land do we actually use? Imagine a 125 square mile city of one million people. How much space does each individual in that city occupy? A simple answer could be derived by dividing the total number of people by the total land within the city. This would equate to .000125 square miles per person, or twelve and a half people per acre.

This answer would be incomplete, of course. Beyond the city limits, the residents of the city require many additional acres of land to support their needs. Distant farmlands supply meat, grains, vegetables and fruit to the city's residents. A nearby landfill takes its refuse. Small sections of forest scattered over the globe supply lumber and paper to each office and household within the city. Plantations from Columbia to Kenya send coffee beans, bananas, cocoa, and sugar. Mining companies and manufacturing plants mine and process gold, steel, copper and other minerals from natural areas and send finished products for purchase within the city. Soon, it becomes obvious that the city residents are sitting atop far more land than the 125 square miles represented by the city's political boundaries. Each individual is using far more land than one-twelfth of an acre.

How Much Land We Use Versus How Much Land Nature Has to Offer

What if it were possible to determine the total space on the globe that supplied an individual with his or her consumption needs? It is not possible, usually, to identify the exact tree that went into an individual writing tablet, or the farmlands from which a particular quarter pound burger derived. We can, however, create a rough picture of how much land specific population segments require by counting the total resources used by that population, then estimating how much land it takes to produce those resources. The sum total of land required to produce those resources is that population's "ecological footprint." This ecological footprint for the larger population can then be divided by the number of people in the group to give a rough average individual footprint.

According to the authors of *Our Ecological Footprint*, each individual Canadian needed roughly 2.4 acres of garden, crop, forest and pastureland to supply his or her food in 1991.[101] But that is not all. To produce these foods and bring them to market required energy—which required more land (on which sat oil refineries, coal mines, etc.)—bringing the total land required to supply an individual Canadian with food to 3.2 acres. Additional land scattered far and wide supplied a variety of other consumer goods, from packaging to electronic products to motor vehicles. All told, the study concluded that approximately 10.5 acres of the planet were directed toward the exclusive use of each individual Canadian. By comparison, the average American in the mid-1990s had an ecological footprint of 25 acres.[102] The worldwide average is less than one-quarter of the American total.

So how much does nature have to offer? If we divide all of the biologically productive land and sea on the planet by the number of people inhabiting it in 1998, the amount of land per person would amount to 5.5 acres. Of these 5.5 acres, 4.5 are landbased natural and managed ecosystems such as forests, pastures, and arable land. The other acre consists of ecologically productive parts of the ocean, primarily located on continental shelves.[103]

But as the authors of the ecological footprint studies note, it is not safe to assume that all this biologically productive space is available for human use and alteration. There are over 30 million other species on the planet. Many cannot survive on land occupied (in person or through intense management) by humans. The loss of many of these species would have large repercussions throughout the system. How much land should we set aside—as much for our own needs as for the needs of these other species?

A 1987 United Nations study addresses this question. *Our Common Future*[104] (known as "The Brundtland Report" after the Norwegian prime minister who chaired the report commission), offers a conservative estimate that at least 12 percent of the biologically productive space on Earth should be left intact to help maintain global ecosystems. This estimate would shrink the bio-productive space per person to under 5 acres. A global population of 10 billion in 2050 would reduce that space to under 3 acres—less than ⅛ the current space "occupied" by the average American.[105]

Though it would be easy to quibble over the exact numbers produced by these calculations, an overall picture is clear: Skyrocketing consumption is rapidly depleting the Earth's ecosystems, robbing future generations of vital life-sustaining resources. We are currently using far more of the Earth than the Earth has to offer.

ENDNOTES

1. Durning, Alan. *How Much is Enough?* (New York: W.W. Norton, 1992), pp. 21–22.

2. World Wide Fund for Nature (WWF). *Living Planet Report 1999* (Gland, Switzerland: World Wide Fund for Nature, 1999), p. 8.

3. Tuxill, J. *Losing Strands in the Web of Life: Vertebrate Declines and the Conservation of Biological Diversity* (World Watch Institute, 1998).

4. Suplee, Curt. "1 in 8 Plants in Global Study Threatened," *The Washington Post*, 8 April 1998, A01.

5. World Conservation Union (IUCN). *The World List of Threatened Trees* (Cambridge: World Conservation Union, 1998).

6. Hertsgaard, Mark. *Earth Odyssey* (New York: Broadway Books, 1999), p. 202.

7. Stevens, William K. "1999 Continues Warning Trend Around Globe," *The New York Times*, 19 December 1999, A01.

8. The World Resources Institute, The United Nations Environment Programme (UNEP), The United Nations Development Programme (UNDP), and The World Bank. *1998–99 World Resources: A Guide to the Global Environment* (New York: Oxford University Press, 1998), p. 185.

9. Sitarz, Daniel, ed. *Agenda 21: The Earth Summit Strategy to Save Our Planet* (Boulder, Colorado: Earthpress, 1994), p. 2.

10. Ibid.

11. United Nations Development Programme (UNDP). *Human Development Report 1998* (New York: Oxford University Press, 1998), p. 4.

12. The World Resources Institute et al., 140.

13. Hertsgaard, 13.

14. Coale, Ansley J. "The History of Human Population," *The Human Population* (San Francisco: Freeman and Co. for Scientific American, 1974).

15. Population Reference Bureau (PRB). *World Population Data Sheet* (Washington, D.C.: Population Reference Bureau, 1999).

16. Ibid.

17. Ibid.

18. The World Resources Institute et al., 185–86.

19. Ibid., 152.

20. Durning, 29.

21. Ibid., 26–28.

22. Durning, 28.

23. The World Resource Institute, 2.

24. Durning.

25. Durning, 22–23.

26. Durning, 36.

27. Durning, 35.

28. Durning, 36.

29. Hertsgaard, 244.

30. Wackernagel, Mathis, and William Rees. *Our Ecological Footprint.* (Gabriola Island, British Columbia: New Society Publishers, 1996).

31. The estimate of four extra planets represents a recalculation from the two extra planets cited in *Our Ecological Footprint.* Wackernagel et al. "National Natural Capital Accounting with the Ecological Footprint Concept," *Ecological Economics*, Vol. 29, no. 3, June 1999, pp. 375–390.

32. Hawken, Paul, Amory Lovins, and L. Hunter Loving. *Natural Capitalism* (Boston: Little, Brown, 1999), p. 2.

33. Durning, 74.

34. The World Resources Institute et al., 161.

35. Durning, 38.

36. President's Council on Sustainable Development (PCSD). *Population and Consumption Task Force Report* (Washington, D.C.: President's Council on Sustainable Development, 1996), p. 33.

37. Brower, Michael, and Warren Leon. *The Consumer's Guide to Effective Environmental Choices: Practical Advice from the Union of Concerned Scientists.* (New York: Three Rivers Press, 1999), pp. 4–5.

38. Brower and Leon, 4.

39. Brower and Leon, 4–5.

40. Hawken, Paul. *The Ecology of Commerce: A Declaration of Sustainability* (New York: Three Rivers Press, 1999), p. 4–5.

41. Stern, Paul C., Thomas Dietz, Vernon W. Ruttan, Robert H. Socolow, and James L. Sweeny, eds. *Environmentally Significant Consumption* (Washington, D.C.: National Academy Press, 1997), p. 30.

42. "The Price of Beauty," *Sierra Magazine*, January/February 1998, p. 19.

43. Amey, Earle B. "Gold." In *Minerals Yearbook* (Washington, D.C.: United States Geological Survey, 1998), p. 8.

44. Franklin Associates. *Characterization of Municipal Solid Waste in the United States, 1998 Update* (Washington, D.C.: United States Environmental Protection Agency, 1999), p. 2.

45. Hawken, *Natural Capitalism*, 184.

46. Ibid., 174.

47. Ryan, John C., and Alan Thein Durning. *Stuff: The Secret Lives of Everyday Things* (Seattle: Northwest Environment Watch, 1997), p. 55.

48. Denslow, Julie, and Christine Padoch, eds. *People of the Tropical Rain Forest* (Berkeley: University of California Press, 1988), p. 168.

49. Matthews, Emily, and Allan Hammond. *Critical Consumption Trends and Implications: Degrading Earth's Ecosystems* (Washington, D.C.: World Resources Institute, 1999), pp. 51–68.

50. United Nations Development Programme. *1998 Human Development Report* (New York: Oxford University Press, 1998), p. 54.

51. Hammond and Matthews, 39.

52. United Nations Food and Agricultural Organization. *State of the World's Forests* (Rome: Food and Agriculture Organization, 1997), p. 10.

53. Gardner-Outlaw, Tom, and Robert Engleman. *Forest Futures: Population, Consumption and Wood Resources* (Washington, D.C.: Population Action International, 1999), p. 1.

54. Ibid., 2.

55. Population Action International (PAI). *Why Population Matters* (Washington, D.C.: Population Action International, 1996), p. 37.

56. The World Resources Institute, 187.

57. The World Resources Institute, 54.

58. Hammond, 35.

59. Hammond, 34.

60. Hammond, 34.

61. Abromovitz, Janet N. *Taking a Stand: Cultivating a New Relationship with the World's Forests* (Washington, D.C.: Worldwatch Institute, 1998), p. 29.

62. Dudley and Stolton, 1996, cited in Hawken, 18.

63. Abromovitz, 31.

64. Hammond, 57.

65. Hammond, 58.

66. United Nations Food and Agriculture Organization (FAO). *State of the World's Fisheries and Aquaculture* (Rome: United Nations Food and Agriculture Organization, 1998).

67. The World Resources Institute.

68. Brown, Lester, Michael Renner, and Christopher Flavin. *Vital Signs 1998* (New York: W.W. Norton, 1998), p. 34.

69. United Nations Food and Agriculture Organization.

70. Matthews and Hammond, 57.

71. The World Resources Institute, 55.

72. The World Resources Institute, 58.

73. Alverson, Dayton L. et al. *A Global Assessment of Fisheries Bycatch and Discards* (Rome: United Nations Food and Agriculture Organization, 1994), p. 26.

74. World Resources Institute, 60.

75. Natural Resources Defense Council. *Fish Facts* (World Wide Web Document: Accessed 8 December 1999, www.nrdc.org/nrdc/worldview/fwfaqs.html).

76. *BP Statistical Review of World Energy* (London: British Petroleum, 1995).

77. United Nations Development Programme, 54.

78. Hawken, 21.

79. "Oil, Oil Everywhere . . . Are We Running Out of It or Aren't We?" *Rocky Mountain Institute Newsletter*, Vol. 14, no. 1, Spring 1998, p. 7.

80. Durning, 52.

81. Myerson, Allen R. "U.S. Splurging on Energy After Falling Off Its Diet," *The New York Times*, October 22, 1998, pp. A1, C6–C7.

82. Ibid., C6.

83. Ibid.

84. Ibid.

85. Ibid.

86. Ibid.

87. Beers, Stephen, and Elaine Robbins. "Lights Out: The Case for Energy Conservation—It Works, So Why Aren't We Using It?" *E, The Environmental Magazine*, Vol. 9, no. 1, January/February 1998, p. 41.

88. Myerson, C6.

89. Brown, 50–53.

90. The World Resources Institute, 170.

91. Brown, 50.

92. Dunn, Seth. "King Coal's Weakening Grip on Power," *Worldwatch*, Vol. 12, no. 5, September/October 1999, p. 10.

93. The World Resources Institute, 63.

94. United States Environmental Protection Agency. *Environmental Effects of Acid Rain* (World Wide Web Document: Accessed 7 January 2000, www.ipa.gov/acidrain/effects/envben.html).

95. Sheehan, John. *Acid Rain: A Continuing National Tragedy* (Elizabethtown, NY: The Adirondack Council, 1998).

96. Motavalli, Jim. "2000: Planet Earth at the Crossroads," *E, The Environmental Magazine*, Vol. 10, no. 1, January/February 1999, p. 31.

97. Intergovernmental Panel on Climactic Change. *IPCC Second Assessment Report: Climactic Change 1995* (Cambridge: Cambridge University Press, 1996).

98. United States Environmental Protection Agency. *Climate* (World Wide Web Document: Accessed 27 January 2000, www.epa.gov/globalwarming/climate/index.html).

99. United States Environmental Protection Agency National Vehicle and Fuel Emissions Laboratory. *Annual Emissions and Fuel Consumption for an Average Vehicle, EPA/420/F-97/037* (Washington, D.C.: Environmental Protection Agency, 1997).

100. Berry, Wendell. "Back to the Land," *Amicus Journal*, Winter, 1999, p. 37.

101. Wackernagel, 82–3.

102. Wackernagel, Mathis, et al. "National Natural Capital Accounting with the Ecological Footprint Concept," *Ecological Economics*, Volume 29, Number 3, June 1999, pp. 375–90.

103. Wackernagel, Mathis. "What We Use and What We Have: Ecological Footprint and Ecological Capacity," Centre for Sustainability Studies Universidad Anáhuac de Xalapa, México, and Redefining Progress: San Francisco, 1999.

104. The World Commission on Environment and Development. *Our Common Future* (New York: Oxford University Press, 1987).

105. Ibid.

28
Frithjof Bergmann
"ECOLOGY AND NEW WORK: EXCESS CONSUMPTION AND THE JOB SYSTEM"
(2000)

Imagine that you are on a plane. The person next to you, an older man, starts to write furiously, without looking up, the very minute he flings himself into his seat. Clearly he is not run-of-the-mill; everyone else is dozing or outright asleep. One could say that he is part demon, though a demon who laughs. There is no question that he is possessed. He writes incessantly for hours until the meal is served. As the tray in front of him interferes with his writing, he begins to talk.

It turns out that you are both returning from the same international congress on Excess Consumption. In fact, soon you both realize that you had seen each other in one or another of the sessions. Indeed, eventually you recall that among the many posters in the halls, there had been one of this man, and underneath his face there had been the two words: NEW WORK. He says:

I attended only so as to get across a single thought. What is more, the delegates certainly knew this idea; in fact, they had heard it many times. All the same, for the sake of this one thought I flew across the ocean and took time away from my frantically busy life. And would you believe that whole idea can be expressed in a single moment, in one flash!

I am quite convinced, you see, that everyone, in some fit of exasperation (say, after hearing an announcer shout for twenty minutes about a super-sale on couches) has had the fantasy that—with one fell swoop—the totality of all advertising could be silenced; that the hawking, the hype, the cajoling, the whole tidal wave of insipid, exaggerated muck could be stopped. Oh, the calm, the peace, the wonderful relief we would feel if we were no longer inveigled, manipulated, and harangued. What a return to innocence, to silent nature this would be.

But—and here's the sum and substance of my one thought—we of course cannot abolish advertising—and we *know* it. No, such an effort could not come to more than an explosive, irritable outcry. Even if everybody had a fit of rage at exactly the same time, and we managed to organize a gigantic demonstration—it would not matter how many of us there were. In the end, the whole crowd could only shrug and then go home.

Now, why is that? Because the elimination of all advertising would bring on a catastrophic economic collapse. The desires, the very appetites for the next wave of newly fashioned products, suddenly would no longer be created. No one would even know that these new goods existed. They would pile up in unopened boxes, and not just in the freight yards, but in the streets and alleys, the market squares and intersections.

But still! Who cares about the boxes? Certainly not we, who've come together at this congress. Let the dust settle on them till one could ski in it. No, the much more serious effect would be the massive awful swamp of unemployment. Soup and bread lines; children suffering from hunger. Indeed, the picture of the children tells us why, though we might complain and make mild proposals about advertising, the idea of trying to seriously expunge advertising does not even enter our heads.

Now to me, this single image shows that the customary picture of our economy is askew. Surely we all want hats and shoes and houses and also to eat, but that clutter does not begin to account for the *excess*—the constant leaping up to higher rungs, the white-hot pace the wheels of the machine inside which we are now living have to turn.

And to say that advertising cajoles, titillates, and wheedles, but also browbeats us into wanting extravagancies is of course true. But this ignores a far more telling truth, lying skintight beneath that surface fact: The real reason for our excruciating, never-sated, and forever gobbling appetite or—rather—our need is for what? For *jobs!* Yes. Yes. The force that drives us to churn up the metals of the earth and grind them into heaps of slag and waste is not the appetite of our coddled senses or even the chafing of our finally aroused desires. When it comes to pleasure, our culture is a dolt, a clod with ten unsubtle thumbs. No. We are more like convicts on a galley. We heave and pull our oars at a desperate battle speed because otherwise the supply of jobs will slacken, and the whole of our circus tent will come crashing down around our ears.

Does it not strike you as bizarre inversion that work, which began as the "Great Punishment" after we had been driven out of Eden—irksome, tedious, an outright condemnation—that work is no longer the means we're prepared to suffer for some other end? No. We have devised a contraption, a newfangled squirrel cage that has transformed work into the mysterious and ultimate desideratum—the treasure that heroes now go out to find, to bring home, to their city or state.

This has transformed the act of buying. It has been disconnected from the product and from the pleasure of its later use. What matters is merely the effect of the purchase—the making of space at the end of the assembly line so the next unit can be produced and the flow can continue. So there's the idea as blatantly expressed as you could wish. The purpose of our economy is not pleasure or use or satisfaction; it is not paté or bubble baths or alligator leather shoes. The driving force is to keep us in work.

You can see this still more sharply if you concentrate on the very idea of stimulating an economy. Growth is the economists' equivalent of caffeine or speed. Without it, we will have soup lines. What's extraordinary is that we are so inured to this idea that we no longer notice it. Whether it is more government spending or a cut in taxes or any of the seven other "interventions" (and all are crude, like medicine in the Middle Ages, like bloodletting the weak)—invariably they appear in the context of the need to "create" (note the pretentious nineteenth-century word) more jobs.

The deeper reason for pushing down on the accelerator and thereby using resources and creating filth—is not that the average person in our culture is a self-indulgent, coddled lout, a princess on a pea, unable to sleep unless she is pillowed on 880 different consumer goods. Nothing like it. Why do we not sigh with relief when the economy slows down? Why do we spur and urge and stimulate instead? Because of our need for jobs.

Let me add another twist: If our appetites really were as voracious and as mighty as we say, then the whole exercise of stimulating the economy, of wafting smelling salts and thumping on its chest, would obviously not be needed. It is one more proof that what I call *the poverty of desire* does actually exist: that, at the bottom, people are not voracious; on the contrary, they are passive, depressed, timorous, and subdued.

The people at the congress probably assumed that my idea was simpleminded. But I meant to explain that there is an ambiguity, a doubleness. Yes, there are those who buy too many shoes and too many snowmobiles. Seen from one side, it is wasteful, a disgrace, insolently flaunting their wealth in the presence of the poor. Yet to look down one's long, puritan, ascetic nose upon acts of spending misses the fact that these acts are also necessary, obedient—indeed, downright dutiful.

At the congress, I tried to make it graphic. In effect, I said: suppose you write the two words "Profit Motive" on the wall. These words name the main driving force in the picture to which most of us subscribe. And how sweeping and encompassing and maybe facile it has become by now. For the long list of offenses and crimes that capitalism has committed, without a single lone exception, can all be explained through the Profit Motive. From the beginnings of colonialism and the expansionary wars to the sweatshops in which children died; to the ghastly murderous urban slums; to how we have turned rivers into sewage and rain into acid; to the vulgarities to which the media have addicted us; yes, down to the faked wrestling shows—all of this is the mud churned up by this devil-take-the-hindmost race. And since the clawing for profit is the cause and is to blame, we, who are not in business but instead work, we are victims, passive, dragged along by this monster-force. It is our part to wring our hands in disapproval, to lament or censor and now and then suggest in pitifully ineffectual ways that even profit does not justify some especially ghoulish outrages.

All I am suggesting is the addition of a companion motive: employment. Jobs. To suppose that the two are an isomorphic pair, like two oxen, would be a gigantic mistake. As soon as you allow the Job Motive to come in at all, the drama of history changes abruptly. History is no longer a sweetly edifying moral tale with all the guilt clotted together in one corner and blue-eyed innocence across from it. The scene no longer shows two plainly marked opposing camps; in fact, it is no longer a battle or a fight. In the center now is a great mass of people, and a new category applies to them; that category is not nice, in a word they are *collaborators.*

I know that is an awful, loaded name, but let me take that very context as one more example. Consider Hitler and his ascent to victory by a mass vote—or nearly so. Certainly he had his well-functioning and well-paying alliance with the Junkers and the traditional German heavy-metal industry and thus with Big Money. And there also were the millions who waited six hours in the hot sun to shriek at his rallies, a sound that one could never forget. However, these were not enough. No, the scales tipped only because of the many other millions who were not ignorant, who had accurate apprehensions about what that man eventually could wreak upon the world, but who voted for him nonetheless! Why? What outweighed their fears?

That too is known. Germany was drowning in a morass of unemployment, and our ignorance, our bafflement in the face of joblessness played a great role. For a large proportion of the meek fellow-voters said that a "strong man" like the one with the mustache was really needed, that nothing short of him would be sufficient to cure this weird, ill-understood disease of unemployment. And even now, in 2000, that very same bafflement prevails in many countries and maybe some other strong man (maybe this time he will have curls and wear a business suit) will seem like the only adequate response.

So you see how the two motives, like tongue and groove, fit easily together. Focus on the awful balance, the horror of an equation that these people made. Look at what is in the two scales: on one side a slaughter such that the frozen corpses bulldozed into heaps eventually grew into mountains and on the other: Jobs. That should be an indication of the value that very many place on having work. And that in turn should be a measure of the extraordinary power of the bond, which integrates these people into the social order that promises them jobs. When jobs are at stake, the threat is absolute and total; people will not just go berserk or panic—they may kill.

You do understand, don't you? That the colossal corporations by now possess a monstrous power. You can call it a new form of dictatorship or the arrival of a world government. In one night's financial roulette game, they can destroy the economy of a whole country (Thailand, for example). But these are understatements which miss the point: The power is not exerted from above. What were at some point called "the masses"—not John Doe, but Joe Consumer—are inextricably tied into the system. And tying people into that system are their jobs. Jobs are what buffalo were for some Indians. Out of buffalo they made their shelter and shoes and their bowstrings, and buffalo were what they ate.

And this fact means that "you" and "we"—that is, "you" ecologists and anti-consumer people and "we" New Work people—must be partners. For the last twenty years, we have been arguing that the job system is the all-including fact, and for the last twenty years we have tried to change it. Any effort to reduce consumption or to save a piece of forest or a species of fish is utterly doomed, is radical waste, if we do not address how this will affect the job system. Who doesn't want clean rivers and safe air? But once you threaten their jobs, the people will be against you.

So far the Environmental and the Labor movements have been very far apart. Each side has viewed the other as a threat. Labor, naturally, has wanted growth, and Environmentalists of course did not. So the conflict could not have been more head-on. But my most encompassing point: We are all helpless in the grip of the job system, and Environmentalism has no chance of making any serious difference unless that system is changed. That is our common purpose and our common cause.

To make efforts to protect the environment while leaving the job system in place is like putting your hand over the exhaust pipe of a car while the engine is still running. It will give you the satisfaction of having tried, but it will have made no difference, will burn one's hand, in the end. In that way, we from New Work come at you in dead earnest: Don't be satisfied with gestures and good intentions. If you mean to accomplish deep and lasting differences—both for the environment and in the area of consumption—then make common cause with us. Help us to change the job system.

I know that, on first hearing this, it may sound strange and puzzling, so let me explain. In the framework of New Work we've been developing and applying for the last twenty years, the concept of the "job system" is the central pivot. The vast majority of society has only worked in jobs for approximately two hundred years. Prior to that, the prevailing "work system" was agricultural, wholly different from the job system since then: People did not punch time clocks, did not get hired and fired, did not receive weekly or monthly checks. Small farmers did not have a boss but worked for themselves. In historical terms, the entire job system is a relatively recent invention. It came into being with the Industrial Revolution. What is more, right from the beginning, many different people were quick to point out all its flaws and potential problems. We, in fact, speak routinely of the "pathology" of the job system. And in the end, that is the cardinal point: We see the job system as one possible arrangement. It was problematic from the start, and in the last two hundred years the configuration of problems has gradually but painfully grown worse. So now may be the time to cautiously and carefully phase in a New Work system! That system will be the successor (if you like, the twenty-first-century successor) of the job system, and it will be as different from it as the job system differed from the agricultural one preceding it.

We do not envision an abrupt change let loose upon the world by a conspiratorial group out of small hidden cellars. Far from that. The dynamic already pushing in the direction of New Work is vast and enormously complex, and it is very much already under way. For the last twenty years we have been working in and with these economic and political forces. More specifically, we have been fostering two forms of work that are both explicitly different and indeed juxtaposed to job-work. Both of these forms of work are now in the process of rapid growth. The chances are excellent that these—and, of course, other forms of work—can be developed further and that this evolution also can be steered to some extent till a critical mass is achieved. As with so many other developments, what was formerly mainstream at some point becomes marginal. Other forms of work will gradually wax, and the now dominant form of work, job-work, will recede until a new gestalt, a new complexion, a new system will have congealed or emerged.

Let me explain that these two forms of work are only pieces. A dramatically different relationship to the environment and to consumption will be achieved only in a configuration in which these pieces interact, or in the coherent whole that could arise from them.

Our name for the first form of New Work is *High-Tech-Self-Providing*. As the name implies, it is a form of providing directly for oneself, which means right away that it is not working for a boss (there, you already have the key distinction from jobs), and it is also not working for a market but immediately for one's own consumption. One can talk for half an hour about what it has in common with farming, but it is also at the same time removed by miles from the labor of haying or of shoveling manure, just as it is not the same thing as growing one's own parsley or making home-cooked jam. Most people already practice various stepping stones to High-Tech-Self-Providing. The most common, banal, and ubiquitous of these is the pumping of one's own gas in service stations. It is in some sense high-tech, since it became possible only with pumps controlled by computers, and it is clearly doing something for oneself—providing a service that was formerly rendered by others. Getting cash out of an ATM without ever seeing a bank teller is another by-now equally humdrum example, not yet of High-Tech-Self-Providing but of the bridge that could bring us there. So, too, are vending machines, computerized forms of payment, and so forth. All of these taken together are a mere nothing compared to the very much larger realm of services we perform for ourselves—not mainly in the public sphere, but instead right in our own home, in the bedroom corner where we keep our PC.

I put it this way intentionally, because the formulation suggests a deeper principle of quite singular and so far ill-understood importance: namely the gradual emergence, or even the revelation of a second new face that technology is able to wear. Most of us associate computers with the impersonal, the anonymous, that which is hostile to the emotional, the subjective, the private life. The inversion of this is now just beginning to appear: namely (paradoxically) very "Hi-" advanced technology not in the service of the big market or the Goliath corporations but the *reverse!* It is technology that provides a counterforce toward the inward, the personal, the domestic, the emotional, and the humane. To recognize that possible development, that conceivable future, and to help foster and steer it is very much what we propose.

The small minority beginning to make active use of the Internet are, I think, just at the juncture where they have started to develop a feel for this. There was somewhere far in the past, the emancipation from something as mundane as somebody else's typing (i.e., from the secretary who possessed this skill). By now there is far too much to exhaustively list: from planning vacations to servicing one's own bank account, to the not just ordering but (increasingly) also the printing of articles and books, to finding information about diseases and disabilities, to teaching and educating oneself in virtually limitless ways. A good many of us have started to practice Hi-Tech-Self-Providing in all these areas in an almost somnambulistic way. But it may be socially, culturally, and politically even more explosive and revolutionary than we have so far allowed ourselves to dream—and that, in spite of the deluge of hype about it.

Let me suggest three plausible further developments of this thrust: First, make clear to yourself that using a computer to merely drive a printer may some day be held up as an example of just how doltish and hidebound we were. A printer is only one of a myriad of possible machines a computer can guide and control. (Walk through a car factory, and you will see.) Since machines are becoming cheaper, more versatile, and far more "intelligent," the idea of connecting our computers to machines that make things (clothes, shoes, watches, jewelry, cell phones) is not far-fetched, and on the contrary, may be around the next corner.

Second, to make things in the space of one's own private home would cramp it, would put ten kinds of restraints on it. These machines will still be far too expensive for individual private possession. By contrast, working together with others in one space would obviously have a string of advantages beyond the sheer cost, from having somebody else's assistance to simply having the fun of working together instead of alone. So locating these machines in a neighborhood Center for New Work people could use them as they now would a library or a copy shop. Some of the political and social implications of this would be that great numbers of people could make use of these computers, machines and the Internet—and could thus, for instance, buy goods much more cheaply over the Internet. These people now have neither the skills nor the computers to do this. (Among the great number of functions performed by neighborhood Centers for New Work would be providing bridges across what some call the digital divide for the approximately 80 percent that are so far excluded.)

Third, the cost of items is what will matter. So far the Internet is contested territory—a wrestling match between Goliath corporations who want to extend their control to this new domain, and a large and motley crowd of micro-entrepreneurs (sometimes musicians, poets, or video artists, but also a great array of more conventional small-business venturers), who all pull in the direction of fulfilling the democratic, or populist vision, an initial hope attached to the Internet. The winning of this battle may be cardinally important, and ironically the small people, the poor, the Davids may win it through their use of "free enterprise." In a nutshell: Right now, books ordered from Amazon.com are not cheaper than those ordered from Borders. But this fact is a scandal, for savings are possible if one does not use a store or employees. Conceivably, enough small entrepreneurs, coming up from the bottom, could use the Internet to underbid the large companies and thus bring the prices down. (Small Internet outfits have the capacity to sometimes underbid large companies; this might be the Molotov cocktail the Internet has presented to the "Wretched of the Earth.")

Just these three developments, joined and working together, would have a sizable effect on the environment and on our patterns of consumption. Clearly, if something like 60 or 70 percent of services and goods are created (through the use of Hi-Tech) in the neighborhood instead of transported 3,000 miles, then the exhaust fumes from trucks will be reduced. The enormous waste involved in the processes of mass production would be lessened: There would not be the piles of excess, from clothes to shoes to cars that haplessly did not connect with a buyer. Still, there is a fourth development to help bring the other three into sharper focus and thereby give a far more vivid sense of just how big the difference would be.

It comes to this: The customary prognosis of how the factory of the future will look—gigantic halls with mile-long rows of robots that all bend forward like tall birds, with hardly any people interspersed between them—may be incorrect. One person in a white coat with a clipboard every quarter of a mile is the fantasy we have. At this point it seems likely—not certain, but possible—that events will take a different turn basically because of a quantum leap in technological sophistication. Robots that perform only a single task represent a low level of intelligence. One would need numbers of long rows of these low-IQ robots. But that is not true of the next generation. These will be by orders of magnitude more flexible, adjustable, and (above all) more intelligent. One of these robots will be able to perform the sum of the segmented discrete tasks that so far required the assembly line. So, factories with long lines may soon belong to the past.

The conception that has been evolving during the last few years is radically different from what many thought: The actual manufacturing of all the parts—for anything, whether it be a car, a refrigerator, furniture, or cell phones—may in the future occur in extraordinarily small shops. There will be no more than one or two of these next-generation robots in any one shop. The most startling and (from our perspective) most telling change is that this will be *all* that is needed!

Large assembling facilities are fearfully expensive and in the near future one may abandon them, just as one has "outsourced" so much else. If one remembers that this outsourcing included levels of hierarchies, large segments of management, and also much that dealt with distribution, one can begin to see how the whole tends toward a coherent development that is now close to reaching a goal: That goal could be small, decentralized, highly sophisticated neighborhood plants, which would (naturally) be connected through computers. Any order, for whatever one is buying, would go from one's own computer to the relevant network of small plants. The parts arrive and could be assembled in one's own home or garage or, better yet, in the next neighborhood center.

Clearly, this scheme eliminates large chunks of the "manufacturing system" to which we have become accustomed. The very landscape would have a different look: Not only would the giant factories be gone, but also the high-rise administrative, bureaucratic buildings, as well as much of the architecture for sales showrooms and to store spare parts and facilitate repairs. Repair shops are already in a sharp process of contraction.

To grasp the full impact this could have, you must combine this new system of "digital" manufacturing with the concept of neighborhood centers for Hi-Tech-Self-Providing. In other words, add to the disappearance of the just-described architecture the fact that a great variety of services but also the making of a vast array of things (from Christmas cards to cloths to furniture to jewelry) could happen in these centers. What effect on the environment and on consumption could this have?

Still, this is only one of the emerging forms of New Work. Let me describe the second, wholly different form: If you have heard anything at all about New Work—if you have read some piece in a newspaper or heard a radio interview—then the one sentence you probably have run across is that "People should do work that they really, really *want* to do." Well, our name for that form is "Paid Calling," and it is far from a footnote; it is actually a good half of the structure of the whole of New Work. Right now let me only say this much: That species of work again has its foundation in the mud of the everyday, namely, in the fact that many people experience their work like a mild disease—*It will pass. It's Wednesday already, and I'll make it to Friday somehow.* The idea of making it possible for everyone, not just an elite, to at least part of the time do work that constitutes a Paid Calling was simply to set up the most pitched and pointed head-on contrast to this—i.e., in contrast to work as a mild disease. From the beginning and for the duration of the last twenty years, we aimed at assisting people into work as juxtaposed to this as we could manage. Succinctly, to help them into work that would be the best, the optimum for them—appropriate to their talents, their worldview; fitted to their private lives, to their values; fitted above all to their desires, to what they really, seriously, and deeply want. Not work that is a mild disease, but work far better than many therapies: that gives more strength, more vitality, and greater health.

Let me emphasize one central point: Namely, that the structure of this form of work is the mirrored opposite of that of job-work. In job-work I market myself to someone else and hope that he can make use of me for *his* plans. The essence of a Paid Calling is that the origin and the impulse for the work arises from within me, and not on my surface, but as close to the core of me, as close to the place "where I live" as can be achieved—that I work from the very heart and core of my soul.

Naturally, we insisted that this kind of work was (at least often) separate from job-work, that as a category it was intended to represent an addition, a new and further species of work. Of course, it was understood all along that for this form of work one would be paid, and (indeed) not a miserly amount, but well. That it had to make an economic, a material difference, was to us a self-understood precondition (exactly like in the case of High-Tech-Self-Providing). Otherwise it plainly would be of no consequence. (That is part of what is meant by attempting to phase in a different work system: If it did not produce material and economic changes, it would have no right to the word "system"; it would only be flimflam, wool pulled over tired people's eyes.)

In an effort to drive this point deliberately to a clarifying extreme, we consistently underscored that there are a number of ways in which paying for this species of work could be arranged. That was part of our larger, more basic stance: that what we were proposing was easy. Early on, we suggested that a corporation like General Motors could pay (and maybe, even be made to pay) a sum for every workplace that is ration-

alized or engineered away. A sum that would allow one worker to perform work that she or he seriously wanted to do. Later we concentrated
more on the analogy to foundations: Why should only professors and
artists receive fellowships? Why not anyone at all who has the capacity
to perform valuable work? More recently we have been suggesting that
government programs should not push people into picking up litter
along the edges of highways, but instead would assist people to perform
the most creative and productive work possible for them to achieve.

The situation we aimed at from the start was that a premium be
placed on the development of talents and the having of ideas. If someone
has an idea, a task that she or he seriously wants to perform, and if the
person and the task meet some obvious required conditions—if it, indeed, "adds value" (though "value" broadly defined)—then in a society
with the barest minimum of sense, such a person should be well paid.
It is a matter of regaining some bare shreds of a sane perspective: We
obviously pay millions to reams of people who do not produce anything
of serious value. (Go through the halls of any number of corporate or
government bureaucracies, and you will see them doodling on their
desks.) There also are the billions for the three weekly great mergers.
And beyond that, the legendary and much discussed trillions that multiply simply by wandering from one computer to another computer that
happens to be halfway around the world. To pretend that a society such
as ours cannot pay people for the most creative kinds of work is simply
grotesque. It should be finally understood that the claim to be paid for
work is stronger than any other—arguably even stronger than the claim
to be assisted in a circumstance of ill health or old age.

I hope you understand. Our basic idea is to gradually loosen the stranglehold of the job system through the fostering and phasing in of these
two forms of work that are clearly not job-work and not part of that
system. If you allow me, I will very quickly sketch a model so as to give
you a simplified description of how these parts interact and form a new
coherent whole that could be the work system of the twenty-first century.

Imagine a splendid-looking Buckminster Fuller–like glass dome in the
middle of a neighborhood. Among its many other functions, this dome
is also a greenhouse; all manner of vegetables and flowers are grown
there in the most advanced, perma-culture ways. But in that dome are
also several of the next-generation robots I described. So the dome is
also a manufacturing site. In another corner are numerous computers
staffed with trained assistants so that everyone and not just a few can
High-Tech-Self-Provide themselves with a variety of services but also
goods. Naturally, there is also a restaurant, space for performances and
plays, and—needless to say—hosts of children, for this dome also is
their school. In short, a lively place, its general appearance suggests an

ultra-modern railway station from which trains for a more cheerful future leave every hour round the clock.

Every person living in this New Work neighborhood would participate in the three kinds of work I just described. Assume it to be two days each, and people will spend two days Hi-Tech-Self-Providing and two days doing job-work (for example, in the small sophisticated manufacturing plant), and two days they will pursue a "Paid Calling."

Let me try to give an overview of the more-than-90-degree angle by which the whole thrust of consumption would be turned if we did manage to cross over into a New Work society and culture. Take first the ground floor of the structural economic changes: The provision of most services and the manufacturing of most goods from neighborhood centers would result in such immense simplifications, streamlinings, and reductions of waste that the resistance to it will no doubt be great. Indeed, the reduction in job-work would be so very large that the pressure to introduce something like New Work to offset it would grow by leaps and bounds. In sheer magnitude, the difference is as great as the old industry of Pittsburgh or Detroit versus the new industry of the California coast. But with tenacious organized support, it nonetheless could happen, simply because huge economic forces push that way: Small plants with greatly enhanced intelligent machines are more economical and more competitive than the hulking dinosaurs still in use.

Add the gamut of cultural changes that would also help bring consumption down: First among these would be the dissipation of a specific kind of rage. What I mean is the fury of frustration about work that builds up in many who serve in the job system. I used to observe this in Flint: workers coming out of the plants and going on buying sprees with the paycheck they had just received—out of the rage they felt about their work. They would buy to avenge themselves, to prove their superiority at least to things, to merchandise. They felt humiliated by the life they led and by the work they had to do, and they got even by buying ostentatious things. Their contempt showed. They would not even take their purchases inside their homes, leaving the merchandise on their front lawns in the rain.

A second such cultural change could be summarized through the analogy to a hydraulic system. In quite a number of recent films, the ultra-tough, young, high-up executive gets asked why he is climbing up the money ladder from rung to rung. He (Michael Douglas) answers: "It's one way to keep score." That is close to accurate. Closer still would be: "It's the only way to keep score that still remains." The truth behind this is broad: Work has drowned out much of what used to be the rest of life. As work covered more territory, it also became less satisfying—for all the multifarious reasons that get boiled down into the one word *stress.* So, what is a person to do? It resembles a hydraulic system: As the area from which some pleasure or nurturance can be gotten constricts, the lust, the greed, goes exponentially up. Buying is not just the only measure; it is the only thing one can still do. One sits immobilized high on the flagpole of one's conspicuous consumption.

The converse of this could be illustrated with anyone who passionately loves their work, and we could think typically of an artist, a scientist, or an inventor. Their passion for their work is often so intense that they become indifferent to the blandishments of the materialistic world. If more people had a chance to practice High-Tech-Self-Providing and could go beyond this work for pay at something that was indeed their *calling,* then many of the goods which they now buy would pale by comparison. They would buy less, not from frugality or asceticism, but from *discrimination*—having acquired a taste for "finer things."

Consumerism is also a last resort. One buys with one's last breath. If there are other pleasures, particularly the gorgeous, sumptuous, enthralling pleasure of work that one seriously wants to do, then the pleasures with which trinkets wave will feel like ashes on one's tongue.

The third cultural change addresses our relationship to things. Of the vast majority of things we buy, we say: "Easy come, easy go." They are discarded as perfunctorily as they are acquired. This is an awful waste of resources, but it also means that we are unattached, adrift, like an astronaut whose tubes and wires have been cut. High-Tech-Self-Providing would change that. If we returned to a style of life where many things would again be made by ourselves, only this time with far less biblical sweat and with far more assistance from the most sophisticated and advanced technologies, we would give of ourselves to the things we make. They would embody our talents, our taste, a stretch of our time; they would be a piece of ourselves, and our relationship to them would be like a fragment of that to our children.

Try to visualize the landscape beginning to take shape: There are small decentralized neighborhood manufacturing shops and nothing else, since all else has proved dispensable, uneconomical, and a waste. And there are also neighborhood Centers for New Work, where people as a group advance, on the one side, toward greater self-reliance and, on the other side, toward work they "really, really, want to do." Surely there is some hope in that, but there's still the monster problem, which brought me to this conference in the first place: the problem of forced growth.

Remember that one of the modes of execution in the Middle Ages was to be dragged to death by horses. That is what's happening to us. We are on the ground, our wrists are tied together, and the panicked horses of the combined corporate job system race with us through a field of stones. Of all evils, this is the most serious one, and the concept of New Work was created as a response to it.

To see how, imagine a New Work neighborhood or community in economic straits. To make it concrete, assume they have some years of experience in High-Tech-Self-Providing, that for several years many of them have been working, very much part-time, in the small local plant that makes components for electric batteries for mopeds. For one reason or another, the market for their batteries has begun to sag and they are in economic trouble. How do they proceed?

Most obviously and also most important, their Self-Providing is in place! Their dependence on their jobs is wholly different from the total dependence in which we live now. They are very like farmers used to be—when farmers were still farmers and not agribusinessmen. They could far more easily weather a dry period than someone who is fired overnight. Their jobs represent only a fraction of their work, and the income they derive from it is only the equivalent of what farmers made of their cash crops.

But they also have behind them years in which they developed their inventiveness, their ingeniousness in improvising. High-Tech-Self-Providing has thoroughly trained them in that. One of the first decisions they might make is to compensate for the losses with a greater proportion of Self-Providing. Maybe they have so far not made their own shoes. So they do some research with the assistance of the Local Center for New Work and find that this can be done (which, at this writing, is indeed the case). This might not only reduce their expenses; it might at the same time be the seedling for the next enterprise they grow. Many of the surrounding neighborhoods might have reached a similar point and might want to buy from them the training or assistance needed to make one's own shoes.

That still leaves out of account the other side of New Work: Every one in the whole community has gone through several stages of finding out what kind of work they "really, really want" to do. That, too, has trained them in many skills and has strengthened their inventiveness. An obvious strategy would be to take stock of the great array of their past endeavors and to ask which of this variety could be put to an economic, or money-making, use. Decisive here is that very little would go a long way: If one is already at a level of 80 percent self-providing, then the equivalent of one additional job would be enough for five.

And there is yet another side. They have all trained themselves in the gestation of ideas, and the presumption is that they live in a society in which valuable ideas are encouraged and supported in a colorful variety of ways, so any number of them might seek support for one of their "callings," and—in exchange for that—relinquish their claim to one of the currently endangered part-time jobs.

The crux is that they can weigh and balance strategies against each other. That they are not automatically coerced into bribing a new entrepreneur to set up another plant. This is the quintessential, cardinal-red pivotal point I wanted to make at the conference: The indispensable condition for any Economic Freedom is the freedom to say *no* to a new technology, *no* to a new line of products, *no* to a yet more concocted line of "services," *no* to Goliath corporations—even when they dangle the promise of jobs.

Do you begin to see how New Work would loosen the stranglehold that I have talked about from the beginning? You could run through the entire gamut of the illustrations I have given. Maybe the big mouth of advertising could, after all, be muzzled, and maybe the consequent piling up of trinkets would be a catastrophe that would send us screaming through the streets. Maybe we would face it with equanimity, and experience it as another step in our gradual liberation. If so, it would be proof that the force of the behemoth—the combined corporate and job system—in the direction of more growth and more waste had begun to be tamed.

Ooops! More or less, just in time. So we're cleared for the final approach. So fasten your seat belt now. Sorry if this was not the restful flight you expected to have. One last sentence, if you permit. Consumption would be a totally different thing if only people had something in which to believe, that you and everybody already knows. But that's what New Work is for. If the immense ocean of marvelous human energy now being wasted would instead be put to some halfway intelligent use, we would not only consume substantially less, we could create, we could produce with that energy a from-the-ground-up different culture. And you should work with us on that, on achieving a more humane, a more intelligent, more cheerful culture (the Marxists forgot about that), but also a culture that will be more sensuous and far more flamboyant. You know that we could have this—it's as close to us as we are right now to the ground—but I know. Enough! Good-bye. Good-bye. I will stop—and go back to the writing of my very long, very thick book.

PERMISSIONS

We are grateful for permission to reproduce the following copyrighted material:

ABOUT THE EDITORS

Douglas B. Holt is assistant professor in the department of marketing at the University of Wisconsin–Madison. His research has explored how consumption works to reproduce class and gender boundaries, the characteristics of consumer culture in the postmodern economy, and the commodification of the ghetto. He is currently investigating how marketers and advertisers use market research data to construct consumers. Holt is a member of the editorial boards of the *Journal of Consumer Research*, *Poetics*, and *Marketing Theory*. He holds a Ph.D. in Marketing from Northwestern University.

Juliet B. Schor has taught at Harvard University since 1984, and is currently senior lecturer on women's studies. She is also professor of the economics of leisure at Tilburg University, The Netherlands. She is the author of *The Overworked American: The Unexpected Decline of Leisure* (Basic Books, 1992), *The Overspent American: Upscaling, Downshifting and the New Consumer* (Basic Books, 1998), and, most recently, *Do Americans Buy Too Much?* (Beacon Press, 2000). She is a member of the board of directors of the Center for a New American Dream.

Breinigsville, PA USA
06 January 2010
230218BV00002B/2/P

9 781565 845985